Characteristics of and Strategies for Teaching Students with Mild Disabilities

FIFTH EDITION

Characteristics of and Strategies for Teaching Students with Mild Disabilities

MARTIN HENLEY

Westfield State College

ROBERTA S. RAMSEY

Norwich University

ROBERT F. ALGOZZINE

University of North Carolina at Charlotte

PEARSON

Boston   New York   San Francisco
Mexico City   Montreal   Toronto   London   Madrid   Munich   Paris
Hong Kong   Singapore   Tokyo   Cape Town   Sydney

KH

Executive Editor: *Virginia Lanigan*
Series Editorial Assistant: *Scott Blaszak*
Marketing Manager: *Kris Ellis-Levy*
Production Editor: *Annette Joseph*
Editorial Production Service: *Modern Graphics, Inc.*
Composition Buyer: *Linda Cox*
Manufacturing Buyer: *Andrew Turso*
Electronic Composition: *Modern Graphics, Inc.*
Photo Researcher: *Larissa Tierney*
Cover Administrator: *Linda Knowles*
Cover Designer: *Suzanne Harbison*

Library of Congress Cataloging-in-Publication Data
Henley, Martin
    Characteristics of and strategies for teaching students with mild disabilities / Martin
Henley, Roberta S. Ramsey, Robert F. Algozzine.—5th ed.
        p. cm.
    Includes bibliographical references and index.
    ISBN 0-205-45764-9
    1. Learning disabled—United States. 2. Mainstreaming in education—United States.
3. Behavior modification—United States. I. Ramsey, Roberta S. II. Algozzine, Robert.
III. Title.

LC4705.H46 2006
371.9—dc22   2005045368

Photo Credits
p. 1, Mike Peters/Silver Burdett Ginn; p. 44, Getty Images Inc. - PhotoDisc; p. 81, Stockbyte; p. 125, Getty Images Inc. - PhotoDisc; p. 174, Nicola Sutton/Getty Images, Inc. - PhotoDisc; p. 215, David Buffington/Getty Images, Inc. - PhotoDisc; p. 247, Doug Menuez/Getty Images, Inc. - PhotoDisc; p. 280, Creatas/Dynamic Graphics; pp. 314, 346, David Buffington/Getty Images, Inc. - PhotoDisc; p. 374, David Mager/Pearson Learning Photo Studio.

Printed in the United States of America

10 9 8 7 6 5 4 3   RRD-VA 10 09 08 07 06

2/8/07

To
Margaret, Bobby, Kathryn and
Michael, Randy, and Carl

CONTENTS

4   Students with Behavioral/Emotional Disorders   125

7   Learning and Teaching   247

8   Instructional Modifications   280

PREFACE

This book is written for general and special education majors who want to learn how to effectively teach students with mild disabilities. Aside from speech and language problems, mild disabilities are the most common disabling conditions found in schools. The mild disabilities include mild mental retardation, emotional/behavioral disorders, and learning disabilities. Students with mild disabilities spend the major portion of their school day in general education classrooms. This means that the responsibility for educating these students is shared by general and special educators. The emphasis on inclusion makes it imperative that general and special educators share a common knowledge base about the nature and needs of these hard-to-teach students.

Our purpose is to provide in a single volume a comprehensive overview of educational practices that influence the identification, placement, and teaching of students with mild disabilities. No other text details both characteristics of and strategies for teaching students with mild disabilities. Our emphasis on characteristics separates this text from others in the same genre. Too often key issues that influence the placement and teaching of students with mild disabilities are muddled by misinformation. One such issue is eligibility criteria. One of the most troublesome aspects of special education today is the misidentification of students as mildly disabled. In some cases students with legitimate disabilities are overlooked. In other instances problem learners are called mildly disabled without sufficient supportive evidence. It is crucial that both general and special educators develop a clear understanding of the types of learning problems that characterize students with mild disabilities. Many special education programs sag under the weight of misplaced students and unfulfilled expectations.

The first part of this book addresses the characteristics of students with mild disabilities. Chapter 1 explains the basic principles of special education, including its history, legal mandates (including No Child Left Behind and IDEA '04), and descriptions of various types of disabling conditions. Chapter 2 details those reasons and highlights similarities and differences found within the three mildly disabling conditions. Chapters 3 through 5 present detailed information on each of the three mild disabilities, including practical teaching strategies for each. Although some states subscribe to a cross-categorical approach when serving students with mild disabilities, the reality is that learning problems are addressed by educators and parents in terms of one of the specific mild disabilities of mild mental retardation, learning disability, or emotional/behavioral disorders. There are many reasons for this shifting back and forth between using and not using categorical terms to discuss students with mild disabilities.

The second part of this book describes effective teaching practices for students with mild disabilities. The research basis for instruction of students with mild disabilities indicates that effective teaching works for all youngsters regardless of the reason for their learning problems. Although categories of disabilities help determine eligibility for special education and provide direction for the prevention of mild disabilities, teaching concerns are best addressed cross-categorically. Such classroom practices as cooperative learning, peer tutoring, career education, and social skills instruction are equally effective for all learners, including those with mild disabilities.

Chapter 6 explains how to organize and implement inclusion programs. Chapter 7 looks at teaching from the point of view of the learner, and Chapter 8 highlights instructional modifications. Classroom management practices are detailed in Chapter 9. The emphasis is on actions by the teacher that prevent discipline problems, and information on such classroom management practices as behavior modification and life space crisis intervention is presented. Chapter 10 extends the classroom management discussion to an analysis of social skills instruction. The final chapter, 11, describes the value of family-school cooperation. It describes programs for helping families and gives an overview of issues that surface when a family discovers that a child has a mild disability.

This book is organized with the needs of the reader in mind. Visual organizers highlight how concepts tie together. Figures and tables summarize information. Anecdotes help the reader get a feel for events that affect the lives of youngsters with mild disabilities. Case studies provide models for problem solving. We have attempted to achieve a writing style that is readable without sacrificing content. Many issues relating to the education of students with mild disabilities require thoughtful analysis. As in most educational concerns the "right" answer is elusive. Our goal is to present an honest and straightforward picture of the issues that confront teachers and families as they strive to provide mildly disabled students with the education they need to live successful lives.

We owe sincere thanks to our families, who supported us during the writing of this fifth edition. As always we are in debt to our college students who, in their quest for knowledge and practical solutions, have pushed us to expand our awareness. We owe special thanks to our editor, Virginia Lanigan. Her encouragement and support were instrumental in allowing this project to reach a successful conclusion. We also thank Scott Blaszak, editorial assistant, and the reviewers who provided helpful comments on the book: Moniqueka E. Gold, Austin Peay State University; Paul R. Malanga, University of South Dakota; Carol Robinson, Indiana State University; and Dawn R. Speidel, West Liberty State College. Finally, we want to thank our college and university colleagues who provide us with both inspiration and challenge. We are keenly aware that in the final analysis the value of our work rests on their judgment. We hope we have met their expectations.

CHAPTER

1 Foundations of Special Education for Students with Mild Disabilities

ADVANCE QUESTIONS

Answer the following questions as you read this chapter:

1. What factors led to the development of special education?
2. What are the key principles that drive special education today?
3. Why do some students receive special education?
4. Who is eligible for special education?
5. What are mild disabilities?
6. What are the advantages and disadvantages of classifying students for special education?

Chapter Web

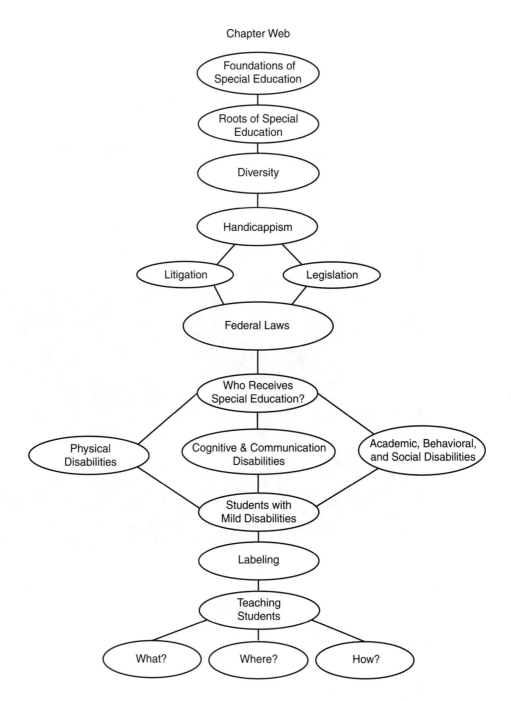

7. How do school personnel decide what special education services are appropriate for students with mild disabilities?
8. What are some key differences between general and special education?

Vignette: Jake, Mary, Felipe

Jake always seems to be one step behind the other students in his seventh-grade class. Despite the slowness that is a part of Jake's performance and social development, his teacher enjoys having him in class. Because Jake is talkative with a good sense of humor, many of his schoolmates enjoy helping him. Jake's teacher likes teaching him because he responds favorably to efforts to help him develop new skills. Jake's classroom performance is similar to many students with mild mental retardation.

Jake's class contains a mixture of students who are easy to teach and students who are hard to teach. Mary is one of the difficult kids. When she was younger she was diagnosed as "hyperactive," and she was put on medication to control her behavior. She comes from a home where both parents work hard to maintain a comfortable lifestyle. There is a lot of pressure put on Mary to succeed. Both of her parents are upwardly mobile professionals. Mary does not trust adults and often takes her anger out on her classmates. When she is not physically disrupting the classroom, Mary is socially withdrawn, isolated, and unhappy. Mary's teacher believes that Mary has emotional problems.

Felipe is also difficult to teach—not because of what he does, but because of what he does not do. Felipe does not read or write as well as his seventh-grade classmates. He has never done well in reading, but his scores on ability tests and tests of achievement in other areas (e.g., mathematics) have always been average when compared to his peers. Now that Felipe is in junior high school, his difficulties are particularly troublesome, because he is expected to read and complete homework assignments in English, history, science, psychology, and economics. Felipe appears to have a learning disability.

Each of these students, Jake, Mary, and Felipe, is difficult to teach. They are constantly at risk of failing, and they are potential school dropouts. Jake, Mary, and Felipe have mild disabilities that are interfering with their progress in school.

Now that you have read the vignette about Jake, Mary, and Felipe, see how many problem-solving questions you can answer. For those questions you cannot readily answer, try to find some additional information to use in answering them as you read the chapter. The experiences of Jake, Mary, and Felipe are typical of students with mild disabilities.

1. What should be done to help students like Jake, Mary, and Felipe?
2. Who should teach them?
3. Should public schools provide special education services for students with learning and emotional problems?
4. What expectations would you have for students like Jake, Mary, and Felipe if you were teaching in their junior high school?

5. What is a mild disability?
6. Should students with mild disabilities be included in classes with students without disabilities?

Every classroom contains students like Jake, Mary, and Felipe. Helping students with learning problems is part of the motivation that stimulates many to become teachers. As one experienced teacher put it, "some teachers like the underdog." The purpose of special education is to help students achieve success in school. Special educators and their general classroom peers want to see all students stay in school, graduate, and succeed in life; but because of differences between the two systems of education, they sometimes work at cross-purposes. When special and general educators communicate and share responsibility for educating students with special needs, everybody benefits.

The Roots of Special Education

Origins of the United States's national education system date from the colonial days. Early schools educated a select, limited segment of the population—white, male children of upper class families (Smith, Price, & Marsh, 1986). Before 1815, schools serving this small proportion of school-aged youth were primarily church sponsored.

Public support of schools by local taxation began during the first half of the nineteenth century. Children previously excluded from schooling—middle class, poor, female, or culturally different—were included. During the mid-nineteenth century, states began enacting compulsory education laws (e.g., Rhode Island in 1840, Massachusetts in 1852). A change in the values and economic thinking of our society was reflected by this Common School Movement.

These early common schools educated students of all ages in the same classroom. In the one-room schoolhouse, students of different ages, different abilities, and different backgrounds learned side by side. Horace Mann, the architect of American public education, believed universal education was the great equalizer. Cremin (1961) characterized this early vision.

> Mann's school would be common, not as a school for the common people—for example, the nineteenth-century Prussian Volksschule—but rather as a school common to all people. It would be open to all, provided by the state and the local community as part of the birthright of every child. It would be for rich and poor alike, not only free but as good as any private institution. It would be nonsectarian, receiving children of all creeds, classes, and backgrounds. (p. 10)

Mann's humanitarian ideal began to take hold, and by 1860 a majority of the states had established public school systems. Throughout this period of rapid growth, Mann advised that instruction be adapted to meet the needs of children who differed in temperament, ability, and interests.

As the United States grew, the one-room schoolhouse was replaced by graded elementary, middle, and high schools. Explicit academic requirements were established for each grade level of the common public school. Students were taught a specific curriculum, and that curriculum was organized into graded units. Educators believed that grouping students by age would make the task of teaching easier (Sarason & Doris, 1979; Ysseldyke & Algozzine, 1982). Achievement was determined by how well children learned the predetermined, graded curriculum. This curriculum-centered characteristic of the new schools made it difficult for many children to keep pace (Smith, Price, & Marsh, 1986; Ysseldyke & Algozzine, 1984).

Immigration and compulsory school attendance broadened the school-aged population to a larger, more diverse membership. Cultural and ethnic differences in students created a mismatch between teacher expectations and student performance. Some children adapted to school and learned; others dropped out. Many children worked in factories; others took to the streets. Few of the absent students were missed. Little concern was shown for children with learning problems and what we now refer to as "at-risk youth."

The influence of social reformers, such as Jane Addams, encouraged the establishment of alternative instructional programs for "special cases." The superintendent of the Baltimore schools wrote, "Before the attendance laws were effectively enforced there were as many of these special cases in the community as there is now; few of them, however, remained long enough in school to attract serious attention or to hinder the instruction of the more tractable and capable" (Van Sickle, 1908–1909, 102).

Early public educational programs offered two choices. Students either received and profited from instruction in lock-step, curriculum-centered classes, or they were placed in special classes. Many administrators believed that these first special education programs were proper preparation for institutionalization. In a speech to the National Education Association, E. R. Johnstone stated that the special education class

> must become a clearing-house. To it will be sent the slightly blind and partially deaf, but also incorrigibles, the mental deficients, and the cripples. . . . The only thing to do is to give them the best of care and training possible. Keep them in the special classes until they become too old for further care in school, and then they must be sent to the institutions for safety. (Johnstone, 1908, 114–118)

A few early special programs were set up for children with specific disabilities, such as deafness or blindness. However, many early public school special classes were repositories for diverse youngsters who did not fit into the regular classroom. In 1899, Elizabeth Farrell described students in her first special education class in New York City:

> The first class was made up of the odds and ends of a large school. There were the over-age children, the so-called naughty children, and the dull, and stupid

children. They were taken from any and every school grade. The ages ranged from eight to sixteen years. They were the children who could not get along in school. They were typical of a large number of children who even today are forced directly or indirectly out of school; they were the children who were interested in street life; many of them earned a good deal of money in one way or another. While some of them had been in trouble with the police, as a class they could not be characterized as criminal. They had varied interests but the school, as they found it, had little or nothing for them. (Farrell, 1909, 91–96)

From the first decades of the twentieth century until the mid-1970s, students who did not fit in general education classes were ignored, placed in isolated special classes, or transferred to state institutions. In Pennsylvania, for instance, legislation provided for the exclusion of specific children from school. Children evaluated as uneducable because of below-average IQ scores were assigned to the Department of Public Welfare for training in state-run institutions. Most notable about the process of classifying and rejecting students who didn't fit the standard public school curriculum was the lack of due process in educational decisions.

In 1970, the Task Force of Children Out of School studied the Boston Public School System. The Task Force report—*The Way We Go to School: The Exclusion of Children in Boston*—found over ten thousand students excluded from public school classrooms because they didn't match school standards for the normal student. Patricia Reilly, age sixteen, was told to leave school because she was pregnant. Kathy Fitzgerald, age nine, was excluded from public school because she had a seizure disorder (i.e., epilepsy). Richard, eleven years old, was placed in a special class for the retarded because he was emotionally disturbed and no other program was available. These children were denied the right to an appropriate education because they were different. In 1974, Congress estimated that over a million school-aged youngsters were denied a proper education in America's schools.

The experience of being treated differently because you do not fit into society's vision of what is normal and accepted, because you are seen as different, is a difficult one. Like the experience of being called names and treated poorly because of where your parents come from or the perception others have of your heritage, it is an old one. Many move to the "land of opportunity," to "the other side of the tracks," to "the better part of town," or to "a good school" to overcome criticism, discrimination, and mistreatment and to build a "better life" for themselves and their children. They hope to reclaim the dignity they are entitled to as human beings and citizens of a country where dreams and ideals of individualism, equal opportunity, nationalism, and success prevail and are the basis for fundamental human rights and continuing social responsibilities. Too often it just doesn't work out that way. Too often, differences and diversity that should be celebrated are the source of disparaging remarks, continuing intolerance, and disenfranchising treatment.

How could a nation based on equal opportunity for all its citizens support discriminatory practices toward children? The answer is found in attitudes. Prejudice, like creeping shadows, can take many forms. The public school system mirrors our society. Schools reflect the attitudes and prejudices of teachers, administrators, and parents. Students with disabilities have special needs, and those special needs have been used as a rationale to exclude them from mainstream life in American schools.

Education once intended for a small, elite sector of the population is now mandated for all children. During the past century, the curriculum-centered format of public schools has remained static while the needs of students have changed significantly. School dropouts, discipline problems, low achievement, and increased referrals to special education are a concern to educators and the public at large. Diversity of students, simply defined as the condition of being viewed as different, is at odds with a system of education that requires conformity and assimilation of an unyielding curriculum.

Smith-Davis (1989a) identified some important events and acts of legislation that enhanced diversity. The *Brown v. Topeka Board of Education* decision in 1954 radically altered the national school population. This landmark case, acted upon by the U.S. Supreme Court, decreed that "segregated but equal" school facilities for black and white schoolchildren were discriminatory and unconstitutional. *Brown v. Topeka Board of Education* reversed a prior decision rendered in *Plessy v. Ferguson* in 1894 that legalized separate schools based on racial lines.

The Civil Rights Act of 1964 gave support to advocates who pushed for the inclusion of students with disabilities in public schools (Smith-Davis, 1989a,b; Smith, Price, & Marsh, 1986; Ysseldyke & Algozzine, 1990). Mainstreaming, a term used to promote the integration of school-aged youth with disabilities into classrooms with their peers without disabilities, followed on the heels of successful efforts to deinstitutionalize programs for adults and children with disabilities. Placement of youth and adults with moderate and severe disabilities within community settings dramatized their capability to live normal lives. These changes diversified the student population in the nation's schools and emphasized the need for schools to accommodate children with special learning needs (Ysseldyke, Algozzine, & Thurlow, 1983). Yet changes in public school practices toward students with disabilities have been slow to come. For instance, the steady increase each year in youngsters identified with mild disabilities and placed in special programs is testimony to the intractability of a system of education that looks first to blame the student for failure.

Diversity

In 1987, 47 percent of the workforce was comprised of white Americans; by the mid-twenty-first century 85 percent of new workers will be people of color. In the year 2020 almost half of the school-aged population will be young people of color (Pallas, Natriello, & McDill, 1989). This "browning of America" is a reality that signals profound change in our American culture. Multicultural education, with its attendant emphasis on gender, race, and bilingualism is aimed at preparing today's youth for a future characterized by diversity. Ford (1992) defines multicultural education as school "practices and policies that transform the school so that male and female students, social class, racial, and ethnic groups will experience an equal opportunity to learn" (p. 108).

Advocates for multicultural education believe that all students should learn to adapt to the reweaving of our country's social and economic fabric. The purpose of multicultural education is to restructure schools so that students will acquire the knowledge, attitudes, and skills needed to function in an ethnically and racially diverse nation and world (Banks, 1993, 27). How this is to be accomplished is a matter of some dispute. Some educators argue that textbooks and curricula should emphasize the contributions and lifestyles of such diverse groups as gays, women, and people of color. Others oppose curricula that give equal time to such topics as homosexuality or replace traditional Western European thinking with "Afrocentric" texts and learning materials.

A diversity issue that affects all populations is lack of equal rights for women. Even though men and women have equal ability, men continue to make higher salaries and have easier access to promotion. Stereotypes about women begin in infancy, with pink birth ribbons signifying daintiness and beauty. These initial views are strengthened throughout childhood through toys, sports, and leisure activities. Consider a nine-year-old boy who chooses ballet over baseball, or a ten-year-old girl who wants to play football. These youngsters will face opposition and ridicule as they attempt to oppose gender barriers. Look around your education classes. If you are an elementary or early childhood major you probably have five times more females than males in your class. Why do more women than men select education as a major? An analysis of explanations will highlight some of the gender barriers girls and women must overcome in order to achieve an equal position in our society.

As the debates continue about how diversity issues should be dealt with, the major hurdle to the educational progress of many people of color continues to be poverty. Hu-DeHart (1993) succinctly illustrates the chasm that separates rich and poor in America, "Today 1% of the population of the U.S. has 'gained control' of more of the nation's wealth than the bottom 90%. This situation parallels the stark and painful inequality in much of the Third World" (p. 51). Multicultural proponents point to inequities of school funding as evidence that today's poor schoolchildren (many of whom are minorities) are at a distinct disadvantage in their preparation for tomorrow's workplace. Property taxes fund schools. Children who live in destitute communities are unable to break the cycle of poverty because their education is as bleak as their neighborhoods.

Placement of students in special education programs represents one of many multicultural problems that confront our schools (Winzer & Mazurek, 1998). African American children, particularly males, are overrepresented in special education programs for students with mild mental retardation and behavior disorders. Paradoxically, females and children with limited English proficiency (e.g., Hispanic) are underrepresented in special education programs. This trend of over- and underrepresentation means that many African American children may be inappropriately placed (see Lloyd Dunn's remarks in the chapter on mild mental retardation), while females and Hispanic students who require special education are overlooked. The uneven distribution of students in special education has created a confusing picture about the educational needs of females of all races, African-Americans, Hispanics, and Native Americans.

In an optimistic future scenario, America will be built on a strong foundation of respect for individual differences. The positive outcomes of multicultural education could help alleviate sexism and racism. In such a society all individuals regardless of gender, ethnic origin, sexual preference, or disability will have an equal opportunity to succeed. As educators, the choices we make now will determine our ability to adapt to fundamental changes in American society.

Handicappism

Advocates for individuals with disabilities use the word "handicappism" to refer to the perception that a person is incompetent because of a physical or psychological impairment. When asked about their most difficult adjustments, adults with disabilities invariably comment about dealing with stereotypes. For example, friends and neighbors may refer to Elise Jones, who has a visual impairment, as "poor, blind Elise!" Condescending remarks about individuals with disabilities may be masked as sympathy, but the message is a clear illustration of handicappism. In fact, Elise's visual impairment is only a part of her individuality, not the sum total of what Elise is as a person.

Sooner or later, most of us will experience a disability. Old age, injuries, or illness are inescapable aspects of the human condition. Although the idea that at some point in your life you will experience a disability might seem remote, the simple truth is that we are not talking about infrequent or isolated cases. The number of U.S. citizens with disabilities is equal to the combined population of New York City, Los Angeles, Chicago, and Miami.

Individuals with disabilities are people first and people with a disability second. The label assigned to their disability should not be used to replace all their other characteristics. Franklin D. Roosevelt guided the United States through the Second World War from the vantage point of a wheelchair. Einstein was considered too slow to attend school with his peers. Thomas Edison had a learning disability. These extraordinary people were not limited by their disabilities. Throughout this book, we highlight the individual first and the disability second by our phrasing "student with a disability." We do this because language shapes expectations and expectations shape actions. Our persistent theme is that students with mild disabilities are more like their peers than different from them. This is the most important lesson you can learn from reading this book. Your language, your expectations, and your actions when you teach students with mild disabilities will determine their success or failure. Remember, a disability is a problem that can be overcome; don't handicap your students by limiting your expectations for their personal and academic growth.

Litigation and Legislation

Prior to the early 1970s, handicappism, the notion that individuals with disabilities were severely limited in their ability to learn, was the predominant educational perspective. Most notable about this view was that the lack of due process afforded students when educators either excluded them from school or placed them in dead-end special classes. Due process is a constitutional right guaranteed by the Fourteenth Amendment. During the 1970s, concern about the legal rights of students with special needs spurred several significant class action suits that challenged school evaluation and placement practices. A class action suit is litigation on behalf of a class or group of individuals. For example, when a small group of students who were classified as mentally retarded won a class action suit, all other students with mental retardation within the court's jurisdiction benefitted.

In *Diana v. California State Board of Education* (1970), the issue of Mexican American student overrepresentation in special classes for students with mild retardation was addressed. The plaintiffs were nine children who came from homes where Spanish was the primary language. The class action suit alleged that Mexican American students had been improperly categorized as mildly retarded on the basis of invalid IQ testing. In a consent agreement, the opposing parties agreed that schoolchildren should be tested in their native language. This case laid the groundwork for future lawsuits based on cultural bias in educational evaluations.

The following year, 1971, fourteen families sued the State of Pennsylvania on the basis that their children with mental retardation were denied equal access to a public education. This case, *Pennsylvania Association for Retarded Children (PARC) v. Commonwealth of Pennsylvania,* was prompted by the state policy of denying a public education to youngsters with mental retardation. During the legal proceedings, parents described their futile attempts to fight a system that arbitrarily and callously excluded their children from school.

BOX **1.1**

Americans with Disabilities Act

The year 2000 represented a milestone for the nation's disability community, July 26 marked the tenth anniversary of the Americans with Disabilities Act (ADA). The ADA guarantees access, accommodation, and removal of barriers to help people with disabilities fully participate in society. For people with disabilities, the ADA is analogous to the Civil Rights Act of 1964. This law has provided individuals with disabilities a declaration of liberty from the days when they had little hope of competing on a level playing field with their peers without disabilities. It provides the foundation of nondiscrimination against people with disabilities in the areas of employment, state and local governments, public accommodations, and telecommunications.

HIGHLIGHT **1.1**

Francis

Francis enjoyed going out to eat with his friends. However, he often encountered difficulties because few restaurants were accessible to his wheelchair. Curbs, narrow doors, stairs, and small public restrooms were all obstacles for Francis. One evening Francis and his friends were ordering dinner. When the waitress came to Francis, she asked one of his friends, "What would he like to eat?" The waitress assumed that because Francis was in a wheelchair he was incapable of ordering his own dinner! Just as physical obstacles impaired Francis's ability to live a normal life, so did stereotypes by well-meaning but thoughtless people. A disability is born but society handicaps.

Nancy Beth Bowman was expelled from kindergarten because she wasn't toilet trained. The fifteen-year-old daughter of Leonard Kalish was never allowed to enroll in school. It cost him $40,000 to have her educated in private schools. The parents of David Tupi said their son was expelled from school without notice. One morning the school bus just stopped coming to pick him up. The three-judge panel, in a consent decree, ruled that the state could not predetermine educability. In their decision the judges stated that Pennsylvania must:

1. Admit all children with mental retardation into public school.
2. Place students with mental retardation in regular classrooms when possible.
3. Make all school records accessible to parents.
4. Provide preschool programs for children with mental retardation when such programs were available to nondisabled children.
5. Precede all placement decisions with a hearing to allow parental participation and consent.

The PARC decision emphasized the due process rights of parents to review and challenge placement decisions regarding their children.

In *Mills v. The Board of Education of the District of Columbia* (1972), litigants challenged the exclusion of children identified as mentally retarded, emotionally disturbed, learning disabled, visually impaired, hearing impaired, and physically disabled from Washington, D.C., schools. As in the PARC case, Mills demonstrated the unconstitutionality of school exclusion procedures. Both the *PARC* and *Mills* "right to education" cases highlighted the right of students with disabilities to due process in educational decisions.

By 1973, thirty-one similar court cases constituted a groundswell of political activism on behalf of students with disabilities (Taylor & Searle, 1987). It was clear to Congress that schools could no longer be allowed to violate the Fourteenth Amendment rights of students with disabilities. The Fourteenth Amendment states that "no state shall make or enforce any law which shall abridge the privileges or immunities of citizens of the United States; nor shall any state deprive any person of life, liberty, or property without due process of law."

Federal Laws

No otherwise qualified individual with a disability . . . shall, solely by reason of her or his disability, be excluded from participation in, be denied the benefits of, or be subjected to discrimination under any program or activity receiving Federal financial assistance . . . . [Language of Section 504 of the Rehabilitation Act: 29 U.S.C. 794(a) (1996)]

Section 504 is a brief but powerful provision of the Rehabilitation Act of 1973 that extends to individuals with disabilities the same kind of protection extended to individuals discriminated against on the basis of race and gender (Huefner, 2000). Originally targeted at employment discrimination, the scope of Section 504 is broad, addressing protection in many areas (e.g., public school education, higher education, social services, health care, transportation). Because most school districts in the country accept federal funds, public education was greatly influenced by Section 504.

The relationship between Section 504, the Americans with Disabilities Act (ADA), the Individuals with Disabilities Education Act, and the No Child Left Behind Act is presented in Table 1.1. Basically, any person with a disability (i.e., physical or mental impairment that limits major life activities) is eligible for Section 504 assistance. This group is broader than the group eligible for federal assistance under IDEA and special education guidelines (i.e., all students with disabilities receiving assistance under IDEA are eligible for 504 support, but not all students receiving assistance under 504 are eligible for support under IDEA).

Individuals with Disabilities Education Act

The culmination of many years of struggle on behalf of children with disabilities occurred on November 29, 1975, when President Ford signed Public Law 94–142, the Education for All Handicapped Children Act (EHA). This landmark federal legislation mandated a free, appropriate education for students with disabilities aged 3 to 21. The EHA has been called the "first compulsory special education law," and much of what happens in special education today is a direct response to the provisions embodied in it (Ysseldyke, Algozzine, & Thurlow, 2000). Since first enacted, the EHA has been amended to further emphasize the rights of individuals with disabilities and their families. Today EHA is known as the Individuals with Disabilities Education Act (IDEA). Despite the name change and other amendments, the basic rights and provisions it afforded students with disabilities and their families have remained largely the same: the right to an individualized education program, the right to protection in evaluation procedures, the right to due process, and the right to education in the least restrictive environment.

text continues on page 16

TABLE 1.1   Scope of Key Legislation Affecting Students with Disabilities

---

Individuals with Disabilities Education Improvement Act (IDEA) (2004)

The education act to reauthorize federal financial assistance to state and local education agencies to guarantee special education and related services to eligible children with disabilities.

Who Is Protected?	Children ages 3–21 who are determined by a multidisciplinary team to be eligible within one or more of thirteen specific categories of disability and who need special education and related services. Categories include autism, deafness, deaf-blindness, hearing impairments, mental retardation, multiple disabilities, orthopedic impairments, other health impairments, serious emotional disturbance, specific learning disabilities, speech or language impairments, traumatic brain injury, and visual impairment.
Responsibility to Provide a Free Appropriate Public Education (FAPE)?	An FAPE is defined to mean special education and related services. Special education means "specially designed instruction, at no cost to the parents, to meet the unique needs of the child with a disability. . . ." Related services are provided if required for the students to benefit from specially designed instruction. States are required to ensure the provision of "full educational opportunity" to all children with disabilities. IDEA requires the development of an Individualized Education Program (IEP) document with specific content and a required number of specific participants at an IEP meeting.
Procedural Safeguards	IDEA requires written notice to parents regarding identification, evaluation, and/or placement. Further, written notice must be made prior to any change in placement. The Act delineates the required components of the written notices.
Due Process	IDEA delineates specific requirements for local education agencies to provide impartial hearings for parents who disagree with the identification, evaluation, or placement of a child.

No Child Left Behind Act (2002)

Signed into law in 2002, this new law contains sweeping changes in the Elementary and Secondary Education Act. The Act contains four basic education reform principles.

Responsibility to Provide a System for Educational Accountability	States create their own standards for what students should learn in each grade. Beginning in 2002–2003 states began testing students in grades 3–5, 6–9, and 10–12. By 2005–2006 tests must be administered in grades 3–8 in math and reading. All students including

(continues)

TABLE 1.1   Continued

	those with mild disabilities are to be held to the same curriculum and assessment standards.
Who Is Protected?	Federal aid is contingent on an increase in proficiency in math, reading, and science among all students. States must maintain goals and assess results for various categories of students based on poverty, ethnicity, disability, and limited English proficiency.
Procedural Safeguards	Students attending Title I schools that fail to improve have the option to attend a better school in the same district.
Due Process	Schools have more flexibility in allocating resources and teacher professional development. Students who choose to attend persistently failing schools can use Title I funds to obtain supplemental educational services from public or private sectors.

Americans with Disabilities Act of 1990 (ADA)

A civil rights law to prohibit discrimination solely on the basis of disability in employment, public services, and accommodations.

Who Is Protected?	Any individual with a disability who: (1) has a physical or mental impairment that substantially limits one or more life activities; or (2) has a record of such an impairment; or (3) is regarded as having such an impairment. Further, the person must be qualified for the program, service, or job.
Responsibility to Provide a Free Appropriate Public Education (FAPE)?	Not directly. However, (1) ADA protections apply to nonsectarian private schools, but not to organizations or entities controlled by religious organizations; (2) ADA provides additional protection in combination with actions brought under Section 504 and IDEA. Reasonable accommodations are required for eligible students with a disability to perform essential functions of the job. This applies to any part of the special education program that may be community-based and involve job training/placement.
Procedural Safeguards	The ADA does not specify procedural safeguards related to special education; it does detail the administrative requirements, complaint procedures, and the consequences for noncompliance, related to both services and employment.
Due Process	The ADA does not delineate specific due process procedures. People with disabilities have the same remedies that are available under Title VII of the Civil Rights Act of 1964, as amended by the Civil Rights Act of 1991.

TABLE 1.1   Continued

Thus, individuals who are discriminated against may file a complaint with the relevant federal agency or sue in federal court. Enforcement agencies encourage informal mediation and voluntary compliance.

Section 504 of the Rehabilitation Act of 1973

A civil rights law to prohibit discrimination solely on the basis of disability in programs and activities, public and private, that receive federal financial assistance.

Who Is Protected?	Any person who (1) has a physical or mental impairment that substantially limits one or more major life activities, (2) has a record of such an impairment, or (3) is regarded as having such an impairment. Major life activities include walking, seeing, hearing, speaking, breathing, learning, working, caring for oneself, and performing manual tasks.
Responsibility to Provide a Free Appropriate Public Education (FAPE)?	Yes. An "appropriate" education means an education comparable to that provided to students without disabilities. This may be defined as regular or special education services. Students can receive related services under Section 504 even if they are not provided any special education. Section 504 does require development of a plan, although this written document is not mandated. The Individualized Education Program (IEP) of IDEA may be used for the Section 504 written plan. Many experts recommend that a group of persons knowledgeable about the students convene and specify the agreed-upon services.
Procedural Safeguards	Section 504 requires notice to parents regarding identification, evaluation, and/or placement. Written notice is recommended. Notice must be made only before a "significant change" in placement. Following IDEA procedural safeguards is one way to meet Section 504 mandates.
Due Process	Section 504 requires local education agencies to provide impartial hearings for parents who disagree with the identification, evaluation, or placement of a student. It requires that parents have an opportunity to participate in the hearing process and to be represented by counsel. Beyond this, due process details are left to the discretion of the local education agency. It is recommended that districts develop policy guidance and procedures.

Source: Adapted from ERIC Digest E537, Henderson, K. (1995).

By law, school personnel must prepare an **individualized education program** (IEP) for every student receiving special education services. The IEP must include certain information about the child and the educational program designed to meet his or her unique needs. In a nutshell, this information is (U.S. Department of Education, 2000):

- **Current performance.** The IEP must state how the child is currently doing in school (known as present levels of educational performance). This information usually comes from the evaluation results such as classroom tests and assignments, individual tests given to decide eligibility for services or during reevaluation, and observations made by parents, teachers, and related service providers. The statement about "current performance" includes how the child's disability affects his or her involvement and progress in general education.

- **Annual goals.** These are goals that the child can reasonably accomplish in a year. Goals may be academic, address social or behavioral needs, relate to physical needs, or address other educational needs. The goals must be measurable—meaning that it must be possible to measure whether the student has achieved the goals.

- **Special education and related services.** The IEP must list the special education and related services to be provided to the child or on behalf of the child. This includes supplementary aids and services that the child needs. It also includes modifications (changes) to the program or supports for school personnel—such as training or professional development—that will be provided to assist the child.

- **Participation with students without disabilities.** The IEP must explain the extent (if any) to which the child will *not* participate with children without disabilities in the general class and other school activities.

- **Participation in state and district-wide tests.** Local educational agencies must measure student progress with state- or district-wide assessments used for students without disabilities.

- **Dates and places.** The IEP must state when services will begin, how often they will be provided, where they will be provided, and how long they will last.

- **Transition service needs.** Beginning when the child is age 16 (or younger, if appropriate), the IEP must state what transition services are needed to help the child prepare for leaving school.

- **Discipline.** When disciplining students with disabilities, a school must determine if the behavior was a result of the disability before taking action.

By law, students with disabilities and their families are guaranteed rights of **due process.** This means that these students and their families have the same Fourteenth Amendment rights enjoyed by all citizens. School personnel cannot change the educational placement of students with disabilities without the informed consent (i.e., written permission) of the students' parents or guardians.

Parents are also entitled to independent assessments and impartial hearings when decisions about their children are being made. If needed, states must provide mediation services to resolve disputes with families regarding special education services.

By law, students with disabilities must be educated in the **least restrictive environment**. This means that students with disabilities should be educated to the maximum extent feasible with students without disabilities. Students with disabilities receive special education in a variety of settings. Some are enrolled full time in general education classes and receive only indirect services from special education personnel. Some students with mild disabilities are pulled out of their general education classes daily to go to resource rooms for special education services. Still others are enrolled in self-contained special education classes but, to the maximum extent possible, attend general education classes for part of the school day for certain kinds of instruction. For example, a student might be enrolled in a special class but attend a general education class for instruction in math, music, art, or physical education. Figure 1.1 lists key provisions of IDEA. In addition to IDEA, other significant federal legislation promotes the rights and services for individuals with disabilities. The mandate for a free, appropriate public education for adults with disabilities is also paralleled in the Vocational Rehabilitation Act of 1973 (P.L. 93–112). Section 504 of this act made it illegal for institutions or organizations that receive federal funds to discriminate against citizens with disabilities.

FIGURE 1.1 **Major Provisions of IDEA**

Due Process Provisions
Right to examine all pupil records
Right to independent assessment of pupil
Right to written notice of any program change
Right to impartial hearing on any school decisions

Protection in Evaluation Provisions (PEP)
Right to individual assessment before placement
Right to assessment with appropriate instruments
Right to unbiased assessment and team decisions

Individualized Education Program (IEP) Provisions
Right to written statement of present functioning
Right to written statement of goals
Right to written statement of services expected
Right to written statement of expected time frame
Right to participate in program development

Least Restrictive Environment (LRE) Provisions
Right to education in general education classroom to the maximum feasible extent

In 1990, Congress amended the EHA in several significant ways. The Individuals with Disabilities Education Act (IDEA) (Public Law 101–476) replaced the original title of the law. The name change reflects the need to emphasize the person first and the disability second. Amendments in IDEA included an expansion of related services such as therapeutic recreation, social work services, and rehabilitation counseling. Transition services were mandated to be written into individual education plans (IEPs). Transition services begin at age sixteen. These services coordinate rehabilitative services—for example, supported employment and independent living—beyond the school years. The purchase or leasing of customized equipment to support educational services (e.g., computers, wheelchairs, adaptive equipment) is also authorized by this federal law. The Individuals with Disabilities Education Act adds students with autism and traumatic brain injury to the list of populations provided special education.

By now it should be clear that legal mandates to educate and provide services to individuals with disabilities have been the driving force to provide equal opportunities for all school-aged children. The Individuals with Disabilities Education Act is continually being reviewed in state and federal courts. For example, overrepresentation of African American students in special classes and the use of IQ tests to identify African-Americans and Latinos as mildly retarded have been scrutinized by federal courts. Such key provisions as "appropriate education" and "nondiscriminatory assessment" also have spurred important judicial decisions. Table 1.2 lists some court cases that have shaped refinements of special education services to students with mild disabilities.

Unreported in the special education data are at-risk students who may or may not have received some type of compensatory education. At-risk is the name used for students who fall through the cracks between special education and general education. Unless a student is found eligible under IDEA for learning disabilities, behavior disorders, or mental retardation (or other exceptionality listed in IDEA), the youngster is not required to have an individualized educational program. The 2004 reauthorization of IDEA allows schools to use up to 15 percent of special education funds for underperforming students in general education classrooms.

Several categories of children with disabilities are at risk. Even though they have a condition or a documented disability, they may not be eligible for special education as defined in IDEA. For instance, a child with an emotional disorder may not meet the federal criteria for "intensity and degree."

Many students are protected under Section 504 of the Rehabilitation Act and the Americans with Disabilities Act (ADA). However, they are not covered by the stringent procedural safeguards available under IDEA. The safeguards include the right to remain in the current placement, nondiscriminatory evaluation, an individualized educational plan, an impartial determination as to the appropriate placement, and other due process protections (Rothstein, 1995).

Youth with social maladjustments (e.g., incarcerated youth) do not qualify for special education under IDEA unless a disability is documented. There is disagreement over whether to identify or even attempt to separate youth with

TABLE 1.2   Selected Judicial Decisions Since Passage of Public Law 94–142 Focus on Students with Mild Disabilities

1975   *Issac Lora et al. v. The Board of Education of New York et al.* Nondiscriminatory assessment procedures must be used when placing minority students with emotional problems in special education programs.

1976   *Frederich L. v. Thomas* (Philadelphia). Class action suit that reaffirmed the right of students with learning disabilities to have appropriate education programs.

1979   *Larry P. v. Riles* (California). Intelligence tests banned in California when assessing African American students as mildly retarded. Disproportionate numbers of African American students were placed in special classes for the mildly retarded.

1981   *Luke S. and Hans S. v. Nixe et al.* (Louisiana). Prereferral interventions, curriculum-based assessment, and direct classroom interventions were mandated for students with mild disabilities.

1982   *Board of Education of the Henrick Hudson School System v. Rowley.* This Supreme Court decision clarified "appropriate" education by determining that the intent of P.L. 94–142 is to open the doors of public schools to students with disabilities, not to provide opportunities for students to reach maximum potential. Due process procedures to determine an appropriate education were reaffirmed by the Court.

1984   *Smith v. Robinson.* Supreme Court decision that restricted the ability of students and their families to recover legal fees incurred in due process hearings. This decision was negated in 1986 when Congress passed the Handicapped Children's Protection Act, which restored the courts' authority to award legal fees to parents who succeed in lawsuits or administrative hearings.

1984   *Marshall et al. v. Georgia.* Judge Edenfiel ruled that the overrepresentation of African Americans in special classes was not discriminatory. In his view, lower socioeconomic conditions rather than discriminatory assessment and placement practices was the reason African American students were placed in programs for the mildly mentally retarded. This was the first court case that highlighted the need to include a measure of adaptive behavior within the classroom as part of the criteria for determining mild mental retardation.

1985   *Burlington v. Department of Education, Massachusetts.* The Supreme Court found that parents had the right to public school reimbursement of private school tuition if the public school program rejected by parents was inappropriate.

1988   *Honig v. Doe.* Supreme Court decreed that school systems may not unilaterally exclude children with disabilities from the classroom for dangerous or disruptive behavior. Any programmatic changes because of behavior disturbances must follow due process procedures outlined in P.L. 94–142. In drastic situations the school can suspend a student for up to ten days.

1989   *Daniel R. R. v. State Board of Education.* District and appeals court upheld hearing officer's decision that general education curriculum was beyond abilities of a student with retardation and that he would receive little benefit from mainstreaming. The courts found that for some children placement in general education environment would not provide a free appropriate education.

1990   *Moore v. District of Columbia.* Reversing an earlier decision, federal appeals court ruled that prevailing parents were entitled to recover attorney fees when a final resolution of their special education dispute came at the administrative hearing level.

(continues)

TABLE 1.2   Continued

1993   *Zobrest v. Catalina Foothills School District.* The court held that provision of a sign language interpreter in a parochial school was not an entitlement under IDEA; the decision was reversed in a finding that services of an interpreter were part of a general government program that distributed benefits to any child qualifying for services regardless of the school the student attended.

1997   *K.R. v. Anderson Community School Corp.* The Seventh Circuit court decided that a student with severe disabilities was not entitled to a publicly funded personal assistant while attending a parochial school. The ruling set forth that under the IDEA, students with disabilities who choose to attend religious school need not receive the full range of services they would receive if they attended public school, but they must receive some services.

1999   *Cedar Rapids Community School District v. Garret F.* During the school day, Garret required services of a specially trained nurse because of his health needs. The school district, believing that they were not obligated under IDEA to provide continuous nursing care, refused to provide the services. The Supreme Court held that the school district had to pay for the nursing services required by Garret when he was at school.

2003   *Lewisville Independent School District v. Charles W. and Gay W. ex rel. Charles W.* The Fifth U.S. Circuit Court of Appeals determined that an intellectually superior seventh grader with pervasive developmental disorder received FAPE, despite the parents' belief the child could make better grades and should attend a private school for children with disabilities. The court determined that his IEP was individualized, addressed all his special needs, and resulted in both academic and nonacademic progress.

2004   *C.J. v. Indian River County School Board.* The court agreed with the hearing officer's determination that a student presenting with bipolar disorder and oppositional defiance disorder was not eligible for special education since there was no support for a finding of emotional disturbance. While the student exhibited behavior and feelings that were inappropriate under normal circumstances, the behaviors were intermittent in the school setting. The student's behavioral problems, suspensions, and hospitalizations did not interfere with her learning and she performed well, above average in most of her classes. Unilateral placement in a residential facility was largely for noneducational reasons.

social maladjustments from other youth who meet the federal definition of emotional disturbance.

Another category of children who require significant assistance in schools, but for whom there is no category in special education, are those with attention deficit/hyperactivity disorders. In order to assess public opinion about whether attention deficit/hyperactivity disorders (ADHD) should be a separate special education disability, the 1990 amendments to IDEA required that the Department of Education solicit comments about the issue. It was decided that this condition would not become a separate disability category under IDEA. Several reasons were given, including the fact that many youngsters with ADHD qualify for special education services as learning disabled. Some youngsters with ADHD receive special education services under the category "Other Health Impairments."

Youth who are addicted to drugs and alcohol are protected under IDEA only if they qualify for special education and related services under one of the disability categories. These students, like other categories described, are at risk, and while they do not qualify for special education under IDEA, they are entitled to protection under Section 504 of the Rehabilitation Act or the Americans with Disabilities Act, referred to as ADA. Only the slow learner is not protected under IDEA, Section 504, or the ADA.

What determines whether a person is entitled to protection under Section 504? The individual must meet the definition of a person with a disability, which is

> any person who (i) has a physical or mental impairment which substantially limits one or more of such person's major life activities, (ii) has a record of such an impairment, or (iii) is regarded as having such an impairment.

If the person meets the definition of a person with a disability under Section 504, "reasonable accommodations" must be made by recipients of federal financial assistance. Public school systems receive this assistance, so teachers must make accommodations that are educationally beneficial for these students. The usual remedy when a violation of Section 504 is proved is the termination of federal assistance, which means loss of federal funding to the school system.

No Child Left Behind Act

On January 8, 2002, President Bush signed into law the No Children Left Behind Act (NCLB). This reauthorization of the Elementary and Secondary Education Act set challenging new academic standards for the education of America's youth. The act is based on four education reform principles:

1. Stronger school accountability is needed for student improved learning.
2. Local schools need increased flexibility in order to respond to specific student needs.
3. Expanded options should be made available to parents.
4. Teaching methods should have a strong positive research basis. (www.nclb .gov/next/overview/index.html) (Retrieved 3/20/2003)

Throughout the 670-page document a central theme is repeated—schools and teachers are accountable for the academic achievement of *all* students including those who receive special education services. Some highlights of NCLB in relationship to special education students are:

1. Students with disabilities must be included in each state's new accountability system.
2. State plans must be coordinated with the Individuals with Disabilities Education Act.

3. Academic standards apply to all students including those with disabilities.
4. Special education students must meet each state's proficient level of academic achievement by 2014.
5. States must report graduation rates for students with disabilities and at least one other academic indicator.

Who Receives Special Education?

In the United States, school-aged children with disabilities are entitled to a free, appropriate public education. It is illegal to discriminate against individuals with disabilities. An individual cannot be denied an education or a job because of a disability. *Special education is mandated to provide services to students who have been identified as unable to progress effectively in the general classroom as a result of that disability.* It is important to note that the presence of a disability alone is not sufficient reason to initiate special education services. Special education is warranted only after all attempts to help a youngster within the confines of the general classroom have proved ineffective.

In the first textbook dealing with the "education of exceptional children," Horn (1924) observed that mental, temperamental, and physical differences were the bases for some students needing special education. Today, many states organize their special education departments along similar categorical lines. A category is a descriptor or label assigned to a group of students. Although the names of the categories vary slightly from state to state, special education is generally provided for children within each of the following categories:

1. Students with visual impairments or blindness.
2. Students with hearing impairments or deafness.
3. Students with deafness and blindness.
4. Students with orthopedic impairments.
5. Students with multiple disabilities.
6. Students with language or speech impairments.
7. Students with learning disabilities.
8. Students with behavior disorders or emotional disturbances.
9. Students with mental retardation.
10. Students with autism.
11. Students with traumatic brain injury.
12. Students with developmental delay.
13. Students with health impairments.

Physical Reasons for Needing Special Education

Special learning needs in areas of physical abilities (e.g., seeing, hearing, moving) are the basis for several categories of students with special needs. Most of us take normal vision and hearing for granted. The expression "20/20 vision" is used to describe normal visual functioning. Vision is measured by having people read letters or discriminate objects at a distance of twenty feet. The task is not difficult for most people. There are people, however, who must stand closer to see what others see easily from twenty feet away. These differences in visual functioning are the basis of deciding whether a student is blind or visually impaired. There are also people who even at a louder volume cannot hear what can easily be heard by the majority. Between normal hearing and deafness are various degrees of hearing loss, and it is these differences in degrees of hearing that are the basis for another category of exceptional students (i.e., deaf or hearing impaired).

How different does vision or hearing have to be before a person is considered blind or deaf? A person who, even with correction (e.g., glasses), must be twenty feet from a target that a person with normal vision can see at two hundred feet or more is considered blind. People with corrected vision better than 20/200 but not better than 20/70 are considered *visually impaired*. Ability to hear is measured along two scales: intensity and frequency. Intensity or loudness is measured in decibels (dB), and frequency or pitch is measured in hertz (cycles per second). Moores defines deaf and hard of hearing in terms of the effects on hearing loss:

> A deaf person is one whose hearing is disabled to an extent (usually 70 dB or greater) that precludes the understanding of speech through the ear alone, without or with the use of a hearing aid. A hard of hearing person is one whose hearing is disabled to an extent (usually 35–69 dB) that makes difficult, but does not preclude, the understanding of speech through the ear alone, without or with a hearing aid. (Moores, 1982)

For practical purposes, deafness means the absence of hearing in both ears; people with deafness have great difficulty hearing conversational speech without the assistance of a hearing aid. People with hearing impairments experience significant difficulty in hearing.

There are other disabling conditions that are of a physical nature. For example, *arthritis* is a measurable inflammation of a joint that limits movement. *Cerebral palsy* is impaired motor function due to brain damage; it produces difficulties in motor control that are observable in movement of large and small muscle groups. *Seizure disorder* (i.e., epilepsy) is also a brain disorder that results in convulsive episodes and periods of unconsciousness. Other health impairments include severe orthopedic problems that adversely affect educational performance and limit strength, vitality, or alertness. Special education may be provided to people with physical differences caused by congenital anomalies (e.g., spina bifida) as well as other general health and physical problems (e.g., heart disease, asthma, diabetes, traumatic brain injury, autism).

Cognitive Reasons for Needing Special Education

Differences in intellectual performance or mental abilities are the bases for identifying a special need. To be considered mentally retarded, an individual must demonstrate subaverage intellectual functioning and delayed social development. Intelligence tests are frequently used to determine if an individual's intellectual performance is below that of peers. Students with scores from 75–50 on an intelligence test fall within the mild range of mental retardation. Students with more complex forms of mental retardation are categorized as mildly, moderately, severely, or profoundly disabled. Besides the differences in severity linked to IQ scores, students with moderate to profound mental retardation usually have communication and health problems. We refer to these students as having a developmental disability because they have serious physical and medical complications that are identified by a physician at birth or soon afterwards.

Students with intellectual disabilities demonstrate deficits in adaptive behavior (i.e., social development). Adaptive behavior generally refers to the way in which an individual functions in his or her community. As with intelligence tests, adaptive behavior evaluations are based on age-group comparisons. Formalized inventories of functional abilities (such as dressing oneself, using the telephone, or independently moving about the neighborhood) help educational evaluators determine adaptive behavior. Any determination of mental retardation must include a measure of intelligence and a measure of adaptive behavior skills.

Just as there are students with low intelligence test scores, there also are students whose intellectual performance is above that of their classmates.

HIGHLIGHT 1.2

Evan is a fourteen-year-old resident of a Catholic residential facility for youngsters who require child care in Syracuse, New York. Tall and athletic, Evan is a leader among the other boys. Mark Costello, a first-year child care worker, describes his response to Evan's invitation to come see the puzzle he has just completed.

As Evan led me over to a card table sitting in the middle of the living room, it was obvious how proud he was of his accomplishment. Eager to lavish him with praise, I looked down at the table to see the three-hundred jigsaw pieces carefully connected after many evenings of effort. Pride quickly turned to confusion, however, when it became apparent that the picture was face down on the card table.

"What picture, Mr. Cos?" Evan asked.

"Do you see the picture on the top of the box the pieces came in, my friend?" I asked.

"Sure, what about it?"

"Well, that picture is now upside down on this card table and you old buddy, have just completed one heck of a tough task."

While the other boys were trying to read Evan's reaction to this perplexing bit of news, I began to internalize my first real lesson about the significance of mental retardation. Naive but determined, he had stuck to a task few if any youths of normal intelligence could tolerate. Was this just a glimpse of his true potential? How hard it was that night to convince Evan of how proud we were of his somewhat tarnished accomplishment.

Historically, giftedness was determined by high IQ test scores. This approach is no longer favored by many educators because intelligence tests sample too narrow a range of abilities. Creativity, musical talent, leadership skills, and problem-solving abilities are a sample of talents not measurable through intelligence testing. More recently, experts in the field of giftedness recommend a multidimensional approach to establishing criteria for identification of students with special gifts or talents. According to Renzulli, Reis, and Smith (1981), in order to be identified as gifted, students should demonstrate:

1. High ability including measured intelligence evaluation.
2. Creativity in the development and implementation of innovative ideas.
3. High task commitment—perseverance or diligence.

Students with special talents are not disabled; consequently, they do not receive federally mandated special education. Four groups of students are underrepresented in gifted education programs: culturally different, female, disabled, and underachieving (Patton, Kauffman, Blackbourn, & Brown, 1991).

How different do measures of intelligence have to be before an individual is considered mentally retarded or gifted? Differences in scores on intelligence tests and measures of adaptive behavior are evaluated in the same way as differences in scores on hearing, vision, or physical performance tests. Standards for normal intelligence and adaptive behavior are set by testing large groups of individuals. Professionals then set criteria for retardation or giftedness that are based on differences from mean intelligence or adaptive behavior ratings. For example, the common standard for normal performance is a score of 90–110 on an intelligence test; scores below 75 or above 130 are generally considered indicative of mental retardation and giftedness. It is important to remember that special education services for students identified as gifted are not mandated by federal legislation. Figure 1.2 traces the normal curve distribution of IQ scores.

Academic Reasons for Needing Special Education

With the categories of mental retardation and gifted, it is assumed that the individual's performance on achievement tests will be consistent with the performance on intelligence tests. This means that if a student obtains a high score on an intelligence test, high performance on an achievement test is also expected. If students perform poorly on intelligence tests, it is expected that their achievement test scores will also be low. There are students whose performance on achievement tests is not consistent with their performance on intelligence tests. When the difference between ability (e.g., intelligence test performance) and achievement (e.g., reading, math) is significant, the student may be identified as learning disabled. Students with learning disabilities comprise one-half of the entire special education population.

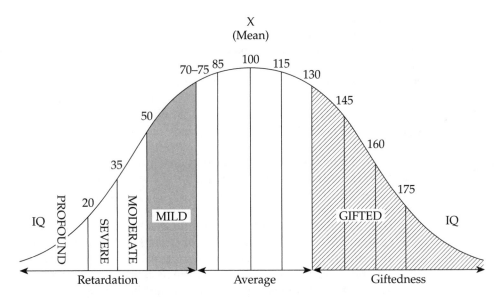

X
(Mean)

FIGURE 1.2   **Normal Curve Distribution of IQ Scores**

How different do scores on ability tests and scores on achievement tests have to be before a student is classified as learning disabled? Although officials of the federal government have provided guidelines for use in identifying students with learning disabilities, no specific criteria have been provided for judging when discrepancies between ability and achievement are severe enough to call a student learning disabled.

Students are considered eligible for special education if they meet guidelines spelled out in state regulations. Due to a lack of consistent criteria between and within states, it is likely that many students in special education programs for students with learning disabilities are misidentified. African American students are underrepresented in the learning disability category.

Communication Reasons for Needing Special Education

Just as there are differences in the reading, writing, and mathematical skills of students, there are also differences in the ways students speak and express themselves. Some people speak clearly, enunciating each part of their speech. Others speak quickly, making it difficult for listeners to understand them. Some children use speech as a means of making their desires, feelings, and opinions known. Others are less adept at verbalizing personal needs. There are accepted ages at which children are expected to demonstrate the use of various forms of communication. For example, most children understand approximately one thousand words, combine their words into simple sentences, and understand concepts related to language (e.g., on, off, later) by the time they are two years old. By the age of seven, children are expected to use culturally acceptable grammar when speaking; language at this age is much like that used by family and friends. Differences in language and communication skills are measured by performance on tests and classroom observations of student interaction. Differences in language development and communication skills are commonly observed in children of all ages. When these differences adversely affect educational performance, the individual may be entitled to special services provided for students with language impairments.

How different does language have to be before a student is considered language impaired? Many students in this category receive special services for such problems as lisping, stuttering, and mispronunciation of individual words (e.g., they say "wabbit" instead of "rabbit," "pasketti" instead of "spaghetti," or "bud" for "bird"). Some of these students have voice tones that are too low, too high, too nasal, too harsh, or too hoarse. There are no absolute standards for determining when an individual's speech is "too" nasal or "too" harsh or when it will adversely affect educational performance. When speech mannerisms cause difficulties for the listener, a student may be referred for speech therapy. Some teachers are more adept than others at understanding differences in the language produced by their students. Similarly, the context in which speech occurs influences the judgments made about it. Recent government figures indicate that there are more students in this category than in any other besides learning disabilities. This is probably not surprising for a category based on differences in speech clarity or tone.

Behavioral–Emotional Reasons for Needing Special Education

Just as standards for normal intellectual performance have evolved within the educational system, standards for how students should act in school and society also have evolved. Standards for normal behavior are based more on what is judged acceptable in a specific setting than on judgments about how an individual performs on a test. Demonstrating intellectual performance that is sufficiently above or below normal is the basis for being identified as gifted or mentally retarded. Demonstrating unacceptable behavior in school is the basis for being identified with behavior disorders or emotional disturbance.

Just how different does behavior have to be before a student is considered behaviorally disordered or emotionally disturbed? Based on what you have learned about the other conditions of special education, your answer may be "behavior that is significantly different from the behavior of their peers." You are right, but you will have trouble explaining behavioral differences. There are no numerical standards for normal behavior. There are no tests to measure the normality of behavior. Classroom observations by teachers carry the most weight in identifying students with emotional/behavior disorders. However, what is acceptable behavior for one classroom may not be acceptable in another, and what is acceptable behavior for one teacher is not necessarily acceptable for another.

Many students with emotional problems sit undetected in general education classrooms. While one percent of students receive special education services because of emotional disturbance, mental health experts estimate that from six to ten percent of the school-aged population have an emotional problem serious enough to warrant mental health care. Chief among these emotional problems are depression, post-traumatic stress disorder secondary to abuse and attention deficit disorder with hyperactivity (Forness, 2001).

How Many Students Receive Special Education?

Since 1976–77, the Department of Education has maintained a database on the number of children with disabilities served in special education programs. In 1990, several of the disability category labels were revised: learning disabled was changed to specific learning disabilities, mentally retarded became mental retardation, and hard-of-hearing and deaf were combined to become hearing impairments; in subsequent regulations, multihandicapped was changed to multiple disabilities.

Approximately six million students aged 3 to 21 receive special education services in public school or private settings (Twenty-fourth Annual Report to Congress, 2002). In thinking about the number of students involved, consider that it is about the same as the total full-time undergraduate enrollment in all United States colleges and universities. The number of students who receive special education is more than the combined population of North Dakota, South Dakota, Montana, Nevada, Idaho, and Wyoming.

There has been a steady increase in the number of students aged 6–21 receiving special education services. In 1992, 4,499,824 school-aged students were placed in special education programs. By 2001 the overall figure had increased to 5,775,722 students. (See Table 1.3.) Including the 599,678 students aged 3 through 5 who received preschool services, the total students in special education in 2001 amounted to 6,375,400. The average cost to educate a student with a disability is $12,639 per year (U.S. Department of Education, 2002). Reasons for the increase in students identified as having special needs include the following:

1. A high swing in the poverty rate, resulting in more children coming to school with problems.
2. An increase in cultural and linguistic diversity in the schools.
3. An increase in the numbers of students identified with specific learning disabilities.
4. The addition of new categories of students eligible for special education.
5. Variations in school referral and evaluation procedures.

Special education's growth has increased the demand for special education teachers (U.S. Department of Education, 1999).

The growth of special education services has caused other problems. For example, school personnel have to decide how to pay for the increasing num-

TABLE 1.3 Number of Students Ages 6 Through 21 Served Under IDEA During 1991–92 and 2000–01

Disability	1991–92	2000–01	Percent Change in Number
Specific learning disabilities	2,247,004	2,887,217	28.5
Speech or language impairments	998,904	1,093,808	9.5
Mental retardation	553,262	612,978	10.8
Emotional disturbance	400,211	473,663	18.4
Multiple disabilities	98,408	122,559	24.5
Hearing impairments	60,727	70,767	16.5
Orthopedic impairments	51,389	73,057	42.2
Other health impairments	58,749	291,850	396.8
Visual impairments	24,083	25,975	7.9
Autism	5,415	78,749	1,354.3
Deaf-blindness	1,427	1,320	–7.5
Traumatic brain injury	245	14,844	5,958.8
Developmental delay	—	28,935	—
All disabilities	4,499,824	5,775,722	28.4

Note: Reporting in the autism and traumatic brain injury categories was optional in 1991–92 and required beginning in 1992–93. Table does not include students aged 3–5.

Source: U.S. Department of Education, Office of Special Education Programs, Data Analysis System (DANS).

bers of students. Since the cost of educating students with special needs may come at the expense of educating students in general education, school personnel face hard choices when allocating funds. The growth of special education is directly attributed to passage of the Individuals with Disabilities Education Act, which mandates a "free and appropriate public education" for all students with disabilities.

For years many school districts organized their special education programs along categorical lines (e.g., emotionally disturbed, learning disabled). Recently public schools have made a greater effort to include students with disabilities in general education classrooms. The "inclusion" movement is based on the premise that students with disabilities will make better progress if they are allowed to learn alongside their nondisabled peers. The 1997 re-authorization of the Individuals with Disabilities Education Act (IDEA) stated that special education students should be educated in general education classrooms to the maximum appropriate extent. Inclusion efforts continue to show results. During the 1984–1985 school year, only twenty-five percent of students with disabilities aged 6–21 spent more than 80 percent of their day in general education classrooms. By 1998–1999, almost half of all students with disabilities spent more than 80 percent of their time in general education classrooms (U.S. Department of Education, 2001). However, the inclusion trend is not without problems. Forty-two percent of general education teachers feel inclusion is "not workable" due to deficiencies in teacher attitude, teacher preparation, and administrative support (Henley, 2004).

Students with Mild Disabilities

Students with mild disabilities are those typically categorized with learning disabilities, mild mental retardation, or emotional/behavioral disorders. Students with language or communication impairments is another large category of mild disabilities; however, because their difficulties are treated by speech clinicians rather than teachers, we have not included information about them in this book.

The term *mild disabilities* is not used to imply that these students do not have serious learning problems or that their problems are less important than those of other students. We think the term has come to be used for this group of students because many of their characteristics overlap and many of them can be educated in general education classrooms.

According to the definition included in the Individuals with Disabilities Education Act, 1990 (U.S. Department of Education, 1990), students with learning disabilities exhibit a disorder in one or more of the basic psychological processes involved in understanding or using spoken or written language. These may be manifested in disorders of listening, thinking, talking, reading, writing, spelling, or arithmetic. Learning disabilities include conditions that historically have been referred to as perceptual handicaps, brain injury, minimal brain dysfunction, dyslexia, and developmental aphasia. They do not include learning problems due primarily to visual, hearing, or motor handicaps, to mental retardation, emotional handicaps, or environmental disadvantages.

Students with mild mental retardation are those with impaired intellectual and adaptive behaviors and whose development reflects a reduced rate of learning. If a student's IQ score is 50–75, and the student's socialization skills are uniformly below age expectations, an evaluation of mild mental retardation is likely.

Students with emotional/behavior disorders are those who exhibit persistent and consistent problems that interrupt their own or others' learning. Sometimes these students are referred to as emotionally disturbed. The term "behavior disordered" is more descriptive of this population of students. Using the term "emotionally disturbed" implies that we know *why* the student is unable to adapt to classroom routines—he or she has an emotional or psychological problem. In fact, this is often not the case. Many students are referred for special education because they are impulsive, distractible, or hyperactive. These behaviors can be caused by any number of factors that have no connection with a student's emotional development. Neurological factors, diet, allergies, delayed development, and ineffective teaching are some explanations for students' inability to control their behavior in a classroom.

We recognize, however, that many students with behavior disorders do, in fact, have emotional problems. There is often overlap among students identified with behavioral disorders and emotional disturbance. Even if the primary cause of a student's behavior problems is diet or allergies, the reaction of others to the disruptive behavior can affect that student's emotional development. Moreover, a student may have an emotional problem and demonstrate no overt behavior disorders. This is a particularly acute problem with adolescents who may be withdrawn or depressed but mask their emotional distress with good grades.

Students classified with learning disabilities, mild mental retardation, or emotional/behavioral disorders account for more than two-thirds of all students with disabilities (U.S. Department of Education, 2001), and they share many characteristics. For example, students with learning disabilities often have problems with reading comprehension, language development, interpersonal relations, and classroom behavioral control (Lerner, 2000). These same characteristics are common in teacher descriptions of students with mild mental retardation and behavioral disorders.

If you find that these characteristics can also be found in students who do not receive special education services, you are correct. It is a thin and sometimes arbitrary line that separates students with mild disabilities from other students. Many classroom problems are interactional: the result of a mismatch between teaching and learning style. The behavior, expectations, and attitude of the general classroom teacher is a key component in determining whether a student is referred and evaluated as having a mild disability. For example, some characteristics of learning disabilities, such as dyslexia (i.e., an impairment in reading ability), are neurologically based; other characteristics, such as distractibility, can be based on teacher perception of student performance. A student with dyslexia will be dyslexic in every classroom; on the other hand, a student identified as distractible and hyperactive in one teacher's classroom may have less difficulty attending in another classroom. How can this happen? Some teachers are more adept at engaging students in their schoolwork than others. In special education, we have learned never to underestimate the power of good teaching to "cure" a mild disability.

Whether or not it helps students with mild disabilities to be categorized is controversial. Over the years, each of the three subgroups of mild disabilities have been separated by distinct identification criteria, different teaching methods, teacher certificates linked to a single disability, and different special education placements. Each category is represented by separate professional organizations and advocacy groups. The American Association for Mental Retardation and the Council of Children with Behavior Disorders are two examples of category-specific organizations. Researchers develop expertise within a single category of mild disabilities and report their findings in journals that specialize in mental retardation, learning disabilities, or behavior disorders.

Yet students who are placed in different categories of mild disabilities share many common traits. Lack of interest in school and low motivation are two traits displayed by many youngsters categorized as having a mild disability. It is also clear that instructional practices proved effective for students in one category of mild disabilities can be useful with students within another category. Such instructional strategies as peer tutoring, whole language, and cooperative learning can help students learn regardless of how their mild disability is categorized.

There are advantages and disadvantages to classifying students by specific categories of mild disabilities. Special educators sometimes use the term "labeling" to describe this categorization process. Is it a good idea to label students? We will present the facts about both sides of this issue. Ultimately you will need to make your own professional decision about labeling students with such terms as mental retardation, learning disabilities, and behavioral disorders. Whether or not to place a student into a mild disability category is an issue you will be faced with throughout your career as a teacher.

Labeling

Students identified as having problems in school either will meet eligibility criteria for special education services or will be unofficially labeled with such negative adjectives as "lazy," "unmotivated," "slow learner," or "behavior problem." In the latter case, neither the teacher nor the student will get help. The student will remain in general education and most likely continue to fail in school. There is an increased probability that the student will eventually drop out of school (see Figure 1.3).

In most states, a student is identified as requiring special education when school evaluation data match the student with a specific disability category that is outlined by state education regulations. This classification process assumes that assigning a student a categorical name implies knowledge about the characteristics of the student's learning problem. This categorical approach to providing help has been roundly criticized by many educators who claim that labeling a student does more harm than good. What students are called determines what services they receive and where they will receive them. Because this classification process alters the school experience of many students, professionals have researched and described the advantages and disadvantages of the labeling associated with it.

Advantages of Labeling

The advantages of labeling were more obvious in the formative years of special education (mid-1940s to early 1970s) than they are now. For instance, without the category of learning disabilities, advocates for these children would have had no rallying point to promote educational programs. Imagine how ineffective scientists would be in raising money for cancer research if we had no name for it. The advantages of labeling can be summarized as follows:

1. Federal and local funding of special education programs are based on categories of disabilities.

FIGURE 1.3   Children with Disabilities Remain at Risk

Although it is true that special education has created a base of civil rights and legal protections, children with disabilities remain at risk of being left behind.

- Young people with disabilities drop out of high school at twice the rate of their peers.
- Enrollment rates of students with disabilities in higher education are still 50 percent lower than enrollment among the general population.
- Most public school educators do not feel well prepared to work with children with disabilities. In 1998, only 21 percent of public school teachers said they felt very well prepared to address the needs of students with disabilities, and another 41 percent said they felt moderately well prepared.
- Of the six million children in special education, half of those who are in special education are identified as having a "specific learning disability." In fact, this group has grown more than 300 percent since 1976.
- Of those with "specific learning disabilities," 80 percent are there simply because they haven't learned how to read. Thus, many children identified for special education—up to 40 percent—are there because they weren't taught to read. The reading difficulties may not be their only area of difficulty, but it's the area that resulted in special education placement. Sadly, few children placed in special education close the achievement gap to a point where they can read and learn like their peers.
- Children of minority status are overrepresented in some categories of special education. African American children are twice as likely as white children to be labeled mentally retarded and placed in special education. They are also more likely to be labeled and placed as emotionally disturbed.

Sources: U.S. Department of Education, 2004; U.S. Department of Education, 2002.

2. Labeling enables professionals to communicate with one another because each categorical label conveys a general idea about learning characteristics.
3. The human mind requires "mental hooks" to think about problems. If present categorical labels were abolished, a new set of descriptors would evolve to take their place. There is ample evidence of this in the evolution of the term "mildly retarded."
4. Labeling the disability spotlights the problem for the general public. Labeling can spark social concern and aid advocacy efforts.
5. Labeling may make the nondisabled majority more tolerant of the disabled minority. In other words, the actions of a child identified as having mental retardation might be tolerated, whereas the behavior of a nondisabled child would be criticized.
6. Labeling has led to the development of specialized teaching methods, assessment approaches, and behavioral interventions that are useful for teachers of all students. (Hallahan & Kauffman, 1982)

Disadvantages of Labeling

Because of the Individuals with Disabilities Education Act, students with disabilities have made significant gains in public schools. These advances have been accompanied by problems inherent in officially designating someone abnormal. Make no mistake about it—these labels stick. Once a child is categorized with mental retardation, behavioral disorders, or learning disabilities, that information will be forwarded to every new teacher in the child's cumulative folder. Along with the label comes the stigma of being considered deficient. For this reason alone, assigning a student to a category for special education purposes is a fateful step that should not be taken unless all other options have proved unsuccessful. The disadvantages of labeling are summarized as follows:

1. Labels shape teacher expectations. Imagine what your reaction would be if the principal informed you that the new student in your class is mildly mentally retarded. Studies on teacher expectations have demonstrated that what teachers believe about student capability is directly related to student achievement.
2. All children have some troubling behaviors. Labels can exaggerate a student's actions in the eyes of a teacher. A teacher may overreact to behavior of a labeled child that would be tolerated in another.
3. Labels send a clear message: the learning problem is with the student. Labels tend to obscure the essence of teaching and learning as a two-way street. Some students placed in a mild disability category have nothing wrong with them. They are the unfortunate recipients of ineffective schooling.
4. Labels perpetuate the notion that students with mild disabilities are qualitatively different from other children. This is not true. Students with mild disabilities go through the same developmental stages as their peers, although sometimes at a slower rate.
5. Teachers may confuse the student with the label. Labels reflect categories of disabilities. Categories are abstract, not real, concepts that are general enough to incorporate many different individuals. Almost two million students are identified as learning disabled, but as individuals, each is a unique human being. When a student is placed in a category, a teacher who knows some of the characteristics of a category may ascribe all known characteristics to each labeled child. This is stereotyping. Stereotypes handicap students when teachers rationalize low achievement by citing characteristics of the label. An example is the teacher who explains away a teaching–learning problem by stating, "We can't really expect Mary to remember too much math because she is mildly retarded."
6. Students cannot receive special education services until they are labeled. In many instances, the intervention comes too late. The need to label students before help arrives undermines a preventive approach to mild learning problems.

7. Diagnostic labels are unreliable. Educational evaluation is filled with quirks. States use different descriptive criteria for the same categories; many evaluation instruments have questionable validity and reliability; specific labels go through trends (for example, at one time learning disabilities was considered a white, middle class affliction, while African American students were overrepresented in the mild mental retardation category).
8. Labels often put the blame (and the guilt) for a student's learning problems squarely on the parents' shoulders. In many cases, this is unjustified because students may be mislabeled or teachers may not fully understand the many different causes of mild disabilities.

Focus on What to Teach Students

The purpose of the Individuals with Disabilities Education Act is to ensure that all students with special needs receive a free and appropriate education. Congress did not define what it meant by the term "appropriate." The legislators recognized that there is no one instructional approach that is best. Instead they viewed "appropriate" as a process rather than a product. Whether or not a program is appropriate is based on the ability of the school system and parents to work out a mutually acceptable individualized education program.

Individual Education Program

An individualized education program (IEP) must be written for each student receiving special education. Special education includes many services related to classroom instruction, such as transportation, occupational therapy, counseling, and adaptive equipment. Assessed instructional needs of each student determine the areas for which an IEP is developed.

Each school district may develop its own IEP format as long as the required information is included. The IEP must be developed within a meeting by participants stipulated by legislation. The IEP Team is a group of individuals composed of:

1. The student's parents or guardians.
2. At least one general education teacher (if the child is, or may be, participating in the general education environment).
3. At least one special education teacher, or, where appropriate, at least one special education provider of such child.
4. A representative of the local educational agency who is qualified to provide, or supervise the provision of, specially designed instruction to meet the unique needs of individuals with disabilities; is knowledgeable about general curriculum; and is knowledgeable about the availability of resources of the local educational agency.

5. An individual who can interpret the instructional implications of evaluation results.
6. At the discretion of the parent or the agency, other individuals who have knowledge or special expertise regarding the student, including related services personnel as appropriate.
7. Whenever appropriate, the student.

In the case of students with mild disabilities, the IEP is usually determined by the portion of the general education curriculum with which a student is having difficulty. A student with a learning disability might have an IEP that emphasizes reading and mathematics. A student with a behavior disorder would have an IEP that emphasizes self-control and adjustment to classroom routines. An adolescent with mild mental retardation might have an IEP that describes vocational goals and objectives.

Focus on Where to Teach Students

When Congress passed the Individuals with Disabilities Education Act, the media hailed it as the mainstreaming law. This caused considerable concern among teachers and administrators who feared mainstreaming would lead to dumping students with disabilities into general classrooms. Newspeople inadvertently misled the public. The term "mainstreaming" is not mentioned in the law. Congress believed that students with disabilities should be educated with students without disabilities whenever feasible. The law states that students should be educated in the least restrictive environment. The intent of the least restrictive environment mandate is to assure that students are not segregated because of their disabilities and to give them every opportunity to have a normal school experience. More restrictive settings, such as self-contained special classes and residential programs, should be utilized only when a student's needs are so complex that he or she would not receive an appropriate education in a less restrictive environment. Evelyn Deno's *Cascade of Services* (Figure 1.4) provides a visual representation of the relationship between least and most restrictive settings. Level I is least restrictive. Each succeeding level establishes more distance between special and general education services.

It is the responsibility of each school system to provide a continuum of educational services ranging from least to most restrictive. We will briefly describe the types of special education services you can expect a school system to provide.

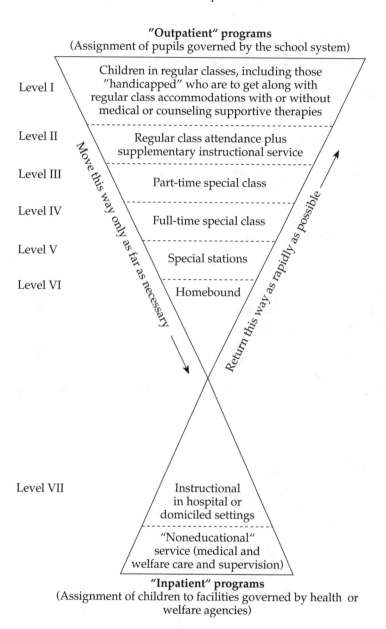

"Outpatient" programs
(Assignment of pupils governed by the school system)

Level I — Children in regular classes, including those "handicapped" who are to get along with regular class accommodations with or without medical or counseling supportive therapies

Level II — Regular class attendance plus supplementary instructional service

Level III — Part-time special class

Level IV — Full-time special class

Level V — Special stations

Level VI — Homebound

Move this way only as far as necessary

Return this way as rapidly as possible

Level VII — Instructional in hospital or domiciled settings

"Noneducational" service (medical and welfare care and supervision)

"Inpatient" programs
(Assignment of children to facilities governed by health or welfare agencies)

FIGURE 1.4   Cascade of Services

Source: "Special Education as Developmental Capitol" by E. Deno, *Exceptional Children 37,* 229–237. Copyright © 1970 by the Council for Exceptional Children. Reprinted with permission.

General Education Classroom Placement

Placement in the general education classroom with supportive services (e.g., materials, consultation, team teaching) is the least restrictive environment in the hierarchy of services. If a student spends less than 21 percent of the school day outside the regular classroom receiving special instruction, the federal government defines the placement as a regular classroom. Students with learning disabilities usually spend most of their day in the regular classroom. Speech clinicians, social workers, special education teachers, and school psychologists may consult with the regular classroom teacher on student needs and progress.

Resource Room Placement

Resource rooms are commonly referred to as pull-out programs. The resource room is a special education classroom located within the student's school. A youngster goes to the resource room on a scheduled basis to receive tutorial help from a special education teacher. Students may spend from 21 to 60 percent of their school day in a resource room. Typically, resource room teachers teach fundamental skills and/or tutor students in the academic subjects that were the source of the referral. It is the resource room teacher's job to take a lead role in the development and implementation of IEPs for students placed in this setting. The majority of students who receive resource room help remain in the regular classroom for most of their school day (U.S. Department of Education, 2002).

Special Class Placement

Special classes are self-contained programs located in a public school system. They are sometimes called segregated programs because only students with disabilities are enrolled. Students are usually grouped in special classes by categories of disability. The special class is the most criticized of special education placements when it is used for students with mild disabilities. Although students with learning disabilities are not usually placed in special classes, students with mild mental retardation and behavior disorders are sometimes placed in these programs.

Special Day School Placement

Alternative high school programs, special education early childhood programs, and private day programs are examples of special day school placements. Students are transported to these special education programs at the school system's expense. Public school systems sometimes contract with private vendors to provide special education services for students with low-incidence disabilities such as autism or multiple disabilities. In addition to the disadvantages inherent in segregation, students who attend special day school programs may spend lengthy amounts of time being transported from home to program and back home again.

Homebound Programs

Students who are ill or require intensive medical services are educated by itinerant teachers at home. With the passage of P.L. 99–457 in 1986, incentives were created to develop individualized family service plans for infants and toddlers with disabilities at home. P.L. 99–457 (Handicapped Infant and Toddler Program, Part H) amended the Education for All Handicapped Children Act to extend special education services to preschoolers in 1991–92.

Other Domiciled Settings

Some hospitals have their own special education programs. Only a small percentage, less than 1 percent, of all special needs learners are restricted to hospital care (U.S. Department of Education, 1999). More than 450,000 adolescents are incarcerated in correctional facilities across the country each year (Margolis, 1988). Many of these young people are from minorities and uneducated. If a special need is identified, an incarcerated youth up to age twenty-one has

---

HIGHLIGHT **1.3**

An Educational Oasis on Rikers Island

In the halls of the Adolescent Reception Detention Center on Rikers Island, there are rapists and muggers, murderers and thieves awaiting judgment. But when Sharon Jones looks at the teenagers there, she sees mechanics and writers, printers and scientists. "Whatever they might be to other people, to me they're students," said Ms. Jones, principal of the Rikers Island Educational Facility, a surprising oasis of order, possibility, and education for young men who mostly never before appreciated the value of school and who mostly never before bothered to attend. Ms. Jones believes that if the offenders at Rikers Island are not educated, "you might as well set

a permanent place with them in a prison mess hall." The school has a newspaper and a literary magazine that is printed in the school's print shop. There are seven computer labs and an auto shop. And there is no violence.

"I was really into autos back at home, but I had the bad influence of my environment and I let it rule me," said Danny, awaiting trial at Rikers Island. "Then I see my teacher in here and I think, 'Oh man, I really made a mistake with my life.' But if there was no auto shop here, I don't think I would learn any lesson being incarcerated because I would have nothing to keep me interested" (Fein, 1995).

the same right to special education services as students in the public school system. In their book *Special Education in the Criminal Justice System* (1987), Nelson, Rutherford, and Wolford suggest that this population is underserved and that there may be a higher prevalence of mild disabilities among prisoners than the general population. Within the past few years, some special educators have argued that an adjudication of delinquency (i.e., socially maladjusted) may be a disability in itself (Benson, Edwards, Rosell, & White, 1986; U.S. Department of Education, 1999). Correctional facilities include prisons, jails, and detention centers. DiGangi, Perryman, and Rutherford (1990) reported that 42 percent of offenders in a state juvenile facility required special education.

Residential Programs

When a student requires intensive, around-the-clock treatment, residential programs are an option. Residential placements are expensive, however, and it can cost a school system over $50,000 a year to send one student to a residential facility for a year. One program for students with severe disabilities in Providence, Rhode Island, presently costs in excess of $135,000 a year. Ironically, the funding mechanisms in some states actually create incentives for such restrictive placements by providing reimbursements that increase in proportion to time in a special education program.

Blackman reported that in Illinois "it frequently costs a school district less money to send a child to a private day, often a residential school, than educating the child within the school district" (Blackman, 1989, 461). Illinois has set aside money to fully reimburse school districts for room and board costs incurred as a result of residential placements. Despite the additional expense, residential placements cannot match the quality of public school special education programs. Private school teachers are often uncertified or inexperienced. They work longer hours (usually through the summer) and for less pay than public school teachers. Union representation, a sine qua non of public school life, is virtually nonexistent in private, residential facilities. In 1997, less than 1 percent of students with special needs were placed in residential programs (U.S. Department of Education, 1999).

Focus on How to Teach Students with Mild Disabilities

The laws and court decisions that mandate an appropriate educational program for youth with disabilities are equally beneficial for general education students. Working together, general and special educators can improve the education of all students. Some special educators have proposed a merger of general and special education. They believe that the splintering of educational services in schools has diminished efforts to help difficult-to-teach students (Stainback, Stainback, &

Forest, 1989). If the ideal is the establishment of an appropriate education for students with disabilities, can this be accomplished in the general education classroom with collaborative efforts of general and special educators? The movement to educate all students together has addressed this concern and is discussed in more detail in Chapter 6, The Inclusive Classroom.

Both general and special educators are aware that we are in a state of transition as we conceive the best strategies for helping students with mild disabilities. Therefore, the future focus may shift from where (setting) and why (rights) students are placed in special education to a focus on *how* to educate successfully those students who are difficult to teach. Smith-Davis (1989a) defined the following factors as critical in making these decisions: (1) curriculum, (2) instruction, (3) methods, (4) materials, (5) options, (6) alternatives, and (7) instructional roles and relationships. In order to understand how these factors can make a difference in the realm of general education, it is necessary to understand the current status of the field.

Comparing General and Special Education

Many students end up in special education, not so much to meet unique individual needs but because special education is one of the few services available to help children unable to meet general education requirements (Sarason & Doris, 1979; Ysseldyke & Algozzine, 1982; Ysseldyke, Algozzine, & Thurlow, 2000). This practice neglects preventive efforts to solve classroom problems. Often, the only way a teacher can get help for a student (or for herself) is to refer the youngster for special education evaluation.

There are differences between the two systems of general and special education. Basically, special education is adaptive to the individual needs of students. Concepts such as individualization, specialization, heterogeneity, and lifelong learning are among those that drive practices in special education. In contrast, general education is group-oriented, global, norm-referenced, and presents standardized curriculum.

Since 1975, special education has grown as a subsystem of general education. This growth has tended to accentuate differences between the two systems. Students have received special services, but not without cost. The stigma of being identified as deficient, along with a loss of general classroom instructional time, has pushed some students with mild disabilities further down the ladder of school success. If general and special educators can find ways to work together, the combination of knowledge and expertise will benefit all students. The following chapters will focus on the unique characteristics of students with mild disabilities. Using this knowledge as a base, in ensuing chapters we describe those strategies that can help general and special educators work more closely to assist students with mild disabilities in reaching their fullest potential.

Summary

Special education serves students with disabilities. Students with mild disabilities constitute the majority of students in special education programs. These students have problems and characteristics that make success in school difficult without special assistance. Students with mild disabilities have problems that are basically educational in nature. Today, more than two-thirds of the students served in special education programs are classified with learning disabilities, mild mental retardation, or behavioral disorders.

Early special education programs sometimes consisted of isolated special classes or custodial placements that left much to be desired in terms of good instruction and sound educational practices. With the advent of Individuals with Disabilities Education Act (IDEA), and its subsequent supplements and amendments, special educators focused on providing appropriate education for students with mild disabilities. As a result of this monumental legislation, students who receive special services are entitled to education that is as much like normal as possible. Cooperation between general and special educators is the best strategy for ensuring the success of educational interventions for students with mild disabilities.

ACTIVITIES

1. Based on what you have learned in this chapter, answer the following questions:

   a. How did schools come to deal with the disabilities, that Jake, Mary, and Felipe presented in the vignette at the beginning of this chapter?

   b. How would IEPs for Jake, Mary, and Felipe be similar?

   c. How would their IEPs be different?

2. Play the labeling game. Cut strips of tagboard that can be stapled to cloth or plastic strips and tied to one's forehead. Write labels on the strips like "cheerleader," "jock," "brain," "clown," "leader," "trouble-maker," "critic," "learning disabled," "gifted," and so on. In order to play the game, the labels are laid face down and randomly drawn by the group leader. He or she ties one to each participant's forehead without the person seeing what his or her label is before removing it. Playing this game brings about an awareness of how we label each other and how other people's reactions label us as well.

3. Simulate a planning conference between a special education teacher and a general classroom teacher. Select a hypothetical student and describe how this student functions in domains like academic achievement, language development, social skills, adaptive abilities, and so on. Have the teachers offer ideas and suggestions about remediating and accommodating the student within and between the two classrooms.

4. Visit an elementary, middle (or junior high), and high school. Arrange an interview with the principal, assistant principal, and/or guidance counselor. Ask about the special education programs at each of the schools. Which services are available? How restrictive are each of the special education settings?

5. While at the school, visit a general education classroom. Observe students while they are working. Are the students academically engaged? Is their behavior appropriate to the learning task? Can you identify any who are having learning or behavior problems?

CHAPTER

2 Overview of Students with Mild Disabilities

ADVANCE QUESTIONS

Answer the following questions as you read this chapter:

1. What is the difference between noncategorical and cross-categorical identification of students with mild disabilities?
2. Students with mild disabilities have which generalities in common?
3. How do the learning and behavioral disabilities of students considered mild versus severe compare?
4. What are organic and what are environmental causes of mild learning and behavioral disabilities?
5. Who is served under Part B of the Individuals with Disabilities Education Act? Who receives Public Law 99–457, Part H services?

Chapter Web

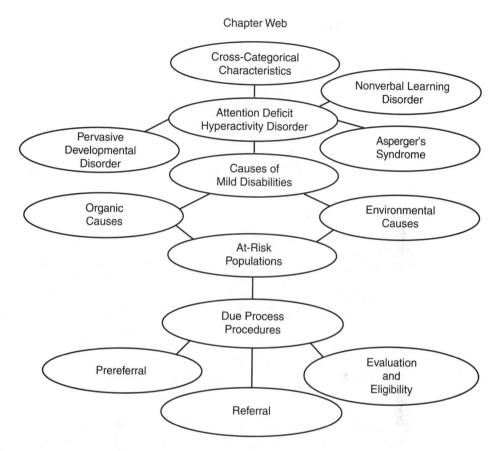

6. What are the characteristics of Asperger's Syndrome, ADHD, Nonverbal Learning Disorder, and Pervasive Developmental Disorder?
7. Who are the special populations at risk of educational and school failure? Describe these two main groups of students.
8. In which instructional settings are students with mild intellectual, learning, and behavioral disabilities primarily taught?
9. Explain the due process procedure that must be followed when making decisions about who will receive services in special education.
10. List student behaviors required for success in the general education classroom.
11. What are some effective strategies for modifying classroom instruction?

Students with mild disabilities are those who are served in special education in the categories of learning disabilities, mild mental retardation, or emotional/behavior disorders. These students are referred to as having a mild disability because many of their special learning needs and characteristics go undetected until they reach school age. The majority spend some time within general education classrooms. Others receive special services in a special education classroom one to several periods a day. Whether you are a general or special education teacher, you will have students with mild disabilities in your classroom.

Vignettes: Tale of Three Students

Karl's third-grade teacher reported that his academic abilities were significantly delayed. In reading, Karl had difficulty blending letter sounds and recalling content from reading and listening. Mathematics was also a problem for Karl, although he experienced some success with basic facts. He did have difficulty mastering reasoning and problem-solving skills. His teacher estimated that he was two to three years behind his classmates in academics. Karl's teacher also reported that he had poor social skills. Working cooperatively with classmates and controlling impulses were two areas in which Karl experienced difficulty. His teacher stated that Karl's "immaturity" and social withdrawal were a source of frustration to her. His IQ was sixty-nine. Karl has been identified as a student with mild mental retardation.

Jackie was in constant trouble because she did not turn in assignments or complete work in class. Her fifth-grade teacher reported that her academic performance suffered due to her incomplete work. Jackie was a source of frustration to her teacher and family. Although Jackie's teacher tried to handle most discipline problems herself, she sent Jackie to the principal's office an average of three times per week. Jackie's teacher described her as "sullen and hostile." When she was in these moods, she talked out in class, refused to work, and became disruptive. Jackie had been involved in several fights in school and on the bus; one was enough to get her suspended from school. Jackie was identified as a student with a behavior disorder.

José was eight years old. His IQ was 110. His teacher reported that José had average intelligence and a good understanding of spoken language. He was extremely verbal and often engaged in long conversations on a variety of topics; however, José's performance in spelling and written language was comparable to students who were three years younger than he. He was unable to reproduce letters legibly. Although he readily recognized each letter of the alphabet, he had difficulty both remembering what the letters looked like and executing the motor patterns necessary to form each letter. When José was given a set of letters to copy, his written product was often illegible. José's fine motor coordination and memory difficulties extended into the area of arithmetic. He understood mathematical concepts but had difficulty reproducing numbers and remembering basic facts. His academic performance in math was approximately two years below his peers. José has been identified as a student with a learning disability.

Answer the following problem-solving questions about the three students in the vignettes, Karl, Jackie, and José.

1. Can you identify differences between the three students?
2. What are the social and adaptive differences shown by Karl, Jackie, and José?
3. How could these learning and behavior differences influence decisions regarding the least restrictive environment and an appropriate educational

plan?
4. Are Karl, José, and Jackie more similar or different in terms of their educational needs?

Cross-Categorical Characteristics of Students

Special education labors under the weight of two contradictory beliefs. The first is that each student is unique in his or her individual learning needs. That is why all students are required by law to have an individual education program. The second belief is that there are homogeneous groups of mild disabilities that can be described, classified, and remediated. The categorical assumption led to the formulation and separation of mild mental retardation, behavior disorders, and learning disabilities into distinct categories of mild disabilities. We can see the results of this bipolar perspective in the debate over whether students with mild special needs are best served in special education or general education programs.

It's reasonable to categorize students with developmental disabilities (e.g., autism) because at the more severe learning level, behavioral characteristics and etiological roots are identifiable. But at the mild level, there is overlap between learning and behavioral characteristics of students. Historically, certain characteristics have been attributed to students with mild disabilities. Recent changes to IDEA allow states to identify students 9 or younger as "developmentally delayed." Table 2.1 shows categorical descriptions of students with mild disabilities. These characteristics are not descriptive of individual students. They are general characteristics of mild mental retardation, learning disability, or emotional/behavioral disorder.

Table 2.2 identifies generally accepted instructional strategies for students with mild disabilities across the three categories of mild retardation, emotional/behavioral disturbance, and learning disabilities. The categorical view of students with mild disabilities begins to unravel when researchers investigate what happens in special education classrooms.

Hallahan and Kauffman (1982) stated that differentiated instruction matched to characteristics of specific mild disabilities is largely nonexistent. The authors observed:

> Anyone, who happens to look in on each of three special classes or resource rooms for mildly disturbed, mildly retarded, or learning disabled children is not likely to see very different teaching techniques being used. . . . The appropriate teaching strategies and the materials used are very nearly the same for each of the three areas. (Hallahan & Kauffman, 1982, 435)

Similarly, Ysseldyke et al. (1982) suggested that a student diagnosed as having a learning disability may *not* require instructional treatment different from

TABLE 2.1 Generally Accepted Categorical Descriptions of Students with Mild Disabilities

	Mild Mental Retardation	Emotionally Disturbed (ED) Behavioral Disordered (BD)	Learning Disabled
Cognitive	Subaverage intellectually. Eligibility criteria: 2 SDs below the mean (50–75 IQ); often demonstrate short memory span, difficulty transferring learning, inability to project beyond the present situation, poor reasoning skills, poor abstract thinking, attention deficits.	Average to low-average intelligence scores; behavior interfaces with test scores.	Average or above average intellectually. Mental processing dysfunctions affect thinking and learning abilities.
Academic	Delayed academically. Demonstrates expectancy of failure, has slow learning rate, repeats unsuccessful strategies or behaviors, does not attempt new tasks.	Behavior interfaces with school achievement. Weak, average, or superior academic performance.	Have processing deficits. Lack generalization skills, demonstrate learned helplessness, work slowly on tasks, may or may not have developed coping skills.
Adaptive	Eligibility criteria specifies poor adaptive skills. Hyperactive, low tolerance/frustration, easily fatigued, moral judgment comparable to mental age. Delayed community-family adaptive skills.	Discipline problem. May have anxiety, fears, physical pain. May be unhappy or depressed.	Learn to compensate for deficiencies. Dependency needs. Outer-directed.
Social	Socially and emotionally immature. Unfavorable self-concept. Lacking in self-esteem. Susceptible to peer influences.	Poor peer relations. Disruptive behavior/conduct problems. May be shy/withdrawn or aggressive. Disturbing behavior demonstrated in various settings. Often elicit emotional responses in others.	Lack social insightfulness. Poor self-esteem. Susceptible to peer influences. Often feel inferior but want acceptance.

TABLE 2.1   Continued

	Mild Mental Retardation	Emotionally Disturbed (ED) Behavioral Disordered (BD)	Learning Disabled
Perceptual-Motor	Delayed developmental skills affect perception and motor abilities.	Intact perceptual and motor skills generally.	Impaired perceptual and motor abilities. Eye–hand coordination problems. Awkward. May lack orientation skills.
Language	Speech/language delayed or deficient. Poor social communication.	Spoken content problems (e.g., profane, argumentative, disrespectful language).	Receptive, integrative, and expressive language difficulties. Deficient processing abilities. Poor social communication.
General Characteristics	Manifest problems adapting to the environment. Lag behind in most academic areas. Perform best at physical/motoric skills.	Display behavior that is persistent and incompatible with cultural norms to a significant extent. May have concomitant academic deficits.	Manifest specific learning problems in one or two academic areas. May have concomitant negative behavioral manifestations.

Note: These characteristics have historically been attributed to each category. Individual students' profiles will vary considerably.

that of youngsters with mental retardation or emotional/behavioral disorders. The authors also state that many students without disabilities can benefit from specialized instruction designed for students with mild disabilities.

Generalities about Mild Learning Disorders

Some generalities can be made about students with mild disabilities—who they are and who they are not.

- **Students with mild mental retardation, learning disabilities, and emotional/behavior disorders are the largest subgroup of students receiving special education services.**

TABLE 2.2   **Summary of Instructional Strategies by Functional Domains**

	Mild Mental Retardation	**Behavior Disorder**	**Learning Disability**
Cognitive	Identify stage of cognitive development. Match teaching style to student level of development and learning style.	Make lessons relevant by connecting to meaningful experience outside of school.	Teach metacognitive, "how to learn" skills. Teach study skills.
Academic	Provide early childhood education. Teach thinking/problem-solving skills. Teach functional/career skills.	Focus on enhancing motivation to learn. Provide emotional support. Build on student experiences.	Teach students self-monitoring strategies. Analyze products and performance for learning disability clues.
Language	Emphasize intuitive skills and high interest in reading. Use systematic analysis of skills and progress. Respect cultural differences.	Emphasize congruent communication: "sane" and "I" messages. Accept student feelings; promote expression of feelings.	Utilize alternatives to phonics such as whole language and right-hemispheric activities. Identify specific language processing deficits and teach coping skills.
Social	Emphasize activities to build confidence and self-esteem. Teach social skills.	Establish a proactive behavior management program. Teach social skills.	Teach social perception skills. Teach social behavioral skills.

Since 1976, a prevalence figure of 11 to 12 percent for special education students has been reported by the U.S. Department of Education. We estimate that of the number of students identified, those with mild disabilities are approximately 75 to 90 percent of the total special education population. The population of students with mild disabilities receiving special education constitutes approximately 9 percent of the total school population.

■ **Students with mild disabilities are identified during school years.**

Mild disabilities are usually unrecognizable before entering and after exiting school. The physical appearance of these students is like that of students without disabilities. There are no differences in facial features or body dimensions. Students with mild disabilities are, in almost all respects, physically normal children who have encountered learning problems. Consequently, they remain unidentified until entry into public school, and they mesh into the mainstream of society upon leaving school. Acquaintances and employers usually don't make a connection between social and work difficulties and the fact that, at one time, an individual received special education services.

■ **Evaluation of mild retardation, emotional/behavior disordered, and learning disabled is unreliable.**

Education is not precise in pinpointing students with mild disabilities. Consider a scenario in which a virus would be identified by different criteria in the various states. An infected child traveling cross-country would be diagnosed as sick in one state and healthy in the next. Despite the difference in diagnosis the child would still be ill.

This is the problem with mild disabilities. Because there are no consistent state criteria, some students are accurately diagnosed while others are misevaluated as false positives or false negatives. A false positive means that some students are incorrectly identified as having a mild disability, whereas, with a false negative, some students who have a mild disability are overlooked.

Unreliable evaluations are complicated by the diversity of behaviors that are subsumed under the category learning disabled. Everybody has trouble in school at one time or another. As James Ysseldyke, an authority on special education assessment practices, pointed out, at one time or another 80 percent of all American schoolchildren could be identified as having a learning disability.

Similar troublesome problems are observed across these categories when we must determine which mild disability category fits a student. An analogy could be that of a preschool child attempting to put geometric shapes into the right holes of a container. When the particular objects do not fit into any of the holes, he just pounds on them or pushes harder to make them go in. Perhaps a hypothetical student with mild disabilities is like a square shape (Figure 2.1). We try to shove her into the circle representative of mild mental retardation, or, seeing at least two straight sides, we try to push her into the triangle representative of learning disabilities. If that does not work, then we try the behavior rectangle because, even though it does not have all sides equal, it does have four sides like a square. The child may not have the exact dimensions of the category, but she is similar enough to all three that we figure if we just try hard enough, she can make a fit with one of them.

Common characteristics of students with mild disabilities are listed in clusters in Figure 2.2.

■ **Students with mild disabilities are those who are most likely to be taught in a general education classroom inclusion program.**

Special education services for students with mild disabilities are usually provided in the general classroom and/or in a combination of general and special

"*Oh dear, some of these kids don't **fit** into the categories.*"
"*No problem — — we'll just stuff 'em in.*"

FIGURE 2.1   School Category Machine
Illustration by Lois Creech.

education services. For these students, the key issue is the effectiveness of the education they are receiving in both types of classrooms.

For every study that presents gains by students with mild disabilities in general education classrooms, there is a contradictory study that demonstrates gains through services from placement in resource rooms (Fuchs & Fuchs, 1986; Marston, 1988; Villa, Thousand, Stainback & Stainback, 1999; Henley, 2004). Educators are attempting to refocus this murky picture by shifting the viewfinder from where students are educated to what teaching methods work best. In subsequent chapters, you will find that many strategies that work well with students in general education are just as useful for teaching students with mild disabilities, and vice versa. Good teaching is a constant that cuts across both special and general education.

- **Similar instructional strategies work with both general and special education students.**

FIGURE 2.2 **Common Characteristics of Students with Mild Disabilities**

The following characteristics will vary from one student to another but are generally the same across the categories of mild mental retardation, behavior disorders, and learning disabilities. They are clustered under psychological, educational, and social characteristics.

Psychological Characteristics

- Mild disability undetected until beginning school years
- Cause of mild disability is difficult to detect
- Physical appearance the same as students in full-time regular education
- Poor self-concept

Educational Characteristics

- Lack of interest in school work
- Prefer concrete rather than abstract lessons
- Weak listening skills
- Low achievement
- Limited verbal and/or writing skills
- Right hemisphere preference in learning activities
- Respond better to active rather than passive learning tasks
- Have areas of talent or ability that are overlooked by teachers
- Prefer to receive special help in regular classroom
- Higher dropout rate than regular education students
- Achieve in accordance with teacher expectations
- Require modifications in classroom instruction
- Distractible

Social Characteristics

- Experience friction when interacting with others
- Function better outside of school than in school
- Need adult approval
- Have difficulties finding and maintaining employment after school
- Stereotyped by others
- Behavior problems exhibited

Effective instructional approaches that have found common ground among teachers of students with mild disabilities as well as general educators include cooperative learning, peer tutoring, social skill instruction, metacognitive strategies, career education, technology, and behavior modification. Students within all three mild disabilities categories participate in inclusion programs where they are instructed together in large or small groups with their general education peers. Similar behavior management approaches are used with all students with mild disabilities including functional behavior assessment, positive reinforcement, and positive behavioral supports.

Attention Deficit Hyperactivity Disorder

Attention deficit hyperactivity disorder (ADHD) is an example of a condition that cuts across categories. Some youngsters with ADHD do not receive special education services, some receive special education services under the category of "other health impaired," while still other youngsters with ADHD are categorized as emotionally disturbed, behavior disordered, or learning disabled.

Whether or not a youngster with ADHD is provided with special education can depend on several factors, including how rigorous parents are about getting services, how disruptive the student's behavior is, and how distractability problems affect the student's academic progress. If the problem is perceived as primarily academic, the student might be classified as learning disabled. If the problem is perceived as primarily behavioral, the student might be classified as behavior disordered or emotionally disturbed. If the condition does not interfere with academic progress, no special education services are provided. ADHD often coexists with other childhood problems such as dyslexia, depression, bipolar disorder, and anxiety disorder (Gilbert, 2000).

The prevalence of coexisting learning disabilities and ADHD is approximately 25 percent (Fowler, 2002). Learning disabilities may occur more often with ADHD-IA, primarily students with attention problems, than with students with ADHD-HI, primarily hyperactive (Figure 2.3). Lerner et al. (1995) estimated that 40 to 60 percent of ADHD students have coexisting oppositional defiant disorder (ODD), while approximately 20 to 30 percent of students develop the more serious conduct disorder (CD). The *Diagnostic and Statistical Manual of Mental Disorders (DSM-IV)* published by the American Psychiatric Association specifies the following guidelines for determining if ADHD is present:

- Onset of symptoms occurs no later than 7 years of age.
- Symptoms are present in two or more situations.
- Symptoms do not occur exclusively during the course of a pervasive developmental disorder, or schizophrenia or other psychotic disorders, and is not better accounted for by a diagnosis of a mood disorder, anxiety disorder, dissociative disorder, or personality disorder.
- Symptoms have been present for the past 6 months.

ADHD is a presumed neurobiological disorder involving a network of brain structures that control inhibition and focus attention (i.e., frontal lobe, caudate nucleus, and thalamus). While research in etiology continues, evidence to date suggests that ADHD has a genetic factor and is likely caused by a chemical imbalance in the brain. Individuals with ADHD have difficulties with the brain's executive functions, which include planning, staying focused on a task, over-

FIGURE 2.3   Diagnostic Criteria for Attention Deficit Hyperactivity Disorder (ADHD)

The diagnostic criteria for attention deficit hyperactivity disorder (ADHD) was revised in the fourth edition of *The Diagnostic and Statistical Manual of Mental Disorders* published by the American Psychiatric Association. Three types of ADHD are specified.

1. **ADHD-IA.** *Primarily inattentive.* This subtype refers to children who have primary problems with attention.
2. **ADHD-HI.** *Primarily hyperactive and impulsive.* This subtype refers to children who primarily display behaviors of hyperactivity and impulsivity.
3. **ADHD-C.** *Combined.* This subtype refers to individuals who have attention problems and exhibit symptoms related to hyperactivity and impulsivity.

In order to be diagnosed, each type requires that the person display at least *six of the following nine symptoms.*

ADHD-IA Subtype. Symptoms of inattention.

- Fails to give close attention to details, makes careless mistakes.
- Has difficulty sustaining attention.
- Does not seem to listen.
- Does not follow through or finish tasks.
- Has difficulty organizing tasks or activities.
- Avoids or dislikes tasks requiring sustained effort.
- Loses things needed for tasks.
- Is easily distracted by extraneous stimuli.
- Is often forgetful in daily activities.

ADHD-HI Subtype. Symptoms of hyperactivity or impulsivity.

Hyperactivity

- Fidgets with hands or feet, squirms in seat.
- Leaves seat in classroom or other situations.
- Runs about or climbs excessively.
- Has difficulty playing or engaging in leisure activities quietly.
- Talks excessively.
- Acts as if "driven by motor" and cannot sit still.

Impulsivity

- Blurts out answers before questions are completed.
- Has difficulty waiting in line or awaiting turn in games or activities.
- Interrupts or intrudes on others.

ADHD-C. Combined Subtype.

Sources: American Psychiatric Association, 1994; Lerner, 1997.

riding emotional impulses, and short-term memory gaps. While some students are successful because they persevere with school tasks, students with ADHD have difficulty attending to tasks that they find frustrating or uninteresting. Impulsive and inattention characteristics of ADHD are presented in Chapter 4. While hyperactivity often appears to diminish with age, problems with attention can continue through adulthood. The following three disabilities, like ADHD, often are included as mild disabilities, although the category assigned will vary with individual students.

Pervasive Developmental Disorder

Pervasive Developmental Disorder (PDD) is a term used to describe a group of neurological and biological conditions. These conditions are characterized by delays in social, communication, and cognitive development. Pervasive Developmental Disorders include Asperger's Syndrome (High Functioning Autism), Childhood Disintegrative Disorder (Heller's Syndrome), Hyperlexia, Rett's Disorder, and Pervasive Developmental Disorder, Not Otherwise Specified. Autism is the main PDD recognized and studied. In fact, the terms Autism and Pervasive Developmental Disorder are often used interchangeably. *Autism* (usually a general term) and *Autistic Disorder* (a specific term) do not necessarily mean the same thing to all people. Autistic Disorder is a severe and pervasive form of PDD. Moreover, there is no clear understanding about how these disorders are caused. Conner (2003) states that causation theories include biochemical, electrophysiological, and structural differences within the brain. Recent studies have implicated abnormal levels of neurotransmitters (serotonin or dopamine), phenylketonuria, epilepsy, ventricular enlargement, and brain stem abnormalities.

Two diagnostic categories are listed in the Diagnostic and Statistical Manual of Mental Disorders (4th ed.). These are:

- **Autistic Disorder**—considered the primary disorder in which most children are diagnosed. This diagnostic category has specific criteria and symptoms which are fairly similar from one child to the next.
- **Pervasive Developmental Disorder, Not Otherwise Specified**—a category for children who meet the general description for Pervasive Developmental Disorder, but not the criteria for Autistic Disorder. (Conner, 2003)

The majority of children with Pervasive Developmental Disorder exhibit behaviors in the moderate range (somewhere between mild and severe). Those with the most severe impairments are usually diagnosed with Autistic Disorder. Diagnosis of the most pervasive form, Autistic Disorder, may involve profound mental retardation, cerebral palsy, and a pattern of severe impairments across intellectual, adaptive, social, language, and motor functioning. The least pervasive forms of Pervasive Developmental Disorder are characterized by less severe impairments in one or a few areas, such as expressive or receptive language (Conner, 2003).

Educational Strategies for Pervasive Developmental Disorders

Early intervention is essential. During early years, the child's brain is adapting and changing. Parental support and appropriate educational services must be obtained in order to provide for appropriate early intervention. The child needs to interact with nondisabled youngsters in settings where inclusion can take place.

Conner (2003) has laid out what might be considered an effective treatment approach. It is based upon the individual child's intellectual functioning. For the lower cognitive functioning children, the following curriculum is suggested: self-care skills, a reasonable degree of compliance to directions or simple rules, the acquisition of basic social and affectional behaviors, communication skills which assist in expressing needs and wants, appropriate play with peers, and the reduction of harmful behaviors. For the higher cognitive functioning children, it is suggested that an emphasis be placed upon acquiring age-appropriate expressive language, providing opportunities for mainstreamed social interaction with nondisabled peers, and a focus upon developing skills and behaviors expected of all preschool and lower-elementary-aged children.

Asperger's Syndrome

One type of Pervasive Developmental Disorder is *Asperger's Syndrome*. Asperger's Syndrome (AS) is generally recognized as a neurological and biological disorder, characterized by normal intelligence and language development, but accompanied by autistic-like behaviors and marked deficiencies in social and communication skills. The autistic-like behaviors include restricted and repetitive patterns of behavior, interests, and activities. These children have trouble making transitions or changes and thus prefer sameness. They seem to experience difficulties in determining appropriate body space and in reading nonverbal cues (body language). They are often overly sensitive to sounds, tastes, smells, and sights (see Figure 2.4).

By definition, persons with AS have normal intelligence and some exhibit exceptional skills and/or talents in specific areas. Because individuals with AS perceive the world differently, their behaviors often seem odd or unusual. They excel in literal language usage. Most are unable to apply this rich vocabulary in social or pragmatic settings. They seem to perceive the world differently due to their neurobiological differences. This leads to behaviors which often seem "odd" or "eccentric." Unfortunately, these behaviors are sometimes seen as intentional or bad.

Asperger's Syndrome contrasts with Autism or Autistic Disorder in that there are no clinically significant delays in language, cognition, self-help skills, or

FIGURE 2.4   Diagnostic Criteria for Asperger's Disorder

1. Qualitative impairment in social interaction, as manifested by at least two of the following:

   ■ Marked impairments in the use of multiple nonverbal behaviors such as eye-to-eye gaze, facial expression, body postures, and gestures to regulate social interaction.
   ■ Failure to develop peer relationships appropriate to developmental level.
   ■ A lack of spontaneous seeking to share enjoyment, interests, or achievements with other people (e.g., by a lack of showing, bringing, or pointing out objects of interest to other people).
   ■ Lack of social or emotional reciprocity.

2. Restricted repetitive and stereotyped patterns of behavior, interests, and activities, as manifested by at least one of the following:

   ■ Abnormal preoccupation with one or more stereotyped and restricted patterns of interest that is abnormal either in intensity or focus.
   ■ Rigid performance of routines or rituals that do not appear to have a function.
   ■ Stereotyped and repetitive motor mannerisms (e.g., hand or finger flapping or twisting, or complex whole-body movements).
   ■ Persistent preoccupation with parts of objects.

3. The symptoms cause clinically important impairment in social, occupational, or personal functioning.
4. There is no clinically important general language delay (the child can speak words by age two, phrases by age three).
5. There is no clinically important delay in developing cognition, age-appropriate self-help skills, adaptive behavior (except social interaction), and normal curiosity about the environment.
6. The patient does not fulfill criteria for Schizophrenia or for another specific pervasive developmental disorder.

Sources: American Psychiatric Association, 1994; Kirby, 2003.

in adaptive skills, other than social interaction. Some professionals refer to Asperger's Syndrome (AS) as High Functioning Autism and others describe it as a Nonverbal Learning Disability. AS is named for a Viennese physician, Hans Asperger, who described a pattern of behaviors seen in some young boys in a paper published in the 1940s. We now know that this syndrome is more prevalent in males. AS was added to the DSM-IV in 1994. Because it was virtually unknown until this time, many persons originally diagnosed with ADD or ADHD have been re-diagnosed with AS. Likewise, AS shares many of the characteristics of High Functioning Autism (HFA), Nonverbal Learning Disability (NLD), or Pervasive Developmental Disorder, Not Otherwise Specified (PDD-NOS); therefore, many individuals diagnosed with one of these have been re-diagnosed or found to have a dual diagnosis.

Lois Freisleben-Cook (2003) provides a more "down-to-earth" description of persons diagnosed with AS. They have a wonderful vocabulary and often talk like "little professors"; however, their literal vocabulary does not usually convert into socially appropriate speech in a pragmatic sense. Motor dysfunction is often reflected by clumsiness. In social interactions, persons with AS may demonstrate gaze avoidance and actually turn away at the same moment when greeting another. Most would like to socially interact with others, but must be taught appropriate ways of doing so. Because the characteristics are often very similar, the educational strategies given earlier in this chapter for ADHD and PDD can be effectively used with individuals with AS.

Nonverbal Learning Disorder

Nonverbal Learning Disorder (NLD) is a type of PDD known as a neurological and physiological impairment originating in the right hemisphere of the brain. Similarly to other types of PDD, individuals with NLD experience early vocabulary and speech development, remarkable rote memory skills, attention to detail, development of early reading and spelling skills. In addition, persons with NLD tend to have eloquent verbal expressive abilities and strong auditory retention (NLDline, 2003; Nonverbal Learning Disorders Association, 2003).

There are primarily four areas in which persons with NLD have dysfunctional abilities. These include motoric, visual-spatial-organizational, social, and sensory skills:

- Motoric. Lack of coordination, severe balance problems, and difficulties with graphomotor skills.
- Visual-spatial-organizational. Lack of image, poor visual recall, faulty spatial perceptions, difficulties with executive functioning,[1] and problems with spatial relations.
- Social. Lack of ability to comprehend nonverbal communication, difficulties adjusting to transitions and novel situations, and deficits in social judgment and social interaction.
- Sensory. Sensitivity in any of the sensory modes: visual, auditory, tactile, taste, or olfactory. (NLDline, 2003, 1)

Misdiagnosis of NLD is prevalent. This is partly due to the fact that many individuals with PDD develop secondary neurobiological disorders—anxiety disorders, panic disorder, obsessive-compulsive disorder, post-traumatic stress

---

[1] Definition of executive functioning: Neuropsychological functions including, but perhaps not limited to, decision making, planning, initiative, assigning priority, sequencing, motor control, emotional regulation, inhibition, problem solving, planning, impulse control, establishing goals, monitoring results of action, self-correcting. From www.behavenet.com/.

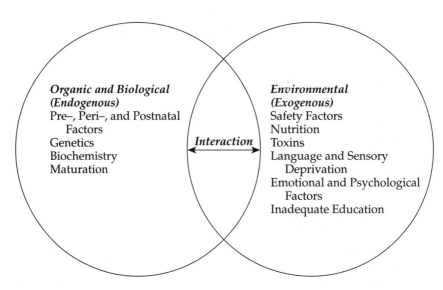

FIGURE 2.5   Common Causes of Mild Disabilities

disorder, phobias and depression, as well as suicidal tendencies. Once again, early intervention is very important.

Causes of Mild Disabilities

There are two categories of causes for mild intellectual, behavioral, and learning disabilities—organic (biological) and environmental (Figure 2.5). In the chapters on mild mental retardation, behavior disorders, and learning disabilities, we discuss organic and environmental causes and what the literature states about them.

Under the category of organic are included pre-, peri-, and postnatal factors, genetic factors, and maturational lag. These are the contributors that originate within the body. We include under environmental reasons for mild disabilities factors such as poverty, nutrition, toxins, language differences, sensory deprivation, emotional problems, and inadequate education. Although some environmental factors (e.g., toxins) cause organic dysfunction, the point of origin is environmental.

The more severe the disability, the sooner the problem is identified. In fact, it is not unusual for a parent of a child with a developmental disability to learn of this at birth. The appearance of the infant may differ from that of normal babies, with enlarged head circumference, tell-tale facial features, or inadequate response to visual or auditory stimuli. Several medical tests are now in use with expectant mothers to provide information about possible abnormalities in their unborn fetus. These include ultrasound scans (the recording of tissue densities by sound waves), amniocentesis (examination of amniotic fluid and culturing of fetal cells), chorionic villus biopsy (examination of fetal cells in placental tissue), fetoscopy (the surgical placement of an endoscope into the uterus), and blood analysis (analyses of embryonic cells that migrate from the fetus into the mother's bloodstream).

As mentioned earlier, however, mild learning and behavior disabilities are usually not discovered until children enter school. The schedule and routines of classroom life serve as a backdrop to compare children's ability to cope with various academic and social demands. Such mild learning problems as distractibility or delayed social development become apparent when students are unable to sit for lessons or follow classroom routines.

As a teacher of students who have learning or behavioral difficulties, you may never know for sure the origin of their learning problems. Attention deficit hyperactivity disorder, for example, has been attributed primarily to minimal brain dysfunction; but allergies, developmental lag, emotional problems, and lead poisoning can also cause impulsivity and hyperactivity. For individual students, the cause may be any one of these or a combination of causes.

Fortunately, educational intervention is not contingent on identifying and curing the cause of a problem. Educational intervention begins with the identification of a student's strengths and weaknesses in thinking, behaving, concentrating, using language, and functioning in other areas. Once an educational assessment profile of an individual student is compiled, teachers can select any one of numerous educational strategies to enhance learning. No one plan works for all students even though their functional problem may be the same. For example, one student who is identified as hyperactive may respond to a behavioral intervention program that uses positive reinforcement or encouragement to extend the student's ability to concentrate. Another student with hyperactivity may flourish in a classroom that provides indirect instructional methods, such as learning centers and peer tutoring, while still another might respond best to medication.

An informed understanding of causal agents can prove beneficial in the identification of students who are at risk for developing learning or behavioral difficulties. For instance, students who live near toxic waste discharge run a high risk of developing a disability (Croser & Seiter, 2003). Better knowledge about etiology provides educational programs with information to prevent learning problems. An example is the Head Start preschool program aimed at ameliorating the effects of poverty, such as inadequate nutrition and lead poisoning.

Determination of causes can also:

- Provide a better understanding of the child for family members and educators.
- Provide justification for government programs aimed at preventing disabilities.
- Enable better communication among various human service agencies.
- Suggest a particular treatment approach (e.g., diet instead of behavior modification).

- Provide information that may facilitate referrals outside the educational system.
- Enable more accurate prognosis. (Smith, Price, & Marsh, 1986, 58)

Organic Causes

Pre-, Peri-, and Postnatal Factors.   Mild learning, intellectual, and behavioral disabilities may be the result of prenatal, perinatal, and postnatal problems. Learning problems have been traced to the following prenatal conditions:

- Maternal endocrine disorders (e.g., hypothyroidism, diabetes)
- Maternal–fetal blood type incompatibilities (i.e., Rh factor)
- Maternal age, reproductive readiness, and efficiency
- Maternal cigarette smoking
- Maternal drug and alcohol abuse
- Rubella
- Radiation exposure
- Anoxia
- Accidents (Pasamanick & Knoblock, 1973)

Infants born of mothers who have consumed alcohol during pregnancy may develop fetal alcohol syndrome. This disability is characterized by mental retardation and other serious learning problems. Prenatal and postnatal growth deficiencies are present in approximately 50 percent of babies born to mothers classified as severely and chronically alcoholic, with an unknown number of babies affected by a lesser degree of alcohol abuse during pregnancy and nursing (Smith, Price, & Marsh, 1986; Umbreit & Ostrow, 1980). *Abstinence from alcohol consumption during pregnancy is recommended by obstetricians.*

Researchers have attributed various pre- and postnatal factors to mild disabilities. Maternal malnutrition can harm the development of the fetus's central nervous system and modify the growth and biochemical maturation of the brain (Hallahan & Cruickshank, 1973; Silver, 1989). Secondary cigarette smoke and substance abuse by nursing mothers have been reported as cumulative, postnatal toxins (Silver, 1989; Smith-Davis, 1989a,b).

Genetics.   There is some evidence that dyslexia, a type of learning disability that impairs a student's ability to read, occurs in family lineages. Schizophrenia, a severe emotional disturbance, also appears to have, in some instances, a genetic component. Some forms of mental retardation leave unmistakable genetic tracers. Riley–Day syndrome is an inherited form of mental retardation that occurs principally among people with Jewish backgrounds. Marfan's syndrome is a rare, inherited disorder that causes visual impairments and mild mental retardation.

As neuroscientists and geneticists become more adept at chromosome and gene identification, they will unravel the mystery of why some individuals develop learning disabilities and other mild learning disorders. In the meantime, the code word is caution when making assertions about an individual's innate, inherited characteristics. When any disorder appears with regularity in different generations of the same family, environmental influence cannot be dismissed as a causal factor. Home life, readiness for school, adequacy of teaching, motivation, and attitude toward learning are the deciding factors in a large number of cases of students with mild learning disorders.

Biochemistry. Despite its durability, the human body is a delicately balanced organism. The way our body functions depends on how well approximately 100,000 different chemicals work together. In order for the body and mind to function in unison, these chemicals must mesh in rhythmic patterns that assure optimum performance of all body organs. An imbalance in one area, such as glucose metabolism, will adversely affect mood, perception, and thinking. In the flurry of educational evaluations that precede a determination of special education services, physiological reasons for a learning problem are often overlooked. Vitamin deficiencies, allergic reactions, and abnormal mineral levels (e.g., iron deficiency) are just a sample of biochemical explanations for why students fail to develop normal learning and socialization skills.

It is also possible that many behaviors that are considered disturbing in school are stress related. Hans Seyle (1975) defined stress as the nonspecific response of the body to a demand. By this he means that regardless of the type of stressor experienced, the biochemical reactions of the body are the same. The student who views reading as a threatening activity or who perceives the teacher as hostile may instinctively resort to a flight or fight response. Withdrawal, apathy, resentment, moodiness, and anger are nonverbal responses to stress that are common both inside and outside the classroom. The ability of the teacher to identify physical signs of a youngster in distress (e.g., eyes with dilated pupils or increased muscle tone of the body) is important because many students do not have the verbal facility to describe feelings like panic, tension, and anxiety. Students with behavior disorders, in particular, are apt to act these feelings out rather than communicate them verbally.

Educators, both general and special, have been reluctant to accept biochemical explanations for learning problems. There are two reasons for their indisposition. First, possible biochemical causes for learning problems are difficult to track down. Hair analysis, for example, can pinpoint mineral deficiencies, but the procedure requires expertise that is outside the range of most family physicians. Second, educators, in general, simply do not accept biochemical explanations for learning problems because the evidence is largely anecdotal. For example, while Feingold's (1975) and Crook's (1980) research on how specific foods can cause allergic reactions and learning problems caught on with parents, educators remained unimpressed. School menus, which weekly offer schoolchildren large doses of preservative-laden and chemically treated foods, graphically illustrate a lack of concern about biochemical contributors to learning problems.

Maturation.   Although it is common knowledge that children physically de-velop at different rates, parents and educators sometimes overlook the fact that children's nervous systems follow the same idiosyncratic pattern as height and weight. Differences in development are not uniformly equal. Small children in a classroom may have quick reflexes, while larger children may lag behind others in the ability to coordinate movement. This developmental lag is normal and, eventually, as the students' nervous systems mature, they will be on an equal physical footing with others in the class. Developmental delay is more serious with some children, presumably because there is an irregularity in the physical development of their nervous system.

Much is written about developmental lag and mild learning and behavior disorders in relationship to recent brain research. Within the brain, some reason-ing abilities are localized in specific areas. For instance, in most individuals the language center of the brain is in the left frontal and temporal lobe of the neo-cortex. A slight anomaly to a small area of the brain can be responsible for prob-lems in such abstract skills as calculating and reading. Often these problems are detectable only in a formal learning environment, such as a classroom.

Hynd and Hynd (1984) contend that developmental anomalies exist in all brains. Not all brains develop in the same way (e.g., time stages, growth sections), and not all parts of the brain develop uniformly within a single individual. These researchers contend:

> While it is easy for psychologists and educators to conceive of separate distribu-tions for IQ, reading achievement, math achievement, personality, and so on, it seems almost impossible for these same professionals to conceive of a separate dis-tribution of neurological development. It is almost as if an assumption is made that everyone was born with a perfect unblemished cerebral cortex. (Hynd & Hynd, 1984, 491)

This statement has several implications. First, rather than assuming that stu-dents with mild disabilities have organic deficits, consider the possibility of developmental lag that, given time, can "catch up." Second, educational modifi-cations can stimulate development in schoolchildren while maturation proceeds. Third, if all brains are "blemished" in some fashion, learning disabilities may be contextual. In school the context is verbal skills. Thus students with language-based learning disabilities stand out, while students with deficits in musical or artistic abilities would be overlooked.

Environmental Causes

Environmental factors can enhance a child's learning potential or retard progress. The most rapid developmental growth in physiological, intellectual, emotional, motor, and linguistic functioning domains occurs during preschool years (Healthy Children Project, 2005).

Safety Factors.   Physical safety is necessary for the healthy growth and devel-opment of any child. A complicated delivery, early injury, illness, or falls and accidents can be traumatic and show their effects as the child develops learning readiness. Harmful events can occur even under well-supervised medical and familial conditions. Nevertheless, accidents frequently occur during times of inadequate supervision at home, on the playground, and even in school.

Nutrition.   Many different children are at risk of learning problems as a result of poor nutrition. Poor children, children of teenagers, migrant children, and children in rural areas are most likely to develop learning and behavior problems as the result of poor nutrition. Some of the symptoms of a lack of a proper diet are listlessness, irritability, fatigue, and inability to concentrate. Although poor nutrition slows metabolism and restricts the functioning of the central nervous system, the effects are reversible. The most prevalent nutritional disorder in the United States today is iron deficiency. Mothers of iron-deficient children tend to be younger, less educated, poor, and depressed. Iron-deficient children have short attention spans and behavior problems. Drinking cow's milk rather than mother's milk or formula can harm infants. Uneducated families who are unable to afford formula sometimes feed their infants cow's milk or sweetened beverages such as carbonated colas.

Feingold (1975) proposed the elimination of food additives and natural substances called salicylates by adherence to a special diet called the Kaiser-Permanente (KP) Diet. Though unproved in curbing hyperactivity and learning disabilities in controlled studies, parents and teachers have attested to beneficial effects from use of the elimination diet with children with learning and behavior problems (Mayron, 1979). Allergies, which come about as abnormal responses to substances within the environment (e.g., food, chemicals, inhalants, dust, mold, selective foliage), have been associated with learning and behavior problems. It is estimated that 60 to 80 percent of this nation's population has suffered an allergic reaction to food at some time during their lives (Mayron, 1979). Cott (1972) supported megavitamin therapy (i.e., massive use of vitamins to eliminate deficiencies associated with learning and behavior problems); however, success in using large doses of vitamins to treat learning and behavior problems has not been substantiated in independent studies (Silver, 1975). Other dietary deficiencies correlated with learning and behavior disorders include deficiencies in protein, zinc, magnesium, and calcium.

The cumulative aspect of nutritional effects is most aptly illustrated and summarized by Crook (1980) (see also Figure 2.6):

> If you don't use the right kind of fuel in your automobile, it won't run properly. It may sputter, jump, jerk, and knock. Similarly, the poor performance of the inattentive, overactive child is often caused by improper "fuel": too much sugar and other junk food and insufficient amounts of essential nutrients, including complex carbohydrates, essential fatty acids, vitamins, and minerals.

Toxins.   Environmental pollution is a contributory source for mild disabling conditions. Toxins found in the environment that have a strong likelihood for causing intellectual, learning, and behavioral problems include hydrocarbons (from coal,

FIGURE 2.6   Cars and Kids Don't Run on Bad Fuel

Illustration by Lois Creech.

petroleum, and natural gas) (Mayron, 1979), lead (from such sources as paint, plaster, automobile exhausts) (Smith & Patton, 1989), and mercury (from factory-contaminated waterways) (Peterson, 1987). Contamination from toxic waste sites and landfills contribute to learning problems as well. A follow-up study of 425 children treated for lead poisoning in the Chicago inner-city area reported 39 percent with neurological damage, 54 percent with recurrent seizures, 38 percent with mental retardation, and 13 percent with cerebral palsy (Wallace, 1972). Oil and chemical spills continue to be studied for negative effects on development and learning.

Although high doses of radiation are known to be deadly, effects from low-level radiation are not so easily determined. Pregnant mothers, however, are advised to avoid unnecessary dental, chest, and other body X-rays because of possible damage to the developing fetus. Electromagnetic radiation in radio frequency wavelengths has been implicated as a possible cause of hyperactivity and underachievement (Mayron, 1979). And, though not well understood, evidence has linked radiation from fluorescent lights and televisions to learning and behavior problems (Smith, Price, & Marsh, 1986). In addition, the pollution of air, soil, and water has resulted in the contamination of many foods. Animal products are especially apt to contain insecticides and other toxic substances. These toxic substances may place a further burden on a child's developing immune and nervous systems.

Language and Sensory Deprivation. Intellectual learning and behavioral development is retarded by the absence of sensory, linguistic, and cognitive stimulation. Children learn through interaction within their environment (Piaget, 1950). During infant and preschool years, overlooked health problems such as ear infections can hinder involvement in activities that are important to the development of academic readiness. Regular trips to the pediatrician or family physician are necessary to detect subtle hearing and visual difficulties. Unfortunately, many poor or uneducated parents are unable to provide preventive health attention for their children.

Children can develop verbal language problems when adequate models are unavailable to them during early years while speech is forming (Smith & Patton, 1989). Deficits occur in homes where there is language deprivation. For example, if a primary caregiver does not initiate speech or respond to a youngster's speech efforts, the child's language will suffer. Sometimes bilingual confusion exists. Adverse effects in the academic setting may be countered in classrooms where respect for diverse language forms (e.g., bilingual, African American and Anglo-Saxon derivatives) is shown, while instruction continues in standard English (Bryen, 1982).

Emotional and Psychological Factors. Many children with mild learning, intellectual, and emotional disorders exhibit lack of self-esteem, insecurity, low frustration tolerance, and impulsive behavior. Home life that at an early age is unstable, abusive, or psychologically stressful, contributes to poor emotional and social development of the young. Furthermore, some children are slow to respond to maternal bonding and nurturing. Sometimes these children will not allow themselves to be comforted during stressful times (Ainsworth, 1989).

Mary Ainsworth studied infant-mother bonding at twelve months of age. Ainsworth found that infants respond differently to their mothers. In an experiment called the "strange situation," Ainsworth analyzed infant reaction when the mother left them in an observation room. Securely attached infants cried when the mother left and greeted the returning mother with pleasure. Avoidant infants gave the impression of independence and did not seem to be affected by the mother leaving or returning. Insecurely attached infants clung to mother and cried profusely when mother left. However, upon return of the mother, insecure infants resisted all attempts to be soothed and would angrily arch away from mother's comforting embrace.

Without intervention, these attachment patterns persisted. Insecure and avoidant infants often become problem children. At age two, they tend to lack self-reliance and show little enthusiasm for problem solving. From three to five, they have poor peer relations and little resilience. At six, insecure and avoidant children are apathetic and unmotivated. Ainsworth has found that teachers tend to treat securely attached children in age-appropriate ways. Teachers tend to excuse and infantilize insecurely attached children. With avoidant children, Ainsworth found, teachers are controlling.

Ainsworth's research is valuable because it highlights the interactional aspect of social–emotional growth. Significant adults in a child's life, whether they are parents or teachers, help mold a youngster's personality by the way they respond to his or her behavior. A teacher who ignores a child because "she just wants attention" or gets angry at a child who is "immature" is unwittingly contributing to the development of the offensive behaviors. Child abuse, inconsistent nurturing, neglect, and poverty all play a role in contributing to the development of avoidant and insecure children. The effect of an early unnurturing or depriving living environment may result in youth who lack motivation for learning and are unconcerned about others. Further unacceptance may be shown by teachers who have a differing value system coupled with intolerance for youth who are disturbing in the classroom.

Inadequate Education.   Negative expectations for students with mild learning and behavior problems are handicapping factors in the classroom. Poor instructional programming, disorganized teaching practices, and low expectations for educational outcomes of children with mild disabling conditions contribute to learning difficulties. Hallahan and Kauffman (1994) include the following teacher behaviors as contributors to school failure: insensitivity to individuality, requirement of conformity to rules and routines, inappropriate and inconsistent disciplinary practices, reinforcement of inappropriate behaviors, and emphasis upon student inadequacies.

Insufficient development of prerequisite readiness skills occur both in home and school environments. The absence of intellectually stimulating experiences and lack of exposure to materials that will be used in school contribute to academic delay (Smith & Patton, 1989). Lack of readiness for school coupled with desultory teaching in school almost guarantees school failure.

Populations at Risk

Infants, Toddlers, Preschoolers

When the Individuals with Disabilities Education Act (IDEA) was written, Congress understood that early intervention is effective for young children with disabilities and through IDEA authorized several programs to establish a coordinated service-delivery system for children with disabilities from birth through age 5.

Under Public Law 99–457, at the state's discretion, infants and toddlers, ages birth to 2, are eligible for early intervention services if they are currently experiencing developmental delays or are at risk of having such developmental delays. Preschoolers, children aged 3 to 5, are entitled to special education if they have developmental delays in physical, cognitive, communication, social, emotional, or adaptive development. In 2001, 599,678 preschoolers received special education services (U.S. Dept. of Education, 2003).

IDEA defines children with disabilities as those

> with mental retardation, hearing impairments including deafness, speech or language impairments, visual impairments including blindness, serious emotional disturbance, orthopedic impairments, autism, traumatic brain injury, other health impairments, or specific learning disabilities . . . who, by reason thereof, need special education and related services.

Two significant developments outside of IDEA have begun to impact on the way in which preschool services are provided. One of these is the Americans with Disabilities Act (ADA) and the other is the concept of "developmentally appropriate practice." The ADA mandates that preschoolers with disabilities can not be excluded from a public day care or kindergarten facility because of a disability, and that reasonable accommodations are to be given children with disabilities according to need. The ADA became effective in 1992. The ADA is discussed later in this section as we talk about school-aged children with disabilities.

At-Risk School-Aged Youth

School efforts to help at-risk students have focused almost exclusively on children and youth from low socioeconomic backgrounds. The term *compensatory education* is used to describe federal programs that are targeted for disadvantaged children who are at risk of academic failure.

About 25 percent of school-aged youth needs significant assistance to benefit from education, but only about half or 12 percent of these fit the IDEA definition (Rothstein, 1995). Two criteria must be met in order to qualify for special education. A youngster must:

1. qualify for one of the disability categories listed in the law.

2. The presence of a disability alone does not necessarily mean that special education assistance is needed, if the student is making adequate educational progress.

The 12 percent reported by Rothstein as requiring significant assistance in order to benefit from education and who do not qualify for special education are considered "at risk." Some receive reading and math assistance from compensatory education programs—such as Title 1. Some are referred to as "slow learners" or "underachievers." Others have chronic discipline problems or are frequently truants. All have a high probability of becoming school dropouts.

Students at risk is a generic term that describes a range of problems of school-aged youth. Low achievement, retention in grade, truancy, and behavior problems are indicators that a student may be at risk of school failure. Approximately 15 percent of all high school students leave school before their graduation date; thus, after infants, the most vulnerable at-risk population is adolescents. A student is at risk when failure is likely to occur—either in school or in life. Whether or not a youth is at risk is a function of the family and community as much as school actors. Problems linked to family and society include drug abuse, deficient school readiness skills, emotional problems, absenteeism, and family turmoil. Retention, low achievement, behavior problems, and absenteeism are school variables that are characteristics of students at risk.

School Dropouts

The annual dropout rate for students with disabilities ages 14 to 21 is 5.1 percent. Students with behavior disorders have a higher rate than any other type of disability. Older secondary students are more likely to drop out than younger secondary students, although the latter group has a sizable proportion of students who also dropped out of school. Students with disabilities who drop out are less likely than those without disabilities to eventually earn a high school diploma.

Warner (1991) studied factors that influence retention. Schools and communities can apply some of these findings to assist at-risk students who might be potential dropouts.

- Students who received individual attention such as tutoring or counseling were more likely to remain in school.
- Smaller classes, tutoring, and other services increased the chances that students would succeed in general classes.
- Students in general classes were less likely to have high absenteeism or to be retained in grade if classes were small or if they had help from an instructional aide.
- Students who received job-specific vocational education performed better in school and at work than those who did not, had significantly lower absen-

teeism, and were significantly less likely to fail a course, miss school, or drop out.
- Students who socialized with other students outside of school and were involved in extracurricular activities were less likely to fail a course, miss school, or drop out.

When a student is identified as at risk of education failure the educational response has often been to place the student in a special education program rather than a compensatory education program. For instance, since the passage of the Individuals with Disabilities Education Act, the number of all learning disabled students has increased beyond all reasonable expectations. However, as Slavin (1989b) points out, labeling students "learning disabled" is no guarantee that their problems will be remediated.

> This increase (in learning disabled students) represents the entry into the special education system of low achievers who would not have been served in special education in the past. In other words, special education has assumed a substantial burden in trying to meet the needs of students at risk of school failure. Yet research comparing students with mild handicaps in special education to similar students left in regular classrooms finds few if any benefits for this expensive service. (Slavin, 1989b, 15)

A better response to at-risk students is to identify effective teaching practices from all sectors (general, compensatory, and special education) and use these methods with all students receiving education in the mainstream (for example, cooperative learning based on planned student groupings, and peer tutoring work

HIGHLIGHT 2.1

Jerome is sixteen years old. He has barely scraped through school. His reading and calculating skills are on par with those of an average ten-year-old. Each year his teachers promote him, hoping that their successor will have more luck in teaching Jerome. Jerome's poor academic skills are counterbalanced by his leadership ability. The other students look up to him because he is tough but kind. In the inner-city school Jerome attends, this is a charismatic combination. When Jerome leaves school at the end of the day, he walks home through a maze of drug dealers, winos, and storefronts girded with iron gates. His mother would like to move Jerome and his two sisters to a nicer neighborhood, but her salary as a fast food restaurant worker barely provides the family with rent and food money. Jerome is street-wise, and lately he has begun to make extra money by selling crack. All his teachers agree that Jerome is a good kid, who, with a few opportunities, could be a success; but, in educational jargon, he is a functional illiterate. Jerome is at risk of graduating from high school unable to read a newspaper.

with students who are accelerated, average, at-risk, and have mild disabilities). Unsuccessful teachers need to be retrained in effective teaching practices. Teachers must be willing to work with a broad spectrum of students, including those identified as at risk or with a mild disability. The gray area between students with mild disabilities and at-risk students may have been expanded by 1997 changes to IDEA, which permit states to use "developmental delay" as eligibility criteria through age nine, rather than a specific disability category. Experience with noncategorical criteria suggests that absent the accountability of having to substantiate a specific mild disability the numbers of students placed in special education will increase.

Perhaps the most difficult challenge is to convince teachers that their responsibilities to youth do not end at the schoolhouse door. Most of the problems of at-risk students begin in the home and community. Teachers who make home visits and who value parental participation in school activities are capable of understanding the needs of at-risk students more clearly than teachers who have little interest in their students' lives outside of school.

Problems with Learning

Identification of Learning Problems

Identification of a student's learning problem occurs when comparisons are made within the general peer population about a student's academic or behavioral characteristics. Teachers hold expectations for student behaviors, and those who exhibit behaviors that differ significantly are singled out. Salend and Lutz (1984) identified student behaviors required for success in the general classroom. These behaviors are grouped into the following major areas:

1. *Interact positively with other students.*
   Work well with others.
   Respect feelings of others.
   Play cooperatively.
   Share materials and property.
   Avoid fights.
   Refrain from stealing.

2. *Follow class rules.*
   Remain quiet while others are talking.
   Use appropriate language.
   Tell the truth.
   Keep hands and feet to self.
   Use time wisely.

3. *Display proper work habits.*
   Follow directions.
   Seek assistance when appropriate.

Initiate assignments independently.
Attend to task.
Persist at difficult tasks.
Attend regularly.
Have materials ready.

Students with mild disabilities are identifiable by academic and social behaviors that deviate from those of their classmates; however, these students are not always so obvious. Imagine three groups of children working on an assigned worksheet. Students in one group appear to be concentrating on what they are doing, and are busily writing answers on a worksheet. In the second group, students are working on task, concentrating, and recording answers about 50 percent of the time. Students in the third group are off task, staring into space, or jesting with each other while they ignore worksheets on their desks.

Students at the far right end of the continuum are displaying disturbing academic and social behaviors at a high rate, duration, or intensity; these students are easily identified by their nonconforming behaviors. It would make things simpler if a certain portion of the continuum could be designated as representative of the characteristics and traits of students who are special education candidates. Unfortunately, identification of students with mild disabilities is not this simple. Imagine that some of the students at the left side of the continuum appear to be working appropriately, but closer inspection shows no rhyme or reason for the answers they are writing. Others appear to be working on task, but are drawing doodles on their worksheets.

These students often fall further and further behind. Their learning problems are not as noticeable, and they are tolerated by the teacher. Students like these are often told to pay attention, listen, and try harder. Because they have no obvious disability, they are mistaken for being lazy or apathetic. These children are at risk because if they are not identified as deviating from the norm in their learning, they are likely to fall increasingly further behind age-mates in school.

Prereferral Intervention

Once a student is identified as being at risk academically or socially, remedial interventions are attempted within the general classroom. (See Figure 2.7.) Federal legislation requires that sincere efforts be made to help the child learn in the general classroom. The concept of general education intervention is based on a redistribution of the resources of special education toward more immediate problem solving in general education (Pugach & Johnson, 1989b). This preventive approach to learning problems is discussed in more detail in Chapters 6 and 9 (The Inclusive Classroom and Classroom Management).

In some states, school-based teams of educators are formed to solve learning and behavior problems in the regular classroom. These informal problem-solving teams have a variety of names that include concepts of support (school support teams, student support teams), assistance (teacher assistance teams, school assistance teams, or building assistance teams), and appraisal (school appraisal teams) (Pugach & Johnson, 1989b).

Regardless of what the teams are called, their purpose is similar. Teacher assistance teams are created to make professional suggestions about curricular alternatives and instructional modifications. These teams may be composed of a variety of participants, including regular education teachers, building administrator, guidance counselor, special education teacher, and the student's parent(s).

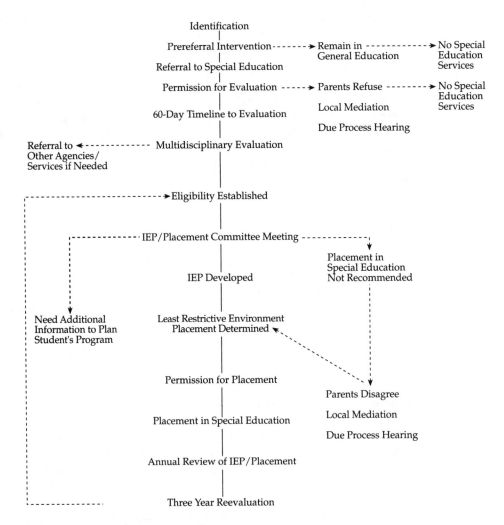

FIGURE 2.7   Due Process Procedures

Source: Georgia Department of Education.

The team composition varies based on the type of referral, the needs of the student, the availability of educational personnel, and state requirements.

Modifications are tried in an attempt to accommodate the student in the general classroom. Modifications are based on the presumption that learning problems can occur because of a mismatch between teaching and learning style. Students have different learning styles (see Chapter 7, Learning and Teaching). Whereas one student might benefit from phonics instruction, another student could be baffled by the system of blending sounds to make words. The second student might excel at a reading approach that emphasizes children's literature rather than phonics-oriented basal readers. Effective instruction recognizes differences in how students learn. The strategies shown in Table 2.3 for modifying regular classroom instruction are effective with students at risk, students with mild disabilities, and students without learning problems.

Implementation and results of any intervention that is tailored to meet the unique needs of a student should be documented. Anecdotal records, test results, and samples of work help team members assess progress during regularly scheduled meetings. Thus, appropriate changes within the classroom environment and teaching approaches are attempted prior to or in lieu of special education referral. At this time, focus remains on what can be done in the regular classroom to assist

---

TABLE 2.3   Strategies for Modifying General Classroom Instruction

Strategy 1	Provide active learning experiences to teach concepts. Student motivation is increased when students can manipulate, weigh, measure, read, or write using materials and skills that relate to their daily lives.
Strategy 2	Provide ample opportunities for guided practice of new skills. Frequent feedback on performance is essential to overcome student feelings of inadequacy. Peer tutoring and cooperative projects provide nonthreatening practice opportunities. Individual student conferences, curriculum-based tests, and small group discussions are three useful methods for checking progress.
Strategy 3	Provide multisensory learning experiences. Students with learning problems sometimes have sensory processing difficulties; for instance, an auditory discrimination problem may cause misunderstanding about teacher expectations. Lessons and directions that include visual, auditory, tactile, and kinesthetic modes are preferable to a single sensory approach.
Strategy 4	Present information in a manner that is relevant to the student. Particular attention to this strategy is needed when there is a cultural or economic gap between the lives of teachers and students. Relate instruction to a youngster's daily experience and interests.
Strategy 5	Provide students with concrete illustrations of their progress. Students with learning problems need frequent reinforcement for their efforts. Charts, graphs, and checksheets provide tangible markers of student achievement.

the student. Special education labels are not considered—only modifications that might help the student to progress in the general classroom.

Referral to Special Education

Referral is the process through which a teacher, a parent, or some other person formally requests an evaluation of a student to determine eligibility for special education services. Ramsey (1995a) lists six factors that may influence a decision to refer. The factors are: (a) student characteristics, such as the abilities, behaviors, or skills that students exhibit (or the lack of them); (b) individual differences among teachers in their beliefs, expectations, or skill in dealing with specific kinds of problems; (c) expectations for special education assistance with a student who is exhibiting academic or behavioral learning problems; (d) availability of specific special education programs; (e) parents' demand for referral or opposition to referral; and (f) institutional factors that may facilitate or constrain teachers in making referral decisions.

Fewer students are referred when school districts have complex procedures for referral, lengthy paperwork is required, special education classes are filled to capacity, psychological assessments are backlogged for months, or building principals and other site administrators do not fully recognize the importance of special education services. It is important that referral procedures be clearly understood and coordinated among all school personnel.

Multidisciplinary Evaluation and Eligibility

If instructional modifications in the general education classroom have not proved successful, a student may be referred for multidisciplinary evaluation. The evaluation is comprehensive and includes norm- and criterion-referenced tests (e.g., IQ and diagnostic tests), curriculum-based assessment, systematic teacher observations (e.g., behavior frequency checklist), samples of student work, and parent interviews. The results of the evaluation are twofold: to determine eligibility for special education services and to identify a student's strengths and weaknesses in order to plan an individual education program.

Eligibility is based on criteria defined in federal law or state regulations. Identification of a mild disability occurs in many states when a student's evaluation results correspond with established eligibility criteria for learning disabilities, mild mental retardation, or behavior disorders. As mentioned previously, there is variation in state eligibility criteria.

Evaluation by a multidisciplinary team is the means by which eligibility criteria is determined. A variety of professionals including a speech-language pathologist, school psychologist, special education teacher, and guidance counselor can be involved in the multidisciplinary evaluation. The wording in federal law is very explicit about the manner in which evaluations must be conducted and about the existence of due process procedures that protect against bias and discrimination. Provisions stated in the law include:

1. Testing of children in their native or primary language.
2. Use of evaluation procedures selected and administered to prevent cultural or ethnic discrimination.
3. Use of assessment tools validated for the purpose for which they are being used (e.g., achievement levels, IQ scores, adaptive skills).
4. Assessment by a multidisciplinary team utilizing several pieces of information to formulate a placement decision.
5. Rule out lack of appropriate instruction in reading.
6. Use processes that determine if student responds to scientific, research-based intervention.

According to the law, parents *must:*

1. Be notified before initial evaluation or any change in placement by a written notice in their primary language describing the proposed school action, the reasons for it, and the available educational opportunities.
2. Consent, in writing, before the child is initially evaluated.
3. Consent, in writing, to classification and placement in least restrictive environment.

Parents *may:*

4. Request an independent educational evaluation if they feel the school's evaluation is inappropriate.
5. Request an evaluation at public expense if a due process hearing decision is that the public agency's evaluation was inappropriate.
6. Participate on the committee that considers the evaluation, placement, and programming of the student.

All students referred for evaluation for special education should have on file the results of a relatively current vision and hearing screening. This will determine the adequacy of sensory acuity and ensure that learning problems are not due to a vision and/or hearing problem.

Evaluation methods correspond with criteria for special education disabilities. For example, a multidisciplinary evaluation for a student being evaluated for mild mental retardation would include the individual's intellectual functioning, adaptive behavior, and achievement levels. Other tests are based on developmental characteristics exhibited (e.g., social, language, and motor).

A student evaluated for learning disabilities is given reading, math, and/or spelling achievement tests, an intelligence test to confirm average or above-average cognitive capabilities, and tests of written and oral language ability. Classroom observations and samples of student work (such as impaired reading ability or impaired writing ability) also provide valuable indicators of possible learning disabilities.

Eligibility for services in behavior disorders requires documented evidence of social deficiencies or learning deficits that are not due to intellectual, sensory, or physical conditions. Therefore, any student undergoing multidisciplinary evaluation for this categorical service is usually given an intelligence test, diagnostic achievement tests, and social and/or adaptive inventories. Results of behavior frequency lists, direct observations, and anecdotal records collected over an extended period of time often accompany test results.

Additional information frequently used when making decisions about a child's eligibility for special education include:

- Developmental history
- Past academic performance
- Medical history or records
- Neurological reports
- Classroom observations
- Speech and language evaluations
- Personality assessment
- Discipline reports
- Home visits
- Parent interviews
- Samples of student work

If considered eligible for special education services, the child's disability should be documented in a written report stating specific reasons for the classification decision.

Periodic reevaluations of a student's progress are required by law and serve the purpose of determining the growth and changing needs of the student. During the reevaluation, continued eligibility for services in special education must be assessed, using a range of evaluation tools similar to those used during the initial evaluation. All relevant information about the student is considered when making a decision about continued eligibility. The development of the Individual Education Program (IEP) is described in Chapter 8.

Summary

Students with mild disabilities are those who receive services in special education for learning disabilities, emotional/behavior disorders, and mild mental retardation. Regardless of the category in which they are receiving services, these students have similar learning needs. In fact, unless you are informed about each one's specific exceptionality classification, you may not know whether a particular student is identified as mild mentally retarded, learning disabled, or behavior disordered. Because of this, some states now deliver services under cross-categorical systems. Students with mild disabilities are generally more alike than different.

Generalities can be made about mild disabilities. Students with mild mental retardation, learning disabilities, and behavior disorders are the largest subgroup of students receiving special education services. In fact, the total group of students with mild mental retardation, emotional/behavior disorders, and learning disabilities comprise the majority of the total special education population. Second, students with mild disabilities are served primarily during their school-aged years. Mild disabilities are often unrecognized before and after school years. Third, the categories for mild mental retardation, emotional/behavior disorders, and learning disabilities are unreliable. As demonstrated with ADHD, many psychological, educational, and social characteristics overlap. Although many students with mild disabilities receive special education services, there are some who are incorrectly identified as having a mild disability and others who have a mild disability but are overlooked. Finally, students with mild disabilities are most likely to be placed in the general classroom. Effective collaboration between general and special education teachers is vital.

Causes for mild disabilities can primarily be subdivided into two major categories: organic (biological) and environmental. Particularly vulnerable populations of at-risk students are identified: infants, preschoolers, and adolescents. Existing and new compensatory education and special incentive programs can offset school failure. The inability of some students to keep up and make successful progress within our educational system results in an increased number of school dropouts at the secondary level.

A series of mandated steps must occur before a student can be delivered services in special education. The full sequence of procedural steps includes identification of learning problem, prereferral intervention, referral, evaluation, eligibility and classification, development of an individualized education program, placement, and reevaluation. An individual education plan (IEP) is developed and the student is placed in a special education program that the multidisciplinary team agrees is the individual's least restrictive environment.

ACTIVITIES

1. Visit a school and observe students with mild learning, intellectual, and emotional/behavioral disabilities. Interview the teacher about the characteristics you identify after having read this chapter. Compare your findings about these students with those of Karl, Jackie, and José, in the vignettes.

2. Invite a teacher from an early intervention program or Head Start program to visit your class. Prepare questions about the identification and services for at-risk infants, toddlers, and preschoolers.

3. Have a panel discussion about pros and cons of categorical understanding of students with mild disabilities versus a cross-categorical perspective.

4. Inquire about services on your college/university campus for students with mild disabilities. Which students have services and how are the services provided? Are there students with disabilities who do not have services?

5. Invite a general education teacher and special education teacher to come to one of your classes. Ask them to comment on categorical versus cross-categorical approaches to teaching students with mild disabilities. In addition, ask these teachers to talk about inclusion versus resource room delivery of services to students. If the teachers are using the inclusion model, are they involved in consultative or co-teaching approaches? Ask them to explain how they implement the various models.

6. Conduct a campus survey. What are students' attitudes about persons with learning disabilities, persons with mild mental retardation, and persons with emotional/behavioral problems?

CHAPTER 3

Students with Mild Mental Retardation

ADVANCE QUESTIONS

Answer the following questions as you read this chapter:

1. How has IQ testing influenced social and education practices in the United States?
2. What is mild mental retardation?
3. What are the causes of mild mental retardation?
4. Why is adaptive behavior important in defining mild mental retardation?
5. What does the "six-hour retarded child" mean?

6. Why is there an over-representation of African American males in special education programs for students with mild mental retardation?
7. What are the cognitive, social, language, and academic characteristics of students with mild mental retardation?
8. How can teachers improve the functional, social, and academic skills of students with mild mental retardation?

Chapter Web

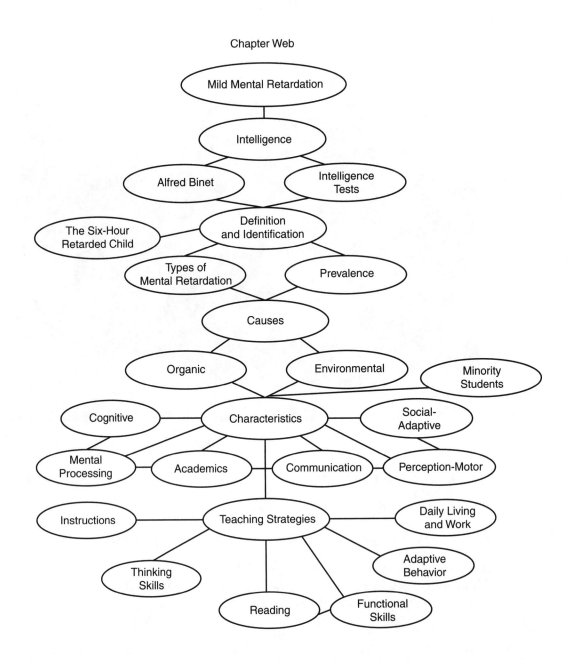

Vignette: Larry

Larry was nine years old. Each day he boarded a yellow school bus for a half-hour journey to George Washington Elementary School. When he arrived at school, he walked past a series of cheery, primary-grade classrooms and entered a small room at the end of the hall. In this, the special education classroom, Larry struggled with reading and arithmetic. He had difficulty sitting still and attending to lessons. Because of his distractibility, he was a constant discipline problem. Despite these negatives, Larry's schooling provided him with a safe and secure routine for five hours a day.

Larry, his mother, and his two-year-old sister shared a single room in a rundown tenement, which was also inhabited by drug addicts and prostitutes. Hunger, anxiety, and depression were a way of life for Larry in this bleak world. Even a trip down the hall to the communal bathroom was a hazardous journey. Larry never knew his father. His mother tried to make do on their welfare check, but it barely provided enough money to live on. She tried several times to find a full-time job, but she was handicapped by her lack of formal schooling.

Larry was one of many children who strained the resources of the city's social and educational services. His teacher described him as "depressed" and "apathetic." "Even when he smiles," she reported, "his eyes are sad." Larry was evaluated as a student with mild mental retardation soon after he began school at George Washington Elementary School six months ago. Larry's chaotic and insecure life made the prognosis bleak. His teacher felt that school could offer Larry an orderly environment, a nutritious lunch, and emotional stability. "I don't know if Larry will ever learn to read," she admitted, "he has been in three different schools in the past two years, and I doubt if he will be here much longer." This teacher's remarks underscore how unfavorable social conditions can overwhelm the best educational intentions.

Now that you have read the vignette about Larry see how many problem-solving questions you can answer. If necessary refer to other sources of information about the effects of poverty on the quality of life of children. See, for example, *Savage Inequalities* (1991) and *Amazing Grace* (1995) by Jonathan Kozol.

1. What can teachers do outside of school to promote the social welfare of young people?
2. What kind of social programs can you identify in your community that offers assistance to homeless youth?
3. What can teachers do in school with students like Larry? Is Larry's situation an isolated case?

Intelligence

Over 600,000 students with mental retardation participate in special education programs throughout the country (U.S. Department of Education, 2002). Most of these students, approximately 89 percent, are students with mild mental retardation. Although many students with mild mental retardation are Caucasian, minorities, especially African Americans, are over-represented.

Because of their lack of success in school, students with mild retardation lose confidence in their ability to learn. Motivation is a persistent problem for teachers. Although individual students differ significantly, generally students with mild mental retardation exhibit problems in academics and social adjustment. Such specific problems as distractibility, weak verbal skills, and speech disorders are common to this population. In appearance, these students are normal. Most are not identified as having a mild disability until they enter school and begin to fall behind their age-mates in learning. After they leave school, these young people merge with the general population. In the mainstream of society, they usually leave the label "mentally retarded" behind them.

In 1968, Lloyd Dunn was president of the Council for Exceptional Children, the nation's largest professional special education organization. During a speech at the Council's annual conference, Dunn urged educators to reevaluate their view on students with mild mental retardation. He criticized special education placements that tracked students into dead-end special education programs. Dunn characterized students with mild retardation as children of poverty who were denied equal access to educational opportunity in regular classrooms. He called for the elimination of self-contained special education classes for students identified as mildly retarded. Dunn stated that the label "mildly retarded" was used by educators to explain away the school's inability to educate African Americans, Native Americans, Latinos, and other nonstandard-English-speaking students. Dunn was particularly forthright in his condemnation of the use of intelligence testing to categorize hard-to-teach students.

> Again the purpose has been to find out what is wrong with the child in order to label him and thus make him eligible for special education services. In large measure this has resulted in digging the educational graves of many racial and/or economically disadvantaged children by using the WISC or Binet IQ score to justify the label "mentally retarded." This term then becomes a destructive, self-fulfilling prophecy. (Dunn, 1968, 9)

Dunn's speech alerted educators to the need to reexamine practices for diagnosing and educating students with mild retardation. The use of intelligence (IQ) tests to identify students with mild retardation and the educational practices that follow are so closely knit that an understanding of one is virtually impossible without knowledge of the other (Zucker & Polloway, 1987).

Alfred Binet

In 1904, Paris school officials asked Alfred Binet and his colleague, Theodore Simon, to identify students in need of special education. Binet was a fervent believer in the power of education, and he agreed to the project because he saw an opportunity to improve school services for slow learners. Previously, Binet had attempted to measure intelligence of schoolchildren by following the accepted "objective" method of calculating head size with a tape measure. He soon found that the pseudo-science of "craniometry" could not provide information to accurately select students who needed special education. The differences he found in head sizes of students designated by teachers as the smartest or dullest was insignificant.

When presented with the task of screening large numbers of schoolchildren for mental retardation, Binet changed tactics and decided to follow the practical strategy of presenting youngsters with problems in abstract reasoning. He tested students on a variety of tasks, including counting money, classification, and choosing "pretty" faces drawn on cards. Binet's procedure was empirical; that is, he did not start from a theory of intelligence, rather he experimented with an array of tasks until he was satisfied that he could derive a "mental level" that would indicate a child's potential for school achievement. Because of the high priority placed by schools on verbal skills, items on Binet's original test emphasized language-based cognitive skills. This accent on language skills as a primary indicator of intelligence still persists in IQ tests today.

Intelligence Tests

The turn of the century in the United States was a time of rapid cultural and social change. Vast numbers of immigrants provided industry with cheap labor. As slums, teeming with thousands of poor immigrants, sprang up in major cities, social reform became a national necessity. While educators tried to cope with students who were different, some United States psychologists focused their attention on the relationship between intelligence and social status. In Vineland, New Jersey, Henry Goddard founded the New Jersey Institute for Feeble-Minded Boys and Girls to investigate the influence of heredity on intelligence. After a visit to Paris in 1907, Goddard imported Binet's intelligence scale and used it to classify residents into categories of mental deficiency. To the already existing groups of "idiot" and "imbecile," he added a new term, "moron," to describe the highest functioning level of mental retardation. It was the moron or "feebleminded" group that became the centerpiece of Goddard's research.

In 1912, Goddard set out to detect feebleminded immigrants. He selected Ellis Island as his research site. Goddard intended to use the intelligence test to detect individuals who would, he believed, spread pauperism and crime. Each day thousands of immigrants poured through the massive disembarkation building in New York harbor. Goddard sent two associates to test immigrants as they passed through customs. Candidates for testing were selected by visual inspection. Goddard believed that an individual's posture, facial characteristics, and dress provided clues about his or her mental ability.

Goddard's associates administered intelligence tests to twenty-two Hungarians, thirty-five Jews, fifty Italians, and forty-five Russians. When the scores were tabulated Goddard found that 83 percent of Jews, 80 percent of Hungarians, 79 percent of Italians, and 87 percent of Russians were feebleminded! He dismissed language as an explanation because the Jews had been tested by a Yiddish-speaking psychologist, and their scores were as low as the other groups. Goddard did not consider testing conditions a contributing factor, rather he concluded that many immigrants were genetically inferior (Gould, 1981).

Goddard's views on the genetic character of "feeblemindedness" were reinforced by his infamous Kalikak Study (1912). Goddard claimed to have traced the offspring of a Revolutionary War soldier, Martin Kalikak, to an impoverished community located in the Pine Barrens of New Jersey. He claimed that these uneducated and dirt-poor residents of this isolated area were the descendants of a sexual liaison between Kalikak and a "tavern wench." Goddard compared the intellectual abilities and economic lives of the Pine Barren residents with the legitimate descendants from Kalikak's marriage. The legitimate Kalikak clan produced lawyers, business professionals, and doctors. The illegitimate Pine Barren descendants were characterized as sexually immoral, alcoholics, and mentally retarded. Goddard's research provided powerful arguments for the heritability of mental retardation. In 1981, Goddard's study was discredited because he failed to consider environmental factors (Taylor & Searle, 1987). Stephen Jay Gould (1981) discovered that the photographs displayed in Goddard's research had been retouched to give the Pine Barren residents a sinister and dimwitted look.

Other psychologists, including Lewis Terman, continued Goddard's work with intelligence testing and came to the same conclusions about the heritability of feeblemindedness in Mexicans and African Americans. After the publication of his "Stanford–Binet Intelligence Test," Terman, in a speech at Harvard University, made his ultimate claim for the role of intelligence testing and social engineering.

> In the near future intelligence tests will bring tens of thousands of these high grade defectives under the surveillance and protection of society. This will ultimately result in curtailing the reproduction of feeblemindedness and in the elimination of an enormous amount of crime, pauperism, and industrial inefficiency. It is hardly necessary to emphasize that the high grade cases, of the type now so frequently overlooked, are precisely the ones whose guardianship it is most important for the State to assume. (Kamin, 1977, 47)

Politicians gave Terman's notion of guardianship a macabre twist by initiating a number of state sterilization laws. In 1907, the Indiana legislature passed a law that allowed the state to sterilize prisoners and orphans. Beginning with the preamble, "Whereas heredity plays a most important part in the transmission of crime, idiocy, and imbecility . . . ," this, the first of many state sterilization laws, was passed amid high hopes of controlling the spread of mental retardation.

It was the "high grade defectives," or the feebleminded, identified through intelligence tests, that were the primary targets for sterilization. In a 1911 sterilization law, Iowa listed criminals, rapists, idiots, the feebleminded, imbeciles, lunatics, drunkards, drug fiends, epileptics, syphilitics, and moral and sexual perverts as primary targets for sterilization. Any adult who was institutionalized or any child who became a ward of the state was a potential candidate for sterilization. From 1907 to 1972, over 60,000 "social misfits" were sterilized in the name of social reform (Houts, 1977; Taylor & Searle, 1987; O'Brien, 1999).

By the 1930s, Binet's procedure for measuring intelligence was fully Americanized and in the process distorted. Instead of a measure to identify students for special education, the IQ test was used as an "objective" measure of innate intelligence. Binet's concept of environmental stimulation to increase intelligence was turned inside out as low IQ became synonymous with intractable dullness.

Between 1928–29, 65,000 intelligence tests were administered in Los Angeles elementary schools. Youngsters whose scores ranged from 75 to 50 were placed in special classes for the "educable feebleminded" (Hendrick & MacMillan, 1987). Immigrant and minority children were placed in segregated special classes at a higher rate than their middle-class, white peers.

The tenacity with which educators clung to the IQ test as a valid measure of intelligence is remarkable. When pressed, most scholars admit that IQ tests don't measure intelligence. There is no correlation, for instance, between an individual's IQ and success in life after school. But the IQ test still serves the purpose for which it was originally intended by Binet. Intelligence test scores are reasonably good predictors of school achievement, and, for this reason, until a more efficient method is developed, IQ remains the most frequently used standard for identifying students with mild retardation.

Definition and Identification

Professionals use a number of different terms to refer to students with mental retardation: educably mentally retarded, cognitively delayed, and intellectually disabled. Two primary characteristics are needed to identify mental retardation: limited intellectual functioning and adaptive behavior impairments that adversely affect life outside school. Limited intelligence is indicated by a score that is at least two standard deviations below the mean on a standardized intelligence test. Adaptive behavior refers to an individual's adjustment to everyday life such as a five-year-old boy dressing himself or a ten-year-old girl participating in a competitive game.

The American Association on Mental Retardation (AAMR) is an organization of professionals dedicated to improving the lives of individuals with mental retardation. The AAMR definition is the most widely accepted guideline used in identifying individuals with mental retardation. According to the AAMR, mental retardation is

> a disability characterized by significant limitations both in intellectual functioning and in adaptive behavior as expressed in conceptual, social and practical adaptive skills. This disability originates before age 18. (AAMR, 2002, 1)

The following four assumptions must be considered when applying the AAMR definition.

- Valid assessment considers cultural and linguistic diversity, as well as differences in communications and behavioral factors.
- The existence of limitations in adaptive skills occurs within the context of community environments typical of the individual's age peers and is indexed to the person's individualized needs for supports.
- Specific adaptive limitations often coexist with strengths in other adaptive skills or other personal capabilities.
- With appropriate supports over a sustained period, the life functioning of the person with mental retardation will generally improve.

Some states have developed their own definitions of mental retardation, and the federal government has slightly modified the AAMR definition as well in IDEA. State criteria for identifying mental retardation does not have to follow either the AAMR nor IDEA guidelines. However, all states recognize the need to evaluate mental retardation in terms of both intellectual and adaptive behavior.

Dever and Knapczyk offer the following instructional definition of mental retardation:

> A person with mental retardation is someone who requires specific training in skills that most people acquire incidently and which skills enable people to live in the mainstream of the community without supervision. (p. 26)

Rather than focusing on an individual deficiencies in intelligence and adaptive behavior, this definition underscores the benefits of teaching.

The theme that students with mental retardation are capable of learning is a major premise of this text. What a teacher believes about a student's capabilities is more important than any other single instructional variable. Several years ago one of the authors was chatting with a special education teacher. "The problem with my students," the teacher said, "is that they forget things so easily." "I taught them addition facts before the Christmas holiday, and when they came back to school they had forgot 50 percent of the material." "I guess that is what you have to expect," she continued, "when you teach the mentally retarded." The teacher went on to describe how little progress her students were making. Rather than recognizing that all students forget taught information, this teacher had given up on her students and herself. No student is so disabled that they cannot learn one more thing. Good instruction trumps problems in learning every time.

Mental retardation is reflected in difficulties in learning and in performing certain daily life skills as a result of substantial limitations in conceptual, practical, and social intelligence. Limitations in intelligence are usually interpreted as scores of 75 or below on one or more individually administered intelligence tests.

Test scores and other information are reviewed and evaluated by teams of school professionals. However, limited intelligence alone is an insufficient basis for identifying mental retardation—the individual also must demonstrate limited adaptive skills in social and practical skills (see Table 3.1).

The Six-Hour Retarded Child

The need to ascertain a youngster's adaptive behavior outside of school before making an educational diagnosis of mild mental retardation was highlighted by the research of Jane Mercer (1973). In an eight-year study in Riverside, California, Mercer found that the majority of youngsters identified as mildly retarded were poor. When Mercer examined classification of students by race, she found a disproportionate number of Mexican Americans and African Americans placed in special classes for the mildly retarded. Mercer coined the term *six-hour retarded child* to describe the students in her research. At home and in the community, the six-hour retarded child was considered normal; in school, the same child was considered retarded. Why was there a discrepancy in views? Mercer concluded that the schools failed to take a youngster's adaptive functioning outside of school into account. In Mercer's judgment, the lack of attention to socialization skills outside of school resulted in the mislabeling of many minority students. Mercer's research highlighted the need to take adaptive behavior into account before making an evaluation of mild mental retardation.

Types of Mental Retardation

It is important to discriminate between mild mental retardation and other types of mental retardation. One demarcation point is IQ score. An IQ range from 50–75 indicates mild mental retardation. As IQ scores move below 50, the degree of

TABLE 3.1   **Adaptive Skills**

Social	Practical
Interpersonal skills	Meal preparation
Responsibility	Housekeeping
Self-esteem	Transportation
Gullibility	Dressing
Follow rules	Taking medication
Avoid victimization	Money management
Obeys laws	Telephone use
Naiveté	Personal hygiene

Adapted from *Mental Retardation: Definition, Classification and Systems of Support* (10th ed.) by AAMR Ad Hoc Committee on Terminology and Classification, 2002, Washington, DC: American Association on Mental Retardation.

mental retardation is more severe. Students with IQs below 50 usually demonstrate observable physical and behavioral anomalies. Educators use the continuum "moderate to severe mental retardation" when discussing students with IQs below 50.

Within the mild range, the majority of students are not identified as mentally retarded until they enter school and begin experiencing academic and social difficulties. The etiology in these cases is difficult to determine, but a significant number of such students are poor. A combination of factors related to poverty, such as lack of adequate health care, exposure to toxins in the environment, and paucity of early childhood educational experiences, are often cited as contributing factors.

According to Armor (2003) the major risks to a youngster's IQ are eight family factors: parental IQ, cognitive stimulation of child, parental caring, nutrition (e.g., breast feeding), family structure (two parents versus never-married mother), mother's age at first child, number of children in the family, and child's birth weight. Commenting about key factors in treating mild mental retardation, Armor said:

> if we are really serious about improving IQ of low-socioeconomic-status children, we must look hard at programs that aim to change family behaviors or, at least, to supplement parenting behaviors for infants. The best example of the latter approach is Early Head Start, which does the best job so far of emulating some of the critical parenting behaviors. (p. 33)

Some students with mild mental retardation have obvious organic impairments that are detected at birth or soon afterwards (e.g., Down syndrome). These are identified in about 25 percent of individual cases. The type of mild mental retardation described by Armor is referred to as non-specific or socioeconomic mental retardation. Organic mild mental retardation, such as Down Syndrome, is also referred to as clinical mental retardation. Intelligence test scores for students with socioeconomic retardation usually fall in the mild range. Intelligence scores for students with clinical mental retardation can range from mild to profound levels as measured by intelligence tests. See Table 3.2 for comparison of socioeconomic and clinical mental retardation.

Children with clinical mental retardation are identified at birth or soon after because of obvious physical anomalies such as hydrocephalus (i.e., pressure on the brain from cerebrospinal fluid) or spina bifida (a defect in the bony arch of the vertebra protecting the spinal cord). There are over 350 inborn errors of metabolism that can lead to mental retardation. Students with clinical mental retardation usually have multiple disabilities—for example, communication and health impairments. Their condition is chronic, and they often require lifelong rehabilitation services with independent living, employment, or mobility. Clinical mental retardation cuts across all socioeconomic levels. Prevention and early intervention are the most effective strategies to reduce the deleterious effects of clinical mental retardation. Genetic counseling and amniocentesis are methods of detecting clinical mental retardation before birth.

TABLE 3.2 Comparison of Socioeconomic and Clinical Mild Retardation

Socioeconomic Mental Retardation (Non-Specific)	Clinical Mental Retardation (Organic)
Primary cause is environmental	Primary cause is biological
Normal physical appearance	Physical anomalies
Subtle health complications	Obvious health complications
Identified after beginning school	Identified at birth or soon afterwards
Developmentally delayed	Developmentally disabled
After school, able to merge into the general population	Disability is chronic and often requires lifelong support
Higher prevalence among poor with African Americans over-represented	Cuts across all socioeconomic and ethnic groups
Subject to misidentification	Demonstrates clearcut medical diagnostic criteria
Not recognized as a disability in all countries	Universally recognized as a disability

Prevalence

Ten percent of all students with disabilities ages 6–21 are identified with mental retardation. There is variation among the states in the numbers and percentages of students identified. For example, one survey reported that students with mental retardation ranged from about 3 percent of students with disabilities in Alaska and New Jersey to over 20 percent in Alabama, Arkansas, Georgia, Kentucky, Massachusetts, and Ohio (Ysseldyke & Algozzine, 1995). Reasons for this variation include assignment of students with mild learning problems to categories other than mental retardation (e.g., learning disabilities), differences in adaptive behavior criterion, and variations in IQ score cutoff points.

A recent change to IDEA allows each state to identify students from the age of six to nine as "developmentally delayed." In all likelihood this new classification will prompt a decrease in prevalance figures for students with mild mental retardation as school systems switch to the more descriptive and less stigmatizing term.

The issue of terminology has been a central clinical and political issue in the field of mental retardation. "Moron," "imbecile," and "idiot" were considered humanitarian classifications by the scientific community during the early twentieth century. Until the 1970s, "mongolism" was the clinical term used by researchers and lay people alike to identify individuals with Down syndrome. This crossover between mental retardation and ethnicity encoded in "mongolism" was no accident. The view that minorities were intellectually inferior extended beyond "feeblemindedness" to clinical forms of mental retardation as well. As Gelb (1997) observed, "the typological logic of scientific racism was a major influence on the social sciences in the late nineteenth and early twentieth centuries" (p. 449).

Baroff (1999) argued for "general learning disorder" on the grounds that it is a less offensive term than "retarded." He noted that adults with mental retardation don't like the term, and that "retard" is a common insult. The American Association on Mental Retardation recently suggested the term "intellectual disabilities." Lower (1999) disagreed on the grounds that intellectual disabilities would create confusion among researchers and practitioners. It is inevitable that professionals will search for less denigrating terminology. More than any other disability, mild mental retardation is a lightning rod for social, political, and educational debates. Without a clearly defined nomenclature that is accepted by all educators prevalence figures will be unreliable and social policy will detour around intellectual debates about accurate identification of students for special education services.

Causes of Mental Retardation

Intellectual and adaptive behavior deficits are caused by a variety of different factors. Two conditions cause mental retardation. These include organic problems prior to, during, and after birth, and environmental problems that result in delays in development. A summary of organic and environmental causes is presented in Table 3.3; more detailed information is presented in the following sections.

Organic Causes

Although we describe two groups of causes—organic and environmental—the boundary between them is not always clear. For example, because drugs have an effect on the unborn child similar to the effects of infections and genetic disorders, we have grouped them with organic causes. It could also be argued that drugs are part of serious environmental circumstances that are common for some families living in poverty and therefore should be included with other environmental causes. The edges are blurred but the problems are clear-cut.

Drugs.   From the moment of conception, a child is vulnerable to influences that can stunt normal development. A pregnant mother's health is a crucial determiner of a healthy child. Whatever a pregnant woman puts into her body will eventually be absorbed into fetal tissue. Alcohol and cocaine are especially dangerous to the fetus. Even small amounts of these drugs pose a threat to the fetal nervous system, especially during the first trimester of pregnancy.

Drug abuse cuts across all socioeconomic levels and poses an immediate threat to the nervous system of an unborn child. Because drug abusers neglect their bodies in general, the fragile nervous system of the fetus may be jeopardized by malnutrition, iron deficiency, or anoxia. Newborn infants of drug abusers often

TABLE 3.3   **Summary of Causes of Mental Retardation**

Organic Causes	Environmental Causes
Drugs	Toxins
Infection	Diet
Genetic	Inadequate health care
	Environmental deprivation

are addicted to whatever drug the mother was using. The National Institute on Alcohol Abuse and Alcoholism estimated that annually 1,500 of three million newborns will be born with fetal alcohol syndrome (FAS). Thousands of other children will have some of the characteristics of FAS, including prenatal and postnatal growth deficiencies, mental retardation, and fine-motor impairments. Low birthweight (less than 5.5 pounds) can lead to a variety of health problems, including mild retardation. Teenage pregnancies and inadequate prenatal care, for instance smoking, can result in low birth weight.

Infections.   Several forms of mild retardation are caused by maternal infection. Retardation can result from the mother's being infected with rubella (German measles). The effects can range from mild to severe mental retardation. Toxoplasmosis is caused by a protozoan infection of a pregnant woman. The protozoa is sometimes found in cat litter. Toxoplasmosis can cause mild to severe mental retardation, along with a variety of health problems. Cytomegalic inclusion disease is caused by a viral infection. The child's intelligence can range from normal to severely retarded. Cytomegalic inclusion disease can also cause visual and hearing problems. Microcephaly often accompanies this disease. Kernicterus is a form of neonatal brain damage that is caused by the destruction of fetal red blood cells in utero. The principal cause of kernicterus is Rh incompatibility, but drugs, infections, and enzyme abnormalities have also been identified as etiological factors. Although mild mental retardation is sometimes present, such other symptoms as disturbed speech articulation and athetoid cerebral palsy can lead to a misdiagnosis of mild retardation in an individual with normal intelligence. Children who run high fevers for an extended period of time are also at risk of brain damage that can result in mild mental retardation.

Genetics.   In the past, many pediatricians and educators assumed that children with inherited mental retardation disorders were moderately to severely retarded. Although this may sometimes be true, it is a mistake to assume that inherited mental retardation exists at any specific level—mild, moderate, severe, or profound. Inherited disorders are genetic in origin. Some are found in specific ethnic groups. For example, Riley–Day syndrome occurs principally within Semitic groups. Autonomic nervous system function is impaired, and children are usually small with poor coordination. Emotional problems are common, but intelligence can range from above normal to moderate mental retardation.

Approximately 5,000 infants are born with Down syndrome each year in the United States. Infants with Down syndrome are born to women over 35 years of age in approximately 80 percent of cases. Women over the age of 35 have babies with Down syndrome in about 1 out of every 400 births. In 95 percent of cases Down syndrome is caused by a chromosome imbalance resulting in three number 21 chromosomes instead of two. Mental retardation can range from mild to severe. Down syndrome is one of the most common forms of clinical mental retardation. Since the institution of preschool special education programs, children with Down syndrome, as well as other inherited disabilities, have demonstrated an increased ability to learn and participate in age-appropriate activities. Some Down syndrome children score in the normal range on IQ tests.

Fragile X syndrome occurs in 1 of 1,000 males; however, many cases may go undiagnosed. This sex-linked disorder occurs in males four times as often as females. Individuals with fragile X do not produce a protein, FMRP, which is crucial in nerve cell function and learning (http://waisman.wis/edu/www/rr0998.html). The name "fragile X" is derived from a break in the long arm of the X chromosome. Characteristics of fragile X syndrome may include delayed language development, hyperactivity, mood disorders, a long narrow face, and prominent ears. Other forms of inherited mental retardation include Prader–Willi syndrome, Marfan's syndrome, oral facial digital syndrome (OFD, Type I), and Klinefelter's syndrome. Each of these clinical forms of mild mental retardation is complex in its educational, medical, and psychological symptoms. Seizures, behavior disorders, metabolic problems, organ dysfunctions, motor problems, speech disorders, and emotional disturbance can combine in any number of ways in specific individuals (Lemeshow, 1982).

One of the greatest difficulties for children with clinical mental retardation is overcoming the social stigma of their physical appearance. Children with Down syndrome, for instance, might be placed in self-contained special classes based on the fact that they look "retarded." Limited expectations for success, along with isolation from nondisabled peers, can become a self-fulfilling prophecy of failure for these youngsters. Adolescence, with its emphasis on being attractive and popular, can be a particularly painful period. The aphorism "nature disables but society handicaps," aptly describes the constant struggle of these children for acceptance by their peers without disabilities.

Environmental Causes

The majority of students with mild retardation are poor and have no observable organic impairments. Poverty contributes to mild mental retardation by limiting access to experiences that lay the foundation for educational achievement and good health. Consequently, mild mental retardation is as much a social as an educational problem. A combination of factors contributes to mild mental retardation among the poor. Because it is difficult to pinpoint a specific cause, these youngsters are referred to as having socioeconomic or non-specific retardation. African Americans and Hispanics constitute the highest ethnic percentage of students with mild mental retardation, and 33 percent of African Americans and 30 percent of Hispanics live in poverty (Center on Budget & Policy Priorities, 2000). See Table 3.4 for government established poverty guidelines.

Toxins.   Lead and other heavy metals, such as mercury, poison children through inhalation, ingestion, and skin contact. The toxin is absorbed by central nervous system tissue, where it can cause a variety of learning problems. Lead poisoning causes irritability, listlessness, clumsiness, and distractibility. Verbal and attending skills are most vulnerable to lead's toxic effects. A child can get lead poisoning by drinking from water pipes that are soldered with lead. Lead is found in plaster and paint. Children are exposed to lead from carbon monoxide exhaust in automobiles and factory emissions. The National Center for Disease Control estimated that 890,000 U.S. children ages 1–5 have elevated blood lead levels, and more than one-fifth of African American children living in housing built before 1946 have elevated blood levels (www.cdc.gov/nceh/lead/faq/cdc97a.html). A blood test can detect elevated levels of lead.

Although all children are exposed to lead in some form, poor children are most susceptible to lead poisoning. Old, dilapidated buildings and houses are often covered with lead paint. Major highways, circling over inner-city ghettos, spew hydrocarbons into the air. Eventually the lead soaks into the soil, which remains contaminated for decades. Children playing in yards or playgrounds near highways and factories are at risk of lead poisoning. Table 3.5 lists vulnerabilities of school-aged children.

TABLE 3.4   Poverty Guidelines, 1999

Size of Family Unit	Forty-eight Contiguous States ($)	Alaska ($)	Hawaii ($)
1	8,240	10,320	9,490
2	11,060	13,840	12,730
3	13,880	17,360	15,970
4	16,700	20,880	19,210
5	19,520	24,400	22,450
6	22,340	27,920	25,690
7	25,160	31,440	28,930
8	27,980	34,960	32,170
Each Add'l Person	2,820	3,520	3,240

Source: Children's Defense Fund, 2000.

TABLE 3.5   **Vulnerabilities of School-Aged Children**

Age	Vulnerabilities	What to Look For
2–6 years	Brain, lungs, small intestines, immature detox capacity	Pesticides, floor level air pollutants, lead, mercury, allergens
6–12 years	Brain, lungs	Air pollutants, arts & crafts, pesticides
Adolescent	Brain, lungs, rapid growth, sexual maturation	Occupational hazards, drug abuse, air pollutants, arts & crafts, trade school hazards, pesticides

Adapted from Mental Retardation: Definition, Classification and Systems of Support (10th ed.) by AAMR Ad Hoc Committee on Terminology and Classification, 2002, Washington, DC: American Association on Mental Retardation.

Diet. A proper diet is necessary for normal growth and development. Nutrition is most important during fetal, neonatal, and early life, when body cells are dividing, organs are forming, and developmental reflexes are beginning. Lack of proper nutrition in early development can contribute to growth retardation, intellectual delay, and behavior disorders. Winick (1976) found that undernutrition is a widespread problem in the United States, particularly among low-income African Americans, Native Americans, and Hispanics. Although research has not proved that malnourishment alone causes mild mental retardation, it is evident from studies of Third World children that there is a significant relationship between proper nutrition and normal development (Edgerton, 1979).

Health. A number of overlapping health issues put poor children at risk. The lack of adequate health services for poor children is well documented. Infant mortality rates and percentage of low-birth-weight infants is higher among the poor, as are teenage birth rates. Low-birth-weight infants are underdeveloped and vulnerable. Children born to teenage mothers confront a host of environmental and developmental difficulties, including diminished learning opportunities, inadequate nurturing, and frequent illness. A child born to an unmarried, teenage, high school dropout is 10 times as likely to grow up in poverty as a child born to an intact family. Mothers who lack health insurance are less likely to seek out medical advice. Some youngsters only see a doctor when their illness is so severe that they require emergency room care. Among these youth, common childhood ailments such as asthma, ear infections, fevers, and infectious diseases fester without the benefit of medical intervention. The sum total of these environmental risk factors can contribute to cognitive delay, which upon entry to school can result in a diagnosis of mild mental retardation.

Deprivation. The cultural gap between the lives of poor children and the middle-class standards of school puts these youngsters at a disadvantage. This is particularly true in the case of minorities, especially non-English-speaking students. Most discouraging are the conditions that many American youth must adapt to within areas ravaged by poverty. Consider the following description reported by Jonathan Kozol in his guided tour of East St. Louis (1991).

> East St. Louis begins at the Monsanto fence. Rain starts falling as we cross the railroad tracks, and then another set of tracks, and pass a series of dirt streets with houses that are mostly burned out shells, the lots between them piled with garbage bags and thousands of abandoned auto tires. . . . The waste water emitted from the sewage plant, according to a recent Greenpeace study, "varies in color from yellow-orange to green." The toxic substances that it contains become embedded in the soil and the marshland in which children play. Dead Creek, for example, a creek bed that received charges from the chemical and metal plants in previous years, is now a place where kids from East St. Louis ride their bikes. The creek, which smokes by day and glows on moonless nights, has gained some notoriety in recent years for instances of spontaneous combustion. . . .
>
> "Nobody in East St. Louis," Ahmed says, "has ever had the clout to raise a protest. Why Americans permit this is so hard for somebody like me, who grew up in the real Third World to understand. . . ."
>
> "I'm from India. In Calcutta this would be explicable, perhaps. I keep thinking to myself, 'My God! This is the United States!'" (p. 17)

When considering the negative effects of poverty, it is clear that mild mental retardation is as much a social as an educational problem.

Poor children may begin school with delayed language development, inadequate reading readiness, and short attention spans. Some are latchkey children: when they finish school for the day, they return to empty homes where they must care for themselves. The gut-wrenching reality of poverty is that formal education has little meaning to a youngster whose daily existence is a struggle for survival.

In *The Longest Mile* (1969), Rene Gazaway documented the inexorable slide toward mental retardation in isolated, rural Appalachian communities, or "hollows." In Duddie's Branch, Gazaway found rampant illiteracy, malnutrition, disease, and isolation. The culture was so impoverished that for some time Gazaway thought that many adults were mute. In the course of a day, a typical family exchanged no more than a half dozen words. Children under six showed little curiosity or imagination. They spent most of the day together without the benefit of adult guidance or playthings. Gazaway provided the following description of a youngster's life in Duddie's Branch:

> Hollow parents are completely indifferent to the expanding demands for more formal and informal educational experiences. Not one child from Duddie's Branch has ever seen a sandbox. None has played with finger paints, puzzles, or blocks. Their "toys" consist of broken bottles, sharp metal, discarded tin cans. Ask them about Goldilocks, and they will look at you in bewilderment—they never heard a fairy tale. I made a bean bag from an old rag and asked some of the older boys to catch it. They had difficulty. With an old string ball and a heavy stick, I tried to involve them

in batting practice. I was unsuccessful. Not only do games fail to interest them, they are almost completely unable to participate in most activities. They could not be taught to whistle, or even sing a simple tune. (Edgerton, 1979, 55)

Gazaway went on to describe the inability of these children to count, draw a geometric shape, discriminate right from left, or identify pictures of common animals. In this community, characterized by disease, hunger, lack of stimulation, neglect, and minimal verbal interaction, few children could be expected to score over 70 on an IQ test. Duddie's Branchers were trapped in an unchanging cycle of mental retardation. Adults with mild mental retardation parent children who will soon become retarded themselves, and the cycle continues.

Since *The Longest Mile* was published in 1969, both state and federal government combined have infused millions of dollars into highway construction to relieve the isolation of Appalachia. But a high rate of school dropouts continues to sustain functional illiteracy and undermine political initiatives. Hampered by an inability to do simple arithmetic calculations, read a recipe, or fill out a job application, functionally illiterate parents struggle to provide their children with the basic necessities. A national survey in the state of Kentucky reported that 30 percent of the adults in Appalachian counties were functionally illiterate (Kilborn, 2000).

For children of poverty, success or failure will hinge on the teacher's ability to adapt to the students' needs. This begins with an understanding of a youngster's life outside of school. When a student can see a connection between life in and outside of school, then there is a reason to learn. There are too many distractions on the streets for disadvantaged youngsters to sit still for eighteen years of unmeaningful schooling. The identification of a youngster as mildly retarded ensures the delivery of special education services. Yet provision of special education is no guarantee of success. Rather, it is the quality of these services that will make a difference. The task for both regular and special educators is to convince disadvantaged youngsters that there is a good reason to persevere in school.

Disproportionate Representation of Minorities

African American boys continue to be identified as mildly retarded at a higher rate than their overall attendance in the public schools. Among adolescents, African American students accounted for 21 percent of the total number of students in special education programs, and they represented 16 percent of students in general education (Wagner et al., 2003). The intersection of poverty, racism, and questionable diagnostic procedures presents a complex problem for educators. Are minorities over-represented in special education programs because of their higher poverty rate or are diagnostic procedures culturally biased? Educators have argued both sides of this thorny issue since Dunn drew national attention to the problem in his address to the Council for Exceptional Children in 1968.

Only the most ardent political advocate would argue that over-representation of minorities is purely discriminatory in origin. Many minorities live in poor urban and rural areas. The deleterious effects of poverty are bound to hinder normal development of many youngsters and result in special education placement. Between 1983 and 1996, numbers of students identified as mentally retarded declined from 13.3 percent to 11.3 percent among families living *above* the poverty line. During the same time span, students identified as mentally retarded and living *below* the poverty level increased from 17.4 percent to 18.4 percent (Fujiura & Yamaki, 2000). Recent population-based studies have found "no increment risk associated with racial/ethnic group beyond the overlap with poverty and family" (Fujiura, Yamaki, & Czechowicz, 1998).

Friend & Cook (2000) summarized concerns about over-representation of African Americans. Although African American students represent 14.8 percent of all the students in school ages six to twenty-one, they represent 19.8 of all students served as having disabilities defined by IDEA. The disproportionate representation of this group is particularly striking in: (1) the mental retardation category, in which African Americans represent 33.8 percent of all those identified; (2) the emotional disturbance category, in which African Americans represent 26.7 percent of those identified; and (3) the developmental delay category, in which African Americans represent 25.5 percent of those identified. (p. 92)

The case for discrimination is supported by further evidence that despite the legal mandate for multidisciplinary assessments, limited-English-speaking youngsters continue to be tested in English. Despite widespread knowledge of the "six-hour retarded child" phenomena, some school districts still identify students as mildly retarded without gathering additional information on adaptive behavior outside school. Finally, concerns about the cultural fairness of IQ testing continues to spark serious reservations. For example, a judicial decree in California prohibited IQ testing of African American students when making an educational assessment for mild mental retardation (*Larry P. v. Riles*, 1979). As long as IQ tests remain the primary assessment tool for determining mild mental retardation, arguments about both validity and cultural fairness will persist.

Characteristics

The following sections describe learning characteristics of students with mild mental retardation. The first, cognitive, reviews the research on the development of thinking skills. The next section, on mental processing, describes how students with mild retardation interpret, store, and use sensory information. The section on *academics* explains how students with mild retardation succeed or fail in school. The *communication* section describes the relationship of language ability to school achievement. The *perception/motor* section explains how attention and memory influence learning. Finally, the section on *social–adaptive* skills discusses the special problems of living with the label "mildly retarded." Through a review of each of these sections you will find that students with mild retardation are more similar

HIGHLIGHT **3.1**
A Profile of Poverty

In a large northeastern city, one elementary school encapsulated the miserable union of poverty and inadequate schooling. The neighborhood around the school resembled the aftermath of a battle scene. Shop windows were boarded, abandoned automobiles lined the streets, and the stamp of despair was etched in the faces of middle-aged men hunched in doorways. The school playground looked like a suburban landfill. Mattresses, old tires, and appliances were piled high amid broken bottles and overfilled garbage bags. Any child who played in this area risked serious injury. The outside of the school resembled a fortress with heavy metal doors and wire-mesh windows. It was a cheerless yellow building covered with graffiti.

Teachers, the majority of whom were white, punched time cards and talked of weekends away from the chaos of the inner city. In one classroom the teacher made several tentative attempts to get his sixth-grade charges to sit down and have a group lesson. After it was clear that no one was listening, he sat down with two students in the corner of the room and helped them with some math problems. The rest of the "class" wandered around or amused themselves with solitary activity. A teenage girl doodled on the blackboard. She carefully drew an arm with a clenched fist. A hypodermic needle jutted from the bulging biceps. Another girl stared into the tiny holes of an oval pencil sharpener attached to the wall. For fifteen minutes she slowly turned the handle as she peered inside, occasionally giggling to herself. When queried about the total disorder, the teacher's response was plain, "I'm just happy they come to school, at least they are safe for a while; anything after that is a bonus."

to than different from students without disabilities. Variations between learners with mild retardation and other students are differences in degree of ability rather than differences in kinds of ability.

Cognitive

What is intelligence? This is a question that continues to confound scholars in science and education. While scientists study the brain, educators study the mind. Neuroscientists calculate that the brain is composed of a hundred billion neurons, with 500 trillion connections between these microscopic carriers of information. At the molecular level of brain function, thoughts are electrical impulses coursing through neural networks at the speed of light. Teachers in classrooms, psychologists in research laboratories, and employers in business provide ample descriptions of the thinking abilities of individuals with mild retardation. These descriptions of thinking skills vary depending on the point of view of the observer. For example, a teacher might describe problems with abstract material, while a psychologist will report a subaverage mental level. An employer, meanwhile, might complain about difficulty following directions.

Within the context of everyday life, a suitable definition of intelligence is the ability to adapt to the demands of specific settings and individuals. This social-systems view of intelligence, with its emphasis on adaptation, is different from the psychometric (i.e., IQ) concept of intelligence that prevails in schools. In the former, intelligence is a function of survival and of getting along with others; in the latter, intelligence is a score on a test.

Psychometry is the measurement of intellectual ability by mental tests. Mental tests provide an intelligence quotient (IQ) and mental age (MA) but present limited information about how an individual thinks. Because the first mental test devised by Binet was meant to screen slow students, revisions of the original intelligence test continue to focus on school-related skills. For example, the Wechsler Intelligence Scales for Children-Revised (WISC-R) measures verbal and performance skills, including information questions, arithmetic, memory, and speed in putting together puzzles. To judge intellectual capacity based on performance on fourteen subtests on the WISC-R (or its latest revisions) provides a limited view of the nature of intelligence.

Sternberg (1990) described student cognitive ability in terms of thinking styles. Many learning problems could be eliminated, according to Sternberg, if teachers examined more carefully the mismatch between their teaching style and their students' thinking style. He maintained that any subject can be taught in a way that is congruent with a student's thinking style. Students who prefer what Sternberg calls the "executive" thinking style like to be told what to do and are good at recalling facts. These students make a good match with teaching methods that emphasize memorization and objective examinations. On the other hand, students who are more "legislative" in their thinking respond best to learning tasks that require imagination, planning, and creative problem solving. Teachers might confuse thinking style with quality of intelligence. When a "legislative" thinking student is taught by an "executive" style teacher, the student is at a disadvantage. According to Sternberg, teachers need to pay closer attention to the differences in how their students think.

Multiple Intelligences

Howard Gardner (1991) described a more inclusive view of intelligence. Gardner postulated eight forms of intelligence (see Figure 3.1). According to Gardner, each person acquires the ability to use all of the eight forms of intelligence; however, there is variability in the relative growth of intelligence among individuals. For example, lawyers have strong linguistic intelligence, but compared to surgeons their spatial intelligence is probably weaker. The eight intellectual faculties develop as a result of the interaction of heredity and experience. Standard intelligence tests measure only a segment of linguistic, spatial, and logical-mathematical intelligence abilities. Gardner's view of intelligence opens up the possibility that in some instances students identified as mildly retarded might have abilities that are not measured and, as a result, burgeoning skills are

FIGURE 3.1   Multiple Intelligences

Musical Intelligence
Bodily-Kinesthetic Intelligence
Logical-Mathematical Intelligence
Linguistic Intelligence
Spatial Intelligence
Interpersonal Intelligence
Intrapersonal Intelligence
Naturalist Intelligence

overlooked or underdeveloped. For example, standardized tests, which many consider to be the key to improving education, primarily measure a narrow range of skills and facts. These tests ignore core intelligence faculties outlined by Gardner such as musical, interpersonal, and naturalist intelligence. Gardner's views on intelligence have major implications because his theory suggests revisions in both curriculum and testing.

Traditional schooling rewards students with good verbal skills. Within the traditional classroom the three most common ways that students acquire and demonstrate knowledge are listening, reading, and writing. While the value of these skills are undeniable, sitting in every classroom are several students whose intellectual strengths are in areas other than language. Gardner's advocacy of multiple intelligence underscores the adage—it's not how smart you are, it's how you are smart.

Gardner's work has generated excitement among educators who suspect that the problems some students experience in school have more to do with a mismatch between instruction and learner than learner inadequacies. The educational implications of Gardner's work have transformed classrooms from passive to active centers of learning. Rather than spending prolonged periods of time sitting at desks students are up and moving about the room. Open-ended activities that have practical uses such as student-directed newspapers and research are emphasized in the multiple intelligence classroom. Teachers encourage student reflection. Rather than emphasizing right and wrong answers teachers ask students to follow the thinking processes that lead to their conclusions. Students explore their own unique forms of expression through music, art, and dance.

Insights about multiple intelligence have sparked innovative teaching methods that capitalize on student strengths. A high-school history teacher incorporated multiple intelligence into a unit on American history by allowing students to choose their own presentation formats.

- Writing and performing skits about the Lewis and Clark expedition (verbal/linguistic and interpersonal intelligence)

- For a project on John J. Audubon painting watercolors of birds and other wildlife (visual–spatial and naturalist intelligence)
- Devising a working telegraph (logical–mathematical; kinesthetic intelligence)
- Creating an American history board game (visual/spatial intelligence)
- Delivering a eulogy on Davy Crockett (existential and verbal/linguistic intelligence)
- Role playing a historical figure and speaking to the class in character (intrapersonal and verbal/linguistic intelligence) (Lambert, 1997, 5)

The cognitive theory of Jean Piaget (1950) offers another method for understanding the development of thinking. Piaget's theory describes four phases of intellectual development. Each phase is distinctively different in terms of *how* the individual perceives and interprets information. The *sensory-motor* stage is the initial phase of mental development. It begins at birth and typically develops through infancy. (All age indicators are only approximations. There is a good deal of variability in when individual children move onto the next stage of development.) As its title suggests, learning is linked to sensory input and evolving motor abilities. During this stage, the infant organizes and constructs a sense about how the world operates through imitation and play.

The second stage of cognitive development, the *preoperational*, begins around age two. At this point the child develops the ability to think symbolically through language, deferred imitation, games, and art. Ideas are tied to perceptions. For example, a pile of leaves that is scattered may appear to be "bigger" to a four-year-old than if the leaves were pushed close together because it covers more space. The preoperational thinker's view of the world is still characterized by the egocentrism of infancy. For example, clouds are alive because they move, and the sun sets, as a four-year-old put it, "because kids get tired."

During the primary school years (ages seven to eleven), most children are *concrete operational* thinkers. A child can mentally manipulate such symbols as numbers and words, but the child's thoughts are still tied to concrete here-and-now experiences. The opportunity to experiment with materials, to select topics of interest, and to investigate relationships, coupled with an increased need to share ideas verbally, characterizes thinking during this stage.

Formal operations is the final stage of cognitive development. Piaget described the onset of this stage around adolescence. At the formal stage, the young adult has developed the ability to reason logically, to analyze, and to search for solutions among an array of possibilities.

Cognitive research with individuals with mental retardation demonstrated that their reasoning abilities are better characterized as developmentally delayed than deficient (Henley, 1985). Stafford and Klein noted in their comprehensive review of cognitive research:

An important aspect of Piaget's orientation is that it enables one to shift from the deficit notion . . . to understanding where the retarded may be in terms of developmental structures. This positive view enables us to look at what retarded children are rather than what they are not; what they know rather than don't know. (Stafford & Klein, 1977, 308)

The major impact of Piaget's view of intelligence is that children interact and view their world in a distinctively different manner depending on their stage of cognitive development (Figure 3.2). The application of cognitive developmental theory to the instruction of learners with mild retardation requires a close look at what goes on in classrooms. Piaget described learning as interactive. Children require opportunities to learn through trial and error. They use language to compare perceptions and make adjustments to their egocentric view of life. A teacher-directed, sit-still-and-listen classroom does not match the cognitive abilities of children at the sensory-motor, preoperational, or concrete stage of intellectual development.

Reid (1978) analyzed education methods from a Piagetian perspective and observed that many education techniques work in opposition to the natural abilities of students. Rigidly sequenced curricula, concern for the "right" answer, drill, and memorization are formal operational strategies that overshoot the cognitive strategies of students who are at the preoperational or concrete operational stage of thinking. The neglect of educators to consider underlying developmental processes in their teaching can create a conceptual gap between the curriculum and the mediating cognitive structures of the student. The overall effect can be a loss of motivation and continued dependency on adults to provide information and solutions to problems. Educators who view the cognitive development of learners with mild retardation from a Piagetian perspective modify classroom activities to match the learning capabilities of their students.

Mental Processing

Thinking is a complex process. Suppose a stranger asks you for directions. As you picture a route in your mind, the visual center of your occipital lobe is activated. Then you mentally translate your vision into a series of steps while your left hemisphere analyzes each part of the stranger's journey. Words take shape next, and instantaneous messages flash back and forth between the parietal lobe and frontal lobe. The mouth region of the motor cortex fires signals to your tongue, jaw, and larynx. Finally, as you speak, the auditory cortex of the temporal lobe tracks your words and sentences to ensure that you are accurately describing the correct route.

This brief illustration describes the multiple tasks the brain performs in "processing" the steps of a simple communication. When a deficit exists in these processing skills, even everyday tasks can become overwhelming. Much of the pioneering research on processing skills was done using patients who had suffered brain injuries. Researchers would pinpoint the damaged area of the brain, determine what processing skill was impaired, and draw a conclusion that the damaged area was responsible for that specific processing disability. With individuals

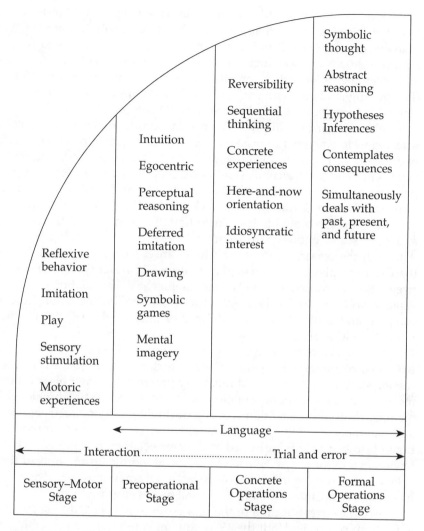

FIGURE 3.2 Piaget's Model of Cognitive Development

Source: Adapted from Wyne, M., and O'Connor, P. (1979). *Exceptional Children, a Developmental View.* Lexington, MA: D.C. Heath.

who had no obvious brain damage, judgments about deficits in processing skills were hypothetical. Ellis (1963), for example, theorized that individuals with mental retardation were deficient in some processing skills and had normal abilities in others. The challenge for researchers was to determine which processing skills were intact and which were deficient.

The previous section on cognition described the developmental view of how students with mild mental retardation think. Researchers who espouse the developmental view of mild mental retardation report a slower rate of cognitive development rather than specific deficits in mental processing. It is likely that the developmental and deficit theories are to some extent both correct. Present research methodologies are muddled by divergent statistical procedures and grouping of subjects by mental age rather than type of mental retardation (i.e., putting students with socioeconomic and clinical mental retardation in the same category because they have similar IQ scores).

When researchers discriminate mental retardation by etiology, a clearer picture begins to emerge. For instance, research conducted on students with mental retardation with an organic etiology, such as Williams syndrome, Prader–Willi syndrome, and fetal alcohol syndrome, produced evidence of diverse mental processing problems not found in students with socioeconomic mild mental retardation (Dykens & Kasari, 1997; Uecker & Nadel, 1998).

Advances in biotechnology, including PET scans, magnetic resonance scans, and CAT scans, allow neuroscientists to observe the thinking brain in action. Although the research costs for such advanced equipment are still prohibitive, these technologies are certain to play a future role in clarifying the relationship between mental processing skills and intelligence. The mapping of the human genome will add to this body of knowledge by allowing future researchers to compare and contrast thinking abilities of students based on genetic markers rather than IQ scores.

Testing is a common method for identifying processing deficits of students with mild retardation. However, many tests that are used to measure mental processing skills have validity and reliability problems. Teacher observations are the most common source of information about mental processing problems. Deficient memory skills, short attention span, distractibility, and impaired abstract thinking are commonly attributed to students with mild retardation. Yet teachers' observations of student actions are biased by their expectations for "normal" classroom behavior. In a classroom, where students spend inordinate amounts of time sitting, listening, and writing in workbooks, even small amounts of bored or distracted behavior can be misinterpreted as a "mental processing" problem.

Accurate identification of the processing skills needed to succeed in school is far from complete. Until the 1970s, attempts to evaluate processing skills and deficits were hindered by overreliance on the need to infer abilities from samples of behavior. Sometimes the behaviors were answers to questions on a test; at other times the behaviors were actions in the classroom. The difficulty with these indirect assessments of processing skills is that there were other factors, such as teacher bias and inadequate theory, that distorted judgments about processing skills.

With positron emission tomography (PET scans), neuroscientists can directly observe the brain in action. Through the use of computer-enhanced imagery, physicians are able to observe the brain of a patient in the act of thinking. A radioactive tracer in the bloodstream lights the computer projection of the patient's brain in vivid colors that correspond to the part of the brain that is engaged. When the patient is talking, the left frontal lobe and motor cortex are highlighted in red. When the patient is listening, the left temporal lobe projection turns red and surrounding inactive brain tissue is colored a dim blue on the computer monitor. Although this procedure is too expensive to use in schools, the knowledge gained from PET scan research on mental processing and learning is certain to benefit researchers in their work with all students.

Academics

In some ways the classroom experience for students with mild mental retardation has changed, in other ways it has remained the same. Twenty years ago students were labeled "educable mentally retarded" and placed in self-contained special education classrooms or state sponsored training schools. While the label "educable mentally retarded" has been dropped, in most school systems the placement of students in self-contained classrooms still persists, particularly within inner-city school districts (U.S. Department of Education, 2002).

In the past students with mild retardation were often exposed to a "watered down" curriculum. Special education teachers would present the regular school curriculum but at a slower pace, with emphasis on drill and repetition. Students subjected to this tedious instruction frequently failed to show any significant gains in academic skills. Failure brought on motivational problems and a high dropout rate. Researchers began to detect a characteristic phenomenon, which they referred to as "learned helplessness." Students lost faith in their ability to learn and gave up when a task seemed difficult. Over the past ten years two new approaches to curriculum for students with mild mental retardation have emerged with an emphasis on functional and thinking skills. (More information about these approaches is included in the section on Teaching Strategies.)

An equally vital academic strategy is early childhood education. Two types of early childhood programs play a significant role in alleviating conditions that contribute to mental retardation: programs that target children at risk because of poverty and programs for developmentally disabled and delayed children provided through IDEA. Early childhood programs that target poor children, such as Head Start, provide health, family training, and educational services to preschool children. Entrance criteria for Head Start is based on income guidelines; entrance criteria for special education early intervention programs is based on the identification of a disability.

Over the years a strong research base has substantiated the positive effects of early childhood programs to stimulate cognitive development of high-risk disadvantaged youth and students with disabilities. For example, a longitudinal study of early childhood for poor children, the Carolina Abecedarian Project (Ramsey, 1998) reported numerous benefits when they compared project young adults (21 years) with individuals who had not participated in early childhood programs. Included among the positive findings were higher scores on tests of cognitive ability, enhanced language development, higher academic achievement in reading and math, and increased enrollment in post-secondary school education. Young people at risk of socioeconomic mild mental retardation clearly benefit from early childhood preschool experiences as do children with clinical mental retardation. Various studies have demonstrated an increase from 13 to 20 points in measured IQ of children enrolled in early childhood programs as compared to non-participating peers (Kotulak, 1996).

Communication

Robert Ornstein, the neuroscientist, once observed that students are not judged on how well they use their brains, but on how well they use their mouths. Rational thought involves more than verbal abilities. The neocortex of the human brain is divided into two halves, the left and right hemispheres. For most individuals, the left hemisphere is the language center. In the left frontal, parietal, and temporal lobes of the brain, mental activity is expressed through listening and speech. The right hemisphere is the creative, intuitive part of the brain. While the left hemisphere solves problems through analysis, the right hemisphere integrates information and searches for holistic solutions. Neither half is superior to the other; both work together to produce rational thought.

The majority of school activity, including reading, speaking, and writing, requires a preponderance of left-hemisphere language skills. Therefore, a preschool child who is not provided with such language activities as bedtime stories, listening to music, and guided conversations with adults is at a distinct disadvantage upon entering school. Because so many students with mild retardation are poor, minorities, and speak English as a second language, their opportunities to develop the language skills required for a successful school experience may be limited.

Secondary teachers expect students to follow oral directions, recall information from lectures, locate information in textbooks, and take notes. In elementary classrooms, students are expected to listen to the teacher, answer questions correctly, read silently, and write. The one-sided emphasis on verbal skills favors the middle-class child and handicaps the poor child. Disadvantaged learners may not begin school with the middle-class language background that is a prerequisite for successful classroom participation.

Language Deficient versus Language Different.   Bernstein (1961) described poor children's language as a "restricted code," which was ill-suited for subtle shades of thought or meaning. Poor children, he said, were unprepared for rational thought when parents dealt with them in an authoritative, impulsive manner. Thus the disadvantaged child fails to learn such abstract concepts as causality and long-range planning. Bernstein's view of the deficient language development of poor children was used by some educators in this country to explain the inadequate school performance of poor African American children.

Bereiter and Englemann (1966) believed that a deprived environment retarded speech and that deficient speech led to deficient thought. School failure was the cumulative result. The "language deficient" perspective of African American children's speech focused attention on remedial efforts to teach them "White Standard English." For instance, DISTAR, a sequentially structured preschool program, was used to teach language development to poor inner-city children. The TV show "Sesame Street," which is designed especially with poor children in mind, adopted the deficient-language hypothesis by teaching new vocabulary, labeling objects, and presenting basic school readiness skills.

The assumption that poverty causes deficient language, which leads to deficient thinking skills, was challenged almost immediately by researchers in the field of psycholinguistics. Robinson (1965) found that the "restricted code" hypothesis is a better description of poor children's performance than of their competence. From his studies Robinson discovered that poor children choose to speak in dialects that are accepted by their peers even when they are capable of more elaborate, middle-class speech. To test his hypothesis, Robinson asked a group of lower- and middle-class students to write a letter to a friend and to a school administrator asking for a favor. Whereas the informal letters reflected the children's social class speech patterns, the formal letter to the educator contained few elements that could be attributed to lower-class language deficiencies. Robinson concluded that when poor children choose to use more elaborate middle-class language, they can do so. Farley (1986) found that students with mild retardation were capable of age-appropriate, fluent writing.

Lobav, Cohen, and Lewis (1968) reported that poor and middle-class students are more alike than different in the way their language develops. Lobav carefully scrutinized how disadvantaged African American children learned to speak. He found that their language, which he described as "Black Standard English," progressed through a logical sequence of syntax and structure. Lobav reported that the speech of his subjects followed a normal pattern of development. Their language was not deficient, only different from white middle-class language. The "language different" hypothesis advocated by Ginsburg (1972) highlighted the structural and functional conflicts between how poor children speak and the expectations placed on them by schools embedded in middle-class language. One example of structural conflict is the use of "White Standard English" in reading texts. A student might encounter difficulty when the teacher expects the child to pronounce words as they appear in the text. Functional conflicts occur when, as Robinson noted, students persist in using speech in school that is accepted by peers because to do otherwise would be considered unmanly.

The proposition that "Black Standard English" is a legitimate dialect was carried one step further in 1996 when the Oakland, California, school board unanimously declared "Ebonics" a language. The Ebonics controversy was fueled by attempts to solicit federal funds for Oakland schoolchildren based on the premise that they should receive assistance in the same way any non-English-speaking youngster would via bilingual classes. The Ebonics movement divided African American leaders. Some felt validation of Black Standard English would be the first step to improve scholastic achievement. Others, including the political activist Jesse Jackson, said that legitimizing Ebonics would limit the ability of African American students to compete against people with fluent verbal skills. The debate faded after both federal and state officials opposed funding that would support Ebonics in California classrooms.

English as a Second Language.   When English is a second language, it is difficult to determine whether mild disability exists. Language assessment of non-English-speaking or limited-English-proficient students is improving, particularly for Spanish-speaking youngsters. Still, it is difficult to identify a language deficit in a bilingual or non-English-speaking youngster. Assessment of language disorders analyzes a variety of skills, including auditory discrimination, articulation, verbal expression, and comprehension of complex relationships. According to Langdon "the purpose of testing a non-English- or limited-English-proficient student is to determine his or her proficiency in the native language and to compare it with the performance in the second language, when appropriate" (Langdon, 1983, 39). The objective is to determine whether lack of proficiency in English is due to a general language disorder or is a reflection of normal difficulties in learning a new language.

As numbers of non-English-speaking students strain the resources of public schools, determining the source of academic problems will continue to challenge educators. For instance, in California, there are 90 distinct language groups and nearly 400,000 limited-English-proficient students in public schools (Cegelka, Lewis, & Rodriguez, 1987). When these students fail to progress satisfactorily, standard testing procedures used to identify mild mental retardation will almost certainly indicate a disability, unless special measures are used to take language differences into account. This is because most standardized tests of intelligence primarily assess language skills. Misdiagnosis can take two forms: false positive and false negative. In the former, students are incorrectly assessed as mildly retarded, whereas in the latter situation, mild learning problems are overlooked.

To accurately assess a language disorder among non-English-speaking students, both languages are assessed by a clinician who is fluent in each. Assessment instruments are translated into the student's native language, and, if a language disorder is found, remediation begins in the student's native language (Langdon, 1983). Figure 3.3 contains a list of tests that have been translated into Spanish.

The itinerant lifestyles of many of non-English-speaking students make it difficult to assess mild retardation and other disabling conditions. Baca and Harris (1988) estimated approximately 80,000 migrant children in need of special education. They concluded that only 8,000, or 10 percent, of these children receive special education services. Because of limited English proficiency, poverty, and inadequate health conditions, migrant children are especially vulnerable to mild mental retardation. In a study of migrant education, Barresi (1984), found that:

1. Only 10 percent of children with mild disabilities were identified.
2. Identification occurs late in the school career.

FIGURE 3.3   Tests Used by School Systems that Are Translated into Spanish

Bilingual Syntax Measure
Ber-Sil
Dos Amigos Verbal Language Scales
Del Rio
Leiter International Performance Scale
Language Assessment Scales
SOMPA
WISC-R
Boehm Test of Basic Concepts
Carrow Test of Auditory Comprehension of Language
Peabody Picture Vocabulary Test
Woodcock–Johnson Psychoeducational Battery
Bender–Gestalt
PEOPLE
Austin Spanish Articulation Test
Columbia Mental Maturity Test
Raven Progressive Matrices
Woodcock Language Proficiency Battery

3. Students were placed in the wrong special education programs.
4. Gaps in services existed because of different administrative procedures between school districts. (Baca & Harris, 1988)

The number of culturally and linguistically diverse students will continue to increase in our nation's schools. Urban schools, in particular, will be faced with increased numbers of underachieving students with cultural and language differences. Schools need to keep pace with the changing student population. If teaching techniques do not change to take into account such meaningful circumstances in children's lives as their language and culture, special education will become inundated with children identified as mildly disabled. Many of these children will not have intellectual deficiencies. Rather, they will be the product of an educational system that was unable to adjust to the changing needs of its student population.

Perception/Motor

Perception is a combination of attention, memory, and thinking. As an illustration, without looking, list the names of the authors of this textbook. Even though you look at the cover of this book on a regular basis (at least your professor hopes this is the case), you probably found naming each author a difficult task. Perception begins with selective attention. You can look at many features of your environment day after day (e.g., the color of the walls in your classrooms), but if you do not concentrate and willfully commit the sensory input to memory, your brain will not encode the information, and it will be forgotten.

Familiarity, interest, color, and movement are a few of the factors that influence perception. As infants mature, they learn to discriminate specific details from a background of competing stimuli. This figure–ground discrimination is an essential perceptual skill for successful school performance. Students with poor figure–ground discrimination skills may have trouble selecting individual letters from a line of words, become confused by oral directions, or become distracted by movement in a classroom.

According to Hebb (1966), early childhood experience plays a key role in the development of perceptual skills. Hebb theorized that environmental stimulation accelerates the growth of brain tissue and connections among neurons in the brain. Conversely, environmental deprivation will adversely affect brain tissue development and subsequent mental processing of information in later years. In applying Hebb's theory to children with mild mental retardation, Wyne & O'Conner noted,

> Some have argued that Hebb's theory, which stresses sheer experience to stimulation and variation in perceptual stimulation early in life, fails to account for deviant cognitive development of disadvantaged infants who grow up in slum conditions, absolutely bombarded with stimulation. On the contrary, this may not be at all inconsistent with Hebb. Hebb's theory is built on the proposition that repeated stimulation is necessary for learning to occur, and that selective attention to those stimuli is crucial. It is now thought that some children growing up in such intense slum conditions may be so bombarded with stimuli of all kinds as to force them to tune out much of it from their awareness, and that this may be part of their cognitive deficit—the failure to selectively attend. What appears to be inattentive, off-task behavior in school aged disadvantaged children may have its origins in a disruptive, noisy, disorienting environment in infancy. (Wyne & O'Conner, 1979, 237)

Inadequate teaching is often overlooked as a contributor to presumed deficits in attention and memory. Students who are expected to maintain attention during dull and repetitious lessons are unlikely to remember what they read or heard only moments before. Ineffective teachers use general characteristics of students with mild mental retardation as a rationale for individual learning problems. A vicious cycle of low expectations and unsuccessful learning evolves when teachers use mild mental retardation as an explanation for a student's learning difficulty. A teacher who remarks, "Well, Susan simply can't retain concepts because she's mildly retarded," is overlooking the significant role of effective teaching in helping students learn. Teaching that includes active student involvement with learning tasks, guided practice sessions, and systematic error-correction procedures will produce successful results that can overcome deficits in organizing perceptual information (Algozzine & Maheady, 1986).

The ability to coordinate perception with movement is a fundamental skill required for learning. The fact that he named the first phase of intellectual development the sensory-motor stage is a clear indication of the importance Piaget attached to early perceptual-motor experiences. Lack of perceptual-motor stimulation at a young age may delay intellectual development. The delay can be so subtle that negative consequences may be overlooked until the school years, when a youngster is compared to peers in such tasks as reading, writing, and physical education.

Perceptual-motor problems can manifest themselves in a variety of ways, including poor coordination and inadequate fine-motor skills. Research on motor-skill performance of students with mild mental retardation consistently reports difficulties with such activities as running, throwing, and jumping (Dobbins & Rarick, 1977; Holland, 1987). Poor performance in physical education classes can negatively affect student self-confidence and motivation to persevere. Conversely, physical education and recreational skills can promote student self-confidence by enhancing awareness of body coordination and performance. Such programs as Outward Bound and rope climbing increase perception and attention skills of students while providing them with challenging and successful experiences.

Social/Adaptive

Categorical labels, such as mental retardation, reinforce the tendency to classify students in terms of the single dimension ascribed by the label. The social needs of students with mild retardation may be overlooked because their "problem" is viewed in terms of subaverage intellectual functioning. Yet there is nothing retarded about the emotions of these students. Students identified with mild retardation have normal feelings. They want to be liked, accepted, and valued as human beings. Their self-esteem is strongly influenced by their status and day-to-day activities in school (Dupont, 1978).

Many students spend a significant portion of their day out of the mainstream of normal school activities. A study of students with mild retardation in northern Illinois found that more than 90 percent of the students were in regular classrooms less than half the day (Polloway et al., 1983). The stigma of spending most of the day in a special education classroom, isolated from normal school activities, can have a corrosive effect on a youngster's self-esteem. Like all other students, youngsters with mild mental retardation want to be liked and accepted, yet studies of regular education students' perceptions report nonacceptance or rejection of students identified as mildly retarded (Kuveke, 1983).

The majority of students with mild disabilities are identified by an educational assessment after entering school. At the precise time in their young lives when they are most in need of success, these youngsters experience failure and the added indignity of being identified with such labels as learning disabled or mildly retarded. The stress of dealing with school failure, peer rejection, and segregation as a learner with mild retardation can cause students to lose faith in themselves as competent individuals. Failure in school leaves a strong impression. Educators use the term "learned helplessness" to describe students' lack of confidence in their own abilities. When Reynolds and Miller (1985) compared students identified as mildly retarded with nondisabled students, they found the special-needs students showed significant signs of depression and learned helplessness. The findings suggest that students with mild retardation are vulnerable to emotional disturbance because of their failure in school and their prolonged exposure to peer disapproval (Epstein, Cullinan, & Polloway, 1986).

Wehmeyer, Kelchner, and Richards (1996) found that many adults with mental retardation have difficulty acting autonomously. Subsequently, they are unable to manage their lives and are limited in pursuing quality-of-life experiences. They lack what researchers call "self-determination." Everyday experiences such as paying a bill, returning an item to customer service, or asking a friend to socialize can seem overwhelming. Such students exit or graduate high school handicapped in their ability to find work, live independently, and enjoy everyday experiences that many of us take for granted, such as riding a bus to the mall. In order to encourage self-determination, Wehmeyer and Schwartz (1997) recommend that teachers "provide activities that optimally challenge the student and promote autonomy by supporting student initiation of activities and allowing choice." (p. 254).

Wehmeyer et al. (1996) identified ten components that characterize self-determination:

- choice making
- decision making
- problem solving
- goal setting and attainment
- self-observation skills
- self-evaluation skills
- self-reinforcement skills
- positive attributions of efficacy
- self-awareness
- self-knowledge

While many students with mild mental retardation demonstrate inadequacies in self-determination, increased interest in behavioral difficulties demonstrated by students with specific types of clinical mental retardation present the possibility of distinctive patterns. For example, Dykens and Kasari (1997) reported that children with Prader-Willi syndrome exhibit distinctive maladaptive behaviors including overeating, food obsessions, and sleep disturbances. Students with Prader-Willi syndrome also exhibit an increased tendency to argue, be stubborn, and have tantrums than comparative groups of students with Down syndrome and socioeconomic mild retardation. Social disinhibition and difficulties modulating reciprocal relationships are common behavioral difficulties experienced by students with Williams syndrome, another type of clinical mental retardation (Dykens & Rosner, 1999). As research continues to identify maladaptive characteristics common to specific subtypes of clinical retardation, educators can better target curriculum priorities in order to provide students with appropriate behavioral supports and socialization learning activities.

Placement decisions are often based on educator perception of student social functioning. Hughes et al. (2002) postulated that the reason that less than 10 percent of students with mental retardation are educated primarily in general education classrooms is the "narrow repertoire of social interaction behavior" (p. 533). Researchers' observations within informal school settings, such as lunchroom and hallways, indicate that without interventions students with mental retardation infrequently interact with their non-disabled peers. Differences in how students socialize verbally were observed in both groups of students. For example, general education students stayed focused on a topic longer than disabled students, also, students with mental retardation engaged in more inappropriate motor activity during conversations. This research builds on many studies that have emphasized the need for specific social skill training coupled with planned interventions such as school "buddy" programs, peer tutoring, and incorporation of social skill curriculums within the academic program.

Teaching Strategies

Students with mild mental retardation often need assistance to connect academic learning to real-life experiences (i.e., functional skills) and adjust how they approach learning activities (i.e., school adaptive behavior). They need assistance learning the content and skills that many of their peers learn without special educational activities (Ysseldyke & Algozzine, 1995). Of course, many of their characteristics overlap with those of students with learning disabilities or emotional disturbance. Therefore, many of the approaches used to improve basic academic skills (e.g., reading, writing, and arithmetic), communication (e.g., language and speech), and behavior (e.g., attention to tasks, disruptiveness) of these other students are also useful when working with students with mild mental retardation. Effective teachers of students with mental retardation set high expectations and focus instruction on functional activities designed to promote success with real-life problems. A summary of general interventions used by teachers with students with mental retardation is presented in Figure 3.4. Some general principles of effective teaching, general procedures for improving thinking skills, teaching reading, school adaptive behavior, leisure, and work skills are discussed in the following sections.

Instructions

Given the array of students with different language skills and backgrounds who populate classrooms, and the amount of listening that students are expected to do, teachers face a formidable challenge when instructing their students. Teachers, however, are sometimes unclear in their lessons. An analysis of teacher talk by Nelson (1988) found that false starts, repetitions, lack of clarity, and abstract language were common aspects of teacher talk. Students with mild retardation may have attention and memory deficits that further impair their ability to understand teachers' explanations.

FIGURE 3.4 **General Interventions for Teaching Students with Mild Mental Retardation**

1. Expect to see progress; mild mental retardation is not a permanent, unalterable condition.
2. Many students come to school without readiness skills: don't assume they know what you are talking about.
3. Identify a student's level of cognitive functioning (i.e., preoperational, concrete, operational), and match teaching approaches to learner's characteristics.
4. Always connect abstract ideas to life experiences.
5. Avoid dull, repetitious work. Provide novelty in lessons.
6. Provide maximum opportunities for learning in the least restrictive environment.
7. Remember that the label "mentally retarded" is demeaning and promotes stereotyping.
8. Keep in mind there is more to intelligence than the narrow range of skills assessed by IQ tests.
9. Insist on a measure of adaptive behavior before a student is evaluated as mentally retarded.
10. Provide students with functional, career-oriented learning experiences.

Robinson (1989) recommended the use of advance organizers to help alert students to important material. She proposed the following guidelines for the use of advance organizers:

1. Alert students to the transition to a new activity.
2. Identify topics or activities students will do.
3. Provide an outline or other organizational framework.
4. Clarify teacher expectations for student participation.
5. Provide background information regarding how this lesson relates to previous activities.
6. State the concepts to be learned.
7. Give examples of concepts.
8. Highlight the relevance of topic.
9. Introduce new vocabulary.
10. Specify the desired general outcomes of the activity.

These ten steps provide the student with a direct and simple framework for listening and understanding teacher expectations for successful classroom participation. They are highly effective with many students with mild retardation.

Student memory can be enhanced through the use of verbal rehearsal and self-questioning. Rehearsal requires the student to repeat directions silently several times. This strategy can help a student follow teacher directions. Self-questioning is a strategy useful for all students. After a passage is read or a lesson is taught, the student reviews key elements by asking:

What is the story (lecture) about?
Who is in the story (lecture)?

Where did the events take place?

When did they take place—in what order?

Why is this information important or useful? (Robinson, 1989, 150)

Teaching requires clarity. Many students, including those with language differences or deficits, need help in listening and remembering. The simple technique of asking students what they learned in class today can help a teacher determine what students do or do not understand.

Thinking Skills

Documented evidence continues to point to effective decision-making and problem-solving skills as an academic weakness in students with mild mental retardation. Concerns about these critical cognitive abilities have provided an impetus for development of cognitive curriculums.

Guided teaching of thinking skills is a general procedure used in educating students with mild retardation. Goldstein (1974) advocated the direct teaching of problem-solving skills. A major hurdle for many individuals with mild retardation is adapting to the social demands of life after school. Goldstein's Social Learning Curriculum utilized a "logical inductive strategy" to teach students a hierarchical procedure for problem solving. Within this system, students learned to label, detail, infer, predict, verify, and generalize.

Goldstein's approach is significantly different from the traditional teacher-directed lessons so often encountered in academic programs for students with mild retardation. In a teacher-directed lesson, the teacher:

1. tells the student what is to be learned;
2. tells the student what to do;
3. calls on students to respond;
4. evaluates student answers; and
5. corrects wrong answers.

In a teacher-directed lesson, each step is controlled and monitored by the teacher. Goldstein believes that teacher-directed lessons undermine student confidence in their own thinking abilities.

Students with mild retardation are sometimes characterized as field dependent in their thinking. This means they do not trust their own perceptions or judgments. They are easily influenced by peers and authority figures. By emphasizing individual problem solving, critical thinking programs such as Goldstein's logical–inductive strategy can help develop self-reliance and improve the reasoning abilities of students with mild retardation.

Reuven Feurenstein's Instrumental Enrichment Program teaches thinking skills by providing learners with strategies for using such cognitive skills as analysis, categorization, and inference. Students develop tools and habits of thinking that allow them to process information, see connections, visualize spatial and temporal relationships, and increase their reasoning ability (Feurenstein, 1980). Through a process of mediated learning teachers use paper and pencil exercises that focus on specific cognitive functions. Students receive feedback through self-correction, peer interaction, and teacher's assessment. Feurenstein's systematic method requires training in mediation practices and an introduction to cognitive and affective factors that effect student performance. Advocates of Feurenstein's methods claim that they effectively ameliorate cognitive problems experienced by students with varying disabilities including autism, mental retardation, and attention deficit disorder.

Reading

The teaching of reading by phonics is an example of a left-hemispheric approach to language development used in schools. Phonics teaches the sounds of letters, how those sounds blend to make syllables, and the combination of syllables to make words. In the reverse procedure—decoding—students are expected to decipher new words by sounding out each letter to complete a whole word. This auditory, analytical, sequential approach to reading is fine if it takes advantage of preexisting language abilities, but what about the child who does not master the phonics approach? For students who lack good auditory and analytic abilities, phonics and eventually reading can be difficult to master.

Marie Carbo found that economically disadvantaged readers tend to be tactile-kinesthetic learners. Their approach to reading is best described as "global." These students have excellent visual and integrative skills that enable them to acquire sight vocabularies. They demonstrate an intuitive awareness of word patterns. Carbo observed that "global learners learn to read most rapidly through such activities as writing stories, reading books of their own choosing, engaging in choral reading, writing and performing in plays, and listening to tape recordings of interesting and well written books" (Carbo, 1987b, 432). The global reading style described by Carbo is an example of right-hemisphere abilities and is an apt description of the approach to learning observed by teachers of disadvantaged, underachieving students (Dennison, 1969; Kohl, 1967).

Mandelbaum (1989) reviewed best practices in teaching reading and found that a combination of functional reading lists with interesting reading material best met the needs of students with mild retardation. Several principles of effective teaching summarized by Mandelbaum are:

1. *Demonstrate Rather than Tell.* The teacher and student discuss, read, and answer questions together about a story on the student's reading level.
2. *Provide for Successful Practice.* Make sure students use reading materials that will sustain at least an 80 percent success rate.
3. *Use Direct Instruction.* Teacher-led group instruction should demonstrate the skill to be learned, provide practice with feedback, and allow for independent student practice.
4. *Plan for High Levels of Task Involvement.* Reading in unison, choral reading, and high-interest readings improve fluency and comprehension.

5. *Ignore Errors that Do Not Matter. All errors are not equal.* Every word does not have to be read correctly. Focus only on errors that change the meaning of a sentence. Provide sufficient time for a student to analyze a word and decode.

6. *Give Independent Assignments that Relate to the Lesson.* Most workbooks and dittos focus on isolated skills unrelated to stories. Avoid the drudgery of worksheets unless relevant and necessary.

7. *Integrate Subject Matter.* Use themes or webbings to cluster concepts.

8. *Measure Behavior Change.* Plot and graph reading improvement in terms of median of number of words read correctly each minute.

9. *Provide Opportunities to Learn Achievement Formats.* Formats vary widely, and students need practice with the procedures that will be used to evaluate their skills.

Functional Skills

Students with mental retardation respond to the same instructional methods as other students. They may require more time to achieve satisfactory levels of performance and typically require special instruction and extra practice to generalize what they have learned to settings other than the classroom. Sometimes they simply need to be taught how to approach academic tasks. For these students, basic academic skill instruction must go beyond basal readers and traditional worksheets. Effective teachers of these students design instructional and practice activities so that they relate to functional use in everyday life, including home and community living. Ysseldyke and Algozzine (1995) provide a detailed set of tactics for improving these functional skills; some of them are summarized with others from Smith, Finn, & Dowdy (1993) in Table 3.6.

TABLE 3.6   Summary of Functional Skill Interventions

Functional Skill Area	Intervention Description
Reading	Have students use community signs, local store directories, local restaurant menus, newspapers, local street signs, yellow pages, and other everyday materials for reading practice.
Mathematics	Have students use newspaper advertisements, mail-order catalogs, menus, and other everyday materials for basic skill and problem-solving practice. Use real objects and manipulatives often when teaching math concepts.
Writing	Have students keep diaries of school events, local news stories, classroom visitors, and other everyday activities for writing practice.
Listening	Use real objects or pictures to teach sounds or names. Give students directions to follow in sentences that require movement around the room or manipulation of real objects. Read directions to students and have them make the object described in the directions.

Recall that according to a widely accepted view of intelligence, children interact differently depending on their stage of development (see Figure 3.2). This means that using concrete objects and manipulatives helps many children learn concepts more easily. It also means that while some students pass through the concrete stages of learning more rapidly than others, the need for these stages is extended for students with mental retardation and other developmental disabilities. Some ideas from Smith, Finn, & Dowdy (1993) for ways to extend instruction in important areas of mathematics are illustrated in Table 3.7.

TABLE 3.7   Instructional Activities for Extending Learning in Mathematics

Goal: Classifying objects based on characteristics or unique features

- Have students place blocks into groups based on size, color, texture, shape, name, or other attributes.
- Have students place small toys into groups based on size, color, texture, function, or other attributes.
- Have students sort coins, paper money, school supplies, books, or other common objects.

Goal: Learning one-to-one correspondence

- Have students match sets of different objects using numbers to create sets (3 coins = 3 bottle caps).
- Have students match sets of objects with numbers used to represent them (3 coins = 3).
- Have students find as many target sets as possible in a large group of objects (all groups of 3 similar objects in a set of 100 or more).

Goal: Ordering objects on the basis of some characteristic

- Have students arrange a box of pencils from shortest to longest.
- Have students arrange coins from smallest to largest in size.
- Have students arrange sports team members from shortest to tallest.

Goal: Learning that order doesn't change relationships between objects

- Have students combine sets of items to represent relationships.

4 dimes + 3 dimes = 7 dimes	4 clips + 3 clips = 7 clips
3 dimes + 4 dimes = 7 dimes	3 clips + 4 clips = 7 clips
7 dimes – 4 dimes = 3 dimes	7 clips – 4 clips = 3 clips
7 dimes – 3 dimes = 4 dimes	7 clips – 3 clips = 4 clips

Adaptive Behavior

Adaptive behavior refers to the ability to be independent and socially responsible (Reschly, 1989). This means that students with mental retardation require a curriculum that teaches social skills, self-direction, and health and safety information. Effective teachers of these students design instructional and practice activities that they need to succeed in school and other adaptive life experiences. Most incorporate the following teaching procedures (Meese, 1994):

1. They carefully select skills that maximize the likelihood of a student's success.
2. They provide clear statements of the skills to be learned and reasons for learning them.
3. They demonstrate the new skills using a variety of methods (e.g., videotapes, films, live demonstrations), models (e.g., high status peers, siblings), and situations.
4. They provide plenty of examples and nonexamples of expected behaviors.
5. They provide opportunities for practice under their supervision so students can receive supportive and corrective feedback and avoid practicing errors.
6. They provide recognition and rewards for successful demonstration of newly learned skills.

Some specific activities for improving adaptive behavior skills are summarized in Table 3.8.

TABLE 3.8   Summary of Adaptive Behavior Interventions

Adaptive Behavior Area	Intervention Description
Social Skills	Have students take part in role-playing activities related to using appropriate social skills. Have them practice greeting friends, exchanging information, engaging in small talk, and other social and communication skills. Reward them for doing so.
Self-Direction	Teach students how to ask for help in school and community settings. Provide practice using these skills in small groups and real-life situations.
	Have students keep track of occasions in which they made a decision on their own, and discuss the outcomes of what they did. Share alternatives between and among classmates.
Health and Safety	Have students role-play emergency situations and generate, discuss, and practice alternative solutions.

Daily Living and Work Skills

Self-care, including activities of daily living and being successful at a job, are important adaptive behavior skills that are the focus of instruction for students with mild retardation. Self-care skills include managing personal finances, caring for personal needs, buying clothing, food, and other personal items, and getting around in the community. Job-related skills include following directions, being punctual, beginning assignments promptly, staying on task, and completing assignments; these are sometimes addressed with functional academic interventions.

Here are some ways to improve self-care skills:

1. Teach students to differentiate coins and other money.
2. Teach students to make and receive change.
3. Have students practice physical fitness activities.
4. Have students practice personal grooming skills.
5. Teach consumer economics.
6. Teach traffic and safety rules.
7. Teach students to use public transportation.

Here are some ways to improve work skills:

1. Teach students that attendance and punctuality are important.
2. Reward students for being on time and for high attendance.
3. Have students record their own attendance.
4. Reward students for completing tasks on time.
5. Have students keep records of completed assignments.
6. Have students complete job applications.
7. Provide rewards after completion of smaller tasks.
8. Set liberal standards for task completion.

Students with mild mental retardation experience difficulties in many areas of school and life functioning. There is no magic in instructional activities that work with these students. In many ways, what effective teachers do with them is just like what they do with everybody else. And, whenever necessary, they modify what they do to accommodate the special learning needs of their students. With this type of instruction, students with mild or moderate mental retardation can learn to overcome many of their problems and can be successful and productive in school and life experiences. A key here is the importance of high expectations and functional curriculum goals.

Summary

Mild mental retardation is both a social and an educational problem. The majority of children identified as mildly retarded are poor, with African Americans over-represented in many states. While many students with mild mental retardation have no identifiable organic or neurological problems, the health-threatening conditions of poverty clearly put poor children at greatest risk. The deleterious effects of such factors as low birth weight, deficient diet, and improper prenatal care can be offset by health and educational intervention for children and their families. There are two types of mild mental retardation: socioeconomic and clinical.

Characteristics of children identified with mild mental retardation can vary from one state to another. Although the American Association of Mental Retardation published guidelines for identifying mild mental retardation, individual states establish their own criteria. Consequently, the prevalence of students identified as mildly retarded varies from state to state. This means that some students who need special education services may go without, and other students without disabilities receive services.

Students with mild retardation are characterized by slower cognitive development; academic deficiencies, especially in reading; and deficits in adaptive behavior. Because success in school depends so much on verbal skills, some students—poor children and children from non-English-speaking families in particular—encounter difficulties. An individual student may demonstrate specific learning problems in mental processing, social adaption, and perception. However, students with mild retardation show a great deal of variability in learning characteristics, and generalizations about their abilities or disabilities can lead to stereotypes and negative teacher expectations.

Students with mild retardation score in a range of 50 to 75 on IQ tests, and they have deficits in social skills outside the school setting. Quality of educational programming depends on the teacher's ability to motivate students who have a history of school failure. Academic programs that emphasize functional skills provide adolescents with a reason to stay in school. Younger children learn best when teachers match instruction to their cognitive abilities. Programs that attempt to remediate specific deficiencies, such as poor memory, through drill and repetition fail to consider the point of view of the learner. Students with mild retardation need practice in developing their own thinking abilities. School programs that help students with mild retardation gain confidence in themselves as learners are most successful in helping them to adapt to life after school.

The cycle of destitution that has characterized mild mental retardation throughout the past century will be broken when disadvantaged learners graduate from school with employable skills. Education is the best offensive strategy in the war on poverty. When regular and special educators work together to keep learners in the mainstream of school life, teacher and student expectations for success are enhanced. As Lloyd Dunn eloquently pointed out, the interests of poor children are not served by labeling them retarded and relegating them to isolated special education classrooms. Ultimately it is the quality of educational programming, not the label pinned on the student, that determines success or failure.

ACTIVITIES

1. Visit a special education classroom that serves students with mild retardation. Observe the students at work. How many students are in the classroom? Draw a diagram of the physical arrangement of the classroom. Observe the bulletin boards and other displays in the classroom. What topics are emphasized? Are students working in large groups, in small groups, or individually?

2. While visiting the special education classroom, ask for a private time to talk with the teacher. Try to find out what type of curriculum guide he or she uses. Which subjects are primarily taught? Is career education an integral part of the curriculum? Are social skills taught? Are functional skills included?

3. Investigate the professional organizations in the field of mental retardation. Two national organizations are the Division on Mental Retardation of the Council for Exceptional Children (1920 Association Drive, Reston, Virginia 22091) and the American Association on Mental Retardation (1719 Kalorama Road NW, Washington, D.C. 20009). Write to these organizations for their literature. Try to determine their purposes, who their members are, and what services are offered to members.

4. Are there local or state branches of the national professional organizations for mental retardation? If there is a local organization, arrange to visit one of their meetings. Ask a member to visit your class and talk with students about the purpose of the organization, membership composition, and services offered to members.

5. Visit the campus library. Locate the special education journals that focus on mental retardation. These journals include the *American Journal on Mental Retardation, Education and Training in Mental Retardation*, and *Mental Retardation*. Look for articles about intellectual disabilities and mental retardation in major special education journals like *Exceptional Children* and *Teaching Exceptional Children*.

4 Students with Behavioral/Emotional Disorders

ADVANCE QUESTIONS

Answer the following questions as you read this chapter:

1. What types of students are included in the category of behavior disorders?
2. What are some of the main components of definitions of behavior disorders?
3. How many students are included in the behavior disorders category?
4. What causes behavior disorders?
5. What are some characteristics of students with behavioral/emotional disorders?
6. What strategies are used by teachers of students with behavior disorders?
7. What can teachers do to improve social and emotional problems?
8. What aspects of cultural diversity are important to consider when meeting the needs of students with behavior disorders?

Chapter Web

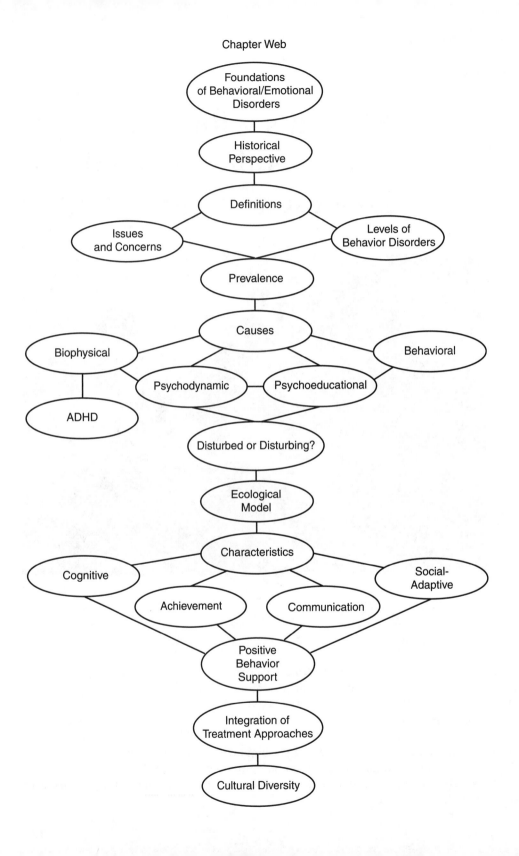

Vignette: Fred Peterson

Fred Peterson has been a teacher for over twenty years: each of his classes has had at least one problem student. This year it was Selena. Selena could always find a way to avoid schoolwork. For example, one day Fred told the class to begin work on the math sheet he had provided each of them. "Excuse me, Mr. Peterson," said Selena. "Can I go to the bathroom?" Fred had a policy of letting students move freely throughout the school, so he let her go. About fifteen minutes later, she returned and asked if she could wash the blackboards. Fred mentioned it was probably a better idea to start on her worksheet. At this suggestion, Selena grew angry. She walked up to Fred, balled the worksheet in her fist, and threw it at Fred. "Do your own damned worksheet," she shouted, and she ran out the classroom door.

Alan is a senior in high school with decent grades. He is on the basketball team, and he has a lot of friends. Lately he and a few buddies have started smoking marijuana on the way to school in the morning. Alan maintains that after twelve years of boring classes, it's fun to go to "high" school. Ms. Hildago, his homeroom teacher, can tell when Alan has been smoking. His eyes are red and glassy. She has tried talking to Alan privately but to no avail. Alan either denies he smokes or walks away. Alan's behavior in his classes is erratic. He jokes around, makes snide comments, or just spaces out. Ms. Hildago is hesitant to discuss Alan's situation with the principal because she's afraid Alan will be expelled.

Alice has been teaching kindergarten for ten years, but she has never had a class like this one. Several youngsters have attention problems caused by alcohol use by mothers during pregnancy. Raymond, although talkative and outgoing, is unable to handle scissors or even extra fat crayons. Louis gets a sticker just for sitting still for ten minutes. He is constantly careening around the room, bumping into other children, and starting fights. Fay tries hard to do well, but she can't follow directions. She is frequently confused about what she's supposed to be doing. Alice is unable to give Fay all the individual attention she requires.

Now that you have read the vignette about some teachers of students with problem behaviors, see how may problem-solving questions you can answer. For those you cannot readily answer, try to find some additional information to use in answering them as you read the chapter. The experiences of Fred Peterson, Ms. Hildago, and Alice are typical of teachers of students with behavior disorders.

1. What should be done to help students like Selena, Alan, Raymond, Louis, or Fay?
2. Who should teach them?
3. Do all schools provide special education services for students with behavior disorders?
4. What expectations would you have for students like Selena, Alan, Raymond, Louis, or Fay if you were teaching them?
5. Should students with behavior disorders be included in classes with students without disabilities?

Experiences like these illustrate the kinds of "problems" that cause students to be identified with behavior disorders. Disturbing behaviors, noncompliance, or an inability to adjust to classroom routines are common reasons for students to be referred for special education. Each year, Phi Delta Kappa, a national education organization, commissions a Gallup Poll of the public's attitudes toward education. In all of the surveys, discipline (i.e., controlling disruptive behavior) is a major concern.

At one time or another, every teacher has a student who has conflicts with rules for proper behavior in school. The decision to evaluate a student for special education services on the basis of classroom behavior is a matter of frequency and intensity of the disturbing actions. The more "acting out" the behavior, the more likely a student will be referred for special education. The following behaviors are those most likely to attract unfavorable attention in the classroom:

1. Exhibits physical and verbal aggression toward classmates (fighting, instigation of arguments).
2. Exhibits verbal aggression toward teacher and the other authority figures (profanity, negative names).
3. Refuses to cooperate in classroom group activities.
4. Intentionally damages classroom materials.
5. Uses classroom materials to create disruptive sounds and noises.

A student who is shy or withdrawn may have serious emotional difficulties but if she continues to follow classroom directions and completes her schoolwork, her problems may be overlooked. Depression and suicide are too common among today's schoolchildren to be ignored. Latchkey children (children who return home from school to empty houses), students with learning disabilities, and students experiencing chronic family problems are particularly vulnerable. Guetzloe summarized the causes of suicide among children:

> Any problem that contributes to feelings of depression, worthlessness, helplessness, or hopelessness has the potential to trigger suicidal behavior in a vulnerable individual. Among the many factors that have been cited as contributing to youth suicide are isolation, alienation, loss, physical or psychological abuse, disturbance in peer relationships, substance abuse, rejection, incarceration, disorganization, availability of weapons, fear of punishment, fear of failure, knowledge of suicide, and humiliation. (Guetzloe, 1988, 26)

U.S. Surgeon General David Satcher stated that one in 10 children suffers from mental illness (Satcher, 2000). Among special educators there is concern that not enough is being done to help students with emotional problems. This concern is equally shared by general classroom teachers who spend a large portion of their day trying to manage youngsters' behavior. Table 4.1 lists at-risk factors associated with emotional problems.

TABLE 4.1 In School At-Risk Indicators of Emotional Problems

Internalized Emotional Problems (Depression, Suicidal)	Externalized Emotional Problems (Aggressive, Confrontational, Socially Maladjusted)
Anxiety	
Lacks friends	Chronic discipline
Incomplete work	Lack of empathy or compassion
Mood swings	Gang attachments
"Learned helplessness"	Angry outbursts
Interest in cults	Poor academic performance
Inordinate attraction to fantasy	Conflicts with authority figures
Indolent	Bullying
Bully victim	Frequent absences
Frequent absences	Physical aggression
Inappropriate affect (e.g., crying)	Damaging property
Obsessive/compulsive behaviors	Obscene language
Shyness	Ignore teacher warnings

Outside of School At-Risk Indicators of Emotional Problems

Premature birth
Maternal depression
Poverty
Neglect, physical, sexual, or emotional abuse
Foster home placement
Chronic discipline problem
Frequent temper tantrums
Loss of appetite/overeating
Long periods of isolation watching TV or on computer
Sleep disturbances/nightmares

Source: Compiled from Gresham, F.M., MacMillan, D.L., Bocian, K. (1996). "Behavioral earthquakes:" Low frequency, salient behavioral events that differentiate students at-risk of behavior disorders. *Behavioral Disorders* 21(4), 277–292.

Foundations of Behavior Disorders

Hyman and D'Alessandro (1984) highlighted the complex interaction of environmental and individual factors that contribute to student behavior disorders. They found that causes often rest outside the student's ability to control. Their assessment still has value today.

Included among environmental causes are inadequate parenting, overcrowding, racism, lack of employment, overexposure to violence through television and other mass media, peer pressures, and specific social, political, and bureaucratic factors that ignore the needs of the young. Schools contribute to behavior problems through ineffective teaching, poor school organization, inadequate administrative leadership, inappropriate curricula, overuse of suspensions, and other punishments. Within the individual student, Hyman and D'Alessandro cited inborn traits, such as neurological impairments, that may disrupt interactions with others, ultimately causing behavior disorders. Poor self-esteem and frustration with learning are also student responses that accelerate behavior disorders. When attempting to understand students' problems, we must also take into account the troubled systems (family, school, community) that interact with and shape children's development (Apter, 1982; Erickson, 1998). Placing students in a special education program will produce mixed results if, at the end of the school day, youngsters return home to an abusive father, a tormented mother, or a neighborhood permeated with drugs and violence.

There is a fine line between normal and abnormal, right and wrong, mental illness and mental health. Often the force that pushes an individual into one or the other of these categories does not originate in their own behavior. Others with whom they interact are instrumental in shaping, defining, managing, and manipulating our feelings and behavior. This is the crux of the human dilemma. We need to interact with others to grow and learn, yet the nature of those interactions, which are often shaped by forces outside our control, help determine the kind of person we will become.

Behavior disorder, emotionally disturbed, anti-social, mental illness, and *conduct disorder,* are some terms professionals use to explain special needs of students who cannot cope with the social demands of school or society. Over the years, special education has accumulated a large body of research on the causes and treatment of students with behavior and emotional difficulties. Before we discuss these different conceptual models, we examine the historical roots of behavior disorders and their treatment.

Historical Perspective

Human history is replete with strange stories of how deviancy has been dealt with. There was a time when the treatment of insanity was worse than the condition. Early medicants believed that by boring holes in the head (a method called trephining), the devil or other evil spirits would be released and leave the body. Hippocrates first classified mental problems using mania, hebephrenia, and melancholia as terms to describe separate conditions. He also is credited with offering the first theory for the cause of mental problems, blaming an imbalance of body fluids for strange behavior (Rhodes & Tracy, 1972a,b).

Throughout the ages, theories of causation of mental illnesses or emotional disturbances ranged from witchcraft to science. One of the first environmental causes of mental illness was identified in the Middle Ages, when it was discovered that hatters were driven "mad" from the mercury they used to condition felt. When mercury use was discontinued, so was the incidence of "mad hatters." As Restak (1984) noted, "Over the centuries, schizophrenics have been burned at the stake, chained in dark dungeons, starved to death, and drowned" (p. 273). Discoveries that vitamin B6 deficiencies and syphilis caused mental illness helped move mental treatment out of the shadows and into the medical laboratory. About

1890, Kraeplin identified an advanced form of mental illness that he called "dementia praecox." This term was used to refer to adult mental illness, and the classification system surrounding it became the forerunner of the scientific classification system that is in place today (Algozzine, Serna, & Patton, 2001). After Kraeplin introduced dementia, a psychologist, DeSantis, recommended that a new term be designated for the childhood version of this mental condition. He suggested "dementia praecocissima," and the study of childhood emotional problems was given a life of its own.

Shortly thereafter, another psychologist, Heller, observed a severely debilitating, degenerative condition in infants characterized by a loss of motor and language abilities. This condition was labeled as Heller's syndrome. In 1943, Leo Kanner observed odd, stereotyped behaviors in young children. The children, although uncommunicative and aloof, appeared to have average or above average intelligence. This condition became known as early infantile autism. By 1952, the American Psychiatric Association produced a document listing the major types of mental disorders. Childhood disorders did not appear in the first *Diagnostic and Statistical Manual* (*DSM-I*), but the second edition (*DSM-II*) contained a category titled Behavior Disorders of Childhood and Adolescents. Students with behavior disorders do not exhibit the kinds of severe debilitating conditions that were first identified by early psychologists and physicians. Such disabilities as childhood schizophrenia and autism still exist; however, they are severe disabilities and are not included in our discussion of mild disabilities.

Definition and Identification

Professionals use a variety of terms to describe students with emotional and behavioral problems. Classroom teachers use terms based on observations combined with judgments about classroom behavior. Frequently used are such terms as *immature, hyperactive, needs attention, inappropriate,* or *withdrawn.* Psychologists are more clinical in their approach. Using the *Diagnostic and Statistical Manual of Mental Disorders Fourth Edition* (DSM-IV-TR) (American Psychiatric Association, 2002) as a reference, psychologists match student behavior to specific criteria for such conditions as adjustment disorders (e.g., difficulties dealing with a stressful event), impulse control disorders (e.g., unable to control feelings of rage), and mood disorders (e.g., severe swings in mood or behavior). Figure 4.1 lists some of the specific disorders that may be used to justify a special education placement. Keep in mind that not only does a disorder have to be identified but that there must be evidence that the disorder is interfering with academic progress. For example, a student who is being treated with medication for depression might be able to maintain satisfactory grades and thus not qualify for special education services.

The Individuals with Disabilities Education Act provides the following set of guidelines for determining if a student is eligible for special education services for emotional disturbance.

FIGURE 4.1   Synopsis of Selected Behavioral and Emotional Disorders in Children

Opposition Defiant Disorder—a pattern of negativistic, hostile and defiant behavior lasting at least six months. Included among eight listed behaviors are: often losing temper, often angry and resentful, deliberately annoys people. (Four or more of the eight behaviors must be present.)

Conduct Disorder—A repetitive and persistent pattern of behavior in which the basic rights of others or major age-appropriate social norms or rules are violated. Specific behavioral criteria is listed under the following: aggression to people and animals, destruction of property, deceitfulness or theft, serious violation of rules.

Attention Deficit Hyperactivity Disorder (ADHD)—There are three types of ADHD inattention, hyperactivity-impulsivity, and combined. Each type has a list of symptoms that persist for six months or more. Inattention is characterized by six or more of nine traits including difficulties with sustained attention, listening, following directions, memory, and finishing tasks. Hyperactivity-inpulsivity is characterized by six or more of nine traits including fidgeting, excessive talking, constant moving, impatience, and interrupting others.

Asperger's Syndrome—a developmental disorder that is characterized by unusual preoccupation with a topic that excludes other interests. Behavioral traits include repetitive routines, oddities in speech, inappropriate social behavior, and uncoordinated motor movements.

Bipolar Disorder—Bipolar disorder is characterized by mood swings from elation to sadness. Changes in energy and behavior mirror mood swings. Some signs of the manic stage include extreme irritability, increased energy, euphoric mood, spending sprees, and increased sexual drive. During the depressed phase individuals express feelings of guilt, worthlessness, and helplessness. Normal sleep routines are impaired and appetite is adversely affected. Mood swings are interspersed with normal moods. Diagnosis is based on how often (three or more times a day) mood swings each day and within a week. Children and adolescents experience very fast mood swings.

Early-Onset Depression—Almost one-third of six- to twelve-year-olds with depression develop bipolar disorder within a few years. Some of the signs of early-onset depression are chronic sadness, withdrawal from friends, poor school performance, frequent physical complaints, lack of energy, changes in eating and sleeping habits, and increased agitation.

Source: Compiled from The National Alliance of Mental Health fact sheet *(www.nami.org)*, Retrieved 12/20/04; The National Institute of Mental Health fact sheet *(www.nimh.nih.gov)*, retrieved 12/20/04; and the National Institute of Neurological Disorders and Stroke *(www.ninds.nih.gov)*, retrieved 12/19/04.

The term (i.e., emotional disturbance) means a condition exhibiting one or more of the following characteristics over a long period of time and to a marked degree that adversely affects a child's educational performance.

- An inability to learn that cannot be explained by intellectual, sensory, or health factors.
- An inability to build or maintain satisfactory interpersonal relationships with peers and teachers.
- Inappropriate types of behavior or feelings under normal circumstances.
- A general pervasive mood of unhappiness or depression.

■ A tendency to develop physical symptoms or fears associated with personal or school problems.

The term includes schizophrenia. The term does not apply to children who are socially maladjusted, unless it is determined that they have an emotional disturbance [July 1, 1999.34 C.F.R. 300.7(c)(4)]. States are not mandated to use the federal criteria to identify students, however many do so. Many special educators are critical of the federal definition, but to date no suitable replacement has been crafted.

Issues and Concerns

Unfortunately, the criteria fall short of being a conceptually clear representation from which to develop meaningful identification procedures and treatment practices. For example, how do we identify "an inability to learn which cannot be explained by health factors," or what constitutes a "general pervasive mood of unhappiness"? And what about students who perform in school but still have emotional problems? Morse put it this way:

> Note that a definition including educational performance leaves out those who have no school problems or problems that do not affect achievement, and this can be a significant number. The idea that all disturbed children must have an educational problem in behavior or achievement is a significant error. The other error lies in implying that when children have problems in school, these problems are primarily school related. The fact is that problems are often generated outside the school environment and brought to school. (Morse, 1985, 43)

Perhaps most contentious to some special educators is the omission of "socially maladjusted students" from the ranks of students who qualify for special education services. In addressing this problem, the Executive Committee of the Council for Children with Behavioral Disorders had this to say:

> This exclusion of the socially maladjusted from special education seems to be based on several assumptions. These include: (a) There is a significant population of youngsters whose antisocial behavior is more related to a general social phenomenon than a specific handicapping condition; (b) it is possible to consistently differentiate such students from those who are truly handicapped by virtue of their behavior; and (c) it is important that special education not automatically incorporate a group specified as "in trouble" by other systems, such as the juvenile justice system. (Executive Committee of the Council for Children with Behavioral Disorders, 1987)

The position of the council is that an adjudication of delinquency does not mean a disability is present. However, some students with delinquent behavior do have mild disabilities, and they have an equal right to federal services mandated by Congress for all school-aged youngsters (U.S. Department of Education, 1997, 1998, 1999). Indeed, comprehensive surveys of incarcerated youngsters indicate that mild disabilities are more prevalent among youthful offenders (Nelson, Rutherford, & Wolford, 1987; Rutter et al., 1998).

The lack of clear direction in determining who receives special education services for behavioral or emotional problems is highlighted by a survey that found states use a total of 17 different terms to describe this population (Knitzer, Steinberg, & Fleisch, 1990). Most state definitions used to refer students with behavior or emotional difficulties tend to have several general similarities. They suggest that the disturbances or disorders that exist within the student's behavior patterns cause academic and social problems that in turn affect the youngster and peers. Although these state definitions help professionals to know who should be identified as requiring special education, the actual process of identification is not facilitated by any one definition in particular. Most definitions do not have clearly stated operational criteria that can be dovetailed into a special educational assessment.

Levels of Emotional/Behavioral Disorders

A systematic application of operational criteria should result in the identification of two types of troubled children. The TYPE I (Student with a Behavior Disorder) is characterized by the types of behavior problems found typically in public schools. This student may be a problem in school but not at home. The behavior may be a response to an inappropriate or unmotivating school environment, and it may be responsive to positive environmental strategies. The TYPE II (Emotionally Disturbed Student) may be characterized by the more comprehensive form of disturbance typically not found in general classrooms. This student's behavior will be problematic at home and school, and it may exhibit itself with regularity in both favorable and unfavorable environments. The behavior will not be immediately responsive to environmental management strategies. The behavior may be traced to organic inadequacies, as in the case of youth with childhood schizophrenia. A possible diagnostic comparison between TYPE I and TYPE II students with emotional and behavioral disorders based on the suggested operational criteria is presented in Table 4.2.

Hallahan and Kauffman (1977) suggested that the conditions referred to as learning disabilities, behavior disorders, and mild mental retardation are similar disabilities. The characteristic behaviors of each condition are also similar (Neisworth & Greer, 1975). Whereas the TYPE I behavior-disordered child may be similar in many respects to students with learning disabilities and mild mental retardation, it would seem that the TYPE II child with a severe social–emotional disturbance would be unique.

Prevalence of Emotional/Behavioral Disorders

Of the 5,775,722 students with disabilities (ages 6 through 21) receiving special education services in 2000–2001, 473,663 were included in the category of emotional disturbance, reflecting about a 2 percent increase per year over the preceding ten-

TABLE 4.2   Comparison of TYPE I Behavioral and TYPE II Emotional Disturbance

TYPE I (Behavior Disorders)	TYPE II (Clinical Emotional Disturbance)
General class has not been beneficial; but, placement there is a preferred goal.	General school placements have not been successful; outside placements common.
School counseling services often prove beneficial.	External counseling services are typical.
Common behavioral problems evident in assessment records	Clinical diagnoses and problems recorded
Problems often reported in only one classroom or only at school	Problems evident at home, school, and in other environments
Evidence that interventions are effective with selected problem behaviors	Evidence that problems are very resistant to common interventions

year period (U.S. Department of Education, 2002). This represents about 8 percent of the special education students and about 1 percent of the general school-age population. The overall prevalence of this group of students has been relatively constant over the last ten years (Ysseldyke, Algozzine, & Thurlow, 2000). There is considerable variation from state to state in the percentage of the school-age population identified with EBD. Prevalence figures can range from about 2 percent in some states to less than 0.5 percent in others. Forness (2001) reported that the majority of students with emotional problems sit undetected in general education classrooms.

The prevalence of students with emotional/behavioral disorders (EBD) tends to fluctuate considerably depending on several factors. The nature of the definition and criteria used to identify students has a major impact on the rate of identification and numbers of identified students; for example, when the Bower definition was originally used, the rate of occurrence of behavior disorders was estimated to be 10 percent (Reinert, 1976).

Rubin and Balow (1971) found that 41 percent of the students they studied were identified chiefly by their inability to meet the demands of school behavior expectations. Their findings are analogous to Jane Mercer's description of the "six-hour mildly retarded student." (See Chapter 3, Students with Mild Mental Retardation). The results of the Rubin and Balow study indicated that some students may be regarded as disturbed or behavior disordered by their teachers in school. Outside of school, their behavior is adaptive to the demands of their environment.

The "six-hour" behavior disordered student, identified by Rubin and Balow, is an illustration of the widening cultural gap between poor children and the demands of school. As an illustration, consider a ten-year-old who lives in a ghetto neighborhood. What are the environmental conditions that this youth must deal with on a daily basis? The widespread reports of violence, drug use, and gang membership in poverty-stricken neighborhoods suggest that survival dictates an aggressive attitude. A ten-year-old who cannot take care of himself could quickly become prey to any passerby who fancied his sneakers, jacket, or money. In order to survive, our ten-year-old must learn to stand up for himself; he must project an image of toughness and nonchalance in the face of danger.

Now let's project this same street-wise youth into a fifth-grade classroom. His teacher has just demanded to know why he didn't complete his homework. The youth is trapped between the demands of the adult authority and the expectations of his classmates, who eagerly await his response. Our ten-year-old is no fool, he knows that his mettle is inadvertently being challenged by the teacher, so he replies, "Do your own homework." The teacher's authority has been challenged, and the teacher responds by sending the young rebel to the principal, who suspends him for the rest of the day. A cycle of hostility is now perpetuated that could lead to a special education referral because of a behavior disorder.

Kelly, Bullock, and Dykes (1974) reported teacher-perceived prevalence rates of 12.6 for mild behavior problems, 5.6 for moderate problems, and 2.2 for students with severe emotional disturbance. This general ratio has been reported elsewhere (Glidewell & Swallow, 1968). Paul and Epinchan (1991) cite more current research that indicates a prevalence rate of 11 percent of the total school population. This amounts to an estimate of six to eight million students with behavior and emotional disorders (EBD).

Sex is an important factor in prevalence reports. Boys consistently outnumber girls. One interpretation of these data is that girls are better adjusted than boys. It is far more likely, however, that cultural experience plays a significant role. Boys tend to develop aggressive ways of expressing emotional problems, whereas girls learn to express anger and hostility in a more covert fashion. Promiscuity, drug abuse, and depression are not the type of disturbed behaviors that teachers see, but that doesn't mean that they don't exist.

Between 1977 and 1995, there was a 45 percent increase in students with behavior disorders identified nationwide (U.S. Department of Education, 1996). Several factors indicate that the prevalence will continue to escalate.

Item: One out of every five children grows up in poverty. Poverty contributes to broken homes, proliferation of drugs, violence, and homelessness. Millions of American children will be required to adapt to desperate environmental demands. The same behaviors that are adaptive on the streets will be disruptive in school.

Item: We are becoming a multilingual nation. While schools attempt to deal with the steady increase in non-English-speaking students, the cultural gap between home and community continues to widen. Students are alienated from the affairs of schooling, and this alienation is acted out in classrooms.

Item: Inner-city schools continue to present the greatest challenge to educational reform. The social and emotional turmoil that infects these schools requires the best teachers available. However, few young people who enter the teaching profession want to risk their psychological or physical safety teaching in ghetto schools. Without a massive infusion of educational and social support, inner-city schools will become hotbeds of chaos.

Item: Violence and neglect permeate the lives of many American children (see Figure 4.2).

The psychological and emotional fallout from children's violent lives presents an overwhelming challenge to American policymakers. However, there is no national agenda with the specific aim of creating safe havens for children. According to the *National Needs Analysis in Behavior Disorders* (Grosenick & Huntze, 1979), "The most glaring concern that exists in the area of behavior

FIGURE 4.2   At-Risk Factors of Youth in the United States

- Over 900,000 children were confirmed victims of abuse and neglect in 1998.
- Black and Native American children are significantly over-represented among abuse and neglect victims—double their proportion in the national population.
- Three to ten million children witness family violence each year.
- Young children are most at risk for being abused and neglected. Infants represent the largest proportion of victims; almost 40% of victims are under age 6.
- A history of family violence or abuse is the single most significant contributor to delinquency.
- Children who witness domestic violence may display the following symptoms: sleep disorders, headaches, stomach aches, diarrhea, ulcers, asthma, enuresis, and depression. Such complaints are identified as reactions to stress.
- Children of women who are battered have high rates of poor school performance, truancy, absenteeism, and difficulty concentrating.
- Children who witness domestic violence experience symptoms such as anxiety, aggression, temperament problems, depression, low levels of empathy, and low self-esteem. Lower verbal, cognitive, and motor abilities are also documented as symptoms in children who witness domestic violence.
- Juveniles make up 71% of all sex crime victims reported to the police.
- In 1998, firearms killed 10 children every day. Of these, 2,184 were murdered, 1,241 committed suicide, and 262 were victims of accidental shootings.
- Between 1979 and 1998, gunfire killed nearly 84,000 children and teens in America—36,000 more than the total number of American soldiers killed in Vietnam.
- Not all children exposed to violence suffer significant harmful effects. Resilient factors include a protecting family member, a caring teacher, and supportive peers. Resilient factors also include a child's internal capacity to cope with stress.

Compiled from *America's Children: Key National Indicators of Well-Being,* by the Federal Interagency Forum on Child and Family Statistics (1999) and *A Month of Mental Health Facts: Fact-of-the-Day,* by the New York University Child Study Center (2001).

disorders is the staggering number of children with behavior problems who remain unserved" (Apter, 1982, 7).

To summarize, almost 500,000 students are identified as requiring special education due to behavioral or emotional disturbance. Seventy percent of students are diagnosed with conduct disorder. Anxiety disorder and depression disorder follow in prevalence (Greenbaum et al., 1998). Yet many children go unserved because their behavior is not disruptive in the classroom or their behavior does not fit categorical criteria for special education. America's children and youth are in a state of emergency. As children become more vulnerable, the need for effective educational and community programs will continue to grow.

Attention Deficit Hyperactivity Disorder

Since hyperactivity was first described in 1902 by Dr. George Still as "an abnormal defect of moral control," it has been one of the most discussed behavior disorders encountered by teachers and parents. The *Diagnostic and Statistical Manual of Mental Disorders*, or *DSM IV*, describes hyperactivity as a symptom of attention-deficit hyperactive disorder (ADHD). According to the *DSM IV*, the onset of hyperactivity occurs before age seven, persists for at least six months, and must include a subset of some of the following symptoms: fails to give close attention to details, often does not seem to listen to what is said, often fidgets with hands or feet or squirms in seat, and often talks excessively.

William Cruickshank (1986) described two types of hyperactivity: sensory hyperactivity and motor hyperactivity. Distractibility is one of the primary characteristics of sensory hyperactivity. A student with sensory hyperactivity has an exceedingly short attention span, sometimes less than a minute. The student's attention is literally tugged back and forth by the visual and auditory stimuli of classroom activity. Unable to discriminate figure–ground relationships, either visually or auditorily (i.e., separating object from background), this student encounters severe problems with the simplest task. The printed page of a book, with its angled letters, spaces between letters, and pictures, is a visual mine field for a student with impaired figure–ground ability. The student is unable to stay focused on the sequential arrangement of letters and words.

According to Cruickshank, students with motor hyperactivity "seem to fall apart at the seams." They are constantly twisting, squirming, bending, and manipulating anything they can get their hands on. Hallways, playgrounds, or other open spaces, with the abundance of stimuli, cause the hyperactive student to overreact by running, yelling, and generally making a nuisance. Requesting such a student to sit still for ten minutes is asking the nearly impossible. Needless to say, a student with sensory and/or motor hyperactivity is a severe test of a teacher's patience and creativity. Cruickshank (and many other researchers) believes that hyperactivity is a neurological disorder that is outside a youngster's ability to control. With estimates of hyperactivity ranging from 3 to 10 percent of school-aged students, it is plain to see how the problem of hyperactive students would attract teachers, pediatricians, and parents to treatment with drugs.

The *DSM-IV* criteria describe three types of ADHD:

- ADHD primarily of the hyperactive-inattentive type
- ADHD primarily of the hyperactive-impulsive type
- ADHD of the combined type

Teachers, parents, and health professionals often work with children and young adults exhibiting behaviors related to activity, inattention, and impulsivity. The developmental variation commonly observed in these individuals is presented in Figure 4.3 and a variety of intervention methods are part of the special education they receive when properly diagnosed and treated.

FIGURE 4.3 Development Variation in Hyperactive Behaviors

Inattention

Developmental Variation

Young children have short attention spans that increase with age.

Inattention should be appropriate for the child's level of development and does not indicate a problem if it does not impair functioning.

Common Development Presentations

In early childhood, the child has difficulty attending, except briefly, to a storybook or quiet task such as coloring.

In middle childhood, the child may not continue with a task that he or she does not want to do such as read an assigned book or do some homework, or complete a household chore.

The adolescent is easily distracted from tasks that are undesirable to perform or complete.

Other Information

Infants and preschoolers usually have very short attention spans and normally do not persist with activities for long periods of time.

Diagnosing inattention is difficult in very young children.

Attention span varies greatly with interests and skills.

Inattention may be more an indication of interest or skill than a marker for a behavior problem.

Impulsivity

Developmental Variation

Young children are normally very active and impulsive; some need constant supervision to avoid injury.

Constant activity may be stressful to adults who lack energy or patience to tolerate their behavior.

(continues)

FIGURE 4.3   Continued

During school years, activity may be high during play situations and impulsive behavior may occur with peer pressure.

High levels of hyperactive/impulsive behavior do not indicate a problem if they do not impair functioning.

Common Developmental Presentations

In early childhood, the child runs in circles, doesn't stop to rest, may bang into objects or people, and asks questions constantly.

In middle childhood, the child plays active games for long periods of time and may do things impulsively, especially when excited.

The adolescent engages in active social activity for long periods of time and may be involved in risky behavior with peers.

Other Information

Activity and impulsivity normally increase with hunger and fatigue.

Activity and impulsivity normally increase in new or anxiety-provoking situations.

Activity and impulsivity should be judged in the context of the expectations of others; when expectations are unreasonable and caregiver stress levels are high, perceived levels may be exaggerated.

Activity levels for some children are high from birth and continue to high throughout development.

Source: Adapted from American Academy of Pediatrics (1996). *The Classification of Child and Adolescent Mental Diagnoses in Primary Care.* Elk Grove Village, IL: Author and American Academy of Pediatrics (2000). Clinical practice guideline: Diagnosis and evaluation of the child with Attention-Deficit/Hyperactivity Disorder. *Pediatrics, 105,* 1158–1170.

Many hyperactive students are treated with Ritalin, a stimulant. Ritalin is classified as a Schedule II drug, meaning that it is regarded as an easily abused drug. Its manufacture is regulated by the Drug Enforcement Administration. Kohn (1988) reported that three-quarters of a million children are receiving the drug because of ADHD. Ritalin helps some students to concentrate by activating areas of the brain that help focus attention, plan, and organize thoughts. Barkley (1977) found that approximately 75 percent of children with ADHD who take Ritalin or other psychostimulants showed short-time improvement, but found evidence still lacking to support long-term positive results. A recent synthesis of research literature by Swanson et al. (1993) sorted out expectations for effects of stimulant medication on children diagnosed with ADHD (Figure 4.4).

Some possible negative effects of stimulant medication are:

1. Some students don't improve and others worsen.
2. Although concentration may improve, the linkage with improved academic achievement has not been firmly established.

Figure 4.4   Effects of Psychostimulant Treatment for Children with ADHD

Temporary Management of Symptoms

Decrease in overactivity
Improved attention
Decrease in impulsivity

Associated Improvements

Improvement in deportment
Improvement in social interactions
Improvement in academic productivity

Other Observations

Response to medication cannot be predicted from neurological signs, biochemical
    markers, or physiological measures.
Side effects are infrequent.
Higher-order thinking processes and skills show scant improvement.
There is no long-term improvement in adjustment.

3. Placebos often (up to 40 percent of the time) work as well as Ritalin.
4. Physical side effects such as stunted growth, elevated blood pressure, facial
   tics, insomnia, and weight loss have been reported.

   Underlying the pros and cons of drug treatment for hyperactivity is the more
basic question—is there a safer, more effective method for helping students control their hyperactivity? In some instances the problem may be the classroom.
When students labeled as hyperactive are placed in school programs that promote
movement and concrete activities, problems of hyperactivity may diminish. These
classrooms utilize learning centers and small-group activities. Students with hyperactivity are able to learn because the routines of the environment allow them
to move around and manipulate materials.

   Other more controversial approaches to decreasing hyperactivity in students with ADHD include elimination diets to remove allergens and decrease
of sugar consumption. Evidence to support diet therapy is largely anecdotal.
However, widespread testimony by parents and professionals about the effect
of food on behavior is difficult to ignore. Reports like the following are commonplace:

   A nurse described the effect of nitrates, a common food preservative, "I can always
   tell when my daughter (seven-year-old) has eaten a hot dog or baloney sandwich.
   She is off the walls, and it takes at least an hour for her to calm down." A college

professor reported the effects of sugar on his six-year-old daughter, "Forget giving her dessert before bedtime. Just peanut butter on apple slices will keep her bouncing out of her bed and awake till 10:00 P.M." (Henley, 1986; 1990)

Table 4.3 lists commercial foods that contain minimal amounts of sugar and preservatives. Many are part of dietary treatments prescribed for some children with behavior disorders.

Emotional factors can also play a role in hyperactive behavior. Life in a dysfunctional home, where a youngster is continually exposed to chaotic living situations and warped family ties, will raise a student's stress level. The normal reaction to stress is flight or fight. For a student who is experiencing chronic stress, flight in the form of hyperactive behavior may be a futile attempt to adapt to an unpredictable life style.

Over the years, educational strategies have run the gamut from controlling techniques such as elimination of extraneous stimuli coupled with behavior modification to focusing on the "whole child" by monitoring diet, identifying stress factors, and allowing guided movement in the classroom (Armstrong, 1998). The rise of Ritalin use and other stimulants to control ADHD has spawned a cottage industry of books, pamphlets, and research monographs that extol the benefits and disadvantages of medication. In 1993, the United States consumed three times the amount of Ritalin used throughout the rest of the world (Valentine, 1994). Frankenberger (1998) synthesized the often contradictory findings regarding stimulant medication use. The following are some of the claims about stimulant medication and the research findings:

- *Stimulant medication has a positive effect on cognitive functioning.* A review of 84 studies found stimulant medication sometimes improved short-term cognitive functioning in laboratory tests, but the results were inconclusive in terms of classroom behavior. Other researchers found no improvement in cognitive functioning.

- *Stimulant medication has a positive effect on achievement.* Results are mixed. Short-term gains have been documented. Best results are when medications have been used in conjunction with remedial teaching. Many studies found no improvement in achievement.

- *Stimulant medication has a positive effect on reading achievement.* As compared to overall achievement, the results with reading seemed somewhat more promising. Two studies documented improvement, two studies showed no improvement, and one study documented temporary improvement.

- *Stimulant medication has a positive effect on behavior.* Behavior appears to be most positively influenced by stimulant medication. In one reported study, 75 percent of hyperactive students improved. Many anecdotal reports by teachers and parents support the positive effect of stimulants on hyperactive behavior. However, such negative side effects as weight loss, interrupted sleep, and loss of appetite are also commonly reported.

TABLE 4.3 **Partial List of Foods Commonly Found in Supermarkets that Are Free of Artificial Coloring, Flavoring, and Preservatives**

Cereals
Cheerios
Quaker Oats, Puffed Rice, and Puffed Wheat
Post Grape Nuts
General Mills' Kix
Kellogg's Raisin Bran

Crackers
Hi-Ho
Krispy Saltines
Premium Saltines
Cheese-Its
Nabisco Graham Crackers (not Honey Graham)
Pepperidge Farm Cookies

Ice Cream
Ben & Jerry's
All Natural Hendries
All Natural Breyers
All Natural Dolly Madison
All Natural Stop & Shop

Canned Juices
100% juices such as: pineapple, grapefruit, cranberry, apple, tomato. Check label to be sure that no sugar, coloring, etc., added.

Salad Dressing
Walden's

Popsicles, etc.
Hood's Orange (all natural)
Welch's Grape
York Peppermint Patty Sticks

Frozen Waffles
Golden Harvest (at Stop & Shop and Shop Rite)

Sausage
Jones or fresh ground

Soda
Seven-Up
Soda water
Country Club Ginger Ale

Jelly
Smuckers
Polaner

Candy Bars
Reese's Peanut Butter Cups
Mound's
Almond Joy
York Peppermint Patties
Planter's Peanut Bars
Bit-O-Honey

Frozen Juices
Juicy Juice
Minute Maid orange juice and lemonade
Stop & Shop Lemonade
Welch's Grape Juice
Many brands of orange juice—look at label

Gum
Wrigley's

Cocoa
Swiss Miss Cocoa Mix
Hershey's Pure Cocoa

Peanut Butter
Smucker's
Teddies

Mayonnaise
Cain's

Spaghetti Sauce
Prince

Sharp Cheese
"Helluva" Good Cheese

Margarine
Shedd's Willow Run
Natural food store margarine (colored with carotene, which is natural)

Hot Dogs (without nitrates)
Wild Wind

Maple Syrup—100% Pure
Vermont Maple Orchards

Educational Strategies for ADHD

Whether stimulant medication is administered or not, the classroom teacher still needs to improve the achievement of students and help them learn to cope with some of the deleterious outcomes associated with hyperactivity, distractability, and impulsivity. What follows is a brief synopsis of educational strategies used by general and special education teachers to help students with ADHD.

■ *Cognitive Behavior Modification (CBM).* The objective of CBM is to teach students problem-solving strategies and self-control techniques. Students are instructed in a step-by-step procedure to monitor and direct their behavior. For example, students are taught to deal with conflict by (1) calming down before reacting impulsively; (2) identifying feelings and expressing feelings in an appropriate manner; (3) setting positive goals for themselves; (4) thinking of alternative solutions to problems; (5) trying a plan and evaluating results (Greenberg, 1998). The overall goal is for students to spontaneously think through situations in which they feel the impulse to act quickly.

■ *Social Skills Training.* Students with ADHD develop impulsive habits that interfere with their ability to manage interactions with peers and adults. The purpose of social skills training is to rectify social skills deficits through direct and indirect instruction. This proactive approach seeks to change students' disruptive behavior by focusing on teaching new skills rather than the reactive approach of trying to eliminate bothersome behaviors. For example, a student who acts out impulsively might benefit from learning to verbalize his or her feelings (i.e., proactive), rather than being sent to timeout each time the offending behavior occurs (i.e., reactive). Social skills curriculums (see Chapter 10) employ a variety of instructional techniques including modeling, step-by-step scripts, classroom meetings, reinforcement, and emphasizing social skills embedded in the regular curriculum, for example, using science to teach how to anticipate consequences or using children's literature to teach conflict resolution.

■ *Contingency Management.* Based on principles of behaviorism, students are rewarded when they demonstrate socially appropriate behavior. Contingencies can also include negative consequences for inappropriate behavior. Positive consequences can include praise or tangible rewards. Reprimands or ignoring the behavior are examples of frequently used negative consequences. Teachers must be vigilant to ensure that negative consequences are logical and match the inappropriate behavior. For example, a logical consequence for throwing food in the cafeteria is eating lunch alone in the classroom for three days rather than doing additional homework. Other applications of behavior theory to ADHD include token economy, response cost, and contingency contracting.

■ *Structured Activity and Movement.* Planned classroom activities that allow students to move about, converse with others, and interact with concrete materials help students with ADHD sustain attention and reduces the stress of trying to constantly restrain motor activity. Some frequently used techniques are learning centers, planned student interactions, art, music, kinesthetic activity, games, and authentic learning experiences such as teaching ratios by making orange juice from concentrate. (Reif, 1998)

■ *Self-Management Strategies.* Students with ADHD lack organizational skills for sustaining attention and completing projects. Direct instruction in time management helps students learn to divide a task into subunits. By monitoring due dates incrementally, teachers help students set realistic time lines and avoid procrastination. Helping students learn how to organize materials is another key self-management strategy. Filing papers, scheduling, keeping notes in binders, and periodical inventory of materials are frequent self-management organizational objectives. Teaching study skills such as active reading (i.e., writing down questions and comments rather than simply highlighting), webbing of chapters, reviewing key topics and subtopics, and developing test taking skills are helpful strategies.

■ *Classroom Accommodations.* The physical layout of a classroom is the single most important element in focusing attention. Textbooks with shiny paper are particularly problematic under fluorescent lights. Also, the hum and the flickering of fluorescent lights is a distraction. They should be replaced with incandescent lights. Soft, classical music in the background can be soothing. "Natural" sound recordings can have a similar effect. Student seating should be adjusted to cut down distractions from high-traffic areas. Sitting at tables may present a problem for some students. Carrels with side panels help eliminate visual distractions. Some teachers report that overhead projectors help cut down on visual distractions by reducing the "clutter" that sometimes fills up chalkboards (Flick, 1998). Directions should be given slowly with frequent requests for the student to provide restatements. When worksheets are used, students benefit from fewer problems to complete, lined paper helps with handwriting, and computer software offers myriad possibilities from word processing to games that reinforce academic skills.

Causes of Behavior Disorders

The search for understanding the causes and treatment of behavior and disorders has followed many roads (Erickson, 1998). Each distinctive field of knowledge—biophysical, psychodynamic, psychoeducational, and behavioral—has contributed, in a synergistic fashion, to an overall understanding of behavior disorders (see Table 4.4). During the early years of special education, theorists tended to pitch their tents in a single conceptual camp. They fortified their encampments with rigorous defenses, and with equal vigor hurled conceptual assaults at each other. Thus graduate students would burn the midnight oil as they debated the relative merits of Bettelheim's psychodynamic view versus Skinner's behavior modification techniques for treating troubled children.

The term "behavior disorders" is a victory of sorts for the behaviorists. Its acceptance outside the behavior modification camp indicates that psychologists and

TABLE 4.4   Summary of Causes of Behavior Disorders

	Biophysical	Psychodynamic	Behavioral	Psychoeducational
Emphasis	Biological and physical systems	Stages of psychological development	Behavior antecedents and consequences	School adaptation and behavior change
Etiology	Genetics, nutrition, biochemistry, neurology	Conflict in development, traumatic experiences	Learning systems, conditioning, reinforcement, punishment	Conflict in development compounded by expectations
Diagnosis	Identify area(s) of biological or physical dysfunction	Identify critical phases in development or insight into origins of conflict	Identify controlling conditions within learning trials	Identify controlling influences in development
Assessment	Medical and physical exams	Psychological exams	Observations	Observations
Instruction/ Treatment	Medical and physical treatments	Psychological counseling	Behavior therapy	Reeducation
Goals	Correcting system dysfunctions	Reduction of conflict	Arranging conditions of learning	Individual and system change
Some Major Figures	Rimland Feingold	Freud Erikson Redl Bettelheim	Pavlov Skinner	Hobbs Long Morse Wood

educators agree it is a faulty leap in logic to ascribe an emotional causation to all disruptive behavior. The first model we address, the biophysical, makes a clear case for understanding that behavior disorders can occur when something goes wrong with the delicate mechanism of a child's body.

Biophysical Causes

Throughout history, physical and biological factors have been identified with some of the conditions that are part of the broad classification known as behavior disorders (Erickson, 1998). Researchers have linked genetics and emotional disturbance; Schwartz (1979) pointed out that evidence exists to support the role of heredity in shaping behavior and personality. This conclusion is based on findings that sex-linked differences are evident in many types of behavioral disorders. For example, hyperactivity, antisocial behaviors, and conduct disorders are more commonly identified in boys than in girls.

Thomas and Chess (1977) followed several groups from childhood to adulthood and found that their behavior patterns were relatively constant. About 40 percent were made up of the "easy child" whose characteristics included adaptability, high tolerance for frustration, and positive responses to change. The "difficult" child (about 10 percent) was characterized by irregular biological functions, negative behaviors, poor adaptability, and negativism. The "slow to warm" child was characterized by limited responsiveness, flat emotional responses, and unsatisfactory interpersonal relations. These findings were presented as support for the position that behavioral characteristics are predicated on biophysical differences among people.

The popularity of psychoactive drugs to treat behavior disorders is testimony to the widespread acceptance of the biophysical approach. Physicians prescribe drugs, and they rely on parents and others to monitor the effects those drugs have on problem behaviors. School personnel are in a crucial position to monitor a successful drug therapy program. Teachers maintain consistent contact in situations that allow for comparisons of student behavior, so observations by teachers are exceptionally valuable. The drug-monitoring process requires systematic observations and recordings of a student's behavior at various points during the school day.

Interest in using drugs is based on general knowledge about the ways chemicals influence behavior. For example, the amino acid tryptophan is converted into the neurotransmitter serotonin by chemical reactions that are regulated by enzymes (e.g., tryptophan hydroxylase); serotonin is believed to influence aggression, depression, and normal sleep patterns (Restak, 1984).

Stimulants, such as methylphenidate hydrochloride (Ritalin), dextroamphetamine sulfate (Dexadrine), and magnesium pemoline (Cylert), as well as antihistamines, such as diphenhydramine hydrochloride (Benadryl), are used to treat problem behaviors related to overactivity. Antidepressants and antianxiety drugs, such as imipramine hydrochloride (Tofranil), oxazepam (Serax), and chlorpromazine hydrochloride (Librium), are used to control problem behaviors related to mood disorders.

Experiments with lithium, a drug originally used to treat gout, indicated a calming effect with aggressive animals. In the laboratory, Siamese fighting fish, rats, and mice showed decreased hostile behavior when treated with lithium. Outside the laboratory, experiments with lithium have demonstrated interesting and controversial results with aggressive prisoners. In an experiment in the maximum security prisons at Vacaville and Sacramento, California, twenty-seven inmates were administered lithium. Although diverse in family backgrounds and personalities, the inmates were similar in their recurrent violent behavior and quick tempers. Restak described changes in both prisoner behavior and attitude after nine months:

> The results showed a decline in disciplinary action for violent behavior. Among fifteen of twenty-two subjects, the number of disciplinary acts for violent behavior were reduced. Even more interesting than the decrease in violence, however, were the reports offered by several prisoners in Dr. Tupin's study. One man stated,

"Now I can think about whether to hit him or not." Another said, "I have lost my anger." Each of the Lithium dosed prisoners demonstrated an increased capacity to reflect on the consequences of his actions, a quality Dr. Tupin refers to as a "more reflective mood." (Restak, 1984, 142)

Stimulants, minor tranquilizers, and anticonvulsants commonly used for children with behavior disorders are presented in Appendix B. Each class of psychoactive medication includes generic and brand name drugs, common dosages, expected effects, and side effects. Whenever students are given drugs to treat behavior disorders, the underlying premise is that chemical body processes are being altered. Imbalances in the biochemical system are believed to be the source of the problem. Drugs are prescribed by physicians to bring abnormal body chemicals into proper levels of balance and thereby change behavior. The more disturbing the behavior, the greater the likelihood that drug treatment will be accepted as a needed procedure. In the case of students with mild behavior disorders, the use of drugs can and has created controversy.

Psychodynamic Causes

Some educators believe that problems related to personality development are the cause of social and emotional problems of children and youth (Rhodes & Tracy, 1972a,b). Generally, these professionals have received training from psychiatrists and psychologists who believe that the inner conflict principles first developed by Sigmund Freud can be used to explain and treat behavior or emotional problems. The psychodynamic view describes the evolving personality in terms of the relationship between three strong intrapsychic forces: id, ego, and superego. The id is the pleasure seeking, impulsive force that is dominant in childhood. The superego is the conscience—it represents moral and ethical beliefs. The ego mediates between the id and the superego. The ego shapes judgments about reality. The ego guides actions by taking into account the natural consequences of behavior. The id, ego, and superego act as a system of checks and balances on individual behavior.

Consider the following illustration of the id, ego, superego relationship. A teenager walks through a shopping mall and sees a Swiss Army knife sitting on a counter. His impulse (id) is to pick the knife up and put it in his pocket. His conscience (superego) tells him it is wrong to steal, but his id is winning the battle. "I'll go to church and it will be okay," he thinks. Meanwhile his reality-testing instincts (ego) tell him to look around. He sees several mirrors arrayed along the store walls. Now the struggle is on between id and ego. The teenager walks away without the knife because he decides the knife wasn't worth the risk.

Freud described neurosis (emotional disturbance) as a conflict between the ego and the id. The person is at war with himself. The goal of psychodynamic treatment is to bring the id, ego, and superego into harmony. As Freud explained, "A man should not try to eliminate his complexes but get into accord with them; they are legitimately what direct his conduct in the world" (Seldes, 1985, 151). Over the years Freud's theory has been expanded and modified by some of the greatest thinkers in the field of psychology. A list of contributors to psychodynamic theory reads like a *Who's Who* of twentieth-century thought—Carl Jung, Alfred Adler, Erik Erikson, Anna Freud, Erich Fromm, and Bruno Bettelheim are just a sample of the writers and therapists who were heavily influenced by psychodynamic theory.

Fritz Redl and David Wineman were two of the first practitioners to successfully apply psychodynamic principles to the treatment of aggressive youth. In *Children Who Hate* (1951), Redl and Wineman described how the self-control (ego development) of adolescents collapsed under the impact of specific environmental or psychological triggers. Redl and Wineman cataloged twenty-two separate self-control challenges that all children need to cope with in order to continue their emotional development. Using colorful language such as "gadgetorial seduction" and "warfare with time," Redl and Wineman presented a roadmap for identifying self-control weaknesses in specific youngsters. Their descriptions of ego functions provide classroom teachers with a clinical model for anticipating when and where a student will lose self-control (Henley, 1987).

The psychodynamic point of view underscores the need to understand *why* students are disruptive. It emphasizes the connections between how a student feels and how a student acts. The classic psychodynamic treatments are play therapy for children and individual psychotherapy for youth. For educators, who saw the value of psychodynamic principles, it was necessary to develop treatment procedures that would be useful in the classroom, where teachers must manage groups of children. Psychoeducational treatments were born out of the need to merge behavior management with psychodynamic theory.

Psychoeducational Causes

Proponents of the psychoeducational perspective believe that problem behaviors result from underlying psychological disturbances, and that adaptive behaviors must be learned for successful accommodation in schools. Knoblock presented a succinct description: "A psychoeducational framework assumes that behavior is caused, that there are reasons why children act as they do. Early psychoeducators like Berkowitz and Rothman believed that children's feelings were the source of observed behaviors. Now it is recognized that behaviors should be analyzed in the context of specific environments as well. . . ." (Knoblock, 1983, 107). There is a balance between concern for causes of behavior and acquisition of adaptive skills in the psychoeducational treatment model.

This integrated philosophy is illustrated in the principles of Project Re-Ed (Hobbs, 1966):

1. Students should be kept busy in school; successful completion of purposeful activities is central to reeducation.
2. Students should spend as much time as possible in positive, therapeutic environments; neighborhood schools with supportive personnel are preferred in efforts to reeducate students with behavior problems.

3. Supportive teacher–student interactions are a key to establishing academic success; teachers learn this by working with students in positive relationships.

Psychoeducators believe the student–teacher relationship is the fundamental building block for change. Out of this relationship comes mutual trust and a willingness on the part of both teacher and student to accept the needs of each other. Behavioral and emotional difficulties are viewed developmentally. Using cognitive and emotional developmental milestones as a guide, the psychoeducator attempts to identify developmental strengths and weaknesses. Classroom accommodations are made that capitalize on student abilities in order to move a youngster along the normal developmental continuum. Self-concept development, the teaching of social skills, and normalization of a youngster's school experience are all components in the psychoeducational treatment model.

Some social development programs, including *Life Space Crisis Intervention* (Long et al., 2001), and *Teaching Self-Control: A Curriculum for Responsible Behavior* (Henley, 2004) have translated psychoeducational principles into functional systems for assessment, goal setting, and teaching. These models assume that all students have the internal resources to change, and that appropriate environmental supports can nourish and maintain student emotional growth. These treatments assume that change begins within the individual and that the ultimate goal is to teach students to accept responsibility for their own behavior. A counterpoint to the psychoeducational treatment approach is the behaviorist model, which focuses almost exclusively on the manipulation of environmental conditions to shape student behavior.

Behavioral Causes

During the 1960s, educators and psychologists recognized the importance of behavioral principles of learning. The key points of behavioral theory and practice can be summarized as follows:

1. Behaviorists view inappropriate and appropriate behavior as learned. Behavior is a response to a person's interaction with the environment.
2. Learning occurs when environmental conditions reinforce a specific behavior. Learning takes several forms, including imitation, modeling, and operant conditioning (i.e., consequences that shape behavior).
3. Inappropriate behavior is learned through environmental conditioning and new, appropriate behaviors can be learned with proper arrangement of the conditions of learning.
4. Effective implementation of behavior treatments in classrooms requires observable descriptions of behavior to be changed, targeting of new behaviors, systematic application of reinforcers, and collection of pre- and postdata to determine treatment effectiveness.

Behaviorists do not attempt to understand behavior problems using psychological constructs (e.g., id, ego, superego), nor do they ascribe hypothetical causes (e.g., inner conflict) to behavior. In explaining behavior, behaviorists prefer to deal with observable actions (e.g., what happens before and after the behavior) rather than theoretical (e.g., arrested development) explanations. The emphasis on observable, known causes for behavior rather than possible, unknown causes has been a catalyst to replace the term *emotionally disturbed* with the classification *behavior disorders* in many states. Whereas the former term implies we know the reason for a behavior (i.e., disturbed emotional development), the latter makes no claim about causality but simply points to a problem associated with an individual's behavior. To clarify reasons for the behavior, the behaviorist would conduct a functional behavioral assessment to identify variables that cause it. To design an effective intervention, the behaviorist would systematically control all or some of these variables and observe changes in the behavior. This process of applying principles of behavior theory is known generally as behavior modification or applied behavior analysis. Operant conditioning is a form of behavior modification used to change student behavior in the classroom. Operant conditioning is based on the premise that actions are shaped or changed by their consequences. The operant is the behavior (e.g., listening, hitting, laughing), while the consequences (e.g., praising, punishing, or ignoring) either reinforce or eliminate the operant.

Individuals can modify their own behavior. Cooper, Heron, and Heward provide the following example of behavior, which is modified by the consequences it produces.

> When an infant moves her arms through space, setting in motion the mobile dangling in her crib, she is literally operating on her environment. The mobile's movement and sound are stimuli produced by the child's behavior, consequences of her batting at the toy with her hands. If continued observation of the baby reveals an increased rate of arm swinging when the mobile hangs in her crib, her behavior would be described as an operant. (Cooper, Heron, & Heward, 1987, 21)

Behavior can be modified spontaneously, for example, when a student invents a shortcut to solve math problems. Or behavior can be shaped systematically, for instance, when a teacher awards tokens for finishing classroom tasks. Behavior can also be modified ineffectively, as when a teacher's verbal reprimands reinforce acting out behavior. The principles of operant conditioning are always the same—the key is knowledgeable application. Many teachers, both special and regular education, use operant conditioning practices in their classrooms on a regular basis.

Schroeder and Riddle (1991) list the basic components of operant conditioning. The following is an adaptation of their definitions.

1. *Positive reinforcement*: presenting a consequence that increases the probability of a behavior in the future. Example—a student who shares toys in a play area of a classroom because of favorable reaction from other children.

2. *Punishment*: presenting or withdrawing a consequence that decreases the probability of a behavior in the future. Examples—a reprimand (i.e., presenting a stimulus) or keeping a youngster in class during recess (i.e., withdrawing a stimulus) in order to stop disruptive classroom behavior.

3. *Negative reinforcement*: increasing the probability of a behavior by removing an unpleasant consequence. Example—students who complete homework for five consecutive days are excused from taking a weekly math quiz. Negative reinforcement is often confused with punishment. Example—a student is sent into the hall for disrupting the class. The teacher is negatively reinforcing the misbehavior when the child continues to act up in the future in order to avoid an unpleasant classroom activity (Cooper, Heron, & Heward, 1987, 25).

4. *Extinction*: decreasing the probability of a response by withholding a previously reinforcing stimulus. Example—classmates don't laugh when a student makes a sarcastic comment in class.

5. *Differential reinforcement of other behavior (DRO)*: decreasing the probability of a response by reinforcing the omission of it; sometimes referred to as omission training. Example—a student who is disruptive is given a token for every five minutes the behavior is not emitted.

6. *Satiation*: decreasing the probability of a response by reinforcing it excessively. The reinforcer no longer maintains the behavior. Example—a teacher uses a novel reading series to encourage student effort. In a short while, student effort diminishes as the novelty wears off.

Often the above treatments are used in combination to shape behavior in the classroom; for example, a teacher might use both positive and negative reinforcement to encourage a youngster to comply with classroom rules. Positive reinforcement could take the form of verbal praise immediately following the desired behavior, and negative reinforcement would consist of a decrease in corrective comments from the teacher. A comprehensive elaboration of each component of operant conditioning is outside the scope of this book. For more details, we suggest *Behavior Management from Theoretical Implications to Practical Applications* (2nd ed.) by Macy (2004), Thomson Wadsworth.

Disturbed or Disturbing?

When a student is disruptive in a classroom, does that mean that the student has a disability or are there alternative explanations? Consider the following behaviors: talking out of turn, swearing at the teacher, throwing objects, running out of the room, or refusing to do an assignment. Those behaviors are commonplace in chaotic classrooms, but they occur infrequently in classrooms where teachers demonstrate effective group management skills.

Frederic Jones (1987) studied teacher–student interactions in hundreds of elementary and secondary classrooms. Many of his observations were done in inner-city schools and alternative programs for students with behavior disorders. One might expect Jones to report many examples of behavior disorders such as hostility, impulsiveness, or aggression. He didn't. Jones and his colleagues characterized the majority of student activity as "massive time wasting." Students walked around the room, "goofed off," and talked whenever they felt like it. In poorly managed classrooms, these behaviors occurred every twenty seconds. In well-managed classrooms, the same behaviors were noted once every two minutes. Jones found that teachers in poorly managed classrooms lost 50 percent of their instructional time dealing with disturbing behaviors (Charles, 1989). Jones concluded that many disruptive behaviors were symptomatic of mismanaged classrooms.

The classic study by Wickman (1929) is the first major investigation that attempted to identify specific behaviors that educators perceived bothersome or disturbing in their work with children. Behaviors identified were characterized as those that offended moral standards (e.g., stealing, cheating, untruthfulness) and challenged teachers' authority (e.g., defiance, impertinence). Ramsey (1981) analyzed thirty-three replications that followed this seminal study and concluded that classroom orderliness and recognition of authority are of primary importance to teachers so that they can do their job, which is to teach students.

The notion that teachers can cause behavior problems is underscored by Jacob Kounin's research. Kounin (1977) found classroom disruptions were correlated to teacher expertise. Kounin reported that the following teacher behaviors contributed to discipline problems: making verbal comments about minor disturbances such as dropping a pencil, getting sidetracked by a single student's behavior, forcing students to do boring and repetitious activities, and becoming angry or punitive when students misbehaved. Conversely, Kounin observed that teachers positively influenced appropriate classroom behavior by smooth transitions between lessons, keeping track of all student behavior in the classroom at the same time, and providing novelty in lessons. Teachers who were liked by their students had the least behavior problems.

The interactional perspective of disturbing/disturbed behaviors underscores the need to evaluate both the individual and the setting. Behavior is a function of the individual interacting within the environment. While disturbing behavior may begin with the individual student, the way in which the teacher responds is crucial in preventing further problems. Organization of classroom space, routines, and lessons influence student behavior. Imagine a seven-year-old youngster with ADHD attempting to conform to a classroom where students are expected to sit quietly at their desks and complete assignments consisting of workbooks and ditto exercises. In this classroom, the student is handicapped by her learning problem. She is unable to sit still and concentrate. Why force a student to do something that is outside her limits? Suppose we move the same student into a classroom where she can walk around and work at learning centers that feature manipulative materials. In the latter classroom, our seven-year-old is no longer restrained and she is engaged in concrete tasks that match her developmental abilities.

When a student's behavior is properly evaluated, the context within which the behavior occurs is examined. Special education has historically provided individual services for students rather than classroom support to the regular classroom teacher. The entire special education service delivery system is geared to find something wrong with the student. Yet for years special educators have recognized that disturbance is often in the eye of the beholder. In 1967, William Rhodes remarked that behavior is often more "disturbing" than "disturbed." He contended that disturbance is a function of where and with whom a student interacts (Rhodes, 1967; 1970).

School records and case histories brim with examples of the influence of adult expectations and perceptions on the lives of students classified as behaviorally disordered or emotionally disturbed. For example, Hewett and Taylor (1980) provide the following description of a "disturbed" student.

> We worked with an adolescent boy with an IQ of approximately 80. He has the misfortune to be born into a family of extremely high achievers who expected him to go to Princeton University. He was attempting an academic program in high school and failing miserably. From his father's point of view, he was just lazy. His mother babied him. His older brother teased him. His teachers criticized and demeaned him. He stayed up long hours to study but couldn't keep up. His health began to suffer. Finally, he became deeply depressed and attempted suicide. Fortunately, following this episode, a careful examination of this boy's ecosystem (home, family interactions, community, school, teacher behavior) resulted in greater understanding on the part of all parties concerned. (Apter, 1982, 72)

In analyzing this story, it is difficult to identify the source of the problem. Did the family's expectations and behaviors produce the student's problems? Did his behavior and expectations influence others' perceptions of him? Would he be a problem in another family? Would he be a problem with other teachers? The complex nature of human interactions clearly leaves the source of the disturbance unresolved in this case study. And, this is true for most students with behavior disorders as well. Table 4.5 illustrates how four different theories influence analysis and treatment of disturbing behavior.

The Ecological Model

When trying to understand students with behavior and emotional problems, one can get caught up in the chicken or the egg paradox. Does the behavior problem lead to negative responses from others, which ultimately result in an emotional disturbance? Or are the behavior problems caused by an emotional disturbance? Or is the student simply a disruptive individual without an emotional problem? These questions may seem to be rhetorical verbal games best suited for clever banter; but, in fact, how teachers and administrators view students and determine the answers to these questions can mean the difference between a student getting special education services, no help at all, or becoming a school dropout.

TABLE 4.5   There's Always a Reason for Behavior: Four Theoretical Explanations

Behavior: Sixth grader Manuel frequently disrupts class through attention-seeking behaviors such as making sarcastic remarks and inappropriate jokes.

Theoretical Perspective	Hypothetical Explanation
Psychoeducational Theory	Manuel is frustrated by his attempts to develop friendships. His attention-seeking behavior is an awkward attempt to gain other students' acceptance. This social–emotional conflict typically surfaces in insecure students during adolescence.
Behaviorist Theory	Each time Manuel makes a wisecrack the other students laugh and snicker. Their response serves as positive reinforcement for his disruptive behavior.
Biophysical Theory	Manuel lives in a run-down area of town. The state freeway bridge runs almost directly over his subsidized public housing unit. Over the years lead has gradually accumulated in Manuel's nervous system. Manuel's impulsivity is caused by lead poisoning.
Psychodynamic Theory	Manuel's self-control problems are triggered by situations that remind him of past failures. Most of his inappropriate remarks occur in situations where he is expected to read. He is insecure about his weak reading skills. This insecurity increases his anxiety which he acts out through impulsive behavior.

Source: Henley, M. (2005). *Classroom Management: A Proactive Approach.* Englewood Cliffs, N.J.: Prentice-Hall. Reprinted with permission.

What is conspicuously absent from the general–special-education connection is a focus on prevention, which we discuss in more detail in the chapters on classroom management. More help for the classroom teacher would improve classroom management practices. Community centers would provide mental health and networking services for troubled families. More attention to the needs of children in general would produce a concentrated effort to mobilize national attention and resources to battle such childhood perils as loneliness, fear, abuse, addiction, and school failure.

The view that treatment of behavior disorders must take into account all features of a student's life (including school, family, and community) is called the ecological model. Educators who embrace the ecological perspective believe that in order to understand troubled children, we need to consider all facets of their lives.

From this outlook emotional disturbance is not seen simply as the necessary result of intrapsychic conflict (psychodynamic model) nor as the inevitable product of inappropriate social learning (behavior modification model). Instead, according to the ecological model, disturbance resides in the interaction between a child and critical aspects of that child's surrounding environment, that is, the child's system.

> More specifically, ecological theorists believe that what we know as emotional disturbance or behavior disorders actually result from discrepancies between a given child's skills and abilities and the demands or expectations of that child's environment. (Apter, 1982, 2)

The ecological model emphasizes the need for comprehensive preventive systems within and outside school to make adjustments in the parts of a student's life that can cause behavior disorders. As Apter (1982) acknowledged, change strategies should be aimed at increasing competence instead of reducing deficits. Well-baby clinics, parent effectiveness training, community development programs, sex and drug education programs, and teenage counseling programs are examples of change strategies that focus on prevention while increasing the competence of young people (Heller & Monahan, 1977).

Clearly the ecological model cannot work without community and political support. The long-range view of looking at troubled social systems requires a broad based constituency. It requires a commitment to social change and social policies that are often not shared by politicians or the populace in general. The road to social change is riddled with pitfalls.

A case study in the pitfalls of prevention is illustrated by the work of Spencer Holland, a psychologist at Morgan State University in Baltimore. Holland recommended educational intervention specifically aimed at African American male students. African American males have the highest dropout rates, get the lowest grades, and exhibit more discipline problems than any subgroup of students. Holland argued that lack of adequate male role models was a primary cause of troubles encountered by African American males.

> The most common reasons cited for the academic and social failings of young black males are that such boys come from poor, single-parent, female-headed households; that they have no positive male role models; and that they view the (school) as feminine and not relevant to their daily lives. (Chmelynski, 1990, 16)

One extension of Holland's reasoning is that referral for special services for behavior problems may be related to females teaching males. Teacher ratings of behavior are the most influential component in school evaluations of behavior disorders. Teachers rate boys as "acting out" more often than girls, and boys are more likely to be evaluated as having a behavior disorder (Walker, Ramsey & Gresham, 2004). When one matches the over-representation of boys in the category of behavior disorders with the over-representation of females among teachers, a likely hypothesis is that referrals for social and emotional problems are gender related.

Some schools, influenced by Dr. Holland's work, took a hard look at gender issues in classrooms. Several school systems responded to this problem by providing African American male students with positive male role models. African American businessmen, professionals, and tradesmen volunteered as role models for students in Baltimore, Detroit, Miami, Milwaukee, San Diego, and Washington, D.C., schools. The role models tutored students, took them on field trips, and provided them with the male mentoring that was conspicuously absent in the youngsters' lives.

These volunteer programs proved so popular that school officials in Dade County, Florida, and Detroit considered starting African American male academies. The possibility of schools just for African American male students quickly produced widespread critical reactions. Specters of sexism and segregation raised by the National Organization of Women (NOW) and the National Association for the Advancement of Colored People (NAACP) caused many advocates to reconsider education programs that single out only African American boys. Proponents of the programs contended that the situation for young African American males was so dire that radical measures were in order. Holland argued that whereas African American girls have role models in their mothers and teachers, boys searching for role models in their inner-city neighborhoods find that the only successful males are drug dealers or criminals (Chmelynski, 1990). As this case study of prevention illustrates, it is easier to refer a disruptive student for special education services than it is to try to change school practices or redirect social policies.

The advantage of the ecological model is that it focuses attention on the interactional aspects of behavior disorders. David Witcher was a teacher at Batchler Middle School in Bloomington, Indiana; his comments in the August 1988 issue of the Council for Children with Behavior Disorders newsletter are revealing:

> For the past eight years, I have been a public school teacher in special education programs for so-called emotionally handicapped children and adolescents. Even after working on over a hundred cases, I still cannot tell why one student qualifies for my special services while another does not.

As long as ineffective teaching practices continue and urgent social issues are ignored, many students whose behavior problems could be prevented will be classified with behavior disorders and placed in special education programs.

Characteristics

Students with behavior disorders exhibit a wide variety of characteristics (Erickson, 1998). A description of functional characteristics is somewhat hampered by the differences in professional perceptions of these youngsters. We all interpret what we see, hear, and understand in terms of the assumptions we hold about the world around us. Keep this in mind when you hear professors and teachers discussing students with behavior disorders. A professional who is solidly in the behaviorist camp does not recognize feelings as important aspects of a student's behavior. If a behaviorist were to describe the functional priorities of a youngster, feelings would be at the bottom of the list. At the same time, a professional who is devoted to the psychodynamic treatment approach would describe a youngster's functional abilities in terms of interpsychic conflicts between id, ego, and superego. The observable actions that are the foundation of the behaviorist treatment model are minimal in the psychodynamic view. A key point to remember is the power of the observer (i.e., teacher, professor, psychologist) of student's behavior to determine if a behavior is disturbing or disturbed.

Students with serious emotional disturbance are identified by their severe deficits in perception, communication, and behavior. Such behaviors as delusions and lack of affect are marked examples of the extreme behavioral disturbances in seriously emotionally disturbed students. Students with mild behavior disorders are quite different. Before they entered school, the majority of these youngsters seemed capable of adapting to the social demands of formal education. (We hope at this point this theme sounds familiar.) Basically students with behavior disorders exhibit behaviors that interfere with productive interpersonal relationships; they are unable to adapt to classroom routines; and they cause classroom disruptions. These students have behavioral excesses or differences that make regular school progress difficult to achieve without special education.

Consider this example: Mrs. Stone, a junior high school teacher, has just passed out a sheet of math problems to be completed by each of her students. Frank's response is clearly excessive. He looks at the paper, throws down his pencil, and angrily states, "What do you think I am, a genius or something?" After this preamble, he proceeds into a harangue supported by four-letter words and no-holds-barred attacks on Mrs. Stone's professional and personal integrity. He ends up with an ultimatum suggesting that "nothing or nobody" can make him do the worksheet.

In this episode, we see grist for everybody's theoretical mill. Frank's behavior is clearly inappropriate, and a behaviorist would work to eliminate outbursts and reinforce appropriate school behaviors. The psychodynamic-oriented professional examines the relationship between Frank and Mrs. Stone. Counseling might be directed at helping Frank cope with females in authority positions. From a psychoeducational point of view, Mrs. Stone is setting Frank up for failure by using typed dittos when Frank is developmentally unable to handle such abstract work. Classroom modifications that include work-related functional skills and supported employment would be directed at changing Frank's attitude toward school. The biophysical model suggests that we examine Frank's medical history. Perhaps he is allergic to ditto fluid, and the fumes set off impulsive and aggressive behavior.

In the following sections, we describe functional characteristics on which most all professionals agree regarding mild behavior disorders. The brevity of this section is testimony to the need of professionals to consolidate theoretical models in order to present a less fractured and more comprehensive description of students with behavior disorders.

Cognitive

Students classified with behavior disorders usually score in the low average range (75–100) on standardized tests of intelligence. Some professionals argue that emotional problems can cause individual students to perform poorly on intelligence tests. Anyone who is accustomed to taking standardized tests readily reports feelings of anxiety prior to and during testing. For children with minimal ability to cope with stress, an IQ test can be overwhelming. These students will give up, guess wildly at answers, or refuse to continue.

Students with behavior disorders proceed through the same stages of cognitive development as other children: sensory-motor, preoperational, concrete, and formal. Selman (1980) applied Piaget's developmental scheme to social perception, and he suggested that children go through four stages before they are fully capable of socialized thought. Paul and Epanchin summarized Selman's model:

> First, the child is in a fully egocentric state and is unable to differentiate the points of view of others. Second, the child can consider other people's ideas in a rudimentary way and realizes their thoughts can be different from his own. However, he has difficulty understanding exactly what the differences are. Third, although the child cannot consider others and his own perspectives simultaneously, he can sequentially consider first his own perspective and then another's perspective. Finally, the child is able to think about both perspectives at the same time in an integrated manner, as well as having a "third person" perspective in which he can figuratively step back from the interaction and examine both sides' point of view. (Paul & Epanchin, 1991, 195)

As children develop cognitively they are more capable of understanding a situation from another's point of view. They recognize how their behavior affects others. They are able to identify their own feelings, and they empathize with the feelings of others (Erickson, 1998).

Students with behavior disorders are delayed in their social–cognitive development. They literally forget their own contributions to conflict. Their memories seem to evaporate when they are asked to recall how their actions contributed to a classroom disruption (Henley & Long, 1999). They seem to be able to recall only the behavior of others while they remain steadfast in their own innocence. These students cannot apply past experiences to present situations. As often as a student will experience peer retribution for teasing or belittling others the student does not change tactics that goad others into retaliation. They don't understand how their behavior affects others in a negative way. Students with social–cognitive delay are unable to learn from the experience of others, and they possess minimal strategies for solving social problems. If another youngster is disapproving, the student with emotional and social problems will maintain a fixed and predictable response such as a temper tantrum, sulking, scapegoating, or fighting.

These students need practice in developing social problem-solving skills. Included among these needed skills are anticipating consequences, learning from past experiences, and understanding how their behavior affects others (Henley, 2004).

Academic

Many students with behavioral and emotional difficulties don't like school. Some professionals believe these students fail because they have not developed academic survival skills (e.g., finishing tasks, following directions, adjusting to classroom routines). Other professionals maintain that emotional problems (e.g., anxiety, low self-esteem, depression) prevent students from doing well. Although researchers tend to focus on independent variables, for example, task engagement, in reality a given student could be limited by all the above characteristics.

For the classroom teacher, the main difficulty is motivation. These students have limited faith in their ability to learn. Their whole school experience has been testimony to their inadequacies. Because their behavior has been a consistent liability, they have internalized feelings of worthlessness. This makes learning a formidable task. Suppose you were on a ski slope taking your first lesson, but you were absolutely convinced you were going to fall. How far do you think you'd make it down the slope without falling? When it comes to learning, students with social and emotional difficulties are always falling down.

More than anything else these students need success in school. Learning requires risk-taking and a willingness to change; students with social–emotional problems have spent much of their lives resisting change. Sameness, even if unpleasant, provides security. For a student with behavior disorder, learning to read can be a fearful experience. Reading may mean loss of control because it is change, and if one thing about a person's life changes, what is next? Fritz Redl and David Wineman (1951) called this resistance to change "newness panic." The student is overwhelmed by apprehension when confronted with new or different experiences. This makes teaching students with behavior disorders difficult.

A secure classroom environment is the first priority. Unless psychological and physical safety is maintained, the student will be overcome by real or imagined threats. The ensuing anxiety will disrupt learning. Next, the students need to derive some personal meaning from school activities. As we discussed in the previous section, students with behavior disorders are egocentric. Schoolwork that relates to their day-to-day lives enables students to personalize their learning. Teachers can make learning relevant by emphasizing students' interests, using humor and developing functional lessons to teach skills. Activities such as rope climbing and challenge courses help to develop risk-taking behavior and enhance self-confidence. Finally, students need reminders of their progress. Positive feedback about emerging skills helps to consolidate gains and encourages perseverance.

Think of student development as a series of upward spiraling circles. Be prepared for regression following progress. This natural cycle of growth and backsliding is normal (Long, 1986). When teaching students who have social and emotional problems, it is easy to overlook how far they have come. Others who have a long-range view, such as administrators or counselors, can help keep intermittent reversals in perspective.

Many special education teachers are cloistered with eight to ten students in a single classroom. These teachers are expected to bring their students up to grade level, while also teaching them how to behave properly. This is a difficult task. Students are put in special education programs because they need to learn new behaviors. In a special class, there are no models for appropriate behavior. Regrettably, the reality of the situation is that the teacher is "keeping the lid on" a group of youngsters that other teachers won't tolerate in their classrooms. The burnout rate among teachers of students with behavior disorders is extremely high.

Despite the negative programmatic aspects of self-contained classrooms, these socially isolating environments serve the administrative purpose of making the problem go away. Unless the emphasis in regular classrooms changes to preventive discipline and the teaching of prosocial behaviors becomes a legitimate part of the curriculum, the label "behavior disorders" or "emotionally disturbed" will continue to be a one-way ticket into segregated, self-contained special education programs.

Communication

For students with behavior disorders, words are both sword and shield. Their verbal outbursts of hostility outrage others, while their facile excuses keep them, in their own minds, free of responsibility. The inability to communicate feelings in a socially appropriate manner results in resentment and misunderstandings between these students and others. Resentment, fear, apprehension, and other tumultuous feelings are acted out rather than discussed. At the same time, students with behavior disorders can use language in finely executed performances of manipulation. Students who are hostile know just what to say to get others to respond in kind. For example, students who whine and complain cause others to withdraw from them.

Like a crafty salesperson, troubled youngsters solicit feedback that reaffirms their position. The more angry or caustic the teacher or student response, the more secure a youngster is in the knowledge that others are indeed out to get him. The student with emotional disturbance needs negative feedback to keep his world steady and predictable. Why change one's behavior if it is clear that others are unable to change theirs? As long as teachers threaten, criticize, and shout, a student with a behavior disorder remains in control. The student pulls the strings, and the adults and peers in the classroom put on the show.

Ginott believed teachers can short-circuit this closed system of emotional turmoil through "congruent communication." Charles (1989) defined congruent communication as "a harmonious and authentic way of talking in which teacher messages to students match the students' feelings about situations and themselves" (Ginott, 1971, 57). Students need teachers to model communication methods that highlight verbal expression of feelings in appropriate ways. For example, Ginott advocated "sane messages." When addressing student disruption, sane messages describe the situation rather than criticizing the student. Sane messages give students the opportunity to assess a situation and to understand why a be-havior is disruptive. Sane messages describe the area of concern rather than blam-ing, preaching, or criticizing students. As an illustration, two students are arguing about who is first in line; an "insane message" is, "You two are always causing trouble; both of you sit down and wait for everybody else to leave." In this situa-tion, the students may feel attacked, and they have no opportunity to learn from the situation. A contrasting sane message would be, "When you act like that it takes longer for all of us to get to lunch; you have to take turns." The explanation provides insight into *why* the teacher is disturbed and describes a more acceptable behavior.

According to Ginott, through modeling, the teacher helps students to ex-press their feelings and communicate their needs. "I messages," for example, help students understand that teachers do indeed have feelings. Statements like "I am disappointed" or "I am angry" are better than "You are a nuisance" or "You ruin everything for everybody else." Teachers accept and acknowledge feelings when they avoid negative communication modes such as sarcasm and verbal insults. One of Ginott's more novel observations is the perils of praise. Praise creates a de-pendence on others for approval. Judgmental praise such as "You are a good girl" or "I really like the way you are acting" reinforces the need to look to others for self-worth. What of the student on the other side of the room who was equally "good"? Ginott underscores the need for teachers to understand that for every student who stands in the spotlight, twenty or so are going to feel left out. Charles (1989) has summarized Ginott's main points:

1. Good classroom discipline begins with the teacher's self-discipline.
2. Use sane messages when correcting misbehavior.
3. Teachers at their worst attack and label student characters.
4. Teachers should model the type of communication they expect from stu-dents.
5. Anger and other feelings should be expressed in sane ways.
6. Avoid sarcasm and be judicious with praise.
7. The best teachers build self-esteem and help students to trust and express their own feelings.

Social–Adaptive

A student is referred for special education services for a behavior disorder when a teacher notes frequent and chronic behavior that is markedly different from peers. Difference in behavior is based on teacher expectations and judgments. Authoritarian teachers prize student behavior that is compliant and conforming. Teachers who depend on workbooks, dittoes, and other repetitious instructional materials view students who don't "stay on task" as disturbing. Teachers who encourage students to ask questions, express their opinions, and partici-pate in group discussions would more likely view a passive and quiet student as disturbing.

Behavior should not be separated from the context in wr judged. Apter emphasized the interactional aspect of behavior d commented that ". . . what we know as emotional disturbance or ders actually result from discrepancies between a given child's skill and the demands or expectations of that child's environment" (Apter student who is loud and aggressive may be disturbing in school, b streets he could be a leader. Students who are unable or unwilling to adap expectations of classroom life are most likely to be referred to special educa

Achenbach and Edelbrook (1981) distinguished between internalizing externalizing behavior problems. Internalized problems are those manifest when a student turns inward because of emotional or social conflict. Anxiety fears, social withdrawal, and immaturity are examples of internalized problems. Aggression, noncompliance, and open hostility are examples of externalized behavior problems; they are more obvious (and get more attention) because they are disruptive.

Externalized behaviors, because they are the most difficult to deal with, are more frequently used as indicators of behavior disorders. Although all children may fight, bully, or argue, students classified with behavior disorders engage in these behaviors repeatedly. Teachers refer students because they find disciplinary measures are ineffective in controlling or minimizing externalized behaviors. Though less frequently noted, such internalized behaviors as poor self-esteem, moodiness, depression, and social withdrawal are also difficult to change. Internalized students are often overlooked in teacher's judgments about who has an emotional problem.

As children pass through developmental stages of social maturity, they acquire self-control skills that help them to restrain their impulses, assess social reality, manage group pressure, deal with stress, and solve problems in relationships. Impulse maintenance includes the ability to deal with frustration, to self-regulate behavior, and to understand that temptations are accompanied by consequences. When assessing social reality, youngsters need to be realistic about rules and routines, evaluate the effect of their behavior on others, take responsibility for their possessions, and remain reasonable about such gratifications as praise and attention. Group pressure skills include staying calm when others have lost control, managing competitive challenges, and participating in and furthering group activities. Stress management requires coping with anxiety, adjusting to new situations, separating past trauma from present events, and accepting responsibility for actions. Finally, social problem-solving skills include learning from experience, noting one's effect on others, and drawing inferences from others' experiences (Erickson, 1998; Henley, 2004). (These skills are discussed in more detail in Chapter 8.)

The less capable a student is in each self-control skill, the more likely the youngster will encounter social problems in school. Teachers who understand that the misbehavior they encounter in the classroom is based on frustration or stress are likely to demonstrate what Fritz Redl and David Wineman (1951) referred to as "symptom tolerance." Simply stated: when teachers don't personalize disruptive

163

disturbing and disturbed behavior.

s, and discipline practices that may contribute to behavior

sical causes for disturbing behavior.

sroom routines before going along with drug treatment.

otional growth. Work to develop a trusting relationship with a

odification in a systematic fashion. Don't use behavior modification as a way

alizing punishment.

Make a home and neighborhood visit of each student in your class and determine adaptive skills required for environments outside of school.

8. Present lessons in a format that connects to the personal experience of your students.

9. Assess the impact of such real-life issues as teenage pregnancy, drugs, and depression on your students.

10. Model the language and behavior that you want to foster in your students.

behavior but try to understand not only the behavior but the child as well, dealing with the behavior is easier. When teachers believe a child is intentionally being disruptive or mean or selfish, it is difficult to squelch the adult impulse to "put the kid in her place"; "show him who is boss"; or "not let the kid run all over me." No child chooses to be unhappy in school. Every child wants to be liked and admired. By working to understand the students you deal with, you will find the best way to deal with their behavior. Some general suggestions for teaching students with behavior disorders are presented in Figure 4.5.

Positive Behavior Support

Positive Behavior Support (PBS) is a schoolwide system that defines, teaches, and encourages appropriate behavior in children. In schools that have been successful building PBS systems, the following procedures have been established (cf., Colvin, Kame'enui, & Sugai, 1993; Lewis & Sugai, 1999; Sugai & Horner, 1999; Todd, Horner, Sugai, & Sprague, 1999).

1. Identify a small number of clearly defined behavioral expectations and present them as positive, simple rules. For example:

   ■ Follow all adult directions promptly; or
   ■ Be respectful to yourself and others.

2. Teach the behavioral expectation to all students in the school using the same instructional formats applied to other curriculum content: Present the gen-

eral rule, discuss the rationale for the rule, describe and rehearse positive examples ("right way"), describe and model negative examples ("wrong way"), and provide opportunities for students to practice the "right way" until they demonstrate fluent performance.

3. Acknowledge appropriate behavior on a regular basis using formal systems (e.g., tickets, rewards) or social events (e.g., Friday Fun-Time). When teachers are successful in creating a positive behavior learning environment, there interactions with students are "positive" four times as often as they are "negative."

4. Establish clear procedures for providing information to students that their behavior was unacceptable. Students, teachers, and administrators all should be able to predict what will occur when behavioral errors are identified.

According to Sugai and Horner (2001), schools that adopt a schoolwide PBS approach have the following features:

- An agenda of primary prevention has priority and is visible schoolwide.
- All students and staff members are taught the schoolwide expectations and received regular and frequent opportunities to practice them and to be positively acknowledged when they use them.
- A majority (> 80%) of students, staff, and families can state the schoolwide positive expectations and give a specific behavioral example for each.
- Positive schoolwide behavioral expectations are defined, taught, and encouraged for all students using a range of positive and negative examples.
- Most contacts between teachers and students are prosocial (positive and preventive) rather than corrective and punishing (i.e., 5–8 positives for every negative interaction).
- A full continuum of PBS is available for all students at the school and district levels.
- Behaviorally competent personnel are readily available.
- A function-based approach serves as the foundation for addressing problem behaviors.
- All staff members actively participate in the implementation of schoolwide PBS approach.
- Accurate and consistent implementation of PBS practices by all staff members is emphasized.
- The school administrator is an active participant and leader in the PBS effort.
- A schoolwide leadership team guides the systemic adoption and sustained use of research-validated practices.
- School data are reviewed at least monthly to guide decision-making and planning.

Positive Behavior Support interventions are proactive and designed to prevent problem behavior by altering a situation before problems escalate while concurrently teaching appropriate alternatives (Safran & Oswald, 2003). When *universal schoolwide interventions* are designed for all students, positive effects can also be achieved for individuals with severe difficulties. Positive Behavior Support also can be applied as *secondary-level interventions* with small groups of students and in specific settings such as hallways, playgrounds, and cafeterias or as *tertiary level interventions* with individual students experiencing chronic difficulties. While research offers several guiding principles, individual schools must collaboratively shape PBS to fit their own unique needs; the key factors to be included are using collaborative team problem-solving and research-based interventions, using multiple data sources for planning and evaluating, and using positive strategies to reduce punitive disciplinary practices.

Students with behavior disorders receive special education because they have emotional and social problems that require attention from teachers, parents, and other professionals if they are to be successful in school (Ysseldyke & Algozzine, 1995; Erickson, 1998). **Emotional problems** stem from unproductive personal ways of managing stress or activities (e.g., inappropriate types of behaviors or feelings, tendency to develop physical symptoms or fears). For example, one child's response to having to wait for the school bus might be to become impatient while another's might be to become very anxious. Low self-esteem and limited self-control are common emotional problems of students with behavior disorders. **Social problems** are unproductive ways individuals respond in situations involving interactions with other people (e.g., inability to maintain satisfactory interpersonal relationships). Disruptiveness is a common social problem of students receiving special education for behavior disorders.

Effective teachers of students with behavior disorders use a variety of approaches for establishing discipline in their classrooms, managing behavior, and improving emotional and social problems. Four widely accepted discipline models, and specific activities for improving selected emotional and social problems are discussed in the following sections. Many of these same models, principles, and activities are also effective for improving the behavior of students with mental retardation and learning disabilities.

Discipline

Discipline is a key part of any educational program. For many people, discipline means punishment, but this is a common misconception. There are three types of discipline: (a) avoiding inappropriate behavior—preventive discipline, (b) assisting students when they first show signs of misbehavior—supportive discipline, and (c) controlling or redirecting misbehavior when it occurs—corrective discipline. For effective teachers, discipline means teaching rules or a code of conduct for appropriate behavior, practicing them, and providing recognition and reward for doing them (Meese, 1994). The underlying beliefs, primary focus, and goals for students of some widely accepted discipline programs are presented in Table 4.6. In each case, the overall goal is to teach students responsibility and respect, to develop a positive classroom environment, and to help students meet basic needs and avoid behavior problems.

TABLE 4.6 Summary of Discipline Models

Model	Characteristics
Cooperative Discipline *Albert, 1994*	Students must be valued and opportunities for behavioral responsibility must be shared. Keys include identifying goals of misbehavior, intervening early, building self-esteem, and involving students, colleagues, and parents. Goals include successful completion of school tasks and functioning as a contributing member of the school group.
Discipline with Dignity *Mendler & Curwin, 1994*	Dignity of students must be valued and improved regardless of their behavior. Values underlying desired behaviors are internalized through problem solving, prevention planning, and student involvement in discipline process. Goals for students include believing they are capable and successful, knowing they are cared about, recognizing they can influence other people, and practicing helping others.
Kids Are Worth It! *Coloroso, 1994*	Self-discipline will develop if students are treated with respect, given responsibilities and choices, and permitted to experience reasonable consequences. Focuses on showing students what they have done wrong, giving them ownership of the problem, and identifying ways to solve it. Goals include providing students with six "critical life messages" each day: I believe in you, I trust you, I know you can handle it, you are listened to, you are cared for, and you are very important to me.
Positive Classroom Discipline *Jones, 1994*	Classroom management must be positive and gentle, must set limits, and must build cooperation. Reducing disruptions, teaching students to internalize control, structuring classrooms, setting limits, using incentive systems, and managing behaviors outside the classroom are keys to effective discipline. Goals include self-regulation, cooperation with peers, and making positive contributions to the group with learning as the reward.
Unified Discipline *Algozzine, Audette, Ellis, White, & Marr, 2000*	Classroom management occurs on a school-wide basis with unified attitudes, expectations, consequences, and roles serving as key implementation. Goals include singular sets of rules across grade levels, standardized consequences for rule violations, and clearly defined responsibilities for teachers, administrators, and staff within a school.

Improving Emotional Problems

Students with behavior disorders respond to the same instructional methods as other students. They may exhibit more disruptive behaviors than some of their peers and, often, they need to be taught simple rules for self-control and conduct that their peers learn without instruction. Effective teachers of these students design instructional programs to include direct instruction in skills related to improving their emotional problems.

Improving Social Problems

Students with behavior disorders are among those many teachers least prefer to teach. This is largely because of what they do in the classroom. Disruptiveness is among their primary negative characteristics.

Integration of Treatment Approaches

When you look in classrooms, you will probably see evidence of many approaches used in combination. For example, one student may be taking medication to control hyperactivity; other students may be participating in a behavior modification system designed to reinforce work completion. The teacher is likely to have the room organized in a manner that encourages student participation through learning centers or discussion groups. You may see many self-concept materials on display. One or two of the students may be in counseling either in school or after school at private agencies.

If you were to look at the teacher's lesson plans or the students' IEPs, you should see goals and objectives that center on improving interpersonal skills and reducing behavior problems. You would also see academic textbooks and other instructional materials that are the same as those used in regular classrooms. Finally, if you observed the teacher working with the students, you would see the same type of positive teaching behaviors you would expect to see in any classroom—special or regular. The differences that have come to be identified with some students are a function of assumptions people have about the nature of behavior disorders. This perspective is evident in the diversity of definitions that are used to describe troubled students in our schools.

Cultural Diversity

Diverse home values, family traditions, and general cultural experiences are important considerations for teachers and other professionals working to improve the lives of all children with disabilities (cf. Dyches, Wilder, Sudweeks, Obiakor, & Algozzine, in press; Obiakor, 1994; 1999; 2001; Utley & Obiakor, 2001; Ysseldyke, Algozzine, & Thurlow, 2000). Prevalence within cultural groups and adaptation within families with multicultural backgrounds are important to consider when meeting the needs of students with behavior disorders.

Distribution of Behavior Disorders. The prevalence of behavior dis
is reflected in the numbers of children who are served under the Individu
with Disabilities Education Act (IDEA) of 1997 and rates of service differ (see
Table 4.7) among cultural groups (cf. U.S. Department of Education, 2002). For

TABLE 4.7   Percentage of Students Ages 6 Through 21 Served Under IDEA by Disability and Race/Ethnicity, During the 2000–2001 School Year

Disability	American Indian/ Alaska Native	Asian/ Pacific Islander	Black (Non-Hispanic)	Hispanic	White (Non-Hispanic)	All Students Served
Specific learning disabilities	56.3	43.2	45.2	60.3	48.9	50.0
Speech or language impairments	17.1	25.2	15.1	17.3	20.8	18.9
Mental retardation	8.5	10.1	18.9	8.6	9.3	10.6
Emotional disturbance	7.5	5.3	10.7	4.5	8.0	8.2
Multiple disabilities	2.5	2.3	1.9	1.8	1.8	2.1
Hearing impairments	1.1	2.9	1.0	1.5	1.2	1.2
Orthopedic impairments	0.8	2.0	0.9	1.4	1.4	1.3
Other health impairments	4.1	3.9	3.7	2.8	5.9	5.1
Visual impairments	0.4	0.8	0.4	0.5	0.5	0.4
Autism	0.6	3.4	1.2	0.9	1.4	1.4
Deaf-blindness	0.0	0.0	0.0	0.0	0.0	0.0
Traumatic brain injury	0.3	0.3	0.2	0.2	0.3	0.3
Developmental delay	0.7	0.6	0.7	0.2	0.6	0.5
All disabilities	100.0	100.0	100.0	100.0	100.0	100.0

Source: U.S. Department of Education, Office of Special Education Programs, Data Analysis System (DANS). U.S. Department of Education (2002). *Twenty-Fourth Annual Report to Congress on the Implementation of the Individuals with Disabilities Education Act.* Washington, DC: Author. [Table II-5, p. II-22]

for the 2000–2001 school year, White students made up 62.3% of the
served; 19.8% were Black; 14.5% were Hispanic; 1.9% were Asian/Pacific
; and 1.5% were American Indian/Alaska Native (U.S. Department of
on, 2002). While the rank ordering of the top five disability categories
arly identical for all racial/ethnic groups, students from some racial/eth-
oups were overrepresented or underrepresented in specific disability categories when compared with the IDEA student population as a whole. For
example, the percentages of Asian/Pacific Islander and Hispanic children receiving services for behavior disorders were lower than the percentages observed
for all IDEA students. Further,

> when compared with the average percentages for all students with disabilities,
> the percentages of Black students receiving services for behavior disorders were
> higher, and the percentages receiving services for specific learning disabilities or
> speech/language impairments were lower. Among Hispanic students, the per-
> centage receiving services for specific learning disabilities was higher than that
> for all students with disabilities, and the percentages receiving services for be-
> havior disorders, other health impairments, or mental retardation were lower.
> The percentages of Asian/Pacific Islander students receiving services for speech/
> language impairments or autism were higher than those for all students with
> disabilities, and the percentages receiving services for specific learning disabili-
> ties or behavior disorders were lower. As is the case for Hispanic students, the
> percentage of American Indian/Alaska Native students receiving services for spe-
> cific learning disabilities was higher than that for all students with disabilities,
> and the percentage receiving services for mental retardation was lower. The per-
> centages of White students in most disability categories were all close to those
> for the IDEA student population as a whole, but the percentages of White stu-
> dents in the other health impairments category was higher. (U.S. Department of
> Education, 2002, II-23)

Multicultural Family Adaptation. Family adaptation researchers are just beginning to recognize culture as an important variable for exploration (Bennett,
DeLuca, & Allen, 1996; National Research Council, 2001; Seligman, 1999). For example, African American families whose religions strongly influence their family
traditions may appraise disability positively. "The optimism and belief that all
children are important typifies African American culture and is reflected in family functions and reinforced in church and religious beliefs" (Rogers-Dulan &
Blacher, 1995, p. 234). Within the Native Hawaiian culture the spiritual orientation
toward life may influence families to think that having a child with behavior disorders is "normal" and that this child is a valued member of the community, regardless of disability. The Native American assimilation of individuals with
disabilities into the mainstream culture is reflected in the absence of native language "labels" or "classifications" for disabilities such as autism. Rather, descriptive statements are commonly used such as those by some Navajos including,
"she runs away," or "he gets excited," or "he's in his own world" (Connors &
Donnellan, 1998, p. 171).

Social support is defined as the community supports and resources "that the family may use to cope with a stressor situation" (McCubbin, McCubbin, Thompson, & Thompson, 1998, 20). Social support may include people, such as family and friends, and organizations, such as schools, churches, parent and sibling support groups, and medical services. Social support mediates the effects of the stressor on the health of the family (see McCubbin, McCubbin, Thompson, & Thompson, 1998). The strong familial support needed to raise a child with behavior disorders is found in many cultures. Native Hawaiians share a common concern for the well-being of all individuals in the tribal structure, which encompasses the immediate and extended family (McCubbin, McCubbin, Thompson, & Thompson, 1998). Similarly, the foundation of the family structure in Filipino American families is built upon cooperation and family support and allegiance, where individual desires are sacrificed for the benefit of the family (McCubbin, McCubbin, Thompson, & Thompson, 1998). Many individuals within the African American culture perceive caregiving for a dependent member as a responsibility to be shared among siblings and extended family members (Pruchno, Patrick, & Burant, 1997). Fear of stigma has also been reported in African American families (Pruchno, Patrick, & Burant, 1997), who tend to access services provided by professional organizations less frequently than the majority culture (see Pruchno et al., 1997) and only after relying on family, friends, religion, and church support. The concept of "familismo" in Hispanic families relates to strong family cohesion. This familial cohesion may circumvent the use of professional services if family values conflict with standards of the majority culture (Blacher, Lopez, Shapiro, & Fusco, 1997). When Latino mothers of children with disabilities believe in their spiritual role as "sacrificing mothers," and if they receive strong support from their extended family, they may take upon themselves the responsibility of raising their child with little organizational support (Bailey, Skinner, Rodriguez, Gut, & Correa, 1999).

Little is known about how multicultural families appraise their family situation when raising a child with behavior disorders or about how these families gain support. Some hypotheses may be made based on information related to raising children with other disabilities. For example, the appraisal of emotional/behavior disorders may vary among racial groups and is likely to be more extreme than those reporting their perceptions of raising a child with some other disabilities. When professionals in the field of behavior disorder ascertain how families from various cultures appraise their children and understand how they perceive their need for and access to social support, more effective treatment and education of multicultural students with behavior disorders may occur.

Summary

Behavior disorders in students are one of the three prevalent mild disabilities identified in schools. Students are referred for special education programs when their behavior is perceived to be disturbed or disturbing. Teachers like Fred

Peterson, Ms. Hildago, and Alice often report that these students are among the most difficult to teach. There are no absolute standards to judge the presence of normal or abnormal behavior. Frequently, judgments represent opinions about the appropriateness of behavior in a specific classroom. Normality and abnormality are relative concepts that are derived from the interaction of the actor, the observer, and the environment. Reactions to behavior vary according to the skills, expectations, and tolerance of the teacher. A signal indication of the relativity inherent in the category of behavior disorders is the variance in state prevalence figures and differences in state criteria for identifying students.

Over the years, the study of emotional and behavioral problems has been based in four theoretical viewpoints. The biophysical perspective emphasizes the relationship between body chemistry and behavior. The psychodynamic is concerned with feelings, family history, and relationship building. The psychoeducational framework is developmental in nature. It integrates clinical insights in behavior with practical methods for managing behavior. The behaviorist position views observable behavior as the critical element. Treatment strategies are focused on modifying environmental factors that reinforce appropriate behavior.

A synthesis of these models highlights the interactional nature of behavioral and emotional disorders. The ecological model promotes the notion that children are influenced by many different environments and that any attempt to help children with social or emotional problems must focus on all key elements in a youngster's life.

ACTIVITIES

1. Arrange to speak with some teachers like Fred Peterson, Ms. Hildago, and Alice who work with students with behavior disorders. Ask them to describe the behaviors of the students with whom they work. How do these behaviors differ from those of general students? Ask them to talk about special interventions that might be done in general and special education classrooms. What recommendations would each of them make about teaching both social and academic skills?

2. Make a list of disruptive behaviors and ask educators at your school to rate them as disturbed or disturbing behaviors. Are some behaviors rated both disturbed and disturbing? Ask if the degree, intensity, and/or duration has an effect upon the perception of whether a particular behavior is rated as disturbed or disturbing.

3. Investigate the professional organization in the field of behavior disorders. The national organization is the Council for Children with Behavioral Disorders of the Council for Exceptional Children (1920 Association Drive, Reston, Virginia 22091). Write to this organization for its literature. Try to determine its membership and the services offered these members.

4. Find out if there are state and local branches of the national Council for Children with Behavioral Disorders. If there is a local organization, arrange to visit one of the meetings. Arrange a meeting with a member to discuss the organization's purpose, membership composition, and services.

5. Look for journals that discuss techniques for working with students with behavior disorders, like *Behavior Disorders, Programming for Adolescents with Behavioral Disorders, Behavior Therapy,* and *Journal of Emotional and Behavioral Problems.* Read several articles, from different journals if possible, and discuss techniques you find about working with students with behavior disorders in general and special education classrooms. Talk about approaches suggested for academic and social skills training. Discuss suggestions about collaboration with other educators, support personnel, and parents.

6. Read a book about individuals with emotional or behavioral problems. A list of these books would include titles such as *Dibbs, In Search of Self; I Never Promised You a Rose Garden; Lisa and David; Jordi, One Child;* and *Flowers for Algernon.* What were some aberrant behaviors and what was done to "treat" the story characters? What are some other treatment methods?

7. Observe in a general-education classroom where students with behavior problems are being taught. Make a list of the behaviors that differentiate these students from others in the class. Notice how the teacher deals with them.

5 Students with Specific Learning Disabilities

ADVANCE QUESTIONS

Answer the following questions as you read this chapter:

1. What are the most common terms used to describe learning disabilities today?
2. Why do you think students with learning disabilities were "misclassified"?
3. How has brain research contributed to our knowledge of learning disabilities?
4. What are believed to be causes of learning disabilities?
5. How is learning disabilities defined? What are some concerns about the federal definition?
6. What is the prevalence of learning disabilities? Can you explain the relationship between identification criteria and the numbers of students who receive special education?
7. What are the primary characteristics of students with learning disabilities?

8. What are the general interventions and instructional procedures used by teachers of students with learning disabilities?
9. What are some specific activities that teachers use to improve academic and interpersonal skills of students with learning disabilities?
10. What are some suggestions that might be helpful to college students with learning disabilities?
11. How can teachers and faculty assist college students with learning disabilities?

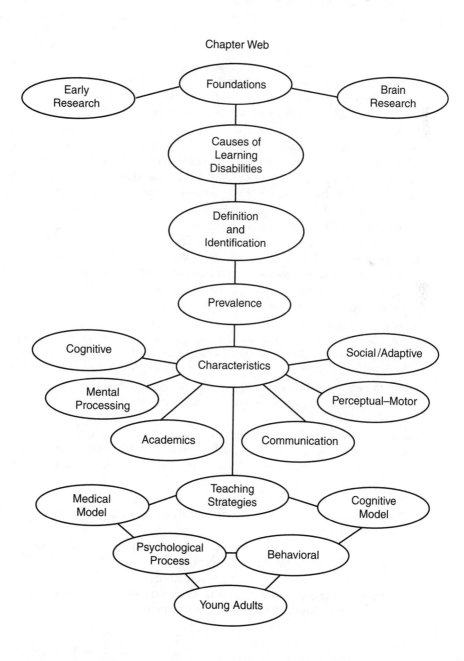

Chapter Web

Vignette: David

David, an active and friendly child, progressed through preschool with some minor behavior problems. His year in kindergarten was without incident, and his parents recalled that he was excited and happy to be going to school. He was particularly fond of the learning games and activities that the teacher had the children play.

It was surprising then, when during first grade, David displayed ambivalence about school. Some days he seemed excited about going. On other days, he cried to stay home. David's parents talked with his teacher about his scratchy-looking printing and his problems with reading and spelling vocabulary words. The teacher always assured them that David was ahead of the class in math, and in fact, the teacher was impressed with the way in which David could add and subtract numbers in his head.

By second grade, it was apparent that David was unable to associate sounds with letters of the alphabet. The letters he wrote down for his spelling words showed little relationship to the sounds that the words made when spoken. Interestingly, David was still well ahead of his classmates in math. He did make careless mistakes aligning numbers when writing them down during seatwork. His teacher said that he needed to space his numbers more carefully so that he wouldn't make addition or subtraction errors. And if he would just try as hard in reading and spelling as he did in math, he would do fine.

When David entered third grade, he was unable to read or spell on grade level with his classmates and was making poor grades in these subjects.

Finally, in fourth grade, David's teacher referred him to the prereferral assistance team for prereferral interventions. The team studied David's learning capabilities and performance, and made suggestions about ways in which David could best learn. Instead of using phonics and trying to teach him sound–symbol relationships, the team recommended a sight approach. In addition, David's teacher used line cues to help him in his number spacing in math so that his numbers didn't get out-of-line and appear so confusing to him. The teacher talked with David's parents about his pattern of school problems and asked them to confirm that David's hearing was all right. These techniques seemed to help, but David needed more intense instruction using similar types of learning strategies. (Refer to Figure 5.4 and Table 5.4 for ideas about special instructional strategies.) Thus, David's teacher referred him for a special education evaluation.

Now that you have read the vignette about David, see how many problem-solving questions you can answer. For those that you cannot readily answer, think about them as you read the chapter. David's story typifies that of other youngsters with learning disabilities.

1. Why do you think that David's attitude toward school became more negative each year?
2. Why was David having difficulties with spelling and reading? Why was math a better subject area for him?
3. How was David's handwriting affecting his school work?
4. How did the prereferral assistance team assist David's teacher in working with him? How did their suggestions help?

Foundations of Learning Disabilities

Of the current disability categories named in the Individuals with Disabilities Education Act, learning disability is the fastest growing and most controversial condition. Since 1975, millions of students have been identified as "learning disabled" and treated in public schools and clinical programs by educators, psychologists, and physicians (Coles, 1989; Lyon, 1996). In fact, about one-half of the approximately 6 million students with disabilities reported in the 6 to 21 age group are served as specific learning disabled (U.S. Department of Education, 2002).

In almost every public school classroom, there are at least two students identified as learning disabled. According to the National Institutes of Health, learning disabilities affect one in seven people (The Coordinated Campaign for Learning Disabilities, 2000).

The study of learning disabilities can be traced to several diverse disciplines including psychology, medicine (i.e., ophthalmology, optometry, otology, neurology, neuropsychology, psychiatry, pharmacology), speech and language pathologists, linguistics, and education (Lerner, 2003; Lyon, 1996). Researchers and practitioners in all of these specialized fields have made important contributions to the study of learning disabilities. Paradoxically, these diverse contributions have played a role in confusing our understanding of specific learning disabilities.

Because each profession tends to view phenomena from a distinctive perspective, it is difficult to get professional agreement about what a learning disability is and how it should be treated. To a pediatrician, a learning disability is a mild neurological disorder. To an otologist, a learning disability is an auditory discrimination problem. To a teacher, a learning disability is a reading, writing, or math deficiency. To an ophthalmologist, a learning disability is a visual tracking problem. To a pharmacologist, a learning disability is a metabolic disorder. To a speech and language pathologist, a learning disability is a deficit in vocabulary and syntactic development. Each of these professionals will evaluate, describe, and treat learning disabilities in terms of his or her own professional point of view. Much of the confusion can be cleared up by recognizing that there are many types of learning disabilities. Throughout the past forty years, many different terms have been used to indicate a learning disability (Table 5.1).

One type of specific learning disability is dyslexia, an impairment in reading ability. Students with dyslexia have difficulty decoding phonemes. A youngster who reads "saw" for "sew" *may* have dyslexia. It is important, however, not to jump to conclusions too quickly about the diagnosis of dyslexia. It is common for children to mispronounce letters and numbers as their nervous systems are maturing. Many educators believe dyslexia is caused by crossed signals in the area of the brain that interprets and gives meaning to words. A mild neurological impairment is the most widely accepted explanation for the cause of a learning disability.

Terms used to identify specific learning disabilities typically begin with the prefix *dys*, which means an impairment in a particular ability, as in *dysfunctional*

TABLE 5.1   Terms Used to Describe Learning Disabilities over the Past Forty Years

Attention Deficit Disorder	Perceptual Handicap
Minimal Brain Dysfunction	Behavior Disordered
Hyperactivity	Hyperkinesis
Educationally Handicapped	Impulsive
Strauss Syndrome	Strephosymbolia
Dyslexia	Word Blindness
Psycholinguistic Disorder	Multisensory Disorder
Neurologically Handicapped	Slow Learner
Reading Disability	Dyscalculia
Dysgraphia	Dysphasic
Organic Brain Dysfunction	Puzzle Children
Minimal Cerebral Palsy	Neurologically Immature
Developmentally Delayed	Mildly Handicapped
Hypoactivity	Language Disordered
Delayed Learner	Neurophrenia
Congenital Alexia	Diffuse Brain Damaged
Association Deficit Pathology	Organicity
Primary Reading Retardation	Maturation Lag

(Table 5.2). Mild neurological dysfunction cannot be proved by a standardized test. A neurological examination (including a detailed medical history, an examination of cranial nerves, an assessment of motor function, and an electroencephalogram [EEG]) *may* be able to confirm a neurological basis for a student's learning problems.

Other types of learning disabilities are more generalized in terms of behavior or cognitive difficulties. Students who are hyperactive or distractible are sometimes called learning disabled. Students who are disorganized and have difficulty following directions may be identified with learning disabilities. Poor coordination, problems with short-term memory, perceptual problems, limited concentration, speech deficits, inadequate verbal skills, and problems with becoming easily frustrated are just a sample of characteristics that have been attributed to learning disabilities.

Distinguishing the student with learning disabilities from the underachiever is a major challenge facing educators today. In recent years, almost 5 percent of the school population of students aged 6 to 17 received special education services because of a presumed learning disability. While the U.S. Department of Education has consistently stated that a range of 2 to 3 percent is a more reasonable prevalence figure for learning disabilities, the actual number of students identified across the nation and served in the specific learning disabilities category continues to increase. Many students may be misclassified with specific learning disabilities, while others remain unidentified.

TABLE 5.2 **Specific Learning Disabilities**

Each of these specific learning disabilities is generally believed to be caused by an impairment in nervous system functioning.

Dyslexia	A language-based reading disability. The individual has trouble understanding words, sentences, and/or paragraphs.
Dysgraphia	Difficulty forming letters correctly or within a defined space. Mirror writing is a severe form of this impairment.
Dysacusis	Impairment in understanding and deriving meaning from speech
Dyskinesia	Clumsiness or poor coordination.
Dyscalculia	A mathematical disability in which a person has difficulty solving arithmetic problems and grasping math concepts.
Dyslogia	A linguistic disturbance characterized by faulty formation or expression of verbal ideas.
Dysphasia	An impairment in the ability to produce or comprehend language. It can affect either written or spoken language function.
Dysnomia	Difficulty in searching for and thinking of a word to express a thought or idea.
Dysrhythmia	Poor rhythm or the loss of ability to move with rhythm.
Auditory and Visual Processing Disorders	Sensory disabilities in which an individual has difficulty understanding language in these modalities despite normal hearing and vision.
Nonverbal Learning Disability	Well-developed verbal and auditory abilities accompanied by difficulties in coordination, visual–spatial organization and social relationships.
Hyperlexia	Precocious reading ability with concurrent difficulties in communication and social skills.

Reification

Reification refers to the tendency to believe a problem is explained because it is named. In a relatively brief period of time, the field of learning disabilities has emerged as a major explanation for underachievement in school. Its historical antecedents are rooted in neurological research on brain injury and brain dysfunction. Its contemporary growth has branched out into education, linguistics, psychology, and medicine. Like an apple tree, learning disabilities, with the benefit of lots of attention, has grown quickly. But the growth is wild, and the fruit is spotty. The time has arrived to do some pruning. Simply identifying a student as having dyslexia is not enough. Unless school systems become more adept at varying instruction to meet individual needs and the different learning styles of students in the general classroom, students identified with learning disabilities will continue to flounder.

Early Research on Learning Disabilities

Barsch was one of the first professionals to point out the need to look more closely at learning disabilities as a possible explanation for the failure of some children to make adequate progress in school.

> The failing learner is no longer a statistic of minor significance. Academic failure, learning inefficiency, anxiety barriers, dismissals, expulsions, dropouts, reading retardation, and a host of other problems are rampant on the educational scene. The percentages of failing students is increasing annually. . . . The problem is immediate upon the educational terrain: the confrontation is compelling and vibrant and the pressure for action is inescapable. (Barsch, 1968, 7, 10)

Barsch's remarks, which appeared in the first issues of the *Journal of Learning Disabilities*, signaled a shift toward considering the possibility that some problem learners had a learning disability. Barsch's comments linked 30 years of research with brain injured individuals to remedial services for students in public schools.

Misclassified Mentally Retarded Students.   In the 1950s, Samuel Kirk discovered that a number of persons had been misclassified as mentally retarded at the Wayne County Training School in Northville, Michigan. Kirk could not justify classifying these pupils as having mental retardation for several reasons. First, the intelligence quotient (IQ) scores of these students were too high; second, after intensive remediation in reading, they made extraordinary progress. Similar gains were rarely made by their counterparts with mental retardation.

> All of the children I taught . . . were classified as mentally retarded. In all of these cases my purpose was to show through the results of remediation that these children should have been classified as learning disabled instead of mentally retarded, since they were normal in some respects but had specific disabilities. (Kirk, 1976, 260)

Many of these individuals eventually left the institution and became self-supporting (Kirk, 1976). These misclassified individuals inspired Kirk to do further research to determine the nature of their disabilities. Kirk's findings paralleled earlier research on patients with brain injuries. In the early 1930s, Kurt Goldstein had observed perseveration, figure–ground confusion, and forced responses to stimuli in adults who had suffered brain injury (Goldstein, 1942).

Heinz Werner (1944) and Alfred Strauss and Laura Lehtinen (1947) followed similar research avenues. They identified and described exogenously brain damaged (i.e., point of origin of disability outside the body) children with mental retardation. The disabilities of these children could not be traced to genetic causes. Their behavior was characterized as perceptually disordered, impulsive, distractible, and repetitive. This condition became known as Strauss syndrome. Later, during the 1960s, William Cruickshank (1967) was instrumental in changing the focus of research from exogenous retardation to minimally brain damaged (MBD) children with normal intelligence. Cruickshank's identification of Strauss syndrome characteristics in children with average intelligence was a pivotal turning point in the study of learning disabilities (Figure 5.1).

Supporters of Learning Disabilities.   The movement to gain recognition for children with Strauss syndrome took a giant step forward in 1963 when Kirk proposed the term *learning disability* in a speech at a special-education parents' conference. Previously, professionals had used many different terms to identify the same children. By using the term *learning disabilities* as an umbrella concept to cover children who had been variously called minimally brain damaged, perceptually handicapped, minimally brain dysfunctional, or language delayed, advocates were able to join forces and push for federal legislation to provide remedial school services for those students.

Critics of Learning Disabilities.   The category of learning disabilities evolved as a means of addressing a condition that did not fit into preexisting classifications

---

FIGURE 5.1   **Strauss Syndrome, Characteristics of Brain Damaged Children**

These are general behaviors that Strauss and Werner believed characterized brain-injured children. These characteristics influenced the later work of William Cruickshank with nonretarded children and led to treatment in classrooms that were devoid of distractions. Study carrels, which are still found in many resource rooms, are artifacts of instructional programs that were designed to focus the attention of students who exhibited Strauss syndrome characteristics.

---

1. Forced responsiveness to stimuli—Any noise or movement distracted the child: a pencil dropping on the floor, the sound of cars driving outside a window, a student passing by. This is different than distractibility caused by boredom.

2. Pathological fixation—The child perseverated. Once engaged in a motor task, the child repeated movements over and over. An example is a student who rubs a hole in a work sheet with an eraser. Perseveration can affect thinking, talking, or movement.

3. Disinhibition—Excessive motor activity. Now commonly referred to as hyperactivity. Strauss found that children with brain damage were attracted to specific features of objects. The "bounciness" of a ball or the "jabbiness" of a pencil would seduce the child into bouncing or jabbing.

4. Dissociation—The child was unable to integrate or see the "whole picture." For example, a student would have difficulty seeing how the parts of a puzzle fit together. The child was disorganized. This integration problem inspired Werner's famous Marble Board experiments where students were asked to repeat patterns of red and black marbles on eleven inch squares with ten lines and ten holes to each line. Children who were unable to copy the patterns were identified as dissociated in their conceptual reasoning.

Source: Derived from Farnham-Diggory, 1978, and Bruner, Cole, and Lloyd, 1978.

of exceptionality (e.g., mental retardation, emotional disturbance). Some educators think that the label is a convenience because students with learning disabilities usually have average intelligence, no sign of emotional disturbance, and come primarily from middle class backgrounds. The critics believe that the identification of a learning disability is a way for students to get special education services without anyone being held accountable for the problem. The student is blameless because the problem is assumed to be neurological in nature. Parents are blameless because the learning problem is not caused by inadequate parenting. Finally, teachers are blameless because the students' presumed neurological impairment, rather than inadequate instruction, is the reason for school failure.

Coles (1989) suggested that the term *learning disabilities* is popular because it explains and justifies poor school performance by focusing upon presumed characteristics and attributes found within the child. Bartoli (1989) proposed that instead of leaning on neurological dysfunction solely, we also should consider the child's learning curriculum, classroom dynamics, our means of testing student progress, the overall school climate, teacher-parent relationships, family socioeconomics, and the values of the community. In other words, we need to look at the child's whole learning situation and environment.

Brain Research

The human brain weighs less than five pounds, and it can store more information than all the libraries of the world. In appearance it resembles a soft, wrinkled walnut. It communicates with itself through ten billion neurons and a hundred billion neuron connections (Restak, 1984). Neuroscientists approach the study of the brain with the same awe most of us reserve for space travel and exploration of the universe. We have much to learn about brain function, thinking, and learning disabilities. Modern technology, through the use of computerized axial tomography (CAT) scans and positron emission photography (PET) scans, can provide a detailed picture of brain function in living patients. Unfortunately, these medical techniques are far too complex and expensive to be helpful to school evaluation teams.

It is possible to detect brain anomalies in persons with severe learning disabilities. In 1861, Paul Broca, a French neuroanatomist, exhibited the brain of a deceased patient who had a severe communication impairment. His intelligence was average and he showed no indication of emotional disturbance. Broca called his patient "Tan-Tan" because those were the only words the man could utter. Tan-Tan understood speech and communicated through gestures. Only Tan-Tan's speaking ability was impaired. The brain Broca exhibited had observable damage in a circumscribed two-inch area of the left hemisphere, including the lower portion of the frontal lobe, the lower portion of the parietal lobe, and the upper part of the temporal lobe. Broca convinced his colleagues that Tan-Tan's speech impairment (known today as aphasia) was the result of an insult to the brain. Broca was one of the first contributors to the theory that language ability is localized in the left hemisphere of the brain (Restak, 1984).

The Russian psychologist Aleksandr Luria believed, as Broca did, that certain mental abilities were localized in specific areas of the brain. For instance, visual images are centered in the occipital lobe in the brain. Any damage to the occipital lobe will result in a visual impairment. Luria's work on memory, particularly with his most famous patient "S," documented the relationship between visual imagery and memory.

Luria's work with patients who suffered from dyscalculia (impaired ability to do arithmetic) demonstrated how defects in spatial logic, mathematical planning, and calculating could be traced to defects in specific areas of the brain. For example, Luria presented the case of an artillery commander who lost the ability to add, subtract, divide, and multiply after a bullet wound. Surrounding brain tissue was unblemished and other mathematical skills, such as counting and logic, were unaffected. In another illustration, Luria described a female patient who was unable to plan how to solve sequential problems. She became confused when given a three-part problem like: a boy is eight years old; his father is thirty years older; and the mother is ten years younger than the father—how old are they? Luria reported that this patient's thinking ability improved after surgical removal of a brain tumor (Farnham-Diggory, 1978; Restak, 1984).

Specific areas of the brain control discrete cognitive functions (Figure 5.2). Robert Sperry's (1968) work with split-brain patients detailed the different ways that the right and left hemispheres of the brain process information. Sperry studied individuals whose corpus callosums were severed by surgery in order to diminish uncontrollable seizures. The corpus callosum is the bundle of nerves that connect the left and right hemispheres of the brain. It is the line of communication that allows the hemispheres to communicate with each other. Sperry found that the left hemisphere is specialized for dealing with things in sequence; the right hemisphere deals with things all at once. The left hemisphere is often characterized as the logical, verbal, analytical half of the human brain. The right hemisphere is characterized as the intuitive, holistic, visual half of the brain.

Robert Ornstein, who studied under Sperry, found that his subjects were right- or left-hemispheric oriented; that is, they had a preferred mode of thought. Using EEG measurements of electrical activity in individuals from different occupations, Ornstein discovered that artists relied more on their right hemisphere even when the task required left hemisphere capabilities. The opposite was true of lawyers; that is, even when the task required right hemispheric thought, the lawyers tended to process the information through their left hemisphere. Ornstein concluded that the hemispheres are specialized for information processing and that individuals gradually develop a hemispheric preference.

Ornstein also found that the hemispheres of most right-handed people are specialized for specific types of thought along the lines outlined by Sperry. But left-handed individuals, according to Ornstein, sometimes do not follow the standard left-right hemisphere localization of function. According to Ornstein:

> Left-handers often show a reverse specialization, in which some information is processed in the opposite hemisphere from the one used by right-handers. Some

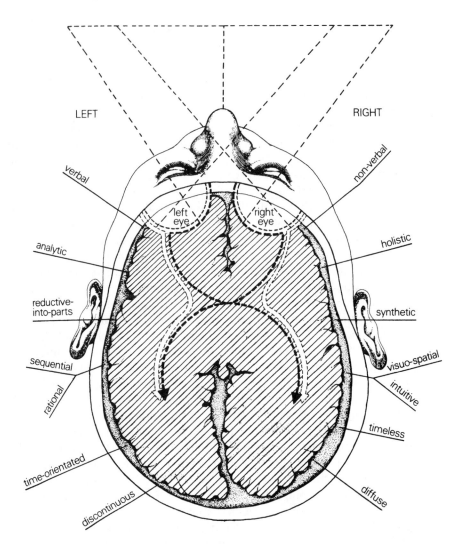

FIGURE 5.2 **Areas of the Brain**

Source: Charles Hamptden-Turner, *Maps of the Mind*. London: Mitchell Beazley, 1981. Reprinted with permission.

left-handers appear to have brains organized like those of right-handers, while others show no specialization at all. Ambidextrous people seem to have the least specialization of all the groups we have tested. (Ornstein, 1978, 81)

Students with learning disabilities sometimes have a developmental history of mixed dominance (e.g., favoring neither the right nor the left hand). Perhaps the "reverse specialization" that Ornstein discovered in left-handers may provide a clue as to why left-handed children are identified with learning disabilities at a greater rate than right-handed youngsters. In applying his findings to schools Ornstein observed:

> Even a casual look at the results of hemisphere research shows that the ways of thinking that seem to be primarily the province of the left hemisphere are used extensively in the basic subjects of the school curriculum. The realization that schools spend most of their time training students in what seem to be left hemisphere skills, and that most educators and taxpayers regard what seem to be right hemisphere skills as frills, has caused many people to wonder whether our educational system is unbalanced. (Ornstein, 1978, 82)

Ornstein's research indicated that there may be a mismatch between how students process information and how information is presented by teachers. If some students have a preferred mode of right hemispheric thinking, they will be at a distinct disadvantage in classrooms where the teacher relies heavily on sequenced learning, verbal skills, and analysis of problems (i.e., left-hemispheric material). This supposition is supported by the work of Sally Smith (1980) at the Lab School, a special school for students with learning disabilities in Washington, D.C. Smith has found that her students respond to activities in which the arts (right-hemispheric thinking) are used to teach academic skills. Smith's observation that ". . . the child with the hidden handicap of learning disability also has a hidden talent in an artistic area because he has learned unique ways of looking at things," sounds very much like Ornstein's description of individuals who prefer right-hemispheric modes of thought.

New evidence from the National Institute of Mental Health (NIMH) (1996) shows that most learning disabilities do not stem from a single, specific area or hemisphere of the brain. Rather, difficulties occur when attempting to bring together information from various regions of the brain. These difficulties stem from subtle disturbances in brain structures and functions. For example, a recent study sponsored by the National Institute of Mental Health (NIMH) found an absence of functional linkages between the occipital lobe, which recognizes letters, and the angular gyrus in the left hemisphere, which processes language. Interaction between these regions enables an individual to read (www.nimh. nih/gov/events/prlefdy.htm) (Retrieved August 6, 2003).

The NIMH stated that some disturbances in brain structures begin before birth. During pregnancy, the fetal brain develops from a few all-purpose cells into a complex organ made of billions of specialized, interconnected nerve cells called neurons. During this evolution, things can go wrong that may alter how the neurons form or interconnect (NIMH, 1996).

Brain development continues throughout pregnancy and is therefore vulnerable to disruptions. If the disruption occurs early, it may be fatal to the fetus, or the infant may be born with mental retardation or other disabilities. Disruptions can occur from such occurrences as maternal diseases, trauma, and heredity. If the disruption occurs later, when the brain cells are becoming specialized, errors may occur in the cell make-up, location, or connections. Some of these "errors" are thought by scientists to contribute to learning disabilities. In 1999, scientists identified the first gene linked to dyslexia. While not considered the only gene that contributes to dyslexia, the discovery confirms a genetic basis for some cases. They mapped the gene DyX3 to chromosome 2 by studying a large Norwegian family in which 11 of 36 members had dyslexia (*New York Times*, Sept. 7, 1999).

Causes of Learning Disabilities

IDEA does not recognize environmental, cultural, or economic factors as primary reasons for a learning disability; however, these factors do impact upon youth and can cause subsequent disorders. For example, a child born into an impoverished environment may have parents who are economically deprived and educationally deficient. Lack of knowledge about nutrition, or the ingestion of harmful substances (e.g., paint with lead or mercury) can result in delayed development or neurological damage. Insufficient prenatal or inadequate perinatal care, as well as maltreatment of postnatal diseases or trauma (e.g., infections) are contributors to learning disorders. Thus, detrimental environmental factors and biological conditions are interrelated (Smith et al., 1986).

Many of the organic origins of mental retardation can overlap as possible contributors of specific learning disabilities and behavior disorders as well (Ramsey, Dixon, & Smith, 1986). For example, postnatal disorders of encephalitis and meningitis can result in attention disorders, behavior disorders, and mental retardation. Hyperactivity, visual impairments, and deafness can be caused by measles or whooping cough. Anoxia, or oxygen deprivation, can cause brain damage, with resulting learning or behavior disorders. Furthermore, genetic factors may precipitate learning disabilities.

Silver (1989) reported findings from a study of children with learning disabilities who were attending the TRI-Services' Center School in Chevy Chase, Maryland; the Chelsea School in Silver Spring, Maryland; and Pine Ridge School in Williston, Vermont. He calculated that the frequency of learning disabilities was 4.5 times higher among adopted children—according to his study, 17.3 percent of adopted children versus 3.9 percent of biological children. He reported that many adopted children are born out of wedlock to indigent young women. Such mothers are likely to receive less adequate nutritional and medical care during pregnancy and insufficient emotional support. Pregnancies of young, indigent mothers are usually stressful, and Silver concluded that the mother's tension and anxiety could adversely affect the fetus. Children born to such mothers are slow to mature and sometimes develop learning disabilities.

The fact that learning disabilities tend to turn up in families, some even generations apart, indicates a genetic link. Many times educators have identified learning problems in children only to find that one of their parents had the same problem in school. For example, a young boy is identified as having a problem linking phonetic sounds to letters they represent. It turns out that the boy's father had the same problem when he was trying to learn to read during early grades. Or a girl has difficulty expressing herself, and it so happens that her mother has always had this problem. A parent with an expressive language disorder might talk less or use distorted language. In this situation, the child acquired the same problem due to environmental reasons because her mother was a poor language model from which to learn. Of course, it could have also been genetic. In this case, it is difficult to say which was the primary cause—environment or genetics.

Definition and Identification

In 1975, Congress delayed the passage of the original federal special education law several months while it wrangled with experts and parents over a suitable definition for a learning disability. The expression that a camel is a horse created by a committee aptly applies to the federal definition of a learning disability. It appeases everyone but pleases no one. It is vague in some parts and too specific and exclusive in others. According to the latest federal guidelines implemented under the Individuals with Disabilities Education Act, "specific learning disability" means

> a disorder in one or more of the basic psychological processes involved in understanding or in using language, spoken or written, which may manifest itself in an imperfect ability to listen, think, speak, read, write, spell, or do mathematical calculations.

The term includes such conditions as perceptual handicaps, brain injury, minimal brain dysfunction, dyslexia, and developmental aphasia. The term does not include children who have learning problems that are primarily the result of visual, hearing, or motor handicaps, of mental retardation, of emotional disturbance, or of environmental, cultural, or economic disadvantage (P.L. 101–476).

Major Concepts and Key Phrases

The federal definition for learning disabilities has been criticized because it is broad-based and includes undefined terminology. It is helpful to understand the thoughts and concerns that existed when the major concepts and key phrases were first proposed and put into practice in 1975.

Basic Psychological Processes. This phrase has yet to be specifically defined but refers to the processing functions that any learner must have intact in order to receive, integrate (i.e., organize, associate, store, retrieve), or express information. It infers that learning problems of students in this category are of a neurological nature and that development is uneven due to subtle disorders of mental processing. Chalfant and Scheffelin (1969) describe "mental processes" as sensing information by listening, looking, or touching; integrating sensations

HIGHLIGHT 5.1
What Is a Learning Disability?

In order to help you understand the difficulty in defining a learning disability, we are going to give you a brief quiz. First question—what is a table? Nice going—you figured that out without much trouble. When you can see, feel, and eat off something, it's not hard to define. Let's try another. What is the wind? That's a little harder. You can't see the wind, and you don't use it very often (except for some kite flying or sailing if you're fortunate); but you can feel the wind, and it's a common part of life. But did you give a specific definition or did you just describe what it means to you? The more abstract a concept, the further removed from direct experiences (our senses), the harder it is to come up with one definition. Let's extend this thinking to one more question. What is eternity? Now there's an abstract concept. We'll have to accept a lot of different views on this one. We have the same problem with the term "learning disabilities." It is a very abstract idea, and it is interpreted in many different ways.

through such cognitive functions as attention, discrimination, memory, integration, concept formation, and problem solving; and responding through speech or body movements.

Language-Based. The federal definition states that the disorder is language-based and occurs in learning situations that involve oral language, listening comprehension, written composition, writing, spelling, reading (e.g., vocabulary, word-attack skills, decoding, comprehension), or arithmetic (e.g., calculation, reasoning, general problem solving). Due to each student's specific processing deficit, uneven abilities are manifested in these language-based areas highlighted in academic tasks.

Inclusion Clause. The federal definition specifically includes examples of presumed central nervous system deficits like perceptual handicaps, brain injury, minimal brain dysfunction, dyslexia, and developmental aphasia. These deficits are representative of more severe disabilities, and are not typically identified during educational assessment of students with mild learning disabilities.

Exclusion Clause. The federal definition excludes mental retardation, emotional disturbance, visual impairments, organic hearing dysfunctions, and motor disabilities as primary causes of learning disabilities, even though these conditions can coexist with learning disabilities. According to the definition, a learning disability cannot be attributed to conditions such as environmental, cultural, or economic disadvantage. This part of the exclusion clause is particularly perplexing because it is difficult to determine whether a student's underachievement is due to a subtle central nervous system disorder, delayed developmental growth, inadequate teaching, or a lack of environmental opportunities.

Because the federal definition is ambiguous, criteria were established to complement and to spell out a *functional* method for determining whether a student has a learning disability. Consider the following:

a. A multidisciplinary team may determine that a child has a specific learning disability if:

1. The child does not achieve commensurate with his or her age and ability levels in one or more of the areas listed in paragraph (a) (2) of this section, when provided with learning experiences appropriate for the child's age and ability levels, and

2. The team finds that a child has a severe discrepancy between achievement and intellectual ability in one or more of the following areas:

i. Oral expression;

ii. Listening comprehension;

iii. Written expression;

iv. Basic reading skill;

v. Reading comprehension;

vi. Mathematics calculation; or

vii. Mathematics reasoning.

b. The team may not identify a child as having a specific learning disability if the severe discrepancy between ability and achievement is primarily the result of:

1. A visual, hearing, or motor handicap;

2. Mental retardation;

3. Emotional disturbance; or

4. Environmental, cultural, or economic disadvantage. (U.S. Office of Education, 1977, 65081–65085)

These criteria are referred to as the "severe discrepancy formula" because they focus attention on the gap between a youngster's academic achievement and intellectual ability. Simply stated, the assumption is that a severe discrepancy between intelligence and achievement indicates a learning disability. Because both intelligence and achievement can be measured by testing, the discrepancy formula has been widely used. Widespread acceptance of the discrepancy formula has not solved all the problems in identifying students with learning disabilities. Two key aspects of discrepancies require closer inspection.

Intellectual Ability.   For many years, William Cruickshank, a pioneer in the field of learning disabilities, argued against assuming that only children with average or above average intelligence have learning disabilities. The way the present discrepancy formula is written, it appears as though students with mental retardation or other disabilities cannot have learning disabilities. It is not uncommon to hear teachers define a student with learning disabilities as a youngster with *average* intelligence who is underachieving. This is misleading, and the results show up in educational programming. As an illustration, a child with Down syndrome has a clear neurological impairment, but rarely does one hear learning disabilities discussed as an explanation for academic problems. Any learning problems a student with Down syndrome has with reading or math are attributed to mental retardation. The possibility that the student might have dyslexia or some other specific learning disability can be overlooked.

Achievement

As Farnham-Diggory (1978, 5) pointed out, "A learning disabled child is presumably not up to a 'grade level' that can be specified in terms of test scores. Grade-level work is what 50 percent of the children in a particular grade are doing." If grade-level measures are accurate, half the class will always have a discrepancy between their ability and achievement. This leaves us to ponder what a *severe* discrepancy is. According to Smith (1991), 57 percent of the states provide guidelines on how to quantify severe discrepancy. Two or more years below grade level is common. Some states use three or more years below grade level. In almost half of the states, the meaning of "severe discrepancy" is left in the hands of local school systems. Lerner (2000) pointed out that a one year delay in reading at age six could be more severe than a three year delay at age sixteen.

The Discrepancy Problem

Too many referrals to special education programs are a major problem that has evolved from the discrepancy notion. Many students are under grade level. If teachers take "below grade level" to mean that students need special education, referrals are quick to follow. This often leads to students being mistakenly placed in special education.

The 2004 reauthorization of IDEA (P.L. 108–446) addressed concerns regarding overidentification of students when the discrepancy formula was used to determine a learning disability. The new bill stated that

> a local educational agency shall not be required to take into consideration whether a child has a severe discrepancy between achievement and intellectual ability in oral expression, listening comprehension, written expression, basic reading skill, reading comprehension, mathematical calculation, or mathematical procedures. (Council for Exceptional Children, 2004, 14)

Instead of utilizing IQ and achievement tests to determine if a learning disability exists, the language in IDEA suggests that school systems use scientific, researched teaching methods as an intervention. If there is no progress then a determination of a learning disability is acceptable.

Response to Intervention.   Scanlon et al., (2003) summarized the pros and cons of what some educators call the "Response to Intervention" (RTI) approach. Some of the potential positive aspects of RTI are: students will get systematic instructional help sooner rather than waiting until after the student has a lengthy history of failure; there will be an emphasis on data based and monitoring of student progress; theory and practice will be more closely aligned as school systems utilize research based interventions; the discrepancy formula is particularly ineffective in identifying learning disabilities in adolescents and girls. Drawbacks to the RTI approach include: no research based instructional approaches are sufficiently validated; learning disabilities will be correlated with low academic achievement; the push for reading proficiency will cause educators to overlook learning disabilities in other areas such as math and oral expression; implementation and monitoring will be particularly difficult to accomplish in secondary schools.

Prevalence of Learning Disabilities

Prevalence of learning disabilities depends upon multiple factors. Reliable figures are difficult to obtain. Only generalities about the numbers of students identified and served can be stated. Numbers of students depend upon methods and criteria used for identification and classification (Lerner, 2003). As a result, the number of students classified as learning disabled varies from state to state (Algozzine & Korinek, 1985). Much of this variation is a result of differences in the eligibility guidelines used by states (Algozzine & Ysseldyke, 1987). The more stringent the criteria, the fewer students with learning disabilities are identified. Therefore, a student determined eligible for services in one school district or state might not meet the requirements in another.

Since 1977, the U.S. Department of Education published statistics reporting the numbers and percentages of children and youth receiving special education and related services. These statistics are based upon student-count data submitted by states and territories. A continued trend of increases in the category of learning disabilities is attributed to:

1. The broad and vague wording of the federal definition for specific learning disabilities.
2. Social acceptance and preference for the learning disabilities classification (rather than mental retardation or behavior disorders).
3. Differing criteria used by states for qualification for services. (Sigmon, 1989)

Added to this list of possible reasons for the increase in numbers are reasons offered by Lyon in 1996:

4. Financial incentives to identify students for special education.
5. Inadequate preparation of teachers by colleges of education, leading to over-referral of students with any type of special need.

The list constitutes "questionable reasons" for the increase. "Sound reasons" for the increase in numbers of students identified for specific learning disabilities include better research, identification of girls with learning disabilities, and a broader definition of disability in reading, which focuses on phonemic awareness (or lack of). Recent research indicates that a disability in basic reading skills is primarily caused by deficits in phonemic awareness, which is independent of any ability versus achievement discrepancy. Lyon (1996) maintains that deficits in phonemic awareness can be identified in late kindergarten and first grade using inexpensive and straightforward reading testing measures.

The field continues to be plagued by disagreements about the definition of specific learning disabilities, diagnostic criteria, assessment practices, treatment procedures, and educational policies. It appears there is much truth in the statement made by Ysseldyke, Algozzine, and Thurlow that "learning disabilities is whatever society wants it to be" (1983, 145).

Characteristics

Each student with learning disabilities has unique characteristics, just as does each student with any other disability and as do students without learning disabilities. Student characteristics can be categorized within functional domains. These domains include cognitive abilities, processing skills, academic achievement, communication development, perceptual–motor skills, and social-adaptive skills. All domains interact; no functioning areas operate independently.

Each student needs to be viewed holistically. If one part of an auto malfunctions, the rest of the vehicle will not function properly. Compensations can be made, but the malfunctioning part affects the overall service the car gives; for example, have you ever tried to go somewhere only to find that your car would not start because the battery was dead? You quickly learned that the best-performing engine will not function at all because the starter would not turn over. You may have used a jumper cable to start your car—which means you were able to temporarily bypass the main problem. But sooner or later, the battery had to be replaced. People with learning disabilities are a heterogeneous group of individuals who have deficits in one or more of the functional domains. The problem can be bypassed or overlooked for a period of time—but sooner or later, the specific disorder has to be addressed.

Students with learning disabilities do not have an easily identifiable problem. We cannot assume that the problem simply resides within the student. We have to look at all of the interactive components within the child's learning environment; for example, what task is the child being required to perform? If it is above his or her functioning level or if instruction is inappropriate, the student may fail. Curricular and task components should be analyzed as assiduously as learner behavior. Learner characteristics by functional domains are presented in Table 5.3, along with general instructional interventions for students with learning disabilities. We will have more to say about teaching in sections that follow.

TABLE 5.3 Teaching Students with Learning Disabilities

	Cognitive	Academic	Adaptive	Social	Perceptual/ Perceptual Motor	Language
Learner Character-istics	Normal or above aver-age intelli-gence.	Uneven pattern of academic perfor-mance.	Some de-gree of field de-pendency.	Susceptible to distrac-tion. Social impercep-tion.	Difficulties with learn-ing modali-ties and eye–hand coordina-tion. In-adequate gross or fine motor skills.	Difficulty in reading or lan-guage skills.
Instructional Intervention	Adapt in-struction to individual cognitive abilities.	Identify entry-level skills for each aca-demic area.	Emphasize indepen-dent strate-gies for learning.	Teach self-manage-ment skills. Make so-cial skills training sit-uational.	Adjust in-struction to individual learning styles and physical capabili-ties.	Provide opportu-nities for language stimulation activities.

Cognitive

There is overlap between cognitive functioning, intellect, and processing of infor-mation. Cognitive refers to a wide spectrum of thinking skills (e.g., memory, analysis, deduction). Jacobs (1984) defines cognition as the active process of men-tal awareness and thinking. Some of these skills are sampled by an intelligence test.

Children without disabilities approach learning by asking themselves ques-tions, organizing information, and using environmental cues. This process of thought is called metacognition (Ryan, Short, & Weed, 1986). Students with a learning disability typically do not acquire the skills of learning how to think through problems naturally. These students can be taught how to organize their thoughts through metacognitive training.

Students with deficient metacognitive strategies may appear to be passive learners or apathetic. Some teachers describe students with learning disabilities as dependent, lazy, impulsive, or disorganized. A negative cycle occurs when a stu-dent's academic progress is limited by his or her inadequate metacognitive strate-gies. The youngster becomes soured and turned off toward learning, and teachers come to think of the child as unmotivated. This cycle of failure can be changed by teaching metacognitive strategies (Levine, 1990; Torgesen, 1977).

Metacognitive training teaches students *how* to learn (Tarver, 1986). Deshler et al. (1983) suggested teaching students study skills like scanning, outlining, note taking, time management, and questioning. Tarver (1986) said metacognitive training includes instruction in various (1) self-monitoring strategies (e.g., self-questioning, self-interrogatives, self-checking); (2) self-instructional strategies; and (3) executive strategies (e.g., selecting the strategy most appropriate to the task or problem at hand).

Lloyd (1980) emphasized the positive benefits of using self-instructional training. This involves training in use of self-verbalization to apply academic strategies. The student is taught to ask himself or herself: "Am I paying attention?" "What is the problem asking me to do?" "What is my plan for solving this problem?"

According to Deshler, Schumaker, and Lenz (1984), cognitive skills interact with academic achievement. Their view is supported by factors such as the high number of students with learning disabilities who (1) reach an academic plateau of fourth- or fifth-grade level in the tenth grade, (2) have not passed minimal competency tests, and (3) are school dropouts. Most of these students are unable to generalize what they have learned across subjects or settings. The fact that these students are reported to be less satisfied with their personal social lives and continue to live with parents after school years supports the contention that they lack the cognitive tools necessary for life after school.

Mental Processing

Processing skills relate directly to cognitive skills. A problem may occur in one or more of the perceptual neuro-pathways activated during learning. In school, these perceptual neuro-pathways are primarily visual and auditory. Educators use terms such as visual discrimination, auditory memory, visual closure, auditory sequencing, and auditory blending to describe the interplay between how a student perceives something and the mental processing that must occur in order to understand it.

The mental receptive processing utilizes subskills that are essential to learning. These include attending to task and being able to discriminate what is heard or seen (Ramsey, 1995a). Attending has to do with being able to focus selectively. As students read or listen, they must select which facts and concepts are important and which are less critical or relevant. Students with learning disabilities are likely to miss cues (Levine, 1990). Distractibility is sometimes confused with attending. The problem is not lack of attention, rather the problem is the inability to focus attention on a single stimulus. Instead of reading a book, a student is attracted to coughing, a pencil dropping, or a door opening.

In order to read, a child must be able to perceive individual phoneme sounds and to correspond these sounds with letter symbols. Students must also learn to associate groups of letters with English language sounds, store numbers with quantities, store words with definitions, along with other memory recognition and recall tasks as they progress through school. Over the school years, memory becomes increasingly automated. Learning higher skills depends upon effortless recall of previously learned skills (Levine, 1990). Thus, the importance of practice as students learn and attempt to further learning is evident. Lokerson (1996) states that it is not unusual to hear parents of children with specific learning disabilities proclaim, "My child made all As and Bs in earlier grade levels. Why is he or she having problems now?"

Discrimination refers to the ability to differentiate one stimulus from another (e.g., an object, an item, a sound). When asked to identify the letters "m" and "n," the child must visually perceive that there are two humps in "m" and only one in "n." Children learn to discriminate by color, shape, pattern, size, position, and brightness. Eventually students must be able to visually discriminate letters and words to learn to read. This requires more intricate visual processing skills than some students with learning disabilities may have. Figure 5.3 lists typical problems students with visual learning disabilities encounter when reading and spelling.

Academics

The decline of the academic status of students with learning disabilities has been the focal point of much research (Deshler, 1978; Koppitz, 1972–1973). The impact that delayed developmental cognitive functioning has on academic progress was addressed in a study by Speece, McKinney, and Appelbaum (1986). They concluded that students with learning disabilities, even though they showed average

FIGURE 5.3   Typical Reading and Spelling Patterns of Students with Visual Processing Difficulties

- Confuse letters that differ in directionality (b-d, p-q)
- Confuse with words that can be reversed (was-saw)
- Limited sight vocabulary; unrecognizable from word configuration
- Lose place reading, especially when moving gaze from the end of the line on the right side to the beginning of the next line on the left side
- Omit letters and words because they were not visually noted
- Insert and substitute letters erroneously as well as omit them
- Have difficulty learning irregular words that cannot be sounded out phonetically
- May find it easier to read words when learning to spell them first
- Sometimes experience difficulty recalling the shape of letters when writing them
- Spell phonetically but inaccurately (cof-cough; bisnis-business)
- Can spell difficult phonetic words but not simple irregular phonetically spelled words

intelligence on tests, did not catch up with their peers after three to four years of remedial services.

The disparity between academic performance and intellectual ability characterizes students with learning disabilities. The federal definition specifies academic areas in which learning disorders are manifested during school experiences. Reading, mathematics, spelling, and writing are listed.

Learning disabilities may occur in the following academic areas:

1. Spoken language: Delays, disorders, or discrepancies in listening and speaking.
2. Written language: Difficulties with reading, writing, and spelling.
3. Arithmetic: Difficulty in performing arithmetic functions or in comprehending basic concepts.
4. Reasoning: Difficulty in organizing and integrating thoughts.
5. Organization skills: Difficulty in organizing all facets of learning. (NICHCY, 2000, 18)

Instructional procedures need to match the learning style of students in order for them to achieve success in learning to read (Ratekin, 1979). Since reading skills are necessary in every subject area (e.g., science, history, geography), Wong (1985) suggests that learning strategies be combined with teaching school subjects. Palinesar (1982) suggested, for example, that reading comprehension can be improved by teaching students self-monitoring strategies, such as reciprocal questioning and summarization skills (i.e., metacognition). However, to use self-questioning skills, a student must have an adequate knowledge base in the particular subject matter. The acquisition of knowledge may be hampered due to inattention, decoding problems, vocabulary deficiencies, poor reading comprehension skills, and inadequate instruction in content areas (Wong, 1985).

Edge and Burton (1986) cite studies in which many students with learning disabilities are able to perform such computational skills as adding, subtracting, multiplying, and dividing, but they lack the ability to use these computational skills in problem-solving situations. These authors further point out that students need to know how to apply computational skills to financial situations that occur in everyday life.

Spelling disorders have been studied by a number of researchers. A major type of difficulty is the incorrect utilization of standard rules in a phonics approach to spelling. Boder and Jarrico (1982) refer to these errors as phonetically inaccurate (PI). PI spelling errors contain inaccurate phoneme-grapheme (i.e., sound-symbol) correspondences. Letters of the alphabet (i.e., symbols) that correspond with phonemic sounds are not used in the spelling of words. Cicci (1983) concluded that these errors must reflect an underlying language disorder. Horn, O'Donnell, and Leicht (1988) determined that an excessive number of PI disorders is characteristic of persons with learning disabilities; however, other factors, such as inattention and carelessness, might also contribute to this problem. Eighteen percent of the young adult sample population with learning disabilities in this study were characterized by PI spelling and deficient speech sound perception. Much is currently being written about phonetic problems and difficulties that children with learning disabilities are experiencing when learning to read (Levine, 1990; Lyon, 1996. See Figure 5.4).

Communication

Language disorders usually interfere with academic achievement, not only in subject areas like reading, spelling, language arts, and mathematics, but also in listening, thinking, and expression. Recall that language is identified as the broad-based disorder in learning disabilities in the federal definition:

> Specific learning disability means a disorder in one or more of the basic psychological processes involved in understanding or in using language spoken or written, which may manifest itself in an imperfect ability to listen, think, speak, read, write, spell, or to do mathematical calculations. (U.S. Department of Education, 1997)

Language is a complex phenomenon. It refers to the ways in which a person receives, comprehends, and transfers thoughts to another person and to oneself. Five components are traditionally identified in the study of language: phonology,

FIGURE 5.4   Typical Reading and Spelling Patterns of Students with Phonetic Processing Difficulties

- Lack ability to analyze the sequence of sounds and syllables in words; often the sounds become reversed in words
- May misunderstand phrases in songs and rhymes like "Hosé, can you see?" for the first line of our national anthem
- Poor ability to remember individual sounds or sequences of sounds
- Difficulty blending individual sounds into words
- Difficulty substituting sounds in one word for sounds in another word, whether in initial, final, or medial position (e.g., man-fan; cat-cut; tan-tag)
- Experience problems remembering sounds of individual letters and sounds represented by regular and irregular letter combinations
- Unable to quickly retrieve letter sounds while analyzing words so that the beginning sound of a word is forgotten by the time the individual recalls the last letter of the word (naming problem)
- Limited sight vocabulary because the student has difficulty memorizing words without being able to use phonetic cues
- Guesses at unfamiliar words rather than using word-analysis skills
- Spelling attempted more by sight than by ear
- Correct spellings occur primarily with words that the individual can visualize
- Bizarre spellings occur, because phonetic patterns cannot be applied
- Extraneous letters and omitted syllables occur when spelling

morphology, syntax, semantics, and pragmatics. Youth with learning disabilities may have difficulties with basic speech sounds (phonemes), units of meaning (morphemes), sentence structure (syntax), relationships between words, grammatical forms, and underlying meaning (semantics), and everyday context usage (pragmatics).

In the receptive channel, phonology refers to how well one can discriminate speech sounds. Proficiency, or lack of it, is observed as a child attempts to form letter–sound associations. In the expressive channel, phonology refers to the production or articulation of speech sounds. Misarticulation is a major problem area in verbal expression for many children (Bryen, 1982; Lund & Duchan, 1988). Morphology refers to the linguistic structure of words and how word units (i.e., prefixes, suffixes, tense, and comparative endings) change the meaning of the word. Syntax includes grammatical usage of word classes, word order, and transformational rules for the variance of word order. In other words, syntax refers to the arrangement of words within sentences. Semantics relates to the understanding and use of word meanings and vocabulary, respectively, when viewed in terms of receptive (listening and reading) and expressive (speaking and writing) abilities. Receptive and expressive skills in semantic functioning include vocabulary, categorization, ability to define, identification of synonyms and antonyms, and detection of ambiguity or absurdity. Pragmatics is the practical application of language. It is concerned with the way language is used to communicate rather than with its structure.

Perceptual–Motor

The ability to process (or use) information received through the sense organs of the body is necessary for learning. Deficits within this functioning domain may stem from the perceptual realm and underlie cognitive and motoric functions. For example, a child may incorrectly copy simple geometric designs. If she cannot see her errors, a problem might exist in her perceptual (input) mechanism, whereas a child who can acknowledge her errors but cannot correct them may have a deficiency in her motoric (output) mechanism. Likewise, a child who is unable to write on a paper at his desk what he sees on the chalkboard or in a textbook may be experiencing cross-modal difficulties. The difficulty rests in the ability to transfer from one modality to another (e.g., visual to motor, auditory to expressive). Keep in mind that the perceptual–motor hypothesis described above is only one of the several possible explanations for a child's behavior.

According to Jacobs (1984), perception, memory, and attention are integrative processes and are used collectively to obtain information from the environment and make it meaningful. Perception is the differentiation of distinctive features with filtering of irrelevant information. Attention is affected by a person's capacity to organize and make sense of information (Reid & Hresko, 1981b). Memory is dependent upon attention and how well information has been received and associated with experience. Perception, attention, and memory are necessary prerequisites for learning. Jacobs suggests that each individual uses unconscious metacognition strategies to organize and remember new information.

Some students with learning disabilities have coordination problems. They may appear awkward or clumsy when attempting ordinary childhood activities like riding a bicycle, skipping, and jumping rope. Children with learning disabilities usually develop these skills, but later than their age-mates. Problems with fine motor skills may become apparent when these children are cutting with scissors and manipulating small objects. Motor problems are most evident in school during physical education and during handwriting and art activities (Lewis & Doorlag, 1987).

Dysgraphia is a term that describes the impaired handwriting skills some children demonstrate when attempting to form letters of the alphabet. The child can see accurately what to write but cannot manage correct writing movements (Bush & Waugh, 1982). An example is mirror writing. Each letter is symmetrical but backwards. This condition is not to be confused with children who have poor handwriting skills of a temporary nature due to late maturation or those who write poorly due to carelessness or lack of practice.

During the formative years of learning disabilities research (1950s–1960s), perceptual–motor differences in underachieving children with average intelligence were considered indicators of a minimal brain dysfunction. When hard-to-teach children were unable to match peers in such tasks as copying geometric shapes, researchers believed that a learning disability represented by perceptual–motor processing difficulties was present. Treatment programs were developed based on the premise that the presumed perceptual–motor dysfunction would be remediated by having students practice such worksheet tasks as connecting dots, tracing lines, and finding hidden objects in pictures. Perceptual–motor training declined in the early 1970s when basic assumptions of this approach were unsupported by research. Perceptual–motor training failed to improve academic skills, and tests used to identify perceptual–motor dysfunction were found to be unreliable.

Social/Adaptive

Social skills underlie one's ability to adapt to the environment. Students with learning disabilities demonstrate adaptive behavior problems through such difficulties in school performance as lack of self-control, poor self-esteem, and inadequate interpersonal relationships. Adaptive behavior skills shape friendships, communication, and vocational choices (Weller et al., 1985). Social competence comprises an umbrella of social skills that one needs in order to be accepted in social situations (Hops, 1983; McFall, 1982). A socially adept person selects appropriate skills in particular circumstances and uses social skills in ways that lead to positive outcomes (Deshler & Schumaker, 1983; Larson & Gerber, 1987). Taking appropriate actions and making appropriate responses in social situations requires the use of adequate social perception, social knowledge, and social performance. Some individuals with learning disabilities lack the ability to perceive

TABLE 5.4   What to Look for: Some First Signs of Trouble Keeping Up with the Flow of Expectations

	Language	Memory	Attention	Fine Motor Skills	Other Functions
Preschool	Pronunciation problems Slow vocabulary growth Lack of interest in story telling	Trouble learning numbers, alphabet, days of week, etc. Poor memory for routines	Trouble sitting still Extreme restlessness Impersistence at tasks	Trouble learning self-help skills (e.g., tying shoelaces) Clumsiness Reluctance to draw or trace	Trouble learning left from right (possible visual confusion)
Lower Grades	Delayed decoding abilities for reading	Slow recall of facts Organizational problems Slow acquisition of new skills Poor spelling	Impulsivity, lack of planning Careless errors Insatiability Distractibility	Unstable pencil grip Trouble with letter formation	Trouble interacting (weak social skills) Trouble learning about time (temporal–sequential disorganization) Poor grasp of math facts
Middle Grades	Poor reading comprehension Lack of verbal participation in class Trouble with word problems	Poor, illegible writing Slow or poor recall of math facts Failure of automatic recall	Inconsistency Poor self-monitoring Great knowledge of trivia Distaste for fine detail	Fist-like or tight pencil grip Illegible, slow, or inconsistent writing Reluctance to write	Poor learning strategies Disorganization in time or space Peer rejection
Upper Grades	Weak grasp of explanations Foreign language problems Poor written expression Trouble summarizing	Trouble studying for tests Weak cumulative memory Slow work pace	Memory problems due to weak attention Mental fatigue	(Lessening relevance of fine motor skills)	Poor grasp of abstract concepts Failure to elaborate Trouble taking tests, multiple choice (e.g., SATs)

Source: Levine, M. D. Learning Disorders and the Flow of Expectations. *Their World,* 1990.

social situations correctly, show deficiencies in social "know-how" skills, and fail to act appropriately. These students require instruction in the use of social skills (Wojnilower & Gross, 1988).

Several factors have been suggested as contributors to social problems of children with learning disabilities. Carlson (1987) reported studies that showed those with learning disabilities have processing deficits in social comprehension and misinterpret social situations. Specific cognitive functions may be affected in some persons with learning disabilities that cause an impaired ability to understand or empathize with another person's feelings, make inferences about social cues, or predict and evaluate consequences for social behavior (Schumaker & Hazel, 1984). Students sometimes misinterpret information from their environment and misperceive social cues (Fine, 1987). Both are problem areas related to perceptual and cognitive deficiencies. Such students adopt an egocentric perspective and exhibit an inability to shift the focus away from themselves (Derr, 1986). An overwhelming number of studies indicate problems including social competence, personal failure in social interaction (Bryan, Donahue, & Pearl, 1981), and peer relationships (Bruininks, 1978; Bryan, 1974).

Researchers report that delinquent behaviors and antisocial acts characterize a significant number of adolescents with learning disabilities (Bryan, Werner, & Pearl, 1982; Larson & Gerber, 1987; McConaughy, 1986). Even as children, these youngsters evidently lack the skills and inner control to handle age-appropriate tasks and to manage their own behavior (McWhirter, McWhirter, & McWhirter, 1985). Because of this, they may receive negative feedback from family and neighbors. Messages like this lessen feelings of self-worth (McConaughy, 1986). Thus, by adolescence, it is not surprising when students with learning disabilities exhibit behaviors that are out of step with prevailing values (see Table 5.4).

Zigmond, Levin, and Laurie (1985) reported tardiness, absenteeism, and off-task behavior by high school students with learning disabilities. Ysseldyke and his colleagues (1982) observed no differences in the classroom behaviors of elementary nonlearning-disabled children and those with learning disabilities. Contrary to this finding, other researchers found that children with learning disabilities, when compared to nonlearning-disabled elementary students, spend more time off-task (McKinney, McClure, & Feagans, 1982) and engage in more non-task-related behaviors (Sherry, 1982).

Strategies for Teaching Students with Learning Disabilities

Students with school achievement problems have been around for a long time and a variety of teaching strategies have been proposed. Contemporary intervention practices stem from four major theoretical models: the medical model, the psychological process model, the behavioral model, and the cognitive/learning strategies model (Poplin, 1989). In general, treatment models evolve in response to how the problem of learning disabilities is conceptualized. Authorities within each model highlight different student characteristics. Early conceptualizations and corresponding treatment practices were based on the assumption that underlying causes of learning failure were neurological.

Medical Model

During the late 1940s and 1950s, the medical model emphasized diagnosis and treatment of neurological symptoms. Diagnosis included: (1) thorough reviews of case histories, (2) extensive anecdotal records, (3) tests of neurological functioning (involuntary motor reflexes), (4) lists of characteristic symptoms, (5) intelligence tests, (6) electroencephalogram (EEG) tests, and, often, (7) the administration of medication. Students typically attended private facilities or institutions where they were taught in a structured, stimuli-free environment. These early programs misclassified students with learning disabilities as mentally retarded or brain-damaged (Wiederholt, 1974). The specific category of learning disabilities was unknown to these early researchers.

Interventions based on the medical model focus on correcting or compensating for physical or neurological problems. In the area of learning disabilities, this is evident primarily in the use of psychoactive medication and dietary control programs to improve students' attention in the classroom (see Table 5.5). Teachers' responsibilities in these programs are primarily evaluative. If a student in your room is on medication or a special diet to control his or her behavior, you should find out as much as possible about the expected effects and potential side effects of the treatment. You should provide frequent feedback to parents and physicians regarding changes in the student's behavior. You should also check with your principal and school nurse to determine whether any special procedures are required or guidelines available for teachers with students on medication or special diets.

Psychological Process Model

In the 1960s, emphasis shifted from the medical realm to the psychological arena. This was due to three primary factors: (1) the recognition of the existence of students with disabling conditions within the public schools, (2) insufficient evidence that neurological examinations could reliably differentiate neurologically impaired youth from the normal population, and (3) a lack of evidence that neurological interventions alleviate school learning problems (Coles, 1989; Poplin, 1989). Treatment, however, continued to be given in controlled and structured pull-out programs or special classes. Emphasis was placed upon remediation of perceptual skills. Teachers were trained in methods for educating students with minimal brain dysfunction. They focused on changing behaviors described by such terms as distractibility, inadequate figure–ground discrimination, and impulsivity. Psychological process tests and remediation materials proliferated. In 1971, Newell C. Kephart described the student with perceptual disabilities in the preface of his book, *Slow Learner in the Classroom*.

TABLE 5.5   Medical Interventions for Students with Learning Disabilities

Common	Medications
Ritalin	Generic name is Methylphenidate. Intended effects include improved academic and behavorial performance, heightened ability to focus, increased attention span. Potential side effects include tolerance over a period of time, flushed face, dry mouth, nausea, and drowsiness.
Dexedrine	Generic name is Dextroamphetamine. Intended effects include less classroom restlessness, increased attention span and focusing capabilities, improved academic and behavorial performance. Potential side effects include loss of appetite, loss of sleep, headaches, stomachaches, dizziness, and apathy.
Cylert	Generic name is Pemoline. Intended effects include improved classroom behavior, improved academic performance, and increased attention span and focusing capabilities. Potential side effects include tolerance over a period of time, loss of sleep, flushed face, dry mouth, apathy, and drowsiness.

Dietary Programs	
Elimination Diet	Controls food additives such as artificial flavors, preservatives, and coloring, thought to be responsible for hyperactivity and other behavior problems.
Sugar Control	Without dietary control, blood-sugar and energy levels drop after eating, creating problems in learning. Eating patterns are controlled to reduce effects of low blood-sugar levels.
Megavitamins	High dosages of vitamins are prescribed as a way to improve and control body chemisty.
Allergy Control	Removal of allergens in attempt to bring about changes in behavior that result from them.

He does not see what we think we show him; he sees something different. He does not hear what we think we are saying to him. He does not make the connections as we do between bits of information which we think we are presenting in such a beautifully organized fashion. His central nervous system is treating these items in a different way. (Kephart, 1971, 23)

Helmer Myklebust was recognized for his work in determining a relationship between neurological disorders and language development. He coined the term "psychoneurological learning disorders." This term refers to students with reading and other language impairments. He maintained that if the central nervous system is dysfunctioning, there may be a learning disorder of one or more of the following types (Myklebust, 1964; classroom problems by the authors).

1. Perceptual disturbance: Inability to identify, discriminate, and interpret stimuli. (Classroom problem: Poor recognition of everyday sensory experiences [e.g., reading letters, following directions].)

2. Disturbance of imagery: Inability to recollect common experiences although they have been perceived. (Classroom problem: Deficiencies in recalling words and other information provided.)
3. Disorders of symbolic processes: Inability to express experiences symbolically. (Classroom problem: Children with aphasia, dyslexia, dysgraphia, dyscalculia, and language disorders have difficulty using letters and numerals.)
4. Conceptualizing disturbances: Inability to generalize and categorize experiences. (Classroom problem: Problems classifying ideas.)

Teaching methods that evolved from this orientation emphasized three primary approaches to correcting processing problems (Lerner, 1985): (1) Strengthening the areas of processing deficits (e.g., students with visual processing problems were provided exercises designed to improve visual processing skills); (2) Using processing strengths to overcome problems (e.g., students with auditory processing problems were taught using primarily visual approaches); or (3) Strengthening weak areas and using strong areas simultaneously.

Behavioral Model

In the 1970s educators became disillusioned after seeing only slight progress being made by students who were assessed and taught by psychological process model methods. Test results were unsuccessful in differentiating students with learning disabilities from their low-achieving peers, and psycholinguistic and perceptual process training models were unable to provide evidence of improved ability to perform academic tasks. The behavioral model emerged from a need for social skills training coupled with a general lack of academic achievement in regular classrooms.

Proponents of the behavioral model proposed direct instruction of academic and social skills. Prerequisite processing abilities were minimized in delivery of special education services. The remediation of inadequate sensory processes was replaced by a functional approach to teaching. Programmed texts, short-term objectives, task analysis, and criterion-referenced tests were developed as educational materials during this decade (Poplin, 1989). The purpose of these materials was to provide the classroom teacher with a practical, sequenced approach to academics.

Improving Behavior.   Norris G. Haring, while director of the Children's Rehabilitation Unit at the University of Kansas Medical Center, argued for the use of behavior modification because it deals with observable behaviors and deemphasizes mental types of remediation. According to Haring, achievement-oriented behaviors increased when events (i.e., reinforcers) were arranged to follow targeted behaviors (Haring & Phillips, 1962). Careful arrangement of reinforcers, Haring maintained, was a more practical way to teach students with learning disabilities.

Ogden Lindsley taught the use of "precision teaching" i tings while at the University of Kansas. According to Lindsley (1 teaching is a type of instruction that directly measures student perform daily basis. Students are administered probes (i.e., skill samples) each da correspond to their instructional objectives. These frequent measurements pro vide a systematic method for planning instruction. In addition, Lindsley en- couraged the use of contingency management, which is similar to behavior modification. Contingency management is an "if–then" type of arrangement that incorporates carefully selected reinforcers to follow specified target behaviors.

Behavior modification, precision teaching, and contingency management were transferred from the laboratory setting into the classroom in an effort to identify observable and measurable student behaviors. The goal was to teach by contingency (i.e., an "if–then" type of reinforcement) rather than concentrating upon undetectable neurological causes. By looking at task requirements, adding contingencies, and observing the learners' responses, behaviorists believed that students could be more effectively taught. Observable behaviors related to learn- ing (such as staying on-task, being in seat, or raising one's hand to talk) were tar- geted for reinforcement.

Improving Academic Achievement. During the 1970s, studies of brain func- tioning, which were characteristic of the medical model, were replaced by mea- surements of academic achievement. The academic model rejected the concept of mastering mental processing skills as prerequisites to academic achievement. The academic achievement advocates remained the primary force in teaching students with learning disabilities in the 1980s. The notion that instruction for students with learning disabilities should focus upon acquisition of academic skills and the application of these skills into everyday functioning skills became widely ac- cepted among special educators. Still, the academic remediation approach had its limitations. It was characterized by critics as teacher-directed and student-passive. Critics maintained that behavioral treatments bred student dependency. Poplin (1989), for instance, felt that students should develop autonomous ways of learn- ing in order to adequately prepare for self-sufficiency after school.

Cognitive Model

Teaching students how to learn, how to manage their own behaviors in the learn- ing environment, and how to generalize information from one setting to another is a present-day emphasis in learning disabilities. Initiated in the early 1970s, this approach is called *metacognition*. The metacognition movement was derived from previous research in psychological processing dysfunctions, information process- ing, cognitive psychology, metacognitive theory, tenets of general education, and self-reinforcement principles in behaviorism. Metacognition ties together the past with the present. Cognitive strategists recommend that students be taught "strat- egy behaviors" necessary to perform academic tasks.

...ts emphasize a self-monitoring approach to learning. Self-
...ng, self-correcting, self-evaluating, and self-reinforcing are
...ive strategies. Students are taught such learning skills as
...g time, memorizing, studying, and generalizing conceptual
...one setting to another. Teaching students "how" to learn is
...& Hresko, 1981). Presently, two cognitive/learning strategy
...nate: cognitive behavior modification and the cognitive strategy

Co... *ehavior Modification.* Donald Meichenbaum at the University of Waterloo... in Ontario, Canada, is a primary contributor to the cognitive behavior modification (CBM) approach. Meichenbaum (1977) emphasized teaching students a variety of self-instructional strategies (e.g., self-questioning, self-checking), a variety of self-guidance strategies (e.g., "What do I have to do? I have to find the main idea in this paragraph."), and a variety of executive strategies (e.g., reflection about one's own array of strategies and selecting the strategy most appropriate to the task at hand). The goal is to train students to use verbal statements and images that prompt, direct, and maintain their behaviors (Lovitt, 1989).

In Meichenbaum's "What's my problem? What's my plan?" problem-solving program, students are taught to verbalize statements of self-correction, self-evaluation, and self-reinforcement (Meichenbaum & Goodman, 1971). Hallahan and Kauffman (1982) outlined Meichenbaum's self-instructional procedure:

1. *Cognitive modeling.* The adult model performs a task while verbally instructing himself.
2. *Overt, self-guidance.* The student performs the same task by imitating instructions spoken by the model.
3. *Faded overt self-guidance.* The student softly repeats the instructions spoken by the model.
4. *Covert self-instruction.* The student performs the task while silently instructing himself.

Tarver (1986) theorizes that gradual fading of speech from overt (outward) to covert (inward) will change the student's spoken language into the inner language that typically regulates thought. According to cognitive behavior modification advocates, modeling and imitations of inner language improve thinking skills.

Cognitive Strategies. Another type of metacognitive approach teaches such study skills techniques as scanning, outlining, taking notes, and time management. The model is derived from cognitive psychology and information processing literature. The cognitive strategy model incorporates theories based on student learning styles, cognitive styles, thinking skills, and cognitive behavior modification research. Torgesen (1977) hypothesized that passive learning is a characteristic of many students with learning disabilities. Thus, cognitive strategy researchers addressed how students approach learning.

Metacognition

Knowing how one knows, metacognition, is also stressed in the cognitive strategy model (Wong, 1979). Brown (1978) summarized metacognitive processes as including the identification and analysis of the task at hand, the reflection on what one does and does not know about the situation that may be necessary for solving the problem, the designing of a plan for dealing with the problem, and the monitoring of one's progress toward solving the problem. Other assumptions in the cognitive strategy model are: (1) the learning strategies students need are relatively stable across learners and tasks, (2) the act of verbalizing a strategy assists learning, and (3) knowing how one learns is advantageous to further learning (Poplin, 1989). The following guidelines detail Meichenbaum's (1985) techniques for teaching metacognitive strategies:

1. Teachers need to adopt metacognitive outlooks. They should have the attitude that self-instructional thinking skills exist and can be taught.
2. It is important that teachers be aware of their own metacognitive skills and make students aware of these. Teachers let students down when they fail to assist them in developing the metacognitive skills that they themselves find effective.
3. Teachers need to conduct a task analysis of the skills to be taught. This requires reducing the desired metacognitive skills into a series of simpler sub-skills.
4. Teachers must be aware that generalization of the learned metacognitive skills will not simply occur; learning opportunities that cut across various settings (e.g., home, community, work) must be employed.

A major criticism of teaching students with learning disabilities is that many do not learn generalization and maintenance skills (Lovitt, 1989; Poplin, 1989). What is taught in one training site or classroom has not been proven to carry over sufficiently to other settings or circumstances. When skills do not carry over, maintenance, or sustained use of them, diminishes. Some suggestions for assuring generalization include tasks that place responsibility for learning on the student. These include (1) student self-instruction, (2) student self-rehearsal, (3) practice in multiple settings, (4) dividing skills into manageable portions, (5) student self-monitoring, (6) teacher feedback about performance, (7) skills taught to mastery level, and (8) teacher reinforcement of skills acquired.

Contemporary thinking about best practices for teaching students with learning disabilities combines academics with cognitive learning strategies. In other words, it is important that teachers focus upon academic skills; however, this can be effectively accomplished through teaching students how to learn, how to manage their own behaviors in school, and how to generalize information from

FIGURE 5.5 Suggestions for Teaching Students with Learning Disabilities

1. Teach the student to organize materials and assignments. Use lists to establish work priorities. Teach study skills.

2. Help the student to think through steps in completing a task. Use questions such as the following as a guide: "How much time do I have to complete a task? What materials will I need? Who can I ask for help?"

3. Overlook such minor errors in written work as spelling and handwriting. Emphasize quality of ideas and perseverance.

4. Provide right-hemispheric activities such as art, drama, and images to represent ideas. Don't overemphasize such left-hemispheric functions as verbal reasoning, logic, and sequential arrangement of ideas.

5. Provide emotional support to help ease the frustration of a learning disability.

6. Provide options during tests such as untimed or oral exams. List answers to multiple-choice questions vertically rather than horizontally.

7. Give clear and concrete directions. Have the student repeat instructions back to you.

8. Link new ideas to the student's experience.

9. Use multisensory materials. Repeat concepts, but use novel presentations rather than drill.

10. Collaborate with parents.

one setting to another. Some suggestions for teaching students with learning disabilities are presented in Figure 5.5.

Young Adults

It was once thought that the problems encountered by children with learning disabilities ended upon reaching adulthood. It has become evident that a learning disability persists as individual lives evolve.

Up until 1960 there was little research, limited personnel, and few teacher training programs specifically for youngsters with learning disabilities in the public schools. But, due to parent advocacy groups, the Association for Children with Learning Disabilities was formed. This eventually led to the Specific Learning Disabilities Act of 1969, which authorized teacher training and research. Finally, in 1975, the passage of Public Law 94–142 occurred, which federally mandated special services for learning disabled students (Smith, 1983).

It was not until the 1970s that the need for providing college programs for students with learning disabilities was recognized. Gertrude Webb at Curry College in Milton, Massachusetts, was one of the first to develop college services for those with learning disabilities. Her pioneer efforts and the development of the Program of Assistance in Learning at Curry College inspired other colleges and universities to develop similar programs (Mangrum & Strichart, 1984).

For many students who manage to survive high school academics, college is increasingly becoming a goal (Osman, 1979; Ramsey, 1996; Treible, 1996). As stated previously, the belief at the onset of the learning disabilities era was that these children would eventually outgrow their disability. As it became obvious that this condition was ongoing, more pressure was put on colleges to serve their needs.

Section 504 of the Rehabilitation Act of 1973 (P.L. 93–112) (refer to Chapter 1) has had vast importance for college learning disabilities programs. The requirement states that colleges receiving federal assistance may not discriminate against any qualified individual.

> No otherwise qualified handicapped individual in the United States, shall solely by reason of handicap, be excluded from participation in, be denied the benefits of, or be subjected to discrimination under any program or activity receiving federal financial assistance.

The Americans with Disabilities Act (P.L. 101–336) extended these provisions into private colleges and universities.

Characteristics

The characteristics and special needs of learning disabled young adults in college differ little from the characteristics and needs they had when much younger. The domains discussed in this section include cognitive, language, perceptual motor, academic, work/study habits, and social/affective.

Cognitive. The college student with learning disabilities may have difficulties with sequencing, understanding abstract concepts, reasoning, short- and long-term memory, organization, and generalizing (Mangrum & Strichart, 1984). Difficulties are often experienced in processing information. These can occur in the receptive, associative, or expressive learning modalities (Ramsey, 1995a).

Language. The weaknesses children with learning disabilities experience in receiving, processing, and acquiring language skills continues to be a problem (Smith, 1983). The young adult may have trouble grasping what is spoken, expressing appropriate vocabulary, understanding words in context, clear and precise written expression, sentence structure, punctuation, and written composition (Mangrum & Strichart, 1984).

Perceptual Motor. Educators working with students with learning disabilities at colleges report that perceptual motor problems continue. These students may have trouble locating information and performing tasks that require motor coordination. One particular problem they may encounter is the form in which tests may be given. For example, tests that require students to fill in circles or to grid in answers may penalize students who actually know the information that is being tested but cannot perform the fine motor tasks required to show evidence of their knowledge (Hobbs, 1982).

Academic.   Because of deficits in basic skill areas, the student with learning disabilities may have difficulties reading required material, spelling, handwriting, and math (Mangrum & Strichart, 1984).

Work and Study Habits.   Smith (1979) reports that the college student with learning disabilities may continue to have problems organizing and budgeting time, completing work and getting work started, and establishing long- and short-term goals. This student may also suffer from test anxiety (Mangrum & Strichart, 1984). Note taking may present a serious problem as well (Roberts, 1983).

Social and Affective.   The social difficulties experienced by youngsters with learning disabilities continue to follow them into adulthood. They have difficulties establishing good relationships with others, reading body language, expressing their own feelings, and relating to authority figures (Mangrum & Strichart, 1984). Social implications of behavior problems extend beyond academic programs. A national survey revealed that 44 percent of incarcerated adolescents had a history of learning disabilities (McConaughy, 1986).

Likewise, young people with learning disabilities frequently suffer from poor self-concepts and tend to feel insecure and frustrated with life. They may have difficulties meeting responsibilities, curbing impulsive behavior, and maintaining motivation (Mangrum & Strichart, 1984).

Alternative Strategies

Some of the higher education services offered students with learning disabilities include:

1. Assessing students to determine deficit areas, in order to provide appropriate services.
2. Using tape recorders for lectures.
3. Providing students with an outline as an aid for organizing content.
4. Photocopying class notes.
5. Allowing testing modifications (e.g., administered orally, additional time, less items).
6. Purchasing textbooks in advance so they can begin reading earlier.
7. Using taped textbooks.
8. Securing tutors to help students understand and master the content of subject areas.
9. Having another student take notes.
10. Offering special courses to students according to their needs. These might include writing courses, typing, study skills, or instruction in college survival.

FIGURE 5.6   Suggestions for Faculty Who Teach College Students with Learning Disabilities

1. Provide students with a detailed course syllabus the first week of class.
2. Clearly spell out expectations before the course begins (e.g., grading, material to be covered, due dates).
3. Start each lecture with an outline of material to be covered in that period. At the conclusion of class, briefly summarize key points.
4. Speak directly to students, and use gestures and natural expressions to convey further meaning.
5. Present new or technical vocabulary on the chalkboard or use a student handout. Terms should be used in context to convey greater meaning.
6. Add stories and examples to illustrate or provide examples to information being taught.
7. Role play, act out, draw, or utilize some other media or activity to build meaning to conceptual material.
8. Give assignments BOTH orally and in written form to avoid confusion.
9. Announce reading assignments well in advance for students who are using taped materials.
10. Help students find community resources, like The Talking Book Center (affiliated with the National Organization for the Blind) where they can get tape-recorded reading materials (e.g., textbooks, newspapers, magazines).
11. Facilitate use of tape recorders for notetaking by allowing students to tape lectures.
12. Make use of self-correcting materials, which provide immediate feedback.
13. Provide study questions for exams that demonstrate the format, as well as the content, of the test. Explain what constitutes a good answer and why.
14. If necessary, allow students with learning disabilities to demonstrate mastery of course material using alternative methods (e.g., extended time limits for testing, oral exams, taped exams, individually proctored exams in a separate room).
15. Let students use a simple calculator, scratch paper, a thesaurus, and/or a speller's dictionary during exams and formal writing exercises.
16. Provide adequate opportunities for questions and answers, including review sessions.
17. Modify the amount of practice work required when needed.
18. Be sure students are being taught by you, or by someone else at the college, skills relating to how they can more efficiently and effectively:
    a. study,
    b. manage time,
    c. take notes,
    d. proofread their work,
    e. take a multiple-choice, true-false, or essay test,
    f. cope with stress, and
    g. engage in decision-making and problem-solving.
19. Encourage (or require) students to use campus support services (e.g., pre-registration, assistance in ordering taped textbooks, alternative testing arrangements, specialized study aids, peer support groups, diagnostic consultation, study skills training, and academic tutorial assistance.
20. Capitalize on each student's strengths.
21. Provide opportunities for success in a supportive atmosphere to help build self-esteem.
22. Allow flexibility in classroom procedures.

11. Using microcomputers with word processing programs. Some also have word-check programs, which would help with spelling errors when writing research papers and other composition projects. (Ramsey, 1995b; 1997)

Looking to the Future

There needs to be an ongoing effort to provide services within colleges to young adults with learning disabilities. These services need to be focused upon helping them cope more effectively with academic learning and study techniques, as well as vocational preparation concerns. Social skills interventions need to emphasize interactions with instructors, peers, and personal development. Maintaining effective communication is essential (Ramsey, 1997). See Figure 5.6 for teaching suggestions.

Summary

The search for appropriate terminology that would identify learning disabilities continues to challenge educators. The first terms used to describe this population emphasized medical and neurological processing deficits. The most popular and widely accepted name was *minimal brain dysfunction,* or *MBD.*

In 1962, Kirk suggested the name *learning disabilities.* This new classification was intended to distinguish persons with learning disorders and average intelligence from other exceptionality categories, especially mental retardation. Many students were identified as mentally retarded during the 1940s and 1950s, because the category "learning disabilities" didn't exist. The classification was adopted following Kirk's use of the term to link together students with average intelligence and presumed mild neurological disorders.

The current federal definition of learning disabilities was formulated in 1968 by the National Advisory Committee on Handicapped Children. This definition served as the basis for the Learning Disabilities Act of 1969, and was subsequently included in the Individuals with Disabilities Education Act. Thus, this definition is widely used in providing appropriate public education to students who are eligible for services because of a learning disability. The operational part of the federal definition is referred to as the discrepancy clause.

The prevalence of learning disabilities is reported by states to be between 2 and 5 percent of the school-aged population. The number of existing cases eludes accuracy because methods and criteria used for identification differ from state to state. In lieu of data reported by respective states showing otherwise, federal estimates have remained at 2 percent.

Characteristics of students with learning disabilities are classified by developmental domains of functioning. These functioning domains include cognitive skills, academic achievement, language and communication development, perceptual and perceptual–motor skills, and social–adaptive skills. Students with learning disabilities demonstrate learning difficulties in at least one of these functioning domains.

From the 1940s into the twenty-first century, treatment models continue to evolve in response to theories about the causes of learning disabilities. For example, the medical approach of the 1940s and 1950s advocated the use of heavily structured and controlled learning environments to offset presumed neurological deficits. Programs were developed during the 1960s that attempted to ameliorate perceptual deficits. This approach is called the psychological process approach. Interaction between the learner and the environment was the major emphasis during the 1970s. This is the behavioral approach. Arranging the environment, reinforcing appropriate behavior, and using systematic instructional approaches in the teaching of academic skills are components of this model. Contemporary thinking states that it is important to teach academics, but it is also necessary to teach students how to learn, how to manage their own behaviors in school, and how to generalize information from one setting to another. Cognitive/learning strategies models emphasize the need to produce self-sufficient, independent learners for a lifetime.

ACTIVITIES

1. What are some teaching strategies that David's fourth-grade teacher used to help accommodate his learning? Why were these helpful? What other interventions could she have used?

2. Examine typical reading and spelling patterns of students with visual or auditory processing difficulties listed in Figure 5.4 and Table 5.4. Do you reconize any of David's learning problems? Are there other processing patterns that David's teacher might find helpful to identify?

3. Arrange to speak to several special educators who work with students with learning disabilities. Ask them to describe the ways in which a learning disability is manifested by their students. How do they function in school compared to regular grade-level peers?

4. Ask the educators in the third activity to discuss strategies and instructional approaches that they use with students who have learning disabilities. Ask the educators to talk about special interventions they would recommend for these students.

5. As an extension to activities three and four, ask the special educators to describe ways in which each of them works with other educators, support personnel, and parents. How do they collaborate effectively with general classroom teachers and support personnel like guidance counselors, social workers, school nurses, and building principals? What things do they do to build relationships with parents?

6. Invite a college student or an adult (professional) with a diagnosed learning disability to come speak with your students. Ask the person to talk about ways in which they have learned to make accommodations and/or modifications in order to be successful.

7. Conduct an activity to help students determine if they have more of a left or right hemispheric preference. Follow up with an activity that helps them to identify their preferred mode of learning—visual, auditory, or haptic.

8. Organize your students into "a class reading lesson." Divide the class in half. Give half of the class a reading passage that appears to them like it might to a student with a learning disability. The other half of the class needs to be given the reading passage in a normal format. Discuss with the class later how it felt for both groups of students—those with an assumed learning disability and those assumed normal in reading skills.

9. Look for journals that discuss techniques for working with students with learning disabilities, like the *Journal of Learning Disabilities, Learning Disabilities Quarterly, Learning Disability Focus,* and *Remedial and Special Education.* Read several articles from different journals if possible, and discuss techniques about working with students with learning disabilities in general and special education classrooms. Talk about approaches suggested for academic and social skils training. Discuss suggestions about collaboration with other educators, support personnel, and parents.

10. There are two major professional organizations as well as a major parent-professional organization in the field of learning disabilities: The Division for Learning Disabilities of the Council for Exceptional Children (1920 Association Drive, Reston, Virginia 22091); the Council for Learning Disabilities (P.O. Box 40303, Overland Park, Kansas 66204); and the Learning Disabilities Association (4156 Library Road, Pittsburgh, Pennsylvania 15234). Write to these organizations for their directories and literature. Determine the purposes, membership, and services offered by these organizations.

11. Find out if there are active state and local branches of these national organizations in your area. If there is a local organization, arrange to visit one of those meetings. Try to determine concerns that the group is currently addressing in your community. Ask a representative from the group to visit your class and speak about the organization's purpose, membership composition, and service.

12. Join the Student Council for Exceptional Children. Find out when and where the annual state CEC conference is going to be held, and suggest that the local chapter send representatives. Volunteer to attend as a representative, and while at the conference, attend the meeting for the Division for Learning Disabilities.

13. Write a proposal to give a presentation at the state CEC conference. Share teaching aids that you have made in your methods course, or student teaching. Practicing teachers and other teachers-in-training enjoy seeing and hearing about new ideas. Remember that this gives you a "foot in the door" for an interview for a teaching position upon graduating, as many people within your state will remember you. It also gives you something of a professional nature that you have done to list on your resume or vita!

ADVANCE QUESTIONS

Answer the following questions as you read this chapter:

1. What comparisons can you make between least restrictive environment, mainstreaming, and inclusion?
2. What are four steps for setting up an inclusion program?
3. How do collaborative consultation and cooperative teaching support inclusion?
4. How have court cases influenced inclusion?
5. Describe co-teaching.
6. Discuss role responsibilities in the collaborative consultation and cooperative teaching models.

7. How would you organize a peer tutoring program?
8. What is cooperative learning and how would you use cooperative learning in the classroom?
9. What are some common issues that general and special educators deal with?

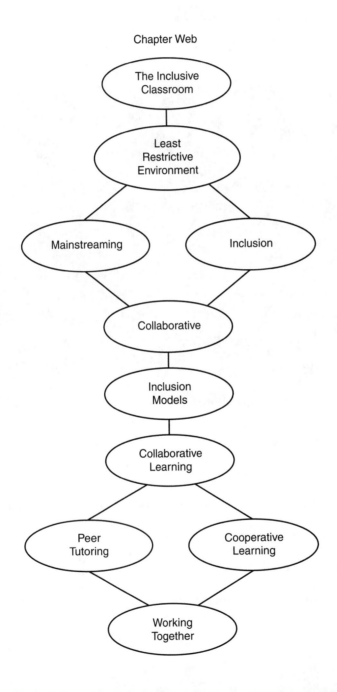

Chapter Web

10. How do educators (teachers, principals, guidance counselors, support staff, etc.) effectively work together in a unitary manner? Discuss the Reauthorization of IDEA and how the law supports this collaboration.
11. How does The Responsive Classroom inclusion program work so effectively in The Kensington Model?
12. In what ways does classroom organization contribute to active teaching strategies such as cooperative learning projects, learning centers, and peer tutoring?
13. How are special needs students included in assessments? What are some suggested ways of performing alternative testing?

Vignette: Marsha

Light streamed through the unfinished attic's bay window of her aunt and uncle's house. The sun's rays lined the floor beside the straight rows of chairs filled with cousins and teddy bears in Marsha's "classroom." Marsha always dreamed of becoming a teacher, so playing school was her favorite activity when visiting her cousins during the summer. An old standing chalkboard, a few pieces of chalk and an eraser gave Marsha all the materials she needed in order to "teach" her students. In her play schoolroom the rows were straight and neat. Her students were quiet and ready to learn.

One day, many years later, Marsha's dream came true. She graduated from an elementary education/early childhood program and found a teaching job. And, as in the early play days, the rows in her classroom were neat, straight, and quiet.

As several years passed, Marsha enjoyed teaching but was troubled each school year by two or three students who seemed to require more than the others. John constantly got up to sharpen his pencil. Susie read below grade level but was excellent in math. It was almost impossible to read Bob's stories because of poor handwriting and spelling.

Circumstances required Marsha to move. It was hard to get a teaching job. One day her telephone rang and she was asked if she would consider a position in a learning-disabilities resource room. Marsha could teach out of field for one year. If she wanted to remain at that job, she had to become certified in learning disabilities. She loved her new job and soon became certified.

As the year progressed, Marsha discovered that the training she had received in elementary education was perfect for teaching the academic skills needed by her students in special education. She now had many students like John, Susie, and Bob. With her help, they were much more successful in their homerooms. What was troubling now was how "divided" the students' attentions were by being removed from their homerooms. No matter how closely Marsha and the classroom teacher collaborated and planned, the students were always missing something in the other classroom.

After several years as a resource teacher, a self-contained fourth through sixth grade learning-disability classroom position became available. No longer would the students' attention be divided. Marsha was successful in mainstreaming many students. The students loved going into a regular classroom for math or science. Everyone was fairly happy until the county decided to redistrict special education. Marsha's unit was moved across town.

Marsha stayed at her school and was given a third-grade classroom. She found that her training in learning disabilities was now invaluable to her work with students in her regular classroom. She is considered an excellent teacher and was given the honor of being voted "Teacher of the Year" at her school. Thanks to her dual training in general and special education, Marsha knows how to individualize instruction for students whom she finds to be a very diverse group of children. Students like John, Susie, and Bob are successful in cooperative groups, with peer tutors and modified instruction.

Sunlight streams into Marsha's third-grade classroom. The sun's rays fall straight across the floor and mingle with the array of desks set in clusters of varying shapes and sizes. From those scattered desks comes the chatter of happy, actively learning, and enthusiastic students. Marsha's childhood dream came true.

A poem written by Marsha was published in a special education teachers' competency test study manual. In this poem, Marsha very aptly and vividly describes the diverse, unique characteristics of the third-grade students in her regular classroom. Her poem is printed here for you (see Box 6.1).

1. Did you want to someday become a teacher early in life?
2. Which are the at-risk students and the special education students in Marsha's poem?
3. How would you describe today's diverse classrooms?
4. Are there opportunities for inclusion and collaboration in Marsha's general education classroom?

Marsha's poem illustrates the heterogeneous group of students found in so many general education classrooms across the nation. In addition, her poem highlights the diverse population of students which might be found by a teacher in a general classroom. Finally, her poem shows the dedication of many of today's teachers, and the training that so many seek in order to do the very best job for their students.

Mainstreaming, least restrictive environment, and *inclusion* are three important terms that appear regularly in special education literature and conversations. Each term has a distinct meaning, yet all three share one similarity. All of them relate to efforts to integrate students with disabilities with students who do not have disabilities.

During the early years of compulsory education in our country, students with disabilities either did not attend school or were placed in segregated learning environments, such as self-contained special education classrooms, special schools, or institutions. The at-risk children and special education students described in Marsha's poem were virtually nonexistent in general education classrooms during this time. Each of us wants to be viewed as normal. When students are categorized and placed into self-contained special classrooms, they are often viewed as incompetent by their peers and eventually by themselves.

Over the years, educators have discovered ways of integrating students with disabilities with those without disabilities. Even those with the most severe disabilities have been integrated or "mainstreamed" during nonacademic times, such as lunch, recess, and assembly. The Individuals with Disabilities Education Act requires educators to teach students in the least restrictive environment. For many, this is a general education classroom (see Figure 6.1). For others, their least

BOX **6.1**

A Special Child—Me
(Ode to My Teacher)

Written by Marsha Sykes, General Classroom Teacher
Pine Castle Elementary School, Orange County School System, Orlando, Florida

I'm a special child . . . you know—that quiet
    one in your room.
Or maybe I'm the loud one—or the sad one
    filled with gloom.

It really doesn't matter—but I'm in your
    room this year.
It's sometimes hard to spot me—but WHY?—
    is not too clear.

I cry out in frustration—or my silence is
    TOO serene.
I get attention when I'm noisy—you KNOW
    I'm on the scene!

You might find me in a corner—where I'll
    really try to hide.
My dad's an alcoholic—he beat Mom last
    night . . . I CRIED!

Maybe I'm from that broken home—my Mom
    works hard, you see.
My homework, friends, behavior—a lot's left
    up to me!

I've been tested—I'm a GENIUS!—but
    you've always known that's true.
The school psychologist just told Mom—my
    IQ's one-forty-two!

I'm laughed at 'cause I make mistakes—my
    classmates call me dumb.
I TRY and TRY—but I guess they're right—
    my IQ's eighty-one!

And then there's me—I'm SLD!—to you I'm
    not amusing!
The line goes right—but I go left!—this world
    is so confusing!

I might not see—I might not hear—my
    English might be broken.
My speech teacher's proud of me—I correctly
    pronounced "quotient!"

I'm "AVERAGE," have two parents—though
    rare—I fit the "norm!"
Ironically . . . I'm the one STANDARD
    curriculum's designed for!

YES, I'm in your class of twenty-six! But I'm
    SPECIAL, can't you see?
It takes HARD WORK and SPECIAL
    SKILLS to teach a child like me.

Your job's so tough—so much to do—you
    must spread yourself so THIN!
Counseling, parenting, advising, teaching—
    how will it ALL fit in?

Whole language, exciting math and science,
    sex ed . . . YOUR JOB'S IMMENSE!
I don't know how you'll do it all—BUT
    TRY—MY HOPE'S INTENSE!

And so, if in your daily plans—SKILLS AND
    CONCERN for ME, you provide,
I'll grow . . . I'll learn . . . I'LL LOVE YOU
    SO—AND YOU'LL SEE ME BEAM
    WITH PRIDE!

Source: Ramsey, R. S. (1995). Preparatory Guide for Special Education Teacher Competency Tests—revised. Available: 5435 Woodruff Farm Road, MBE #118, Columbus, GA 31907-1395.

Least Restrictive

↑	I	1. Full-time general class/
¦	N	room placement with
¦	T	support services.*
¦	E	2. Resource room (pull-out)
¦	G	program for part of the
¦	R	day, and general education
¦	A	placement without special
¦	T	education services the rest
¦	E	of the day (Mainstreaming)
¦	D	

¦	S	3. Full-time placement in
¦	E	self-contained special
¦	G	classroom in regular
¦	R	school.
¦	E	4. Special day or alternative
¦	G	school program outside
¦	A	of regular school.
¦	T	5. Homebound/Hospital.
¦	E	6. Residential facility.
↓	D	7. Correctional facility.

Most Restrictive

* Inclusion

FIGURE 6.1   Continuum of Special Education Placements

restrictive environment is a separate educational setting, such as a self-contained special education classroom or resource room.

Least Restrictive Environment

The emphasis on keeping special education students in general education classrooms comes from the "least restrictive environment" provision of the law. When students are educated in the least restrictive environment, they are taught in classrooms that most closely approximate a normal learning situation. For many students with mild disabilities, the least restrictive environment is a general education classroom. For students who require more intensive remedial help, the least restrictive environment would be part-time resource room instruction with the majority of their school day spent in the general classroom. When students with special needs are placed in full-time special classes or alternative special education programs, they are in the *most* restrictive environment. Their opportunities to associate with nonspecial-needs children are severely limited.

When a student with a mild disabling condition is placed in a special education program, there is a presumption that it is a temporary situation. Placement in a special education program is no badge of distinction for child or parent. Indeed, if parents suspected that, once identified as having a special need, their youngster would be permanently tracked in special education, it is unlikely that they would be so cooperative and eager to have their child receive special education services.

When students with disabilities are kept out of the mainstream of normal school life, it underscores the differences between them and students without disabilities. Indeed separate special education programs are sometimes classified by such categories of disabilities as emotionally disturbed, mentally retarded, or behavior disordered. When a student is grouped with eight to ten other "behavior disordered" students, taught in a program by a teacher who is trained in "emotional disturbance," and isolated in a special classroom that is located in a secluded area of the school, it is unlikely that the student will either feel or act "normal." Table 6.1 details placements for students with disabilities.

The intent of the least restrictive environment provision of the law is to assure that a student's special education program is as normal as possible. Each school system is required to provide a continuum of special education

TABLE 6.1   Percentage of Students Ages 6–21 with Disabilities Served in Different Educational Environments

Disabilities	All Students with Disabilities	1999-2000 School Year			
		Served Outside the Regular Classroom			
		< 21 % of the Day	21–60% of the Day	> 60% of the Day	Public Separate Facility
Specific learning disabilities	50.4	48.3	67.4	39.2	9.9
Speech or language impairments	19.2	35.5	4.6	5.0	2.5
Mental retardation	10.8	3.2	11.3	26.9	23.3
Emotional disturbance	8.2	4.5	6.8	13.3	32.9
Multiple disabilities	2.1	0.5	1.4	4.5	16.8
Hearing impairments	1.3	1.1	0.9	1.5	3.6
Orthopedic impairments	1.3	1.2	1.0	1.7	2.3
Other health impairments	4.5	4.2	5.2	3.8	2.1
Visual impairments	0.5	0.5	0.3	0.4	1.1
Autism	1.2	0.5	0.6	2.9	4.9
Deaf-blindness	0.02	0.01	0.01	0.05	0.2
Traumatic brain injury	0.2	0.2	0.2	0.4	0.3
Developmental delay	New category; data not yet compiled				

Source: U.S. Department of Education, Office of Special Education Programs, Data Analysis System (DANS).

placements. Figure 6.1 lists special education programs for learners with special needs ranging from least to most restrictive environments. Once the bold line is crossed, a student is out of the mainstream, and the prospects for return to a normal school experience are bleak. (This might be a good time to return to Chapter 1 and review the descriptions of each type of special education placement.)

Mainstreaming

Mainstreaming means returning students to general education classrooms without special education services. Many articles and essays describe the advantages of mainstreaming; for example, students with mild disabilities develop better academic and socialization skills when they are educated in well-organized mainstreamed classrooms (Guralnick & Groom, 1988; Wang & Baker, 1986). Yet there are reports about failed mainstreaming and teacher concerns for students who are "over their heads" or "lost" in general classrooms. As Susan Ohanian states, it takes more than good intentions and administrative fiat to make mainstreaming work. In the following excerpt from "P.L. 94–142: Mainstream or Quicksand," she highlights the folly of unplanned mainstreaming endeavors.

> When following the mandates of P.L. 94–142 we need to figure out just what it means to mainstream children "to the maximum extent appropriate to their needs." Many school districts lump all children with learning problems together in a sort of academic twilight zone. The educable mentally retarded [i.e., students with mild mental retardation], the low normal, the learning disabled (whatever that means this week), and the emotionally disturbed are all sent off to regular English, science, social studies, and mathematics classes—until the situation becomes too traumatic either for the child or for the teacher. I always figured my district had to see blood before it would demainstream a child. (Ohanian, 1991, 219)

Mainstreaming works if benefits are accrued by students with special needs, general education students, and their teachers. A general education teacher who is asked to take a youngster with a mild disability into her classroom might legitimately ask, "What's in it for me and my students?" After all, is it fair to ask general educators to teach special education students at the expense of the other students? An educational program that does not have something for everybody is headed for failure. Teachers, administrators, and parents will not tolerate the education of a minority of students if it takes away from the learning of the majority.

Wang and Baker's (1986) meta-analysis of eleven empirical studies on mainstreaming indicated that mainstreamed students consistently achieved better than nonmainstreamed students with comparable disabilities. The paradox of students with special needs doing better in general rather than special education programs can be explained by several factors.

1. The research on the ineffectiveness of tracking students by ability groups demonstrates that students perform better academically in heteroge-

neous groups than in homogeneous groups (Lewis, 1990; Massachusetts Department of Education, 1991).

2. Modeling enhances learning. Students naturally imitate their peers. Good peer models provide teachers with success examples that can help encourage students with learning problems to strive harder.

3. Teacher expectations for success go up in relationship to perception of a student's capability. Mainstreamed students may benefit from increased teacher expectations because the student is perceived to be ready to succeed in the regular classroom.

4. Teachers who were used as mainstreaming research subjects may try harder to succeed with their students. The "Hawthorne Effect" (i.e., trying harder to excel because of the perceived special status of being a research subject) is well documented in research annals.

5. How students feel about their abilities has a lot to do with success. Students in special education programs may feel stigmatized. This can affect motivation and perseverance, two crucial elements in school success.

6. Teachers who agree to accept mainstreamed students may be more skilled than their colleagues.

Inclusion

Inclusion is a movement designed to bring special education services into the general classroom. This is a significant change from the traditional practice of having students receive special services in resource rooms or self-contained special education classrooms and then return to general education classrooms without special education support. See Figure 6.2.

Four separate obstacles to effective educational progress are unintentional by-products of separate special education services.

1. *Fragmented instruction.* Students who do not meet eligibility criteria for specific remedial programs "fall through the cracks" and receive no special help. Financial incentives determine program choices. School systems "put the child where the money is with too little regard for educational need." Many who receive special services are put in "pull-out programs," others in self-contained classrooms. Meanwhile, there is a lack of coordination between general and special educators. Consequently remedial and special education students fall further behind in their studies. Each minute they spend in a special program, students miss a minute of regular classroom instruction. Likewise, students who could use extra help are overlooked because their learning problems are not severe enough to qualify for remedial or special education. The present system of general education emphasizes remediation rather than prevention of learning problems.

2. *Dual systems.* Special and general education have separate administrative structures, distinct budgets, and separate training for teachers. The duality of

FIGURE 6.2   **Key Definitions**

Least restrictive environment: Students with disabilities must be placed in appropriate education programs to meet their individual needs. Every effort should be made to place students with special needs in general education programs. Parents and the school system together select from a continuum of special education placements to determine what is the least restrictive setting for a student.

Mainstreaming: Students with disabilities placed in general education classrooms either full or part-time without special education support.

Inclusion: Students with disabilities placed in general education classrooms full-time with special education support services provided.

these systems creates a gap between the general and special educator. Building principals do not feel ownership of special programs because of separate financial, administrative, and decision-making procedures. Special education teachers feel estranged from general teachers because they tutor students in resource rooms or teach small groups of students in self-contained classrooms. The physical isolation of special education classrooms minimizes contact, communication, and mutual problem solving. With these constraints it is difficult to foster a sense of shared responsibility for the instructional needs of special learners. Learning becomes jeopardized when special and regular instruction do not complement each other.

3. *Stigmatization of students.* Schools are social environments. Isolation of students from their peers decreases self-esteem and increases negative attitudes about school. All children want to be accepted and feel they belong. Low expectations for success, failure to persist on tasks, learned helplessness, and continued school failure are some of the negative consequences of separating students into categories of "special needs."

4. *Placement decision as battleground.* The Individuals with Disabilities Education Act is based on the premise that parents have much to contribute in making school-based decisions. Requirements for special programs can place teachers and parents in opposing positions. Parents get stereotyped as "pushy" if they fight to get a youngster into special education and "uncaring" if they don't attend school meetings. The cumulative effects of these misunderstandings are "a series of adversarial, hit-and-run encounters" between parents and educators (Will, 1986).

Stainback and Stainback (1984) recommended a unitary system of education to replace the splintered approach of providing help through regular, special, remedial, migrant, bilingual, and Title 1 education programs.

Several sources spurred the movement toward inclusion. Many parents and professionals argued that inclusion in school is best preparation for inclusion in the community. This point of view was bolstered by research studies such as the one conducted by Baker, Wang, and Walberg (1994) that reported students with disabilities performed better academically in general education u ucation classrooms. Furthermore, the least restrictive environmen federal law clearly intended that students with disabilities be educated nondisabled students to the maximum feasible extent.

The reauthorization of the Individuals with Disabilities Act (IDEA) in required that the general education classroom be the first option in determining where special education services should be delivered and school systems had to justify why a student was not placed in the general education classroom. Some of the documented benefits of including students with disabilities in the general classroom are:

- Students with physical disabilities achieved IEP goals more effectively within inclusive rather than separate special classrooms (Miller, 1996).
- Students who receive special education services in the general classroom do better academically and socially than comparable students in non-inclusive settings (Baker, Wang, & Walberg, 1994).
- The academic progress of students without disabilities is not hampered (Staub and Peck, 1994).
- Documented benefits for students without disabilities include tolerance for individual differences, growth in social skills, improved self-concept and enhanced interpersonal skills (Staub and Peck, 1994).

Within the inclusion model personnel, money, and material resources are reallocated for use in the general education classroom. General education teachers, with support, take on greater responsibility for the education of special populations. One of the major rationales for inclusion is that it provides a better academic environment for students with mild disabilities than either pull-out (resource room) programs or separate special education classes.

Court Cases

When making the decision to put a student in an inclusive setting two legal principles included in IDEA need to be balanced—least restrictive environment and appropriate educational placement. A series of court cases during the 1980s and 1990s provide legal guidelines for how school systems and parents work together to determine the best placement for a youngster. In *Roncker v. Walker* (U.S. 6th Cir., 1983) the court established the "feasibility" principle.

> In a case where the segregated facility is considered superior, the court should determine whether the services which make the placement superior could be *feasibly* (emphasis added) provided in a non-segregated setting. If they can, the placement in the segregated school would be inappropriate under the Act. (cited *CEC Today*, p. 4, 1996)

Roncker v. Walker was influential in highlighting the need for a full continuum of services for students and confirmed that for some students a segregated special was a better placement than an inclusive general education

v. State Board of Education (U.S. 5th Cir., 1989), the court moved
ection and stated that Roncker placed too much emphasis on
it. This ruling broke new ground by deciding that the nonaca-
general education classrooms also need to be taken into account.
ished a two-part test for inclusion. First, the court asked if the ad-
mental aids and services will help a student achieve satisfactory
general education classroom. If the answer is "no," the second test
is whethei ... school has included the student with special needs in general curriculum activities to the maximum extent appropriate. By placing more responsibility on school systems to justify why a student is not included in general
education classrooms, *Daniel R.R.* gave inclusion a legal boost that led to a large
increase of students with special needs placed within inclusive classrooms. An
often overlooked side note to the *Daniel R.R.* decision was that the court stated
that the effect of inclusion on general education students should also be taken into
consideration.

Each of these court cases will continue to be refined by others; however, it is
clear that the mandate for an appropriate education requires that a continuum of
educational placements must be made available to students with special needs. If
parents opt for an inclusion program for their youngster, and the school system
disagrees, it is incumbent on the school system to explain why the general education classroom cannot be modified to accommodate the special needs student.

Organizing Inclusion Programs

Careful planning precedes the implementation of successful inclusion programs.
Inclusion will not work if teachers are coerced to comply or if special and general
educators are not given ample time to plan together. Students cannot be included
with the expectation that simply seating students with mild disabilities next to
other youngsters in a general classroom is a formula for success. There are five
basic strategies that help ensure an inclusion program will work for both teachers
and students. By following the guidelines of communicating with parents, understanding student needs, and evaluating progress, teachers will increase the probability of a successful inclusion program.

Communicate with Parents.   Parents play a vital role in student achievement.
Parents of students with mild disabilities attend individual education program
conferences, participate in decisions regarding type of special services, and ap-
prove placement changes. Lack of communication between teachers and parents
can foster misunderstandings and adversarial positions. Parents are concerned
about their youngster's progress in school. They want to be kept informed and
need to know that the teacher respects their views.

Often the only time parents hear from the teacher is when something is
wrong. A weekly note indicating classroom successes, a home visit, or a monthly

phone call to review student progress can bridge the communication gap between home and school. Parents can provide information on a student's interests, likes, dislikes, and time spent outside of school. When parents feel that the teacher values their input, crossover learning between school and the family is more likely to occur. A productive teacher-parent partnership can be a powerful alliance for change and growth in a youngster's life.

Understand Student Needs. Full-time entry into a general classroom can be an anxiety-provoking experience for a student. Special education programs provide a safe haven from the demands of normal school routines, and special education students may experience "newness panic." Some students withdraw, while others act out in uncharacteristic ways. It is not unusual for a recently included student to regress to disruptive behaviors that the special education teacher thought were eliminated. The first few weeks is not the time to evaluate the viability of the inclusion decision. The included student needs reassurance that a few bumps in the road will be tolerated.

When a student is identified as having a mild disability, it is sometimes difficult to remember that the student has the same developmental needs of other children. Students with mild disabilities are more alike than different from nondisabled students. A student with dyslexia has difficulty reading, but this academic activity is a small slice of a youngster's daily experience. Students with dyslexia play Little League, get into trouble, and sing in church choirs, just like other children. All adolescents share a common need for group approval and independence from authority. These developmental needs are just as immediate in a youngster with an emotional or behavior disorder as with other adolescents. Interpreting a youngster's behavior from a developmental perspective rather than an assigned school label provides a clearer picture of a youngster's actions.

Evaluate Progress. Enormous amounts of time and money are spent by school systems to assess the educational status of children referred for special education. Norm-referenced tests measure how they compare in academics to their peers. Criterion-referenced tests pinpoint specific strengths and weaknesses in academics. Psychological tests attempt to determine whether a student has mild mental retardation, a learning disability, or an emotional disturbance. Observations detail learning styles and student ability to adapt to classroom routines. These are the most common evaluation procedures used to identify and place youngsters in special programs.

The need to evaluate progress for any student participating in an inclusion program does not diminish. However, evaluation methods shift to curriculum-based assessment. Samples of student work, observations of student interaction, and charting of student progress provide detailed evaluative information. Students' individual education programs are reviewed to match learning objectives with classroom work. Evaluation also includes assessment of teaching behavior. Does the teacher provide enough time for the student to answer questions? Are classroom materials adapted to meet student needs? Is the student seated in an area of the room that makes it easier to concentrate and follow teacher directions? Is the teacher providing enough hands-on activities to help students master specific skills? These are a sample of questions that could guide observations of teaching methods in an inclusion program.

Collaboration

Medical patients generally appreciate knowing that their physician has collaborated with other medical professionals about their condition. Perhaps the physician requested a second opinion. Independent views from another professional with a similar background provides reassurance that someone else has given opinions from his or her knowledge and experience. The same is true of building construction. It is reassuring to have another carpenter, plumber, or roofer offer his or her opinion about repairs that may be necessary. Having several car mechanics discuss an automobile's malfunction is also helpful.

Why should it be any different in education? Collaboration should be explained to parents as a school team or committee voluntarily meeting together to review all facets of the child's condition, history, and instructional methods previously used in order to develop the most appropriate plan for the youngster. In order to design this plan and work toward a mutual goal, all participants need to be heard on an equal basis and have their area of experience and expertise heard by all members. This includes the essential data that parents can give the team about their child and his or her background, plus current likes, abilities, skills, and so on. Supporting collaboration in one's school helps to foster an important outlook upon meeting the needs of individual students (Fishbaugh, 1997; Friend & Bursuck, 1999; Friend & Cook, 2000).

The term collaboration and its derivatives (i.e., collaborate, collaborative) are used fairly commonly and interchangeably in education, but the terms can differ in the way they are applied in other areas. Simply stated, *collaborate* means "to work together." The word *collaboration* has taken on the meaning of referring to "the event or act of working together." In education, the term has been primarily applied to "persons who work together in order to make inclusion work" (Friend & Bursuck, 1999; Friend & Cook, 2000). With collaboration, there is an interdependence among participants. The act of collaborating provides support and an opportunity to brainstorm ideas with other members who come from a different orientation or training.

Specifically, a team or committee meet to discuss or to *collaborate* about ways of serving students and their families so that student needs will be met. Educators, parents, and other professionals meet to plan programs and interventions, to monitor student progress, or just to problem-solve issues that come up and affect the youngster with special needs. This meeting is referred to as *collaboration*. In some states like Alabama, classes in which students with disabilities are included are referred to as *collaborative classes*, and the special education teachers who consult or co-teach with the regular classroom teacher are called *collaborative teachers.*

Because of the various ways in which it is applied, the term "collaboration" is sometimes used carelessly. For example, two or more educators discussing a child's progress is not always a form of collaboration. According to Friend and Cook (2000), most people agree that collaboration is "working together in a supportive and mutually beneficial relationship." These authors also offer some guidelines for determining what is true collaboration. They have delineated six defining characteristics, which together add to the above definition and expand it. Collectively, all must exist for true collaboration to exist.

Characteristics of Collaboration

Collaboration Is **Voluntary.**   This first characteristic refers to a person's attitude. The meeting or planning session may be held due to a mandate or requirement of the law, but the voluntary part refers to persons being present and involved because they want to be there, or because they sense the need for them to work with others in order to make it possible for the child's special needs to be met (Friend & Cook, 2000; Mostert, 1998).

Collaboration Requires **Parity** *among Professionals.*   Parity means equality. In this situation, parity means that each person's contribution during the collaborative event is accepted on an equal basis. That doesn't mean that all suggestions should be accepted—just listened to. Each person has equal power in making decisions (Friend & Bursuck, 1999).

Collaboration Is Based on **Mutual Goals.**   All teams or committees generally have specific purposes or reasons for meeting. During collaboration, these are translated into goals. For example, a multidisciplinary special education team meets to determine for what services, if any, a student is eligible. Or having established eligibility, the multidisciplinary team meets to develop an individualized plan (IEP) for the student or decide which educational setting the student should be placed in order to have his or her needs best met.

Collaboration Depends upon **Shared Responsibility.**   Sharing responsibility for making decisions when working together toward a mutual goal does not mean that everyone shares equally in accomplishing the tasks outlined. Responsibility is assumed by persons most related to the tasks outlined (Friend & Cook, 2000; Mostert, 1998).

A school guidance counselor may assume responsibility for meeting with a youngster with an attention deficit hyperactivity disorder (ADHD), both individually and with a regularly scheduled ADHD group. Since the counselor is knowledgeable about this condition, he or she might plan to make suggestions to the special education and general classroom teachers about activities they could effectively incorporate into various parts of the curriculum during the school day. These activities would be those directed toward meeting the child's goals and would be helpful to other students as well.

Collaboration Includes **Shared Resources.**   All members of a collaborative team have different types of experience and expertise that they would be able to share with the group. For example, knowledge about a particular technique might be something that one person would be able to share; whereas, the time and accessibility to the student in order to carry out the technique would be in someone else's realm of knowledge.

Collaboration Means **Sharing Accountability** *for Outcomes.*   All participants or team members are accountable for the outcome (Friend & Bursuck, 1999; Friend & Cook, 2000; Mostert, 1998). The outcome may be positive or it may turn out negative; regardless, all members are responsible and accountable.

Inclusion Models

Every profession has models for putting theories to work. Economists have supply-and-demand models for explaining changes in financial trends. Psychologists use developmental models to explain human behavior. Like a blueprint, a model provides a set of instructions for the application of an idea. Education has many models. There are instructional models, assessment models, and discipline models.

In education, a model is judged in terms of its usefulness. An elaborate model of instruction may be well researched, but if it requires too much teacher time or is too expensive to implement, teachers will look someplace else for ideas. Teachers like practical ideas that increase student competence. A good idea for one teacher may seem esoteric or nonfunctional to another. Teachers adopt models that match their professional philosophy and personal values.

A set of guidelines for inclusion qualifies as a model when it has proved effective in a variety of educational programs. This is no easy task because circumstances vary so much from region to region, system to system, and from school to school. There are two inclusion models used to deliver services to students in the general classroom. The first, the consulting teacher, provides services primarily to teachers, and only indirectly through the classroom teachers to students. The second, the *co-teacher*, supports a method by which the regular classroom teacher and special education teacher plan, teach, and evaluate together. Six co-teaching approaches are demonstrated by video (Burrello, Burrello, & Friend, 1996) and written about in the special education literature (Friend & Bursuck, 1999; Friend & Cook, 2000). The following two topics, consultation and instructional practices, describe inclusion models that have proven useful in many classrooms.

Each approach can stand on its own or be combined with other models and strategies. Ultimately, the choice of an inclusion model depends on how well it matches the needs of students, teachers, and parents.

Consulting Teacher

The consulting teacher model is an alternative to the pull-out approach to special education services (Phillips & McCullough, 1990). Instead of working directly with special needs students (e.g., in a resource room), the consulting teacher plans with the general classroom teacher to facilitate inclusion. Some of the responsibilities of the consulting teacher include observing in the general classroom, sharing materials with the general classroom teacher, demonstrating instructional techniques, coordinating programs, and presenting in-service workshops for general educators.

The consulting teacher provides intervention at the site of the learning problem. Both the student with the learning problem and the instructor with the teaching problem can be helped within the general classroom. Consultation can remedy such disadvantages of pull-out programs as fragmentation of instruction and stigmatization of students. It provides a viable means for educators to jointly own the problem of a difficult learner. Through a process of shared problem solving, collaborative consultation crosses over boundaries that have traditionally separated general and special educators.

Consulting requires careful scheduling and administrative support. Consulting is ineffective if the classroom teacher and consulting teacher do not have adequate time to plan. The building principal controls each classroom teacher's schedule. Administrative support in terms of release time and a nonjudgmental view toward teachers who are working with a consultant are two prerequisites for successful implementation of this model.

Consulting also requires diplomatic communication skills on the part of the consultant and a readiness to cooperate on the part of the consultee. Any "helper" has a power advantage over the person who is being helped. The need for consultation, if not handled properly, can imply weaknesses in the ability of the recipient. Imagine the following scenario. A twenty-four-year-old special education teacher has just completed graduate training as a teacher consultant, and her first assignment is a teacher who is a twenty-year veteran of the public schools. The teacher was selected by her principal because she has a higher than average referral rate for special education services, and the principal wants to establish an inclusion model. It is clear, without drawing out this illustration any further, that a successful outcome is problematic. How will the general classroom teacher feel about this "rookie" observing in her classroom and offering suggestions for changes in instruction? How will the consultant deal with the general classroom teacher's attitude toward outside help? Can consulting work when the general classroom teacher has not directly requested outside assistance?

Consulting works when there is genuine collaboration among all parties (e.g., general classroom teacher, consultant, special services teachers). There are superb and mediocre teachers in both special and general education. For the consulting teacher model to be useful, there needs to be a commitment to sharing of expertise and resources on both sides of the fence (Mastropieri & Scruggs, 2000; Pugach & Johnson, 1989a; Thomas, Correa, & Morsink, 2001). Trust must precede collaborative problem solving. Consultant teachers should be selected from the ranks of the most experienced and respected teachers in a school system. Pinning the title "consultant" on a teacher who lacks the expertise or interpersonal skills to work with classroom teachers will disrupt rather than facilitate mainstreaming efforts. Ultimately, the success of the consulting teacher model depends on a mutual sharing of ideas, methods, and responsibilities between regular and special educators.

Co-Teacher Model

Co-teaching means that the general education teacher and the special education teacher work together in the regular classroom. Both work directly with students and share teaching responsibilities. They co-teach. There are several advantages for this type of service delivery to students with special needs who otherwise might be pulled out of the regular classroom to receive special education.

- The general classroom and special education teachers plan lessons together.
- The general classroom and special education teachers instruct students in the same room.
- Special education teachers work with all students, not just the ones with identified special education needs.
- Regular classroom teachers are given instructionally relevant information about students that helps them to adapt and modify classroom instruction and activities.
- Students with special needs are able to participate in regular class activities because appropriate modifications and accommodations have been identified and put into place.
- Regular classroom and special education teachers have mutually agreed upon roles and responsibilities concerning instruction and classroom maintenance.

Friend and Cook (2000) outlined six basic approaches for co-teaching. A brief description of each is given. Some are more appropriate in some situations than others; each should be reviewed by the co-teachers to see which would be most effective when teaching certain subject content, when leading learning activities, when remediating skills, when working with drill and practice, when working with particular student behaviors, and so on. Each classroom has its own combination of students and student strengths and needs (Vaughn, Bos, & Schumm, 1997; Vaughn, Schumm, & Argulles, 1997).

One Teach, One Observe.   One teacher primarily manages the classroom while the other observes. The teacher who is observing can do data collection, record student learning characteristics, and so on.

One Teach, One Drift.   One teacher instructs the class while the other intermingles among students, offering specialized assistance. Both teachers need to take active and passive roles at some time.

The co-teaching roles of the second teacher in *one teach, one observe* and *one teach, one drift* are both considered supportive roles in these first two co-teaching approaches. In Figure 6.3, these are referred to as *one teach, one support*.

Station Teaching. Both teachers deliver instruction in teaching stations. Students can work independently at the third teaching station or with a volunteer, student, or paraprofessional.

Parallel Teaching. The class is divided in half, with each teacher taking a similar number of students to teach. Each teacher is teaching the same information, but in a different manner. For example, the special education teacher might bring in outlines, highlighted materials, and manipulatives with which to instruct students.

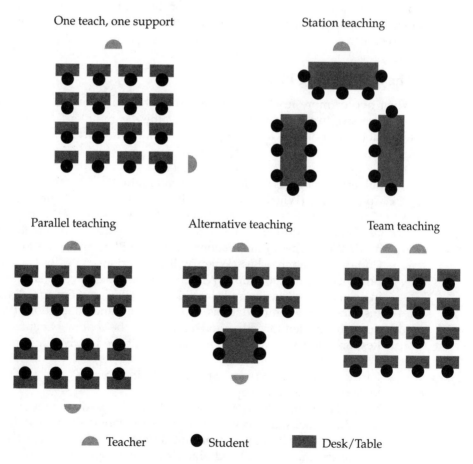

FIGURE 6.3   Co-Teaching Approaches

Source: Friend, M. and Bursuck, W. D. *Including Students with Special Needs: A Practical Guide for Classroom Teachers.* Boston: Allyn and Bacon, 1999, p. 83. Reprinted with permission.

Alternative Teaching.   One teacher manages the major group of students, while the other has a small group pulled aside. The group membership changes according to the purpose of the group, which might be to preview or review material being learned, to provide social skills training, or for enrichment.

Team Teaching.   Two teachers are actively involved in managing instruction with the whole class. Both teachers assume responsibility for teaching subject content areas. Variations to this approach have been around for a long time.

For example, in tag team teaching, one teacher instructs the class in English and then the other teacher instructs math. The first teacher might then teach social studies while the other teacher prepares to teach science. The teachers might each be grading papers or preparing lessons for their subject area while the second teacher is teaching. The students can remain in the same classroom or change classrooms in order for part of the students to receive instruction in one subject area while the other part of the class receives instruction in another subject area.

The Co-Teaching Plan

When two or more teachers work together, there are some topics that need to be addressed and discussed. To work out this "game plan," the teachers need to collaborate about the following topics or concerns (Burrello et al., 1996; Dover, 1994).

- Subject area or class (What is being co-taught?)
- Co-planning (Where, when, and how often will the team collaboratively plan? How will feedback about student progress be discussed?)
- Textbooks and instructional materials (What textbooks and materials will be used? What types of instructional support will be given and to whom?)
- Co-teaching approaches (When will the various types of co-teaching approaches be put into action? What type is needed for various kinds of teaching content and classroom learners? How will classroom space be utilized?)
- Instructional accommodations, modifications, and adaptations (What types might be needed for individual learners for the content being taught?)
- Responsibilities of each team member (What needs to be done, and who will do it?)
- Parity (How will personal space be decided upon? Will the teachers be looked upon as equals by the students?)
- Methods and materials (What materials will be used with the students? Will there be books and materials on diverse functioning levels? Will content be presented according to student functioning levels? What types of materials will be assigned for drill and practice and for homework?)
- Student responsibilities and expectations (What actions and reactions are expected from students? What are the overall setting demands? Will any of these be modified for individuals?)

- Classroom rules and discipline plan (What are the rules? What procedures will be used for enforcing these rules? Is there a difference in teacher tolerance levels?)
- Testing of students (How and when will content be tested or activities assessed?)
- Evaluation of students (Who will grade which papers or assignments? How will student grades be decided upon?)
- Role and responsibilities of the paraprofessional (Will the role and responsibilities of the paraprofessional change as a result of having a co-teacher in the classroom?)
- Substitute plans for each in-class team member (What will happen when a team member is absent?)

Tips to Remember about Co-Teaching

Each co-teacher has his or her own unique areas of experience and expertise. We should not expect regular classroom teachers to know the specialty areas in special education, nor should the special education teacher be expected to be a content expert. Good co-teaching teams do not just happen—it takes good collaborative planning, implementation, and follow-up evaluation (Ramsey, 1998).

- Allow for and respect differences in technique. One teacher may not approach a task exactly like another teacher would. Differences can be looked at in a positive manner.
- Keep a balance of special needs students in proportion to general education students. Special needs and other at-risk students should comprise about 20 to 25 percent of the class.
- Follow the schedule. Other co-teaching arrangements may be planned so everyone's schedule must be held to as much as possible in order not to disrupt plans for another class with another teacher.
- Expect a few problems along the way. Some changes will need to be made as the co-teaching experiences occur.

A Co-Teaching Model

Successful programs like the one developed at Kensington Elementary School, in Springfield, Massachusetts demonstrate that inclusion programs really work (Henley, 2004). Kensington uses the Responsive Classroom program as the major framework within the inclusion program at its school. The Responsive Classroom approach provides practical strategies for teaching students with diverse social and learning abilities, and is well suited for Kensington's school population. The primary teaching components of the Responsive Classroom program are shown in Figure 6.4. The program's emphasis upon developing a community within the classroom and a social skills curriculum meets Kensington's needs.

FIGURE 6.4   The Responsive Classroom Teaching Components

- Morning Meeting—A daily routine that builds community, creates a positive climate for learning, and reinforces academic skills.
- Rules and Logical Consequences—A clear and consistent approach to discipline that fosters responsibility and self-control.
- Guided Discovery—A format for introducing materials that encourages inquiry, heightens interest, and teaches care of the school environment.
- Academic Choice—An approach to giving students choices in their learning that helps them become invested, self-motivated learners.
- Classroom Organization—Strategies for arranging materials, furniture, and displays to encourage independence, promote caring, and maximize learning.
- Family Communication Strategies—Ideas for involving families as partners in their children's education.

Source: Henley, M. (2004). Creating successful inclusion programs. Bloomington, IN: National Educational Service.

Kensington Elementary School is located near downtown Springfield, Massachusetts. With a 92 percent poverty rate and a 22 percent special-needs population, Kensington was recognized as one of five most improved schools in the state in 1999. Throughout this 384-student K–5 school, students with special needs are taught their entire day in general classrooms. The spirit of Kensington Elementary School is emblazoned on the banner that hangs over the front entrance: "Some goals are so worthy it's glorious to fail." This phrase summarizes the key to Kensington's success: dedication to the ideal that all students can learn, and commitment to a community.

A co-teaching approach is used in each classroom. Rather than pulling students out for resource room delivery services, the special education services come to the students. In Kensington's classrooms, teachers work side-by-side. Teachers utilize their individual strengths and to experiment with new ideas. All students, regular and special education alike, benefit from the delivery of instruction by these co-teachers.

During the course of the day, other professionals come into the classrooms to work with students. Support persons include the adjustment counselor, the speech and language teacher, the Title I teacher, and the physical therapist. All make no distinction between special education and general education students.

Teachers enjoy working together, and their efforts have been validated by positive test scores. For example, in the year 2000 administration of state-wide assessment tests, 26 percent of Springfield public school fourth-grade students were proficient in Language Arts, and 12 percent were proficient in Mathematics. In comparison, 48 percent of Kensington's fourth graders were proficient in Language Arts and 37 percent were proficient in Mathematics. The sense of community and the belief that together they are doing good work are the hallmarks of the Kensington success story.

Collaborative Learning

Teachers never cease to puzzle about how to teach students with varying abilities. Students are so different in personality, motivation, work habits, and interests that even the best teachers are challenged to keep all their students involved in learning. The selection of peer tutoring and cooperative learning is based on the flexibility each provides for teaching students who are different. These are a sample of worthwhile instructional practices for maintaining students with mild disabilities in the general classroom.

Peer Tutoring

One of the best ways to learn something is to teach it to someone else. Peer tutoring can be equally effective for students with and without mild disabilities. For example, Maheady, Sacca, & Harper (1988) established a classwide peer tutoring program for fifty tenth-grade social studies students. The students ranged in age from fifteen to seventeen years. Weekly study guides developed by regular and special education teachers were used as the basis for half-hour tutoring periods, three times a week. Progress was measured by weekly quizzes. The researchers reported that the implementation of CWPT (classwide peer tutoring) resulted in an increase in test scores for both special and regular education students.

Peer tutoring places the responsibility for learning on the student. This is a potent change for students with mild disabilities who often become passive learners. With a tutor, students accustomed to sitting alone at their desks waiting for the teacher are directly involved in their learning. Peer tutoring provides individualized instruction. The nonthreatening aspect of peer tutoring encourages students to admit a lack of understanding without concern about adult evaluation. Working with another student provides a youngster with opportunities to discuss, question, practice, and evaluate learning with immediate feedback. Jenkins and Jenkins (1981) described seven steps to implement a peer tutoring program.

1. *Determine which children are to be tutored.* Start small. Begin with four or five students who like to work with other children. Slow development of a tutoring program gives the teacher opportunities to restructure tutoring sessions as needed. Tutoring is not for everyone. Students who are serious behavior problems may not respond well to working with fellow students.

2. *Prepare the school for tutoring.* The principal and teachers who are involved in the program must be convinced that a tutoring program will not disrupt regular school activities. A written proposal outlining scheduling and monitoring procedures will ensure that all participants are clear about each person's role. Accountability is a major issue in schools. The tutoring program developer should reassure the other teachers that time used for tutoring will not detract from the tutor's classroom performance.

3. *Determine a time for tutoring.* Daily sessions of one half-hour produce the best peer tutoring results. Peer tutoring within the classroom does not present the scheduling difficulties that occur when two separate classes are involved. Working out a program between classrooms requires careful negotiation of time and space—two valuable commodities in schools. Establish a set time each day for tutoring sessions. When a program is initiated, adjustments in plans are almost always required. This is a normal consequence of implementing a novel idea. Build in a first week evaluation, with the expectation that adjustments in schedules will be needed.

4. *Inform parents about the program.* Parents are always curious about school programs that vary from traditional teacher instruction. In public schools, even minor changes can have a ripple effect. Some teachers, particularly those who are not involved in the program, may be suspicious of its value. It is best that parents receive written notice about peer tutoring rather than hearing about it from their children or other parents. Such a letter would contain a brief description of the program skills that students will learn, program supervision methods, and evaluation procedures. Invite parents to school to observe the tutoring program in action.

5. *Design lessons and a measurement system.* Decide what content tutors are to teach; then specifically detail tutoring methods. For example, a reading lesson might involve five minutes of listening to oral reading followed by the tutee writing a list of words she found difficult. Then the tutee could write a sentence containing each word. Tutors need clear guidelines for their work. Avoid unstructured tutoring sessions where the students are not sure of their responsibilities. Detailing student progress on daily charts is a recommended procedure for keeping track of program effectiveness.

6. *Conduct tutor training.* Although tutorial skills will vary with age and content, there are some general training needs applicable to all tutors. Each tutor should be clear about punctuality, confidentiality, and positive regard for the tutee. Schoolwork needs to be evaluated in a systematic manner. The tutor will need to understand how progress is measured. Daily charts, percentage of correct answers, or random samples of behavior are examples of data that tutors commonly are asked to maintain.

The tutor will require training. A natural tendency to prompt or do the work for a tutee can be addressed by the teacher modeling proper instructional behavior. The tutor is a helper. This requires the ability to interact in a positive manner. Some key interpersonal skills are active listening and praising good effort. Change behaviors that intimidate or cause the tutee to feel incompetent. Model error correction behaviors that encourage sustained effort.

7. *Maintain tutor's involvement and interest.* Frequent reminders of the tutor's positive contributions can be gleaned from tutee progress charts. Special recognition at assemblies or through the awarding of certificates will serve the dual purpose of rewarding tutors and encouraging other students to be involved with the program. Teaching is no less a difficult endeavor for a youngster than it is for an adult. Periodic group meetings with tutors can provide the program developer with opportunities for refining the program and boosting morale.

Peer tutoring is cost effective, and it provides a student with individual attention. If conducted in a thoughtful and systematic manner, peer tutoring can increase school achievement and motivation of both students.

Cooperative Learning

When students lack control over their learning, motivation to persevere is undermined (Gough, 1987). Cooperative learning is a method of structuring small groups of nondisabled and disabled students so that all the individuals achieve a learning goal through mutual planning and decision making.

Cooperative learning can be used with all age groups to teach any part of the curriculum. Putnam and her colleagues (1989) compared fifty studies of cooperative, competitive, and individualistic learning situations. Cooperative learning produced more instances of positive relationships between students with and without disabilities. Students work in groups and ask questions, share ideas, clarify thoughts, experiment, brainstorm, and find solutions with their classmates (Salend, 2001). Benefits from cooperative learning include: increased student motivation, higher test scores, and enhanced social skills (Johnson & Johnson, 1986; Putnam et al., 1989; Slavin, Madden, & Leavey, 1984; Smith, 1987).

There are four steps to establishing cooperative learning groups in the classroom:

1. *The teacher selects members of each learning group.* Cooperative learning groups are heterogeneous in composition with a balance between males and females, high and low achievers, and active and passive students. A typical group would include three to six students with no more than one student with a mild disability. The balance of the groups is crucial to ensure that each group has strengths to offset individual academic or social weaknesses.

2. *The teacher directly teaches cooperative group skills.* Most students are conditioned to earn grades based on individual work, often in competition with other students. Such familiar refrains in classrooms as, "Pay attention to your own work," or "No talking while we are working" are antithetical to cooperative learning. The teacher who uses cooperative learning wants students to talk and work with each other. Cooperative learning requires such interpersonal skills as the ability to trust and work with others, good listening skills, acceptance and support of others, and the ability to resolve conflicts constructively (Johnson & Johnson, 1990).

Some students may have difficulty making the transition from passive, teacher-directed learning to cooperative learning activities. Roy Smith (1987) found he needed to teach his junior high school students how to work cooperatively. He described six steps for teaching cooperative skills:

a. Identify the specific skills group members will need to demonstrate; for instance, listening or providing information.
b. Help students become aware of the need for cooperative skills.
c. Help students gain a clear understanding of each skill.
d. Provide students with situations in which to practice cooperative skills.
e. Give students descriptive feedback on their performance of each skill.
f. Persevere in practicing the skill. Role playing, group discussions, brainstorming sessions, and observer feedback of group activities are samples of classroom methods that help students acquire and reinforce cooperative group skills.

3. *The teacher assigns cooperative group activities.* There is a difference between small group work and cooperative learning. In typical small group activities, students are given an assignment with little attention paid to how they will work together. A common complaint about small group activities is that a few students do all the work. In cooperative group activities students work together toward a common goal, and the group tasks are equally divided among group members. One approach to subdividing group participation is the "jigsaw" strategy. The group is given an assignment, and each member has part of the materials needed to complete the task; for instance, the assignment could be a group report on drugs. Each student would have a different source of information, such as a medical reference book, newspaper clippings, magazine articles, and an encyclopedia.

Another approach for beginning cooperative groups is to assign each member a specific role to facilitate the group work. One student would be responsible for reviewing suggestions, another would question individual members to elicit their ideas, while a third group member could be responsible for keeping the group on track. When students are experienced in cooperative learning, it is possible to turn virtually any part of the school curriculum into a collaborative learning experience.

4. *The teacher evaluates group efforts.* In cooperative groups, students learn that they sink or swim together. There are two levels of group assessment:

a. Did the group accomplish its goal?
b. How well did the group work together?

Products such as a classroom presentation or tests where individual scores are averaged to give a group score are examples of ways teachers have evaluated group goals. Self reporting by groups or observer feedback on group dynamics can provide information on group interaction. Group evaluation should be criterion-referenced. Before the group work begins, the teacher should clearly outline the criteria used for group evaluation. For example, a cooperative group activity on drug abuse could conclude by members summarizing each other's contributions.

Tateyama-Sniezek (1990) cautions against investing too much enthusiasm in cooperative learning as a tool to increase academic achievement of students with mild disabilities. She points out that more studies need to be undertaken that include students with mild disabilities in cooperative learning groups. Stephens and Slavin (1991) took issue with Tateyama-Sniezek's findings. They pointed out that when group rewards and individual accountability are both included in cooperative learning activities, the outcomes for students with and without disabilities are positive.

Both peer tutoring and cooperative learning groups capitalize on students as classroom resources. The active involvement of students in their own learning enhances mainstreaming efforts by fostering social relationships between students, increasing student motivation, and supporting the acquisition of skills. A poster in the classroom of a teacher who used cooperative learning activities summarizes the impact of collaborative learning strategies. It simply states, "None of us is smarter than all of us" (Smith, 1987, 664).

Working Together

Schools must change in order to meet the demands of the future. Demographic trends indicate increased poverty among students. A growing proportion of students are nonwhite and non-English-speaking, and there is an increase of students from single-parent families. If the schools of the future are to meet the growing demands of hard-to-teach students, changes must occur in present school practices that serve to separate students (and teachers) into groups of "haves" and "have nots."

General and special educators can collaborate to teach all children. There are contact points where key issues faced by regular and special educators rub together. All educators, whether special or regular, must deal with problems of teacher expectations, standardized tests, classroom organization, discipline, and dual systems of administration. The ability of educators to meet these challenges and solve them together will set the course for an improved educational system for the students of the twenty-first century.

Teacher Expectations

Research on effective instruction indicates the powerful effect of teacher expectations, both positive and negative, on student performance. When students are labeled as deficient and put in "special" programs, the message is clear—there is something intrinsically wrong with this student. Labels like mentally retarded and learning disabled become explanations for why a student is difficult to teach. Students are then grouped with other "deficient" learners, and teacher expectations for the group decline. Conversely, when teachers believe that learning problems are temporary hurdles that can be overcome by adapting teaching methods, there is an expectation that success will come with hard work. When teachers have high expectations, the performance of students is enhanced.

But what about teacher expectations of themselves? Two Rand Corporation studies found that positive teacher opinions of their own ability had a beneficial effect on students' learning (Armor et al., 1976; Berman et al., 1977). McDaniel and DiBella-McCarthy described the teaching style of these confident teachers.

> High efficacy teachers maintained high academic standards, had clear expectations for students, concentrated on academic instruction, maintained on-task behavior, and demonstrated "withitness." They combined a secure classroom environment with a strong academic orientation. . . . High-efficacy teachers allocated twice as much time to whole group instruction as did low-efficacy teachers. (McDaniel & DiBella-McCarthy, 1989, 35)

Teachers who believe in their own ability have good group management skills. They encourage student participation and have less discipline problems. Perhaps most important, high-efficacy teachers are problem solvers. They view a student's learning difficulties as a temporary problem, and they try different teaching approaches until they get results. Teacher preparation programs that concentrate on developing high-efficacy skills will provide young teachers with the tools needed to help all learners in the regular classroom.

Classroom Organization

Between kindergarten and twelfth grade a student will spend more than 11,000 hours in school. How much of this time is actually spent learning? According to researchers who have studied life in schools, only a fraction of a school day is allocated to instruction, and students spend even less time engaged in learning activities. Out of a typical 390-minute school day, teachers spend less than half that time teaching. In their survey of second-, third-, and fourth-grade classrooms, Ysseldyke and Algozzine (1984) found that students have few opportunities to do independent work, and they spend a lot of time in such passive activities as listening and waiting.

Students spend as little as 12 percent of their school day questioning, reading, writing, or engaged in some other activity that reflects active learning. Goodlad (1984) reported that a good deal of what goes on in schools is like painting by numbers. The teacher gives directions, and students follow them in robot-like fashion. He described the emotional tone of these classrooms as flat. The climate of these rooms lacked joy and warmth. Goodlad noted that although teachers verbalize the need for students to become independent thinkers, many teachers exhibit a need to control student decision making.

More attention needs to be directed toward how classrooms are organized. When the teacher controls every action, from distribution of materials to collecting lunch money, precious instructional time is wasted. Students must be actively involved in their learning to succeed. Such active teaching strategies as cooperative learning projects, learning centers, and peer tutoring allow teachers to move about the room and guide student learning. By shifting the classroom instructional norm from "frontal teaching" to student-centered activities, teachers can increase instructional time and allow learning to proceed at the student's pace.

Standardized Tests

Chester Finn, past assistant U.S. Secretary of Education in charge of research, characterized standardized testing in America as the "Lake Wobegon" effect. He observed that in the mythical Minnesota town popularized by the humorist Garrison Keillor, all the children are "above average." Finn's comment was prompted by national achievement scores that each year showed a rise in average test scores for all schoolchildren. In their zeal to demonstrate how much their school systems have improved, this statistical paradox has been conveniently ignored by many educators (Fiske, 1988).

Neill and Medina summarized the case against standardized tests.

> At best, standardized testing is hopelessly inadequate for promoting school reform. At worst, such testing will preclude reform. In either case, the continued domination of testing will mean that millions of students—primarily those most in need of improved education—will be dumped into dead-end tracks and pushed out of school. (Neill & Medina, 1989, 695)

The 2004 reauthorization of IDEA mandated that students with disabilities be included in state- and districtwide assessments. These mandates reflect the push for equal access and high standards for all students. They also highlight the need for teachers to be knowledgeable about test accommodations, test preparation, test administration, outcomes, and legal and ethical concerns surrounding high-stakes exams (Washburn-Moses, 2003).

The Council for Exceptional Children (CEC), the primary professional organization for special education, has long supported including students in state- and districtwide assessments. The results of these assessments can help determine if the schools are providing quality instructional programs for the special education students, or if additional resources or professional development are needed to improve the programs.

To ensure that students with disabilities are assessed fairly and appropriately, CEC states that:

- Students with disabilities must be assessed with high expectations.
- Whatever accommodations are necessary to facilitate this must be provided.
- Alternative assessments must be provided for the small percentage of students with the most significant disabilities.
- Individualized decisions must be made within the framework of general assessment, assessment with accommodations, or alternate assessments. (Today, April/May 2003, 1)

The No Child Left Behind Act (NCLB) has given schools additional accountability responsibilities with their students with disabilities. The NCLB Act mandates that a majority of students with disabilities 1) be included in state- and districtwide assessments, and 2) show annual improvement in the test scores of students with disabilities.

"High stakes tests" are a concern to special educators. High stakes testing refers to the requirement that students must pass an exam in order to move from one grade to the next or earn a high school diploma. Presently, twenty-five states require students to pass an exam to receive a high school diploma, and seven require that students pass a test to be promoted to a certain grade level (National Education Association, 2001). This means that students with disabilities *must* be provided with sufficient access to the general curriculum and be given tests which are valid and adequately measure student knowledge, rather than reflect their cultural diversity, linguistic diversity, or disability exceptionality. Middle and high school teachers need to ensure that students are taught course content as well as basic skills, such as reading, writing, and arithmetic.

Assessment reporting must make sure that individual accountability is differentiated from accountability focused upon the school as a whole. School system accountability must never be the sole basis for making individual educational decisions. The IEP team should make the determination about participation in assessment testing based upon individual needs. Teachers, related service personnel, paraprofessionals, administrators, parents, and students must cooperate in the planning, application, and evaluation of an appropriate assessment and accountability system, including its application to students with exceptional needs in order to guarantee its successful implementation (Today, April/May 2003, 5).

Educators should keep in mind that alternatives to standardized tests are available. Curriculum-based assessment, classroom observations, and student portfolios provide more detail about student learning than standardized tests. Evaluation of student performance can improve when assessment paints a picture of student as learner rather than student as test-taker.

Summary

Inclusion, least restrictive environment, and mainstreaming are terms that address the importance of integrating students with disabilities with their nondisabled peers. Inclusion means educating students with disabilities in the general education classroom with special education support. There are two models of support in today's schools used to implement inclusion and these are called collaborative consultation and co-teaching.

The legal mandate for inclusion is based on the least restrictive environment provision, reaffirmed in the latest amendments to the Individuals with Disabilities Education Act. Mainstreaming brings students with and without disabilities together but does not provide the necessary special education support services. All students want to be viewed as normal by peers and teachers. With special education delivered in the general classroom, all students do not have to be pulled out for special instruction in the resource room or placed in segregated "special" programs. Inclusion eliminates the artificial division that is created between students with disabilities and their peers when they are needlessly removed from their general classroom. However, a continuum of special education placements is necessary in order to teach those students for whom inclusion does not work.

Inclusion can be an effective educational intervention. A well-planned inclusion program helps develop both academic and social skills as well as or better than pull-out or self-contained special education programs. Planning an inclusion program includes communicating with parents, understanding student needs, preparing students for a change, and evaluating student progress.

Sound general educational practices such as cooperative learning and peer tutoring work equally well with students with mild disabilities. Consultation strategies offer teachers and students alternative strategies to achieve inclusion programs.

Both special and general educators have a stake in realigning their efforts to teach students with mild disabilities. The inclusion movement breathed new life into mainstreaming efforts by focusing attention on the benefits of merging special and general education efforts for students. It is clear by now that uninspired teaching does as much to create learning problems as do the characteristics of individual students. By focusing attention on ways of enhancing classroom learning environments, educators can best serve the needs of all students.

ACTIVITIES

1. Arrange to meet with several general classroom and special education teachers of students with mild disabilities. Ask them questions about how inclusion works for them. What special needs do students with mild disabilities have in their general and resource classrooms? Are their needs similar? Do the teachers collaborate with each other as they plan for the students' instruction? Do both participate in developing the students' individual education programs?

2. Visit the campus library. Locate major journals in special education. Look for articles on mainstreaming and inclusion. In particular, look for inclusion models and ways in which inclusion concerns have been resolved. Identify articles that present effective ideas about adapting and modifying instruction in the regular classroom.

3. While visiting your campus library, look through journals that publish articles about special education teachers who function as consultants. What would the role of the special education teacher be like in this capacity compared to functioning in a direct service delivery role? How would a special education consultant deliver indirect services to general classroom teachers?

4. Working in small groups, write scripts showing effective and ineffective interactions between general classroom and special education teachers as they collaborate

and plan for students with mild disabilities. Which responsibilities would the general classroom teacher assume? Which responsibilities would be assumed by the special education teacher?

5. In small groups, role play effective collaboration as it should occur in meetings with parents and between teachers.

6. After watching a videotape on co-teaching, divide into small groups and simulate the various approaches.

7. Visit nearby schools with inclusion programs. Note adaptations and modifications in the general education curriculum and in instructional methods and materials.

8. As a variation to number 7, observe in the general education classroom and try to identify which delivery service model is being implemented—collaborative consultation or cooperative teaching. Is a co-teaching approach being utilized? If so, can you identify it?

7 Learning and Teaching

ADVANCE QUESTIONS

Answer the following questions as you read this chapter:

1. How does student perception influence attitudes about school?
2. How does a developmental perspective help teachers understand their students?
3. What is the connection between direct instruction and the effective school research?
4. What is the purpose of precision teaching?
5. What is multisensory instruction?
6. What is the connection between the work of William Glasser and student-centered learning?
7. What is the purpose of teaching students learning strategies?
8. How can recent research on brain function improve teaching?

9. How could task analysis be used to teach multiplication of two-digit numbers?
10. What is a "functional curriculum"?
11. How does a teacher determine what instructional approach to use?
12. How can information about a student's learning style enhance instruction?
13. What is "integrated teaching"?

Chapter Web

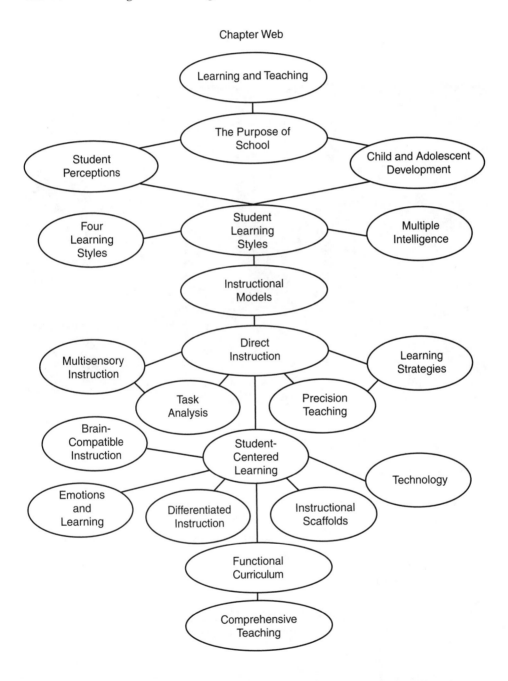

Vignette

Each morning, fifty-five million youngsters troop off to school. They arrive on foot, in cars, and in an armada of yellow school buses. Bells ring; children file into classrooms; the teacher closes the classroom door, calls for attention, and another school day begins. What happens next? Other than sleeping and watching television, no activity demands as much of a youngster's time as school. Even though teachers and students spend almost a thousand hours together each year, our knowledge about what transpires inside classroom walls is fragmentary.

Public school classrooms are oxymorons. They are actually private places. The teacher works alone. The students are there, but they are quiet consumers. Students rarely complain publicly about bad teachers. To whom would they address their complaints? And what would be the purpose? The next day the same teacher would be standing in front of them. This is because teachers have almost total job security. Barring an economic downturn that can lead to layoffs, teachers have the assurance of continuing their profession, with minimum outside interference, until retirement.

Teachers do their best or worst work in virtual isolation from their peers. The act of one teacher observing another teacher in the classroom is so unique that when it happens it is labeled an innovation. Occasionally the seclusion of classroom life is pierced by researchers, and the insights gleaned are informative.

Some teachers spend most of their day standing or sitting in the front of the classroom. Their primary teaching tools are lecture, texts, workbooks, and worksheets. Other teachers appreciate the need for students to be active learners. These teachers mix student-centered learning with direct instruction. They are flexible and are more adept than "frontal teachers" at modifying their instruction to meet the needs of individual students. Teachers who vary their teaching methods are more successful than those who depend on one or two "tried and true" ways of teaching.

Answer the following problem-solving questions about the vignette.

1. Can you recall an elementary school teacher who did most of his or her teaching from the front of the room? Looking back on that classroom experience, how successful was that teacher with students with learning problems?
2. Would you rather be a student in a classroom that featured "frontal teaching" or a classroom that featured student-centered learning? Why?
3. Can you name some specific instructional approaches for individualizing the curriculum for students with learning problems?
4. How do students that you work with in your field-based courses feel about school? Conduct a survey of elementary and secondary students and compare their perceptions of life in classrooms.

The Purpose of School

Ask any teacher what schools are for, and you are likely to get a variety of answers ranging from the basic—"Schools are to teach skills for life," to the enthusiastic—"Schools are to help kids learn about themselves and the world around them." But what about the consumers? What do the students who, from age five to seventeen, spend 12,000 hours in classrooms think about school?

Student Perceptions of School

Noyes and McAndrew (1971) interviewed students throughout the country and asked them, "What are schools for?" A typical response was:

> We go to school because it is the law. They make you stay until you are sixteen, and by then you may as well go on since you probably only have another year or two anyway. The point of it, I guess, is to get a diploma so you can go to college. (Noyes & McAndrew, 1971, 321)

The overall impression made by the students in this study was that the purpose of school was preparation for college. Students did not view school as a place that would meet their personal needs. They gave different versions of the same theme—figure out a way to get through school with the least resistance.

In elementary school, White found that student and teacher perceptions about the purpose of school differ. Whereas teachers value the content of the curriculum, students pay more attention to teacher judgments of their work. In the words of one student:

> . . . you have to have a half-inch margin on your papers . . . you put the headings on the right not on the left, and line it up . . . the cover should be felt if you want an A . . . you can't hand in papers that aren't neat, she'll really mark you down . . . you have to write out "remainder" or it's wrong. . . . (White, 1971, 341)

Students measured their progress by grades rather than what they learned. When he was a special education teacher, one of the authors of this volume had a straightforward reminder regarding the importance of grades to students:

> The director of our program had accepted the teachers' recommendation that we substitute descriptive evaluations for grades. The students participated in assessing their learning. Students met with the teachers to determine if their work in each subject showed improvement. Peter and I had a conference at my desk about his progress. "Do you think your reading has improved?" I asked him. "What do you mean?" he replied. "You know, are you getting better at reading?" I asked. "How should I know," Peter said, "you're the teacher. It's your job to give me a grade so I'll know if I've learned anything."

Peter's comment illustrates the distance between teacher and student perspectives about school. Students are not connected to their learning in the ways adults imagine. They learn the rules of school and how to get by, but curriculum as adults understand it does not have the same meaning to students. Whereas teachers want students to learn, students want to get the teacher's approval, receive good grades, and enjoy the company of their friends. Sometimes they are excited about learning, and sometimes they are bored. At all times, students realize that their fate is essentially in the hands of the teacher. Some students cope with the inequality of power and perform at a level that will satisfy both teacher and parents. Others fall by the wayside. These failures are eventually classified as students at risk, school dropouts, or students with mild disabilities.

What are the characteristics of classroom life that create such a discrepancy between how teachers and students view learning? It should come as no surprise that students view grades as the purpose of their school experience. From the time they receive their first report card until they take the Scholastic Aptitude Test (SAT) in high school, students are continually reminded of the importance of grades. Tests are as indigenous to life in schools as chalk, blackboards, and textbooks.

Some teachers' efforts are best characterized as test- rather than curriculum-driven. These teachers teach to improve test scores rather than to stimulate a love of learning. As long as school-based quizzes and national achievement tests continue as the key measure of success in school, students will concentrate on grades as their most important goal.

Child and Adolescent Development

"What did you do in school today?" When a father asked his six-year-old daughter Margaret this question, she answered, "Well, we had lunch in the cafeteria, we lined up for the bus, and we had folder work on Thursday and we had fun together, me, Brian, all my friends." She added, "That's not all but I forget the rest."

Margaret's response illustrates another major difference between the way in which teachers and students view school. When she thinks about school, Margaret considers its most gratifying aspects—lunch, friends, and a side reference to her studies—"folder work." Children are not miniature adults. There are significant developmental differences between teachers and their students. One developmental distinction is in perceptions of goals.

While adults take the long view, students look at the future from short range. Teachers are concerned with distant goals; students are concerned with here and now. For a five-year-old, twenty minutes is an endless wait. Summer for a twelve-year-old seems to extend into the distance, an uninterrupted progression of sunny days and steamy nights. To the freshman and sophomore, high school appears as if it will never end. Time limits have slight meaning to teenagers who perceive themselves as immortal.

Within this context of time without end, parents and adults pound away at such themes in high school as "You need to learn math in order to get a good job," or they tell primary-grade children, "If you finish your work in twenty minutes, you will get free time at the end of the week." Each of these messages leaves a faint impression on students who are unable to fathom the mystery of work today for tomorrow's reward. Child and adolescent development lend weight to Einstein's view that time is relative. Discipline, grades, and learning are fundamental classroom issues that teachers approach as long-range preparation for work or college, while youngsters jolt forward one day at a time with eyes cast on more substantial concerns, such as watching the clock hands on the wall slowly creep toward dismissal.

Developmental differences between students and teachers are accepted and valued in many early childhood programs, but teachers and administrators sometimes lose track of child and adolescent development. This neglect by school personnel creates a gulf between teachers and students that can have dire consequences. To paraphrase Robert Sternberg (1990), we ignore students' developmental differences at our peril—and theirs.

Part of growing up is learning to take on the perspective of those who are older. Primary-school-aged children learn to be less egocentric as they acquire the ability to perceive a situation from another's point of view. Students in elementary school are here-and-now oriented. It isn't until adolescence that students can begin to think about future goals.

Developmental needs dictate priorities to students, and these priorities can put a student in conflict with adults. For the teenager, relationships, intimacy, and getting a driver's license are major concerns. Adolescence is a time of "grandiose ascension." Teenagers fly high above the mundane matters of the everyday world as they experience new mental and physical abilities they never imagined they would possess (Bly, 1990). Many teenagers perceive parents as "old fashioned" and too strict. When bad things happen, teenagers are reluctant to face them head-on. Denial is a useful defense mechanism for skipping over the hardships of a family's divorce, a mother's addiction, or a father's neglect. This is why depression and drug abuse are such developmental hazards for adolescents. Adolescents are more likely to act out their emotional struggles than to reflect or talk to others.

In high school, acceptance by one's peer group can be more pressing than getting homework done. The teenager confronts the social dilemma of breaking free from the bonds of adult authority at precisely the same time that parents and teachers are demanding "responsible behavior." This pulling in opposite directions usually leaves both adults and adolescents perplexed. Even though developmental changes are at times baffling, these changes help explain why the meaning of school is interpreted differently by teachers and students (Hersch, 1998).

Student Learning Styles

In the Lab School, Washington, D.C., teachers use art to develop organizational skills, strengthen memory, and promote academic readiness. Art activities provide Lab School teachers with opportunities to observe a student interacting with many different mediums of expression (Smith, 2005 www.labschool.org). This procedure provides teachers with insights about educational needs and information about how a child learns most effectively. Experimental programs in Oakland, California and Columbus, Ohio resulted in higher standardized test scores in reading and math when teachers incorporated both right and left hemispheric activities in their lessons (Grady & Luecke, 1978).

Marie Carbo reported that the phonics method of learning to read is unsuitable for some children. Phonics is a left-hemispheric oriented instructional strategy. It requires sequential processing and reproducing of sounds. Students must learn to sound out individual letters and then analyze how each sound combines to make a complete word. For a youngster who is right-hemispheric oriented, this predominant left hemispheric strategy is burdensome and could lead to reading failure. Carbo states that ". . . many global/visual students derive little, if any, benefit from phonics instruction because their strong intuitive abilities enable them to perceive the patterns of entire words or phrases with relative ease" (Carbo, 1987a, 56). Notice that Carbo does not describe global/visual (right hemispheric) students as deficient. Their learning style is different. When teachers use only phonics instruction to teach reading, global/visual learners encounter difficulties. It is the mismatch between instructional strategy and learning style that gives the appearance of student inadequacy. Carbo describes global/visual learners as students who do well when: reading books of their own choosing, participating in choral readings, writing their own stories to read, and listening to tape recordings of interesting books. Drill and repetition of such reading skills as decoding bore these children. They perform better with whole language reading instruction.

Although it is clear that some students do have mild disabilities, it is also evident that many students are misidentified as mildly disabled. The problem is not within the student but is caused by the overreliance on a single instructional strategy. This creates a mismatch between student learning style and teacher methods. This sort of standoff is no contest; the student will be placed in special education and the teacher will continue blithely on his or her way heedless to his or her lack of instructional flexibility. The most effective teachers are able to match instructional approaches to learning styles.

Four Learning Styles

Silver, Strong, and Perini (1997) describe four basic learning styles: the understanding style, the self-expressive style, the mastery style, and the interpersonal style. The understanding-style learner is comfortable with abstraction. This student tests well and learns through reason and questioning. The self-expressive learner relies more on feelings and emotions. Metaphors, aesthetics, and discovery appeal to this style of learner. The mastery-style learner is a concrete learner who prefers information presented in a sequential, step-by-step manner. Practical applications help this learner best. The interpersonal-style learner likes social learning conditions. This student is oriented toward helping others and likes concrete, palpable information. Silver et al. provide the following estimations of style incidence: understanding, 18 percent; self-expressive, 12 percent; mastery, 35 percent; interpersonal, 35 percent. These percentages can change because learning styles are not fixed or rigid, but they change as students grow and encounter new experiences both in and out of school. Closely related to the learning-style approach to understanding differences in how students think is Gardner's (1993) theory of multiple intelligence.

Multiple Intelligence

According to Gardner there are eight types of intelligence that students acquire as they mature and interact with their environment: linguistic, logical-mathematical, spatial, kinesthetic, musical, interpersonal, intrapersonal, and naturalist. Multiple intelligence theory explains the rich diversity of abilities that individuals demonstrate in society. Gardner's concerns related to schooling is that two types of intelligence are emphasized—linguistic and logical-mathematical—at the expense of the six others. Students who demonstrate strengths in linguistic and logical-mathematical intelligence have a distinct advantage over other students, who may be just as intelligent, but are unable to demonstrate their abilities within the traditional curricula. The lack of attention to individual differences between students is demonstrated by one-size-fits-all teaching methods. Gardner said, "What I argue against is the notion that there's only one way to learn how to read, only one way to learn how to compute, only one way to learn about biology. I think that such contentions are nonsense" (cited in Checkley, 1997, 10).

Multiple intelligence emphasizes student movement. Rather than spending prolonged periods of time sitting at desks, students are up and moving around the room. They are engaged in learning stations, group projects, and small-group instruction. Open-ended learning activities that have practical uses such as student-directed newspapers and research activities are highlighted in the multiple intelligence classroom. There are opportunities for socialization as students learn together in pairs or small, cooperative groups. Teachers put a premium on student reflection. Right and wrong answers are not as relevant as the thinking processes that lead students to a particular conclusion. Music, art, and dance are prized as an end and a means to help students explore their own unique forms of expression. Above all, the multiple intelligence approach respects the different ways in which students learn.

The following illustration from a high school social studies class illustrates one teacher's approach to incorporating multiple intelligence methods in her lesson (Lambert, 1997, 53). At the end of a unit on early American history students were allowed to choose presentation formats. The student projects included:

- Writing and performing skits about the Lewis and Clark expedition (verbal, linguistic, and interpersonal intelligence).
- Painting watercolors of birds and other wildlife for a project on John J. Audubon (visual-spatial intelligence).
- Creating a working telegraph (logical-mathematical and bodily-kinesthetic intelligences).
- Developing a board game (visual-spatial intelligence).
- Delivering a eulogy on Davy Crockett (interpersonal intelligence).

- Role playing a historical figure and speaking to the class in character (intrapersonal, verbal-linguistic, and visual-spatial intelligences).

Identifying students' learning style is a good beginning for instruction, but teaching is not a mechanical activity. We cannot fit students to instruction like so many eggs nestled in a carton. To some extent all students need control over their environment, as well as teacher-directed whole group instruction and assistance in how to learn.

Rather than emphasizing the "right" way to teach, learning style literature underscores the fact that students are different. Student learning style is a unique blend of individual development and life experience. Teachers who understand learning styles respect the capabilities of their charges. The literature on learning styles provides a sharp contrast to the traditional school norm of student conformity to a single standard of instruction or behavior. As John Holt remarked, "Children are not only extremely good at learning, they are much better at it than we adults are. As a teacher it took me a very long time to find this out" (Holt, 1977, 232). By utilizing an array of instructional models, the teacher builds a bridge between the student and the curriculum. Research on multiple intelligence and learning styles helps us to grasp the complexity of learning and to appreciate the need for teachers to remain flexible when deciding how to teach individual students.

Instructional Models

Trying to find the best way to teach is a major goal for educators. Educational journals brim with debates about which system of instruction is most effective for teaching reading, math, writing, and appropriate behavior. The search for the best way to teach is tied to many factors. Among these are local leadership, politics, economics, and public support. Education is more like law than like medicine. Absolute cures for educational ills are almost nonexistent. Rather, like law, education must change and adapt to the needs of society; for example, educational policy is shaped at the local level by superintendents, who are hired by school committees. School committees are elected by voters in the community. Consequently, introduction of educational change, along with the necessary budgetary adjustments, must eventually have public support.

Each of the following instructional models has been used successfully with students with mild disabilities and nondisabled students. None is foolproof. The selection of a specific instructional model should come after a careful review of educational goals, schoolwide resources, and student need.

Direct Instruction

Direct instruction, also referred to as mastery learning, refers to a variety of carefully sequenced, teacher-directed methods. The research of Rosenshine and

Stevens (1984) indicated that when teachers follow a hierarchy of instructional steps in their lessons, low-achieving students increase achievement in basic skills.

Direct instruction utilizes teacher demonstration, guided practice, and feedback. According to Larivee (1988), direct instruction includes:

1. *Teacher demonstration*—Provide clear, controlled presentations of new material. Model each step of the material to be learned.
2. *Guided practice*—Follow the demonstration, ask questions, and check student understanding of material.
3. *Feedback*—Circulate among students as they work on independent activities related to the new material. Provide corrective feedback on their work. Use frequent cumulative review.

The work of Madeline Hunter and her Instructional Theory into Practice (ITIP) instructional model is an example of a direct instruction program that has been implemented in thousands of schools throughout the country. Hunter stated that teachers were first and foremost decision makers and teaching decisions should be informed by educational research. Hunter's ITIP system divided teaching into practical lists and sublists that teachers follow as they make decisions about how and what to teach. Hunter organized the teaching act into seven components:

1. Knowledge of human growth and development
2. Content
3. Classroom management
4. Materials
5. Planning
6. Human relations
7. Instructional skills

These components identify the kinds of decisions a teacher makes minute-by-minute in the classroom. Hunter encouraged teachers to use data from learning situations to augment teaching decisions and increase student mastery. Hunter summarized her approach in an interview with Mark Goldberg, ". . . all of the 5,000 decisions a teacher makes every day fall neatly into three categories: what you are going to teach, which we call a content category; what the students are going to do to learn it and to let you know that they've learned it, which we call learning behavior category; and what you as the teacher will do to facilitate and escalate that learning, which is called a teaching behavior category" (Goldberg, 1990, 41).

In their summary of direct instruction for students with mild disabilities, Bickel and Bickel (1986) noted, "Effective teachers take an active role in creating a positive, expectant, and orderly classroom environment in which learning takes place." Teachers' control time management, signal when academic work will begin, maintain a group focus, expect students to be accountable, and provide a variety of instructional tasks. Direct instruction is based on teacher control of instruction and close supervision of student work. It has produced good results in teaching basic skills, and raising standardized test scores. Critics maintain that direct instruction stifles student initiative and that it doesn't teach higher-level thinking skills. Critics also express concern that direct instruction undercuts motivation by reinforcing student dependence on the teacher (Knapp, Turnbull, & Shields, 1990). The following instructional models are teacher directed, and incorporate one or more principles of direct instruction.

Multisensory Instruction

Many students with mild disabilities have severe reading problems. Within the field of learning disabilities, multisensory approaches to teaching reading are well regarded. Multisensory instruction is based on the premise that the more senses involved, the more efficient the instruction. There are many specific reading programs that incorporate multisensory approaches. These programs are often referred to as VAKT instructional methods. This acronym is formed from the first letter of the words visual, auditory, kinesthetic, and tactile. "To stimulate all of these senses, children hear the teacher say the word, say the word to themselves, hear themselves say the word, feel the muscle movement as they trace the word, feel the tactile surface under their finger tips, see their hands move as they trace the word, and hear themselves say the word as they trace it" (Lerner, 2000, 430).

The Orton–Gillingham method is perhaps the best known VAKT instructional approach. This approach was developed during the 1930s by Samuel Orton. Three colleagues of Orton's, Anna Gillingham, Romalda Spaulding, and Beth Slingerland, worked closely with him to develop a reading instruction program that could help dyslexic students. The focus of the program is to teach sounds and letter names. This phonetic approach is teacher directed and carefully sequenced. Orton's approach was primarily tutorial, Slingerland added a whole-class instruction element for dyslexic students, and Spalding extended the VAKT approach to students without disabilities. Spalding's objective was to prevent reading problems (Farnham-Diggory, 1992). The durability of the VAKT approach to reading is testimony to its usefulness with students with mild disabilities and "high risk" learners.

The Wilson Reading Program is closely related to Orton–Gillingham. Students learn encoding and decoding skills through a 12-step, sequenced program. Specifically, the Wilson method focuses on phonological awareness, phonology, and total word structure. The Wilson reading approach is designed for learners after grade three. A distinctive feature of the Wilson method is a sound tapping system to help students differentiate phonemes. The linking of decoding skills with multisensory learning activities provides a strong basis for remediation of reading problems. VAKT-type reading programs present a systematic approach to correcting reading difficulties that are neurological-based auditory processing problems that appear as problems related to phonemic awareness, decoding, and encoding.

Task Analysis

Task analysis is the process of breaking a learning task down into its component parts and teaching each part as a distinct skill. It is often used by sports instructors in teaching such activities as tennis, golf, and skiing. The premise that a hierarchy of subskills underlies mastery of a learning task (e.g., to win a tennis match, to shoot par on a golf course, to ski expert slopes) is the pedagogical foundation of task analysis. By arranging skills in a hierarchy, each skill builds on the next. Task analysis is a sequenced, systematic approach to teaching, which provides opportunities for evaluation of each subskill. When using task analysis the teacher will need to:

1. write a behavioral statement about the learning task (e.g., to be able to divide three-digit numbers with 90 percent accuracy),
2. design an outline of the learning task broken down into a hierarchy of subskills,
3. evaluate student abilities in relationship to each of the subskills before instruction,
4. select materials and procedures for teaching each subskill,
5. provide feedback to students about subskill development,
6. evaluate acquisition of each subskill through systematic monitoring.

Students generally have some prior knowledge and skills when they begin instruction. Teachers who use task analysis define the task that the student will perform, state the conditions under which the task will occur, and show the criterion measurement required for mastery. Task analysis identifies a sequence of skills needed to perform a task successfully; criterion measurements identify whether the student possesses the necessary skills or knowledge for that task. The level of performance that is acceptable is the "criterion level," and it is often specified on the student's individualized education plan (IEP).

Through task analysis, the teacher can plan learning activities in the order in which they need to be learned to reach mastery as indicated on the student's IEP. (See Chapter 8 for a description of IEP development.) The criterion set for determining mastery of the behavioral objective can be measured by using criterion-referenced testing, or some other informal, curriculum-based type of assessment.

Precision Teaching

Ogden Lindsley observed that learning can be enhanced by frequent, self-recorded responses on standardized charts. He encouraged teachers to concentrate on rate of responses instead of percentages of correct responses. Lindsley recommended that teachers teach their students to record their own rate of learning on standardized charts (Lindsley, 1990).

Lindsley designed precision teaching around a framework of behavior modification developed by B. F. Skinner. This framework consists of six basic components:

1. By assessing daily performance, teachers can directly measure performance and monitor learning.
2. Calculating rate of response (i.e., the number of correct responses per minute) establishes a consistent measure of behavior.
3. A standard chart format provides a visual display of performance patterns.
4. Definitions of behavior are descriptive and functional.
5. Analysis of instruction is ongoing.
6. The emphasis is on building appropriate and useful behavior, rather than focusing on doing away with undesired or inappropriate behavior.

> Jamie is a fifth-grade student at Somewhere Elementary School, U.S.A. Five days a week, Monday through Friday, Jamie reads aloud, answers math problems, and spells words dictated by her teacher. Each of these tasks is timed, and Jamie plots her own scores on separate graphs for reading, math, and spelling. A line is extended from the points where other scores have been plotted (Figure 7.1). This procedure enables her teacher to visually track Jamie's learning rate. Jamie and her classmates are participating in precision teaching. Their teacher is measuring their learning performance daily. By seeing the changes in students' learning each day, Jamie's teacher, and others who utilize precision teaching, can adjust their instructional plans as needed (White, 1986).

When students like Jamie are assessed daily, their changes in performance from one timed assessment to the next guide instruction. The more frequently the timed assessments are made, the more often decisions can be made about the effectiveness of instruction for an individual student. Timings are done each day, thus students have sufficient opportunities to demonstrate skills.

Educators traditionally look for accuracy in student responses. Daily timed assessments provide the data to measure both the accuracy and the rate of learning. Wolking (1991) provided the following description of Jamie.

> At the beginning of this unit of study, Jamie answered 20 subtraction fact problems in a minute. She got 13 correct and made 7 errors. Twelve school days later she answered 47 subtraction facts in a minute. On this timing, she got 45 correct and made 2 errors. The learning line for her correct responses showed that she was improving at a rate of 65% per week. The learning line for her error responses showed she was reducing her errors at a rate of about 70% per week. Overall, Jamie's correct responding has improved by 246% (from 13 to 45 per minute correct), and her error responses have decreased by 250% (from 7 to 2 errors per minute) in just twelve school days.

Precision teaching requires plotting scores on a chart so that changes in student learning can be tracked. This chart is a ratio or logarithmic scale, and referred to as the "standard celeration chart." The logarithmic scale displays performance values that are recorded as number of responses per minute. When scores are plotted, an individual's pattern of learning can be seen by drawing a line through the dots. This line of connected points is called a learning line. Generally, the steeper

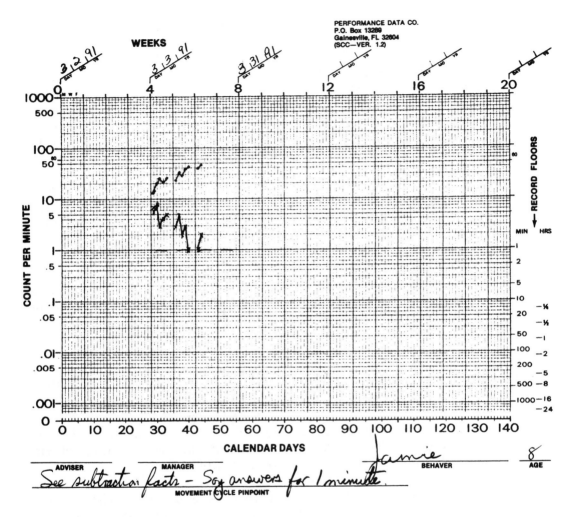

FIGURE 7.1   Precision Learning Chart

Contributed by William Wolking.

the learning line, the faster learning is occurring. Conversely, the more horizontal or flatter the learning line, the slower the rate of learning. The chart is called a standard or celeration chart because the same rate of learning is always displayed by the same slope. Lindsley (1990) recommended students self-monitor by plotting their own data on standardized charts. Two innovative self-monitoring approaches are countoons and software spreadsheets.

Countoons.   Daly and Ranalli (2003) use *countoons* to teach self-monitoring skills to students. They contend that young children can learn to count and record their own behaviors, and seem to enjoy doing so. "When you teach children to do the counting and recording themselves in your classroom, you are teaching valuable skills in self-control, as well as freeing up the time devoted to managing the child's behavior for instruction" (p. 30).

Countoons include a simple cartoon representation of a student's appropriate and inappropriate behavior, a reward contingency, and counting frames for recording data. The representations include a picture of the student doing the appropriate behavior and a picture of the student doing the inappropriate behavior (see Figure 7.2). Any behavior that can be described so a student can count it and that can be pictured simply in a cartoon frame can be used for a countoon. A place is provided for students to circle the number of times they demonstrate the behavior. A "consequence frame" pictures the reward.

There are various ways of creating recording devices for these countoons. A teacher can make a sheet of counting frames which can be copied and cut up so new frames can be added to a countoon for daily data collection. The teacher can also use a file folder and draw the countoon directly onto the inside of the folder. Some teachers use the computer software program Boardmaker (2001) to make countoons. Self-management techniques like countoons appeal to general education teachers who teach in inclusion settings. Both academic and social behaviors can be successfully counted, thus building and reinforcing appropriate behaviors and shaping new ones.

Software Charts. Gunter, Miller, Venn, Thomas, and House (2002) state that "recent simplifications of computer technology software packages have the potential to make it easy for students to record and graph data regarding their academic or social behavior" (p. 30). Gunter et al. (2002) used the Microsoft database software Excel and adapted it for self-monitoring by students.

Gunter et al. (2002) outlined the following self-monitoring steps:

1. Identify the academic or social behavior, the data-collection process, and the extent to which the student can contribute to the data-collection process. For gathering data, students can grade their own worksheets and graph the scores. To determine rate such as words read correctly per minute, an audio recording could be made and someone could provide this data to the student for recording and graphing.

2. On the desktop of a classroom computer, a folder can be created for each student. Within each student's folder are files for different academic areas and for social skills. For example, a student can open his folder labeled Manuel Torres' Data and in it find Excel files for subjects like reading, spelling, and math. Each file contains a teacher-generated Excel spreadsheet with an embedded graph for which the student records his or her data.

3. A desired "celebration" line is calculated. The celebration line allows the student to see if the recorded performance meets the criteria necessary to master the objective in the designated amount of time. This visual feedback is important for determining if criteria have been met.

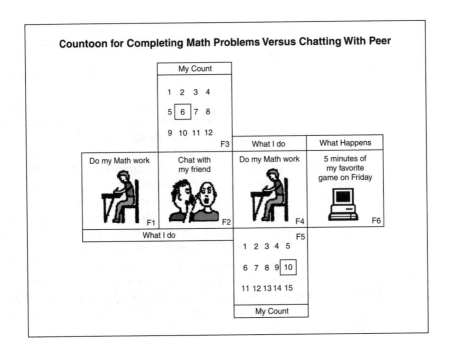

FIGURE 7.2   Countoons

Source: Daly, P. M., and Ranalli, P. (2003). Using countoons to teach self-monitoring skills. *Teaching Exceptional Children 35*(5), 32. Reprinted with permission.

Countoons and software charts promote self-monitoring. The benefits of doing this have been noted over the last thirty years. Moxley (1998) states that self-monitoring by students: (1) provides a clear picture of performance; (2) gives immediate feedback in a clear, visible manner; (3) involves students in selecting behaviors to monitor; (4) enhances communication with parents; and (5) promotes intracomparisons within ones own skills repertoire rather than encouraging inter-competition with peers.

Learning Strategies

A twelve-year-old given the task of remembering a list of objects (e.g., milk, bread, soda, candy) might repeat the words several times in order to commit them to memory. Learning strategies (also referred to as cognitive strategy, cognitive behavior modification, and metacognitive skills) are mental schemes for memorizing, solving problems, planning, or organizing (Pressley & Harris, 1990). Many individuals independently learn these strategies in the normal course of development; others never acquire these strategies on their own. The lack of learning strategy development may be the basis for many of the learning problems encountered by students with mild disabilities.

Alley and Deshler, practitioners in the field of special education, identified learning strategies as ". . . techniques, principles, or rules that will facilitate the acquisition, manipulation, integration, storage, and retrieval of information across situations and settings" (Alley & Deshler, 1979, 13). These authors support the need to teach students how to use learning strategies to improve comprehension and retention of classroom content. Equally important is teaching students how to generalize learning strategies outside of school.

> The adage "Give me a fish, and I can eat for a day. Teach me to fish, and I can eat for a lifetime" summarizes the goal of this approach. The intent is to teach students skills that will allow them not only to meet immediate requirements successfully but also to generalize these skills to other situations over time. (Alley & Deshler, 1979, 13)

Learning strategies help students learn to cope with mild disabilities by providing them with a set of directions for improving their ability to learn. Pressley and Harris present the following guidelines for using learning strategies to improve reading comprehension:

1. Summarize the story. Dialogues and classroom discussions enhance memory of plot and characters.
2. Construct an internal visual representation of the story. This procedure can be enhanced through art activities.
3. Relate student experience to a story.
4. Make up questions about the story while reading. (Pressley & Harris, 1990, 13)

The teaching of learning strategies begins with the teacher modeling the strategy. Students might be assigned an essay, for example, and the teacher would begin by demonstrating how to write an intuitive outline (see Figure 7.3). The purpose of the intuitive outline is to get ideas out before listing them in a sequential outline. An intuitive outline is completed by a student brainstorming by herself. She begins by placing the theme or main idea in an oval, and then writes each idea associated with the main thought on lines that branch out from the center. As

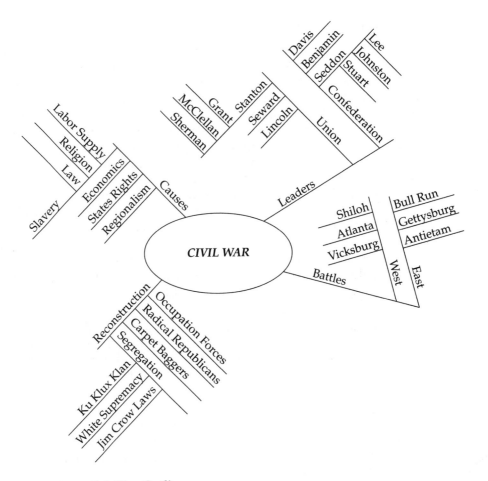

FIGURE 7.3   Intuitive Outline

a new idea comes to mind, it is added to an existing branch or a new branch is started. Just as a tree branches out spontaneously in different directions, the intuitive outline grows to accommodate the natural progression of ideas. This learning strategy (sometimes called webbing) can help solve common problems such as "writer's block" or test anxiety.

Another example of a learning strategy is mnemonics, a system of memory training that helps students remember important concepts by associating ideas to visual stimuli. A student might remember key principles of the U.S. Constitution, for instance, by going for a memory walk down his street and mentally "picking up" due process from the delicatessen, freedom of the press from the newspaper machine, and the right to bear arms from the department store mannequin.

Mann and Sabatino (1985) recommend the following steps for incorporating a learning-strategies approach in the classroom:

1. Describe the strategies needed to solve a classroom problem. (One way to do this is through task analysis—break the solution down into specific steps.)
2. Measure a student's use or nonuse of strategies.
3. Help students implement selected strategies and adjust and revise as needed.
4. Monitor how well the strategy is working.
5. Motivate students to use the strategy. (Scott, 1988, 33)

Selecting the best strategy is a key element in utilizing the learning-strategy approach. Scott (1988) recommends teaching problem-solving skills demonstrated by successful students. She identified concentration, independence, reflection, self-direction, active learning, and persistence as core learning strategies students with mild disabilities could learn to improve their classroom performance. Scott presented a variety of activities to teach each learning strategy to a student. For instance, concentration can be taught by playing chess or other games. Reflection could be taught by having students count to ten before they give an answer.

Story Grammar Marker.   Story Grammar Marker (SGM) is a hands-on manipulative for teaching text structure for oral and written expression. The SGM is designed to be held by the student and teacher while telling, retelling, and writing stories. It is visual, tactile, and kinesthetic, making it a three dimensional graphic organizer. Use of this tool provides students and teachers with a *common language* that connects language and literacy.

Narrative elements of character, setting, problem, feelings, plans, actions, and consequences are represented by icons along a linear linguistic braid. For example, a star represents the "setting" since sailors at night, when lost, look to the stars to see where they are and what time it is. A heart represents the "feeling" of the character relative to the problem and plan.

The teacher can use the SGM with the entire class or a small group to discuss the plot of a story, an episode in a book chapter, a personal experience, or a historical event. When a teacher or student touches an icon, that element of the story is discussed. Connections are made linguistically and visually between the character/setting and the problem (initiating event); the problem, feelings, and plans (critical-thinking triangle); the plans and the actions/attempts; and the attempts and the direct consequence or end of the story.

The visual, tactile, and kinesthetic nature of the manipulative makes it an ideal tool for a variety of learners. The SGM manual contains reproducible maps that serve as graphic organizers modeled after the SGM manipulative. Posters, magnets, an oral/writing activity book, a manual of developmental lessons, a series of card decks, and the ThemeMaker for expository text round out the materials currently available for this link between language and literacy.

Learning strategies teach students how to learn by helping students to organize their thinking and teaching them thinking skills they will use throughout their lives. However, one should be cautious about jumping too quickly on the learning-strategies bandwagon. Much of the seminal work in this area has been conducted under experimental conditions that are unlike classroom conditions. Further research will provide insight into how to teach learning strategies that students can use in different settings; how to integrate learning strategies into the curriculum; and how to design texts to support strategy instruction (Harris & Pressley, 1991).

Student-Centered Learning

In his widely acclaimed book *A Place Called School,* John Goodlad (1984) laments the lack of vigor in United States classrooms. He describes some teachers as "frontal" in their style. By this he meant they seemed rooted to the front of the room, where, like ship captains, they oversee all classroom activity. In describing the culture of school, Goodlad characterizes the teacher as a virtually autonomous person who controls almost every aspect of classroom life. Students labor alone, solitary figures in groups, with little to say about how they spend their days. Many students, Goodlad said, engage in a narrow range of passive behaviors such as listening to the teacher, writing answers to questions, and taking tests or quizzes. Goodlad was not the first educator to describe public schools as havens of autocracy that demand conformity. Demands for changing schools to be more student-centered seem to provide a counterpoint to reform recommendations that insist teachers get back to the basics. For every statement about empowering teachers, such as Hunter's direct instruction model, there is the inevitable reaction to empower students.

Glasser (1985) argued that schools should become more responsive to student needs. According to Glasser, student apathy and unwillingness to participate in classroom activities is a direct response to student impotence. As an illustration, Glasser pointed out that no one has to coerce students to work hard at extracurricular activities. Yearbooks, science fairs, athletics, and debate clubs represent a few manifestations of activities that students engage in with enthusiasm. Glasser maintained that the opportunity to exercise control of extracurricular activities increases motivation and involvement. He articulated four student needs that schools should strive to fulfill in the classroom:

1. Students need to belong. They need to feel a part of a larger community and to feel that they are valued by the group.
2. Students need power. They need to make decisions and have responsibilities.
3. Students need freedom. They need to feel self-reliant and in control of their own destiny.
4. Students need fun. They need to have joy and humor, and they want to work for personal satisfaction.

Notice that none of these needs relates to specific parts of the academic curriculum; rather Glasser is focusing on deeper, developmental needs. It's at the developmental level where student-directed and teacher-directed advocates split. Teachers who formalize student-directed learning in their classrooms assume a developmental view of education. Preschool education is the only sector of public education that holds to a strong developmental outlook. Once students begin first grade and continue through middle and high school, developmental views on how young people learn and what their psychological needs are get mired in a curriculum logjam (Elkind, 1986). Teachers wilt under the pressure to get a student "ready" for the next grade. Achievement tests, basal readers, and an endless array of workbooks provide the grist that students must grind their way through in traditional, curriculum-centered classrooms. In high school, the winds of curriculum pick up pace as teachers bend to pressure to prepare students for graduation and college entrance requirements. The pressure to pass standardized achievement tests increased with the passage of the No Child Left Behind Act (NCLB).

In a student-centered classroom, it is unlikely that students would select the same topics mandated by the school system for each grade. Here lies the dilemma for the student-centered teacher. What is the priority: specific curriculum requirements that are best taught through teacher-directed lessons, or student-centered activities that may overlook content measured in standard tests of achievement? A negotiated solution is workable. Teachers can merge both approaches. Direct instruction on the periodic table is more likely to grab a student's attention after a few experiments in a chemistry laboratory. Classroom discussions about the pros and cons of *Roe v. Wade* can provide the same insight into the judicial system of our country as that covered by a mundane chapter in a social studies text. Cooperative learning projects can cover the same content as a lecture on algebraic equations.

Student-centered classrooms look different than teacher-directed classrooms. Furniture is arranged to enhance student conversation in small groups; cooperative learning and peer tutoring are commonplace. Myriad objects for concrete learning experiences are arranged on tables. While students work, the teacher moves about the room encouraging, providing feedback, and giving directions. Some students are engaged in small groups; others work independently. Work schedules are arranged to allow students to study different topics at the same time. Rote learning, drills, and passive materials such as worksheets and dittos are shunned.

A common misconception of student-centered classrooms is that they are unstructured. A visitor to a student-centered fourth grade might observe the following scene. Adults and students are scattered throughout the room. In one corner, a parent volunteer is listening to three students take turns reading. Along the perimeter of the room, students in pairs are working at several tables that are labeled "math center," "science center," "art center," and "writing center." In another corner of the room, a student is playing a math game at a computer. Two students are cleaning the gerbil cage. Four students are sitting on pillows and reading library books in the "quiet corner." A student teacher is standing in front of the blackboard reviewing fractions with a group of five students. Finally, the visitor spots the teacher in another corner. Around her is a group of seven students. She is doing a phonics lesson. The room is a beehive of activity. People are talking and walking about. Everybody is busy.

To the untrained eye, the scene may appear disorganized, but there is a complex structure that holds everything together. A student-centered classroom requires a well-thought-out plan for moving students from one center to another; materials and themes at the centers need continual refurbishing; volunteers need direction; student progress must be monitored; and the daily schedule must ensure that all students have a blend of direct and indirect learning experiences. A teacher in a student-directed classroom must be capable of supervising several simultaneous activities. The following models incorporate one or more principles of student-centered learning.

Brain-Compatible Instruction

Educators' efforts to solve the mystery about how students think and learn has in the past been hampered by one critical element—our inability to study the human brain in the process of thinking. With the advent of technologies for direct observation of brain function, the brain is slowly giving up its secrets, and the ramifications for educators is enormous. Consider the following information gleaned from the research on brain function and schooling.

■ Students who learn from flash cards will learn better if the card is round. A circle is the most recognizable shape. Circular cards allow students to better focus because the round shape is less distracting than squares or rectangles. (Barron, 2000)

■ Movement is the only experience that unites all brain levels and integrates the right and left hemispheres of young students. Movement increases heart rate and circulation. It provides students with a spatial reference in the classroom, which improves memory. Movement promotes the release of noradrenaline and dopamine. These energizers keep students alert and enhance attention. (Barron, 2000; Jensen, 1998)

■ Thematic instruction improves learning by helping students to identify patterns and build on prior knowledge. Integrating curriculum areas such as the study of rain forests by combining mathematics, music, biology, and geography into a unit helps students learn more effectively than teaching each of the above subjects in isolation. (Wagmeister & Shifrin, 2000)

■ Teach abstract ideas by connecting concepts to students' personal experiences. This helps students link new information into pre-existing neural patterns. For example, a teacher introduced a lesson on ratios by having students make juice from cans of concentrate (i.e., three cans of water for each can of juice). (Westwater & Wolfe, 2000)

■ Analogies, similes, and metaphors enhance learning by linking abstract concepts and visualizations. For example, the terms million, billion, and trillion have no referent in direct experience. Creating visual analogies makes the numbers comprehensible. For example, a four-inch stack of tightly bound 1,000 dollar bills would equal a million dollars. A stack that was a city block long would equal $1 billion. (Westwater & Wolfe, 2000)

- The brain is not wired for long attention spans. Attention is focused in short bursts. Initially, attention lasts for about 18 seconds. The optimum sustained attention span is roughly equivalent in minutes to the age of the student. A first grader's attention span is 6 minutes, sixth grader's 12 minutes, and high school se-niors 17 minutes. Individual lessons should include a variety of components to help students maintain attention. For example, teacher presentation could be followed by student discussion, seat work, group project, and feedback. (Jensen, 1998)

The brain consists of approximately 100 billion neurons. That's a big number that is difficult to grasp. Sylwester explained, "There are about 100,000 hairs on the average human head, so that all of the hair in a population of a million people would be about as many neurons as you have in your brain" (Figgis, 1995). But individual neurons are not the site of most brain activity. It is the connections that develop between neurons (500 trillion by age ten) that powers human thought. Think of individual computers running software on neurons so small that 70,000 could be contained on the head of a pin (Kotulak, 1996). Now connect all of these computers via the Internet and you have an idea of the exponential brain power produced by neural networks. These neural networks are cultivated by experience. As students mature, patterns develop that link neural networks residing in different locales within the brain. It is this chunking or binding of neurons that we refer to as thought. The cultivating and pruning of these pathways goes on throughout life. Sylwester compared the neural landscape to a jungle "where different kinds of neurons and neuronal pathways competed randomly to survive, the way that particular trees or insects do. The message, then, is: for schools to match these messy minds of ours there should be more open-ended work for kids, more conversation, more liveliness—indeed more passion" (Figgis, 1995, 2).

Emotions and Learning

Within the past five years scientists have learned more about the brain than in the previous 100 years. Gradually the fields of neuroscience and education are finding common ground. One of the major insights is recent revelations about how emotions affect thought and learning. These findings are particularly relevant to the education of students with mild disabilities because so many of these students have experienced failure in classrooms. Far more neural fibers project from our brain's emotional center up into the logical/rational areas of the brain than the reverse (Sylwester, 2000). A brain that is faced with a perceived threat is likely to "downshift." This is a biological response that focuses the brain on only what is necessary for survival. When students feel threatened by academic material that carries with it a high anxiety quotient "... their brains perseverate, continuously repeating thoughts or unresolved emotional issues" (Caine, 2000, 59). Anyone who can recall his or her mind going "blank" when confronted with a difficult test question has experienced the downshifting that is commonplace among students who are chronic underachievers in school.

Fatigue, frequent illness, distractibility, and defiance are some of the classroom behaviors observed in "downshifted" students. Students who are exposed to a steady regimen of threatening academic work develop *habitual avoidance habits* often characterized as "learned helplessness." Creating a sense of community and fostering positive relationships in the classroom is one method for countermanding the brain's "downshift" orders. Fostering communal bonds relieves stress and helps students to feel emotionally secure in the classroom. Music, art, drama, and sports help relieve tension and give students opportunities to experience success.

One of the authors worked as a consultant in alternative high school. Students were placed in this program because of severe behavior problems. Getting these young people to attend to academics and to take responsibility for their behavior was a major chore. Yet, while playing basketball during recess these same recalcitrant youths helped each other, managed frustration, and relished the competition. After each game there were smiles, sweat, and satisfaction. The physical education teacher observed that "they seem like different kids!" At least for some of the students who attended this alternative school, the basketball court was a welcome stress reliever from the classroom.

Emotions are unconscious responses spurred by chemical reactions to environmental stimuli. Cortisol, which is released by the adrenal glands, activates a defensive reaction to stress. A stressful school climate can elevate cortisol and eventually destroy hippocampus neurons that are associated with learning. Activities that put students in positive learning states include class discussions, journal writing, stretching, panel discussions, mind-mapping, reflecting, listening to music, dancing, and games (Jensen, 1998). Endorphins are a group of peptides that regulate emotions along the pain–pleasure continuum. They increase euphoria and decrease pain. Exercise, positive social contacts, fun, camaraderie, and a joyful classroom atmosphere activate endorphins and help students tackle difficult academic tasks. Emotions also play a key role in memory retention. Classroom simulations, presentations, role playing, drama, projects, and group collaborations tie learning to emotional contexts, thus enhancing retention of information (Sylwester, 1994). Unexpressed emotions inhibit learning. Students need opportunities to link their feelings to classroom content. Drama, classroom discussions, singing, writing, music, and drawing help build neural connections and inhibit the release of chemicals that interfere with learning such as cortisol, adrenaline, and vasopressin (Jensen, 1998). Emotions direct attention, and attention leads to better learning (D'Arcangelo, 2000). Students who are emotionally involved will learn better than students who are emotionally uninvolved from the content presented. Even mildly stressful situations (e.g., studying for an impending test) support learning better than a neutral state.

Differentiated Instruction

A teacher differentiates his or her instruction by making adaptations which fit each learner's needs, styles, and abilities. Educators who use differentiated instruction are acknowledging that students learn at different rates, that they have different learning styles and strengths, and that they differ in their ability to think abstractly or understand complex ideas. Students can explore the same concept or topic; however, each student needs to have the learning experience tailored to increase his or her learning success. This means that in differentiated instruction, teachers make adaptations in one or more of the following ways:

- Content—what you want students to know and be able to do
- Process—how students are going to learn the content
- Product—how students demonstrate what they have learned
- Resources—the media from which students learn (Benjamin, 2003; Instructional Philosophy and Strategies, 2003)

The role of the teacher in a differentiated classroom is that of a planner and facilitator of learning. Teachers give students as much responsibility for their own learning as they are able to manage. Specifically, teachers:

- Assess students' needs and abilities in a variety of ways (e.g., observation, student conference, diagnostic test of a skill).
- Interpret assessment data to determine students' learning needs and styles.
- Design a variety of ways that students can gather information and explore ideas (listening, reading, viewing—resource-based learning).
- Develop a variety of ways that students can express and share their own information and ideas (e.g., orally, in writing, through a visual representation such as a collage or graphic organizer).
- Provide a variety of options for teacher evaluation and student self-assessment.
- Offer students choices as often as possible:
    - In their learning arrangement (e.g., working independently or in a group).
    - In the ways that they will learn about the concept and the resources they will use to gather their information and ideas (e.g., print resource—fiction or expository; nonprint—audio, video, human).
    - In the ways that they will express, share, or present the ideas and information to others (e.g., oral presentation, visual chart, role play, video production).
- Keep records to chart students' growth related to the curriculum objectives and concepts being developed. (Instructional Philosophy and Strategies, 2003, p. 11).

In summary, teachers and students are essentially both learners. Even though teachers may know more about the subject matter than their students, teachers are continuously learning about the diverse ways in which their students learn. Teachers assess students' attainment levels and readiness skills for learning in a variety of ways. Teachers design learning experiences based on their understanding of students' needs and interests. They then present the material in a differentiated manner, and reassess to determine what individual students have learned.

Some new as well as experienced teachers experience difficulty in planning lessons and in adapting their teaching methods in order to allow for differentiation. In addition, many teachers fail to provide a variety of instructional activities for their diverse group of students. Most of these teachers are "teaching to the middle" in their respective classrooms, without addressing the wide range of student abilities at both ends of the continuum—the accelerated learners and the slower learners. The emphasis in these classrooms is in "keeping everyone together" rather than differentiating instruction to meet individual attainment (Holloway, 2000).

Carol Ann Tomlinson (2000) states that educators can recognize differentiated instruction by the following classroom characteristics:

- Teachers begin where the students are.
- Teachers engage students in instruction through different learning modalities.
- A student competes more against himself or herself than others.
- Teachers provide specific ways for each individual to learn.
- Teachers use classroom time flexibly.
- Teachers are diagnosticians, prescribing the best possible instruction for each student. (p. 2)

Instructional Scaffolds

Students come into classrooms at different levels of understanding and skills inherent in academic subjects. Thus, the learning process is a very personal and individual experience for students, as they construct their own meanings and expand their understanding (Instructional Philosophy and Strategies, 2003).

Instructional scaffolding describes a process in which teachers and students work together to design and to provide support as needed. In fact, instructional scaffolds may be designed for individuals (or for groups) to assist them in learning new skills. Teachers learn to anticipate possible difficulties which students might have. As they move about the classroom and work with students on a one-to-one basis, teachers plan which instructional scaffolds might work with individual students on a temporary basis as they learn the new skill. This may include mini-lessons or breaking down the task into subtasks or steps. It might also include the use of prompts or cues for a temporary period of time. Instructional scaffolds can be designed to help students learn how to identify main ideas and supporting details, ask questions, cooperate in groups, predict, infer, summarize, do research, solve problems and so on (Instructional Philosophy and Strategies,

2003). The scaffold support is given temporarily—only as long as needed. Then later, support may be given at another point in the learning process.

Technology

Individualized Education Program (IEP) teams are required by IDEA to consider whether the child requires assistive technology devices and services. The following distinctions are made for the terms assistive technology, assistive technology devices, and assistive technology services by the U.S. Office of Special Education Programs (2002). Assistive technology (AT) is defined as any tool that helps a student with a disability perform a functional task more easily or more successfully. Assistive technology devices are tools which are provided by school districts when assistive technology services are requested in an IEP. It is stated in IDEA that the AT devices include any item, piece of equipment, or product system, whether acquired commercially off the shelf, modified, or customized, that is used to increase, maintain, or improve the functional capabilities of a child with a disability. Assistive technology services are defined in IDEA as any service that directly assists a child with a disability in the selection, acquisition, or use of an assistive technology device. The services which apply to the classroom teacher, whether a general educator or a special educator, seem to be: (1) purchasing, leasing, or otherwise providing for the acquisition of assistive technology devices by children with disabilities; (2) selecting, designing, fitting, customizing, adapting, applying, maintaining, repairing, or replacing assistive technology devices; (3) coordinating and using other therapies, interventions, or services with assistive technology devices, such as those associated with existing education and rehabilitation plans and programs; and (4) training or technical assistance for a child with a disability, or if appropriate, that child's family.

Special education literature and professional journals are proliferate with ideas and suggestions about technology available for use with special needs students. The following AT devices were selected from a review of this current literature, for possible usage with students in general and special education classes.

WebQuests.　Good teachers use many different strategies to teach students who come to the classroom with differences in readiness, interests, and learning profiles (Albemarle County Public Schools, 2003). When differentiating instruction based on readiness, the learning goals remain constant for all learners; however, learner support, complexity of tasks, and instructional materials are varied according to the individual needs of students. WebQuests are one means of differentiating instruction based on interest. A WebQuest is an inquiry-oriented activity. Teachers can show students how to obtain information from resources on the Internet. Within this process, students can learn how to pursue individual interests while working within common content parameters. Last, students' learning profiles are multidimensional and include individual learning preferences.

Utilizing multimedia and learning centers in the classroom helps to provide information in multisensory and multiple intelligence formats.

Technology can be employed in the process component of differentiated instruction. The process component is "how students learn the content." The following example is given by Albemarle County Public Schools (2003). Differentiated instruction by process may look like this:

> Some students will be using a traditional print encyclopedia to complete a research task in a classroom, while other students use Internet bookmarks collected by the teacher, and still other students use a multimedia encyclopedia that provides audio support. Each of these learning centers may provide the students with the information necessary to answer the question "What are the three branches of the United States government?" but in very different ways. (p. 2)

Widgets.   Miller, Brown, and Robinson (2002) describe how teachers might use what are called "widgets on the web" as a computerized support tool in the classroom. They state that this type of computerized tool is ". . . easy to use, appeals to students, helps them (the students) learn abstract concepts, and can be found on the internet" (p. 24). What are widgets? The authors describe them as small computer programs that are created using an authoring software program, and can be stored on CDs or accessed via the Internet. Widgets are mediation software programs developed to be used by the teacher when interacting with a student in a learning task.

In order to create and develop these widgets, teachers need consider: (1) what concepts they are teaching; (2) what they need to effectively teach these concepts; and (3) what the student characteristics are which would affect the design. Widgets can be used in an individualized manner or projected onto a screen for group instruction (e.g., an LCD projector). They can be paused during instruction to demonstrate, model, or add further elaboration. The authors state that widgets can be designed to tailor what the students need in contrast to programmed computer software that is controlled and sequenced. This instruction can be developed for a broad range of skills and abilities, thus making it appropriate to use with students who have mild disabilities and need instruction tailored to their unique learning needs.

Functional Curriculum

If students with mild disabilities are not anticipating pursuing a postsecondary education, a more practical, applied curriculum may be needed. A functional curriculum includes life skills and teaches them both in the classroom and in the community. When using this approach, basic academic skills are reinforced in a practical manner. For example, math could include paying bills, budgeting, and balancing a checkbook. Reading can be related to assembling appliances, cooking, or home repair. Community-based instruction takes students beyond their traditional textbooks and classroom instruction into the community where they learn skills firsthand and have the opportunity to apply those skills in real life situations. Generally, as students with mild disabilities reach middle and high school years their needs must be evaluated and their curriculum planned accordingly. Polloway and his colleagues (1989) offer the following suggestions for curriculum planning for students with learning problems:

1. *Adult-referenced.* The content should be based on a top-down focus, reflecting curricula alternatives based on successful community adjustment rather than from an elementary-oriented focus upward.
2. *Comprehensive.* Curricula offered to students should include a broad range of topics—generally, a combination of academics, vocational training, social skills development, and life skills preparation.
3. *Relevant.* Students at the secondary level need meaningful programs. A student who can relate academic concepts to his or her own experiences is more apt to understand and then apply the concept.
4. *Empirically and socially valid.* Students must acquire skills that are valuable to them personally, appropriate for the communities in which they live, and meaningful to other members of that community.
5. *Flexible.* Curricula must be flexible enough to accommodate a wide variety of diverse student needs as well as the uniquenesses of different community settings.
6. *Community-based.* Much of the training should occur out of the classroom and in actual community settings to increase the probability that skills will generalize across settings and conditions.

Instead of emphasizing arithmetic problems on worksheets, a functional curriculum teaches budgeting and shopping skills. Although reading is often treated as an isolated "subject," a functional curriculum would teach reading throughout the school day by using such everyday materials as newspapers, magazines, and job applications. Apprentice programs, where high school students spend time in the community working with "mentors" in trades and business, are examples of functional programs that integrate school with on-site job training. Teachers who are successful in implementing functional curricula begin by asking the question, "What do I see this student doing five years from now?"

The Adult Performance Level Curriculum (APL) (Figure 7.4) developed at the University of Texas is an example of a functional curriculum. It contains 42 life skills objectives organized under five major categories: consumer economics, occupational knowledge, health, community resources, and law. The program ranges from elementary to high school and includes reading, writing, speaking, problem solving, interpersonal relationships, and computation skills. Examples of tasks in reading/consumer economics for each level are as follows: elementary— look for ads in the newspaper for toys; junior high school—read an ad for a sale and find the name of the store, location, phone number, and price of the item; high school—read and compare prices of grocery store ads. The purpose of the

	Consumer Economics	Occupational Knowledge	Health	Community Resources	Government and Law
Reading	Read an ad for a sale, locating name of store, location, phone number, and price of item	Read a job description	Locate poison control numbers in phone book	Use phone book to locate recreational program in community	Locate and read list of state and U.S. congressmen
Writing	Fill out a magazine order form completely	Practice writing abbreviations for words	Write a menu for a balanced diet	Write letter to TV station about a program they just cancelled	Fill out voter registration form
Speaking, Writing, Viewing	Discuss saving versus spending money	Discuss reasons why people work	Listen to positive and negative feed-back on personal appearance	Call library to find out if they have a certain book	Discuss why we need to vote
Problem Solving	Use $10 for the evening, which activity would you choose: movies, bowling, or pizza	Decide on job environment: inside, outside, desk, travel, etc.	Role play appropriate behavior for various places (movies, church, restaurant)	Locate the skating rink on a city map and decide the best way to get there	Decide what items have state and/or local tax
Interpersonal Relations	Ask salesperson for help in purchasing jeans	List questions they would ask in job interview	Discuss honesty, trust, and promise; define each	Call skating rink to inquire about hours	Call to find out what precinct you live in
Computation	Compute the sales tax on a pair of jeans	Compute net income	Calculate and compare the prices of hair washing products	Calculate bus fare to and from the teen center	Calculate the cost of getting a driver's license (fee, gas)

FIGURE 7.4   **APL Model of Functional Competency: Examples of Tasks (Junior High School)**

curriculum is to develop student competencies necessary for survival in daily life (Patton et al., 1989).

Everyone must ultimately function in a community setting regardless of the level of schooling pursued or accomplished. This means that life skills preparation is important for all students at all levels of schooling. Many students figure out skills they need as adults through experience. Students with mild disabilities do not have the ability to problem-solve or learn accidentally; therefore, they need to be taught more directly and purposefully (Brolin, 1989; Kokaska & Brolin, 1985; Patton et al., 1989).

Comprehensive Teaching

As long as teachers view direct instruction and student-centered learning as philosophical opposites, the debate about which is the best way to teach will continue indefinitely. A ten-minute slide show on the history of U.S. education would resemble a dance with strobe lights. Following every slide of students frozen in their seats listening to the instructor, there would be a slide picturing students spread around the room involved in different activities. Since the early 1900s the educational pendulum has traced a well-worn track back and forth between direct and student-centered instruction. Teachers who are capable of integrating both approaches into their lessons on a daily basis can attend to the demands of curriculum without forsaking the developmental needs of their young charges.

Glickman (1987) draws a distinction between "effective" schools and "good" schools. Effective schools sponsor teacher-directed learning. They narrow the academic focus. Students are taught in large groups from prescribed instructional objectives. Reviewing, demonstration, checking for student understanding, and frequent tests are standard procedures. Glickman asks the question: Should there be more to school than Scholastic Achievement Test (SAT) scores? And, if a school is effective, does that necessarily mean it's a good school? To illustrate his point Glickman relates the following story.

> A special education teacher recently told me that she had asked her supervisor for permission to take her students on a five-minute walk to a grocery store to observe transactions at the check-out counter. The supervisor immediately asked, "Which specific objectives will this walk accomplish?" The teacher replied, "I don't know. I simply want my students to see transactions involving real money. Besides getting out of the classroom for a while would be fun." Responded the supervisor, "I'm sorry. If it's not one of our curriculum objectives, we don't do it!" (p. 623)

Glickman's point is well made. His concern about the overemphasis of one instructional strategy to the exclusion of others is shared by many educators and researchers. Moreover, Ronald Brandt (1990) observes that teachers have difficulty making changes in their teaching style "like so many compliant windmills on a Kansas prairie." A more comprehensive view of instructional strategies is needed to help teachers integrate seemingly disparate teaching methods.

Harris and Pressley (1991) point out that student-centered and teacher-directed strategies are false dichotomies. Students do indeed need opportunities to construct their own knowledge (i.e., student-directed), but that does not obviate teacher-directed lessons. As Harris and Pressley point out, students will direct their own thinking even when exposed to direct instruction.

> . . . children engaged in the rehearsal of mathematics operations may construct new procedural forms, such as arithmetic shortcuts, while practicing. As students develop skill and proficiency, they do not do exactly what they have been taught. This construction of personalized learning has been well recognized among (learning) strategy researchers. (Harris & Pressley, 1991)

Another element in the discussion of the merits of teaching methods is the uneasy hypothesis that teachers gravitate toward instructional strategies that reflect their personalities. Claudia Cornett observed that teachers tend to choose instructional strategies based on their personal educational philosophies (Cornett,

1983). The research in this area is thin, but there is ample anecdotal evidence that authoritarian teachers prefer teacher-directed strategies, while student-centered strategies are preferred by teachers who have a developmental view on teaching and learning. More research in this area might produce some uncomfortable insights. While researchers labor to determine the effectiveness of specific strategies and college professors promote strategies based on their utility, it may be that teachers select instructional strategies based on conscious or unconscious personal preferences!

Strong and a small group of colleagues (1990) created a framework to integrate five different instructional strategies: ITIP (Hunter's model of direct instruction), learning strategies, student learning styles, cooperative learning, and reading and writing in content areas. Each member of the group identified a basic operating principle that represented the core premise of an instructional strategy. They called these core principles their "declaration of interdependence." From teacher-directed ITIP, they derived the principle that teachers' decisions should be based on verified educational research. From the learning-strategy approach, they highlighted the need for teachers to incorporate reasoning skills in lesson designs. From the research on student learning style, they emphasized flexibility in using a range of instructional strategies. Cooperative learning underscored the social dimension of learning; that is, the sum total of learning in a small group will surpass the learning each student could accomplish working alone. Finally, from the reading and writing across the curriculum literature, they highlighted the need to appreciate the artfulness of teaching.

In order to make use of Strong's integrative model, teachers need to understand how each system works, have knowledge of the learning characteristics of students, and have administrative support for experimentation. Any time a teacher tries something different in a classroom, there is an element of risk. Change is anxiety provoking, and schools are organizations (some would say bureaucracies) that have many built-in mechanisms that resist change. Schedules must be adhered to; school norms must be followed; and principals have most of the power. In a school where teacher-directed learning is the norm, the teacher who attempts to set up student-centered activities is risking failure and ridicule. Without administrative support, teachers must struggle in isolation against the odds. Only in schools where innovation and experimentation are valued will teachers succeed in providing the best of all worlds for their students.

The notion that there is one best way to teach is naive and limiting. Voluminous research that documents that students have different ways of learning should give any teacher reason to pause before wholeheartedly adopting one method of classroom instruction to the exclusion of others.

Summary

Teachers and students sometimes differ in how they view school. While teachers are concerned with long-range successes, students are more concerned about the here-and-now. As children become adolescents, they are often more concerned about peer acceptance than about adult approval. Too often, we ignore developmental differences between students and adults. Teachers like students to adapt to the often unstated norms of public school life; therefore, students with mild disabilities need to learn the hidden curriculum.

Effective teachers are able to use a variety of instructional approaches. In recent years, teachers have found that students with mild disabilities share many of the same learning problems, and that many of the same instructional models are shared by teachers of students with and without disabilities. Educators are realizing that instructional models like precision teaching, direct instruction, student-centered learning, learning strategies, task analysis, and functional skills hold promise for all students. Rather than matching instructional approaches to types of disabilities, teachers are encouraged to match general curriculum strategies to the characteristics, needs, and learning styles of individual students.

ACTIVITIES

1. Prepare a short survey that can be used to obtain perceptions about schools and their purposes. Use it to interview public school students, regular classroom teachers, and special education teachers about their perceptions.

2. Divide into small groups. Each group will be assigned a skill to be taught to pupils. Outline a task analysis for your particular skill.

3. Arrange to speak to several people who work at various jobs in the community. Ask them about specific tasks and responsibilities that the pupils begin acquiring in school (e.g., being on time to school, must be on time to work; being polite and pleasant, customers expect to be talked to politely; and so on). The goal is to help make learning meaningful.

4. Select a theme (e.g., racism), a skill (mathematical), or a concept (science) for a lesson. In cooperative groups design a lesson using each of the following teaching approaches: direct instruction, precision teaching, student-centered learning, learning strategies, and task analysis.

5. Do a Web search of specific instructional models. Contrast the strengths and weaknesses of each.

6. Refer to the No Child Left Behind Act (NCLB). Which instructional models best suit the goals of NCLB? What are the implications of NCLB in terms of teacher preparation?

8 Instructional Modifications

ADVANCE QUESTIONS

Answer the following questions as you read this chapter:

1. How do instructional techniques and modifications for students with mild disabilities compare with those used with general education students?
2. How does classroom time management affect learning? What is the difference between allocated time, engaged time, and academic learning time?
3. What are some features of the physical environment in the classroom which are important for effective instruction to occur?
4. What are some important things to consider when selecting instructional materials?

Chapter Web

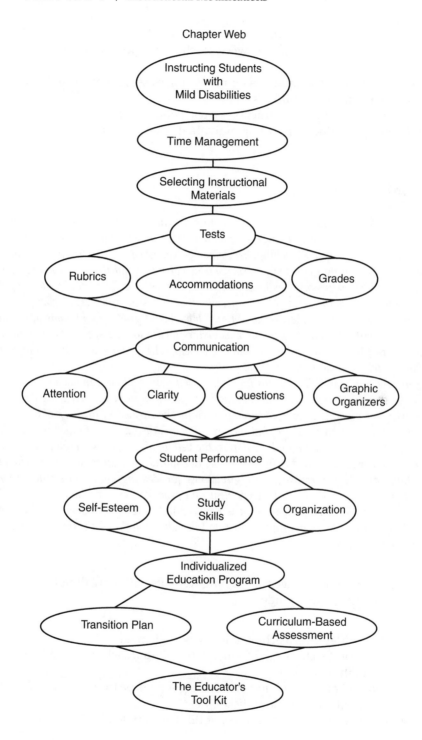

5. What are some testing and grading accommodations?
6. How does good communication between teacher and students contribute to effective teaching?
7. What are some practical suggestions for modifying classroom practices in order to meet the needs of students with mild disabilities?
8. When can curriculum-based instruction be used effectively?
9. What are some guidelines for writing individual education programs?

Vignette: Shirley Allen

It was 3:00 A.M. and Shirley Allen was tossing and turning. Instead of sleeping she was worrying about the conversation she had with Mr. Kane that afternoon. After two years of successful fourth-grade teaching, her principal had asked her to participate in an inclusion program beginning the new fall term. Shirley considered all the additional responsibilities she would be taking on. Her head buzzed with questions. How could she adapt the curriculum to meet the needs of her special education students? What changes would she make in how she used instructional time? How about grading and homework, should she be consistent with all students or make adjustments for the special needs students? She was going to be responsible for helping develop IEPs—how was she going to do that? Fortunately she had listened to old professor Moriarty's warning at the end of her undergraduate course in mild disabilities. "Don't sell your text back to the bookstore at the end of the semester," he said, "someday you are going to need it." Well the time had come. Shirley got up and rummaged through cartons she stashed in the back of her closet. After fifteen frantic minutes she found the text. She breathed a sigh of relief and slowly turned the pages—ah, so many fond memories, the yellow highlighting provided iridescent testimony to her hard earned A in the course. She found the chapter on instructional modifications and began reading. The guidelines for dealing with classroom organization, grading, homework, and IEPs were clear and practical. Half-an-hour later she closed the book with a smile. Apprehension was replaced with excitement over the challenge of setting up her inclusion program. 'I can do this,' she thought as she wearily padded back to bed and dozed off.

Think about the challenges of teaching students with mild disabilities. Use the following questions as a guide.

1. Was Shirley overreacting to her new challenge?
2. How can teachers modify instructional approaches for students with mild disabilities?
3. Should grading and homework assignments be the same or different for students with and without disabilities?
4. What are some main features of IEP development?

Instructing Students with Mild Disabilities

There is a common perception that students with mild disabilities require instructional strategies that are distinctive from effective general education teaching methods. This assumption is based on the "medical model" that characterized the formative years of special education. Just as medicine is geared toward treating diagnosed disorders, the medical model applied to special education was oriented toward matching an educational treatment to specific types of mild disabilities. Students were placed in special education programs based on the assumption that there was something intrinsically wrong with them and that special education instruction would help remediate learning problems symptomatic of specific disabling conditions.

While some mild disabilities, such as dyslexia, are individually based, many mild disabilities are the result of a variety of overlapping issues that are interactional in nature. Poverty, lack of school readiness skills (e.g., mild mental retardation), disorganized classrooms, dysfunctional families (e.g., behavior disorders), and mismatch between instruction and student learning style (e.g., learning disabilities) all contribute to a cycle of school failure that can result in a special education placement.

Jenkins, Pious, and Peterson (1988) wanted to determine whether students with mild disabilities were different from other students. The researchers analyzed differences between students identified as learning disabled and students identified as underachievers. They compared the instructional levels, learning rates, and learning styles of each group. They found more similarities than differences between the two groups of students. Students with and without disabilities had identical achievement levels. Individual students in each group demonstrated considerable overlap in learning rate and instructional level.

> There are not two discrete sets of instructional methods—one set for use with "special" students and another set for use with "regular" students. As used here, instructional methods refer to basic instructional processes, such as the development of behavioral objectives, curricular-based assessment procedures, task analysis, the arrangement of antecedents and consequences, and open education/discovery learning methods. While some methods need to be tailored to individual characteristics and needs, few, if any, can be clearly dichotomized into those applicable only for special students or only for regular students. (Stainback & Stainback, 1984, 103)

Best teaching practices for general education students are also best teaching practices for students with mild disabilities. Teachers in both general and special education have at their disposal instructional strategies to facilitate the learning of students with mild disabilities.

When we talk about students with mild disabilities, underachievers, and other hard-to-teach students, qualitative distinctions among groups are difficult to detect. The challenge for educators is to implement instructional strategies that can change school failure to success for all students.

Time Management

Data about time management are based primarily on research in general education classrooms. Researchers are interested in finding out how learning is influenced by teachers' use of time. Rich and Ross (1989) found that teachers are allocated approximately 55 percent of the classroom day for instruction, but only half of that time, or 25 percent of the entire day, is utilized by students engaged in learning tasks. How is it that out of an entire school day only one-fourth of the time is spent learning?

Jacob Kounin's (1977) research on classroom organization in elementary and secondary schools bears testimony to how time is wasted in classrooms. Kounin found that many teaching behaviors disrupt lessons. He used such terms as "thrusts," "dangles," "truncations," and "flip-flops" to describe common time wasters. "Thrusts" refers to intrusions in lessons. Principal announcements over the loudspeaker are an example of "thrusts" that interrupt lessons and make it difficult for teachers to get back on track. One inner-city school teacher was so distracted by PA announcements that his first action of the new school year was to disconnect the speaker from his classroom wall! This minor act of rebellion nearly cost him his job.

When a teacher leaves a lesson in midair, for example, when a visitor comes to the classroom door. Students may be left with a perfunctory remark like, "I'll be out in the hall for a minute. Turn to page 36 in your workbooks and complete the problems." Kounin called this abrupt change a "dangle." It is the rare group of students who would not take a teacher's momentary absence as an invitation to relax and catch up on some classroom gossip. The ensuing reprimand upon the teacher's return usually wastes more time and creates an unpleasant mood. After such an incident, teacher and students are hard pressed to rejoin the lesson with their original enthusiasm.

Teachers "flip-flop" when they reverse directions in a lesson. Flip-flops may be fostered by strategically minded students who would rather hear how Mrs. Jones spent her summer vacation on Cape Cod than hear a lecture on the "mollusk family." Teacher anecdotes turn into tangents and digressions, which entertain both teacher and students while instructional time is sliced into smaller pieces. When teachers flip-flop, students with mild disabilities become confused and dispirited. The teacher who begins a lesson on multiplication of fractions and then realizes that some review in fractions is needed, may move back and forth too abruptly for students to keep track of the central ideas. Students with weak listening or attending skills will give up and lose the teacher's train of thought.

"Truncations" occur when a teacher abruptly ends a lesson and moves on to something else without alerting students to the change. The conclusion of a lesson and transition to the next topic is one of the most critical parts of instructional time. Many behavior problems occur because of disorganized transitions. Dealing with classroom disruptions is a major time-waster. By moving smoothly from one lesson to the next, the teacher diminishes management problems and focuses students' attention on the next lesson.

Kounin found that teachers who were able to maintain a group focus were most successful in using instructional time. These teachers were able to monitor the entire class without being distracted by minor incidents that could cause the entire class to become diverted, like stopping a class discussion because there is a piece of paper on the floor or because someone isn't paying attention. Such teachers demonstrate "withitness" and "overlapping." They are able to work with an individual student without losing track of the rest of the group. Students describe a teacher who demonstrates "withitness" as having "eyes in the back of her head."

Academic Learning Time

Berliner defines academic learning time (ALT) as "time engaged with materials or activities related to the outcome measure being used (e.g., an achievement test), during which a student experiences a high success rate" (Berliner, 1988, 15). When teachers evaluate students specifically on subjects in which students were engaged, academic learning time will improve. If this sounds confusing, let's look at it from a different point of view.

Suppose a sixth-grade teacher allocates 60 minutes a day to whole language instruction of reading. She has selected this teaching method because she gets high student involvement. At the end of the year, the school system administers a standardized reading achievement test. There is a vocabulary section where students are required to give the meaning of solitary words. Also included are timed reading comprehension sections, which include paragraphs of increasing complexity. The test favors students with strong phonetic skills. Her students are going to do poorly on this test because it is measuring a different set of skills than they were taught. If academic learning time is to improve, then curriculum, instruction, learning, and evaluative measures must mesh. The amount of time a student spends demonstrating a specific skill is important to school success. Teachers who are able to monitor student progress through observation, pre- and posttesting, informal testing, and student portfolios are most effective in enhancing academic learning time. This procedure is called curriculum-based assessment.

Materials that are too difficult impede academic learning time. This is a particularly nettlesome problem for teachers of students with mild disabilities. What do you give a fifteen-year-old, street-wise, inner-city youth, who is on a first-grade reading level to read? How do you reteach fundamental math concepts to eighteen-year-olds who need manipulative materials? One solution is high-interest library books (perhaps with brown paper on the covers) for reading and functional lessons (measuring, check writing, grocery budgets) for mathematics. Students who have failed with the traditional basal texts are not going to improve through drill and repetition with similar materials.

To improve academic learning time, students require opportunities to practice skills in novel situations. They need to see how skills can be generalized, and they need to demonstrate skills in different settings. It doesn't help to teach students to read if they are never going to pick up a book to read for enjoyment or if they don't know how to read the classified section of the newspaper. Berliner illustrates the interrelationship between allocated time, engaged time, and academic *learning time*.

> If 50 minutes of reading instruction per day is allocated to a student who pays attention about one-third of the time (engaged learning) and only one-fourth of the student's reading time is a high level of success, the student will experience only about four minutes of ALT—engaged reading time at a high success level. Similarly, if 100 minutes per day is allocated for reading for a student who pays attention 85 percent of the time and is at a high level of success for almost two-thirds of the time that student will experience about 52 minutes of ALT (academic learning time). (Berliner, 1988, 17)

There are many reasons why students experience lesser amounts of academ-ic learning time. Distractibility, inadequate study skills, emotional problems, disorderly classrooms, and disorganized instruction are samples of the reasons ALT is minimal for students (Copple et al., 1992; Kane, 1994; WestEd., 2000). Students with mild disabilities are placed in double jeopardy when they are pulled out of their classroom for special education services. Unless the resource room teacher is duplicating materials and instructional strategies utilized in the general classroom at the time of the student's absence, academic learning time will be lost day after day, week after week, month after month. This is a strong argument for inclusion.

Selecting Instructional Materials

Teachers are faced with difficult decisions about which instructional materials to select for students, especially those with mild disabilities. When given the choice, Ramsey (1988; 1995a) discovered that teachers most often select materials they (a) are most familiar with, (b) have been trained to use, (c) can find available, and (d) can identify with their teaching style.

Smith (1983) maintained that the most appropriate materials for a teacher to use with students who have learning problems are those which:

- have a logical, hierarchical sequence of instructional objectives,
- are adaptable to a variety of learning styles (e.g., adventurer, ponderer, drifter),
- cover the same objectives in multiple ways,
- pretest to determine where teaching should begin,
- have a built-in evaluation mechanism for determining mastery of instructional objectives,

- allow students to proceed at their own rate and skip objectives they have already mastered,
- have reinforcement activities.

To this list, Ramsey (1995a) adds a few additional criteria for the selection of instructional materials. Stories should contain characters who are the same age, gender, and race as the readers. Young readers will be more interested in reading stories when they see pictures and other illustrations that are representative of themselves, their friends, and their families. Identification with one's culture, gender, and age is important to readers. Likewise, content and vocabulary need to be at their reading levels.

Modification of Materials

Students with mild disabilities sometimes require modifications in materials. One type of modification that is often needed is a reduced number of problems for seat work. For instance, why have Carlos, who works at a pace much slower than his classmates, work out 20 long-division problems when he can show he knows how to do the mathematical operations by answering five of these problems correctly? And when Cathy experiences difficulties with division, why not use error analysis? That is, pinpoint what she is doing procedurally that is causing the same error to occur in several problems. When error analysis is applied, the student has only one calculation error to correct.

Another type of modification is to change the response mode of the questions. For example, the usual way that teachers give spelling tests is by pronouncing words orally and having students write them. Instead, the teacher could give students word choices that are similar and have them underline or circle the correct spelling of words from a multiple-choice format. Or use the cloze procedure where the teacher deletes selected letters which must then be filled in by students. Similarly, the teacher can alter the instruction by having students work at learning centers and use picture directions rather than written sentences. Or use a buddy system whereby one student reads the instructions, and the other performs the tasks.

Reading

Accommodations can be made before, during, and after students read (Figure 8.1). One that can be made prior to the actual reading experience is teaching textbook structure (headings, subheadings, different print, introductory and summary paragraphs). Teach students to understand how and for what reasons these items are employed. Preteaching students the vocabulary words in the context in which they will be read is another way of preparing readers before they actually read. Pair question numbers from a study guide with page numbers on which the information can be found. Use advance organizers to help students look for essential ideas as they read. These can later be used for reviewing what was read and for homework activities (CEC Today, 1997).

FIGURE 8.1   **Instructional Accommodations**

Textual

- Give students an advance organizer, which can also be used for review or for homework.
- Preteach students vocabulary words in the context in which they will read.
- Tape record the text. Recorded text segments should be clear and short. You may want to provide an overview of the selection. Also, give the reader page numbers, and summarize important information periodically.
- Teach textbook structure (headings, subheadings, different print, introductory and summary paragraphs).
- Teach active reading. The student reads a paragraph, covers it, and recites the main point and/or important information in his or her own words.
- Highlight important information.
- Give students a partial outline of important information, to be completed while reading.
- Pair question numbers from a study guide with page numbers on which the information can be found.

Sequencing or Assignment Completion

- Break up tasks into workable and obtainable steps and include due dates.
- Provide examples and specific steps to accomplish the task.
- List and/or post requirements necessary to complete each assignment.
- Check assignments frequently.
- Arrange for the student to have a "study buddy" in each subject area.
- Define all requirements of a completed activity (e.g., your math is complete when all five problems are corrected).

Test-Taking Skills

- Allow extra time for testing.
- Teach test-taking skills and strategies.
- Give alternate forms of the test: oral, essay, short answer, multiple choice, fill in the blank.
- Use clear, readable, and uncluttered test forms.
- Provide a scribe.
- Allow students to take tests on computers.
- Give students the opportunity to practice with the accommodations before the test.

Source: CEC Today, 4(3), September 1997, p. 15.

There are some modifications that can be made to assist readers as they actively read the story or content assigned. One way is to teach active reading. The student reads a paragraph, covers it, and recites the main point and/or important information in his or her own words. Another instructional accommodation is to tape record the text. Recorded text segments should be clear and short. Have an overview of the selection prepared so that the student can review what he or she is going to hear on the tape. Also, while taping, give the reader page numbers and summarize important information periodically.

In order to present content at secondary students' reading and comprehension levels, a teacher might write information presented in textbooks on the blackboard or on an overhead, develop chapter outlines, code paragraphs to chapter questions, and so forth. This is done using magic markers to highlight the main idea, topic, and specific vocabulary words or letters. Another instructional accommodation is to give students a partial outline of important information, and ask them to complete it while they are reading. A review of their responses following the reading exercise is helpful in accomplishing follow-up and provides an after-reading checkup.

Audio Text Recordings. According to Boyle, Washburn, Rosenberg, Connelly, Brinckerhoff, and Benerjee (2002), many middle grade and high school students experience difficulty reading and comprehending assigned textbooks because they have poor reading skills and lack effective learning strategies. In addition, assigned textbooks often have readability levels beyond the abilities of students with mild disabilities. Secondary students must read textbooks independently, demonstrate mastery of content information, and apply previously acquired knowledge to new learning situations. Unlike elementary students, secondary students with learning disabilities and other high-incidence cognitive disabilities must "read to learn rather then just learn to read" (p. 50).

With recent advances in technology, students can now listen to CD-ROM audio recordings of their textbooks. Many have found that traditional books on tape pose several problems. For example, locating a certain page on tape is time consuming, because the tapes have to be approached in a linear fashion. Students have to first find the correct cassette and side, and then fast-forward, rewind, and stop repeatedly as they search for this particular spot, even with embedded "beeptones."

Audio texts have become more efficient due to the introduction of DAISY—compatible digital books, like those offered by Recording for the Blind & Dyslexic. A single CD can hold up to forty-five hours of recorded material, which is about the size of a standard textbook. The CD can be placed into the playback machine, the desired page number entered, and with a press of a button, the machine quickly advances to the requested page. Moreover, the speed of the reader's voice can be adjusted to be heard more slowly or more rapidly.

E-books and Accommodations. E-books are electronic texts containing features that can be classified as accommodations (Cavanaugh, 2002). An e-book comprises three different components: an e-book file, software to read the e-book, and a hardware device with which to read it, such as a computer, laptop, or handheld device. E-books can be created from common forms of electronic text with readily available programs. They are also available through online libraries and bookstores.

E-books are available in a variety of formats. Some are specific for certain computer platforms while others are cross-platform. HTML or text-based e-books can be used in standard browsers. With this format users can adjust text syles, sizes, and colors. They can also search within the e-book, then copy and paste selected text to other programs. Other formats in which e-books are available include Adobe PDF, Rocket, Palm, MS Reader, Mobi, and eBookMan.

In contrast to school textbooks, which cannot be marked in and are somewhat heavy to transport in book bags, e-books are easier to transport, lightweight, have adjustable text sizes, can be highlighted and bookmarked, can be used with note taking, contain interactive dictionaries, and even read aloud. These features allow for many types of special accommodations and adaptations in order to meet the needs of students. The voice output, interactive dictionaries, and note taking are features which provide scaffolding support which many students need.

Speech-Feedback and Word-Prediction Software.   Assistive technology, especially in the form of computer software, can be a valuable tool for many students with special needs (Williams, 2002). Furthermore, according to the author, word processing, speech recognition, and other types of software packages may help students with mild disabilities to participate in classroom writing programs.

The author focused upon the results obtained with a single subject case study. The subject was a student with learning disabilities. Two components were studied: speech-feedback and word-prediction. The Write : OutLoud program supplied the speech-feedback component. It enabled the computer to "read" selected sections of text to students. In addition, this software highlighted each word as it was being read aloud. This component provided scaffolding support for this particular student who often could not remember what he had previously written. The Co : Writer program has word-prediction capabilities and was used for this reason. After a student has typed the first letter or letters in a word, the software will predict the remainder of the word, depending upon supplying a word that would be grammatically correct at this point in the sentence. This program was originally developed to limit the amount of keystrokes required for writers with physical disabilities, but offered the spelling assistance needed by this student with learning disabilities.

Tests

Tests are administered by teachers to find out what students have learned. This in turn helps teachers to know how effective their instruction has been. It is characteristic of students with mild disabilities to function academically at levels lower than their grade placement. Because of this, both testing and grading systems may require modifications.

Ideas for accommodating test-taking skills include allowing extra time for testing in order for the student to be able to process what is being asked and to formulate an adequate response. Teaching students test-taking skills and strategies helps to avoid test anxiety and to build independent thinking, which allows the student to have clear thoughts about the question. When considering oral testing, essay writing, short-answer responses, multiple-choice selections, and fill-in-the-blanks, consider that students vary in their abilities to do better on different question types. Regardless of whatever type of test is selected, it is essential that clear, readable, and uncluttered test forms be developed or chosen. If the test requires writing, perhaps a scribe might be useful if the student has difficulty making written responses. In using a scribe, the teacher is able to find out just what the student knows about the question without the response being confounded by writing difficulties. Another alternative to writing difficulties is to allow the student to take the test using a computer software program or word processor if these would help to make accommodations for the student's area of disability or weakness. It is important that the student be given opportunities to practice whatever accommodation is deemed necessary in order to best find out what the student knows about the area being tested and to avoid his or her being penalized for a disability.

Rubrics

Jackson and Larkin (2002) explain that the original definition for rubric was "marks in red," but today a rubric refers to "a grading guideline or scoring tool to follow in assessment" (p. 40). Rubrics include predetermined criteria for evaluating student work, and provide specific descriptions of teacher expectations for an assigned task (see Figure 8.2).

The following rubric benefits are stated by Jackson and Larkin:

- Students know before beginning an assignment what the expectations for performance will be. The expectations may be assigned by the teachers or may be determined through class discussions.
- Students monitor their own progress as the assignment progresses.
- Students become aware of the quality of work through judging their own and their peers' assignments against the standards set in the rubric.
- Students use the rubric as a final checkpoint before turning in the assignment.
- Students with special needs have the rubric tailored to their learning styles and specific needs. (2002, p. 41)

A number of website resources provide sample rubrics. A tool that can be obtained through the web site http://rubistar.4teachers.org is called Rubistar. A tutorial guides teachers and other users through the process of creating rubrics. Rubrics can be customized for oral projects, products, multimedia, science, research and writing, work skills, and math. For the eighteen months during which they are saved to the web site, the rubrics can be viewed or edited.

Points	1	2	3	4	Total
Title Card or Screen	No title page	Title page is present, but lacks much of the required information	Title page is present but lacks complete information	Title page is present and contains title, author, students' names, and appropriate graphics	
Main Characters	No description of main characters	Incomplete or inadequate description of main characters	Adequate descriptions and character sketches of main characters including a few comparisons among characters	Complete description of main characters including comparisons, contrasts, and complete character sketches	
Setting	No description of setting	Incomplete or inaccurate description of setting	Adequate description of setting including a few visual aids	Complete description of setting. Includes many drawings, maps, and background information	
Brief Summary	Inadequate plot summary	Incomplete plot summary and incomplete or inaccurate story board	Adequate plot summary including some events on a story board	Complete plot summary including story board highlighting major events	
Grading Scale	A=40–44 B=35–39		C=25–34 D=20–24	**Total Points:**	

FIGURE 8.2 Book Report Rubric

Source: Adapted from MidLink Magazine (www.ncsu.edu/midlink/), retrieved January 6, 2005.

Accommodations

Methods for testing students with mild disabilities vary in type, structure, and level of response. Students can be asked to respond to tests and quizzes with written answers, verbal responses, or by demonstration. Learner characteristics often dictate the amount that can be tested at one sitting, the time needed for completion, and whether the testing results can best be achieved by giving group or individually administered tests. Responses should be monitored and expanded from simple recognition and recall to higher-level thinking skills, such as inference, analysis, synthesis, evaluation, and appreciation.

Students with mild disabilities may have short attention spans; therefore, schedule intermittent breaks. Read test directions orally and give an example of the expected correct response. Remind students to review their tests, complete any unanswered questions, and make corrections where needed. For students who have difficulty with traditional tests, alternatives include projects, checklists, discussions, student–teacher interviews, and student-developed portfolios designed to demonstrate student knowledge and understanding of content. Finally, giving brief, frequent tests increases students' opportunities for success. See Figure 8.3.

FIGURE 8.3   Testing Accommodations

Contents of tests should not be altered; accommodations apply to test administration only.

- Segment tests into shorter time periods.

- Space testing over several days.

- Pick the best time of day to administer a test.

- Use enlarged print for visual difficulties.

- Use praise to reinforce perseverance.

- Allow extra time.

- Provide a scribe.

- Allow students to use a computer.

- List multiple choice questions vertically rather than horizontally.

- Use uncluttered test forms.

- Teach test-taking strategies.

- Allow students to practice with accommodations.

- Provide a reader.

- Use alternate test formats, such as oral tests, allowing use of a scribe, or allowing untimed tests.

- Review tests with students to identify test-taking difficulties.

- Provide rubrics for essay tests to give students concrete writing guidelines.

Source: Henley, M. *Creating successful inclusion programs: Guidelines for teachers and administrators.* National Educational Service, 2004. Reprinted with permission.

Grades

Much debate has centered around how the performance of students with mild disabilities should be graded. Carpenter (1985) suggests using the following questions to guide grading decisions: "On what criteria are grades based? What type of medium (e.g., letter grades, pass–fail) should be used? Who should participate in the grading process? How frequently should grades be given?"

Teachers generally include class participation, seat work, tests (e.g., daily, weekly, unit), homework, and special projects in student evaluations. More than one grade could be given to reflect other student attributes, such as effort, attitude, or study skills. Supplement number or letter grades with oral and written information.

A major dilemma for teachers is how to grade work that is completed on the student's functioning level in the general classroom, but not at his or her grade level placement. It is generally agreed that student work that is performed satisfactorily should be reinforced if it is at the student's functioning level and not his or her grade level. One practice is to link grades to the goals and objectives in a student's IEP (Brantlinger & Guskin, 1988). Schulz, Carpenter, and Turnbull (1991) suggest using a criterion-referenced skill list so that specific objectives can be checked as "mastered" or "needs improvement."

Another means of assigning grades is to assign the earned grade and check "working below grade level" on the report card. Yet another way is to reward students with the grades earned but coded with actual functioning levels. For example, a fourth-grade student with mild learning disabilities earns an "A" in reading at the second-grade level (the student's actual functioning level in that subject)—thus an "A2" appears on the student's report card as his grade in that subject.

Special educators are encouraged to meet with general teachers on a regular basis to discuss student progress and achievement. Meetings provide the opportunity to convey to the classroom teacher a clear description of a student's strengths, weaknesses, capabilities, and needs. By doing so, additional data by which to determine grades are provided to the general classroom teacher. Perhaps most important is the inclusion of the general classroom teacher in IEP meetings and decisions. Whenever possible, engage in cooperative grading arrangements so that both general classroom and resource room performances are evaluated. Charting student progress can help illustrate student gains that might otherwise be overlooked. It may help to involve students in their own grading when possible.

Co-grading often occurs when students with disabilities are taught in general education classrooms. The special educator, whether working in an inclusive, consultative, or resource room setting, may make modifications and adaptations to daily work, tests, and homework assignments. Vaughn et al. (1997) suggest that grading procedures and guidelines be discussed and agreed upon during the development of the individualized education plan. They also remind teachers that different grading standards may exist between elementary and secondary level classes. For example, whereas at the elementary level, teachers can consider students' ability and progress, at the secondary level, grading is often done on the basis of established standards.

Special educators are encouraged to meet with general teachers on a regular basis to discuss student progress and achievement. Meetings provide the opportunity to convey to the classroom teacher a clear description of a student's strengths, weaknesses, capabilities, and needs. By doing so, some additional data by which to determine grades are provided to the regular classroom teacher. Teachers need to engage in cooperative grading arrangements so that encouragement and reinforcement for work and effort is given through reasonable accommodations in assessment and grading.

Communication

Effective teaching depends upon good communication between teacher and students (Jones & Jones, 1986). The communication process may break down if the message cannot be heard, understood, or is misinterpreted. When any of these happen, communication exchanges are disrupted.

By using good communication skills, a teacher has more assurance that the intended message is getting across to the students. By being a model of a good listener, a teacher can help students learn to listen and respond appropriately to others. Attention is the prerequisite to listening.

Attention

For some students, special techniques are employed to gain and hold attention (Morsink, 1984; Jones & Jones, 1981; Ramsey, Dixon, & Smith, 1986; Stephens, 1977). For instance, the teacher might first call the student by name when asking a question to assure attending by that individual, conversely the teacher can ask the question before calling the name of a student to create greater interest or anticipation from members of the group. Selecting students at random to answer questions helps to keep everybody alert and listening. Enthusiasm and keeping lessons short and interactive assists in maintaining the attention of those students with attending problems. Some students may be better able to focus their attention when environmental distractions are eliminated or at least reduced and nonverbal signals can be used to draw students' attention to the task. Attending skills can be taught through games that encourage active listening. Arranging the classroom so that all students can see the teacher helps direct attention to the appropriate location. Finally, by paying close attention when students speak, teachers become good models for attending skills.

Clarity

There are many ways in which teachers can improve the clarity of their communication (Gloeckler & Simpson, 1988; Lewis & Doorlag, 1987). One is to give clear, precise directions. Teachers can simplify verbal directions by using shorter sentences, familiar words, and relevant explanations. Asking a student to repeat directions or to demonstrate understanding of them by carrying out the instructions is an effective way of monitoring clarity of expression. In addition, clarification can be achieved by the use of concrete objects and multidimensional teaching aids, and by modeling (i.e., demonstrating) what should be done in a practice situation.

Finally, a teacher can clarify communications by using a variety of vocal inflections. The use of intonation (i.e., stresses on certain words or sounds), and juncture (i.e., spacing of words) can add clarity to a message. For example, pausing before stating key words or stressing those that convey particular meanings helps students.

In situations involving behavior and feelings, the more immediate the feedback, the more helpful it is. Disturbing situations should be discussed as they occur.

> Buddy's father is a salesman and travels during the week. One Sunday evening, he told Buddy all the things that had bothered him during the weekend. His dad did not feel that Buddy had been glad to see him on Friday evening, and he thought that Buddy spent too much time with his friends instead of with him on Saturday and Sunday. Buddy felt that he was being "dumped on" and that his good traits were overlooked, so he withdrew and pouted. Communication ended and nothing was really resolved between Buddy and his dad.

Had Buddy's father talked with him throughout the weekend as things occurred, perhaps his feelings of being left out of his son's life could have been resolved. Had Buddy known how his father felt earlier, he could have reassured him by doing something special with him.

Johnson (1972) gives several suggestions that teachers can use when providing feedback. First, give a student only the amount of feedback that he or she can understand at that time. Overloading a student with feedback reduces chances that the feedback will be used. Second, describe what happened rather than making judgmental evaluations about the situation. For instance, "You need to be sure to pronounce clearly the words at the end of your sentences," rather than, "You don't make a good public speaker." Last, give objective feedback—avoid moralizing. Do not make personal judgments about statements made by the students or their behavior. Instead, give the students descriptive feedback; for example, "Johnny, the rule says you need your pencil and paper ready to begin work," rather than, "You always forget your notebook!"

Questions

Berliner (1979) found that the cognitive thinking level of the questions that teachers ask is typically low rather than high. For example, a lower-level question asks for a literal answer, such as "Who was the first astronaut?" A higher-level question requires a student to apply knowledge, analyze and synthesize information, or make evaluations and interpretations. For instance, "Why do astronauts weigh less in space than on Earth?" requires students to apply their knowledge of gravity. Both lower- and higher-level cognitive questions are relevant and are needed in classroom learning; however, teachers may need to focus on asking more higher-level questions.

Asking lower-level questions encourages student participation and builds factual knowledge. From these bases of knowledge, higher-order questions stimulate and facilitate the development of more sophisticated thinking—such as analyzing or evaluating an idea. In the long run, students achieve considerably more when their thinking is heightened and expanded.

Regardless of the level of a question, Belch (1975) suggests strategies for improving teachers' questioning skills.

1. Ask questions that require more than a yes or no response.
2. Allow sufficient time for students to deliberate the question.
3. Reword or restate questions when students fail to respond or respond incorrectly.
4. Challenge student responses in a professional way. Avoid giving "putdowns" or other belittling responses.
5. Direct questions to all students and not just to volunteers or the brighter ones.
6. Try to sequence your questions. Encourage students to use logical thinking and build one question on another, or build one question on the answer given to a previous question.

Graphic Organizers

Graphic organizers are a specific instructional organization tool which have been used successfully with students in both general and special education classrooms. These students have learning needs which span across a continuum, yet most are expected to learn the same content as their peers.

Many textbooks and curriculum guides provide reproducible graphic organizers; however, Baxendell (2003) states that these often contain too much information for some learners. The author suggests using computer drawing programs or Inspiration 6 (a computer program for creating graphic organizers), in order to design and customize graphic organizers to meet the specific needs of students. To make a main-idea-and-detail chart, Baxendell says to identify the main idea as the central concept and place the details off center. By doing so, the students have a visual reminder of the hierarchical relationship between the concepts. The same approach is used for cause-and-effect diagrams and sequence charts. The use of arrows, lines, and numbers assists students in seeing the flow of ideas. By labeling the relationships and concepts, students can better understand and internalize particular content.

Sequence charts can be used to display the chain of events in various academic areas. Baxendell states, "We use them in reading to review the key elements in a story, in writing to organize 'how to' paragraphs or short stories, and in social studies to create time lines" (p. 50). Students can be assisted in visualizing steps in math multistep word problems or calculations, as well as procedures in scientific experiments. Baxendell also uses the sequence chart in pre- and post-field-trip activities. Before going on the field trip, the chart helps students to anticipate what they will be doing during the day. After returning from the field trip, students (individually, in small groups, or class as a whole) can create their own sequence chart of what they did and learned. An essential component in student understanding of the information is to have all flow going in one direction, either from left to right or from top to bottom.

The most common of the compare-and-contrast graphic organizers is the Venn Diagram. This diagram offers a visual display of the similarities and differences between two or three main ideas, and can be used across the curriculum in most subject areas. For example, in literature, Venn Diagrams can be used to compare characters, stories, genres, problems, and solutions. In science, they can be used to differentiate between animal types or kingdoms, body parts, weather systems, planets, or ecosystems. Social studies, reading, writing, languages, physical education, math—the application to subject matter in all of these areas of the curriculum will be beneficial. The author believes that use of graphic organizers ben-

K	W	H	L
What do we know?	What do we want to find out?	How can we find out what we want to learn?	What did we learn?
Attributes or characteristics we expect to use:			

FIGURE 8.4   KWHL Chart

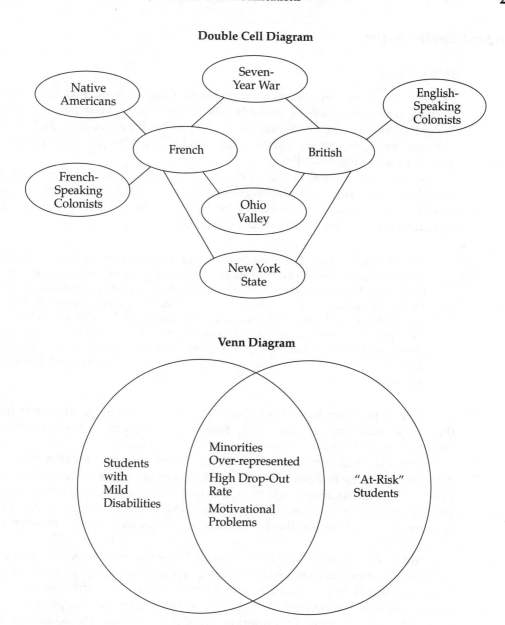

FIGURE 8.4   Continued

efits all learners, especially those in inclusive classrooms, because of the wide spectrum of learner skills and needs. Figure 8.4 provides examples of three types of graphic organizers: a KWHL Chart, a Double Cell Diagram, and a Venn Diagram.

Student Performance

Self-Esteem

Teachers may have stereotyped perceptions of students with mild disabilities; likewise, expectations of these students may be less than what is expected of other students (Coleman, 1985; Siperstein & Goding, 1985). Students often pick up on their teachers' perceptions and develop similar negative stereotypes toward classmates with mild disabilities.

Teachers can serve as positive role models—that is, model positive reactions toward students with mild disabilities in order to create an environment of acceptance and support. Teachers do this by conveying that they want to work with the students and by supporting students' efforts.

> Sara and Juanita have low self-esteem due to their learning problems. Both girls are in their early teens, come from middle-class backgrounds, and are popular with their peers. Sara experiences difficulty comprehending what she has read. Even though she rereads a passage several times, she still has problems answering questions about what she has read. Juanita, on the other hand, has difficulty with written expression. She reads assigned subject content with ease and can tell you what she has read, but cannot write legible responses to short answer or essay type questions. Sara has withdrawn and become quiet in class; whereas Juanita acts belligerent and sassy.

Both of these students would benefit from successes in the areas in which they are experiencing difficulties. By following a few practical suggestions, a classroom teacher can help students such as Sara and Juanita.

First, assign tasks in which the students can succeed, and make certain that the assignments are understood so they can be carried out successfully. Point out something favorable about each student's daily work, and praise efforts, even if progress is small. Whenever offering constructive criticism, recognize the effort that was made and explain the desired outcome rather than just calling attention to shortcomings.

Much of a youngster's self-esteem is tied to social acceptance. Students can make contributions to class discussions by explaining a concept or discussing a topic with which they are familiar. Simulations and role play activities help students to rehearse social responses; cooperative learning provides opportunities to learn with other students. Peer tutoring develops feelings of satisfaction in helping other persons. Grouping students with low self-esteem with classmates who have similar interests enhances social conversation so they can more easily work together on class projects. Providing time for students to share positive accomplishments with classmates and to write daily happenings in a private journal also builds self-confidence.

Encourage students to use computer-based composition so that writing can more easily be edited. Writing on the computer encourages trial, error, and practice. Mark and give credit for students' correct and acceptable work, not just their mistakes and errors (e.g., circle or put checks by correct responses, indicate number correct with a plus symbol).

Study Skills

Knowing how to study is essential to successful performance in school. Students with mild disabilities demonstrate poor study skills (Polloway et al., 1989). Many teachers are either unaware that study skills must be taught to these students or do not know how to teach these kinds of skills (Scruggs & Mastropieri, 1986).

> R.J., a sixth grader, exemplifies this problem. During early elementary school years, R.J. had no problem reading assigned stories, doing basic math operations, and spelling weekly spelling words. Therefore, R.J.'s parents were perplexed when he began bringing home low grades in science and social studies. There was no doubt that R.J. was reading the assigned chapters in his science and social studies textbooks—but he made failing test scores in these subjects. His parents and teacher discovered that R.J.'s lack of effective study skills left him ill-prepared for tests in these classes.

One way to find out if students need to improve their study skills is to ask them questions about their study habits. Stephens, Blackhurst, and Magliocca (1988) recommend using a checklist for this purpose. See Figure 8.5 for the Study Habits Checklist.

Often, students like R.J. read the pages but don't comprehend what the written passages mean. The SQ3R method of study is effective in helping students to

FIGURE 8.5   Study Habits Checklist

_____ Do you have a regular place where you study?
_____ Do you keep a chart that shows the time you spend studying?
_____ Do you have a regular time to study?
_____ Do you keep a homework assignment book?
_____ Do you keep a calendar of tests, reports, and projects?
_____ Do you keep a notebook or folder for each subject?
_____ Do you take class notes?
_____ Do you make notes or highlight material while reading?
_____ Do you review class notes and reading notes regularly?
_____ Do you outline or summarize what you read?
_____ Do you make note of and look up new words?
_____ Do you keep for review all returned papers and tests?
_____ Do you visit and use the library regularly?

Adapted from Stephens, Blackhurst, and Magliocca, 1988, pp. 160–161.

better comprehend what they are reading (Cheek & Cheek, 1983; Mercer & Mercer, 1985; Wallace & Kauffman, 1986). The SQ3R study skill teaches students to:

- survey or scan the material: read the title, first paragraph, subheadings, last paragraph;
- develop questions: change the title and subheadings into questions;
- read the material: find answers to the questions;
- recite both the questions and answers;
- review the material: recite questions and answers daily.

The SQ3R method can be modified and used to help students better understand math problems (Georgia Department of Education, 1989). The student procedure is as follows:

- survey or scan the whole problem to determine what needs to be done;
- change the math problem into a series of questions;
- determine the facts that need to be answered;
- determine processes needed to answer the facts;
- perform computation to solve the problems;
- question the answer by checking the computation.

Reading comprehension is enhanced when students can relate their personal experiences to what they are reading. Since each reader's background will vary, involve students in firsthand experiences (e.g., field trips) when possible. Another method is to stimulate students' thinking about a topic before oral or silent reading begins (Wilson, 1983). Polloway and colleagues (1989, 229) suggest having the teacher introduce a reading selection by saying, "As you read, think about what you would do if you were caught in a flood as Van is in this story." This helps a student personalize a story.

Active reading is encouraged when a teacher initiates a discussion related to the selection the students are about to read. For example, encourage students to comment on a passage by giving their opinions or by having students read a passage and justify or change their original opinions (Polloway et al., 1989). When students make predictions about the story and generate their own questions, their comprehension is improved.

Students with mild disabilities frequently feel overwhelmed with the amount of material they are expected to learn. The teacher can reduce the amount of written work that is presented or assigned (Carbo, Dunn, & Dunn, 1986; Schulz, Carpenter, & Turnbull, 1991). Students can demonstrate mastery of learning material through projects (Lewis & Doorlag, 1987). For example, students can track the position of planets in relation to the sun by constructing a mobile on which styrofoam balls representing the planets are scaled in size and distance from a sun. Projects enhance interest in learning.

Organization

Organization is important for success in the general classroom. Students with mild disabilities often have organization problems. Particular areas in which organization assistance might be needed include: (a) keeping track of materials and assignments, (b) following directions, (c) completing class assignments, and (d) completing homework assignments.

Keeping Track of Materials and Assignments.   *Roberto, a fifth grader, has a problem keeping track of his materials and homework assignments. One day his English teacher gave him a slip of paper that excused him from that evening's homework in her class. He had earned this waiver by receiving good grades on a specified number of prior homework assignments. When handed this paper, Roberto jammed it into one of his pants pockets. The next day, his teacher asked the students to turn in either their homework assignment or their homework waiver. Roberto suddenly realized that he had neither the excuse nor the homework.*

What can be done in the classroom to help students like Roberto learn responsibility? He could keep all of his schoolwork in a large loose-leaf notebook and not in single folders that could be lost. Students with mild disabilities may not have the materials and supplies necessary to begin their classwork. This is especially a problem when students move from one classroom to another for different subjects. These students need to be shown how to organize and plan ahead for classroom needs. One way to help students develop judgment and planning skills is to teach them strategy games like Monopoly, checkers, or chess. Mnemonic devices and lists help students organize priorities (McCoy & Prehm, 1987).

Following Directions.   *Maria has problems following classroom directions. Invariably, Maria answers the wrong set of questions, uses the wrong type of paper, or in some way, exhibits difficulties following directions.*

Before giving directions to students like Maria, have them clear their desks of distracting objects. A cleared desk helps students to focus attention, as does maintaining eye contact while stating directions. Break directions into parts one, two, and three. Provide visual cues. For example, write key words or steps on the chalkboard or on a large chart. Ask students to restate the directions as they understand them. If directions are written, underline or circle directional words. Gloeckler and Simpson (1988) caution against giving directions to a group several times. Students may "tune out" the initial instructions because they have learned that the directions will be repeated. In addition, the instructions may be reworded the second time, and thus become confusing. Encourage students to ask for clarifications if part of the directions are missed or misunderstood.

Students sometimes experience problems in proper sequencing. To assist with this difficulty, keep the number of directions in a sequence to a minimum. Check to see if the student understands the order in which the directions were given. This can be done by listening to him or her repeat the directions in sequence (Gloeckler & Simpson, 1988).

Completing Class Assignments.   *"Class, you have ten more minutes to finish your assignment," said Mrs. Green. Even that won't help Janice, she thought, as she walked by the girl's desk. Look at her paper—she hasn't even written six math problems on it! I wish I knew what I could do to get her to finish her class assignments!*

Some students, like Janice, have difficulty completing class assignments on time. Before looking for strategies that might be helpful with particular students, teachers might analyze how they are going about assigning work. First, is adequate time being given to finish assigned tasks? Not everyone works at the same pace, and some students require more time than others. Therefore, as in Janice's case, Mrs. Green could assist her in pacing her work. After advising students of exactly how much time is being allowed, Mrs. Green could help Janice set a kitchen timer on her desk that shows her just how much time she has spent on a particular assignment, and how much time is left. Or Janice could be given an assignment sheet with two blank clocks, one for the teacher or student to fill in hands to signify time to begin and one for drawing hands to end that task. With either of these time reminders, a reward system for completed work would help reinforce student efforts.

There are several other strategies that help students with mild disabilities complete work. Students need to know exactly when assignments must be turned in. Mini-deadlines set throughout the day alert students periodically to work that is due. Scheduling a brief free-time period before work is due allows some catch-up time if needed.

Completing Homework Assignments.   *Completing homework assignments is a problem for Sheriffo, a fourth grader. It's not that Sheriffo won't do the work—he does what he can. His problem is that the homework assignments given by his teacher cover new concepts he has yet to master. So why don't his parents help him? Well, his father is a sales representative and travels during most week days. His mother works part-time as a nurse at one of the nearby hospitals. The family with whom Sheriffo stays during the evenings while his mom works is so busy with their own activities that no help is possible there.*

The tasks assigned by Sheriffo's teacher are in the category of new tasks— not practice tasks. Because her teacher is overlooking this basic principle, she is handicapping Sheriffo. Students should be assigned only homework that they are capable of completing successfully. Tasks that are too difficult instill feelings of frustration and hopelessness in students.

Cooper (1989a, 7) defines homework as "tasks assigned to students by school teachers that are meant to be carried out during nonschool hours." He states that homework helps students to understand academic work and to remember what they have learned (Cooper, 1989b). More indirectly, homework helps in the improvement of students' study skills, attitudes toward school, and an awareness that learning occurs in other places than school. Other nonacademic benefits, named by Cooper, include the fostering of independence and responsibility. Homework involves parents in the school process, makes them more aware of what their child is studying, and signals support of their child's education.

There can be a negative side to homework. For example, too much work on the same topic leads to boredom. Homework should not deprive a youngster of recreational activities. If parents try to assist their child with homework, their use of different methods from that of the child's teacher can cause confusion. Not understanding what or how to do a homework assignment can result in copying or cheating.

Homework too often accentuates inequities in home environments. For instance, some children do not have quiet, well-lighted places to do their homework; some do not have the necessary materials; and some, like Sheriffo, do not have someone to answer their questions or monitor them.

So what can be done to reap the benefits of homework yet make sure individual student abilities and home situations are considered? First, remember that only practice tasks should be given as homework. Second, when deciding upon the amount of homework, the objective is for the student to practice things learned at school; thus, too much homework, especially if practiced with errors, can be harmful.

England and Flatley (1985) encourage teachers to talk with their students when homework problems arise. They suggest that teachers ask their students whether they need help or if they are confused about a homework assignment. There may be legitimate reasons that preclude completing a particular homework assignment. Some homework do's and don'ts listed by England and Flatley (1985, 36–37) are given in Figure 8.6.

FIGURE 8.6   Do's and Don'ts of Homework

Do try to make homework interesting. For example, practice math by calculating areas of living room, bedroom, and kitchen, rather than solving problems on a drill worksheet.

Do explain the specific reason for homework assignments.

Do listen to what students have to say about specific homework assignments.

Do solicit parent feedback about homework. Remember that parents have to enforce homework and may spend time helping with assignments.

Don't use homework as punishment.

Don't make up spur-of-the-moment homework assignments.

Don't assume that because there are no questions asked about a homework assignment that students understand it.

Don't expect students (even your best students) always to have their homework assignments completed.

Don't give a homework assignment on a topic unless it has been taught in class.

Coordinate homework with parents. One way to do this is to have students keep a special notebook or folder in which homework assignments are recorded. Such a log would include type of assignment, specific instructions, when it was taken home, and when it was completed. Parents might sign the page on which the day's homework assignments are recorded. Keeping a homework log would ensure that parents know each day what their child is assigned for homework. An alternative is to ask parents to sign the actual homework papers, either before they are turned in or after they have been graded and returned to the youngster. Encourage parents to reward successful completion of homework assignments.

Individualized Education Program

In order to qualify for federal funding under IDEA, each state must develop a policy that "assures all children with disabilities the right to a free appropriate public education." The development of a program of *appropriate* special education and related services occurs through the mechanism of an individualized education plan. The curriculum specified in this program must be tailored to meet the needs of the individual student.

The program (i.e., IEP) includes a written statement about a youngster's present education performance, annual goals, a statement of specific services to be performed, dates for initiation and duration of services, and criteria, procedures, and schedules for evaluating whether the goals are being achieved (Figure 8.7). The IEP is developed at a meeting in which the following people are present: the local education agency representative who is qualified to provide or to supervise the provision of special education, the child's teacher, the parents, and the child, if appropriate. Other persons may be included at the discretion of either the parents or the education agency. If this is the first time the child has been evaluated, the evaluator or an individual qualified to address the evaluation must be present (Rothstein, 1995).

The first step in developing an individual program for a specific child is to *assess*. Due to the medical connotation, the term "evaluation" rather than "diagnosis" is used when examining the assessment data that is collected from testing and other informational sources. Testing and other forms of assessment, however, generally occur on a regular basis for each student. Teachers monitor daily growth by informal tests, observations, and other forms of curriculum-based assessment. According to the law, the educational program for each student receiving special education is revised at least once a year. Yearly standardized tests are given to determine progress in content areas taught. The law further requires that each student in special education be reassessed at least every three years.

Transition Plan

This is a part of the IEP that is required for all students who are 14 years of age or older. This plan is written to include skills and services so that the student with

FIGURE 8.7   Essentials of the Individualized Education Program (IEP)

- **Present level of performance**—This statement describes what the student can or cannot do at the present time. This description comes from test results, school records, special evaluations, and the observations of parents, teachers, and the student's multidisciplinary evaluation team. This includes information about the student's efforts to learn and his behavior.
- **Annual goals**—Statements that describe what the student should be able to do at the time of the annual review.
- **Special education and related services**—These are people, programs, and special resources the student needs in order to learn and reach his goals.
- **When and where the special education services will be provided**—This explains how long a student will spend in a special education setting. It also states how long the student will spend in a general classroom setting with nondisabled students.
- **Who will work with the student and keep track of his progress**—This is generally the student's teacher. Other resource and support personnel may be included.
- **Beginning and ending of the special education services**—This describes when the IEP starts and when the next review will take place.
- **Evaluation**—This is completed ongoing until the end of the IEP period. It notes the student's progress and success in meeting his goals. It is the basis for developing the next IEP, if there is one.
- **Signatures**—Parents and teachers involved in developing the IEP may sign their names on the form. The IEP form is a plan for the student's education and is not a binding contract between the educators and the parents. The signatures are documentation of involvement.

special needs can make a more successful transition from one stage of his or her education to another. The plan ultimately helps to ensure that the student is prepared to leave school for adult life.

Those preparing to enter college might have transition plans that include improvement of study skills and test-taking skills, exploration of colleges and their particular services for students with disabilities, and preparation in life skills such as maintaining checking accounts and understanding housing options. For students who plan to work after the school years, the transition plan might include skills like seeking employment opportunities, completing job applications, and developing interview skills. Essential job skills might also be developed such as punctuality, dependability, getting along interpersonally with colleagues at work, and showing respect for supervisors and customers (Friend & Bursuck, 1999). Like IEPs, transition plans must be tailored to individual strengths and needs and they must be updated annually.

Curriculum-Based Assessment

Standardized assessment practices are often criticized for their lack of relevance to instruction. Assessment procedures linked to what is taught in school have re-emerged as promising alternatives to standardized assessment (Blankenship, 1985; Deno, 1985, 1986, 1989; Tucker, 1985; Wesson, 1991; Ysseldyke & Algozzine, 1982).

Advocates of curriculum-based assessment point out the need to target evaluation procedures on content that is taught in the classroom (Algozzine, Ruhl, & Ramsey, 1991). Standardized achievement tests comprise a limited sample of questions that the test-makers believe reflect the classroom's curriculum. If the standardized test-makers are wrong in their hypotheses, the student is evaluated on content she or he was never taught. Curriculum-based assessment is defined as "the practice of obtaining direct and frequent measures of a student's performance on a series of sequentially arranged objectives derived from the curriculum used in the classroom" (Blankenship, 1985, 234).

An illustration of curriculum-based assessment follows:

> Carol, a kindergarten teacher, decided to teach her students a unit on frogs. Before beginning her lessons she asked her students a series of questions about the amphibians. She tabulated their responses. After the unit, she again quizzed her young charges. She found that they could answer 75% more questions about frogs after the unit than before. By evaluating student progress based on their ability to learn the classroom curriculum, Carol was practicing curriculum-based assessment.

Curriculum-based assessment involves repeated measurement of a student's performance on a sequenced curriculum (Research Brief for Teachers, 1988). Counting and graphing are the best means of tracking student progress. For example, a teacher could ask a student to read a passage from a story that seems to match his present reading level. Each incorrectly read word is marked. A final tally reveals that the student knew two-thirds of the words in the story. This 66 percent figure provides baseline data to measure future progress. Every few days, after instruction, the student's progress in reading is again measured. Graphing the results of each measurement provides a visual means of efficiently marking progress.

Curriculum-based data is collected "prior to instruction, immediately following instruction, and throughout the year to assess long-term retention" (Blankenship, 1985, 238). Assessment of student progress in relationship to the classroom curriculum has several uses:

1. Various instructional procedures are evaluated and, if necessary, changed.
2. The data can provide information to support special education referrals.
3. Current performance and goals for individual education plans (IEPs) are written in a straightforward language; this enhances communication between parents and administrators.

Long-Range Goals and Short-Term Objectives.   In education, curriculum-based objectives are developed prior to instruction. The intent of educational prescription is to *prescribe* or develop an individualized education program consisting of long-range goals. Short-term objectives are not required for an IEP. However, short-term objectives provide valuable benchmarks for tracking student progress.

Goals. Goals are projections of how much a student should be able to progress in a subject or behavior in a year. They are referred to as "long range" because of the year's time span.

Objectives. Objectives are "short term" means for reaching each goal. They are similar to the behavioral objectives outlined in a task analysis. The similarity to task analysis is that the objectives lead, in succession, to obtainment of the goal. The objectives are broken into shorter steps than the overall goal, thus, each is attainable in a shorter period of time.

Like behavioral objectives, short-term objectives begin with a verb that states what the student should be able to do in order to demonstrate whether or not he or she has learned what you wanted him or her to learn. The verbs must be observable and measurable, and specific to attainment of the goal for which they are written. Figure 8.8 lists verbs that meet these criteria along with a sampling of some which do not meet the criteria.

FIGURE 8.8   **Verbs for Behavioral Objectives**

Verbs that are observable and measurable

name	contrast
write	analyze
demonstrate	synthesize
solve	label
recite	read
identify	transcribe
differentiate	translate
construct	run
list	spell
enumerate	summarize
compare	participate

Verbs that are not observable and measurable

know	have faith in
understand	inculcate
appreciate	foster
develop an appreciation for	instill
grasp the significance of	show respect for
enjoy	have a positive attitude toward
believe	comprehend

Objectives specify (1) the conditions under which performance is obtained, (2) the learning behavior being performed, and (3) the criterion for success (Mager, 1962). Rather than stating that Alex will decode words at the second-grade level, which is really a global objective or goal, each objective describes specifically one discrete skill that will move Alex closer to the goal. Consider the following example:

Given a written list of one syllable words, Alex will sound each out with 80 percent accuracy.

The condition (i.e., given a list of one syllable words) describes the context for observing Alex. The behavior (i.e., will sound each out) describes the action Alex is expected to perform, and the criteria (i.e., with 80 percent accuracy) identifies how Alex's skill will be evaluated. A list of four to five such objectives would be arranged in a hierarchical fashion, culminating with the stated goal of improving Alex's phonetic decoding skills. Teacher accountability, student progress, and program effectiveness can be scrutinized on a more professional level when instructional objectives are stated in a clear, observable, and lucid fashion. Other examples include:

Conditions

1. Given a list of 20 spelling problems . . .
2. Given 10 math division facts on a worksheet . . .
3. Given a list of 15 vocabulary words . . .
4. Without access to . . .
5. Without the aid of . . .

Criteria

1. With 90% accuracy . . .
2. Not more than 5 errors . . . .
3. At least 3 out of 5 times . . .
4. With 80% correctness . . .

To summarize, a short-term objective

1. states in shorter steps the means by which a goal will be accomplished;
2. begins with a verb that states the specific behavior to be performed;
3. describes conditions under which behavior is expected to occur;
4. indicates a criterion level for acceptable performance.

Once the lesson has been implemented, teachers *reassess*. There are several reasons for reassessing a student following implementation of instruction. Reassessment occurs so that some determination can be made about the amount of progress a student has made in reaching long-range goals and short-term objectives. Reassessment also occurs so that adjustments can be made in the uses of instructional models if necessary. Actually, it is important that assessment occur

TABLE 8.1   Basic Elements of Effective Teaching

Lesson Introduction	Gain student attention. Review previously learned content and ensure students have the prerequisite knowledge and skills. Provide students a purpose for learning the new content.
Instruction and Modeling	Provide accurate, clear, complete, and concise instruction. Model the less objective. Ask frequent and appropriate questions. Include correct and incorrect examples.
Guided Practice	Provide all students the opportunity to demonstrate lesson objective with assistance. Monitor student performance closely. Apply appropriate error correction procedures when needed.
Independent Practice	Provide all students the opportunity to demonstrate lesson objective independently.
Closure	Review and summarize.

Source: Prater, M. A. She will succeed! Strategies for success in inclusive classrooms. *Teaching Exceptional Children, 35*(5), 58–64.

ongoing and accompany daily implementation of instructional programming.

Both the No Child Left Behind Act (2001) and the Reauthorization of IDEA (2004) state that general education teachers need to be well trained and able to work with all of the students in their classrooms, including those with special needs. The excuse often heard in the past that a teacher does not know how to teach children in special education is no longer acceptable. Conversely, knowing how to effectively make modifications and adaptations for students with special needs assures the general education teacher ways of being successful with all of his or her students. (See Table 8.1.)

The Educator's Tool Kit

Many professionals carry tool kits. Carpenters and repair persons have a collection of tools that enable them to perform carpentry and various types of repair work. Lawyers and business people carry their tools of trade in an attaché case. Physicians used to carry a medicine bag when making house calls. We used the tools that mechanics carry in an earlier example when discussing integrative teaching.

One of the authors encourages students in her "methods for learners with mild disabilities" course to construct an educational kit. Many special education teachers now go into the general education classroom to teach students with special learning needs. Others travel from school to school or from room to room in order to teach these students; still others remain in a resource or self-contained classroom of their own. The tools each teacher-in-training makes and places into this kit help that person to be ready with accessible "tools of the trade" to teach students with mild disabilities. The curriculum with which these tools will be used includes mathematics, reading, spelling, and social skills. With the tools assembled, teachers are equipped and prepared to provide meaningful learning experiences for their students.

Each educational kit contains:

Reading

1. A scope-and-sequence or skills hierarchy.
2. A set of basic sight words (e.g., Dolch word list, survival words).
3. A teacher-made gameboard that provides practice and reinforcement for many skills.

Mathematics

1. A scope-and-sequence or hierarchy of skills.
2. Teacher-made number lines, multiplication table charts (wall or student desk size), and an abacus.
3. A teacher-made gameboard that provides practice and reinforcement for many math skills.

Social Skills

1. A set of classroom rules, few in number and positively directed (wall or student desk size).
2. A teacher-made social skills activity that provides role play or simulation opportunities for practicing and reinforcing many social skills.

The construction of tools encourages teachers to accommodate students' learning needs. Commercial materials will not always provide the means for teaching a particular skill to a student; therefore, some teaching aids will need to be tailored and adapted to meet special learning or behavioral needs of many students. This activity not only prepares teachers by having educational tools ready for use with students, but it requires them to give thought beforehand about what they perceive they will be doing in the way of instruction with their students.

Summary

Effective teachers are able to use a variety of instructional modifications. In recent years, special educators have found that students with mild disabilities share many of the same learning problems. There is a growing sentiment that matching specific instructional approaches to student learning characteristics is the best course to take.

Research has addressed students who have low self-esteem, poor study skills, and weak organizational skills perhaps more than other learning problems. These difficulties can be found on a day-to-day basis within most classrooms with students who have learning disabilities, mild mental retardation, and behavior disorders. These particular problems are also identifiable with low achieving and at-risk learners, as well as other nondisabled youngsters. Practical strategies for dealing with these difficulties include affirmation, successful experiences, and direct teaching of organizational skills. The physical layout of the classroom has a significant impact on learning.

Numerous studies have also noted the importance of time management, allocated time, engaged time, and academic learning time. Teachers are effective when they make appropriate modifications in testing and grading practices. Modified tests more accurately assess the achievement of learners with mild disabilities. Student grades should accurately reflect individual progress, even if in small increments.

Effective teaching also depends upon good communication between teacher and students. It is important that student attention be directed toward the instruction being given, that teachers be clear in their instructions and explanations, that teacher feedback be appropriate to the purpose, and that questioning skills reflect good instructional techniques.

ACTIVITIES

1. Discuss a curriculum-based assessment procedure for this course. See how many variations you can develop. Compare curriculum-based assessment for a college course with curriculum-based assessment in a public school.

2. Visit a public school classroom. Observe for an hour and chart how much time is allocated, engaged, and academic learning time.

3. Discuss the physical features of the learning environment visited in activity number 2.

4. List instructional strategies employed that accommodated student strengths and helped to build areas needing to be strengthened in activity number 2.

5. Survey public school students regarding their views on homework. Do they think homework serves a useful purpose? Where do they do their homework? Who helps them? Research the attitude toward homework in Asian countries. Are there similarities? Are there differences?

6. Write a mock IEP on yourself. Discuss the difficulties. Do a survey of special educators. Ask them what they think of IEPs. What are the advantages? What are the drawbacks?

9 Classroom Management

Answer the following questions as you read this chapter:

1. What effects do teacher attitudes have on classroom management?
2. What is proactive discipline?
3. What is positive behavioral support and functional behavioral assessment?
4. What are some commonly used classroom discipline methods?
5. What are some key features of life space interviews?
6. What are some common behavior modification strategies?
7. What is the difference between verbal and nonverbal classroom interventions?

8. How does classroom organization influence classroom management?
9. What are some advantages and disadvantages of using punishment to control behavior?
10. What discipline procedures are required by federal law (IDEA) for students with mild disabilities?

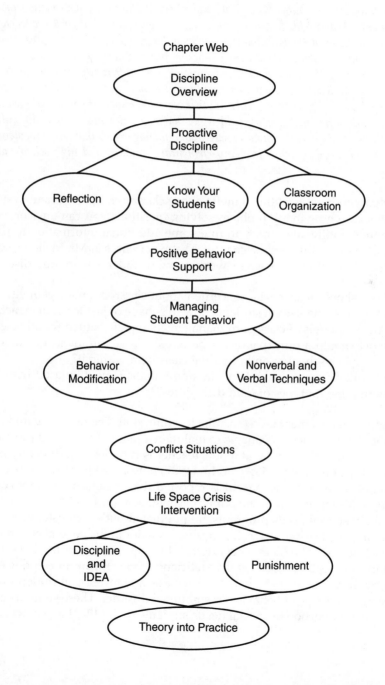

Chapter Web

Vignette: Mr. Mellon

Mr. Mellon has been a principal for 15 years. Each year his teachers have requested "inservice" on classroom management. Over the years, he has provided workshops on discipline, behavior modification, assertive discipline, discipline with dignity, positive classroom discipline, unified discipline, and a mix of other classroom management methods. If you walked into his school on any day in any year, you would observe teachers using a mixture of these methods to manage the complex range of behaviors presented by students with mild disabilities and their classroom peers. You might also observe two teachers implementing the same model, but doing it very differently. If you looked at office referrals for Mr. Mellon's school, you would notice that students in some teachers' rooms are referred more often than students in other teachers' rooms. If you questioned the teachers about these differences, some would argue that some students are more difficult to teach than others. The characteristics of classroom management that are prevalent in Mr. Mellon's school are common in many elementary, middle, and high schools across the country.

Now that you have read the vignette about classroom management systems and discipline, see how many problem-solving questions you can answer. For those you cannot readily answer, try to find some additional information to use in answering them as you read the chapter. The experiences at Mr. Mellon's school are typical of those of many teachers working with students with mild disabilities.

1. Why should teachers be concerned about classroom management?
2. Should teachers teach students how to behave or just teach them academics?
3. Are all models of classroom management equally suited for all teachers?
4. How should a principal or teacher select classroom management strategies to use in a school or an individual classroom within it?
5. Should different methods of classroom management be used with students with different types of mild disabilities?

Classroom management is an essential teaching skill. The most elegant lesson will deteriorate if the teacher is unable to maintain a sense of order and purpose in the classroom. The first signal that a new teacher is experiencing difficulty is usually problems with discipline. Przychodin (1981) notes, "No teacher can teach a class that is out of control, and once it is reported that the teacher cannot control the classroom his reputation in the public eye begins to decline."

Many special needs programs are populated with youngsters who were referred for discipline problems. Disruptive behavior in the general classroom is the fast track to special education services. Although classroom teachers may have tolerance for weak academic skills, deficiencies in self-control can quickly strain teacher patience. Since 1977 there has been a steady increase in students identified as having some type of behavior or emotional disorder. These students constitute the highest proportion of special needs students in the 12–21 age bracket.

Educators have a penchant for labeling behavior problems, and those labels have a way of intimidating even the most sanguine teacher. Such terms as emotionally disturbed, attention deficit disorder, hyperactive, and conduct disordered have a common theme—the youngster needs help with discipline. How is a teacher to manage a classroom with youngsters such as these? The answer actually is quite simple—look behind the label for the child. Labels are deceptive. They obscure the truth by implying that a student is qualitatively different from others. All students, with and without educational labels, have similar needs. Every student needs attention; every student needs success; every student needs recognition.

This chapter will describe behavior management practices that have proved useful with all students. Many of the strategies were designed specifically for youngsters with behavior and emotional disorders. Other strategies were developed within general education. This blend of general and special education discipline practices will provide you with a functional guide for teaching students with mild disabilities.

Not since the influx of immigrants at the beginning of the twentieth century have Americans been so culturally and linguistically diverse. Nearly one-fifth of Americans speak a language other than English (Garcia, 1999). In 2005, according to the Interagency Forum on Child and Family Statistics, 16 percent of children under 18 were Black and 19 percent were Hispanic. The Interagency predicts that in 2020 Black children will constitute 15 percent of children under 18 while the percentage of Hispanic children under 18 will increase to 24 percent (www .childstats.gov, retrieved January 15, 2005).

The teacher who says, "I treat all students the same," and then proceeds to try to get them to conform to a rigid set of behavioral expectations will be continually frustrated. Like Sisyphus, the mythical king whose eternal punishment was to roll a rock to the top of the hill only to have it roll back down again, the educator who presses for obedience will put much effort into a futile task. Young people are resilient and resourceful. They may bend to a heavy hand, but they will end up resenting any system of discipline that overlooks their culture, their personal needs, or their integrity.

Discipline—An Overview

All students, at some time, present behavioral challenges to teachers. Incidents can range from a few cases of noncompliance to serious emotional problems. All teachers, whether general or special education, need a diverse array of classroom management skills to facilitate learning. In their survey of teacher burnout, Feiter and Tokar (1982) reported 58 percent of teachers polled said that student misbehavior was the primary cause of their job-related stress (Baker, 1985, 484). The following remarks by Amanda, a graduate student working toward her M.Ed. in education, illustrate the psychological impact of discipline problems on a beginning teacher.

At the breakfast table last week, I was talking incessantly about how well I was doing in my courses at the college and about how all of the information I was getting about teaching was finally coming together. I was sure that I was soon going to be an English teacher extraordinaire, just like Robin Williams' character in the film *Dead Poet's Society*. My husband was staring at me with his cold, calculating eyes and I knew what was coming; we had this conversation before. "What will you do when some kid acts up in your first class?" he asked, a knowing smile on his lips. "Well that's easy," I said, "I will handle it in as mature and responsible a way as you would expect from someone of my obvious mental stature." And I smiled, but my husband did not. "You'll cry," he said, and then he smiled. (Leverault, 1990)

Every teacher would like a class full of motivated, well-adjusted young scholars. But as Amanda's breakfast conversation with her husband indicates, the more realistic expectation is that public school teaching requires intestinal fortitude as well as good teaching skills.

Students are impressionable human beings with complex life histories. Some urban schools have metal detectors to screen students for weapons. However, there is no method for screening such emotional baggage as hostility or despair. These burdens cannot be checked at the schoolhouse door. Poverty undermines hope. Drug abuse scorches intellectual ability. Dysfunctional families thwart personal development (Menacker, Weldon, & Hurwitz, 1989). Even students who are raised in the best conditions experience emotional ups and downs.

There is no easy life. All young people must grapple with the distress that accompanies growth. The metaphor "growing pains" refers to more than pinched toes from tight fitting shoes. Personal growth requires persistence, mentoring, and opportunity. It is hard work for both student and teacher. Growth is first an emotional and second an intellectual experience. Before students can learn, they need an emotional base of security, trust, and self-confidence. It is the classroom teacher's responsibility to nurture these feelings in some students and teach them to others.

Proactive Discipline

Many discussions about school discipline begin with what the teacher should do after a student is disruptive. Proactive discipline focuses on teacher actions that will decrease classroom disruptions. Proactive discipline is defined as a classroom management system designed to promote student self-control by focusing teacher intervention at the cause of discipline problems and by teaching prosocial skills.

Many proactive teachers use prompts and pre-instructional routines to prevent misbehavior. For example, a teacher was recently observed always reminding his students of one of the classroom rules (i.e., keeping hands and feet to self) before transitioning to a new activity. He explained the appropriate behavior for the upcoming task: "OK, now we are going to start something new. You are going to have to move from your seat to the Life Sciences Center. As we are doing this, please remember Rule #3: Keep hands and feet to self. I know we can all do this." Another teacher used a similar pre-instructional routine to provide structure and prevent misbehavior. For example, prior to taking her students to the Media Center, she reviewed how she expected them to behave in the hallway and how she expected them to behave in another teacher's room. She asked students for examples of how to behave (and how not to behave) and reminded them of the consequences of appropriate and inappropriate behavior. Prompts and pre-instructional routines are simple ways many teachers reduce the likelihood of misbehavior and prevent discipline problems. Other systematic use of proactive discipline requires self-knowledge, knowledge of student strengths and weaknesses, and knowledge of how classroom structure can influence behavior.

Reflection

Kohn (1991) points out that what a teacher believes about the nature of his or her students can have a profound effect on how classroom management is handled. The teacher who believes students need to be taught obedience will emphasize teacher control of student behavior. Many teachers use rewards and punishment as external motivators to encourage conformity. In such classrooms the teacher makes the rules, determines sanctions, and doles out justice. Student behavior is controlled by teacher power.

Authoritarian Discipline

The authoritarian approach to discipline is commonplace in schools and widely accepted. Some parents select schools based on the premise that their children will get "old fashioned discipline." Although authoritarian tactics have admirers and detractors, the use of such teaching practices is rarely controversial. The case of Joe Clark is a notable exception.

Joe Clark was the principal of Eastside High School in Eastside, New Jersey. Each day he patrolled the halls of Eastside with a bullhorn. His motto, "There's only one way—my way," hung on his office door as a stern reminder that Joe Clark was a tough disciplinarian. Before Joe Clark came to Eastside, the school was in chaos. Fights and drug deals were routine in the halls of this inner-city school. Learning was almost nonexistent. Each year Eastside students tallied pathetically low on standardized tests of achievement.

After his arrival, Clark, a retired Army sergeant, quickly took charge. In one incident, he suspended sixty students without notifying the school board. He locked school doors—a fire code violation—to bar intruders. As a result of Clark's tough tactics, 1,900 students either dropped out or were expelled from Eastside. To some, including former Secretary of Education William Bennett, Joe Clark was a hero—an example of a no-nonsense disciplinarian in action. The remaining students at Eastside walked the school hallways without fear, and their standardized test scores improved. Other educators argued that Joe Clark did not solve problems; he merely transferred them from the halls of his school to the streets of his community. After a deluge of positive and negative media attention, Joe Clark resigned. He was commended by President Reagan and a movie was made of his exploits as principal of Eastside. Is Joe Clark a pedagogical hero or villain? He got results, but did the end justify his means?

Albert Shanker, past president of the American Federation of Teachers, believed Joe Clark created more problems than he solved. According to Shanker, punishments, suspensions, and expulsions become necessary when schoolwork ceases to be relevant for students. When students are made to sit still and listen quietly for four to six hours every day, when they are hopelessly behind the rest of the class with no chance to catch up, classroom disruptions are inevitable. Shanker believed many classroom disruptions can be traced to student apathy, student frustration, and lack of student control over daily events. Shanker's wry comment that teachers are the most powerful people in the world "because who else can tell 200 people exactly when they can go to the bathroom?" succinctly captures the essence of discipline codes in some classrooms.

Teacher Values

Classroom management practices are saturated in values (Morse, 1987). Each time a teacher reacts to a classroom disruption, a hidden message is embedded in the teacher's action. Sometimes the message is autocratic, "You need to behave because I say so." With other teachers, the message is humanistic, "I expect you to be responsible for your actions." When teachers act in anger, the hidden message is, "I can't control myself either." This is the most unsettling message of all because students first and foremost need the security of knowing the teacher is in control. When teachers punish students, the embedded message is, "You can't control your behavior, so I must do it for you." Punishment accompanied with anger creates stress among students, and increases the likelihood of further discipline problems (Henley, 2005; Kohn, 1991; Kounin, 1977).

When adults feel secure, they are more capable of responding to the different developmental needs of youngsters. Conversely, insecure adults may feel threatened by disturbing student behavior that is developmentally normal. Rezmierski explains:

> . . . adults who are still struggling to develop a sense of power or autonomy are likely to have difficulty dealing with adolescent children for whom this is a natural developmental struggle as well. Such adults may even have difficulty dealing with their two-year-olds who display what some have called the first round of adolescence. . . . (Rezmierski, 1987, 6)

Nichols and Good (2004) maintain that young people get "a bad rap."

> Research evidence shows that a large majority of adults believe the "average" teenager is "wild, rude, and irresponsible." Though some people may embrace a

more positive view, more by far view the young suspiciously. Even though adults may fiercely love and support the young people they know, when asked about the "average" youths—those they might run into on the street corner, or see in schools across the country—they are more likely to use words such as "lazy" and "out of control." (p. 42)

Teacher Needs

Discipline practices that take developmental phases of youngsters into account emphasize the needs of the students. Some teachers are predisposed toward authority (i.e., power) practices; others are predisposed toward democratic (i.e., co-operation) practices (Algozzine, Ysseldyke, & Elliott, 1997; Lasley, 1989). Before establishing a classroom management system, teachers should understand their own psychological needs. This requires reflection and honesty. Effective discipline is emotionally disengaged from student behavior. Teachers who respond to individual discipline problems with anger, defensiveness, or hostility create stress among all the students in the classroom. This "ripple effect" will either lead to more discipline problems (Kounin, 1977) or produce a group of obedient but frightened learners.

All teachers have pet peeves. Some dislike tattling; others can't tolerate name calling. Fighting is the worst offense in many teachers' minds. *The key action is not the student transgression, but the teacher reaction* (Long and Morse, 1996). Teachers who know themselves are more effective disciplinarians because they don't take misbehavior personally. Such teachers realize that students need to be taught what is expected of them. Canter (1989) says:

> Teachers too often assume that students know how they are expected to behave. Teachers first need to establish specific directions for each activity during the day—lectures, small group work, transitions between activities, and so forth. For each situation, teachers must determine the exact behaviors they expect from them. . . . [Teachers] must teach the students how to follow directions. . . . They must model the behaviors, ask the students to restate the directions, question the students to make sure they understand the directions, and immediately engage the students in the activity to make sure that they understand the directions. (p. 59)

The aim of discipline is to teach students how to behave in a socially responsible manner. Sometimes compliance or noncompliance to classroom routines obscures the real issue. When ten-year-old Jorge consistently argues with his classmates, he is disturbing the classroom, but there is a deeper, more fundamental concern—Jorge lacks the ability to relate with peers. Classroom discipline procedures aimed solely at stopping Jorge from arguing in school miss the point. Jorge needs to learn how to socialize with others both in and out of school. In Chapter Ten, we describe strategies that help teachers manage behavior problems while promoting the development of such prosocial skills as maintaining peer relationships.

Know Your Students

The Phi Delta Kappa Commission on Discipline (1982) had this to say about good discipline practices:

> Educators in well-disciplined schools know that behavior is caused. When misbehavior occurred, the principal and faculty tended to go beyond merely punishing students for the misbehavior. They searched for probable causes and they addressed them. They improved discipline in their schools by taking steps to remove those causes and by establishing activities within their school and community that would result in good behavior. (p. 12)

Discipline is a double-edged sword, it cuts both ways. Students have an obligation to cooperate and allow others to learn. Teachers and administrators have a duty to understand their students and to deal with disruptions in a fair and equitable manner. Teachers who believe students need to learn to be responsible for their own behavior work to help students to develop inner controls. These classrooms are characterized by a respect for student differences. Discipline is approached as a process rather than an end in itself (Henley, 1987). In this context, students are encouraged to develop social skills that will help them to adapt not only to the classroom, but also to the world at large. Cooperation, decision making, and accountability for behavior are skills emphasized by teachers who believe discipline should be a learning experience.

One Teacher's Experience.   Herbert Kohl took his first public school teaching assignment in an inner-city sixth grade. His thirty-six students were academic failures who saw no connection between their lives on the streets of Harlem and the pristine view of America depicted in their textbooks. Over time, Kohl came to recognize that effective discipline began with understanding how his students felt about school and life.

> Each day there were incidents, and ultimately I accepted them as inevitable and impersonal. Alvin's malaise or John's refusal to work were natural responses to an unpleasant environment; not merely my class but a cumulative school environment which meant nothing more to most of the children than white-adult ignorance and authority. There was no simple solution to such discipline problems, and sometimes it seemed necessary to learn to be patient and indulgent with a child who won't behave or refuses to work. A teacher must believe that such problems exist in his classroom because he hasn't found the right words or the right thing, and not that they lie in the heart of the child. (Kohl, 1967, 29)

In Kohl's view, discipline begins with understanding and respect. There is always a reason for misbehavior. Boredom leads to distractibility and inattentiveness. Vandalism is anger erupting in mindless destruction. Impulsivity can signal a learning disability. Teachers who try to understand their students look for the causes of classroom disruptions. They recognize that students are complex human beings with developmental needs that can overshadow reading, writing, and calculating. By looking beyond misbehavior and trying to understand why a student is a discipline problem, a teacher can gain insight into the causes of disruptive behavior (Phi Delta Kappa Commission on Discipline, 1982).

Classroom Organization

A well-organized classroom deters discipline problems. Organization includes the total school attitude toward discipline. The principal takes the lead in establishing an atmosphere of trust and respect. Within the classroom, teachers need to manage individual student behavior in group situations. Groups influence individual behavior, and individual behavior shapes group actions. The manner in which a teacher responds to the group dynamics of a classroom can contribute to or prevent discipline problems.

Effective classroom management requires attention to teacher behaviors that minimize behavior problems. Jacob Kounin (1977) and other researchers have found that teachers prevent discipline problems through their ability to monitor the entire group without becoming distracted by minor incidents that cause the entire class to become diverted. Such teachers demonstrate "withitness" and "overlapping."

"Withitness." "Withitness" is a keen sense of what is happening throughout the classroom (DeLuke & Knoblock, 1987). Two features of "withitness" reduce misbehavior:

1. Select the right student for a desist. When a teacher reprimands the wrong student, the rest of the class assumes she does not know what is going on. Kounin found this "ripple effect" can work to the teacher's disadvantage. Clarity in identifying the correct student and clearly explaining the preferred behavior increases conformity among the rest of the class. Kounin also found that anger, sarcasm, or other roughness in the teacher's reproach upset younger children. The "ripple" effect is most pronounced at the beginning of the school year, and it loses its impact as the year goes on.

2. Attend to the more serious infraction when two problems develop at the same time (Charles, 1989). Taking steps to stop a misbehavior before it "sets off" other students is characteristic of "withit" teachers. These teachers have the ability to judge the "contagibility" of student behavior, and they respond accordingly. For example, Eileen is gazing off into space. The "withit" teacher takes note of her inattention but does not disrupt the smooth work flow of the rest of the class. Planned ignoring or proximity control work best. However, when a serious disruption occurs, verbal desist is warranted.

"Overlapping." "Overlapping" is closely aligned to "withitness." It refers to the ability to monitor two situations simultaneously. Suppose the teacher is working

with a small reading group of seven students, and she lost track of events around the rest of the classroom. This absence of "overlapping" would almost assuredly result in misbehavior. Students with their hands up would be ignored; students who are done with their work would start looking for something else to do; and a mischievous student would have an opportunity to cause a disturbance. The "overlapping" teacher keeps the small group on task while at the same time managing the flow of activity throughout the rest of the classroom.

Maintain a Group Focus.   Virtually all of a teacher's day is spent managing students in groups. Kounin reported that the manner in which teachers conduct their group lessons had a significant impact on discipline problems. Teachers maintain a group focus by encouraging cooperation. For example, during a presentation one student demonstrates at the blackboard, and students in their seats offer suggestions and comments. Students are encouraged to listen, help others, share ideas, and work toward group goals. Well-managed groups have a high rate of student work involvement. Student boredom and indifference to work assignments is a main cause of discipline problems. Tasks that are repetitious and require minimal thought invite discipline problems. As Morse observes:

> If school is not inviting, if the tasks are not clear, interesting, and at an appropriate level, how can we expect students to be on task? Adverse student reactions should be expected when classes are dull, teaching is uninspired, and failure is built in. Their oppositional behavior is a sign of personal growth and integrity. (Morse, 1987, 6)

Teachers who find ways to relate learning to student interests and lives outside of school help students to see value in their lessons. When students understand the purpose of tasks, they can make a connection between teacher expectations and their personal needs; this increases group harmony and minimizes classroom disruptions.

Positive Behavior Support

Positive Behavior Support (PBS) is a schoolwide system that defines, teaches, and encourages appropriate behavior in children. In schools that have been successful building PBS systems, the following procedures have been established (cf. Colvin, Kame'enui, & Sugai, 1993; Lewis & Sugai, 1999; Sugai & Horner, 1999; Todd, Horner, Sugai, & Sprague, 1999):

1. Identify a small number of clearly defined behavioral expectations and present them as positive, simple rules. For example:
   - Come to class prepared.
   - Be respectful to yourself and others.

2. Teach social skills using the same instructional formats applied to other curriculum content: Present the social skill, discuss its rationale, describe and rehearse positive examples ("right way"), describe and model negative examples ("wrong way"), and provide opportunities for students to practice the "right way" until they demonstrate fluent performance.
3. Acknowledge appropriate behavior on a regular basis using formal systems (e.g., tickets, rewards) or social events (e.g., Friday Fun Time). When teachers are successful in creating a positive behavior learning environment, their interactions with students are "positive" four times as often as they are "negative."
4. Establish clear procedures for providing information to students when their behavior is unacceptable. Establish limits with logical consequences.

Positive Behavior Support interventions are proactive and designed to prevent problem behavior by altering a situation before problems escalate while concurrently teaching appropriate alternatives (Safran & Oswald, 2003). When universal schoolwide interventions are designed for all students, positive effects can also be achieved for individuals with severe difficulties. Positive Behavior Support can also be applied as secondary-level interventions with small groups of students and in specific settings such as hallways, playgrounds, and cafeterias or as tertiary-level interventions with individual students experiencing chronic difficulties. While research offers several guiding principles, individual schools must collaboratively shape PBS to fit their own unique needs; the key factors to be included are using collaborative team problem-solving and research-based interventions, using multiple data sources for planning and evaluating, and using positive strategies to reduce punitive disciplinary practices. To summarize, Positive Behavioral Support interventions serve a preventive function by providing antecedent strategies to alter the classroom environment and decrease the likelihood of misbehavior occurring.

Functional Behavioral Assessment

Functional Behavioral Assessment (FBA) is a key component of PBS. The FBA includes the observations and input of people close to the person exhibiting problem behavior. This team observes the person's behavior to identify and define the problematic behavior, determine what actions or events precede and follow the behavior, and identify how often the behavior occurs. The FBA serves as an important part of the process in determining appropriate positive behavioral support plans.

The Individuals with Disabilities Education Act (IDEA) requires that, at a minimum, the FBA be conducted when disciplinary sanctions result in extended periods in which a student is removed from school (i.e., either before or not later than 10 business days after either the first removal beyond 10 cumulative school days in a school year or commencing a removal that constitutes a change in placement). In addition to the IDEA requirements, the FBA gives schools valuable information about the possible causes of problem behavior. Research demonstrates that the process of positive behavioral supports and developing behavioral support plans is more effective when the FBA is conducted prior to developing interventions. The FBA is used to (a) define the problem behaviors; (b) describe the settings under which problem behaviors are and are not likely to be observed; (c) identify the function (the why) of the problem behaviors; and (d) collect information from direct observation to support these outcomes.

Many techniques are available to conduct a functional behavioral assessment. All FBA processes include the following key principles:

■ *Collect information* through informal consultation as well as direct observation. Conversations, questionnaires, checklists, and structured interviews with key persons (e.g., teachers, parents, students) who have contact and experiences with the individual student can offer insights into the contexts or conditions under which the behavior occurs. Direct observations should also be made so that observers can watch the behaviors as they are occurring and note the environmental events (environmental factors, antecedent and consequence events) that may initiate or sustain the behaviors. Specific, concrete behaviors are defined after observational assessments have been performed.

■ *Propose testable explanations* of the student's behavior. A testable explanation is a hypothesis that may explain the relationship between a problem behavior and environmental factors that seem to be associated with its occurrences. Variables observed may include settings or circumstances that seem either to lead to the problem behavior or reinforce it after the fact. The hypothesis should consider the possible functions of the behavior for the student.

■ *Assess the validity of your hypotheses* to confirm the validity of the testable explanations. In general, additional information is collected about the conditions under which the problem behavior occurs and does not occur. This information should demonstrate that occurrences of the behavior and the presence of these conditions are related and predictable.

The results of the FBA should be used to develop an effective and efficient behavioral intervention/support plan. Although the FBA term was introduced formally in IDEA in 1997, there has been a strong history of using FBA for reducing behavioral problems. It is a critical tool for developing effective behavior intervention and classroom management plans.

Felix is an inquisitive, resourceful 15-year-old high school student. He has struggled with behavior problems for years. In middle school, when presented with a difficult or complex assignment, he would complain and refuse to work. When reprimanded, Felix would often run out of the room and, on several occasions, left the school grounds without permission.

Instead of removing Felix from his neighborhood school, the school personnel conducted a functional behavioral assessment to evaluate the reasons for his problem behavior. The team determined that Felix acted inappropriately when he was frustrated with the academic demands. Therefore, the school revised his academic program to meet his individual needs. This included an adapted curriculum with individual and small group tutoring and a revised behavioral support program. The last two years of middle school were a great success for Felix, his family, and school staff.

Managing Student Behavior

Once there was a school administrator who believed he had hit on the perfect plan for classroom discipline. With the assistance of his daughter, who was a graduate student in special education, he embarked on a systematic collection of interventions matched to problem behaviors. His goal was to develop an index card system, compact enough to fit into the top drawer of a teacher's desk. The cards would alphabetically list student discipline problems and briefly explain the correct intervention; for instance, if a student refused to obey, the teacher would flip through the cards, pull out the 3" × 5" labeled "disobedience" and read what to do. His approach was well-meaning, but hopelessly naive. Student behavior cannot be matched to interventions like dominoes. Every student is different and every situation unique. Therefore, teachers need an array of interventions to meet the changing needs of the classroom. Each of the following strategies is research-based (Cooper, Heron, & Heward, 1987; Dreikurs, Grunwald, & Pepper, 1982; Ginott, 1971; Jones, 1987; Redl & Wineman, 1957). Each is useful for eliminating problem behaviors, but none is teacher-proof. Professional judgment determines the best intervention to use at any given time. Classroom interventions anticipate student disruptions and nullify potential discipline problems. Each category of interventions—behavior modification, nonverbal interventions, and verbal interventions—prevents disruptive behavior while maintaining a sense of mutual respect between teacher and student. None will work all the time. Good classroom management requires the ability to select an appropriate strategy from an array of alternatives. It also means being mindful of the types of problems that require attention or as one principal put it, "Knowing the difference between mountains and molehills." When working with students with behavior disorders, teachers and other professionals often group their problem behaviors into two categories: externalizing and internalizing (cf. Walker & Severson, 1999) (see Table 9.1).

Behavior Modification

Behavior modification is regularly used to teach prosocial behavior to students with mild disabilities (Ager & Cole, 1991). Behavior modification programs are data-based. Target behaviors (i.e., behaviors to be eliminated or shaped) are observed and measured. Prior to initiating a program, the target behavior is described in precise, behaviorally concrete terms. Vague behavior descriptors such as "immature," "aggressive," or "cooperative" are replaced with such target behaviors as

TABLE 9.1   Externalizing and Internalizing Behavior Problems

Externalizing Behaviors	
Overt	**Covert**
Fighting	Lying
Disobeying	Cheating
Destroying property	Stealing
Disrupting others	Being truant
Hitting	Being uncooperative
Tantruming	Using drugs and/or alcohol
Bullying	Being passive and noncompliant
Swearing	Being boisterous

Internalizing Behaviors	
Acting anxious	Acting timid
Worrying excessively	Acting bashful
Crying easily	Acting shy
Acting tense	Being self-conscious
Acting shy	Acting aloof
Being sad or depressed	Being easily confused
Lacking self-confidence	Being hypersensitive

"whines," "hits other students," and "shares toys." Baseline data on the frequency of the target behavior are collected for at least a week prior to beginning the program. These data serve as a comparison for determining progress at a later date. Once a target behavior has been selected and counted, the most appropriate consequence is determined (e.g., reinforcement, token economy, extinction, etc.). Next, a schedule to administer consequences is developed (e.g., reinforcement in the form of verbal praise will follow each time a student raises her hand).

The following systems: token economies, contingency contracts, timeout, and cognitive-behavior intervention are well-established in the behavior modification literature and in special education programs.

Token Economies.   A token is a general conditioned reinforcer. Tokens are paired with backup reinforcers such as special privileges or toys from a "class store." A token is given to a student to reinforce a target behavior. At a later time in the day or week, the student can exchange accumulated tokens for the backup reinforcer. The value of tokens is derived from the student desirability for backup reinforcers. For example, without goods to purchase (backup reinforcers), money (tokens) would be useless. Cooper, Heron, and Heward (1987) provide the following guidelines for implementing a token economy:

1. Select a token that is durable and cheap (e.g., rubber stamp, chips, pennies).

2. Be clear about rules and behavior(s) for earning tokens.
3. Whenever possible, use regularly occurring events or privileges for backup reinforcers.
4. Guard against bootlegging of tokens. Hoarding of tokens is often a signal that students don't understand the token's value.
5. Establish a rate of exchange; begin with a low ratio of token to backup reinforcer and increase the ratio as the program becomes successful.
6. Decide in advance how to remove the system.

The efficiency and immediacy of token economies make them an attractive motivation.

Contingency Contracts. A contingency contract is a written agreement between a teacher and student. The contract serves as a positive reinforcer to shape a target behavior. A contingency contract specifies the responsibilities (i.e., the behaviors) of each party and the consequences associated with compliance. Schroeder and Riddle (1991) list five key elements of a contingency contract: detailed privileges and obligations, observable behaviors, sanctions for failure, bonus clauses for consistent compliance, and clear description of methods for administering reinforcers. Contingency contracts are a way of concretely emphasizing student responsibility for behavior. Salend (1987) suggests that responsible behavior can be increased by involving students in making such contractual decisions as determining the target behavior, selecting reinforcers, and evaluating systems.

Timeout. Cooper, Heron, and Heward (1987) describe two types of timeout: nonexclusionary and exclusionary timeout. Nonexclusionary timeout consists of planned ignoring, withdrawal of a specific reinforcer, contingent observation, and the timeout ribbon. Planned ignoring is the removal of such social reinforcers as attention, praise, or verbal comments. Withdrawal of specific reinforcer means that an identified positive stimulus is removed when an undesirable behavior occurs. In one study, researchers turned off classroom music each time students left their seats, thus significantly reducing out-of-seat behavior (Ritschl, Mongrella, & Presbie, 1972).

Contingent observation is the change of seating of a student for a specified period of time following a classroom infraction. During the contingent observation time period, the student is able to observe the activity of the rest of the group, but may not participate. The timeout ribbon is a paired reinforcer. When a youngster wears the ribbon, it is a signal that there are opportunities to receive positive reinforcers. When the ribbon is removed, no reinforcers can be gained.

Exclusionary timeout is the removal of a student to a room outside the classroom for a specified period of time. Release from timeout is contingent on cessation of disturbing behavior. While an effective intervention if used sparingly, exclusionary timeout can be misused and even abused. Procedures for using exclusionary timeout must be spelled out clearly to both students and parents.

Exclusionary timeouts are documented with a timeout log. Such data collection protects against abuse and provides information to determine the effectiveness of exclusionary timeout as a means of extinguishing disruptive behavior.

The aim of timeout is to institute a brief, 5–10 minute isolation of a student from classroom activities because of disruptive behavior. Longer periods of timeout are not recommended for several reasons. Instructional time is lost. The student may prefer the timeout, thus it becomes a positive reinforcer. Removing a student from the classroom may be more disturbing than the behavior that prompted the timeout. Finally, timeout can be unnecessarily punitive (Cuenin & Harris, 1986; C.C.B.D., 1990).

The goal of behavior modification is to increase adaptive behavior and to decrease maladaptive behavior. Behavior modification has a certain intuitive appeal. After all, it's common parenting and teaching practice to reward "good" behavior and punish the "bad." Schools are awash in everyday practices that reflect behavior modification. Students who learn their lessons get good grades. Teachers use stickers and progress charts to encourage students to work harder. Detentions, staying after school, and suspensions are everyday procedures for dealing with students who don't abide by school expectations for proper behavior.

When the normal corrective procedures don't seem to work for a student, it's common for a teacher to step up the reward and punishment cycle through the application of a homespun behavior modification program. Some teachers do this without training in specific techniques. Consequently, errors in treatment undercut the effectiveness of the program and add to the unfortunate judgment that it's the student who is at fault. When teachers begin a behavior modification program, they should keep the seven guidelines listed in Figure 9.1 in mind. Some illustrations of behavior modification methods for improving the behavior of students are presented in Table 9.2. Rewards and creating a positive atmosphere in the classroom are a big part of this approach.

FIGURE 9.1   Guidelines for Behavior Modification Programs

1. Identify and describe the disturbing behavior.
2. Count the frequency of the disturbing behavior.
3. Identify the replacement behavior, if possible with student input.
4. Select a reinforcer that is meaningful to the student.
5. Avoid using sugar foods as reinforcers (e.g., cookies, candy, raisins).
6. Don't take away reinforcers for punishment.
7. Do a postfrequency count of the disturbing behavior after a specified period of time to determine the program's effectiveness.
8. If the program isn't working, don't blame the student; change the plan.

TABLE 9.2   Illustrations of Behavior Modification

Tactic	Illustration
Reward students for reducing out-of-seat behavior	Gather data on the number of times the student is out of his or her seat for ten class periods. Provide a sticker, star, or other token for each class period that the student is out of seat less than average during the data collection phase. Keep track of improvements and discuss them with the student.
Reward appropriate classroom behavior	Provide your class with an opportunity to earn free time based on their behavior. Start a stopwatch at the beginning of a class period. Each time misbehavior occurs, stop the watch and announce to the class that it will start again when appropriate behavior resumes. At the end of the class period, determine the amount of free time that was earned and allow students to select activities for that time period.
Reward appropriate behavior in other students	Look for opportunities to reward other students for appropriate behavior. For example, if a student fails to comply with a request you have made, turn to another student and make a similar request. When the other student complies, provide a reward or special attention for the appropriate behavior.
Ignore inappropriate behavior	The process of withholding attention or reward from previously rewarded behavior is referred to as putting the behavior on extinction. As a general rule, extinction is used for behaviors that are minimally disruptive, attention-seeking types of problems. Often, simply ignoring these behaviors decreases them.
Use contracts to control behavior	Help students set goals for appropriate behavior and then design contracts that detail expectations and rewards for meeting the terms of the agreement.

Nonverbal and Verbal Techniques

An orderly classroom climate is widely acknowledged as a key component of effective instruction. Classroom disruptions are among the greatest obstacles to creating and maintaining a calm and productive classroom environment. A variety of general nonverbal and verbal interventions are available for managing classroom disruptions.

Nonverbal interventions have several advantages over verbal interventions. Silence does not draw attention to the student or inadvertently reinforce the behavior. Classroom activities proceed without interruption when the teacher manages classroom behavior unobtrusively (McDaniel, 1986). Lastly, nonverbal interventions help teachers avoid "power struggles" with students.

Body Carriage.   Frederic Jones (1987) observed teachers in hundreds of secondary and elementary classrooms. He found that teachers conveyed leadership through body language. Posture, eye contact, facial expressions, and gestures conveyed confidence or uncertainty. Students observe teacher body language and make judgments about what they see. Charles summarizes Jones's findings:

> Good posture and confident carriage suggest strong leadership; a drooping posture and lethargic movements suggest resignation or fearfulness. Effective teachers even when tired or troubled tend to hold themselves erect and move with a measure of vigor. (Charles, 1989, 92)

Teachers who convey authority naturally through body language encounter half the behavior problems of teachers in "loud, unruly" classrooms (Charles, 1989, 90).

Planned Ignoring.   Sometimes disruptive student behaviors are intended to attract the attention of the teacher and other students. When teachers ignore attention-seeking behaviors, the audience is eliminated. Planned ignoring works best for minor classroom disturbances. The teacher who interrupts group lessons or activities with a continual stream of admonitions such as "sit still," or "pick up that piece of paper" disrupts learning while drawing attention to the misbehavior. Paradoxically, this "negative" attention can reinforce behavior problems.

Signal Interference.   Every adult has memories of childhood teachers who could quell minor disturbances with a flick of a light switch or a finger raised to the lips. There are numerous nonverbal signals for quieting a class: eye contact, snapping fingers, a frown, shaking the head, or a quieting gesture with the hand. Visual signals do not disturb students and emphasize the teacher's awareness of all activity in the room.

Proximity Control.   Teachers who stand or sit as if rooted to the front of the room are compelled to issue verbal directions in order to deal with disruptions. Teachers who move around the room merely need to stand near a student or gently place a hand on a student's shoulder to stop a disturbing behavior. Teaching while moving has several advantages, rather than being a separate, remote entity, the teacher becomes physically a part of the group; the teacher is able to monitor students more easily; the teacher projects more of a presence because students can't predict where the teacher will be standing at any given moment; finally, standing nearby also reassures students that the teacher is in control.

Removal of Seductive Objects.   Manipulation is a strong channel for learning, and in most instances should be encouraged. However, some students become distracted by objects. Fritz Redl and David Wineman (1951) indicated that the ability to control the impulse to handle, grab, or steal seductive objects was a basic component in the development of self-control. When teachers leave valuables or students leave toys around, youngsters who are prone to "gadgetorial seduction," the objects might disappear. Removing seductive objects decreases the pressure on a youngster's burgeoning self-control system.

Verbal Interventions

Because nonverbal interventions are the least intrusive, they are preferred. Verbal interventions are useful after it is clear that nonverbal interventions have been unsuccessful in desisting a disruptive behavior.

Humor.   It may sound strange to use humor to calm a disruptive student, but it is a very useful technique. Almost every school has a teacher who is capable of defusing discipline problems with a quip or easy comment. Humor is a basic human need. People watch T.V., go to the movies, and pay to watch live performances just to laugh. The teacher who smiles and jokes in the face of adversity sets a strong model for students. A word of caution, however: avoid sarcasm, cynicism, or teasing. Rather than lightening a moment, sarcasm increases tension and creates resentment. Cynicism and teasing breed resentment.

Sane Messages.   When teachers respond to disruptive behavior with anger, they add to student anxiety, which increases the likelihood of further behavior problems (Kounin, 1977). "I" messages let students know how the teacher feels. Such statements as, "I am frustrated because you keep interrupting this lesson," or "I am disappointed because you didn't maintain control when I left the room," describe the situation rather than attacking a student's character (Charles, 1989, 59). • Sane messages are descriptive and model appropriate behavior (Ginott, 1971). Sane messages help students understand how their behavior affects others. They are a direct appeal to change behavior. "Bev, when you talk during silent reading, it disturbs everyone in your group," is an example of a sane message. "Bev, keep quiet," is an example of what Ginott calls an insane message. In the first instance, the reason for a change in behavior is explained to the student. In the second instance, the "insane message," the student feels personally attacked. Such a directive as "keep quiet" or "shut up" may get the intended results, but if the model for expressing needs is abrupt and callous, students will take the same approach in their own conversations.

Restructuring.   Restructuring means changing a lesson or activity that is floundering. When confronted with student disinterest, the best option may be to move onto another activity. Restructuring is part of the decision-making powers of a teacher. One inner-city sixth-grade teacher gave a spelling test every time the class seemed restless and difficult to manage. "It was amazing," he reported; "one minute they are ready to climb the walls, and the next minute they were quietly and dutifully folding their papers and numbering lines from 1 to 20!"

Hypodermic Affection.   Each student from time to time needs a shot of caring. Hypodermic affection lets students know that they are valued human beings. Students get frustrated, discouraged, and anxious in school. Students with mild disabilities, in particular, need encouragement to persevere with tasks at which they have failed in the past. Sometimes a smile, a pat on the back, or a kind word can help a student over a psychological hurdle. Showing interest in a student's life outside of school, and plainly communicating concern are ways of building trust. A trusting relationship between student and teacher is the key to solving all discipline problems.

Praise.   Verbal praise is frequently used to reinforce positive classroom behavior. The aphorism "Catch them being good" describes the most useful approach to praise. For example, some students need attention. Praising their behavior when they are not seeking attention while ignoring disruptive behavior is a useful way to use praise in the classroom. Too much praise can undercut impact; too little praise communicates indifference. Effective praise is directed at student behavior rather than the student personally. "You really are trying hard" encourages student effort. It is a descriptive statement that gives the student guidance in terms of the type of behavior the teacher expects to see.

Ginott (1971) pointed out the "perils of praise." Praise directed at a student personally is condescending and manipulative. A statement such as, "You are a good person to have in my class," implies the teacher is making such judgments about all the students. What about the students who don't get the same compliment? Remember there is always a "ripple effect" in the classroom. Everyone wants to be liked by the teacher. Judgmental praise may make one student feel good, while another may feel rejected. Praise works best when it evaluates behavior instead of the student.

Alerting.   Imagine a group of students during recess playing kickball. They are hot, sweaty, and thoroughly enjoying themselves. All the running around has them excited, and they are eager to continue the game. The teacher looks at her watch and realizes she should have had them back into the classroom five minutes ago. What does she do? One approach is to abruptly end the game and rush the entire group back to class. Abrupt changes will almost assuredly result in behavior problems.

In his extensive research on classroom discipline, Kounin (1977) found the manner in which teachers handled transitions to be a key element in effective discipline. Charles succinctly summarized Kounin's findings: "Teachers' ability to manage smooth transitions and maintain momentum was more important to work involvement and classroom control than any other behavior management technique" (Charles, 1989, 33).

Alerting helps students to make smooth transitions by giving them time to make emotional adjustments to change. This is particularly true for impulsive students or students who are easily frustrated. Alerting takes many forms. One method is to count down the number of minutes before a change will take place. Usually two warnings in five-minute increments is sufficient. Alerting is useful when moving from a high student preference activity (e.g., recess) to a low student preference activity (e.g., grammar lesson).

Accepting Student Feelings.   A student walks into class in the morning radiant with the news that the family will be visiting Disneyland. The teacher is pleased to have such a happy youngster in class for the day. It is a pleasure to accept positive feelings and reaffirm their expression. The next day the same youngster walks into class furious. Her dad has been laid off his job, and the trip to Disneyland is canceled. The student is angry and frustrated. She hates her dad; she hates the teacher; and she hates her schoolwork. These feelings are not so easy to accept and reaffirm. Teachers, who have a one-sided view of student feelings, allow for the expression of positive feelings but are reluctant to accept feelings of distress.

Students need to learn how to express such feelings as anger, frustration, and impatience. Students act out these feelings when they lack appropriate verbal skills. The teacher who attempts to put a lid on student behavior that is embedded in anger or frustration is sowing the seeds of further discontent. Distressful feelings cannot be made to disappear. Suppressed feelings will resurface. By providing opportunities for students to express all types of feelings, teachers reaffirm students. Role playing, class discussions, life space interventions, and journal writing are samples of classroom methods that help students channel difficult feelings into constructive outlets.

Conflict Situations

While all students have "good" and "bad" days, some students have persistent problems in adapting to school expectations and routines. The intensity and duration of student disruptions will determine the severity of the problem. An emotional disturbance can cause a student to act out feelings of anger, hostility, or isolation. For instance, students who engage in attention-getting behaviors don't know how to relate in socially acceptable ways. Many students who receive special education services for behavior problems are identified as emotionally disturbed.

Most of the causes for emotional problems are outside the classroom teacher's reach. Time is a factor no one can overcome. A student's aggressive behavior may be caused by sexual abuse that happened several years earlier. Childhood difficulties, such as separation of parents or death of a loved one, may be overcome in a positive manner by one student or thrust another student into the depths of depression. What then is a teacher to do when confronted with the awesome obstacles presented by a student's troubled life history?

Although a teacher cannot (and should not) pretend to be a therapist, the teacher can utilize therapeutic strategies that have proved useful with students in conflict. One such strategy is the life space intervention (Redl, 1971; Wood & Long, 1991).

Life Space Crisis Intervention

The life space intervention (LSCI) is a technique for turning listening into a plan for student behavior change. If a teacher wants to understand why a student behaves a certain way, the best source of information is the student. The LSCI uses crisis situations to move a youngster toward more constructive behavior. The following five-step procedure summarizes key points of the life space intervention. For a more thorough analysis see *Life Space Crisis Intervention* by Long, Wood, & Fecser (2001).

Step 1. Ventilate Feelings. The LSCI is a conversation between student and teacher. Unlike most such conversations, in the first phase the student does most of the talking and the teacher listens. The LSCI is initiated by the teacher after a specific incident. It requires some privacy. A quiet corner of a classroom might work or if the student is out of control, he or she should be removed from the classroom for the interview.

The teacher begins by allowing the student to ventilate feelings. No moral implications are attached to what is said. The teacher is nonjudgmental and supportive of the student's feelings. Such statements as, "I can see you are angry," or "When Alex said that you must have felt hurt," emphasize empathy and communicate that feelings, even negative ones, are important. During Step 1 of the LSCI, the teacher is accepting. This builds trust and helps the teacher to understand the student perspective.

The student may swear, whine, or blame others. It may seem strange not to correct these "inappropriate" comments. Some youngsters lack the verbal skills to express strong feelings in a socially acceptable manner. Strong language is a symptom of frustration. The intention at this stage is to build trust. The subsequent steps aim at behavior change.

Step 2. Clarify the Incident. Physical signs that the student is beginning to unwind (e.g., relaxed muscle tone; steady, calm breath) will become evident. At this point, the incident that prompted the LSCI is ready to be clarified in two stages.

First, ask the student to explain what happened. The student is likely to place blame on you, other students, other adults, anyone but himself or herself. This is to be expected. The purpose of the LSCI is to help a student learn to accept responsibility for individual behavior. If the student was in the habit of "owning up" to disturbing action, you wouldn't need the life space intervention.

The student's view is significant data. Action is guided by perception. Attempting to correct the student version would eliminate an important source of information. Right or wrong, distorted or clear, the student perspective is a crucial clue in understanding behavior.

Next, the incident is reviewed again, except this time the teacher assists the student to paint a reality-based picture of the crisis situation. The student is prompted to describe the physical scene and chronological time frame. Comments such as, "Where were you standing when Cole threw the eraser?" or, "What happened next?" help the student to recall events. You want to find the central issue. A gentle reminder interjected at this point about how the adult saw events unfold can be helpful, but caution is advised because too much "reality rub" will place teacher and student at odds. The student is reflecting, an unaccustomed practice, and he or she will jump at an opportunity to argue over details, and thus derail the LSCI.

Step 3. Look for Patterns.   Once the central issue is identified, use questions such as, "Has this happened before?" or gentle reminders such as, "Last week it seemed you had the same problem with Sally," to help students gain insight into their own behavior. Many times students with emotional problems will deny their experience. They literally forget past episodes, or they may be unable to learn from experience. The student may be "stuck" in behavior patterns, continually repeating the mistakes of the past.

Up to this point, the LSCI has focused on affective fallout from the incident. Looking for patterns switches emphasis to the cognitive domain. The student may be well-equipped to deny a history of problems related to the incident. Projection (i.e., finding one's own faults in someone else) and rationalization (i.e., explaining away behavior) are well-entrenched defenses against change. Initially it is enough at this stage to get agreement that there does seem to be a problem. Future interviews can continue to explore disturbed behavior patterns.

Step 4. Implement a Plan.   The purpose of the life space intervention is to help a student assume personal responsibility. When a persistent pattern is identified by both teacher and student, the next logical step is to consider alternative ways to deal with the problem. Questions such as "What could you have done rather than knock all of your books off the desk?" or, "Are there any signals we could arrange for the next time you are feeling frustrated?" move the discussion into the problem-solving stage. While the teacher provides supportive or clarifying questions, it is up to the student to do the problem solving. The student needs to "own" the behavior and the solution.

Of course, reality rules of the school and common sense also come into play. A student may be overly zealous in terms of self-imposed consequence. Neither punishment nor "consequences" are part of the solution. The plan is preventive. "Each time I feel frustrated with my work, I'll close my book and count to ten slowly." "Every time I lose my temper I'll put a check in my self-monitoring log." "If I get angry I'll blow off steam by walking around the room."

The intent of the planning stage is to get students thinking and working on their emotional or behavior problems. Student plans are not usually characterized by their elegance. It may be tempting to step in and offer a more reasonable alternative. The student may need to be reminded about such reality concerns as the implausibility of leaving the room when upset. The initial plan might require multiple adjustments, but that is the nature of personal growth. Changing habitual behavior patterns is a difficult endeavor. Whether or not the mechanics of the plan achieve the objective is secondary. The student is learning to take responsibility for behavior. In the long run, there is no more important goal. The final act of the LSCI is for the teacher and student to write the plan and sign it. The "contract" increases commitment and provides a basis for future life space interventions (Fagen, 1986).

Step 5. Transition Back to Classroom Activity. A smooth transition back to classroom activities helps the student save face and establishes a routine for further life space interventions. Wood and Long (1991) suggest preparing the student with the following questions:

> "What is your group doing now?"
> "When you left the group they were writing news reports. Do you think they are still at it?"
> "When you go back to your room, what will they be doing?" (p. 148)

Keep in mind that being removed from the classroom during a crisis situation can be embarrassing. Hard-won gains made during the life space intervention can dissipate if the student or classmates are unable to return to a normal routine. Getting a student returned to work gives the life space crisis intervention a successful closure. The key points of the life space crisis intervention are summarized in Figure 9.2.

Long (1990) describes five uses of emotional first aid: to drain off frustration, to support the management of strong feelings, to maintain communication during stress, to regulate social and behavioral traffic, and to provide umpire service. In this brief episode, Ms. Halpin managed all five. She allowed Andy time and space to ventilate his anger. She helped him deal with his anger by her supportive comments. Instead of punishing him for leaving the room, she maintained communication by remaining nonjudgmental and concerned about his feelings. She emphasized social regulations by giving him five minutes to return to the classroom, and she emphasized his accountability by handing him the stopwatch. Finally, she recognized that she could not solve Andy's problem for him. Like a good umpire, she remained neutral while requiring Andy to return to the classroom.

Life space crisis intervention is directed at helping students make good choices. The technique takes into account the student's point of view and feelings. LSCI provides support and ultimately points the student in the direction of personal accountability. It also adheres to the principle that behavior management should be nonjudgmental and nonpunitive. It helps students to manage their feelings while working toward solutions to behavior problems.

FIGURE 9.2 Life Space Crisis Intervention

Purpose: To Defuse Crisis Situation and Seek Solutions

Step 1. Ventilate Feelings

Teacher behavior: Listens.
Teacher attitude: Accepting, nonjudgmental; allows for ventilation of feelings.
Student behavior: Talks, expresses strong feelings such as anger, hostility, or frustration.

Step 2. Clarify the Incident

Teacher behavior: Asks questions, probes for details of incident.
Teacher attitude: Tries to help student see his or her contribution to the crisis incident.
Student behavior: Attempts to reconstruct a timeline of events that culminated in crisis incident.

Step 3. Look for Patterns

Teacher behavior: Within dialogue helps student to remember similar situations.
Teacher attitude: Problem solving.
Student behavior: Attempts to relate present crisis incident to past problems with adults or peers.

Step 4. Implement a Plan

Teacher behavior: Supports student in searching for alternative ways of handling crisis situations.
Teacher attitude: Helps student take responsibility for actions.
Student behavior: Develops a written contract that describes student solutions.

Step 5. Transition Back to Classroom Activity

Teacher behavior: Discusses what student needs to do in order to rejoin group.
Teacher attitude: Student may need face-saving options or reminder of consequences.
Student behavior: Calmed down and, with support, ready to resume activities.

Discipline and IDEA

The 2004 reauthorization of the Individuals with Disabilities Act (IDEA) created a set of mandates that changed disciplinary procedures for students with special needs. The intent of changes to the law was to modify the perception that a dual system of discipline existed—one for the general education population and another for students with special needs. These changes gave schools more freedom to remove disruptive students whose behavior was not related to their disability. Previously school administrators had to build a case to remove a student to an alternative education setting. The 2004 reauthorization of IDEA allows administrators to remove a student to an alternative placement, and the parents, if they disagree, must appeal the decision. Consider the following scenario.

In 2003, a year before the reauthorization of IDEA, Preston a 15-year-old middle-school student exhibited both academic and behavioral difficulties. Among other things Preston had a record of incomplete work, truancy, and arguing with his teachers. Because of his academic problems Preston's teachers agreed to refer him for a special education evaluation. The evaluation team determined that Preston met the systemwide criteria for a learning disability due to a severe discrepancy between his IQ and academic achievement. (The severe discrepancy formula for determining a learning disability is not recommended in the 2004 reauthorization of IDEA, but this does not change the special education status of students like Preston who were identified with a learning disability prior to the 2004 reauthorization.)

While special education services appeared to help Preston with his academic difficulties, discipline problems persisted. The principal suspended him for fighting several times during the 2003–2004 year. After one more episode of disruptive behavior the principal placed Preston in a temporary alternative program for disruptive students. His parents hired a lawyer who pointed out that because Preston was a student with special needs his placement could not be changed without a "manifest determination" hearing. This time-consuming investigation was mandated by IDEA to determine if a student's misbehavior was related to his or her disability. If the manifest determination found there was no relationship between his learning disability and his behavior Preston was subject to the same disciplinary codes as the general education population. However, if it was determined that his behavior was a manifestation of his disability the school was legally required to follow a series of due-process procedures to ensure that Preston's special education services were not interrupted.

When legislators in 2004 were revamping IDEA it was clear that the complications involved with special education discipline procedures needed to be addressed. Many school administrators complained that mandated legal procedures were too complex. They said that additional hearings, paperwork, IEP revisions, and parental consent had become an overwhelming burden. Delays in fulfilling federal requirements also meant delays in keeping schools safe for all students. While still containing protective due process procedures for students with special needs, the 2004 changes to IDEA were intended to simplify discipline procedures. The following bulleted items include Council for Exceptional Children (2005) highlights of the 2004 IDEA reauthorization in regards to discipline procedures.

■ Language has been added giving school personnel authority, on a case-by-case basis, to consider unique circumstances when determining whether to order a change in placement for a child with a disability who violates a code of student conduct.

■ The length of time that school personnel may remove a student to an interim alternative setting (without a hearing officer) has been changed from 45 days to 45 school days. In addition, school personnel may now remove a student who "has inflicted serious bodily injury upon another person while at school, on school premises, or at a school function" to such an interim placement without a hearing-officer ruling.

- The provisions related to the criteria for determining whether a behavior was a manifestation of a student's disability has been revised to state: "If the conduct in question was caused by, or had a direct and substantial relationship to, the child's disability; or if the conduct in question was the direct result of the LEA's failure to implement the IEP. . . ."

- Timelines have been added for an expedited hearing in matters related to placement during appeals.

- Under the protections for children who are not yet eligible under IDEA, the provisions related to whether or not an LEA should have known that a child was a child with a disability have been changed as follows:

> Current disciplinary provisions require that a parent must put their concerns in writing to school personnel that their child needs special education services, with an exception for a parent who is illiterate or has a disability impacting on their ability to submit concerns in writing. The new bill eliminates that exception related to the parent's ability to put their concerns in writing.

- Under the new bill, an LEA shall not be deemed to have knowledge that the child is a child with a disability if the parent of the child has not allowed an evaluation of the child or has refused services, or the child has been evaluated and it was determined that the child was not a child with a disability.

The Council for Exceptional Children told its members to be cautious in interpreting these new requirements until final federal regulations are issued. The special education organization stated:

> Examples of specific policy areas that will need to be addressed during the regulatory process include: defining "unique circumstances" as they relate to the authority of school personnel to make a change in placement on a "case by case" basis; clarifying the length of time a student may be removed from school, 45 days vs. 45 school days; providing additional information on the revised criteria for determining whether a behavior was a manifestation of a student's disability; and explaining the significance of deleting the definition of "substantial evidence" from the statute. (p. 21) (www.cec.sped.org/pp/IDEA_120204.pdf), retrieved January 10, 2005

Punishment

Punishment is one of the most misunderstood reactions to student actions. One of the factors that makes punitive approaches so appealing is that in terms of short-term goals, they appear to work. Such punishments as checks on a blackboard, "timeout," calls to home, or trips to the principal's office may halt disruptions, but too frequently the gains are temporary. While punishment can temporarily stop misbehavior, it does not change behavior nor does it teach new behaviors (Hyman & D'Allesandro, 1984; Kohn, 1991; Morse, 1987). Punishment is most effective when used sparingly and with students who can make a logical connection between offense and consequence.

Sometimes it's difficult to determine where treatment for disruptive behavior ends and abuse begins. This is particularly true when punishment is couched in scientific jargon. For example the term "negative aversives" is used in special education to label such tactics as blasts of cold water in the face from an atomizer or pinching to thwart disruptive behavior. Whether or not negative aversives are a euphemism for punishment is a matter of some dispute (C.C.B.D., 1990). In Rhode Island, parents of children attending the Behavioral Research Institute defended the use of negative aversives. The Behavior Research Institute served diverse types of behavior disorders from juvenile delinquency to autism. "Negative aversives" ranged from pinches and hot sauces placed in the mouth to blasts of pressurized air on the side of the face, and, ultimately, restraints where a youngster was spread-eagled against a wall face first and held fast by strong cloth bands.

When punishment is used, it should be guided by school policy. Braaten, Simpson, Rosell, and Reilly recommend seven procedural elements to guide the use of punishment in schools:

1. Information about the use and abuse of punishment should be provided to teachers.
2. Teachers should be trained in the use of punishment.
3. Punishment procedures should be approved by the school board and be disseminated to teachers, parents, and students.
4. Records of punishment usage should be maintained.
5. Complaint and appeal procedures should be established.
6. Infractions that warrant punishment should be explained to all students and teachers.
7. Procedures for periodic review of punishment procedures should be implemented. (Braaten, Simpson, Rosell, & Reiley, 1988, 80)

Punishment is commonplace and controversial. Some teachers use it first; others as the last resort. Punishment is effective when used sparingly. Reserve punishment for events or actions that cause physical or psychological harm to students or teacher. Remember if punishment and its antecedent—threats—are used as a primary discipline tactic, there is nothing left to fall back on when those methods fail to achieve the desired results.

Putting Theory into Practice

Rudy is a sixth-grade student. He has been diagnosed as having attention deficit disorder with hyperactivity. He takes medication for his condition three times a day: before, during, and after school. Rudy also meets with the school adjustment counselor for an hour once a week.

Rudy's school behavior is impulsive. He runs in hallways. He often jumps and hits door frames with his right hand like he's dunking a basketball. He is unable to resist misusing such objects as pens, pencils, and paper clips by taking them apart or using them as "weapons." Rudy is also disorganized and frequently fails to complete assignments.

Transition times are difficult for Rudy, especially unstructured times, such as finishing an assignment and getting ready for lunch. When the class makes the transition from lecture to independent work, it takes Rudy several minutes to settle down and begin the task at hand. Often Rudy will get sidetracked into some other type of activity like cleaning his desk.

Socially Rudy cannot work with other students in such activities as group work or cooperative learning. He tends to be disruptive in his group and prevents the other children from completing assignments. Rudy does not anticipate consequences and seems not to care about the effects of his actions on others.

Rudy's problem is twofold: his behavior is disruptive and his social skills are weak. We further discuss social skills and how to help students learn social skills in the following chapter. For now we will concentrate on Rudy's behavior and what to do about his classroom disruptions.

The prevailing expert opinion indicates that Rudy's disorder, attention deficit with hyperactivity (ADHD), is neurologically based. This means that Rudy is not intentionally causing behavior problems. His medication may need to be increased, because his teacher does not report any behavior gains despite two dosages each day. On the other hand, Rudy may be one of those youngsters who does not respond to medication and another treatment may be preferred (see information on diet in Chapter 4, Students with Behavior Disorders).

Remember the school administrator who wanted to develop an index card system matched to each type of behavior problem? He believed there was one solution to each classroom discipline problem. In fact any number of combinations of interventions may fit the problem and provide *positive behavioral support*. Finding what works best with Rudy is trial and error. Try one approach, see how it works, and build on it or try another.

Each time Rudy disrupts the class, the teacher will take him into a corner of the room, which she has set up with a divider to provide some privacy. She will have independent work assignments ready for the rest of the class so she and Rudy can have a few private minutes together. She will provide *emotional first aid* and highlight the effect of Rudy's behavior using *sane messages*. She will encourage Rudy to describe what happened and she will *accept his feelings*. Her goal for these sessions is to maintain communication during stress and to regulate behavior by reminding Rudy in a nonjudgmental fashion that her job is to protect the ongoing classroom programming by using timeout if necessary.

In order to help prevent Rudy's disruptions she will use *alerting* to help him get ready for transitions and she will use several nonverbal interventions such as *proximity control, signal interference,* and *removal of seductive objects* to provide support without drawing attention to his behavior.

His teacher also understands that Rudy needs a more intensive plan to help him learn to control his behavior throughout the day. She will institute a *behavior modification program.* She will do a *functional assessment* of his most disturbing behavior—running through the halls. After gathering this data she finds that three out of every four times the class moves from one area of the building to another she has to correct Rudy's behavior. She will set up a *token economy* with Rudy. Each time he walks through the halls in an appropriate manner she will give him a ticket that he can exchange for a baseball card (baseball is one of his favorite sports) at the end of the day. The use of this *positive reinforcement* will be discussed with the class. This will alleviate negative student feelings about being left out of the reward system. Additionally, for every ten baseball cards Rudy earns, the class will have ten extra minutes of recess. This should help everyone pull for Rudy to succeed. After a month, Rudy's teacher will do another behavior frequency count to see if the positive reinforcement program is taking hold.

The success of the interventions for Rudy will be based on several factors including administrative and parental support. No guarantees go with this behavior plan for Rudy, but the teacher's knowledge of an array of behavior strategies plus her understanding that all behavior interventions require timely adjustments is movement in the right direction.

Summary

Well-managed classrooms facilitate learning. No one can learn in a class that is constantly disrupted by behavior problems. Discipline problems cause stress in both teachers and students. For the novice teacher, classroom management is a major concern. At one time or another all students present discipline problems. While authoritarian discipline tactics hold some appeal, promoting student participation in discipline policies increases their sense of personal responsibility and helps to prevent future behavior problems.

Proactive discipline is based on the premise that many classroom disruptions can be avoided. Teachers who use proactive discipline techniques strive to intervene before a disturbance turns into a full-blown discipline problem. Such teachers are skilled in an array of behavior management tools including behavior modification, nonverbal, and verbal interventions.

ACTIVITIES

1. Arrange to speak with a principal like Mr. Mellon, one who has been working in schools for 10 to 15 years. Ask him or her to describe the classroom management models being used in his or her school. Ask if there are differences in how teachers

implement the model(s) and in how effective the model(s) is (are) in maintaining order in the school. Share the results of your experience with another student in your class or another teacher in your school.

2. Observe an elementary or secondary class. Count the nonverbal interventions the teacher uses in a half-hour. Count the verbal interventions the teacher uses in a half-hour. Analyze the data. Look for classroom rules and other signs of teacher management style. Does the teacher style more closely approximate Canter or Glasser?

3. Watch the video *Lean on Me,* about Joe Clark. Have a class debate; were his tactics positive or punishment-based?

4. Role play a crisis situation using the Life Space Intervention. Discuss the usefulness of LSCI. Ask classroom teachers if they have heard of LSCI; if so, do they use it?

5. Visit a public school classroom. Look for signs of behavior modification practices. Do you think they work?

CHAPTER

10 Teaching Social Skills

ADVANCE QUESTIONS

Answer the following questions as you read this chapter:

1. What is emotional intelligence?
2. Why is social skill instruction needed in some classrooms?
3. What does "character education" mean?
4. How does values clarification fit into a classroom curriculum?
5. What are some specific social skills that comprise self-control?
6. What problem-solving steps would you follow to develop a social skills program for a specific student?

Chapter Web

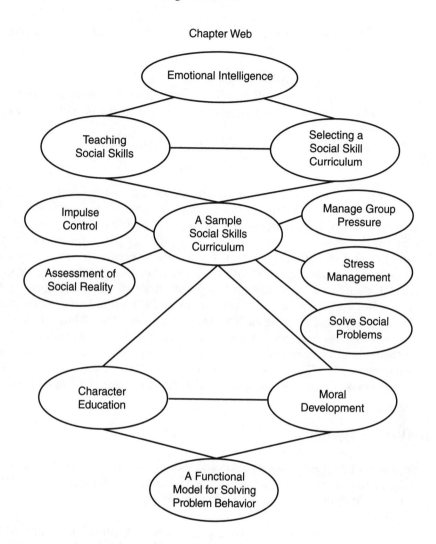

Vignette: Debbie

Debbie is eleven years old and in the fifth grade. Her teacher is concerned about Debbie's social skills. She seems less mature than the other students. Debbie is impulsive and has difficulty following class rules. She gets out of her seat often and always seems to have an excuse to leave the room. In the hallways, cafeteria, and library she often acts up. In the classroom she has difficulty waiting for teacher help. Her teacher believes Debbie needs an evaluation for ADHD and is planning on talking to the principal about it.

Although Debbie likes other students she spends a lot of time alone on the playground. Her classmates shy away from her because she tries to relate to them by gossiping, teasing, or doing favors. She enjoys reading and math and her grades would be much better if she could stay focused on her classwork. Her teacher is fairly traditional, which means she does a lot of frontal teaching. Much of Debbie's school work consists of textbook reading, worksheets, and other "seatwork."

1. What social skills does Debbie lack?
2. Do you think Debbie should be removed from her classroom and placed in a self-contained special education class for students with behavior disorders?
3. What could Debbie's classroom teacher do to help Debbie learn the social skills she lacks?

Consider the challenge of classroom management. The typical classroom teacher engages in 1,000 interactions a day (Jackson, 1968). Less than half of these interpersonal exchanges relate to teaching. The majority of time is spent trying to keep the classroom running smoothly. Maintaining a group focus, minimizing disruptions, and encouraging student participation require the organizational skills of the "one-minute manager" and the human relations skills of a Dale Carnegie. Each student is a unique human being with likes, dislikes, strengths, and weaknesses. Regardless of ability or personality of individual students, the classroom teacher is expected to bring each "up to grade level." The public school classroom is one of the best examples of our democratic tradition. Public education is based on the common school principle that all students should have an equal opportunity to succeed in life. Yet all students do not start out equal. The inequity of student life experiences and student social skills imposes a challenge to teachers.

Emotional Intelligence

Emotional intelligence refers to an individual's ability to monitor emotions and weigh alternatives before acting. Daniel Goleman (1995) explains the relationship between emotional intelligence and social skills:

> Those who are at the mercy of impulse—who lack self-control—suffer a moral deficiency. The ability to control impulse is the base of will and character. By the same token, the root of altruism lies in empathy, the ability to read emotions in others; lacking a sense of another's need or despair, there is no caring. And if there are any two moral stances our times call for, they are precisely these, self-restraint and compassion (p. xii)

Emotional intelligence increases with an individual's ability to consider options before reacting to a stressful situation. Emotionally intelligent individuals control their feelings, rather than letting their feelings control them.

Impulsiveness in childhood is a forerunner of aggression in adolescence and it undercuts social skill development. In the Pittsburg Youth Study (Block, 1995), researchers found that impulsivity is nearly three times more powerful an indicator of delinquency than IQ. When child psychologist Walter Mischel tracked the developmental progress of impulsive four-year-olds into adolescence, he found the teenagers enmeshed in conflict. Impulsive teenagers overreacted. They were easily frustrated, and they provoked fights and arguments with their peers (cited in Goleman, 1995, 80–82). A youngster who is unable to control the impulse to strike out, either in fear or anger, is a walking powder keg. Almost half of the boys identified as bullies in elementary school will have adult felony records by age twenty-four (Brendtro & Ness, 1996).

Impulsive behavior is a survival mechanism that has been passed down to us from our ancient forebears. During the Paleolithic era, an impulsive reaction could mean the difference between life and death. Making quick judgments and leaping to action was the best way to eat and avoid being eaten. The biological root of impulsiveness is located in the amygdala, a bundle of small almond-shaped glands near the base of the brain. The amygdala acts like a switching device. It instantaneously evaluates input from the senses and either forwards signals to the frontal lobe of the neocortex for further scrutiny or mobilizes the body for immediate response. The structure of this neural alert system is unchanged from the time our ancestors dressed in animal skins and slept in caves. Fate and the speed of cultural change has placed us in a fast-paced, complicated world with the brain of a cave dweller as our guide. Everyday life is filled with challenges to emotional intelligence. Frustrations, misunderstandings, and disappointments test our abilities to stay in control. Thinking before acting or speaking is the crux of emotional intelligence (Goleman, 1995; Jensen, 1998).

Emotional circuits may be configured by nature, but they are cultivated by experience. Practiced consideration helps to strengthen the neural pathways between the amygdala and the frontal lobe. For young people who are raised in households or neighborhoods where abrupt and hostile reactions are common, the neural track between the amygdala and the frontal lobe becomes the path least traveled. The amygdala kick-starts an impulsive youngster into action without regard for the consequences. Daniel Goleman calls this an "emotional hijacking." An atavistic reaction to a perceived threat elevates, rather than reduces, danger by turning impulse into aggression. An often cited reason for aggressive behavior is a "knee-jerk" reaction to a perceived slight.

Acting out, aggressive behavior characterizes three-quarters of students placed in special education programs because of a behavior or emotional problem (Report to Congress, 1998). Impulsivity not only characterizes the behavior of many youth with mild disabilities, it also influences how they think about themselves and the world around them. Rather than reflecting on how their impulsive behavior hurts others, aggressive youth rationalize their actions. These rationalizations distort their ability to put their behavior into a proper social perspective. They are unable to see their actions from any other point of view but their own. This "me-centeredness" plays a critical role in their deficient emotional intelligence. Students with behavior disorders in particular utilize self-serving thinking patterns to rationalize their behavior. These "cognitive distortions" serve as a sort of character armor, keeping at bay the slings and arrows of reality (Henley & Long, 1999).

A female jogger was beaten and raped by gang members in Central Park. When interrogated by the police about their motive, the attackers explained that they were "wilding" (i.e., having fun). Several of the guilty youth pointed out that it was the jogger's fault she was attacked, because she should have known better than to be in the park during the evening. Such cognitive distortions twist reality into self-serving observations about victims (Henley & Long, 2003). Thus a car is stolen because the owner "is too stupid to remove the keys"; a student is beat up during recess because "he asked for it"; a delivery man is killed because a young-ster wants a new pair of Nikes.

In her article, "Do Conduct Disordered Gang Members Think Differently?," Beverly Lewis (1992) described "errors in criminal thinking." Included among the rationalizations for their actions, aggressive youth blame their victims and cite causes outside their control, such as poverty and insults (e.g., being "dissed"). Aggressive youth follow their own line of misguided logic, and their egocentric explanations are bereft of social conscience. Such youngsters are de-layed in their emotional intelligence. They maximize the fulfillment of immediate physical needs and desires, and they minimize their responsibility for their action.

Helping students to develop emotional intelligence is a high priority. Rehabilitation efforts over the past half century have produced dismal results. Nearly half of youth who are incarcerated will commit another crime upon release (Brendtro & Ness, 1996). The absence of a comprehensive mental health system in this country, coupled with the staggering number of children (one in six) who grow up in poverty presents a challenging picture for those who would help at-risk youth develop the social skills they need for success.

Teaching Social Skills

Teachers both want and need harmony in classrooms. Learning cannot proceed without cooperation, mutual respect, and caring. The "three R's" of the basic school curriculum has been supplemented with a fourth—responsibility. But, teaching personal and social responsibility to a youngster lacking in emotional in-telligence is a daunting task. The key is prevention. Early intervention in teaching social skills that form a foundation for emotional intelligence will produce more effective results than trying to remediate patterns of violent and aggressive be-havior that have had fifteen or more years to develop.

Many general and special educators agree that social skills instruction has a legitimate place in the classroom. Participation in our changing society requires adaptability and human relations skills. Deficits in social skills have been identi-fied as a source of problems for behavior disordered, gifted, learning disabled, and delinquent adolescents (Davis & Rimm, 1985; Hazel, Schumacker, & Sherman, 1982; Marzano et al., 2003). Gresham (1998) defined social skills train-ing as the process of directly teaching students to develop positive relationships with peers and adults.

Through most of the twentieth century, students graduated from high school and found employment in manufacturing. Factory workers needed to follow directions, tend to repetitive work, and accept company rules. The workplace required obedience and conformity. A worker's value was judged on his or her ability to complete an honest day's labor. However, the blue collar world of work is slowly disappearing from the American scene.

The United States is evolving into a service economy. Many new jobs in the twenty-first century require the ability to handle people instead of machines. Employers want employees who can cooperate with others, solve social problems, and resolve conflicts. Historically, the teaching of these skills was assumed by the family and church. But the changing demographics of U.S. society indicate that traditional means of training children in social abilities need support from the schools.

London (1987) characterized today's children as potential victims of a "psychosocial epidemic." He states that millions of American children are at risk because of rents in the social fabric of childhood. London provides the following statistics: 715,000 children are born to unwed mothers each year; over a million nonsexual cases of child abuse are reported each year; three million fourteen- to seventeen-year-olds may have a drinking problem; half a million children attempt suicide each year, and six thousand die by suicide. Students need help in managing their lives. They need to understand how to make good choices. They need to learn to view problems from the other person's point of view. They need assistance in coping with feelings that drive them to drugs and sex (Garabino, 2000).

Three reasons students have difficulty adjusting to social situations are:

1. The student does not know what are appropriate behaviors.
2. The student may have knowledge of appropriate behavior but may lack practice.
3. Student emotional reactions to situations may inhibit performance of the desired behavior. (cited in McGinnis & Goldstein, 1984, 4)

Lack of social competence is one of the primary reasons that students with mild disabilities have difficulty in regular classrooms (Nelson, 1988). More than one special educator has been chagrined at how a student with mild disabilities seemed to "fall apart" when transferred from a special education program to a full-time regular classroom placement.

Social skills programs are a proactive approach to dealing with behavior problems. Brendtro and Ness (1996) stated that building on strengths, rather than fixing flaws, has been the basis for some of the most significant advances in the treatment of delinquent youth. Jane Addams saw deliquency as a spirit of adventure. Maria Montessori developed inner discipline in slum children. Kurt Hahn nurtured civic spirit through community service. Karl Wilker taught responsibility to youth in Berlin's jails, and then gave them hacksaws to cut off the bars. Janus Korczak developed youth courts with peer governance to teach principles of truth and justice (Brendtro & Ness, 1996, 4).

Some examples of programs that have successfully taught social skills through cooperation include the Capital Offender Program in Texas, which uses psychodrama and role playing to teach empathy to youngsters convicted of rape and murder (Mathews, 1995); the Youth-Reaching-Youth Project, an acclaimed national substance abuse prevention program based on peer counseling (Dietz, 1992); and the Child Development Project (CDP) in California, which is the first long-term school-based project to teach prosocial skills to children. Instructional methods in the CDP focus on giving students control of their learning. Cooperative learning, peer tutoring, and a children's-literature-based program teach students enrolled in the CDP to help one another while they learn. A report published by the *Journal of the American Medical Association* on the effectiveness of the "Second Step" social skills program reported decreases in aggressive behavior and increases in prosocial behavior among 750 second and third graders in King County, Washington (Grossman et al., 1997). The Second Step Curriculum focused on three areas: empathy training, impulse control, and anger management.

Each of these successful programs respects the resourcefulness of young people and involves them as decision makers in their learning. In his article, "Reframing Gang Violence: A Pro-Youth Strategy," Frederick Mathews wrote, "Recognize that young people learn responsibility by having responsibility. Youth need to have a voice with respect to their schools and education, social services, community programs, and in government policy and planning directed towards them." (1992, 27). A survey of teacher attitudes toward social skills training revealed that 82 percent of teachers agreed that social skills training should be a part of the school curriculum. The majority of these teachers believed that outside of the parents the general education teacher was responsible for social skills instruction (Bain & Farris, 1991).

Selecting a Social Skills Curriculum

In one classroom, social skills means following directions, sitting quietly, and working independently. Such a classroom is organized autocratically—the teacher is in charge, and student compliance is prized. Students who have difficulty following this regimen will be identified as having social skills problems. In another classroom, perhaps right across the hall, the teacher encourages students to be self-directed. There is a buzz of activity in the classroom as students work in cooperative learning groups and move from one learning area to another. This classroom is organized democratically with an expectation that students will take personal responsibility for their behavior. In such a classroom a student who lacks the ability to work cooperatively is the deviant. Each teacher has different behavior expectations, a different tolerance level for misbehavior, and different methods of handling discipline problems. This lack of consistency undermines school-based efforts to teach social skills.

The expectation that teachers possess the skills and knowledge to teach social skills without the benefit of guidelines or training is at best an unwarranted assumption, and in some cases just plain naive. In order to teach social skills teachers need a clearly defined curriculum, a method for assessing student abilities, and a model for instruction. Even the most talented teacher would have difficulty teaching science, math, or reading without a curriculum. Curriculums provide goals and objectives, ways of measuring progress, and recommendations for educational activities.

Much time and effort goes into researching school curriculums. The marketing of lesson plans, texts, and tests is a multi-million dollar industry. Yet when it comes to classroom discipline practices, for the most part, teachers are on their own. In one way or another all teachers attempt to teach social skills but there are many different points of view about social skills priorities.

A sound social skills curriculum is research-based. It is derived from a theory or model of human development. It substitutes adaptive skills for nonconstructive behavior both in and out of school. A social curriculum begins with general goals and then delineates observable student behaviors matched to goal statements. Specific objectives provide a basis for evaluation of student growth and program accountability. See Figure 10.1 for a list of some frequently used social skills programs.

FIGURE 10.1   Social Skills Programs

Teaching Self-Control: A Curriculum for Responsible Behavior (2nd ed.), 2004 by Henley, National Educational Service.

Curriculum Strategies: Social Skills Interventions for Young African-American Males, 1997 by Taylor, Praeger Publications.

The Equip Program: Teaching Youth to Think and Act Responsibly Through a Peer-Helping Approach, 1995 by Gibbs, Potter, and Glodstein, Research Press.

Getting Along with Others: Teaching Social Effectiveness to Children: Skill Lessons and Activities, 1983 by Jackson, Jackson, and Monroe, Research Press.

Tribes, A New Way of Learning and Being Together, 1995 by Gibbs, Center Source Publications.

Second Step: A Violence Prevention Cirriculum, Grades 1–3, 1992 by the Committee for Children, Seattle Washington.

Skillstreaming the Elementary School Child: A Guide for Teaching Pro Social Skills, 1984 by McGinnis and Goldstein, Research Press.

Social Skills Activities for Special Children, 1993 by Mannix, Prentice-Hall Trade Books.

Back Off, Cool Down, Try Again: Teaching Students How to Control Aggressive Behavior, 1995 by Rockwell, Council for Exceptional Children.

Improving Social Competence: A Resource for Elementary School Teachers, 1994 by Campbell and Siperstein, Allyn and Bacon.

Reconnecting Youth: A Peer Group Approach to Building Life Skills, 1994 by Eggert, Nicholas, and Owen, National Educational Service.

Second Step: A Violence Prevention Curriculum, Grades 1–3, 1992 by the Committee for Children, Seattle Washington.

The Walker Social Skills Curriculum: The ACCESS Program: Adolescent Curriculum for Communication and Effective Social Skills, 1991, by Walker, Todis, Holmes, and Horton, Pro-Ed.

All social curricula emphasize one key point—scheduling time to teach social skills is a legitimate educational activity. If students are going to change their behavior, they require opportunities to learn new behaviors in an organized and relevant manner. Wood states, "A (social skills) program must have relevance to the student's world beyond the special classroom, and the skills learned in the program must produce satisfying results in personal, real life situations" (Wood, 1986, 12).

Schumacker et al. (1983) posed five questions to serve as a guide in selecting a social skills curriculum:

1. Does the curriculum promote social competence?
2. Does the curriculum accommodate the learning characteristics of the students for whom it is to be applied?
3. Does the curriculum target the social skills deficits of the students for whom it is to be applied?
4. Does the curriculum provide training in situations as well as skills?
5. Does the curriculum include instructional methodologies found to be effective with the population of students for whom it is to be applied? (cited in Walker & Shea, 1991)

Social skills can be taught directly or indirectly. Direct instruction begins with the identification of a specific skill—for example, the social problem-solving skill of learning from experience. For a lesson, a teacher could select a contemporary problem—how to increase drug awareness among schoolchildren. The class is divided into small groups comprised of four students. Each group is given art materials, reference materials, and recent newspaper articles. The students must brainstorm five ways of increasing drug awareness and present their findings to the entire class.

Advocates of direct teaching of social skills develop curricula for both general and special education. Such programs as *Skill-streaming the Elementary School Child* (McGinnis & Goldstein, 1984), *The Responsive Classroom* (2002) and *Teaching Self-Control: A Curriculum for Responsible Behavior* (Henley, 2003) provide goals, instructional objectives, learning activities, and consulting guidelines. The aim of each program is to teach social skills that can be generalized beyond the secure confines of special education programs.

Each of these programs is based on the premise that social skills training of students with special needs requires cooperation between general and special educators. Students cannot be "fixed" in self-contained special education programs and then shipped as finished products into general classrooms. (See Chapter 6 for guidelines about inclusion.) In order to develop appropriate social skills, students with mild disabilities need time to learn with and from nondisabled students. Social skills training requires agreement by general and special educators on specific areas of competence to be developed.

Developmental skills, those that cut across many settings, are preferred to context specific skills. Youngsters must be able to cope with social demands in

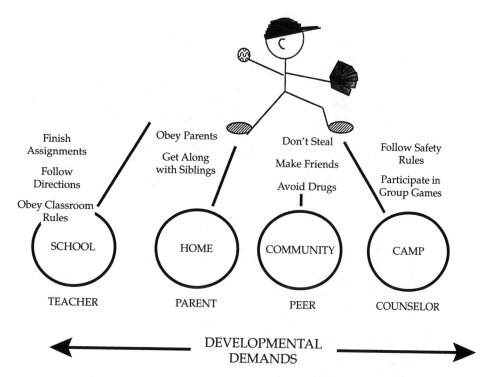

FIGURE 10.2   Development Demands

many different environments. Training a youngster with low frustration tolerance to complete three worksheets is a school context skill. Teaching the same youngster to verbalize rather than act out feelings of frustration is a developmental skill that is useful in many settings (Fagen & Hill, 1987). While following directions, completing assignments, taking notes and other "school survival skills" (Silverman, Zigmond, & Sansone, 1981) are important, unless these skills are embedded in a more comprehensive framework students will leave school without the tools to manage the broader social demands of work, family, and the community (Figure 10.2).

A Sample Social Skills Curriculum

Fagen and Long (1975) defined self-control as the ability to direct and regulate personal behavior flexibly and realistically in a given situation. The work of Redl and Wineman (1951) presented a structural model for describing a self-control curriculum. In their quest to unveil the "anatomy of self-control," Redl and Wineman detailed a list of specific self-control skills that children normally develop as they learn to restrain their impulses and relate to the world at large. Redl and Wineman's detailed descriptions provide the classroom teacher with a paradigm of self-control (1951). As children mature, they must learn to control their impulses, assess social reality, manage group pressure, deal with stress, and solve social problems (Henley, 2003).

What follows is a brief description of the social skills entailed in each of the above areas (see Figure 10.3). The items describe self-control developmental milestones. The descriptions can help the classroom teacher in the following ways:

1. To identify individual student self-control strengths and weaknesses.
2. To anticipate situations when a student might lose control.
3. To establish goals and objectives for a social skills program.

FIGURE 10.3   Self-Control Skills

Impulse Control
Resisting Temptation
Using Materials Properly
Spontaneously Establishing Self-Control
Tolerating Frustration

Assessment of Social Reality
Anticipating Consequences
Evaluating the Effect of Behavior on Others
Appreciating Feelings
Accepting Praise and Affection
Taking Care of Personal Possessions

Manage Group Pressure
Resisting Group Contagion
Maintaining Control Under Impact of Peer Pressure
Adapting to Competitive Challenge
Participating in Group Activities

Stress Management
Coping with Anxiety
Controlling the Floodgates of the Past
Adapting to New Situations
Relaxing

Solve Social Problems
Recalling Disruptive Actions
Learning from Experience
Drawing Inferences from Others' Experiences
Resolving Conflicts

Source: Adapted from Redl and Wineman, 1951; Fagen, Long and Stevens, 1975; and Henley, 2002.

Impulse Control

Impulses are powerful psychological motivators. A student may have an impulse to hit another student or an impulse to throw a textbook in frustration. Impulses are derived from an infant's need for immediate gratification. As children grow and mature, they learn to delay gratification. A student with self-control is capable of restraining impulses. Situations or conditions can strain the impulse control abilities of students and cause classroom disruptions. The following self-control skills are a subset of impulse control:

1. *Resisting Temptation.* As they grow and mature socially, students learn to control the impulses brought on by tempting situations or objects. A student who sees an examination lying on the teacher's desk and resists the urge to pick it up to survey the questions is practicing self-control. Schools are filled with alluring objects. Equipment, toys, and learning materials can present strong temptations to students who lack temptation resistance. Students with emotional problems sometimes steal with no idea about what to do with the object once it is in their possession. One youngster in a program for students with emotional problems was literally seduced by gadgets of any sort. He was so predictable that the teaching staff always knew to go to Peter's "treasure hole" under the schoolyard fence to check for missing items.

Space has its own attraction. Open spaces invite running. Enclosed spaces invite yelling. Field trips, in particular, offer myriad possibilities for disruptive behavior for a youngster who has difficulty curbing impulses.

2. *Using Materials Properly.* Most students understand the purpose of classroom materials. Books are for reading. Erasers are for cleaning chalkboards. Clay is for modeling. Chisels are for scraping wood. Other students use classroom materials as props to act out feelings. An impulsive toss of an eraser across the room at an offensive peer or jabbing an adjacent student with a pencil illustrate how students misuse materials. These students are unable to restrain the impulse to "send a message" with the closest object available. Care should be taken to keep a close watch on materials that could be used to injure another student in a sudden outburst of anger or frustration.

3. *Spontaneously Establishing Self-Control.* Many a substitute teacher has been greeted by a spontaneous, "Oh boy, a sub"; or in other words, "Let the fun and games commence." The substitute teacher scenario is an example of how in certain situations even well-mannered students can fail to spontaneously establish self-control. Controlling one's own behavior when there is no authority figure around to monitor is a sign of maturity and emotional development. Conversely, the absence of spontaneous self-control skills indicates that a youngster is motivated by impulses rather than a sense of social responsibility. Organized classroom activities and routines support the student in maintaining self-control. When schedules indicate a change in routine, particularly from structured to open-ended activities, the impulsive youngster does not have the inner resources

to substitute internal for external controls. Transition times, in particular, challenge the impulse control system of the students.

4. *Tolerating Frustration.* Frustration can be overwhelming for a youngster who lacks impulse control. Such a mundane obligation as waiting for help with a classroom assignment can culminate in a display of anger. When a four-year-old child cries because she loses in a game, that is acceptable. When an unhappy nine-year-old throws a board game aside, sending everyone's pieces flying because someone else bought "Boardwalk," there is a problem. It is quite remarkable to behold how children learn to accept minor frustrations and persevere as they mature. Learning to swim, ride a bike, and play a musical instrument are all building blocks toward perseverance, an essential quality for success in life.

For many children, frustration–tolerance happens naturally and gracefully. Others need to be taught how to handle frustration. Usually low self-esteem exemplified by an "I can't do it" attitude is characteristic of students with low frustration–tolerance.

Assessment of Social Reality

All students learn to take measure of social situations. For instance, behavior that is accepted by one teacher may be forbidden by another. Developing children are remarkably adaptable, and their insight into behaviors that are acceptable and unacceptable is a determinant of how they are accepted by others. Well-adjusted children are capable of maintaining relationships. They interpret social cues and make adjustments in their behavior based on what a situation demands. Deficiencies in their assessment of social reality will result in persistent conflicts with peers or adults.

1. *Anticipating Consequences.* In the classroom, as elsewhere, rules and routines organize activity and keep harmony. Students may not like rules, but they understand why rules are necessary. They know there are consequences for breaking rules. In society, norms substitute for rules, and laws are legislated codes of behavior. Social consequences follow violation of norms, and legal action is the consequence for breaking the law. Students who have an unrealistic notion of rules, norms, and laws interpret them as personal affronts to their integrity or well-being. They resent consequences. Such students, when confronted with consequences for their behavior, may become hostile.

2. *Evaluating the Effect of Behavior on Others.* Youngsters learn that their actions stir up corresponding reactions in others. Without this insight, a student will fail to recognize how personal behavior shapes the way that others act. A youngster who is "mean" to another may show remorse or at least understand why a friend has decided to leave. Some students with behavioral or emotional difficulties are unable to untrack their self-centered thinking. To such a student interpersonal problems are always the fault of others.

3. *Appreciating Feelings.* Students with emotional problems have difficulty accepting the feelings of others. This is not surprising because their own feelings are such a mystery to them. Their ability to identify and describe feelings in themselves and others is deficient. Low self-esteem coupled with a naive grasp of the significance of feelings leaves a student with emotional disturbance at a loss to contemplate his or her own life experience.

4. *Accepting Praise and Affection.* Trust is a basic requirement for social exchange between teacher and student. A student who has difficulty trusting adults will have difficulty forming attachments to others. Expression of care and interest may be reciprocated by hostility or resentment. Many students with emotional problems have well-entrenched defenses against what they consider a hostile world. Such youngsters need to learn to accept and give affection.

5. *Taking Care of Personal Possessions.* A bike that is left unlocked may get stolen. Carelessness in keeping track of assignments can mean coming to school unprepared. Personal responsibility in managing day-to-day activities is important for school success. Students who can manage their daily lives do well in school. Other students need to learn how to organize themselves. They are undermined by their own unintentional carelessness.

Manage Group Pressure

Virtually everything in a classroom happens in a group situation. Group dynamics have a powerful impact on young people both in and out of school. The need to belong and the need to socialize with like-minded people are strong forces that can impel a youngster to make good or bad choices. Why does one youngster join Boy Scouts, while another joins a gang? Why does one youngster look for mystical experience with drugs, and another choose religion? In many cases the answer is the power of peer pressure to shape young people's choices. The ability to handle group pressure is a hallmark of self-control. Students who are overly influenced by peer groups give up control of their lives. These students need to learn how to manage group pressure.

1. *Resisting Group Contagion.* Excitability is contagious. When a class is "out of control," one or more students set off others with their disruptive behavior. Overstimulated students become leaders in pandemonium, and the teacher is hard pressed to restore order. Some students have the internal strength to maintain internal control while others around them are out of control. Meanwhile, other students are swept away by the excitement. Such students need to learn how to appraise situations reasonably and to strengthen their sense of themselves as agents of their own control.

2. *Maintaining Control under Impact of Peer Pressure.* For young people, particularly adolescents, peer pressure is a powerful shaper of attitude and behavior. When confronted with peer pressure, students may be hard pressed to make the types of decisions that adults would advocate. Self-control within groups means being able to steer an individual course of action, even though it may be the opposite of group expectations. By helping students learn to make prosocial decisions despite group pressure, teachers not only enhance classroom management but also provide students with the tools to deal with myriad group pressures outside of school.

3. *Adapting to Competitive Challenge.* Competition is a basic fact of life in our society. Keeping a balanced perspective about winning and losing is necessary to productivity both in and out of school. Winning and losing gracefully require self-control and positive self-regard. Competition in school, both obvious (e.g., tests) and unobtrusive (e.g., art displays), are factors that all students must learn to accept. Resilience, perseverance, and task commitment are basic to success. Students who avoid competition or think of themselves as "losers" need help in learning how to handle competitive challenge.

4. *Participating in Group Activities.* Cooperative group work is prevalent in all levels of society. Learning to help others, resolve conflicts, and share resources are signs of personal growth. Each of these skills requires the ability to "decenter," that is, to consider the other person's perspective. Although these skills develop naturally in some students, others become fixated on their own point of view. This impedes their ability to cooperate and maintain group harmony. Such students need opportunities to learn to set aside their own personal agendas and focus on the concerns of the group.

Stress Management

Stress is the electricity of life. Through a combination of perception and biochemical reactions, stress energizes us to action. Schultz and Heuchen (1983) succinctly state, "All life events carry the potential for introducing stress into a person's life" (cited in Knoblock, 1987, 216). Hans Seyle (1975) define stress as the nonspecific response of the body to any demand, pleasant or unpleasant. For a student, a pleasant prospect, such as anticipating a field trip to the zoo, causes stress just as surely as the unpleasant prospect of going to school without assigned homework.

Learning to manage stress is an important adaptive and survival skill. Perception plays a key role in inducing a stress reaction of fight or flight. Students with emotional disabilities often misinterpret social cues. Overreaction to mild stressors is commonplace with these students. An ordinary task, such as reading aloud in class, can bring on a temper tantrum (i.e., fight) or refusal to perform (i.e., flight). Learning to adapt to stressful classroom situations can help prepare students for life outside of school. Essentially there are four characteristic stressful conditions that challenge the self-control abilities of students.

1. *Coping with Anxiety.* Some students are so ridden with anxiety (painful apprehension or sense of foreboding) that they are unable to decipher reality-based threats from normal expressions of feeling. Their reaction may be to strike out or verbally assault the perceived protagonist. Many teachers have difficulty understanding that overreaction to routine situations, brought on by a student's inability to cope with anxiety, is a symptom of his or her disability. In the section on the life space interview, we emphasized the value of gathering information on how a youngster perceives events in the classroom. Through the use of LSCI and other active listening techniques, it is possible to identify specific stressors that set a youngster off into a fight or flight reaction.

2. *Controlling the Floodgates of the Past.* Fortunately most students have the capacity to separate present events from past unpleasant situations. For example, a student will attempt to persevere in a mathematics assignment despite past difficulties with arithmetic. Given this situation, even a well-adjusted youngster will need support and will at times get frustrated. Students with behavioral disorders have life histories replete with failure or trauma. A minor dose of recall is all that is needed to set off a severe stress reaction.

3. *Adapting to New Situations.* Learning to adjust to unfamiliar situations or people is an essential adaptive skill. Adaptive responses to stress caused by new situations include questions, verbalization of apprehensions, and caution. When students have not learned these adaptive skills, their reactions can be disturbing. Pretenses of familiarity, avoidant behaviors, and unwarranted hostility are samples of how students overreact to new situations or people.

4. *Relaxing.* After a hard day at school, a youngster might look forward to going home and playing with friends. On a rainy day, such a child might pick up a favorite book or get back to completing a model. Relaxation reduces stress. Relaxation is an emotional and biochemical state. Numerous body signs indicate an individual is relaxed: the pulse rate goes down, skin temperature is warm to the touch, breathing is paced and easy. Chronic stress disables the immune system; chronic stress can cause disease. Students with emotional difficulties are rarely able to achieve a prolonged state of relaxation. Even games dissolve into a series of petty disputes. Alone, they have difficulty sustaining solitary activity. Television, alcohol, and drugs are pastimes of youth that are nonadaptive attempts to relax.

Solve Social Problems

Interpersonal problems are difficult to solve. The negotiating of relationships requires the ability to reflect on one's own behavior. One must be able to apply the lessons of the past to present situations. Once a problem is identified, it is necessary to consider various options and eventually choose a course of action. Ultimately, social problem solving requires evaluation of goals and the means to achieve those goals. A student must be able to apply these skills in both individual and group situations. The final achievement is measured by a student's ability to develop and maintain relationships. When a youngster lacks these skills, interpersonal conflicts are frequent, and a youngster becomes isolated by his own futile social gestures.

1. *Recalling Disruptive Actions.* Every teacher and parent is familiar with the refrain, "It wasn't my fault." Denial of personal culpability is normal in young children. As students develop better insight into their own behavior, they begin to accept responsibility for their actions. Students with emotional problems sometimes literally "forget" their own behavior. Redl and Wineman (1951) called this forgetfulness "evaporation of self-contributed links to the causal chain." The youngster is unable to perceive how his or her actions culminated in a classroom disturbance. This lack of recall should not be confused with lying to avoid punishment. Rather the deficiency rests in the inability to perceive personal feelings or behavior clear enough to review a series of events.

2. *Learning from Experience.* Students should be able to apply past experiences to present situations. Learning from past mistakes is a basic strategy for solving social problems. Natural consequences play a significant role in social maturity and development. Children learn to modify their behavior based on reactions from peers: teasing is returned in kind; selfishness keeps others away. Students with behavior or emotional problems may persist in the same social errors regardless of the consequences. Even positive social experiences provide few clues for future behaviors. These students seem unable to learn from their experiences in order to piece together the behavioral steps needed to work out social problems to their advantage.

3. *Drawing Inference from the Experiences of Others.* Some students learn and profit from other students' mistakes or successes. This modeling is a basic style of learning for young people. Adults count on the fact that one youngster may be an example to others. This is the premise behind severe punishment (e.g., expulsions), and it is a premise behind awards and honors. Many youngsters do in fact learn from others and use the experience so gained to guide future actions. A student who cannot learn from the mistakes and successes of others is handicapped by shortsightedness. Adults cringe when they hear a youngster say, "It can't happen to me." The ever increasing numbers of pregnant teenagers and drug dependent youngsters are stern reminders that a key social problem-solving skill is drawing inference from what happens to others.

4. *Resolving Conflicts.* You don't change a lightbulb with a hammer, and you don't solve social problems with aggressive behavior. Many youngsters need to learn conflict resolution, negotiation, and cooperation as social tools. The need for students to be able to appraise social situations and develop peaceful strategies for solving problems has never been greater. Racism and teen violence are commonplace in today's society. Every classroom discipline system should help provide students with the human relations tools needed for functioning as a productive member of a democratic society.

Character Education

Schools are the only places where children are assured constant adult supervision. If today's youngster is to successfully navigate the moral storms that await outside school, they will need adult help. Character education can provide a moral compass. Character education (Kohn, 1991; Lickona, 1988; London, 1987) is a term that best seems to suit the evolving notion that many students need a booster shot of civility and ethics. Proponents of character education stress the teaching of cooperation and mutual respect. Moral development, with its attendant emphasis on caring for others, is emphasized in character education, as is reflection and commitment to moral principles. London lists two primary components of character education: (1) education in civic virtue and in the qualities that teach children the forms and rules of citizenship in a just society, and (2) education in personal adjustment, chiefly in the qualities that enable children to become productive and dependable citizens (London, 1987). Figure 10.4 lists eleven principles of character education.

FIGURE 10.4   Eleven Principles of Character Education

Core ethical values, such as caring, honesty, fairness, responsibility, and respect for self and others, form the basis of good character and should be the focus of character education.

"Character" must be comprehensively defined to include thinking, feeling, and behavior. Knowing the good, loving the good, and doing the good are the ultimate goals of character education.

Character education should be woven into the fabric of school life in a planned, proactive way, and it must be seen as central to the school's mission and purpose.

The school must be a caring community. The daily life of classrooms and all other parts of the school (corridors, cafeteria, playground, school bus), must be imbued with the core values.

To develop character, students need opportunities for moral action. Through repeated moral experiences, students can develop and practice the moral skills and behavioral habits of good character.

Character development and learning should be viewed as inseparable. Effective character education includes a meaningful and challenging academic curriculum that respects all learners and helps them to succeed.

Character education should strive to develop students' intrinsic motivation and commitment to do what is right.

All school staff—teachers, administrators, counselors, coaches, secretaries, cafeteria workers, playground aides, and bus drivers—must be involved in learning about, discussing, and sharing responsibility for character education.

Character education requires moral leadership from both staff and students. A character education committee is often helpful in the initial stages.

Parents and community members should be full partners in the character-building effort.

Effective character education must include an effort to assess progress.

Source: Character Education Partnership, 1997.

Schools that emphasize character education follow different paths in their quest to develop characteristics that exemplify good citizenship. The following examples are winners of the 2000 National Schools of Character awards presented by the Character Education Partnerships, a Washington, D.C.-based national, nonprofit coalition that provides advocacy and leadership for character education.

- Coswold Elementary School, Charlotte, North Carolina—With the motto "Hope means having faith in yourself" as a guide, the school system established a program to recognize character traits among students. School morale went up, and suspensions declined by 40 percent in two years.
- Columbine Elementary School, Woodland Park, Colorado—Beginning with a project to study the culture of Nepal, students' increased understanding of empathy led to support of inclusion programs for students with special needs. The school adopted standards for personal and social responsibility. A 1999 survey indicated gains in students' attitudes toward school and each other.
- Morgan Road Elementary School, Liverpool, New York—Morgan Road used its motto "To grow academically and to become the best people we can be" as inspiration for its Character and Enrichment Committee team to teach character through language arts and literature. Success for increased achievement in math and science was credited to enhanced classroom climate, which increased focused instructional time.
- South Carroll High School, Sykesville, Maryland—Both adults and students are encouraged to be role models for good character. South Carroll established a student leadership program and student SAT scores have risen steadily over the past five years. (ASCD, 1994)

The Child Development Project (Kohn, 1991), begun in 1982 in the San Ramon Valley (California) Unified School District, is an example of a character education curriculum. In the CDP program, children participate in decisions about how classes can become "caring communities." Classroom meetings, cooperative learning, and warm student-teacher relationships are highlighted. A literature-based reading program encourages students to reflect on personal values while learning to read. The CDP program, which was adopted by the Hayward, California, school district, has as its overall goal teaching children to develop self-control. According to Marilyn Watson, an educator in CDP, teachers have learned that you don't need punishment and rewards to have a well-managed classroom. The core of classroom discipline, according to Ms. Watson, "lies in teachers developing positive relationships with their students and helping them to understand the reasons behind the rules."

Character education can be included in any lesson. Lickona describes how a second-grade teacher merged character education with a science lesson. For a science project, the class was incubating twenty chicken eggs. The teacher suggested that the students might want to open one egg to observe embryonic development. Later that day, Nathaniel, seven years old, expressed reservations, "Mrs. Williams,

I've been thinking about this for a long time. It's just too *cruel* to open an egg and kill the chick inside!" Mrs. Williams listened and decided to bring the topic up for a class discussion. Some students agreed with Nathaniel; others wondered how you could kill a chick if it hadn't been born yet. Mrs. Williams gave her students the night to think it over. The next day, the majority decided not to open the egg (Lickona, 1988, 422). This brief episode illustrates a common strategy in character education—values clarification.

Values Clarification

Moral reflection requires understanding one's values. Lickona describes moral reflection in the following way:

> The word reflection refers to a wide range of intellectual activities, including reading, thinking, debating moral questions, listening to explanations by the teacher (e.g., why is it wrong to make fun of a handicapped child), and conducting firsthand investigations to increase children's awareness of the complex social system to which they belong. (Lickona, 1988, 422)

When using values clarification in the classroom, the teacher encourages reflection. The purpose is to guide students in exploring personal values. The teacher does not attempt to impose his or her own value system; rather, opportunities are arranged for students to examine their own values, consider alternatives, and make future choices. Teachers who use values clarification assume that with guidance and freedom, students will identify personal values that reflect the common good. Values clarification can be a proscribed lesson (e.g., class discussion on whether or not to open an egg), or it can be embedded in the flux of daily classroom life. Students are constantly reflecting their values in unconscious ways. Examples of these are:

> Attitudes: "I feel that . . ." "I don't like . . ."
> Aspirations: "One day I'm going to . . . "
> Purposes: "I plan to make a . . ."
> Interests: "I like to . . ." "I enjoy . . ."
> Activities: "After school I'm going to . . ."

Essential to values clarification is questioning. By formulating questions, the teacher can assist the student to understand personal values. Values clarification probes would include questions such as the following:

1. Choosing Freely
   Where do you suppose you first got that idea?
   How long have you felt that way?
   What will you do if you don't succeed?
2. Choosing from Alternatives
   What else did you consider before you picked this?
   How long did you look around before you decided?

3. Reflective Choosing
   What would be the consequences of your choice?
   How much thought have you put into this choice?
   What is good about this choice?
4. Prizing and Cherishing
   Are you glad you feel that way?
   What good is it?
   What do you want?
5. Affirming
   Would you tell the class the way you feel?
   Do people know you feel that way?
6. Acting on Choices
   What is a plan of action?
   Where will this lead you?
7. Repeating
   What are your plans for doing more?
   Has it been worth the time and effort?

Values clarification is aimed at helping students learn how to think through their choices. Caution is advised about making direct statements under the guise of questioning. For example, "You don't really think that is proper behavior, do you?" is a veiled attempt to have a student conform to the teacher's values.

Goals of Character Education

Character educators are proactive in terms of teaching students specific values. For example, Lickona (1991) cited the following goals for character education:

1. To promote movement away from individualism toward cooperative relationships and mutual respect.
2. To foster the growth of moral agency—the capacity to think, feel, and act morally.
3. To develop in the classroom and in the school a moral community based on fairness, caring, and participation—such a community being a moral end in itself, as well as a support system for the character development of each individual student.

Several variations on the above themes appear in other character education models. Edwards (1991) emphasized a modified version of the 1921 Dalton Plan, where students determine their own schedules from subject lab alternatives. The purpose of the Dalton Plan is to teach students to assume responsibility for their own learning in a noncompetitive atmosphere. Kohn (1991) stresses a caring curriculum. He encourages teachers to develop empathetic relationships with their students; to promote cooperation over competition; and to allow students to participate in the governing of the classroom. Each of these conditions, Kohn maintains, increases academic skills by investing students in their day-to-day learning.

Moral Development

The notion of teaching values, moral development, or social skills in the classroom is not a novel idea. Moral development is a cornerstone of Western philosophy. The eighteenth-century philosopher, Immanuel Kant, believed that moral behavior was directed by reason. He provided the following "categorical imperative" to guide reason and actions, "Act only on that maxim through which you can at the same time will that it should become a universal law" (Seldes, 1985, 223). According to the categorical imperative, the rightness of behavior depended on the reasoning behind the act, not the consequences (Benniga, 1988). This focus on the internalization of judgment is what sets advocates of character education apart from teachers who believe students are best trained through external manipulation.

No educator in the twentieth century was a more ardent advocate of character education than John Dewey. In 1909 Dewey published *Moral Principles in Education* in which he advocated the teaching of initiative, courage, judgment, and persistence. He maintained that external control of students instills dependence on the judgment of authority figures. Dewey believed that the purpose of education was to help students develop social consciousness. According to Dewey, concern for the social good required nurturing. Students needed opportunities to help their classmates, participate in classroom decisions, and discuss moral questions.

Classrooms don't have to be inclined toward character education to teach values. All classrooms are saturated in values. Either covertly or overtly, American students for generations have been instilled with values educators believed crucial to success. Consider the following excerpt from *McGuffey's Fourth Eclectic Reader* (1920):

Lazy Ned

" 'Tis royal fun," cried lazy Ned,
"To coast upon my fine, new sled,
And beat the other boys;
But then, I can not bear to climb
The tiresome hill, for every time
It more and more annoys."
So while his schoolmates glided by,
And gladly tugged uphill, to try
Another merry race;

Too indolent to share their plays,
Ned was compelled to stand and gaze,
While shivering in his place.
Thus, he would never take the pains
To seek the prize that labor gains,
Until the time had passed;
For, all his life, he dreaded still
The silly bugbear of uphill,
And died a dunce at last. (cited in Benniga, 416)

Unobtrusive artifacts of values permeate life in classrooms. For example, tests promote competition, while stringent behavior codes demand conformity. Benniga provides insight on the pervasiveness of covert moral education. "Whether or not they offer specific programs, schools provide moral education. In many schools and districts the curriculum in morality is informal and unwritten. It pervades the school and classroom rules (Benniga, 1988). As an illustration, consider the recent change in how scholars depict Christopher Columbus. For years Columbus was portrayed in American textbooks as a prototype of American values. Against all odds, the story goes, he altered our conception of the world and discovered America. He brought Christianity to the native "Indians" and opened the gates to a "new world." So esteemed was Columbus that the Knights of Columbus promoted him for sainthood.

Now compare this traditional tale of Columbus with the view held by some Native Americans. According to Russell Means of the American Indian Movement, Columbus practiced genocide with the fervor of a despot. Under Columbus's administration, Indians living in what is now the Dominican Republic were shipped to Europe as slaves; thousands of others were raped, tortured, and murdered. Recent disclosures of Columbus's misadventures prompted the United Nations to cancel a celebration of his quincentenary. The National Council of Churches stated that the 500th anniversary of Columbus's discovery should be a time of penitence instead of jubilation. Cultural values are shaped by textbook writers and teachers. In the case of Columbus, the atrocities committed against Native Americans were paved over by historians eager to promote Columbus as an icon of American values.

Moral education is as basic to schools as mathematics and reading. What type of moral education do we want to pass on to our students? Advocates of character education believe school should emphasize ethical behavior and civility. These educators prefer cooperation to competition, altruism to individualism, and empathy to egocentrism.

The teaching of character education and social skills is especially relevant for students with mild disabilities. Students with mild mental retardation are characterized by deficits in adaptive behavior; students with learning disabilities have difficulty deciphering social cues; and students with emotional or behavioral disorders act out their emotions in disruptive ways. Teaching students with mild disabilities how to regulate their behavior in socially acceptable ways is a worthwhile goal for educators and parents.

A Functional Model for Problem Behaviors

Teachers in general and special education classrooms are confronted with a variety of behavior problems. Some students, often those with more intense emotional or behavioral problems, require an organized intervention plan. Dealing with chronic disruptive behaviors requires a systematic problem-solving method based on a functional assessment and proactive interventions. The following procedure is a model for responding to persistent classroom disturbances, and it incorporates elements from this chapter and the previous classroom management chapter.

1. *Describe Student Behavior.* Disturbing behavior should be described, not evaluated. Avoid clinical-sounding terms that interpret behavior. Rather than saying that a student is "distractible," describe his behavior; for example, "Steven typically sits still for about five minutes, then he starts sliding books around on his desk, dropping pencils, and talking to other students." Common evaluative comments to be avoided are: hyperactive, immature, aggressive, noncompliant, attention-seeker, and withdrawn. Evaluative terms are too abstract to clearly communicate a problem. A behavior that is "aggressive" to one teacher may be "assertive" to another teacher and "immature" to a third teacher.

Description enhances communication among teacher, parents, and student. It ensures that everybody is talking about the same behavior, and it prevents the misunderstandings that arise when behavior is labeled. Moreover, descriptions of behavior can be counted. Interpretations cannot. You cannot observe "hyperactivity," but you can see and count how many times a youngster gets up from his desk.

2. *Count Behavior.* Educators use a tool called a behavior frequency chart to count behavior (Figure 10.5). This sort of chart is another type of functional assessment described in Chapter 9. Disturbing behaviors are listed next to a series of boxes for each day of the week. Each time a student demonstrates a disturbing behavior, the time is written in the appropriate box. This checklist can be located on the teacher's desk or some other convenient spot in the classroom.

The purpose of the behavior frequency chart is to provide a database for determining the severity of a classroom problem. The more frequent the disturbing behavior, the more likely it is a disturbance in the classroom. The chart gives the teacher an objective way of calculating frequency of the behavior. The data can provide other important information. Perhaps many of the disruptions occur during a specific time of the day; this could provide some insight into its cause. Knowing when a disturbing behavior occurs helps the teacher determine antecedents. For example, the student might be most disturbing after transitions from preferred to nonpreferred activities. Finally, no program can be properly evaluated without initial baseline data. In a few months, do another count to determine whether the intervention program is working.

3. *Empathize with the Student.* All behavior occurs for a reason. Put yourself in the student's shoes. What does he or she feel? A life space intervention (Chapter 9) would be helpful at this juncture to elicit the student's perspective.

Student: _Sylvia_____   Week:_September 7 - 14_

Describe Behaviors	Mon.	Tue.	Wed.	Thu.	Fri.
Verbal taunts directed at teacher	10:00 10:07 10:08 11:15 1:05	9:45 12:57 2:10 2:19	10:12 10:13 10:23 2:19	11:45 11:47 2:29	10:28 10:51 11:12 11:13 11:17
Verbal taunts directed at other students	9:13 12:19 12:20	None	None	11:46 11:51 11:58	None
Moving around the room without permission	10:01 10:08 11:17	2:11 2:21	None	11:45 11:47	10:27 10:53

Comments:

FIGURE 10.5   Behavior Frequency Chart

Consider physiological causes first. Is the student getting enough sleep? How about diet? The average American teenager eats 120 pounds of refined sugar a year. What is your student eating? Is lead poisoning a possibility? When was the last time the student's vision and hearing were checked? Some attention problems are traced to hearing impairments.

What about the student's family? Are there problems at home? Does the student have a home? For that matter, does the student have a family? Don't forget drug and alcohol abuse. Does the student come to school with frequent bruises? Emotional neglect is more difficult to determine than physical abuse, but no less important. Talking to students provides useful information about his or her family and life after school.

Empathizing means trying to understand the problem from the student's point of view. Disturbing behavior in class, if it's serious enough to require a specific plan, will show up outside of school too. Enlist the aid of family members. Empathy alone will not solve the problem, but it will change your perspective. Judgments of the student change from a classroom nuisance, to a real person with a complicated life. Empathizing helps the teacher to depersonalize the classroom disruptions. Approaching the issue with professional detachment ensures that an intervention plan is professionally prepared without anger or resentment.

4. *A Proactive Plan: Behavior Interventions and Teaching Social Skills.* After describing, charting, and counting the disturbing behavior, the next step is to determine the best intervention to curb the disturbing behavior, and to identify a social skill to replace the disturbing behavior.

Teresa, a sixth-grade teacher, has completed a behavior frequency chart on a female student, Sylvia (see Figure 10.5). Sylvia is 12 years old. She is verbal, bright, and impulsive. Sylvia's quick tongue is matched by her fast mood changes. Teresa has counted Sylvia's verbal taunts and sarcastic remarks. They are usually directed at Teresa; and when Sylvia launches these verbal missiles, everything in the classroom stops. Watching Teresa and Sylvia match wits has become a great source of entertainment for the rest of the class.

Through her charting, Teresa sees that Sylvia starts her day out well, then, around 10:00 A.M., she warms to her task of harassing the teacher. By lunch time, Sylvia has made on average five unprovoked and disturbing remarks aimed at Teresa and other students. Sylvia also moves about the room without permission. Empathizing with Sylvia, Teresa considered the possibility that Sylvia might resent her; but why? A conversation in the teacher's lounge with some of the faculty reveals that Sylvia formed a close attachment to Ms. Collins, her fifth-grade teacher. Sylvia asked Ms. Collins to fail her so she could spend another year with her.

Teresa decided to adopt a couple of interventions. First, she would restructure Sylvia's morning. Teresa worked out an arrangement for Sylvia to do peer tutoring each morning in a third-grade classroom from 9:45 to 10:15. Sylvia had no problem with academics, and she had a sensitive side that Teresa hoped could be capitalized on to nurture younger children. Second, Teresa determined to bolster her relationship with Sylvia through hypodermic affection and sane messages. She wanted Sylvia to learn that she was a valued classroom member, but at the same time Teresa knew it was important for Sylvia to understand the effect of her taunts.

Teresa decided to direct her social skills activities toward helping Sylvia assess social reality. Sylvia needed help specifically in evaluating the effect of her behavior on others. The more she thought about it, the more Teresa realized that the other students could learn about how their behavior affects people. Teresa determined to develop a unit for the entire class. She would do values clarification, role playing, cooperative learning activities, and more peer tutoring.

5. *Evaluate the Plan.* How many times do teachers settle on a system for changing student behavior without ever evaluating the plan? In our experience this happens far too often. W. H. Auden had this to say about changing human behavior,

> We would rather be ruined than changed
> We would rather live in our dread
> Than climb the cross of the moment,
> And let our illusions die. (Seldes, 1985, 23)

Changing behavior is a difficult enterprise. A behavior change plan that is elegant on paper can mislead a teacher into overlooking periodic evaluations. Every behavior intervention plan should be evaluated on a regular basis. Three months is a reasonable amount of time to look for some change. Another evaluation requires another behavior frequency count. If there is no decrease in disturbing behaviors, a new plan may be needed. Go back and review the steps outlined in this chapter. Did you miss anything in terms of empathizing with the student? Did you, for instance, fail to talk with family members? Perhaps you need to try some different interventions. If the problem is more serious you might consider life space interventions.

If you are seeing a change in behavior, you hit the mark on your first try. That is a good start. Success in working with a youngster to learn socially adept skills is well worth the effort. Twenty years from now, your students may have forgotten how to multiply mixed numbers; but if they can listen to another person's point of view, you will have left them a valuable legacy.

Summary

Students with behavior problems are handicapped by their lack of emotional intelligence and lack of social competence. Often these youngsters have been identified by the school system as having a mild disability, and sometimes the student is viewed simply as a chronic discipline problem. Regardless of the label, disruptive classroom behavior has a profound negative effect on both teacher and students. Social skills instruction and character education is an educational strategy for helping students with persistent behavior problems learn more appropriate ways of interacting with others. Character education, which overlaps with social skills development, helps students cultivate prosocial values.

Character education and values clarification are two approaches that have been utilized in classrooms for many years in the attempt to shape student attitudes and behavior. When applied to students with behavior problems, social skills instruction is often combined with behavior interventions. The application of a problem-solving approach in order to select specific social skills and behavior interventions helps teachers respond to persistent classroom disturbances in a systematic fashion.

ACTIVITIES

1. Recall your favorite class in elementary or high school. What social skills did your teacher expect you to demonstrate? Did you meet those expectations? What social skills did you develop outside the classroom?

2. In a cooperative learning group, brainstorm ten social skills you think students should learn. Give a rationale for each. Present the results to the class. Discuss similarities and differences in perspective.

3. Have a classroom debate on the question: Is character education a legitimate part of the curriculum?

4. Research old public school textbooks—history, reading, and health would be good choices. Look for values that were highlighted in these texts (e.g., typical American family had mother taking care of children and father working, while Spot just romped around).

5. Review the Redl and Wineman social skills list (Figure 10.3). Select three skills and develop a lesson plan for each.

6. Observe an elementary or secondary classroom for thirty minutes. Record examples of student emotional intelligence. Record examples of student emotional illiteracy. What social skills would incorporate into the observed classroom curriculum?

11 Building Family Partnerships

ADVANCE QUESTIONS

Answer the following questions as you read this chapter:

1. How do social and economic conditions effect the quality of life of children in the United States?
2. What are some barriers to family–school communication?
3. What are some ways that schools have overcome communication barriers that impede parental participation in their youngsters' schooling?
4. What is the emotional impact on family members of having a youngster with a mild disability?
5. What are some ways that parents can gain more information about their role in their youngsters' schooling?

6. How do government-funded programs enhance opportunities for youth?
7. What are some due process rights of parents when a youngster is placed in a special education program?

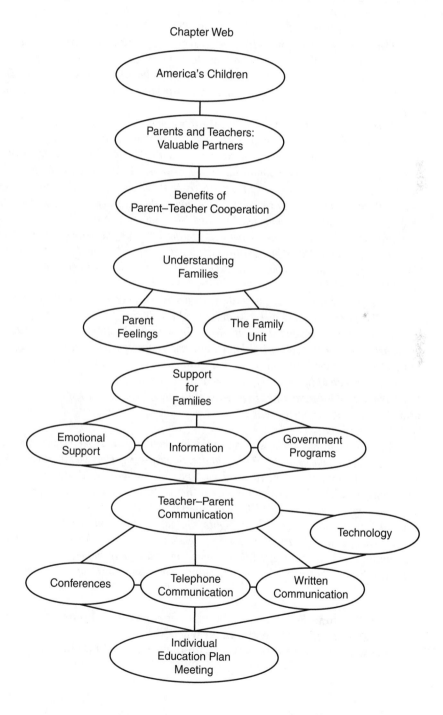

Chapter Web

Vignette: Eileen

Eileen slowly climbed the steps of the run-down, two-family house. She felt apprehensive in this poor neighborhood where every house seemed to need a new coat of paint. As she reached for the doorbell, Eileen reviewed why she was here.

Her student, Alexis, a pretty twelve-year-old, seemed to be compensating for her weak academic skills by playing the role of class clown. Every time Eileen gave an assignment, Alexis had a comment. "You never showed us how to do this," or "This is stupid, why do we have to do it?" were typical of the disturbing remarks Alexis directed at Eileen on a regular basis.

Perhaps this home visit would help. After a moment's hesitation, Eileen knocked on the front door. Within a few seconds the door swung open. Alexis stood in the doorway. "Hi, Ms. Morrison; my mother is in the living room." Alexis led Eileen into a sunny room with blue muslin curtains. Standing with teapot in hand was Alexis's mother. "I'm Mrs. Taylor; I'm pleased you could visit us; Alexis tells me so many wonderful things about you." Eileen glanced at Alexis whose face had suddenly turned three shades brighter. "Please sit down and have some tea," invited Mrs. Taylor. She turned to Alexis, and said, "Go into the kitchen and get some oatmeal cookies for your teacher." "Yes, momma," was the quick reply, and Alexis breezed into the other room. Eileen watched in astonishment. "Is this the same child who has been carrying out a single-handed verbal assault on me in class?" she wondered.

Mrs. Taylor smiled, "It's been difficult for Alexis ever since her daddy died, but she tries hard and she's a good girl." "I'm sorry, Mrs. Taylor. I didn't realize your husband had passed away," responded Eileen. Mrs. Taylor's smile slowly melted away. "Alexis needs help with her schoolwork, I know; but trying to raise her and her younger brother and sister on my waitress salary has been difficult for all of us," said Mrs. Taylor. "Tell me, what can I do at home to help Alexis with her reading? I didn't get past eighth grade, and I want Alexis to earn her high school diploma," continued Mrs. Taylor. Eileen sat down and the two women spent the next hour discussing how together they could help Alexis improve her schoolwork.

As Eileen drove home, she reviewed her home visit. After school, Alexis makes dinner for her seven-year-old brother and nine-year-old sister. Her mother is trying to raise three children on a waitress's salary. They can't afford health insurance. And most surprising of all, Alexis is not the disruptive child at home that she appears to be in the classroom. Eileen smiled to herself. She knew that her classroom strategy for handling Alexis would change. The insights she gained from this visit would help her to better manage Alexis's attention-seeking behavior in school. As she drove toward her condominium in the suburbs, Eileen vowed to make more home visits. An hour in a student's home, she realized, could eliminate countless hours of misunderstanding in school.

1. Do you think Eileen's apprehension about visiting homes in a low-income neighborhood is shared by other teachers?
2. Why don't more teachers visit with their students' families?

3. Do you think school systems should require home visits?
4. What are some reasons for making home visits? What are some reasons for not making home visits?

Eileen's home visit highlights a little-appreciated fact—students' lives do not begin and end at the schoolhouse door. Student experiences outside school have a profound influence on student behavior in the classroom. If a student is having difficulty in school, a home visit can provide a teacher with useful insights into how to handle the problem. In today's public schools there are many communication gaps between students and teachers. Language, cultural, and ethnic differences lead to misunderstandings. Communication is a vital link to bridge this gap. Families are the best source of information about a student's likes and dislikes, emotional peaks and valleys, motivation, and activities outside of school.

America's Children

Children, James Coleman noted, require "social capital" in order to grow, learn, and prosper. Social capital refers to the social networks and adult relationships that nurture children during their development. Coleman found, for instance, a lower dropout rate among students in Catholic schools (3.4 percent) than among students in public schools (14.3 percent). He explained the discrepancy in terms of social capital in the Catholic schools. The community of school and church helped families keep students in school. Because of the additional adult support outside the family, the students attending Catholic schools had a strong incentive to stay in school. Coleman highlighted the bonding together of adults through shared goals and beliefs as a primary source of social capital.

Social capital has steadily eroded since the turn of the century. In early-twentieth-century agricultural society, children were mentored by extended families, neighbors, and community members. Informal relationships between adults outside the family were commonplace. The transformation to an industrial society disconnected children from the lives of adults. Fathers returned home from factories tired from hours of mindnumbing toil on assembly lines. Soon mothers followed fathers into the workplace. The family unit as a source of social capital began to unravel as the pressure to maintain a decent standard of living increased each year. With more time spent in work, adults had less time to spend in community activities such as parent–teacher organizations (PTOs) and Scouting (Coleman, 1987). The overall effect has been an alienation of children from basic nurturing elements in society that were common throughout history. Poverty is the single most crucial factor in determining quality of life for children.

The Children's Defense Fund (2000) reported that in 1999 16.9 percent of children under 18 lived in poverty. African American children have the highest poverty rate (33%), followed by Hispanic children (30%), white children (13%), and Asian/Pacific Islander children (12%). Infant mortality for children born into poverty is 50 percent higher than for children above the poverty guidelines listed by the Department of Health and Human Services (i.e., $16,700 for a family of four living in the contiguous 48 states in 1999). African American children have almost twice the mortality rate of white children—16.5 deaths compared with 6.5 deaths per live births. Poverty and transiency are the two most critical factors influencing the well-being of children in the United States.

Up to 40 million Americans move each year. Mobility is a significant factor in classroom composition. Hodgkinson (2001) reported, "Many teachers have 22 students in the fall and 22 in the following spring, but 20 out of the 22 are different students. Hospitals in these regions spend most of their time taking case histories from strangers. Each Sunday, ministers preach to a congregation, a third of whose members are new" (p. 8). California, Texas, and Florida are the main havens for a million immigrants a year. Sharon Dreyfus, a second-grade teacher in Gaithersburg, Maryland, saw a new face in her classroom every few weeks. Typically the youngster spoke little English and came from a family of recent immigrants. "The biggest challenge is to keep constantly changing the program around to meet the needs of the kids," said Dreyfus. "Not only are they learning a new language, but learning about life in the United States" (Armas, 2001, A5). Other significant demographic data about children include the following:

- Percentage of children born with low birth weight (weighing less than 5½ pounds) continues to rise—7.5 percent is the highest in twenty years. Low birth weight is a leading at-risk indicator for learning problems.
- As children grow older, the quality of their diet declines. A nutritious diet is an essential factor in brain development and learning.
- The percentage of children living with two parents declined from 77 percent in 1980 to 68 percent in 1996. In 1998, 36 percent of African American children lived with two parents.
- Violence among youth has steadily decreased. In 1996, the adolescent firearm mortality rate was the lowest since 1989 for both African American and white youth.

The teenage birth rate has also declined in the 15 to 17 age bracket from 38.7 live births per 1,000 females in 1991 to 32.1 live births per 1,000 females in 1997. Children born to teenage mothers are at risk of developing mild mental retardation (www.childstats.gov). Tragically, government assistance for poor children in the United States falls far behind that provided by other countries. See Table 11.1 for a comparison of the United States and other countries' poverty rate before and after government assistance (U.S. Bureau of the Census, 1995).

Most parents care deeply about their children. A few parents are indifferent and, unfortunately, a small minority of parents actually harm their children. Neglect and abuse are a sad reality in some homes. The Children's Defense Fund

TABLE 11.1   Child Poverty in 17 Developed Countries Before and After Government Assistance

Country	Year	Before Assistance	After Assistance	Percent of Children Lifted Out of Poverty by Government Assistance
United States	1991	26%	22%	17%
Australia	1989	20%	14%	29%
Canada	1991	23%	14%	40%
Ireland	1987	30%	12%	60%
Israel	1986	24%	11%	54%
United Kingdom	1991	30%	10%	67%
Italy	1991	12%	10%	17%
Germany	1989	9%	7%	24%
France	1984	25%	7%	74%
Netherlands	1991	14%	6%	55%
Norway	1991	13%	5%	64%
Luxembourg	1985	12%	4%	77%
Belgium	1992	16%	4%	77%
Denmark	1992	16%	4%	77%
Switzerland	1982	5%	3%	35%
Sweden	1992	19%	3%	86%
Finland	1991	12%	3%	78%

Source: Rainwater, Lee, and Timothy M. Smeeding, 1995, "Doing Poorly: The Real Income of American Children in a Comparative Perspective," Working Paper No. 127, Luxembourg Income Study, Maxwell School of Citizenship and Public Affairs, Syracuse University, Syracuse, New York.

estimated in 1997 that every 47 seconds a child is abused or neglected—a total of 675,000 a year. Early medical and educational intervention for youth should be a national priority. As a society, we are at risk of squandering our most precious national resource—our children. Without a major shift in our national priorities, many youngsters will mature without hope for success in life.

Parents and Teachers: Valuable Partners

Home visits, teacher–parent meetings, and school socials were once common aspects of life in the United States. James Comer's memories of his neighborhood recall a time when the authority of parents was transferred to teachers through proximity.

> When I went into the grocery store with my mother and father in the 1940s, it was a rare day that we did not encounter someone from my elementary school—the custodian, the principal, the secretary, or a teacher. There would always be an exchange of pleasantries and sometimes an exchange about my school behavior or

achievement. The knowledge that my parents knew and appeared to like and respect the people at my school had a profound impact on my behavior. (Comer, 1986, 442)

During the era of the neighborhood school, indirect involvement of parents in school activity was underscored at each chance meeting of teachers and parents at the grocery store, bus stop, park, or library. Trust and mutual respect between school and home was a by-product of close-knit communities. The separation of school and community began in the 1960s with the advent of racial integration through busing. The process of neighborhood-school detachment continued in the 1970s with the middle-class exodus to the suburbs and subsequent regionalization of small town schools. Today, separation of school and family is a pervasive condition. Sometimes the only time a parent has direct contact with the school is when there is a problem. While such measures as school open houses provide some assurance that teachers and parents get an opportunity for personal meetings, these are usually large group activities that preclude personal conversation between parents and teacher.

A common teacher complaint when parents are missing conferences or open houses is that parents "don't care." There are many explanations for parents not attending school functions. Their own education may have left them with negative feelings about school. Perhaps the parent is illiterate or a school dropout. Parents may not have a phone or transportation. There may be a language barrier or a communication problem (the message doesn't reach the parent). A parent might miss a meeting or school function due to an inability to obtain child care. When schools provide child care, parental attendance increases. Parents may be working when meetings are held. Many IEP meetings, for example, are held during the day without regard for parental work schedules.

The isolation of school and family continues at the same time that schools and teachers are being asked to take on responsibilities that used to be the sole domain of the family. Social skill curriculums, character education, and school safety have reordered curriculum priorities. Sex and drug education have become major concerns in schools. In many urban and suburban school districts, Johnny can't read because he's too "high" to care. When schools find ways to work with parents on problems of youth, the results are impressive.

Benefits of Parent–Teacher Cooperation

The National Committee for Citizens in Education (NCCE) found that when teachers maintain frequent contact with parents, students profit. Parent–teacher partnerships produce measurable gains in student achievement. "Some of the major benefits of parent involvement include higher grades and test scores, better long-term academic achievement, positive attitudes and behavior, more successful programs, and more effective schools" (Henderson, 1987, 149). The greater the degree of parental involvement, the greater the likelihood that students will succeed in school. In a review of 53 studies that measured the impact of parent–teacher partnerships, the NCCE did not find a single negative report. The evidence also indicated that students who were at risk for educational failure gained the most from parent–teacher collaboration (Mapp, 1997).

At-risk students include the disadvantaged, the students with mild disabilities, and underachievers. These students are frequently absent from school. Some are behavior problems. Almost all lack the motivation to persevere. By age 16, the at-risk student is a prime dropout candidate. Research on at-risk students indicated that "by the time students are in the third grade we can fairly reliably predict which students will drop out and which will complete their schooling" (Slavin, 1989b, 5). The early onset of school failure underscores the need for close school–family partnerships at the beginning of formal schooling. Successful preschool programs, such as Head Start, place a premium on parent involvement. Disadvantaged students who participate in preschool programs with strong parent involvement components outperform their peers through high school. Despite the documented benefits of parent participation in preschools, the carryover of parent participation in education is uneven. Some educators believe the best place for parents is at a bake sale or car wash. Williams (1988) reported that principals and teachers preferred that parent involvement be limited to extracurricular activities. The educators in Williams's study did not view parent involvement in educational decisions as either useful or appropriate.

Leitch and Tangri (1988) investigated barriers to school–family partnerships in two poor, inner-city, Washington, D.C., junior high schools. Twenty-nine teachers and sixty families participated in the study. The researchers found that a parent from a single-family household was less likely to be involved than one from a two-parent household. The larger the family (six members or more), the more likely the involvement. Extended families, both single- and two-parent, were the most involved. Members of foster families were highly involved. Employment made it difficult for almost half the parents to get to school functions. Among the unemployed, poor health was the most frequent reason for lack of participation. Education did not seem to be a factor; parents who finished and those who did not finish high school were involved on an equal basis.

From the teachers' perspective, their own family responsibilities were factors that impeded setting aside time for parents. Teachers who enjoyed their work tended to value parent involvement more than teachers who were unhappy or disgruntled. Almost half the teachers surveyed blamed parents. Some parental attributes listed by discontented teachers were: unrealistic expectations about the school's role; parental jealousy of teacher's upward mobility; poor parental attitudes about school; large families (although the data showed large families participated more frequently); and lack of parental skills to help with schoolwork. Other teachers listed the following school barriers to parental involvement: absence of school activities, teachers' suspicions of parents, and teacher apathy. All the teachers recognized that changes in society had diminished the parental role. They felt that the schools needed to change to meet the changing social fabric of families and the community.

Leitch and Tangri (1988) reported that parents believed teachers looked down on them. "One parent said that teachers have the attitude, 'I got mine, and you got yours to get' " (Leitch and Tangri, 74). Parents characterized school attempts to get them involved as meager. Parent–teacher organization meetings were the most commonly reported school invitation, although many parents said they never received such notices. The same small group of parents seemed to control most parental activities. Despite the negative attitudes attributed to both teachers and parents, Leitch and Tangri summarized their report by stating that a lack of specific planning about how to organize and utilize parent resources was the major barrier to school–home collaboration.

When administrators and teachers make a commitment to parent involvement, results have followed. In many schools, parents volunteer in classrooms. They sponsor orientation programs, conduct alcohol education classes, welcome new families, arrange for guest speakers, provide library assistance, and much more. The principal is the catalyst in these ventures. The principal allocates resources, persists in parent recruiting efforts, and establishes a school-wide norm that parents are welcome. In order for parent–school partnerships to flourish, parents need to make decisions about school policies. Treating parents as teacher aides and doling out menial tasks works against collaboration. It's not how much time parents spend in school that counts, it's the responsibilities they assume (Sandford, 1987). A well-planned and comprehensive parent–school partnership can have a positive impact on both individual students and the school (Henderson, 1987).

James Comer built school–parent partnerships in approximately 100 urban schools throughout the country. His goal was to create school management teams comprising parents, teachers, and mental health professionals. These schools enhance teachers' knowledge of their students, draw parents into the educational process, especially governance and management, and combine school and community services (Reed & Sauter, 1990). In 1991, The School Development Program merged with the School of the 21st Century to form CoZi, a family support model that enhances families' efforts to participate in their children's schooling (Comer, Zigler, & Stern, 1997). Other such programs throughout the country bear witness to the ability of teachers and parents to work together to improve schools (ASCO, 2000).

In San Francisco and Redwood City, California, Henry Levine's accelerated schools model established specific achievement goals for all elementary-school children. Including parents as educational decision makers is a key component in this program. Joyce Epstein developed other parent involvement models that emphasize reciprocal relationships—the parents within the school and the school within the community. Parent involvement projects share the following values: no child is labeled a potential failure because of social or economic factors; social and physical development of children is as important as academic and cognitive gains; children's development is a shared obligation of school, family, and community. These principles are exemplified in the work of the League of Schools Reaching

Out, a confederation of forty-one urban schools that span thirteen states and Puerto Rico (Davies, 1991).

The League takes an enlarged view on the meaning of parent involvement. The term "parent" is broadened to "family," which may include grandparents, uncles, aunts, and other significant adults in a youngster's life. The League advocates coordinating with social agencies that provide assistance and support to families—for example, agencies that administer housing, mental health, and public health services. Hard-to-reach families are targeted. Included in this group are the non-English-speaking, the unemployed, and the indigent. League members recognize that the families that are least responsive are precisely the ones that most need to get involved with educational affairs. The League of Schools Reaching Out is attempting to revitalize Coleman's concept of social capital by abandoning the deficiency view of urban life and identifying strengths in families. Cultural diversity is prized and families are encouraged to establish their own priorities for school–community partnerships (Davies, 1991).

Just as Eileen's home visit deepened her insight into Alexis and her school behavior, educators throughout the country are learning that families are a teacher's best source of information about students. Families can provide information on developmental, social, and academic problems. Student attitudes toward school are shaped in the home. When families value the educational process, students succeed. If teacher and family are at odds, students are left without direction. But when teachers and families cooperate, they are able to help a student focus on productive goals. Each year teachers begin anew the hope of helping their students grow and learn. Building parental partnerships has proved to be one of the most effective means of turning this hope into reality.

Understanding Families

Cooperation begins with understanding. How does it feel to have a child identified as disabled? What is the impact of a child with special needs on the family? What type of support is available to parents of students with mild disabilities? Parenting is complex and difficult. Parents of children with disabilities must deal with all the tensions and pressures familiar to other families, plus the extra stress of raising a child with special needs.

Parent Feelings

Few children with mild disabilities are identified as requiring special services until they enter school and begin to encounter academic or discipline problems. Suddenly, parents are faced with an array of demands as they attempt to cope with the burden imposed by their child's inability to fit into the normal routine of school life. Excerpts from a family's journal help to convey the feelings experienced by parents whose child became a school "problem."

> September 1995. David began school today. The house seemed so quiet when the three left. David was so happy when he got home. Bubbling away about how much fun it is to ride the bus and have "lots of kids to play with."
>
> October 1995. David's teacher told us that David has no self control. He has been having a lot of trouble getting along with the kids in his class. We spoke to him, but he says it is all the other kids' fault.
>
> May 1996. The complaints about David in school never stop. His teacher says she doesn't know what to do with him. Maybe adjustment to school was just difficult. Maybe first grade will be better.
>
> January 1998. The school called work today and left a message with the switchboard that they need to set up a conference about David's problem behavior. This is just great. Now people at work also know that something is wrong.
>
> November 1998. We just came from talking with the [school] psychologist. He thinks David would be better off if we let him enter a special class. David seems smarter than that, but something has to change. He will be starting in the next few weeks, if some [school] committee says that's what should be done.
>
> December 1998. The meeting of the Committee on Special Education was like the Inquisition. We got there and had to face seven school people. It seemed like they wanted to know everything. The meeting better be confidential and we hope we don't have to go through that again. David is going to the special class in a couple of days. We hope this is the answer, but what does emotionally disturbed mean? What did we do wrong? How can we tell the family about this?

Guilt, denial, anger, and despair are frequently mentioned in professional literature as parental reactions to a child with a disability. The extent to which a parent will experience these feelings is contingent on many factors, including finances, the severity of the disability, the age of the child, availability of child care, and support from family and professionals.

Parents need to be treated as individuals. Each parent has a unique view of his or her child's disability. In order to work effectively, educators need to understand the parent's perspective. This is difficult to do if the parent is pitied or patronized. Trust and respect are essential for communication between parent and teacher. Federal law has made parents key decision makers in determining the type of educational services that will best suit their youngster.

The Family Unit

The universal role of the family is to nurture the young child. Within the family milieu, the child learns the social and intellectual competencies needed to succeed in society. When a family has a child with a special need, all family members are affected. Mother, father, and siblings must learn to cope with the unique stress of living with their child. A child with a disability imposes demands that strain the family's ability to function. Families must cope with several critical periods in the life of a child with a disability (Gloecker & Simpson, 1988):

1. Birth, when parents, usually of children with moderate to severe disabilities, first realize their child is disabled.
2. When the disability is first diagnosed and treatment begins. For parents of children with mild disabilities, this is usually the beginning school years.
3. When the child is placed in a special education program. Placement in segregated special class, pull-out program, or mainstreamed regular classroom can influence parental perceptions about the severity of their child's disability.
4. When the child reaches adolescence, peer acceptance or rejection becomes a central concern.
5. As the child nears the end of the public school years, parents must make transitional plans for their child's future.
6. If by adulthood the son or daughter has not been able to live independently, parents begin worrying about what will happen when their child outlives them.

The family's ability to manage these stress points depends on the severity of the disability, their emotional resources, and the type of support the family receives.

Sometimes the stress can be too much. For example, studies have found that parents of children with mental retardation have higher suicide and divorce rates than families without disabled children (Price-Bonham & Addison, 1978). It also appears that children with disabilities are at greater risk of child abuse (Embry, 1980). In some instances, child abuse or neglect is the cause of the disability. Other problems encountered by families include increased financial burdens, isolation, chronic fatigue, and emotional problems (Gallagher, Beckman, & Cross, 1983).

Coping with the demands of raising a child with a mild disability begins with the husband–wife relationship. Friedrich (1979) found that marital satisfaction is the single best predictor of a family's ability to rear a child with a disability. When husband and wife share the nurturance and physical care of a son or daughter, their marriage can become stronger.

Rick Bennion's comments about his child with mental retardation highlights the need for fathers and mothers to support each other during difficult times.

> Finding out you have a retarded child is somewhat analogous to walking through a mine field. You remain in constant shock and fear as you grope along an uncharted course. The next step is always tenuous, and the lack of a clear-cut path adds to an incessant mental fatigue. For us the initial reactions were, I suppose, rather the norm: Why us? How about a second diagnosis? Is there a miracle cure lurking on the horizon? In the midst of continuous anguish, much solace can be derived from a few words of compassion from friends, loved ones, and particularly each other. No matter how trying, an ongoing dialogue between husband and wife is a must to breach the abyss of despair that envelops your being. (Bennion, 1983, 39)

Gallagher, Cross, and Schartman (1981) studied families who made a successful adjustment to having a child with a disability. Their data suggested that the quality of the husband–wife relationship was an instrumental factor in helping the family cope with stress. Two personal characteristics that the researchers found associated with adjustment were the mother's self-confidence and a "set of supporting values" (e.g., strong religious beliefs).

Working Parents.   The majority of U.S. women are now part of the workforce. This shift in family dynamics presents problems to husbands and wives in their roles as parents. Among some of the problems facing working parents are day care, after-school care, and job responsibilities. Employer sensitivity to the needs of parents is a key factor in how involved they will become in school activities, conferences, or parent organizations. Keep in mind that some parents work evenings and others may work two jobs. Employers who provide employees with flexible short-term leave help promote school–parent relationships. Without an employee-leave arrangement, a parent has to choose between attending a teacher conference and losing a day's pay!

Child care is a pressing problem. Particularly difficult is obtaining child care for older youngsters. Espinoza (1988) reported that in a sample of seventy-nine children aged eight to thirteen years, 42 percent were latchkey children. They were left to care for themselves after school. Parents were anxious about their children returning from school to a home with no adult supervision. An additional 20 percent of the youngsters were supervised by an older sibling, many of whom were just a year or so older. Schools can support working parents by providing after-school child care; arranging evening IEP conferences, and providing an evening telephone service for parent questions regarding homework and other school issues.

Single Parents.   Kathleen McCoy, author of *Solo Parenting: Your Essential Guide* (1987), called single parenting the toughest job in the world. The demographics on single parents indicate that it may be not only the toughest job, but the lowest paying as well. According to the Census Bureau, two-thirds of female-headed families with children under eighteen received some sort of welfare benefits (Zinmeister, 1990). Some researchers and policymakers have dubbed this phenomenon "the feminization of poverty."

Mothers who care for their children alone struggle to make ends meet. Shelter, food, clothing, medical care, and child care are top priorities. Most single mothers work. Two-thirds of single mothers with school-aged children and one-half of single mothers of preschool-age children are employed. The U.S. Department of Agriculture found that almost 10 percent of the average single mother's income goes for child care. Although day care is a necessity for all working mothers, mothers of children with a disability have the combined problem of finding a safe place for their child while they work, and locating someone to provide respite care. The more severe a child's disability, the greater the need for respite. Vadsay noted that 73 percent of single mothers with children who have special needs received some type of social welfare support, but respite care was not included (1986).

Single parents of either sex experience more stress than married couples (Beckman, 1983). Daily chores such as shopping and doing laundry are compounded by nonstop parenting duties. Social isolation, particularly when a child with special needs is involved, increases the loneliness of a single parent. The most obvious impact of single parenting is financial hardship. Parents who must work full time have less time to spend with their children. These families are buffeted by the constant strain of struggling to make ends meet. Older children get recruited as surrogate parents as mothers try to balance impossible schedules. Latchkey children are common in single-parent families. Without a partner to provide emotional support, the parent may be less capable of providing nurturance to a difficult-to-care-for child. This means that normal developmental milestones, such as "the terrible twos" and adolescent rebelliousness, can become the source of severe stress in the single-parent family.

Single parents may cope with their loneliness by relating to their child as an adult friend. Elkind (1982) discovered that single parents are more likely than married couples to treat their children as confidants. Strong emotional bonds can develop between parent and child when that child becomes decision maker, friend, and helper. Children in single-parent families grow up faster than children in two-parent families.

There are negative consequences from relating to a child as an adult friend. The child may be unable to cope with the responsibility of providing emotional support. The parent may become possessive of the child and restrict opportunities for independence. Outside support from friends and other family members can lessen a parent's dependence on his or her child to fulfill the need for companionship.

Many separated or divorced couples continue to share parenting responsibilities. Splitting child-raising schedules is a common practice that ensures that a child will continue to get parenting from both father and mother. The manner in which each parent is able to make the transition from married to separate life while continuing the respective parenting role is a key variable in the emotional development of a child.

Support for Families

Help for families who have a child with a disability can be broadly divided into three categories: emotional support, information, and federal government programs. Emotional support for parents of children with mild disabilities begins with the immediate family, branches out to grandparents and other relatives, and continues with friends and neighbors. Professional support agencies complement "grass root" networks by providing information and services that train families to help themselves. The stronger their support system, the more capable the family will be in coping with the daily stresses of raising a child with a disability.

Federal programs are primarily targeted at low-income families. Poverty continues to play a significant role in the development of mild disabilities, particularly mild mental retardation and behavior disorders. Children without adequate nutrition and health care are at-risk populations. Environmental threats to normal development include heavy-metal poisoning, child abuse, child neglect, community violence, lack of proper educational experiences at home, and drug abuse. Government programs, when funded properly, can prevent and/or remediate medical and environmental conditions that contribute to mild disabilities.

Emotional Support

Parents of children with disabilities often feel alone. Featherstone (1980) reported that "a special loneliness is the most pervasive theme in the stories told by parents of disabled children. This loneliness is nourished from within and without. . . . The two most prominent ingredients of a parent's loneliness are difference—his own and the child's—and isolation" (cited in Stagg & Catron, 1986, 283).

Support groups help parents cope with isolation. When parents have an opportunity to discuss their problems with other parents of children with disabilities, they learn they are not alone. Over the years many self-help, support groups for parents have sprung up in local communities. Sometimes leadership for these groups comes from local professionals; more often parents themselves are the organizers.

Support groups provide parents with an emotional lifeline as they discover that others share their experiences. When parents talk to parents, a sense of comradeship supplants feelings of loneliness and isolation. The Federation of Families for Children's Mental Health, for example, has assisted many family-run organizations in getting started (Bullock & Gable, 1997). Support groups also help parents learn how to use their influence to get the best educational services for their children. Many school systems have parent advisory councils. These advocacy groups are comprised of parents with disabled children and representatives from the local educational agency. They meet on a regular basis to discuss issues pertaining to delivery of special education services in their community. How much influence a parent advisory council has is largely determined by the political activism of member parents. Some typical activities of a parent advisory council include regular review of special education policy in their school system, dissemination of information to parents of special needs children, and the writing of grants to improve educational services for children with disabilities.

Information

Recent federal legislation has enabled parent-organized groups to develop a national networking system. A Federal grant program to support organized parent efforts to provide information and training is the Federation for Children with

Special Needs (www.fcsn.org). The purpose of the Federation is to disseminate information regarding special needs to parents and families.

The National Information Center for Children and Youth with Disabilities (NICHCY, www.nichcy.org) provides educational information and technical assistance to parents, advocates, and professionals. NICHCY maintains a collection of resource publications and fact sheets that help parents locate assistance in their local communities. Since 1922, the Council for Exceptional Children (CEC, www.cec.sped.org) has provided both parents and professionals with support services, including national and regional conferences, journals, and political activism on behalf of children with disabilities. While CEC provides support activities for all types of disabling conditions, other national organizations provide support services for families of children with specific disabilities. Chapters of the Learning Disabilities Association (www.ldanatl.org) and Association for Retarded Citizens exist throughout the country (www.theare.org). These organizations provide parents with information on recent developments in research and teaching children with specific impairments. Parents or educators who wish to contact any of these organizations can get the necessary information from Web sites and state department of education offices.

There are many organizations and agencies eager to help support families. (See Table 11.2 for a list of Internet addresses). Yet each year countless parents

TABLE 11.2 Agencies and Organizations that Support Families

American Association of Mental Retardation www.aamr.org	Internet Resource for Special Children www.irsc.org
American Council of the Blind www. acb.org	Learning Disabilities Associations www.Ldonline.org
American Speech and Hearing Association www.asha.org	Education Development Center www.edc.org
Autism National Committee www.autcom.org	National Educational Service (at-risk and behavior disorders) www.nes.org
Children and Adults with Attention Deficit Disorder (CHADD) www.chadd.org	National Information Center for Children and Youth with Disabilities (NICHCY) www.nichcy.org
Children's Defense Fund–Parent Resource Network www.childrensdefense.org	National Deaf Education Network www.clerccenter.gallaudet.org
Council for Exceptional Children www.cec.sped.org	Office of Special Education and Rehabilitation Services www.ed.gov/offices/OSERS
Federation for Children with Special Needs www. fcsn.org	U.S. Department of Education www.ed.gov

Compiled by Linda Nober, Education Department, Westfield State College.

struggle alone, unaware of the support network that is available to help them. By providing parents with names of local and regional support agencies, teachers can help ensure that their classroom efforts are complemented by help outside of school. Mild disabilities are more than just a school problem. Learning disabilities, mild mental retardation, and behavior disorders are family problems. When families are supported at home, children with special needs have a better opportunity to overcome their impairments in school and in the community.

Government Programs

Because federal grant funding is cyclical and subject to legislative approval, changes in funding priorities and appropriations are frequent. Updated information regarding federal assistance to enhance families involvement in schooling can be obtained through the Department of Education Web site—www.ed.gov. The following is a brief list of important federal assistance programs.

WIC (www.fns.usda.gov). The Special Food Supplemental Program for Women, Infants, and Children (WIC) is a federal grant program for which Congress authorizes a specific amount of funds each year. A family of four that earns $31,593.00 or less annually meets WIC assistance guidelines. The WIC target population are low-income, nutritionally at risk women and children. Specifically included are:

- Pregnant women (through pregnancy and up to 6 weeks after birth or after pregnancy ends). One in four new mothers participates in WIC.
- Breast-feeding women (up to infant's first birthday).
- Non–breast-feeding postpartum women (up to 6 months after the birth of an infant or after pregnancy ends).
- Infants (up to first birthday). WIC serves 45 percent of all infants born in the United States.
- Children up to their fifth birthday.

WIC operates through 2,000 local agencies in 10,000 clinic sites and in 50 state health departments. WIC provides nutritional assistance to pregnant women and children through supplemental nutritious foods purchased at retailers with vouchers, nutrition education and counseling in WIC clinics, and screening and referrals to other health, welfare, and social services.

CHIP (www.cms.nhs.gov/schip). In 1997, Congress enacted the Children's Health Insurance Program (CHIP). Eligible working families are those whose income is too high to qualify for Medicaid, but too low to afford private coverage. More than 90 percent of eligible children live in working families. In most states children age eighteen and younger in a working family of four earning up to $34,100 annually would qualify. The Children's Defense Fund estimated that in

1999, 10.8 million children under 18 lacked health insurance. Of the uninsured, 4.4 million were white, 3.4 million Hispanic, and 2.1 million were African American. Compared with the insured, children without health insurance are four times more likely to have an unmet medical problem, three times as likely to have an unmet dental need, and almost twice as likely to have an unmet vision problem. Lack of health insurance is a leading contributor to mild mental retardation and behavior disorders.

EPSDT (www.familysupport_hsri.org/resources/EPSDT.pdf). Medicaid and Early Periodic Screening, Diagnosis and Treatment (EPSDT) provide health services to families who are unable to afford health insurance. Prenatal care, increased birth weight, decreased neonatal deaths, and fewer abnormalities are some of the benefits of EPSDT for poor children. Screening for lead poisoning is a required component of EPSDT treatment for all Medicaid-eligible children from 24 to 72 months. Childhood immunization programs, which prevent measles, rubella, mumps, polio, diphtheria, tetanus, and pertussis, are funded. As a result of EPSDT, in 1997, an estimated 37,177,000 recipients including low-income persons over 65, disabled, low-income children, and pregnant women received medical assistance (Federal Domestic Assistance Catalog, 1997).

Head Start (www.nhsa.org). Head Start is a federally funded program that provides preschoolers with a range of crucial services. The Head Start educational programs help youngsters learn school readiness skills, thus increasing their chances for academic success when they enter public school. Nutrition and medical screening, including EPSDT and dental checkups, are components of Head Start. Parent involvement is built into every Head Start program. Parents are encouraged to attend parenting workshops on such topics as nutrition and developmental play at home. Some Head Start programs are home-based. Head Start teachers visit youngsters' homes and demonstrate early childhood activities for parents. In 1996, 752,077 children enrolled in Head Start. Children with disabilities comprise 13 percent of the Head Start enrollment (Federal Domestic Assistance Catalog, 1997).

The most notable accomplishment of a Head Start preschool was attributed to the Perry Preschool Program in Ypsilanti, Michigan. By age 19, students who had attended the Perry program "were more likely to have finished high school, were dramatically less likely to have committed a crime, were less likely to be on welfare, and were earning more money" when compared to peers who had not attended the Perry program (Stein, Leinhardt, & Bickel, 1989, 149). Head Start children have demonstrated better school readiness skills, higher verbal achievement, and enhanced social competence when compared to other low-income children (www.nhsa.org/research/bites.htm).

Federal programs make significant contributions to strengthening the ability of parents to improve the health and education of their children. Only the federal government has the financial and political leadership required to make children a national priority. In order to provide for the needs of youth, a new vision of community is needed. A community is a network of people working together toward common goals. This new vision would promote community organizations as extended families. Services such as youth clubs, athletic organizations, schools, mental health clinics, and parent resource centers can help parents and children. All of these ventures are woefully underfunded.

Although we can't turn back the clock to the neighborhood school memories of James Comer, there are many paths to the goal of providing for our nation's children. WIC, CHIP, and EPSDT are based on the premise that children need to be healthy to learn. Head Start integrates health services, parent involvement, and education to help at-risk children succeed in school. Innovative programs and parent involvement provide a decision-making role for parents in schools, establish support for parents to assist children to learn at home, and enhance parent–teacher communication.

Teacher–Parent Communication

Good communication with parents serves three useful purposes. First, it provides teachers with information about their students and parental expectations for school. Second, parents get reliable and up-to-date information to help them make decisions about their child's special education. Finally, when parents and teachers communicate and work together, they develop trust and a sense of shared commitment (Cattermole & Robinson, 1985). Trust helps the school and family support each other and share expectations for student achievement. This is the type of social capital that can make a significant difference in a youngster's life (Bryk & Schneider, 2002).

Communication means more than simply relaying information. The medium of exchange tells parents how the school system feels about them. Schools and teachers who seek minimum parent involvement do the least to attract a parent's attention to important issues. For instance, one school system was obligated by state special education regulations to form a special needs parent advisory board. Instead of sending letters of invitation to parents describing the need for parent participation, the superintendent and special education director squeezed the message on the back of the weekly school lunch menu. As expected, there was minimal parent response. Did this mean that the parents in this school system were apathetic? Of course not, but judgments about parent behavior are sometimes based on such transactions.

Understanding parents of children with mild disabilities requires treating each parent as an individual. Teachers communicate their respect through words and actions. One strategy is to make telephone calls to parents notifying them of their child's positive classroom contributions. This offsets the parental expectation that the only time they will hear from school is when there is a problem.

The following description of an exceptional teacher by a parent highlights the anxiety and hope that parents harbor when they first meet their child's teacher.

I just met a talented and gifted teacher, and I'm still tingling with joy. He invited the parents to a meeting, before the beginning of school, to introduce himself and to discuss the year. I wouldn't have missed it for the world, but I went with fear. What if I didn't like the man? Within half an hour, however, I felt the tension drain from my body to be replaced with excitement. Before me was a talented and gifted teacher. I knew other exceptional teachers before, and this time I could identify the qualities they had in common. (Williams, 1988, 61)

Linda Williams (1988) goes on to describe a teacher who loves to learn, is not afraid to take risks, believes teaching is helping children to learn, conveys the message that parents are important, and respects children. Parents need to know what kind of person is teaching their child.

Conferences

When parents and professionals meet to discuss a child, parents need to feel that they are valued participants. Teachers who treat parents with respect create the best climate for a cooperative partnership. It wasn't long ago that professionals placed the majority of the blame for a child's learning problem on inferior parenting skills. Professionals viewed parents as part of the problem rather than part of the solution. The one-sided view that says, "It's all the parents fault," bred a condescending attitude toward parents of children with disabilities (Gallagher, Beckman, & Cross, 1983). In order to avoid barriers to effective communication, teachers should keep in mind the following pointers outlined by Gloeckler and Simpson (1988).

1. *Parents of exceptional children are more like parents of nondisabled children than they are different.* There are no generalizations about families of children with mild disabilities. Each situation is unique. The majority of special needs children come from families where other children do not have learning problems.

2. *Parents of children with mild disabilities, in general, are not the cause of their children's disabilities.* Mild disabilities have been traced to many sources, including poor instruction, faulty assessment practices, neurological impairments, and poverty. To view parents as the single contributor to a child's disability is misleading and unfair. Teachers may encounter some parents who are inadequate. These individuals need support and help, rather than condemnation.

3. *Parents are interested in their child's welfare and will react positively to those they believe are genuinely interested in their children.* Parents need someone to listen more than someone to tell them what to do. Listening indicates concern and interest in each individual situation. Listening helps professionals to problem-solve with parents. When parents feel their point of view is respected, they are more likely to be open and honest in their conversations.

4. *The family is a social unit.* When a child is identified as having a learning disability, mild mental retardation, or emotional disturbance, each member of the family—mother, father, siblings, and relatives—will have individual reactions.

The interrelationship among family members will have an impact on how a student behaves in school.

5. *Parents have the greatest impact on their own children.* No matter how many professionals are involved with a youngster, the specialist is still the parent. Parents need accurate and full knowledge of their child's status in school. Explanations of classroom actions, test results, and professional judgments should be honest and direct. Describing student actions in descriptive, nontechnical language helps the parent to understand discrepancies between home and school behavior.

An initial parent–teacher conference sets the tone for all future teacher–parent contacts. In order to prepare for a conference, imagine how the parent feels driving or walking to the conference. What will be on his or her mind? Think about feelings that precede a visit to a doctor, dentist, lawyer, or professor. A common concern is that something is wrong. Some parents, particularly those of children with mild disabilities, approach a conference with apprehension. They might be concerned that they appear to be "bad" parents, or they hope the teacher has some magic up his or her sleeve that is going to turn things around for their child. Their schooling may have been a negative experience, so the simple task of walking into a classroom and sitting down with a teacher can be anxiety provoking.

The first step to a productive parent–teacher conference is preparation. The following are some practical suggestions for parent–teacher meetings.

1. *Physical preparation.* Physical preparation means attending to the accoutrements of the conference. Don't sit behind a desk. If you are an early childhood teacher, provide adult-sized chairs. Have concrete samples of student work available to highlight topics you want to cover. Sit at a table that is wide enough to display student work. Be organized.

2. *Mental preparation.* Have a mental or written checklist of specific items you want to review. Avoid using materials, such as test profiles, that require educational jargon to explain. Talk in plain language. If the parent is non-English-speaking, make an attempt to communicate in a way that will help set the person at ease. A smile and cheery "Buenas tardes," for example, can go a long way toward helping a Spanish-speaking parent to relax.

3. *Establish a mood.* Begin a conference with good news. This will set a positive tone and help smooth the waters for any trouble spots that need to be reviewed. Be candid and direct with parents. Honesty helps establish trust. Don't dominate the conference. At least 50 percent of the talk should come from parents. Remember that the purpose of the conference is for both of you to learn about each other. Use active listening skills. Encourage parents to give examples of their concerns by talking about what happens at home. Remember that you are probably the only other adult outside the family that a parent can confide in about his or her child. This is an opportunity for parents, but they need your nonjudgmental support in order to express their concerns. Finally, don't be defensive. If a parent makes what appears to be a negative remark about your teaching or the curriculum, listen to what they have to say. Listening demonstrates respect.

4. *Carryover.* Teachers can use a parent conference to assist parents with their children at home. Many parents would like to do more but they need guidance. Table 11.3 offers ideas for parents to improve their children's school performance. You could give a parent a reading list of children's books, or you might refer a parent to another resource such as the WIC program or Head Start. A teacher's credibility rides on follow-up. After the conference is over, make a careful written record of the conversation. Include suggestions and questions that were discussed, and the type of follow-up you agreed on (Bjorklund & Burger, 1987; ASCO, 2000).

Telephone Communication

School systems that make creative use of telephones can extend educational services to families. For example, the San Diego County Office of Education installed an EdInfo service. It offered seventy-five prerecorded messages twenty-four hours a day in English and Spanish. Funded through a grant from the Wells Fargo Bank Foundation, EdInfo provided families with information on such topics as parents and teachers, tests and testing, drug and alcohol abuse, and special programs (Chrispeels, 1991).

Within the Indianapolis school system, Dial-A-Teacher gave families assistance with homework. This direct access line was staffed by two teams of teacher specialists Mondays through Thursdays from 5 P.M. to 8 P.M. Each five-member team comprised teachers with expertise in specific academic subjects. The specialist teams help parents and students solve difficulties with specific homework assignments.

The "Homework Hotline" was a live, call-in television show carried by two Indianapolis cable systems. The purpose of the call-in show was to provide assistance in mathematics for students in grades one to six. When parents or students made their calls, they talked to teachers who used chalkboards to go over and, if necessary, reteach math concepts.

The Parent Line/Communicator was a computerized telephone message service in Indianapolis that provides families with information on approximately 140 different topics such as parenting skills, adult education, and magnet schools. Fifty messages featured information on drug and alcohol abuse. The line was open twenty-four hours a day. As many as 3,000 calls were made by families each month (Warner, 1991). These innovative programs, sponsored by the Indianapolis School System, illustrate that with a little bit of imagination (and

TABLE 11.3 Helping Parents Help Their Children

1. You Can Help Your Child Mentally by

–praising your child for work well done and for good effort.

–eliminating comparisons of your child to another child.

–showing confidence in your child's abilities.

–being realistic in your expectations of your child.

2. You Can Help Your Child Physically by

–seeing that your child gets adequate sleep.

–providing a schedule or fixed routine for your child to follow during school days.

–seeing that your child has an appropriate diet with limitations on the amount of "junk food" consumed.

–encouraging your child to exercise regularly.

–seeing that your child visits his/her dentist and doctor on a regular basis.

–showing your child a lot of love.

3. You Can Help Your Child Academically by

–talking with your child. Have your child talk about the day's activities or future plans for the weekend or any other subject of interest.

–listening to your child. Responding to questions encourages curiosity and motivation in a child.

–reading to your child and having your child read to you.

–seeing that your child does assigned homework.

–establishing a regular time and place for your child to study.

–providing materials to use while studying (e.g., pencils, paper, dictionary, etc.)

–allowing your child to do his/her own work, but being available to provide assistance if needed.

–taking your child to the library often.

–playing vocabulary games with your child, such as naming common objects around the house and their uses; going to the grocery store and naming fruits and vegetables.

–playing question games with your child. Ask your child questions that begin "What if" or "How will."

–having your child memorize some vital pieces of information, such as a family telephone number, home address, your place of employment, the police emergency number, and other information needed for your child's safety and well-being.

–serving as a positive role model for your child by reading, using appropriate speech, writing notes or letters, watching educational television programs.

4. You Can Help Your Child in Test-Taking by

–ensuring your child gets a good night of sleep so as to be alert during the next day.

–seeing that your child eats breakfast.

–seeing that your child dresses appropriately for outside weather conditions.

–getting your child to school on time (so there will be no last minute problems).

–encouraging your child to do his or her best on the test, but not placing undue pressure on your child.

–demonstrating verbally and nonverbally that you have confidence in your child's abilities to perform well on the test.

5. You Can Help Your Child in Other Ways by

–seeing that your child turns in assigned homework.

–keeping up-to-date on your child's progress in school.

–getting to know your child's teacher(s).

–volunteering to work in a school classroom or making materials for use in the classroom.

–participating in school-sponsored activities.

–reviewing your child's work folder as it is sent home from school.

–supporting the parent-teacher organization of the school that your child attends.

Source: J. Whiting (Child Service Coordinator) and S. L. Aultman (Georgia Learning Resources System Center Director), 1990.

some funding) the telephone can provide families with immediate access to school services. Unfortunately, this scenario is all too common. As Ron Davies points out, "A telephone is a low-cost but crucial piece of equipment to encourage school/family/community connections" (1991, 379).

Written Communication

Newsletters, parent handbooks, and bulletins provide families with information regarding their rights and obligations under the Individuals with Disabilities Education Act. Teachers and administrators usually assume that parents understand this information. Given the importance of parental involvement in special education decisions, it is clearly in the school's best interests to disseminate readable information to parents.

In order to fulfill their obligations, parents need a working knowledge of special education law and regulations. They should understand notification, evaluation, and placement procedures. Parents also must be aware of due process procedures established to protect their rights. Parents should know how to utilize parent advocates. Finally, parents need to understand their role in developing and implementing the individualized education program (IEP).

Roit and Pfohl (1984) assessed the readability of written information disseminated to parents regarding their involvement in special education meetings. The researchers hypothesized that parents did not clearly understand information presented in school information materials. Their supposition had particular significance for parents of students with mild mental retardation and behavior disorders because a disproportionate percentage of these children come from either non-English-speaking or culturally different families. Additionally, Educational Testing Service data on adult literacy indicated that between eighteen and twenty-three million adults cannot read a daily newspaper.

The results of the readability study indicated that large pages filled with small print made reading overwhelming and unappealing. The use of examples, samples, charts, and pictures enhanced the readability of printed materials. The researchers found that bold headings and outlines did not communicate information as effectively as paragraphs that related concepts to specific situations. Finally, Roit and Pfohl recommended organizing the content of printed material into five broad categories: (a) disabling conditions (e.g., what is a learning disability and how does it affect a youngster developmentally, socially, and academically?); (b) normal child development; (c) legal issues and trends in litigation; (d) assessment and placement procedures; (e) the role of parents in the educational process.

Although parent conferences, the telephone, and newsletters represent the traditional approach to school–family communication, educators realize that the electronic media has tremendous potential for interconnecting families and teachers, especially in isolated rural areas.

Technology

In Westfield, Massachusetts, the superintendent had a weekly television show on the local cable public access station. During this show he explained such issues as why school buses ran late and how two new schools would be funded. He interviewed principals and teachers and explained to viewers how public schools compete with other city agencies for shrinking dollars. Local cable access offers educators tremendous opportunities for making contact and educating parents and students alike. Yet television is just one piece in a panoply of electronic devices.

The Internet, C-Span, public access cable, and CNN beam immediate and interactive information into millions of U.S. homes. It appears that the dream of educators—lifelong learning—is about to be fulfilled, but in ways hardly imagined even ten years ago. The classroom has expanded into the living rooms of the United States. Televised college study through distance learning is available in many areas—and can be validated through supervised examinations offered in regional centers or over the Internet.

The tools are available for educators to expand the notion of social capital into social electronic capital. As an illustration, US Vidotel in Houston, Dallas, and Fort Worth offered users a combination of interactive math games, *Grolier's Encyclopedia*, and a directory that lists information about local school systems and educational services. The Internet can provide multiple options for parent involvement. Parents can communicate with teachers and each other via teleconferences. School Web pages provide access to school menus, activities, and volunteer schedules. Interactive Web pages provide tutoring for homework assignments. These electronic systems are not a substitute for face-to-face contact, but they do provide a valuable new link between home and school (Grunwald, 1990). While teachers scramble to find an available telephone (see section on telephone communication), the communication industries are devising new, more profitable ways of bringing electronic communication into U.S. homes. The Internet puts the world at the fingertips of every school child. The U.S. Department of Education provides an array of technology information to assist teachers, parents, and students in using the Internet and other electronic technologies. The Network of Regional Technology Consortia (R*TEC) program is one example. Ten regional offices disseminate information for the effective use of technology in education. Special emphasis is placed on fostering regional cooperation and resource sharing (www.rtec.org). The use of high-tech information systems to facilitate school–home communication requires commitment and imagination. It remains to be seen whether educators can turn Internet possibilities into partnerships between schools and families.

The Individual Education Program Meeting

One of the remarkable aspects of the Individuals with Disabilities Education Act is that parents are required to collaborate with educators to determine the appropriateness of their youngster's individual education program (IEP). The law requires parental involvement in deciding:

1. Type of special services required (e.g., speech therapy, counseling)
2. Educational placement (e.g., full-time regular class with support, resource room, special class).
3. Makeup of the individual education program (e.g., annual goals and objectives).

Students with mild disabilities cannot be evaluated or placed in a special education program without parental consent. If parents do not agree with educational decisions about their youngster, they have the due process right to mediation and appeal. Figure 11.1 lists parental due process rights. The fact that several parent–school disagreements about special education services have reached the Supreme Court highlights the importance of parent–school cooperation.

The IEP begins with the initial referral and concludes with the parents agreeing to special education services outlined in the program. The IEP is a management tool designed to ensure that special education services match a student's individual needs and that special education services are monitored. It contains annual goals and objectives, a statement about a student's educational strengths and weaknesses, and a description of special education and related services. Figure 11.2 lists the basic components of the IEP. The individual education program must be approved by parents before a student can be placed in a special education program.

FIGURE 11.1   Parents' Due Process Rights

1. The right to examine school records.
2. The right to request a special education evaluation.
3. The right to refuse the school permission to do a special education evaluation.
4. The right of child to remain in a general education until parents agree to special education services.
5. The right to request an independent educational evaluation.
6. The right to bring an advocate to all meetings.
7. The right to participate in the development of an individual education program (IEP).
8. The right to disagree with the IEP.
9. The right to appeal decisions made by the school system regarding special education services.
10. The right to review and amend the IEP.
11. The right to have a child educated in the least restrictive environment.

FIGURE 11.2 **Components of an Individual Education Program**

An individual education program (IEP) is a written plan provision of special education services for a student who is disabled.

Each IEP must contain:

1. A statement of the child's present level of educational performance.

2. A statement of annual goals.

3. A statement of the specific special educational and related services to be provided the child, and the extent to which the child will be able to participate in regular educational programs.

4. The projected dates for initiation of services and the anticipated duration of the services.

5. Appropriate criteria and evaulation procedures.

In theory, the IEP meeting provides for maximum parental input into a child's special education program. Unfortunately, the reality is often different. Sometimes, parents are not viewed by educators as colleagues at the meeting. A survey of several hundred families (Lynch & Stein, 1987) reported that 50 percent of parents did not feel they were active participants and only 34 percent of parents made suggestions during the meeting. Sometimes, because of time conflicts, transportation problems, child care needs, or work commitments, parents are unable to attend the meeting. When parents are absent, the IEP is usually mailed to them for their signature.

When parents attend the IEP meeting, a variety of factors impede participation. Consider the following scene. A group of professionals are sitting around a table facing the parents. Each professional takes a turn reporting on the educational failure of their child. The parents are deluged with educational jargon like "subaverage IQ," "deficient adaptive behavior skills," "dyslexic," and "behavior disordered." Education jargon places the parents at a serious disadvantage as they try to follow what is being said. Without an advocate to help the parents sort out what is happening, the parents are in jeopardy of consenting to an IEP that is unclear.

All IEP meetings are not as muddled for parents as the one just described. When educators are sensitive to parents' feelings and take the time to explain what they are talking about, parents have an opportunity to be involved. Educators need to remember that it takes a good deal of resolve for a parent to participate in a meeting that is intended to analyze what is wrong with his or her child. One parent expressed her feelings this way.

The IEP process was something that was really hard for me to accept and get into, because I'm not by nature an assertive person. In a group I don't speak up that much, but as a parent in an IEP conference, I have to. I have to be totally prepared. I may have a lot of confidence in the staff that's working with him; they're all great people. But I have to know what each is doing with Geoff and where they're headed with him. I need to review my concerns when I go to the conference, to speak up, and really be his advocate. I have to do that. I think the parent is the one who has the best whole concept of the child, with regard to where he's been and where he's going. And the parent has a lot to offer the staff members—knowledge and understanding of the child. (Roberts, 1986, 206)

The IEP planning meeting is an important event in a parent's life. By following a few basic guidelines, educators can ensure that the meeting enhances rather than diminishes parent–teacher communication.

1. Before the meeting, tell parents how the meeting will be conducted, who will be attending, and what they can do to be effective participants.
2. Arrange seating so parents are not sitting on one side of a table, "squared off" against the professionals.
3. Avoid general negative statements like "Carlos is eight but has a mental age of five." There is enough valid criticism of educational assessment procedures to warrant tempering of professional enthusiasm for the accuracy of test results.
4. Encourage parent questions after each professional makes a contribution.
5. Be conscious of the group dynamics. Is one person dominating? Are there hidden agendas? Are the professionals communicating their views in plain language? Are parents giving off distress signals with body language? Most important, are parents being given ample opportunity to verbally participate?
6. When the meeting is over, summarize the group's conclusions and indicate one professional that the parents can contact to answer questions that may occur to them on the way home.

In order to ensure an appropriate education for students with disabilities, Congress mandated parent participation in IEP meetings. By encouraging active parental participation, educators not only fulfill their legal responsibilities, they also provide students with their best opportunity for success.

Summary

Teachers and families share a common vision. Both want children to develop the social and intellectual skills needed to function as contributing citizens. Homes, schools, and communities are besieged by the ravages of poverty, drugs, and alcohol. Schools and families need each other. When educators reach out to families and seek their involvement, schools improve, students achieve, and communities grow closer together.

Parents of children with mild disabilities need support and understanding as they deal with the daily stresses of modern life. When a child is evaluated by the school as having a mild disability, it affects all members of the family. This ripple effect in turn influences the family's ability to cope with the demands of parenting and education. There are many organizations that support families. Yet many families struggle on in isolation, unaware of the network of help that is available to them. Parents need opportunities to communicate with others who share their problems. Parents need information about their rights and responsibilities as co-determiners of their child's appropriate education. Successful experiences with the schools are needed in order for parents to believe in their ability to promote their child's education. Most of all, parents need teachers who respect them and value their role in shaping the education of their children.

ACTIVITIES

1. Organize a mock school meeting to which parents have been invited. The purpose of the meeting is to inform parents of students with mild disabilities about the due process guidelines mandated by Public Law 94–142. Half of the class members should act as parents and the other half as school personnel. School personnel can be the building principal, guidance counselor, special education teachers, support teachers (art, music, physical education), and so on. The school personnel should present the guidelines, and then answer any questions the parents might have. Both groups should formulate guidelines they will present and questions they might ask.

2. Divide into teams of four to six students. Each group should simulate two teacher–parent conferences. The first simulation might show ineffective things a teacher might do, such as exhibiting poor planning, having a negative attitude, and so on. The second simulation might show things a teacher can do to have an effective conference with parents. One of the team members could serve as a narrator and describe the things the teacher is doing that lead to an ineffective and then an effective teacher–parent conference. Either the teacher or another student might videotape the conferences for later review and discussion.

3. Divide into "family" groups. Each group will be the parents, siblings, or grandparents of one of the following:

   a. an infant with a developmental delay

   b. a school-age child with a learning disability

   c. a school-age child with mild mental retardation

   d. a school-age child with a behavior disorder

   e. an adolescent with mild mental retardation

f. an adolescent with a learning disability

g. an adolescent with a behavior disorder

Discuss your feelings about various school transitions (e.g., entering school, transferring to junior high, graduating).

APPENDIXES

Appendix A: A Chronology

Appendix B: Commonly Used Psychoactive Medications

Appendix C: Tests

Appendix D: Sample Individualized Education Plan (IEP)

Date	Mental Retardation	Behavior Disorders	Learning Disabilities	Generic to General and Special Education
1799		Jean Itard's attempts to train Victor, the Wild Boy of Aveyron (France). Treatment centered around sensory stimulation exercises coupled with systematic teaching procedures.		
1792		Philippe Pinel appointed head of Bicêtre Hospital of mentally ill in Paris, France. Pinel influenced humane treatment.		
1802			Franz Joseph Gall speculated that specific regions of the brain control certain mental activities.	
1817				Thomas Gallaudet became principal of the first residential school for the deaf and mute persons in Hartford, CT.
1820s	Almshouses erected in America for the destitute, originally designed to provide humane and moral care for the poor; became catchalls for the retarded, insane, ill, and other afflicted.			
1828		Horace Mann influenced authorization of funds for state hospitals for the insane in Massachusetts.		
1831				Samuel Howe became director of the Perkins School, formerly called the New England Asylum for the Blind.
1834				Louis Braille publishes the first Braille code.
1830s & 1840s	Conditions in state hospitals were little better than almshouses. Other forms of treatment included public			Horace Mann set economic and legal foundations of American public education, while Secretary of Massachusetts Board of Education (1837–1848), he wrote bills which became national standard

(continued)

APPENDIX A Continued

Date	Mental Retardation	Behavior Disorders	Learning Disabilities	Generic to General and Special Education
1830s & 1840s *(continued)*		auctions, selling of chattel slaves, and abandonment.		(e.g., lengths of school year, tax base for financial support of schools, standardized teacher training, standardized school curriculum, political selection of school superintendent, and so on). Established first state normal (teacher training) school (1839).
1837	Samuel Howe began a class for training retarded children at Perkins Institute in Boston, Massachusetts.			
1839				The first state normal school opens in Massachusetts. Elementary level teachers receive 11 weeks to one year of preparation.
1842	Edward Sequin was instrumental in founding the first school for care and education of mentally retarded (MR) students in Paris, France.			
1843		Dorthea Dix reported cruel and inhumane treatment to the Massachusetts Legislature (e.g., chains, locks, cages, bloodletting practices). Influenced construction of special asylums some improvement over prisons and poorhouses. Nonexistent rehabilitation and education programs.		
1846		First educational facility (Westborough, Massachusetts) for socially maladjusted youth. Established with reformatory and educational goals in mind; thus called a "reform school."		

Year				
1848	Massachusetts was the first to support state schools for the mentally retarded in the United States.			Depression brought financial strains. Dorthea Dix reveals shocking conditions in asylums.
1850s		Overcrowding doubled clientele of reform school. Custodial rather than instructional services rendered.		
1851	Harvey Willus was the first state-supported school for MR in New York (transferred from Albany to Syracuse in 1855). Other such schools followed in the northeastern and New England states: Ohio (1857); Connecticut (1858); Pennsylvania (1859); Kentucky (1860); Illinois (1865).			
1850s	Edward Sequin believed retardation to be treatable and curable. Environmental factors (e.g., health, diet) considered important.		Paul Broca demonstrated that speech disorders were the result of damage to the frontal convolutions of the brain. He proposed that the functions of the brain's left and right hemispheres were different.	
1860s		Prevailing belief that social deviance was inevitable product of immigrant population, largely poor and uneducated.		
Mid-1860s	Rise of Darwinist thought. Environmental view gave way to emphasis on innate deficiencies. Mood of pessimism became dominant. State institutions became more custodial. Samuel			National Deaf-Mute College opened, later renamed Gallaudet College.

(continued)

APPENDIX A Continued

Date	Mental Retardation	Behavior Disorders	Learning Disabilities	Generic to General and Special Education
Mid-1860s (*continued*)	Howe was discouraged with the results of the Perkins Institute.			
1866		Samuel Howe became discouraged by increased size and bureaucratization of mental hospitals and reform schools.		
1870s		Establishment of "ungraded schools" for mischievous and disruptive children in New Haven, Connecticut (1871); New York City (1874); Cleveland, Ohio (1875).		
1870–1890	Herbert Spencer (Britain) developed a "philosophy of natural selection" (weaker members of society pose threat to future of mankind, thus only the most fit of human species be allowed to survive).			
1875–1900		Classes for socially maladjusted children grew rapidly.		
1887				Anne Sullivan begins work with Helen Keller.
1890s	Increased advocacy efforts for special classes or schools for recalcitrant or mentally deficient children.			More stringent administration of compulsory attendance laws. Educational Commission of the City of Chicago (Hapur Report) urged the establishment of ungraded classes for unmanageable children.
Late 1800s	First public school programs for the MR in Providence, Rhode Island (1896); Springfield, Massachusetts (1897); Chicago, Illinois			

Year		
1896	(1898); Boston, Massachusetts (1899); New York City (1900). Called classes for "backward" children.	
1897	First U.S. psychological clinic for children opened at the U. of PA by Lightner Witmer.	National Education Association (NEA) approves the Department of Special Education.
1898		Alexander Graham Bell states that children with handicaps have a right to education in the public schools. Anti-immigrant attitude perpetuated Social Darwinism.
Turn of Century	Establishment of special classes to cope with children who presented problems for regular classrooms.	
1900		Special class programs for gifted begun in NYC and Worcester, Mass. Day classes are provided children with blindness in Chicago. The first electrical amplifying device is developed for persons with hearing impairments. Term "special education" used by Alexander Graham Bell at the NEA convention.
Early 1900s	MR children frequently assigned to foreign-speaking "steamer" classes; many normal foreign children placed in classes for the mentally deficient.	
1902	Ungraded classes in New Haven, Connecticut, reported to serve three distinct types of children grouped together: incorrigible boys, mentally defective children, and non-English-speaking youth.	
1904	Alfred Binet creates the first paper intelligence test. G. Stanley Hall, founder of the American Psychological Association and originator of child-study movement, published Adolescence, a two-volume study of youth development and adaptation to the environment.	Preparatory schools opened for gifted students in Worcester, Mass. New Jersey's Vineland Training School held summer classes for teachers of students with M.R. Public Law 58–171, promoted circulation of reading materials for persons with blindness.

(continued)

Date	Mental Retardation	Behavior Disorders	Learning Disabilities	Generic to General and Special Education
1905				Maximillian P.E. Groszman became the founder and director of the National Association for the Study and Education of Exceptional Children; was first to use term "exceptional." E. L. Thorndike planned a scale to measure educational achievement.
1907	Indiana passed first sterilization law for mental defectives.			
1908	Henry G. Goddard, while Director of Research at the Training School in Vineland, New Jersey, translated the Binet intelligence scales into English and made adaptations for their use in the United States.	Clifford Beers published personal experiences in mental institutions for a depressive mental disorder. Exposed inhumane and inadequate treatment.		
1909		Elizabeth Farrell helped establish the first special education class in New York City.		
1911	Goddard published own version of the Binet–Simon Test. New Jersey was the first state to pass legislation concerning the education of MR children in the public schools. Defined MR as "three or more years retarded in mental development."			
1911	New Jersey mandated special classes when number of students with MR in district totaled 10 or more.			

1912	Devereau School Founded in Philadelphia for treating youth with mental retardation and emotional disturbance.	
1912	Publication of "The Kallikak Family," which gave fuel to the prevailing eugenics theory. Portrayed the "feeble-minded" as a menace to society and to the future of the human race. Proposed that social undesirables (e.g., criminals, paupers, drunkards) arose from the genetic stock of the mentally deficient.	
1914	Charles Scott Berry set up the first teacher-training program in special education at a residential school for MR in Michigan.	
	St. Louis, Missouri, public school system adopted eligibility standards for special schools for the severely MR and ungraded classes for borderline and backward students.	
1915		Connecticut Board of Education hired Arnold Gesell as first official school psychologist to examine slow-learning children and to devise better methods for their school instruction.
1915		*Laggards in Our Schools* by Leonard P. Ayres, used as one of first special education texts.
1916	Lewis Terman produced the Stanford–Binet Scale of Intelligence.	
1917		James Hinshelwood, a French physician, defined "word blindness" as a condition in which an individual with normal vision is unable

(continued)

Date	Mental Retardation	Behavior Disorders	Learning Disabilities	Generic to General and Special Education
1917 (*continued*)			to interpret written or printed language. Hinshelwood theorized that this difficulty is caused by a defect in the left hemisphere of the brain, the portion that stores memories of words and letters.	
Between 1852 and 1918				Compulsory school attendance required in all states of the Union, beginning with Massachusetts (1852) and ending with Mississippi (1918).
1918	Wyoming appointed State Director of Special Education responsible for MR, crippled, and speech-defective children.			
1919	St. Louis eligibility standards of 1914 were adopted statewide and subsequently adopted by other states.			
Years prior to 1920	Relatively small number of teachers trained to work with mentally or socially handicapped. Most facilities were residential with staff members trained on the premises. Technology was not yet developed for assessing individual differences, and special education was not included in curricula at teacher colleges.			
1920s		August Aichhorn, student of Sigmund Freud, developed residential facility for aggressive, delinquent boys.		Columbia University Teachers College prepared teachers of the gifted.
1922	W.E. Fernald persuaded Mass. to set up statewide system of mental clinics for diagnosing children with MR.			The Internatinal Council for the Education of Exceptional Childeren (CEC) founded with Eliz. Farrell as first president in NYC. Original purposes for establishing the CEC organization included:

Year			
1924	Estimated 43,000 persons with MR reside in institutions; 40 state institutions nationwide in existence.		1) To emphasize the education of the special child rather than his identification or classification; 2) To establish professional standards for teachers in the field of special education; 3) To unite those interested in the problem of the special child.
	American Orthopsychiatric Association founded. Concerned with early prevention and correction of children's behavior disorders.		
1925		Samuel Orton coined the word strephosymbolia (twisted symbols).	Classification of exceptionalities published by John Lewis Horn in the *Education of Exceptional Children*.
1926		Sir Henry Head theorized that disorders in language could not be dichotomized as sensory or motor.	Hollingsworth implemented enrichment programs for the gifted in New York public schools.
1922–1932	MR enrollment in separate facilities within public school systems more than tripled.	Growth of separate facilities within public school systems for deviant children.	
1928			Seeing-eye dogs for the blind are introduced in the U.S.
			Courses in special education offered at 43 teacher training institutions.
1929	Special classes for socially maladjusted frequently called "disciplinary classes." Employed strong arm rather than education or rehabilitation approach.	Samuel T. Orton speculated that one side of the brain dominated the language processes; therefore, he concluded that disabled children who had no demonstrable brain injury had failed to establish hemispheric dominance.	
By 1930	Sixteen states passed legislation regarding education of the mentally handicapped.		U.S. Office of Education established a section of Exceptional Children and Youth administered by Elise Martens.

(continued)

Date	Mental Retardation	Behavior Disorders	Learning Disabilities	Generic to General and Special Education
Early 1930s			Kurt Goldstein observed meticulosity, perseveration, figure-ground configuration, forced responses to stimuli, and catastrophic reaction in adult, brain-injured patients.	
The 1930s	Decrease in special programs for MR and socially deviant youth due to: 1) Less money for special programs; and 2) Dissatisfaction with the quality of education in special classes.			
	Public schools more likely to provide separate facilities for MR children than for any other exceptionality group, especially the northeast and north central states.	Establishment of disciplinary classes for truant and incorrigible youth in the schools.		
	Building principals often experienced difficulty in distinguishing between pupils who were "fit subjects" for disciplinary classes and those who were mentally retarded.			
1932				Thirteen states established a state director in charge of administrative special education services.
1933				The first teaching certificates for special education are issued (Mental Retardation, Deaf, Speech Defective, Partially Sighted, Blind, and Crippled). The International Council for the Education of Exceptional Children was shortened to the International Council for the Exceptional Children (ICEC).
1934				*The Board of Education of Cleveland Heights v. State ex rel Goldman* ruled that the exclusion of a child with low mental functioning, on the basis of tests prescribed by the State Department of Education, was unauthorized.

414

1935	Edgar Arnold Doll publishes the Vineland Social Maturity Scale. New York was the first state to certify school psychologists. Roles consisted largely of evaluating and making recommendations for placement in special services of children viewed as "backward" or MR.	Certification guidelines are established by the American Association of Instructors of the Blind. Talking books on phonograph records are produced.
Late 1930s and Early 1940s		Alfred A. Strauss and Heinz Werner investigated brain-injured, mentally retarded children. Findings led to the identification of the exogenous subgroup of retarded children (externally brain-injured). Grace Fernald used the VAKT (visual-auditory-kinesthetic-tactile) approach in the development of remedial reading programs.
1943	The Sonja Shankman Orthogenic School opened in Chicago under Bruno Bettelheim for children with emotional disturbance.	
1944		Laura Lehtinen collaborated with Strauss to develop teaching procedures. Strauss and Lehtinen coauthored *Psychopathology and Education of the Brain-Injured*
The 1940s-W.W.II years	Use of handicapped (including MR) in many jobs due to able-bodied men being away at war.	World War II years necessitated man power.

(continued)

Date	Mental Retardation	Behavior Disorders	Learning Disabilities	Generic to General and Special Education
The 1940s–W.W.II years (*continued*)			*Child* (1947) in which two interventions were suggested: 1) Manipulation and controlling the environment, and 2) Teaching the child voluntary control.	
1946		Division of Child Welfare in NYC organized "600 schools" for children viewed as emotionally disturbed or socially maladjusted. Despite therapeutic intent, these schools were operated as warehouses for uncontrollable boys and were custodial in nature. Fritz Redl and David Wineman opened Pioneer House, a residential treatment center for severely aggressive adolescents. Developed the Life Space Interview intervention.		
Until Early 1950s	Nearly all schools had policies that excluded children with I.Q.s below the mild range. Parents of these children were expected to educate them at home or place them in state or private residential facilities.	Pearl Berkowitz and Esther Rothman extended psychotherapy into the classroom at Bellevue Hospital in N.Y.		
Early 1950s	Federal funding for teacher preparation in MR enacted.	William Morse designed mental-health milieu in camp setting.		
1948 to 1952 to 1958	Number of children enrolled in special public school programs increased			

Year	
	from 87,000 to 113,000 to over 213,000.
1950	National Association for Retarded Citizens (NARC) first organized in Minneapolis, Minnesota. This organization was considered the primary source of help to families with retarded children, as well as a major information disseminating and legislative lobbying force.
The 1950s	William M. Cruikshank facilitated the transfer of brain-injured research from exogenous retarded children to children with normal intelligence. Cruikshank conducted the Montgomery County Project in Maryland.
1951	Fritz Redl and David Wineman publish *Children Who Hate.*
1953	P.L. 83–531 Cooperative Research Act. Funds earmarked for research with students with MR. B.F. Skinner published *Science and Human Behavior.* Proposed operant conditioning as treatment model for B.D.
1954	Cooperative Research Act of 1954 (P.L. 85–531) authorized support for cooperative research in education; funding was granted for this in 1957.
1955	Helmer R. Myklebust defined language as symbolic behavior (i.e., using words as symbols for expressing ideas and feelings and labeling objects). Strauss and Newell C. Kephart coauthored Vol. II of

(continued)

Date	Mental Retardation	Behavior Disorders	Learning Disabilities	Generic to General and Special Education
1955 (*continued*)			*Psychopathology* . . . in which comparisons were made of research on brain-injured children of normal intelligence with research on mentally retarded brain-injured children.	
1956			Spaulding presented an approach to written language disability called Unified Phonics Methods. Words are pronounced and component sounds are written in accordance with the rules of English spelling. Jerome Bruner coauthored *A Study of Thinking* (Bruner, Goodnow, & Austin) which stressed the importance of studying covert cognitive processes.	All 48 states had established legal provisions for some sort of state assistance, advisory and / or financial, to local special education programs. The degree of involvement and support varied from state to state, and the growth of special education services has not been at the same rate for all types of exceptional programs.
1957			Noam Chomsky gave support to "inner thinking processes."	Public attitude toward education for all children was spurred by general concern of the populace for American education after the Russian launching of Sputnik.
1958 & 1959	P.L. 85–926 and P.L. 86–158 authorized fellowship awards for graduate students intent on careers as teacher-trainers or administrators of the mentally retarded.			
1950s & 1960s	Improved education and training of MR occurred under the Kennedy administration.			

1960	Richard Whelan used token reinforcement methods at the Children's Rehabilitation Unit. Association for the Advancement of Behavior Therapy founded.	CEC publishes first set of professional standards for special education. U.S. Office of Education funds grant for CEC to operate the ERIC Clearinghouse on Exceptional Children. Federal Bureau of Education for the Handicapped (BEH) formed. Encouraged training, research, demonstration, etc.
1960s	Edward L. Thorndike, called the "father of reinforcement theory," believed the connection between stimulus and response represented all learning.	J. M. Wepman postulated that the language "transmission" process is divided into receptive and expressive modes. "Integration" provides for the decoding and encoding of previously learned patterns to give meaning to the stimulus. Emphasized role of recall, transmission (receptive and expressive modes), and integration (the decoding and encoding of previously learned language patterns). Beginnings of educational focus on children with learning difficulties. Ogden R. Lindsley developed a comprehensive set of measuring procedures, called "precision teaching," which includes pinpointing behavior, counting and charting performance, and making instructional decisions based on performance data.
Early to Mid-1960s	Norris Haring and E. Lakin Phillips combined Cruickshank's structured-environment classroom and B. F. Skinner's operant conditioning to develop educational programs for emotionally disturbed children.	

(continued)

Date	Mental Retardation	Behavior Disorders	Learning Disabilities	Generic to General and Special Education
Early to Mid-1960s (*continued*)		The Council for Children with Behavioral Disorders (CCBD) was founded as a division of CEC.		
1962		Nicholas Long became Director of Hillcrest Children's Center, Washington, D.C. (residential school for B.D.). Long trained teachers in psycho-educational principles. Norris Haring and E. Lakin Phillips applied behaviorism in their Arlington Project for educating students with behavior disorders.		
1963	Passage of P.L. 88–164 increased support for training of personnel and extended support for professional training to severe areas of childhood exceptionality, including mental retardation and emotional disturbance; authorized use of funds for research and demonstration projects in field of handicapped education.		Term "learning disabilities" was introduced by Samuel Kirk at a national conference of parent organizations and subsequently adopted. Association for Children with Learning Disabilities (ACLD) was formed as a parent, teacher, professional interest group.	
Mid-1960s			Department of Health, Education, and Welfare sponsored several task forces to study brain-injured children with learning problems. Term "minimal brain dysfunction" (MBD) was introduced.	Host of domestic legislation was enacted at the federal level, aimed at launching "War on Poverty" and achieving the "Great Society."

Year		
1964	Council for Children with Behavior Disorders established as a division under CEC.	
1965	P.L. 89–313 encouraged programs to educate children with disabilities residing in institutions and other state-supported residential facilities.	P.L. 89–10, Elementary and Secondary Education Act, Title VI (ESEA) provided assistance to children in "disadvantaged" areas (including handicapped children). Act was part of the "Great Society's" legislative package and was considered a significant effort to alleviate poverty through schooling. Eleven colleges and universities received funding by the U.S. Office of Education to help support training of personnel in this field. Office of Economic Opportunity (OEO) established to aid the culturally disadvantaged or deprived child.
	P.L. 89–105, added to P.L. 88–164, permitted the construction and operation of research facilities and related programs, including the training of special personnel.	Head Start, an OEO-funded project, along with remedial reading, counseling, and tutorial services was begun.
	National Society for Autistic Children (NSAC) was founded. Was one of the first major parent-interest groups devoted to concerns of the emotionally disturbed child. Organization has sought public school involvement for autistic children and has opposed their placement in private or residential facilities.	Student Council for Exceptional Children (SCEC) is organized.
		A separate Bureau for the Education of the Handicapped (BEH) was created within the U.S. Office of Education. Special Education was included in the top policy-making levels for the first time.
1965	Burton Blatt publishes exposé on institutions "Christmas in Purgatory"	
1967	*Hobson v. Hanson* litigation resulted in finding the "tracking" system in Washington, D.C., to be unconstitutional. Based on standardized test results, children were placed in honors, general, or special programs. Relying on *Brown v. Board of Education*, the court held that assessment measures were culturally biased and sustained an un-	

(continued)

Date	Mental Retardation	Behavior Disorders	Learning Disabilities	Generic to General and Special Education
1967 (*continued*)	justifiable racial separation of students. A disproportionate number of African American children were enrolled in special classes.			
1968	Lloyd Dunn questioned the wisdom of special self-contained class placement for students with MR.	Joint Commission on Mental Health of children estimated at least 100,000 children were in residential treatment institutions for B.D., and 1.5 million children and youth were in need of psychiatric services.	The Division for Children with Learning Disabilities (DCLD) (now Council for Learning Disabilities) was organized as a professional division within the CEC.	P.L. 90–538 authorized the negotiation of grants and contracts with both private and public agencies to establish experimental preschool and early education programs for special needs students.
		Frank M. Hewett designed the "engineered" classroom using developmental sequence of educational goals known as the Santa Monica Project.	The National Advisory Committee of Handicapped Children (NACHC) was formed to develop a definition for learning disabilities. *Journal of Learning Disabilities* was published.	P.L. 90–583 (Handicapped Children's Early Education Assistance Act), established experimental demonstration centers for the education of preschool children with disabilities.
1969			P.L. 91–230, the Specific Learning Disabilities Act of 1969, was passed along with all of the categories of programs and services for educating children with special needs who receive federal assistance. The definition developed by the NACHC under Kirk's leadership was used in this act.	P.L. 91–61, provided the authority to the Secretary of health, education, and welfare to contract a university to develop, construct, and operate a national center of educational media and materials for persons with disabilities.
Late 1960s & 1970s	Skinner defined two types of learned behavior: respondent (involuntary) and operant (voluntary). Transferred work with animals in the laboratory (1950s) to observable, measurable events in the educational arena (1960s and 1970s).			"Right to fair classification" cases filed as action suits. Parents and other interested parties argued that the labeling and placement procedure by which children are processed into special education is culturally discriminatory and a violation of the 14th Amendment's Constitutional guaran-

Early 1970s			tee for due process and equal protection under the law. Jean Piaget's developmental theory suggested that instruction should recognize maturational growth and not require students to perform skills for which they are not ready.
The 1970s	NARC organized effective lobbying forces and succeeded in bringing about massive increases in school services for children previously thought to be "unteachable."	Juvenile justice system dealt with 900,000 youth ages 10 to 17, which was 3 percent of this age group.	
1971	Pennsylvania Association for Retarded Children alleged violations of due process and equal protection under the 14th Amendment of the U.S. Constitution regarding barring of low I.Q children from public schools in that state. Similar "right-to-education" suits initiated in other states.		
1971	Larry P. v. Riles was filed as a class action suit in California on behalf of several African American children who had been placed and retained in EMR classes. Plaintiffs alleged use of racially and culturally biased testing procedures, which violated the Civil Rights Act of 1871 and the right to equal protection under the California Constitution and the 14th Amendment of the U.S. Constitution.		The optacon, an optical scan of a printed page, generates a tactile impression of letters for persons with blindness.

(continued)

Date	Mental Retardation	Behavior Disorders	Learning Disabilities	Generic to General and Special Education
1972	A preliminary injunction was issued by the court halting the use of I.Q. tests in the state of California for placing African American children in classes for the EMR.			P.L. 92–424, mandated a minimum of 10 percent of the enrollment slots in Head Start programs be made available to students with disabilities. *Mills v. the Board of Education* mandated the District of Columbia serve all students with disabilities.
1973		Peter Knoblock promotes open education for disturbed children.		P.L. 93–112, Section 504, specified that no individual with a disability should be excluded from the participation in, be denied benefits of, or subjected to discrimination under any program or activity receiving federal financial assistance.
1974	Carl Fenichel developed the League School in Brooklyn (first day school for psychotic children). Enlisted parents as partners.			P.L. 93–380, Title VI, extended the Education of Handicapped Act. Required states to locate and serve all children with handicaps. Assured an education with one's peers, if possible, and mandated nondiscriminatory evaluation materials. Included in law was Family Educational Rights and Privacy Act of 1974, referred to as Buckley Act. This Act protects the confidentiality of school records and provides procedures to challenge questionable information in student records.
1975		U.S. Senate report (subcommittee to Investigate Juvenile Delinquency, 1975) documented growth of violence and crime in schools.		Public Law 94–142, Education for All Handicapped Children Act (EHA), provided for a free, appropriate public education for all handicapped children, and defined special education and related services. Mandated that an individualized education plan (IEP) or an individualized family services plan (IFSP) be developed for every child found eligible for special education or early intervention.

1975	P.L. 94–142, The Education for Handicapped Childrens Act, is enacted into Federal Law
1976	CEC revised Professional Standards and Guidelines in Special Education.
	The Kurzweil Reader, a prototype translator of printed text into speech for readers with blindness, is invented.
1978	Gifted and Talented Children's Act (Title IX-A), provides funds to state and local education agencies and public and private agencies to meet the needs of gifted and talented students.
1978	Formation of the National Joint Commission for Learning Disabilities (NJCLD).
Late 1970s	The Reagan Administration attempted to deregulate and decentralize all phases of public education; however, most categorical services and mandates regulating special education survived this initiative. Department of Education established by Congress.
1980	U.S. Dept. of Health and Human Services reported 15,000 children ages 14 and under admitted to inpatient facilities and over a quarter million seen in outpatient psychiatric clinics.
	A separate U.S. Department of Education established, removing responsibilities from the Department of Health, Education, and Welfare.
1981	*S-1 v. Turlington* rules that complete cessation of services for students with disabilities is not allowed; expulsion is allowable under some circumstances.
1982	The DCLD membership voted to withdraw from CEC and form an independent organization, the Council for Learning Disabilities (CLD). A cadre of former DCLD members began a new CEC division called the Division for Learning Disabilities (DLD).
1983	Office of Special Education and Rehabilitative Services (OSERS) created under the newly established Department of Education.

(continued)

Date	Mental Retardation	Behavior Disorders	Learning Disabilities	Generic to General and Special Education
1983 *(continued)*				Public Law 98–199 (EHA Amendments) passed. Reaffirmed the federal role in special education by expanding P.L. 94–142 with supported preschool, secondary, and post secondary programs for the handicapped, and support for special education teacher preparation, early childhood education, parent training, and information dissemination.
1985				Children "at risk"—poor, nonwhite, disabled, and female become the focus of education reform.
1986				Public Law 99–457 (EHA Amendments) reauthorized existing EHA, amended PL 94–142 to include financial incentives for states to educate children ages 3 to 5 by the 1990–91 school year, and established incentive grants to promote programs serving handicapped infants (birth to age 2).
1988				The Gifted and Talented Students Education Act of 1988 authorized funding of a National Research Center and demonstration programs to build the nationwide capability to meet the needs of gifted and talented students, especially those from traditionally underserved populations.
1989				Academic standards take the spotlight. The National Council of Teachers of Mathematics is the first to state its curriculum standards.
1990				P.L. 101–336, Americans with Disabilities Act (ADA), gives civil rights protection to individuals with disabilities in private sector employment, all public services, public accommodations, transportation, and telecommunications. Patterned after (and extends) to Section 504 of the Rehabili-

1990 to 1991	tation Act of 1973. Prohibits discrimination on the basis of disability and requires agencies to provide "reasonable accommodations." P.L. 101–392 (Carl D. Perkins Vocational and Technology Education Act) provides resources to improve educational programs needed in order to work in a technologically advanced society. Guarantees full vocational, educational opportunities for all special needs populations. Public Law 101–476, Individuals with Disabilities Education Act (IDEA), reauthorized and renamed existing EHA. This amendment to EHA changed the term "handicap" to "disability," expanded related services, and required individual education programs (IEPs) to contain transitional goals and objectives for adolescents (ages 16 and above, special situations age 14). The exceptionality categories of autism and traumatic brain injury were added.	The U.S. House of Representatives opened for citizen comment the issue of a separate exceptionality category for students with attention deficit disorders. The issue died without legislative action.
1991	National Education Goals 2000 are adopted. Encourages involvement of reform-minded communities, national examinations, and parental choices including private schools.	
1992	Rehabilitation Act amendments establish the presumption that anyone can be employed and increase the focus on vocational rehabilitation services for minorities.	
1994	P.L. 103–239 (School to Work Opportunities Act) promotes collaboration and problem solving by the Department of Education and Labor. Encourages partnership models between school-based and employment-based sites at the local level. Promotes interagency agreements, technical assistance, and services to employers, educators, case managers, and others.	
1995	CEC published its third set of standards for the preparation and certification of special education teachers.	

(continued)

Date	Mental Retardation	Behavior Disorders	Learning Disabilities	Generic to General and Special Education
1997				P.L. 105–17 (Amendment to and reauthorization of IDEA) adds general education curriculum to student's IEP, modifies alternative placement options pending discipline determinations, and modifies transition requirements.
2002				No Child Left Behind Act (NCLB). Reauthorization of the Elementary and Secondary Education Act. Mandates standardized testing of students with disabilities. Sets specific goals for progress in reading, math, and science.
2004				P.L. 108–446 reauthorization of IDEA. Establishes new criteria for identifying learning disabilities and disciplining students with special needs. Reduces paperwork and streamlines due process procedures. Addresses standards for qualified special education teachers.

Bibliography

Cullinan, D., Epstein, M.H., & Lloyd, J.W. (1983). *Behavior disorders of children and adolescents*. Englewood Cliffs, NJ: Prentice-Hall, Inc.

Gearheart, B.R. (1974). *Organization and administration of educational programs for exceptional children*. Springfield, IL: Charles C Thomas, Publisher.

Rhodes, W.C., & Tracy, M.L. (1966). *A study of child variance: Conceptual models* (Vols. 1 & 2). Ann Arbor, MI: University of Michigan.

The Council for Exceptional Children. (1997, May & June). *Teaching Exceptional Children, 29*(5), 5–49.

Appendix B: Commonly Used Psychoactive Medications*

Stimulants

Expected Classroom Effects

Stimulants are the most widely used drugs in the treatment of students with mild disabilities. Their intended effects are to make the students more ready to learn rather than to make the students learn. They have their so-called "paradoxical effect" of decreasing symptoms by increasing behaviors that inhibit hyperactivity, distractibility, and inattention, which often interfere with a readiness to learn.

Stimulants Commonly Used with Students with Mild Disabilities

Dextroamphetamine sulfate. (Dexedrine) is usually administered in 5 milligram dosages (daily at 8 A.M. and 12 noon). Less classroom restlessness, increased attention span, and improvements in social and emotional behavior patterns are the expected effects. Most common side effects are loss of appetite and loss of sleep; less common are headaches with blurred vision, apathy, stupor, tiredness, dry mouth, and drug tolerance over long periods of use.

Methylphenidate hydrochloride. (Ritalin) is usually administered in a single 20 milligram dose in the morning or in two 10 milligram doses in the morning and afternoon; it is generally taken before a meal. Less classroom restlessness, increased attention span, and improvements in social and emotional behavior patterns are the expected effects. Most common side effects are loss of sleep; less common are headaches with blurred vision, apathy, stupor, tiredness, dry mouth, and drug tolerance over long periods of use. Ritalin does not suppress appetite as much as Dexedrine.

Magnesium pemoline. (Cylert) is usually administered once a day in a 37.5 milligram dosage and is considered slower acting than other stimulants. Less classroom restlessness, increased attention span, and improvements in social and emotional behavior patterns are the expected effects. Most common side effects are loss of appetite and loss of sleep; less common are headaches with blurred vision, apathy, stupor, tiredness, dry mouth, and drug tolerance over long periods of use. Cylert is preferred over Dexedrine because it does not suppress most children's appetites as much.

* *Source:* B. Algozzine, *Behavior Problem Management: Educator's Resource Service.* Rockville, MD: Aspen Publishers, 1997.

Minor Tranquilizers

Expected Classroom Effects

Minor tranquilizers are the second most commonly used drugs in the treatment of students with mild disabilities. Their intended effects are to reduce anxiety and agitation associated with some emotional and learning problems. The goal again is to help students become more receptive to instruction.

Minor Tranquilizers Commonly Used with Students with Mild Disabilities

Amitriptyline hydrochloride. (Elavil) is usually administered in varying dosages according to level of problems, but is not recommended for students under 12. Expected effects include antidepressant and sedative action. Most common side effects are sleepiness, dry mouth, blurred vision, nightmares, dizziness when first standing up, and weight gain.

Maprotilene hydrochloride. (Ludiomil) is usually administered in initial dosage of 75 milligrams daily that can be divided; dosages of as low as 25 milligrams are recommended for some. It is indicated for treatment of depressive illness and relief of anxiety associated with depression. Expected effects include antidepressant and sedative action. Most common side effects are sleepiness, dry mouth, blurred vision, nightmares, dizziness when first standing up, and weight gain.

Imapramine hydrochloride. (Tofranil) is usually administered in one 10–25 milligram dose an hour before bed to control enuresis or 75 milligrams once a day for more serious problem behaviors. It is the most widely recognized and recommended antidepressant for children under 12 years of age; there can be as much as a three-week lag before effects are noticed. Controlled bed-wetting and improved emotional and social patterns result in children who are depressed or overly anxious. Most common side effects are dry mouth, urinary retention, blurred vision, tremors, drowsiness, sweating, and some postural rigidity.

Chlordiazepoxide hydrochloride. (Librium) is usually administered in divided doses up to 30 milligrams a day; it is not recommended for children under six. Expected effects include reduction in anxiety, general relaxation, sense of well-being, and general drowsiness. Most common side effects are confusion, skin eruptions, edema, gastrointestinal symptoms, unwanted drowsiness, jaundice, and some changes in electroencephalogram patterns.

Hydroxine hydrochloride. (Atarax) is usually administered in varying doses according to the level of the individual's problems. Expected effects include reduction in anxiety, aggressiveness, and hyperactivity. Most common side effects are tolerance, dependence, and dry mouth.

Meprobamate.   (Equanil) is usually administered 2 or 3 times a day in 100–200 milligram dosages. Expected effects include reduction in anxiety; it is used for its sedative effects. Most common side effects are unwanted drowsiness, dependency, and hematologic disorders.

Deanol acetamid obenzoate.   (Deaner) is usually administered in one 100 milligram dose in the morning. Improved emotional and social patterns result in children who are immature or anxious. Most common side effects are headaches, constipation, insomnia, and skin rashes.

Major Tranquilizers

Expected Classroom Effects

Major tranquilizers are less commonly used than stimulants and minor tranquilizers in the treatment of students with mild disabilities. Their intended effects are to reduce symptoms associated with more severe disabilities, including depression, psychotic behavior, and delusions associated with clinical forms of emotional disturbance. The reduction in symptoms is associated with a more favorable clinical receptiveness for behavioral intervention.

Major Tranquilizers Commonly Used with Students with Mild Disabilities

Haloperidol.   (Haldol) is usually administered in 1 milligram dosages several times a day; it is not recommended for children. Haldol is used to treat mania, paranoia, social withdrawal, and aggressive problems associated with schizophrenia. Most common side effects are skin reactions, jaundice, and impaired vision.

Chlorpromazine hydrochloride.   (Thorazine) is usually administered in 10–24 milligram dosages two or three times a day; it can be increased to 50 milligrams for adolescents. Expected effects include reduction in activity and general reduction in aggressive, negative symptoms commonly seen in seriously disturbed individuals. Most common side effects are skin reactions, impaired vision, and weight gain.

Thioridiazine hydrochloride.   (Mellaril) is usually administered in 10 milligram dosages three or four times a day for preschoolers and in 25 milligram dosages three or four times a day for older children. Expected effects include antidepressive symptoms, reduced anxiety, aggression reduction, and less overall activity.

Most common side effects are sexual dysfunction in males, disturbed color vision, and weight gain.

Anticonvulsants

Expected Classroom Effects

Anticonvulsants are commonly used in the treatment of students with sudden, brief, localized seizures or widespread convulsive seizures associated with epilepsy and some types of mild disabilities. Therapeutic effects do not cure convulsive disorders, but do not control seizures without altering other functions of the Central Nervous System.

Anticonvulsants Commonly Used with Students with Mild Disabilities

Phenobarbital.   (Luminal) is usually administered in 100 milligram dosages and may require as long as 15 minutes to take effect. Expected effects include control of grand mal seizures. Most common side effects are sedation, rashes, slurred speech.

Diphenylhydantoin.   (Dilantin) is usually administered in varying milligram dosages dependent on age of individual, ranging from 50 milligrams for 1–2 year olds to 300–400 milligrams for adolescents. Expected effects include control of grand mal seizures; generally considered drug of choice for most forms of epilepsy (except petit mal seizures). Most common side effects are ataxia, nystagmus, vertigo, blurred vision, confusion, hallucinations, nausea, and urinary incontinence.

Ethosuximide.   (Zarontin) is usually administered in 0.5–1.0 milligram dosages two or three times a day. Expected effects include control of petit mal seizures; generally considered drug of choice for this form of seizures. Most common side effects are gastric distress, nausea, vomiting, anorexia, headaches, fatigue, dizziness, and blood disorders.

Carbamazepine.   (Tegretol) is usually administered in varying dosages relative to diagnosis and age. Expected effects include reduction of psychomotor and grand mal seizures. Most common side effects are drowsiness, double vision, uncoordination, rapid eye movement, nausea, and skin rashes.

Ethosuximide.   (Zarontin) is usually administered in 0.5–1.0 milligram dosages two or three times a day. Expected effects include contol of petit mal seizures; generally considered drug of choice for this form of seizures. Most common side effects are gastric distress, nausea, vomiting, anorexia, headaches, fatigue, dizziness, and blood disorders.

Appendix C: Tests

Frequently Used Achievement Tests

Test	Major Areas	Type of Test		Standardization		Administration	
Name	*Tested*	*Formal*	*Informal*	*Norm-Referenced*	*Criterion-Referenced*	*Individual*	*Group*
Brigance-R Diagnostic Inventories	reading, writing, spelling, mathematics, language, motor skills		X		X	X	
Diagnostic Achievement Battery (DAB)	listening, speaking, reading, writing, mathematics	X		X		X	
Kaufman Test of Educational Achievement (KTEA)	reading, spelling, mathematics	X		X		X	
Peabody Individual Achievement Test-Revised (PIAT-R)	mathematics, reading, spelling, general information	X		X		X	
Wide Range Achievement Test-Revised (WRAT-R)	reading, spelling, arithmetic	X		X		X	
Gilmore Oral Reading Test (GORT)	oral reading	X		X		X	
Durrell Analysis of Reading Difficulty	oral and silent reading, listening, comprehension, word analysis, spelling, handwriting	X		X		X	
Gates-MacGinitie Reading Tests	silent reading, vocabulary, and comprehension	X		X			X

(continued)

Frequently Used Achievement Tests *(continued)*

| Test | Major Areas | Type of Test | | Standardization | | Administration | |
		Formal	Informal	Norm-Referenced	Criterion-Referenced	Individual	Group
Name	*Tested*	*Formal*	*Informal*	*Norm-Referenced*	*Criterion-Referenced*	*Individual*	*Group*
Gray Oral Reading Tests-Revised (GORT-R)	oral reading	X		X		X	
Slosson Oral Reading Test	word reading	X		X		X	
Test of Reading Comprehension (TORC)	reading comprehension	X		X		X	
Woodcock Reading Mastery Tests-Revised (WRMT-R)	reading	X		X		X	
The Boder Test of Reading-Spelling Patterns	reading, spelling		X			X	
Test of Written Language (TOWL)	written language	X		X		X	X
Larsen-Hammill Test of Written Spelling (TWS-2)	written spelling	X		X		X	X
Enright R Diagnostic Inventory of Basic Arithmetic Skills	math computation	X			X	X	X
Key Math-Revised	mathematics	X			X	X	

Frequently Used Intelligence Tests

Test	Major Areas	Type of Test		Standardization		Administration	
Name	Tested	Formal	Informal	Norm-Referenced	Criterion-Referenced	Individual	Group
Coloured Progressive Matrices (CPM)	visual perception and analogous reasoning	X		X		X	
Denver Developmental Screening Test-Revised (DDST)	social, fine motor, gross motor, and language skills	X				X	
Detroit Tests of Learning Aptitude-Revised (DTLA-2)	vocabulary sequencing, detail recognition, and memory	X		X		X	
Detroit Tests of Learning Aptitude-Primary (DTLA-P)	verbal and nonverbal aptitudes, structural and conceptual aptitudes, memory and motor skills	X		X		X	
Goodenough-Harris Drawing Test	conceptual and intellectual maturity and personality characteristics	X				X	X
Kaufman Assessment Battery for Children (K-ABC)	cognitive ability and achievement	X		X		X	
McCarthy Scales of Children's Abilities (MSCA)	general intellectual ability	X		X		X	

(continued)

Frequently Used Intelligence Tests *(continued)*

Name	Tested	Formal	Informal	Norm-Referenced	Criterion-Referenced	Individual	Group
Slosson Intelligence Test for Children and Adults (SIT)	mental ability	X		X		X	
Stanford Binet Intelligence Scale (4th ed.) (SB)	verbal reasoning, quantitative reasoning, abstract/ reasoning, short-term memory	X		X		X	
System of Multicultural Pluristic Assessment (SOMPA)	cognitive abilities, sensory-motor skills, and adaptive behavior	X		X		X	
Wechsler Intelligence Scale for Children-Revised (WISC-R)	general intelligence	X		X		X	
Woodcock-Johnson Psycho-Educational Battery-Revised (WJ-R)	cognitive ability and academic skills in reading, writing, mathematics, and general knowledge	X		X		X	

The column headers above data: Test (Name, Tested) | Type of Test (Formal, Informal) | Standardization (Norm-Referenced, Criterion-Referenced) | Administration (Individual, Group)

Frequently Used Language Tests

Test	Major Areas	Type of Test		Standardization		Administration	
Name	Tested	Formal	Informal	Norm-Referenced	Criterion-Referenced	Individual	Group
The Goldman-Fristoe Test of Articulation (GIFTA)	articulation	X			X	X	
Auditory-Visual Single Word Picture Vocabulary Test-Adolescent (VSWPVT-A)	receptive picture vocabulary		X			X	X
Boehm Test of Basic Concepts-Revised (BTBC-R)	basic relational and space, quantity, and time concepts	X				X	X
Clinical Evaluation of Language Fundamentals Revised (CELF-R)	word meaning; word & sentence structure; recall and retrieval	X		X		X	
Expressive One-Word Picture Vocabulary Test (EOWPVT)	expressive vocabulary	X		X		X	
Expressive One-Word Picture Vocabulary Test-Upper Extension (EOWPVT-UE)	expressive vocabulary	X		X		X	
Peabody Picture Vocabulary Test-Revised (PPVT-R)	receptive single-word vocabulary	X		X		X	

(continued)

Frequently Used Language Tests *(continued)*

| Test | Major Areas | Type of Test | | Standardization | | Administration | |
| | | | | | | | |
Name	*Tested*	*Formal*	*Informal*	*Norm-Referenced*	*Criterion-Referenced*	*Individual*	*Group*
Preschool Language Scale (PLS)	receptive and expressive language; articulation	X			X	X	
Test of Adolescent Language (TOAL-2)	receptive and expressive language, spoken and written	X		X		X	X
Test of Language Development-2-Primary (TOLD-2-P)	receptive and expressive language	X		X		X	
Test of Language Development-2 Intermediate (TOLD-2-I)	receptive and expressive language	X		X		X	
Test of Word Finding (TWF)	accuracy and speed of naming	X		X		X	
The Word Test	expressive language	X		X		X	

Frequently Used Perceptual/Perceptual-Motor Tests

| Test | Major Areas | Type of Test | | Standardization | | Administration | |
Name	Tested	Formal	Informal	Norm-Referenced	Criterion-Referenced	Individual	Group
Test of Visual Motor Skills (TVMS)	visual perception and eye-motor coordination	X		X		X	X
Test of Visual-Perceptual Skills (Non-Motor)	visual perception (all types)	X				X	
Bruininks-Oseretsky Test of Motor Proficiency	motor proficiency, gross and fine motor skills	X				X	
Miller Assessment for Preschoolers (MAP)	sensory and motor abilities; verbal and nonverbal cognitive abilities	X		X		X	
Peabody Developmental Motor Scales (PDMS)	gross and fine motor skills	X				X	X
Marianne Frostig Developmental Test of Visual Perception (DTVP)	visual perception	X				X	X
Purdue Perceptual-Motor Survey	laterality, directionality, perceptual-motor skills	X			X	X	
Wepman Auditory Discrimination Test	auditory discrimination	X				X	

Appendix D: Sample Individualized Education Plan (IEP)

Special Education Department   Type of Staffing
                                Individualized Education Program (IEP)   Initial____
                                                                                          Review____
Student: <u>Jerry Smith</u>   B'date <u>5/15/97</u>   School/Grade <u>Lake Park/3</u>   Date <u>2/23/05</u>

Student Attendance #_____   Parent/Guardian <u>Janet Smith</u>   Work Phone <u>324-1168</u>

Date of Original Program Entry <u>2/23/02</u>   Address <u>1421 McGill Street</u>   Home Phone <u>322-7722</u>

I. Present Level of Performance
Test results indicate average intelligence. Academic performance in reading vocabulary and comprehension below second grade expectancy levels. Parents describe Jerry as well-meaning, but overactive and immature.

II. Prioritized Annual Goals (see attached page(s) for short-term objectives)
1. Jerry will increase his reading comprehension to 2nd grade level, as measured by the Woodcock Reading Mastery Tests–Revised.
2. Jerry will increase his word recognition skills from 2nd to 3rd grade level, as measured by the Woodcock Reading Mastery Tests–Revised.

III. Recommended Special Education and/or Related Services

Service/Program	Implementation Date (Projected)	Hours/Week	Anticipated Duration	Review Date
Resource Room	2/30/05	5 hrs	One school year	2/23/06
_____	_____	_____	_____	_____

Regular Class Placement: <u>25</u> Hours/Week   Transportation: ___Yes <u>x</u> No   Documentation of Attempts to

Adaptive Physical Education ___Yes <u>x</u> No   Involve Parent/Guardian

Committee Members Present: This is to certify that I was invited to   Date   Comment
_____Chairperson   participate in the writing of this IEP & that I   <u>1/10/05</u> <u>note sent home</u>
_____   understand its contents. Due process rights   <u>1/30/05</u> <u>phone call</u>
_____   & procedures have been explained & I have   _____ _____
_____   been provided a copy of these rights. I   _____ _____
_____   understand that a copy of this IEP will be
                                given to me upon my request.

                                                                                 Date   <u>2/23/05</u>

                _____
                Parent/Guardian Signature

Page 2 of 2   Individualized Education Program (IEP)
                                        Short-Term Objectives
                            (Complete at least one objective for each goal)

Student: <u>Jerry Smith</u>   B'date <u>5/15/97</u>   Program: <u>LD Resource</u>   Date <u>2/23/05</u>

                                                Person to Provide Service <u>Nora Clark</u>

Annual Goal: <u>Jerry will increase his reading comprehension to 2nd grade level, as measured by the</u>
<u>Woodcock Reading Mastery Tests-Revised</u>.

Short-Term Instructional Objectives	Criteria for Mastery	Date Reviewed	Method of Evaluation	Mastery Yes	No
1. Given a selected 2nd grade reading passage, Jerry will verbally answer literal and inferential comprehension questions about the content.	80% accuracy	3/15/05	Teacher prepared list of literal and inferential comprehension questions drawn from a reading passage	Yes	
2. Given a selected story from a 2nd grade reading book, Jerry will write correct answers to 8 of the 10 questions.	80% accuracy				

Annual Goal: <u>Jerry will increase his word recognition skills from 2nd to 3rd grade level, as measured by</u>
<u>the Woodcock Reading Mastery Tests-Revised</u>.

3. Jerry will use the context of sentences from a 2nd grade reading passage to identify unknown words.	85% accuracy	4/15/05	Teacher observation	Yes	
4. Given a list of 20 vocabulary words from a selected 3rd grade reading story, Jerry will read 18 correctly.	90% accuracy				

REFERENCES

AAMR Ad Hoc Committee on Terminology and Classification. (2002). *Mental retardation: Definition, classification, and systems of support* (10th ed.). Washington, DC: American Association on Mental Retardation.

Achenbach, T. M., & Edelbrook, C. S. (1981). Behavioral problems and competencies reported by parents of normal and disturbed children aged 4 through 16. *Monographs of the Society for Research in Child Development, 46* (Serial No. 188).

Ager, C. L., & Cole, C. L. (1991). A review of cognitive-behavioral interventions for children and adolescents with behavioral disorders. *Behavioral Disorders, 16*(4), 260–275.

Ainsworth, M. (1989). Attachments beyond infancy. *American Psychologist, 44*(4), 709–716.

Ainsworth, M. D. S. (1978). *Patterns of attachment.* Hillside, NJ: Lawrence Erlbaum Associates.

Albemarle County Public Schools. (2003). *Technology and differentiated instruction web resources* [On-line]. Available: www.lakeland schools.org/EDTECH/Differentiation/home.htm

Algozzine, B., & Korinek, L. (1985). Where is special education for students with high prevalence handicaps going? *Exceptional Children, 51,* 388–394.

Algozzine, B., & Maheady, L. (1986). When all else fails, teach. *Exceptional Children, 52*(6), 287–300.

Algozzine, B., & Ysseldyke, J. E. (1987). Questioning discrepancies: Retaking the first step 20 years later. *Learning Disabilities Quarterly, 10,* 301–312.

Algozzine, B., Ruhl, K., & Ramsey, R. (1991). *Behaviorally disordered? Assessment for identification and instruction.* CEC Mini-library, Reston, VA: The Council for Exceptional Children.

Algozzine, B., Serna, L., & Patton, J. (2001). *Childhood behavior disorders: Applied research and practice.* Austin, TX. Pro-Ed.

Algozzine, B., Ysseldyke, J., & Elliot, J. (1997). *Strategies and tactics for effective instruction.* (2nd ed.). Longmont, CO: Sopris West.

Algozzine, K. (1997). One minute behavior management. In B. Algozzine (Ed.) *Problem Behavior Management: Educator's resource service* (pp. 11:36–11:40). Gaithersburg, MD: Aspen Publishers.

Alley, G., & Deshler, D. (1979). *Teaching learning disabled adolescent: Strategies and methods.* Denver, CO: Love Publishing.

American Psychiatric Association. (1994). *Diagnostic and statistical manual of mental disorders* (4th ed.). Washington, DC: Author.

Apter, S. J. (1982). *Troubled children, troubled systems.* New York: Pergamon.

Armas, G. C. (2001). Schools look for help as Hispanics flood in. *Springfield Sunday Republican.* A5. Springfield, MA: Associated Press.

Armor, D. J. (2003). Environmental effects on IQ: From the family or from the schools? *Education Week, 23*(12), 32–33.

Armor, D., Conry-Oseguera, P., Cox, M., King, N., McDonnell, L., Pascal, A., Pualy, E., & Zellman, G. (1976). *Analysis of the school preferred reading program in selected Los Angeles minority schools.* (Report No. R–2007–LAUSFD). Santa Monica, CA: The Rand Corporation. (ERIC Document Reproduction No. ED 130–243).

Armstrong, T. (1998). To empower, not control! A holistic approach to AD/HD. *Reaching Today's Youth: The Community Circle of Caring Journal, 2*(2), 3–5.

Association for Supervision and Curriculum Development (1994). *Curriculum update.* Alexandria, VA: Author.

Associations of Supervision and Curriculum (2000). Forging school-home links: A new paradigm for parental involvement. *Education Update, 42*(7), 1,4. Available: www.nlda. org/whatis.html

Baca, L., & Harris, K. D. (1988). Teaching migrant exceptional students. *Teaching Exceptional Children, 24*(4), 32–35.

Bailey, D. B., Skinner, D., Rodriguez, P., Gut, D., & Correa, V. (1999). Awareness, use, and satisfaction with services for Latino parents of young children with disabilities. *Exceptional Children, 65,* 367–381.

Bain, A., & Farris, H. (1991). Teacher attitudes toward social skill training. *Teacher Education and Special Education, 14*(1), 49–56.

Baker, E. T., Wang, M. C., & Walberg, J. J. (1994). The effects of inclusion on learning. *Educational Leadership, 52*(4), 33–35.

Baker, K. (1985). Research evidence of a school discipline problem. *Phi Delta Kappan, 66*(7), 482–488.

Banks, J. (1993). Multicultural education: Development, dimensions, and challenges. *Phi Delta Kappan, 75*(1), 22–28.

Barkley, R. A. (1977). A review of stimulant drug research with hyperactive children. *Journal of Child Psychology and Psychiatry, 18,* 137–165.

Baroff, G. S. (1999). General learning disorder: A new designation for mental retardation. *Mental Retardation, 37*(1), 68–70.

Barresi, J. (1984). Interstate migrant council. National policy workshop on special education needs of migrant handicapped students. *Proceedings Report.* Denver, CO: Education Commission of the States.

Barron, M. A. (2000). Surprising truths: The implications of brain research. Barron (2000). *http://nauticom.net/www/cokids/brain.html.* November, 18th.

Barsch, R. H. (1968). *Perspectives on learning disabilities: The vectors of a new convergence.*

Bartoli, J. S. (1989). An ecological response to Cole's interactivity alternative. *Journal of Learning Disabilities, 22*(5), 292–297.

Baxendell, B. W. (2003, Jan./Feb.). Consistent, coherent, creative: The 3 C's of graphic organizers. *Teaching Exceptional Children, 35*(3), 46–53.

Beckman, P. J. (1983). Influence of selected child characteristics on stress in the family of handicapped infants. *American Journal of Medical Deficiency, 88,* 150–156.

Belch, P. (1975). The question of teachers' questions. *Teaching Exceptional Children, 1,* 46–47.

Benjamin, A. (2003). *Differentiated instruction: A guide for middle and high school teachers.* Accessed September 16, 2003 from www.eyeoneducation.com/Merchant2/merchant.mv?Screen=PROD&Store_Code=st

Bennett, T., DeLuca, D. A., & Allen, R. W. (1996). Families of children with disabilities: Positive adaptation across the lifecycle. *Social Work in Education, 18,* 31–44.

Benniga, J. S. (1988). An emerging synthesis in moral education. *Phi Delta Kappan, 69*(6), 415–418.

Bennion, R. (1983). Why us? In Dougan, Isbell and Vayas Associates (Ed.), *We Have Been There.* Nashville, TN: Abington, 32–40.

Benson, D., Edwards, L., Rosell, J., & White, M. (1986). Inclusion of socially maladjusted children and youth in the legal definition of the behaviorally disordered population: A debate. *Behavioral Disorders, 11*(3), 213–222.

Bereiter, C., & Englemann, S. (1966). *Teaching disadvantaged children in the Preschool.* Englewood Cliffs, NJ: Prentice Hall.

Berliner, D. C. (1979). Tempus Educare. In P. L. Peterson & H. J. Walberg (Eds.), *Research on teaching: Concepts findings and implications.* Berkeley, CA: McCutchan Publishing.

Berliner, D. C. (1988). The half-full glass: A review of research on teaching. In E. L. Meyen, G. A. Vergason, & R. J. Whelan (Eds.), *Effective instructional strategies for exceptional children.* Denver, CO: Love Publishing.

Berman, P., McLaughlin, M., Bass, G., Pauly, E., & Zelman, G. (1977). Federal programs supporting educational change. Vol. 7: Factors affecting the implementation and continuation. Santa Monica, CA: The Rand Corporation. (ERIC Document Reproduction Service No. ED 140 432).

Bernstein, B. (1961). Social class and linguistic development: A theory of social learning. In A. H. Halsey, J. Flored, & C. A. Anderson (Eds.), *Education, economy and society.* New York: Free Press.

Bickel, W. E., & Bickel, D. P. (1986). Effective schools, classrooms, and instruction: Implications for special education. *Exceptional Children, 52*(6), 489–499.

Biklen, D., & Zollers, N. (1986). The focus of advocacy in the LD field. *Journal of Learning Disabilities, 19,* 579–586.

Bjorklund, G., & Burger, C. (1987, January). Making conferences work for parents, teachers and children. *Young Children,* 26–31.

Blacher, J., Lopez, S., Shapiro, J., & Fusco, J. (1997). Contributions to depression in Latino mothers with and without children with retardation: Implications for caregiving. *Family Relations, 46,* 325–334.

Blackman, H. P. (1989). Special education placement: Is it what you know or where you live? *Exceptional Children, 55,* 459–462.

Blankenship, C. (1985). Using curriculum based assessment data to make instructional decisions. *Exceptional Children, 52*(3), 233–238.

Block, J. (1995). On the relationship between IQ, impulsivity, and delinquency. *Journal of Abnormal Psychology, 104*(3), 45–48.

Bly, R. (1990). *Iron John: A book about men*. Reading, MA: Addison-Wesley Publishing.

Boardmaker, (2001). *Picture Communication Symbols*. [Computer Software]. Solana Beach, CA: Mayer-Johnson, Inc.

Boder, E., & Jarrico, S. (1982). *The Boder Test of Reading-Spelling Patterns*. New York: Grune & Stratton.

Boyle, E. A., Washburn, S. G., Rosenberg, M. S., Connelly, V. J., Brinckerhoff, L. C., & Banerjee, M. (2002, Nov./Dec.). Reading's SLiCK with new audio texts and strategies. *Teaching Exceptional Children, 35*(2), 50–55.

Braaten, S., Simpson, R., Rosell, J., & Reilly, T. (1988). Using punishment with exceptional children. *Teaching Exceptional Children, 20*(2), 79–81.

Brandt, R. (1990). Overview: Making connections. *Exceptional Leadership, 47*(5), 3.

Brantlinger, E. A., & Guskin, S. L. (1988). Implications of social and cultural differences for special education. In Meyen, E. L., Vergason, G. A., & Whelan, R. J. *Effective instructional strategies for exceptional children*. Denver, CO: Love Publishing.

Brendtro, L. K., & Ness, A. E. (1996). Fixing flaws or building strengths? *Journal of Emotional and Behavioral Problems, 4*(2), 2–7.

Brolin, D. E. (Ed.) (1989). *Life centered career education: A competency based approach*. Reston, VA: The Council for Exceptional Children.

Brown v. Topeka, Kansas Board of Education (1954). 347 U.S. 483, 745. Ct. 98 L. Ed.

Brown, A. (1978). Knowing when, where, and how to remember: A problem of meta-cognition. In R. Glasser (Ed.), *Advances in instructional Psychology*. Hillsdale, NJ: Lawrence Erlbaum Associates.

Bruininks, V. L. (1978). Actual and perceived peer status of disabled students in mainstream programs. *The Journal of Emotional Special Education, 12*, 51–58.

Bruner, J., Cole, M., & Lloyd, B. (1978). *The developing child series*. In S. Farnham-Diggory. *Learning disabilities: A Psychological Perspective*. Cambridge: Harvard University Press.

Bryan, T. H. (1974). Peer popularity of learning disabled children. *Journal of Learning Disabilities, 7*, 621–625.

Bryan, T., Donohue, M., & Pearl, R. (1981). Studies of learning disabled children's pragmatic competence. *Topics in Learning and Learning Disabilities, 1*, 29–39.

Bryan, T., Werner, M., & Pearl, R. (1982). Learning disabled students conformity responses to prosocial and antisocial situations. *Learning Disability Quarterly, 5*, 344–352.

Bryen, D. N. (1982). *Injuries into child language*. Boston: Allyn and Bacon.

Bryk, A. S., & Schneider, B. L. (2003). *Trust in schools: A core resource for improvement*. New York: Russell Sage Foundation.

Bullock, L. M., & Gable, R. A. (Eds.). (1997). *Making collaboration work for children, youth, families, schools, and communities*. Reston, VA: The Council for Exceptional Children.

Burnette, J. (1998). Reducing the disproportional representation of minority student in special education. ERIC/OSEP Digest #E566, ED417–501.

Burrello, L. C., Burrello, J. M., & Friend, M. (1996). *The power of 2: Making a difference through co-teaching*. Elephant Rock Productions, Inc., and Indiana University Educational Series. (Videotape)

Buscaglia, L. (1975). *The disabled and their parents: A counseling challenge*. Thorofare, NJ: Leo F. Buscaglia.

Bush, W. I., & Waugh, K. W. (1982). *Diagnosing learning problems* (3rd ed.). Columbus, OH: Charles E. Merrill.

Caine, R. N. (2000). Building the bridge from research to classroom. *Educational Leadership. 58*(3), 59–61.

Canter, L. (1989). Assertive discipline: More than names on the board and marbles in a jar. *Phi Delta Kappan, 71*(1), 57–60.

Carbo, M. (1987a). Matching reading styles: Correcting ineffective instruction. *Educational Leadership, 45*, 55–62.

Carbo, M. (1987b). Reading styles research: What works isn't always phonics. *Phi Delta Kappan, 68*(6), 431–435.

Carbo, M., Dunn, R., & Dunn, K. (1986). *Teaching students to read through their individual learning styles*. Englewood Cliffs, NJ: Prentice Hall.

Carlson, C. I. (1987). Social interaction goals and strategies of children with learning disabilities. *Journal of Learning Disabilities, 20*(5), 306–311.

Carpenter, D. (1985). Grading handicapped pupils: Review and position statement. *Remedial and Special Education, 6*(4), 54–59.

Casey, A., Skiba, R., & Algozzine, B. (1988). Developing effective behavioral interventions.

In J. L. Graden, J. E. Zins, & M. J. Curtis (Eds.), *Alternative educational delivery systems: Enhancing instructional options for all students.* Washington, DC: National Association of School Psychologists.

Cattermole, J., & Robinson, N. (1985). Effective home school communication—from the parents perspective. *Phi Delta Kappan, 67*(1), 48–50.

Cavanaugh, T. (2002, Nov./Dec.). E-Books and accommodations: Is this the future of print accommodation? *Teaching Exceptional Children, 35*(2), 56–61.

CEC Staff. (March 1997). CEC testifies before Congress, calls for quick IDEA reauthorization. *CEC Today, 3*(8) 1, 7, 9.

CEC Staff. (June 1997). IDEA sails through Congress. *CEC Today, 3*(10), 1, 9, 15.

CEC Staff. (September 1997). Instructional accommodations. *CEC Today, 4*(3), 15.

Cegelka, P., Lewis, R., & Rodriguez, A. (1987). Status of educational services to handicapped students with limited English proficiency: Report of a statewide study in California. *Exceptional Children, 54*(3), 220–227.

Center on Budget & Policy Priorities. (2000). Poverty rate hits all time lowest level since 1979 as unemployment reaches 30-year low. www.cbpp.org/9-26-00pov.htm

Chalfant, J. C., & Scheffelin, M. A. (1969). *Central processing dysfunction in children: A review of the research.* National Institute of Neurological Diseases and Stroke, Monograph #9. Bethesda, MD: U.S. Department of Health, Education, and Welfare.

Charles, C. M. (1989). *Building classroom discipline: From models to practice* (3rd ed.). New York: Longman.

Charney, S. R. (2002). *Teaching children to care: Management in the responsive classroom.* Greenfield, MA: Northeast Foundation for Children.

Checkley, K. (1997). The first seven . . . and the eighth conversation with Howard Gardner. *Educational Leadership, 55*(1), 8–13.

Cheek, E. H., & Cheek, M. C. (1983). *Reading instruction through content teaching.* Columbus, OH: Merrill Publishing.

Children's Defense Fund (1971). *The way we go to school: The exclusion in Boston.* Boston: Beacon Press.

Children's Defense Fund (1990). *Children 1990: A report card, briefing book and action primer.*

Washington, DC: U.S. Government Printing Office.

Children's Defense Fund (2000). Available at *http://www.childrendefense.org*

Chmelynski, C. (1990). All-Black, all-male classes. *The Educator, 12*(10), 16–18.

Chrispeels, J. H. (1991). District leadership in parent involvement-Policies and actions in San Diego. *Phi Delta Kappan, 72,* 367–371.

Cicci, R. (1983). Disorders of written language. In H. R. Myklebust (Ed.), *Progress in learning disabilities.* New York: Grune & Stratton.

Cloward, R. D. (1967). Teenagers as tutors of low achieving children: Impact on tutors and tutees. In V. Allen (Ed.), *Children as teachers: Theory and research in tutoring.* New York: Academic Press.

Coleman, J. (1987, August/September). Families and schools. *Educational Researchers, 31*–38.

Coleman, J. M. (1985). Achievement level, social class, and the self-concepts of mildly handicapped children. *Journal of Learning Disabilities, 18*(1), 26–30.

Coles, G. S. (1989). Excerpts from *The learning mystique: A critical look at "Learning Disabilities". Journal of Learning Disabilities, 22*(5), 267–273, 277–278.

Colvin, G., Kame'enui, E.J., and Sugai, G. (1993). School-wide and classroom management: Re-conceptualizing the integration and management of students with behavior problems in general education. *Education and Treatment of Children, 16,* .361–381.

Comer, J. P. (1986). Parent participation in the schools. *Phi Delta Kappan, 67*(6), 442–446.

Comer, J. P., Zigler, E. F., and Stern, B. M. (1997). Supporting today's families in the elementary school. *Reaching Today's Youth. The Community Circle of Caring Journal, 1*(3), 37–43.

Conner, M. G. (2003, September 7). Understanding and dealing with pervasive developmental disorders. [On-line]. Available: www.CrisisCounseling.org

Connors, J. L., & Donnellan, A. M. (1998). Walk in beauty: Western perspectives on disability and Navajo family/cultural resilience. In H. I. McCubbin, E. A. Thompson, A. I. Thompson, & J. E. Fromer (Eds.), Resiliency in Native American and immigrant families (pp. 159–182). Thousand Oaks, CA: Sage.

Cooper, H. M. (1989a). *Homework.* White Plains, NY: Longman.

Cooper, H. M. (Nov. 1989b). Synthesis of research on homework. *Educational Leadership, 47*(3), 85–91.

Cooper, J. O., Heron, T. E., & Heward, W. L. (1987). *Applied behavior analysis.* Columbus, OH: Merrill Publishing.

Copple, C., Yante, M., Levin, D., & Cohen, S. (1992). *Briefing paper.* Washington, DC: Pelavin Associates, Inc.

Cornett, C. E. (1983). *What you should know about teaching and learning styles.* Bloomington: Phi Delta Kappan. (Phi Delta Kappa Fastback Series #191).

Cott, A. (1972). Megavitamins: The orthomolecular approach to behavioral disorders and learning disabilities. *Academic Therapy, 7,* 245–257.

Council for Children with Behavior Disorders (1990). Position paper on use of behavior education strategies with children with behavioral disorders. *Behavioral Disorders, 15*(4), 243–260.

Council for Exceptional Children. (2003, April/May). Advocacy in action: House Bill on IDEA contains CEC recommendations, but CEC remains cautious. *Today, 9*(7), 4–5, 14.

Council for Exceptional Children. (2003, April/May). CEC says all students must be included in assessments. *Today, 9*(7), 1,5, 14–15.

Council for Exceptional Children. (2003, February/March). Reducing special education paperwork a high priority. *Today, 9*(6), 1, 5–6, 9.

Council for Exceptional Children (2005). CEC provides comments on IDEA proposed regulations. www.sped.org

Cremin, L., (1961). *The transformation of the school.* New York: Vintage Books.

Crook, W. G. (1980). Can what a child eats make him dull, stupid, or hyperactive? *Journal of Learning Disabilities, 13,* 53–58.

Croser, M., & Seiter, M. (Eds.). (2003). *Pollution, toxic chemicals, and mental retardation: Framing a national blueprint for health promotion and disability prevention*: Proceedings of a national Wingspanel summit July 22–24. www.aamr.org/ToxinsandMentalRetardation/pdf

Cruickshank, W. M. (1967). *The brain injured child in home, school, and community.* Syracuse: Syracuse University Press.

Cruickshank, W. M. (Spring, 1986). The learning disabled hyperactive child. *Perceptions, 1,* 7–9.

Cuenin, L. H., & Harris, K. R. (1986). Planning, implementing, and evaluating time out interventions with exceptional students. *Teaching Exceptional Children, 18*(4), 272–276.

D'Arcangelo, M. (2000). The scientist in the crib: A conversation with Andrew Metzloff. *Educational Leadership, 58*(2), 8–13.

Daley, T. C., & Sigman, M. D. (2002). Diagnostic conceptualization of autism among Indian psychiatrists, psychologists, and pediatricians. *Journal of Autism and Developmental Disorders, 32,* 12–23.

Daly, P. M., & Ranalli, P. (2003, May/June). Using countoons to teach self-monitoring skills. *Teaching Exceptional Children, 35*(5), 30–35.

Davies, R. (1991). Schools reaching out. *Phi Delta Kappan, 72*(5), 376–382.

Davis, G. A., & Rimm, S. B. (1985). *Education of the gifted and talented.* Englewood Cliffs, NJ: Prentice Hall.

DeLuke, S. V., & Knoblock, P. (1987). Teacher behavior as preventive discipline. *Teaching Exceptional Children, 19,* 18–24.

Dennison, G. (1969). *The lives of children: The Story of the first street school.* New York: Random House.

Deno, S. (1989). Curriculum-based measurement and special education services: A fundamental and direct relationship. In M. Shinn (Ed.), *Curriculum-based measurement: Assessing special children.* New York: Guilford Press.

Deno, S. L. (1985). Curriculum-based measurement: The emerging alternative. *Exceptional Children, 52*(3), 219–232.

Deno, S. L. (1986). Formative evaluation of individual student programs: A new role for school psychologists. *School Psychology Review, 15*(3), 358–374.

Derr, A. M. (1986). How learning disabled adolescent boys make moral judgments. *Journal, 19*(3), 160–164.

Deshler, D. D. (1978). Psychoeducational aspects of learning disabled adolescents. In L. Mann, L. Goodman, & J. L. Wiederholt (Eds.), *Teaching the learning disabled adolescent.* Boston, MA: Houghton Mifflin.

Deshler, D. D., & Schumaker, J. B. (1983). Social skills of learning disabled adolescents: Characteristics and intervention. *Topics in Learning Disabilities, 3,* 15–23.

Deshler, D. D., Schumaker, J. B., & Lenz, B. K. (1984). Academic and cognitive interventions for LD adolescents: Part 1. *Journal of Learning Disabilities, 17*(2), 108–117.

Deshler, D. D., Warner, M. M., Schumaker, J. B., & Alley, G. R. (1983). Learning strategies intervention model: Key components and current status. In J. D. McKinney & L. Feagans (Eds.), *Current topics in learning disabilities.* Norwood, NJ: Ablex.

Dever, R. B., & Knapczyk, D.R. (1997). Teaching persons with mental retardation: Curriculum developments and instructional methodology. New York: McGraw-Hill.

Dietz, M. P. (1992). Youth-reaching-youth project. *Journal of Emotional and Behavioral Problems, 1*(3), 28–29.

DiGangi, S. A., Perryman, P., & Rutherford, R. B., Jr. (1990). Juvenile offenders in the 90's: A descriptive analysis. *Perceptions, 25*(4), 5–8.

Dobbins, D. A., & Rarick, G. L. (1977). The performance of intellectually normal and educable mentally retarded boys on throwing accuracy. *Journal of Motor Behavior, 9,* 23–28.

Dover, W. (1994). *The inclusion facilitator.* Manhattan, KS: The MASTER Teacher, Inc.

Dreikurs, R., Grunwald, B., & Pepper, F. (1982). *Maintaining sanity in the classroom.* New York: Harper & Row.

Dunn, L. (1968). Special education for the mildly retarded—is much of it justifiable? *Exceptional Children, 35,* 5–22.

Dupont, H. (1978). *Counseling and Human Development.* Denver, CO: Love Publishing.

Dyches, T. T., Wilder, L. K., Sudweeks, R. R., Obiakor, F. E., & Algozzine, B. (in press). Multicultural issues in autism. *Journal of Autism and Developmental Disorders.*

Dykens E., & Kasari C. (1997). Maladaptive behavior in children with Prader-Willi syndrome, Down syndrome, and nonspecific mental retardation. *American Journal on Mental Retardation 102*(3), 228–237 .

Dykens E., and Rosner B. A. (1999). Refining behavioral phenotypes: Personality-motivation in Williams and Prader-Willi syndromes. *American Journal On Mental Retardation 104*(2), 158–169.

Edge, D., & Burton, G. (1986). Helping learning disabled middle school students learn about money. *Journal of Learning Disabilities, 19*(1), 46–51.

Edgerton, R. B. (1979). *Mental retardation.* Cambridge, MA: Harvard University Press.

Edwards, J. (1991). To teach responsibility, bring back the Dalton Plan. *Phi Delta Kappan, 72*(5), 398–401.

Elkind, D. (1982). Parental stresses: Their detrimental effects on the emotional well-being of children. *International Journal of Sociology of the Family, 12,* 275–283.

Elkind, D. (1986). Formal education and early childhood education: An essential difference. *Phi Delta Kappan, 67*(9), 631–637.

Ellis, N. R. (1963). The stimulus trace and behavioral inadequacy. In N. Ellis (Ed.), *Handbook of Mental Deficiency.* New York: McGraw-Hill.

Embry, L. H. (1980). Family support for handicapped preschool children at risk for abuse. *New Directions for Exceptional Children, 4,* 29–57.

England, D. A., & Flatley, J. K. (1985). *Homework-Any why.* Bloomington, IN: Phi Delta Kappa Educational Foundation (Monograph, Fastback 218).

Epstein, M. H., Cullinan, D., & Polloway, E. A. (1986). Patterns of maladjustment among mentally retarded children and youth. *American Journal of Mental Deficiency, 2*(2), 127–134.

Erickson, M. T. (1998). *Behavior disorders of children and adolescents* (3rd ed.). Upper Saddle River, NJ: Prentice Hall.

Erikson, E. (1963). *Childhood and society* (2nd ed.). New York: W. W. Norton.

Espinoza, R. (1988). Working parents, employees, and schools. *Educational Horizons.* Winter, 62–65.

Evers, R. B., & Elksnin, N. (1998). *Working with students with disabilities in vocational-technical settings.* Austin, TX: PRO-ED.

Executive Committee of the Council for Children with Behavioral Disorders (1987). Position paper on definition and identification of students with behavioral disorders. *Behavioral Disorders, 13*(1), 9–18.

Fagen, S. (1986). Conducting an LSI: A process model. *Perceptions,* 4–5.

Fagen, S. A., & Hill, J. M. (1987). Teaching acceptance of frustration. *Teaching Exceptional Children, 19*(4), 49–51.

Fagen, S. A., & Long, N. J. (1975). Teaching children self-control: A new responsibility for teachers. *Focus on Exceptional Children, 7*(8), 1–10.

Farley, J. W. (1986). An analysis of written dialogue of educable mentally retarded writers. *Education and Training of the Mentally Retarded, 21*(3), 181–191.

Farnham-Diggory, S. (1978). *Learning disabilities: A psychological perspective.* Cambridge: Harvard University Press.

Farnham-Diggory, S. (1992). *The learning-disabled child.* Cambridge, MA: Harvard University Press.

Farrell, E. E. (1909). Special classes in the New York city schools. *Journal of Psycho-Asthenics, 13*(1–4), 91–96.

Featherstone, H. (1980). *A difference in the family.* New York: Basic Books.

Federal Domestic Assistance Catalog. (1997). www.gsa.gov/fdac/query fdac.htm.

Fein, E. B. (1995). An educational oasis on Rikers Island. *New York Times,* B 1, January 6, 1995.

Feingold, B. (1975). *Why your child is hyperactive.* New York: Random House.

Feiter, F., & Tokar, E. (1982). Getting a handle on teacher stress. *Educational Leadership, 39*(6), 456–457.

Ferguson, P. M., & Ferguson, D. L. (1987). Parents and professionals. In P. Knoblock (Ed.), *Understanding exceptional children and youth* (pp. 346–388). Boston: Little, Brown.

Feurenstein, R. (1980). *Instrumental enrichment: An intervention program for cognitive modifiability.* Baltimore, MD: University Park Press.

Figgis, J. (1995). A new book about how our brains function. (Interview with Robert Sylwester), ABC Radio National, Education Report Transcript, November 15. *http://www.abc.net.au/rn/ talks/8:30/edurpt/ estories/er151102.htm*

Fine, E. (1987). Are we preparing adolescents with learning disabilities to cope with social issues? *Journal of Learning Disabilities, 20*(10), 633–635.

Fishbaugh, M.S.E. (1997). *Models of collaboration.* Boston: Allyn and Bacon.

Fiske, E. B. (1988, February 12). Standardized test scores: Voodoo statistics? *New York Times.*

Flick, G. F. (1998). 24 ways to manage AD/HD in the classroom without medication. *Reaching Today's Youth: The Community Circle of Caring Journal, 2*(2), 37–40.

Ford, B. A. (1992). *Multicultural education training for special educators working with African-American youth. Exceptional Children, 59*(2), 107–114.

Forness, S. R. (2001). *Schools and the identification of mental health needs.* Report of the Surgeon General's Conference on Children's Mental Health: A National Action Agenda. www.surgeongeneral.gov/topics/cmh/ childrenreport.htm. Retrieved December 19, 2003.

Fowler, M. (2002). *Attention deficit/hyperactivity disorder. NICHY briefing paper.* Washington, DC: National Information Center for Children and Youth with Disabilities.

Frankenberger, W. (1998). Wonder drug or quick fix? *Reaching Today's Youth: The Community Circle of Caring Journal, 2*(2), 11–15.

Freisleben-Cook, L. (2003, September). A more down-to-earth description. In *What Is Asperger Syndrome?* Online Asperger Syndrome Information and Support (O.A.S.I.S.). Available at www.udel.edu/bkirby/asperger/ aswhatisit.html

Freisleben-Cook, L. (2003, September). A more down-to-earth description. In Gonzalez, V., Brusca-Vega, R., & Yawkey, T. (1997). *Assessment and instruction of culturally and linguistically diverse students with or at-risk of learning problems.* Boston: Allyn and Bacon.

Friedrich, W. N. (1979). Predictors of the coping behavior of the mothers of handicapped children. *Journal of Consulting and Clinical Psychology, 47,* 1140–1141.

Friend, M. (2005). Special education: *Contemporary perspectives for school professionals.* Boston: Allyn and Bacon.

Friend, M., & Bursuck, W. D. (1999). *Including students with special needs: A practical guide for classroom teachers* (2nd ed.). Boston,: Allyn and Bacon.

Friend, M., & Cook, L. (1996). *Interactions: Collaboration skills for school personnel* (2nd ed.). White Plains, MA: Longman.

Friend, M., & Cook, L. (2000). *Interactions: Collaboration skills for school professionals* (3rd ed.). New York: Addison Wesley/Longman, Inc.

Fuchs, L., & Fuchs, D. (1986). Effects of systematic formative evaluation: A Meta-analysis. *Exceptional Children, 53*(3), 199–208.

Fujiura, G. T., & Yamaki, K. (2000). Trends in demography of childhood poverty and disability. *Exceptional Children, 66,* 187–199.

Fujiura, G. T., Yamaki, K., & Czechowicz, S. (1998). Disability among ethnic and racial minorities in the United States: A summary of economic status and family structure. *Journal of Disability Policy Studies, 9*(2), 111–130.

Gallagher, J. J., Beckman, P., & Cross, A. H. (1983). Families of handicapped children: Sources of stresses and its amelioration. *Exceptional Children, 50*(1), 10–19.

Gallagher, J. J., Cross, A., & Schartman, W. (1981). Parental adaptation to a young handicapped child: The father's role. *Journal to the Division for Early Childhood, 3*, 3–14.

Garabino, J. (2000). *Lost boys: Why our sons turn violent and how we can save them.* New York: Anchor Books.

Garcia, (1999). *Student cultural diversity: Understanding and meeting the challenge* (2nd ed.) Boston: Houghton-Mifflin.

Gardner, H. (1993). *Multiple intelligences: The theory into practice.* New York: Basic Books.

Gazaway, R. (1969). *The longest mile.* Garden City, NY: Doubleday.

Gelb, S. (1997). The problem of typological thinking in mental retardation. *Mental Retardation, 35*(6), 448–457.

Gelzheiser, L., & Meyers, J. (1990). Special and remedial education in the classroom: Theme and variations. *Journal of Reading, Writing, and Learning Disabilities, 6*, 419–436.

Georgia Department of Education (1989). Revised flow chart. (Correspondence from Dr. Joan Jordan, State Director of Special Education.)

Georgia Department of Education, Program for Exceptional Children. (1986). *Mild mentally handicapped* (Vol. I), Atlanta, GA: Office of Instructional Services, Division of Special Programs, Program for Exceptional Children. Resource manuals for Program for Exceptional Children.

Gilbert, S. (2000). Gains in diagnosing hyperactivity. *New York Times*, June 20, D8.

Ginott, H. (1971). *Teacher and child.* New York: Macmillan.

Ginsburg, H. (1972). *The myth of the deprived child: Poor children's intellect and education.* Englewood Cliffs, NJ: Prentice Hall.

Glasser, W. (1985). *Control theory in the classroom.* New York: Perennial Library.

Glickman, C. D. (1987). Good and/or effective schools: What do we want? *Phi Delta Kappan, 68*(8), 622–624.

Glidewell, J., & Swallow, C. (1968). *The Prevalence of maladjustment in elementary schools.* Chicago, IL: University of Chicago Press.

Gloeckler, T., & Simpson, C. (1988). *Exceptional students in regular classrooms: Challenges, services, and methods.* Mountain View, CA: Mayfield Publishing.

Goddard, H. H. (1912). How shall we educate mental defectives? *Training School Bulletin, 9*, 43.

Goldberg, M. F. (1990). Portrait of Madeline Hunter. *Educational Leadership, 47*(5), 41–43.

Goldstein, H. (1974). *Social learning curriculum.* Columbus, OH: Charles E. Merrill.

Goldstein, K. (1942). *After effects of brain injuries in war.* New York: Grune & Stratton.

Goleman, D. (1995). *Emotional intelligence: Why it can matter more than I.Q.* New York: Bantam Books.

Goodlad, J. I. (1984). *A place called school.* New York: McGraw-Hill.

Gough, P. B. (1987). The key to improving schools: An interview with William Glasser. *Phi Delta Kappan, 68*(9), 656–662.

Gould, S. J. (1981). *The mismeasure of man.* New York: W. W. Norton.

Grady, M. P., & Luecke, E. A. (1978). Education and the brain. (Phi Delta Kappan Series #108). Bloomington: Phi Delta Kappa.

Greenbaum, P. E., Dedrick, R. M., Freidman, K. K., Brown, E. L., Lardieri, S. P., & Pugh, A. M. (1998). National adolescent and child treatment study (NACTS): Outcomes for children with serious emotional and behavioral disturbance. In *Outcomes for children and youth with behavioral and emotional disorders.* M. H. Epstein, K. Kutash, & A. Duchnowdki, (Eds.) Austin, TX: Pro-Ed.

Greenberg, G. S. (1998). Answers to six of them most frequently asked questions about ADHD. *Reaching Today's Youth: The Community Circle of Caring Journal, 2*(2), 16–18.

Gresham, F. M. (1989). Utility of cognitive-behavioral procedures for social skills training with children: A critical review. *Journal of Abnormal Child Psychology, 13*, 411–423.

Gresham, F. M. (1998). Social skills training: Should we raze, remodel or rebuild? *Behavioral Disorders, 24*(1), 21–28.

Gresham, F., MacMillan, D., & Bocian, K. (1996). Behavioral earthquakes—Low frequency salient behavioral events that differentiate students at-risk of behavioral disorders. *Behavioral Disorders, 21*(4), 277–292.

Grosenick, J. K., & Huntze, S. L. (1979). *National needs analysis in behavior disorders.* Columbia, MO: University of Missouri, Department of Special Education.

Grossman, C., Neckerman, H., Koepsell, T., Liu, P., Asher, K., Beland, K., Frey, K., & Rivara, P. (1997). Effectiveness of a violence prevention curriculum among children in elementary school. A randomized controlled trial. *Jour-*

nal of the American Medical Association, 277(20), 1605–1611.

Grossman, H. J. (1973). *Manual on terminology and classification in mental retardation.* Baltimore: Garamond/Pridemark Press.

Grunwald, P. (1990). The new generation of information systems. *Phi Delta Kappan, 72*(2), 113–114.

Guetzloe, E. (1988, Summer). Suicide and depression: special education's responsibility. *Teaching Exceptional Children, 20*(4), 25–28.

Gunter, P. L., Miller, K. A., Venn, M. L., Thomas, K., & House, S. (2002, Nov./Dec.). Self-graphing to success: Computerized data management. *Teaching Exceptional Children, 35*(2), 30–34.

Guralnick, M. J., & Groom, J. M. (1988). Peer interactions in mainstreamed and specialized classrooms: A comparative analysis, *Exceptional Children, 54*(5), 415–425.

Hallahan, D. P., & Kauffman, J. M. (1977). Categories, labels, behavioral characteristics: ED, LD, and ENR reconsidered. *Journal of Special Education, 11,* 139–149.

Hallahan, D. P., & Kauffman, J. M. (1982). *Exceptional children: Introduction to special education* (3rd ed.). Englewood Cliffs, NJ: Prentice Hall.

Hallahan, D. P., & Kauffman, J. M. (1994). *Exceptional children: Introduction to special education* (6th ed.). Boston: Allyn and Bacon.

Hallahan, D., & Cruickshank, W. (1973). *Psychoeducational foundations of learning disabilities.* Englewood Cliffs, NJ: Prentice Hall.

Haring, N. G., & Phillips, E. L. (1962). *Educating emotionally disturbed children.* New York: McGraw-Hill.

Harris, K. R., & Pressley, M. (1991). The nature of cognitive strategy instruction: Interactive strategy instruction. *Exceptional Children, 57,* 392–401.

Hazel, J. S., Schumacker, J. B., & Sherman, J. S. (1982). Application of a group training program in social skills and problem solving to learning disabled and non-learning disabled youth. *Learning Disabled Quarterly, 5,* 398–414.

Healthy Children's Project (2005). www.healthychildrensproject.org/exposures/index.html

Hebb, D. O. (1966). *A textbook on psychology* (2nd ed.). Philadelphia, PA: W. B. Saunders.

Heller, K., & Monahan, J. (1977). *Psychology and community change.* Homewood, IL: Dorsey Press.

Henderson, A. (1987). *The evidence continues to grow: Parent involvement improves student achievement.* Columbia, MD: National Committee for Citizens in Education.

Hendrick, I. G., & MacMillan, D. L. (1987). Coping with diversity in city school systems: The role of mental testing in shaping special classes for MR children in Los Angeles, 1900–1930. *Education and Training in Mental Retardation, 22,* 10–17.

Henley, M. (1985). *Teaching mildly retarded children in the regular classroom.* (Phi Delta Kappan Fastback series #220). Bloomington, IN: *Phi Delta Kappan.*

Henley, M. (1986). Training teachers to manage the feelings and behavior of emotionally disturbed students. Paper presented at the National Adolescent Conference, Minneapolis, MN.

Henley, M. (1987). Ego function and dysfunction: A guide to understanding discipline problems. *The Pointer, 31*(4), 24–30.

Henley, M. (1997). *Teaching self-control: A curriculum for responsible behavior.* National Educational Service: Bloomington, IN.

Henley, M. (2003). *Teaching self-control: A curriculum for responsible behavior.* Bloomington, IN: National Educational Service.

Henley, M. (2004). *Creating successful inclusion programs: A guide for teachers and administrators.* Bloomington, IN: National Educational Service.

Henley, M. (2005). *Classroom management: A proactive approach.* Columbus, OH: Merrill/Prentice Hall.

Henley, M., & Long, N. (1999). Teaching emotional intelligence to impulsive-aggressive youth. *Reclaiming Children and Youth: Journal of Emotional and Behavioral Problems, 7*(4), 224–229.

Hersch, P. (1998). *A tribe apart: A journey into the heart of American adolescence.* New York: The Ballantine Publishing Group.

Heward, W. L. (2003). *Exceptional children: An introduction to special education* (7th ed.). Upper Saddle River, N. J.: Merrill Prentice Hall.

Hewett, F. M., & Taylor, F. D. (1980). *The emotionally disturbed child in the classroom: The orchestration of success.* Boston: Allyn and Bacon.

Hobbs, N. (1966). Helping disturbed children: Ecological psychological strategies. *American Psychologist, 21,* 1105–1115.

Hobbs, N. (1982). Help's on the way for the learning disabled. *Salt Lake Tribune,* 102.

Hodgkinson, H. (2001). Educational demographics: What teachers should know. *Educational Leadership, 58*(4), 6–11.

Holland, B. V. (1987). Fundamental motor skill performance of non-handicapped and educable mentally impaired students. *Education and Training in Mental Retardation, 22*(3), 197–203.

Holloway, J. H. (2000, September). Research link—Preparing teachers for differentiated instruction. *Educational Leadership, 58*(1), 1–3.

Holt, J. (1977). *How children fail.* New York: Dell.

Hops, H. (1983). Children's social competence and skill: Research practices and future direction. *Behavior Therapy, 14*, 3–18.

Horn, J. L. (1924). *The education of exceptional children: A consideration of public school problems and policies in the field of differentiated education.* New York: Century.

Horn, J. L., O'Donnell, J. P., & Leicht, D. J. (1988). Phonetically inaccurate spelling among learning-disabled, head-injured, and nondisabled young adults. *Brain and Language, 33*(1), 55–64.

Horner, R. H. (2000). Positive behavior supports. *Focus on Autism and Other*

Houts, P. L. (1977). *The myth of measurability.* New York: Hart Publishing.

Hu-DeHart, E. (1993). The history, development, and future of ethnic studies. *Phi Delta Kappan, 75*(1), 50–54.

Huefner, D. S. (2000). *Getting comfortable with special education.* Norwood, MA: Christopher-Gordon Publishers.

Hughes, C., Copeland, S. R., Wehmeyer, M. L., Agran, M., Cai, X., & Hwang, B. (2002). Increasing social interaction between general education high school students and their peers with mental retardation. *Journal of Developmental and Physical Disabilities, 14*, 387–402.

Hyman, I., & D'Alessandro, J. (1984). Good old fashioned discipline: The politics of punitiveness. *Phi Delta Kappan, 66*(1), 39–45.

Hynd, G. W., & Hynd, C. R. (1984). Dyslexia: Neuroanatomical/neurolinguistic perspectives. *Reading Research Quarterly, 19*(4), 482–498.

Instructional Philosophy and Strategies. (2003, September). [On-line]. Available: www.sasked.gov.sk.ca/docs/midlsoc/gr8/philos8.html

Jackson, P. W. (1968). *Life in the classrooms.* New York: Holt, Rinehart, & Winston.

Jackson, W. J., & Larkin, M. J. (2002, Sept./Oct.). Rubric: Teaching students to use grading rubrics. *Teaching Exceptional Children, 35*(1), 4045.

Jacobs, L. (1984). Cognition and learning disabilities. *Teaching Exceptional Children, 16*(3), 213–216.

Jenkins, J. R., & Jenkins, L. M. (1981). *Cross age and peer tutoring: Help for children with learning problems.* Reston, VA: The Council for Exceptional Children.

Jenkins, J. R., Pious, C. G., & Peterson, D. L. (1988). Categorical programs for remedial and handicapped students: Issues of validity. *Exceptional Children, 55*(2), 147–158.

Jensen, E. (1998). How Julie's brain learns. In *The Best of Educational Leadership: 1998–1999.* Alexandria, VA: Association of Supervision and Curriculum Development.

Johnson, D. W. (1972). *Reaching out: interpersonal effectiveness and self-actualization.* Englewood Cliffs, NJ: Prentice Hall.

Johnson, D. W., & Johnson, R. T. (1986). Mainstreaming and cooperative learning strategies. *Exceptional Children, 52*(6), 553–561.

Johnson, D. W., & Johnson, R. T. (1990). Social skills for successful group work. *Educational Leadership, 47*(4), 29–33.

Johnstone, E. R. (1908). The functions of the special class. National Education Association Journal of Proceedings and Address of the 46th Annual Meeting, 114–118.

Jones, F. (1987). *Positive classroom discipline.* New York: McGraw-Hill.

Jones, V. F., & Jones, L. S. (1981). *Responsible classroom discipline: Creating positive learning environments and solving problems.* Boston: Allyn and Bacon.

Jones, V. F., & Jones, L. S. (1986). *Comprehensive classroom management: Creating positive learning environments* (2nd ed.). Boston: Allyn and Bacon.

Jones, V., Dohrn, E., & Dunn, C. (2004). *Creating effective programs for students with emotional and behavior disorders: Interdisciplinary approaches for adding meaning and hope to behavior change interventions.* Boston: Allyn and Bacon.

Kamin, L. J. (1977). The polities of IQ. In P. L. Houts (Ed.), *The myth of measurability.* New York: Hart Publishing.

Kane, C. (1994). *Prisoners of time research: What we know and what we need to know.* Washington, DC: National Education Commission on Time and Learning.

Kelly, T., Bullock, L., & Dykes, M. K. (1974). *Teacher perceptions of behavioral disorders in children.* Gainesville, FL: Florida Educational Research and Development Council.

Kephart, N. C. (1971). Foreword. In T. S. Ball (Ed.), *Itard, Sequin, and Kephart: Sensory education, a learning interpretation.* Columbus, OH: Charles E. Merrill.

Kilborn, (2000). Illiteracy pulls Appalachia back, and efforts to overcome it grow. *The New York Times,* July 27th, A1/A16.

Kinsbourne, M., & Caplan, P. J. (1979). *Children's learning and attentional problems.* Boston, MA: Little, Brown.

Kirby, B. L. (2003, September). *What is Asperger's Syndrome?* In Asperger Syndrome Information and Support (O.A.S.I.S.). (Online). Available: www.udel.edu/bkirby/asperger/aswhatisit.html

Kirk, S. A. (1962). *Educating exceptional children.* Boston, MA: Houghton Mifflin.

Kirk, S. A. (1976). In J. K. Kauffman & D. P. Hallahan, *Teaching children with learning disabilities: Personal perspectives.* Columbus, OH: Charles E. Merrill.

Knapp, M. S., Turnbull, B. J., & Shields, P. M. (1990). New directions for educating the children of poverty. *Educational Leadership, 48*(1), 4–8.

Knitzer, J., Steinberg, Z., & Fleisch, B. (1990). *At the schoolhouse door: An examination of programs and policies for children with behavioral and emotional problems.* New York: Bank Street College of Education.

Knoblock, P. (1983). Teaching emotionally disturbed children. Dallas, TX: Houghton Mifflin.

Knoblock, P. (1987). *Understanding exceptional children and youth.* Boston: Little, Brown.

Kohl, H. (1967). *36 children.* New York: New American Express.

Kohlberg, L. (1973). The claim to moral adequacy of a highest stage of moral judgment. *Journal of Philosophy, 70,* 630–636.

Kohn, A. (1988, November). Suffer the restless children. *The Atlantic Monthly,* pp. 90–100.

Kohn, A. (1991). Caring kids: The role of schools. *Phi Delta Kappan, 72*(7), 496–506.

Kokaska, C. J., & Brolin, D. E. (1985). *Career education for handicapped individuals* (2nd ed.). Columbus, OH: Charles E. Merrill Publishing Company.

Koppitz, E. M. (1972–1973). Special class pupils with learning disabilities: A five year follow-up study. *Academic Therapy, 8,* 133–138.

Kotulak, R. (1996). *Learning how to use the brain.* Paper presented at the Brain Development in Young Children: New Frontiers for Research, Policy, and Practice Conference, Chicago, Ill. June 13. *http://www.newhorizons.org/otc_21 chusebrain.html.*

Kounin, J. (1977). *Discipline and group management in classrooms.* New York: Holt, Rinehart and Winston.

Kozol, J. (1991). *Savage inequalities: Children in America's schools.* New York Crown Publishers.

Kozol, J. (1995). *Amazing grace: Lives of children and the conscience of a nation.* New York: Crown Publishers.

Kraeplin, E. (1923). *Textbook of Psychiatry* (8th ed.). New York: Macmillan.

Kunzelmann, H. P., Cohen, M. A., Hulten, W. J., Martin, G. L., & Mingo, A. R. (1970). *Precision teaching: An initial training sequence.* Seattle, WA: Special Child Publications.

Kuveke, S. (1983). School behaviors of educable mentally retarded children. *Education and Training of the Mentally Retarded, 14*(2), 134–137.

Lambert, W. E. (1997). From Crockett to Tubman: Investigating historical perspectives. *Educational Leadership, 55*(1), 51–54.

Langdon, H. (1983). Assessment and intervention strategies for the bilingual language-disordered student. *Exceptional Children, 50*(1), 37–46.

Larivee, B. (1988). Effective strategies for academically handicapped students in the regular classroom. In R. E. Slavin, N. L. Karweit, & N. E. Madden (Eds.), *Effective programs for students at risk.* Boston: Allyn and Bacon.

Larson, K. A., Gerber, M. M. (1987). Effects of social metacognitive training for enhancing overt behavior in learning disabled and low achieving delinquents. *Exceptional Children, 54*(3), 201–211.

Lasley, T. J. (1989). A teacher development model for classroom management. *Phi Delta Kappan, 7*(1), 36–38.

Leitch, L. M., & Tangri, S. S. (1988). Barriers to home-school collaboration. *Educational Horizons,* Winter, 70–74.

Lemeshow, S. (1982). *Handbook of clinical types in mental retardation.* Boston: Allyn and Bacon.

Lerner, J. (2000). *Learning disabilities: Theories, diagnosis, and teaching strategies.* (8th ed.) Boston: Houghton Mifflin Publishing.

Lerner, J. (2003). *Learning disabilities: Theories, diagnosis and teaching strategies.* (9th ed.). Boston: Houghton Mifflin.

Lerner, J. W., Lowenthal, B., & Lerner, S. R. (1995). *Attention deficit disorder: Assessment and teaching.* Pacific Grove, CA: Brooks/Cole Publishing.

Leverault, A. H. (1990). Preventive discipline in the secondary school. Unpublished research paper.

Levine, M. (1990). Learning disorders and the flow of expectations. *Their World.* National Center for Learning Disabilities. Available: *http://www.ldonline.org/ld.org/ld_indepth/general_info/gen-1.html.*

Levinson, E. (1990). Will technology transform education or will school co-opt technology? *Phi Delta Kappan, 72*(2), 121–126.

Lewis, A. C. (1990). Tracking the national goals. *Phi Delta Kappan, 72*(7), 496–506.

Lewis, B. L. (1992). Do conduct disordered gang members think differently? *Journal of Emotional and Behavioral Problems, 1*(1), 17–20.

Lewis, R. B., & Doorlag, D. H. (1987). *Teaching special students in the mainstream* (2nd ed.). Columbus, OH: Merrill Publishing.

Lewis, T.J., and Sugai, G. (1999). Effective behavior support: A systems approach to proactive school-wide management. *Focus on Exceptional Children, 31*(6), 1–24.

Lickona, T. (1988). Four strategies for fostering character development in children. *Phi Delta Kappan, 69*(6), 419–423.

Lindsley, O. R. (1964). Direct measurement and prothesis of retarded behavior. *Journal of Education, 147,* 62–81.

Lindsley, O. R. (1990). Precision teaching: By teachers for children. *Teaching Exceptional Children, 22*(3), 10–15.

Lloyd, J. (1980). Academic instruction and cognitive behavior modification: The need for attack strategy training. *Exceptional Education Quarterly, 1*(1), 53–63.

Lobav, W., Cohen, C., & Lewis, J. (1968). *A study of the non-standard English of Negro and Puerto Rican speakers in New York City.* New York: Columbia University (Research Project No. 3288).

Lokerson, J. (1996). *Learning disabilities.* Council for Exceptional Children, ERIC Clearinghouse on Handicapped and Gifted Children, Reston, VA. (ERIC Digest #E516). Available: *http://www.ldonline.org/ld_indepth/general_info/eric_ldgen.html.*

London, P. (1987). Character education and clinical intervention: A paradigm shift for U.S. schools. *Phi Delta Kappan, 68*(9), 667–673.

Long, N. (1990). Life space interviewing. *Beyond, 2*(1), 10–15.

Long, N. J. & Morse, W. C. (1996). *Conflict in the classroom: The education of at-risk and troubled students.* (5th ed.) Austin, TX: Pro-Ed.

Long, N.J., Wood, M. M., & Fecser, F. A. (2001). *Life space crisis intervention: Talking with students in conflict.* (2nd ed.) Austin, TX: Pro-Ed.

Long, N. L. (1986). The nine psychoeducational stages of helping emotionally disturbed students through the reeducation process. *The Pointer, 30*(3), 5–20.

Long, N., & Morse, W. (1996). *Conflict in the classroom: The education of at-risk and troubled students.* (5th ed.). Austin, TX: Pro-Ed.

Lovitt, T. C. (1984). *Tactics for teaching.* Columbus, OH: Merrill.

Lovitt, T. C. (1989). *Introduction to learning disabilities.* Boston: Allyn and Bacon.

Lower, T. A. (1999). Intellectual disabilities: Have we lost our senses? *Mental Retardation, 37*(6), 498–503.

Lund, N. J., & Duchan, J. F. (1988). *Assessing children's language in naturalistic contexts.* Englewood Cliffs, NJ: Prentice Hall.

Lynch, E. W., & Stein, R. C. (1987). Parent participation by ethnicity: A comparison of hispanic, black, and anglo families. *Exceptional Children, 54*(2), 105–111.

Lyon, G. R. (1996, Spring). Special education for students with disabilities: The future of children. *Learning Disabilities, 6* (1), 1–20. Available: *http://www.ldonline.org/ld_indepth/general_info/future_children.html*

MacKeith, R. (1973). Parental reactions and responses to a handicapped child. In F. Richardson (Ed.), *Brain and intelligence* (pp. 131–141). Hyattsville, MD: National Educational Consultants.

Mager, R. F. (1962). *Preparing educational objectives.* Palo Alto, CA: Fearon.

Maheady, L., Sacca, K. M., & Harper, G. F. (1988). Classwide peer tutoring with mildly handicapped high school students. *Exceptional Children, 55*(1), 52–59.

Mallery, D. (1971). High school students speak—An excerpt. In M. L. Silberman (Ed.), *The experience of schooling.* New York: Holt, Rinehart, and Winston.

Mandelbaum, L. H. (1989). Reading. In G. A. Robinson, J. R. Patton, E. A. Polloway, & L. R. Sargent (Eds.), *Best practices in mild mental retardation.* Reston, VA: The Division of Mental Retardation Council for Exceptional Children.

Mangrum, C. T., & Strichart, S. S. (1984). *College and the learning disabled student*. London: Grune & Stratton.

Mann, L., & Sabatino, D. (1985). *Foundations of cognitive process in remedial and special education*. Rockville, MD: Aspen Systems.

Mapp, K. (1997). Mating the connection between families and schools. *The Harvard Education Letter, 8*(5), Cambridge, MA: Harvard Graduate School of Education.

Margolis, R. J. (1988). *Out of harm's way: The emancipation of juvenile justice*. New York: Edna McConnel Clark Foundation.

Marston, D. (1988). The effectiveness of special education: A time series analysis of reading performance in regular and special education settings. *Journal of Education, 21*, 13–26.

Marzano, R. J. & Marzano, J. S. (2003). The key to classroom management. *Educational Leadership. 61*(1), 6–13.

Massachusetts Department of Education (1991). Tracking: It's bad practice to identify ability groups, educators told. *Massachusetts Education Today, 6*(5), 1, 7.

Mastropieri, M. A., & Scruggs, T. E. (2000). *The inclusive classroom: Strategies for effective instruction*. Upper Saddle River, NJ: Merrill/Prentice Hall.

Mathews, F. (1992). Reframing gang violence: A pro-youth strategy. *Journal of Emotional and Behavioral Problems, 1*(3), 24–28.

Mathews, S. (1995). Juvenile capital offenders on empathy. *Journal of Emotional and Behavioral Problems, 4*(2), 10–12.

Mayron (1979). *Correlates of success in transition of mentally retarded to regular class* (Vols. I and II). Final Report, Pomona, California. Los Angeles, CA: New Psychiatric Institute, Pacific State Hospital. (ERIC Document Nos. EC 081–038 and EC 081–039).

McConaughy, S. H. (1986). Social competence and behavioral problems of learning disabled adolescents. *Journal of Learning Disabilities, 19*(2), 101–106.

McCoy, K. (1987). *Solo Parenting: Your essential guide*. New York: Signet.

McCoy, K. M., & Prehm, H. J. (1987). *Teaching mainstreamed students: Methods and techniques*. Denver, CO: Love Publishing.

McCubbin, H. I., McCubbin, M. A., Thompson, A. I., & Thompson, E. A. (1998). Resiliency in ethnic families: A conceptual model for predicting family adjustment and adaptation. In H. I. McCubbin, E. A. McCubbin, A. J.

Thompson, & J. E. Fromer (Eds.), *Resiliency in Native American and immigrant families* (pp. 3–48). Thousand Oaks, CA: Sage.

McDaniel, E. A., & Dibella-McCarthy (1989). Enhancing teacher efficacy in special education. *Teaching Exceptional Children, 21*(4), 34–38.

McDaniel, T. R. (1986). A primer on classroom discipline: Principles old and new. *Phi Delta Kappan, 68*(1), 63–67.

McFall, R. M. (1982). A review and reformulation of the concept of social skills. *Behavioral Assessment, 4*, 1–33.

McGinnis, E., & Goldstein, A. P. (1990). *Skillstreaming in early childhood. Teaching prosocial skills to the preschool and kindergarten child*. Champaign, IL: Research Press.

McGinnis, E., & Goldstein, P. (1984). *Skillstreaming the elementary school child: A guide for teaching pro-social skills*. Champaign, IL: Research Press.

McGuffey's Fourth Eclectic Reader (1920). New York: H. H. Vail, 38–39.

McKinney, J. D., McClure, S., & Feagans, L. (1982). Classroom behavior of learning disabled children. *Learning Quarterly, 5*(1), 45–52.

McWhirter, J. J., McWhirter, B. T., McWhirter, A. M., & McWhirter, E. H. (2003, May/June). *At-risk youth: A comprehensive response* (2nd ed.). Pacific Grove, CA: Brooks/Cole.

McWhirter, J. J., McWhirter, R. J., & McWhirter, M. C. (1985). The learning disabled child: A retrospective review. *Journal of Learning Disabilities, 18*(6), 315–318.

Meese, R. L. (1994). *Teaching learners with mild disabilities*. Pacific Grove, CA: Wadsworth.

Meichenbaum, D. (1977). *Cognitive behavior modification: An integrative approach*. New York: Plenum.

Meichenbaum, D. (1985). Teaching thinking: A cognitive-behavioral perspective. In S. F. Chipman & J. W. Segal (Eds.), *Thinking and learning skills: Research and open questions* (Vol. 2). Hillsdale, NJ: Erlbaum Associates.

Meichenbaum, D., & Goodman, J. (1971). Training impulsive children to talk to themselves: A means of developing self-control. *Journal of Abnormal Psychology, 77*, 115–126.

Menacker, J., Weldon, W., & Hurwitz, E. (1989). School order and safety as community issues. *Phi Delta Kappan, 71*(1), 39–40, 55–56.

Mercer, C. D., & Mercer, A. R. (1985). *Teaching*

children with learning problems (2nd ed.). Columbus, OH: Charles E. Merrill.

Mercer, J. (1973). The pluralistic assessment project. *School Psychology Digest, 2,* 10–18.

Miller, D., Brown, A., & Robinson, L. (2002). Widgets on the web: Using computer based learning tools. *Teaching Exceptional Children. 35*(2), 24–28.

Miller, E. (1996). Changing the way we think about kids with disabilities: A Conversation with Tom Hehir. *Harvard Education Letter, 10*(4), 5–7.

Miller, L. G. (1968). Toward a greater understanding of the parents of the mentally retarded. *Journal of Pediatrics, 73,* 699–705.

Mills v. *the Board of Education of the District of Columbia,* 348F. Supp. 866 (D.C. 1972).

Moores, D. F. (1982). *Educating the deaf: Psychology, principles, and practices* (2nd ed.). Boston: Houghton Mifflin.

Morrison, J. (1995). *DSM-IV made easy: The clinician's guide to diagnosis.* New York: The Guilford Press.

Morse, W. (1987). Introduction. *Teaching Exceptional Children, 19*(4), 4–6.

Morse, W. C. (1985). *Pursuit of excellence for educating the behavior disordered.* Paper presented at the Midwest Symposium for Leadership in Behavioral Disorders. Kansas City, MO.

Morsink, C. V. (1984). *Teaching special needs students in regular classrooms.* Boston: Little, Brown.

Mostert, M. P. (1998). *Interprofessional collaboration in schools.* Boston, MA: Allyn and Bacon.

Moxley, R. A. (1998). Treatment-only designs and student self-recording as strategies for public school teachers. *Education and Treatment of Children, 21,* 37–61.

Myers, P. I., & Hammill, D. D. (1982). *Learning disabilities: Basic concepts, assessment practices, and instructional strategies.* Austin, TX: Pro-Ed.

Myklebust, H. R. (1964). Learning disorders: Psychoneurological disturbances in childhood. *Rehabilitation Literature, 25,* 354–359.

National Education Association (2001, January). Where the stakes are high for students. NEA Today. In L. Washburn-Moses (2003, March/April). What every special educator should know about high-stakes testing. *Teaching Exceptional Children, 35*(4), 12–15.

National Education Association. (2003, March). Californians offer five big ideas on IDEA. *NEA Today, 21*(6), 1–2.

National Institute of Mental Health (NIMH). (1996). *Learning disabilities: Decade of the brain* (NIH). Available: *http://www.ldonline. org/ld_indepth/ general_info/gen-nimh-booklet. html.*

National Research Council. (2001). *Educating children with autism.* Committee on Educational Interventions for Children with Autism. Division of Behavioral and Social Sciences and Education. Washington, DC: National Academy Press.

Neill, M. D., & Medina, N. J. (1989). Standardized testing: Harmful to educational health. *Phi Delta Kappan, 70*(9), 668–697.

Neisworth, J. T., & Greer, J. G. (1975). Functional similarities of learning disability and mild retardation. *Exceptional Children, 42,* 17–21.

Nelson, C. M. (1988). Social skills training for handicapped students. *Teaching Exceptional Children, 20*(4), 19–22.

Nelson, M. C., Rutherford, R. B., Jr., & Wolford, B. I. (Eds.) (1987). Special education in the criminal justice system. Columbus, OH: Charles E. Merrill.

New York Times (1999). *Scientists find the first gene for dyslexia.* Sept. 7, D1. Reuters News Service.

NICHCY. (2000). *Learning strategies for students with learning disabilities.* Washington, DC: National Information Center for Children and Youth with Disabilities. Available: *www. ldonline.org/ld_indepth/teaching_techniques/ nichcy_interventions_bib.html.*

Nichols, S. L., & Good, T.L. (2004). Why today's young children are viewed so negatively. *Education Week 23*(31), 42.

NLDline News. (September, 2003). *NLD letter and information packet.* Welcome to *NLDline!* Available: www.nldline.com / welcome.htm

Nonverbal Learning Disorders Association. (September, 2003). *What is NLD?* Online Nonverbal Learning Disorders Association. Available: www.nlda / whatis.html

Noyes, K. G., & McAndrew, G. L. (1971). Is this what schools are for? In M. L. Silberman (Ed.), *The experience of schooling.* New York: Holt, Rinehart, & Winston.

O'Brien, G. V. (1999). Protecting the social body: Use of the organism in fighting the menace of the feebleminded. *Mental Retardation, 37*(3), 188–200.

Obiakor, F. E. (1994). *The eight step multicultural approach: Learning and teaching with a smile.* Dubuque, IA: Kendall / Hunt.

Obiakor, F. E. (1999). Teacher expectations of minority exceptional learners: Impact on "accuracy" of self-concepts. *Exceptional Children, 66,* 39–53.

Obiakor, F. E. (2001). *It even happens in "good" schools: Responding to cultural diversity in today's classrooms.* Thousand Oaks, CA: Corwin Press.

Ohanian, S. (1991). P.L. 94–142: Mainstream or quicksand? *Phi Delta Kappan, 72*(3), 217–222.

Olsen, S., Marshall, E. S., Mandleco, B., Allred, K. W., Dyches, T. T., & Sansom, N. (1999). Support, communication, and hardiness in families with children with disabilities. *Journal of Family Nursing, 5,* 275–291.

Ornstein, R. (1978, May). The split and the whole brain. *Human Nature,* 76–83.

Osman, B. B. (1979). *Learning disabilities: A family affair.* New York: Warner.

Paige, R. (2001, October 4). Testimony of Secretary Rod Paige before the House Committee on Education and the Workforce regarding the over-identification of minority students under the Individuals with Disabilities Education Act. Available: www.ed.gov/Speeches/10-2001/011004.html

Palinesar, A. S. (1982). *Improving the reading comprehension of junior high students through reciprocal teaching of comprehension-monitoring strategies.* Unpublished doctoral dissertation, University of Illinois, Urbana-Champaign.

Pallas, A. M., Natriello, G., & McDill, E. L. (1989, June/July). The changing nature of disadvantaged population: Current dimensions and future trends. *Educational Leadership,* 16–22.

Pasamanick, B., & Knoblock, H. (1973). The epidemiology of reproductive casualty. In S. Sapir & A. Nitzburg (Eds.), *Children with learning problems.* New York: Brunner/Mazel.

Patton, J. R., Cronin, M. E., Polloway, E. A., Hutchison, D., & Robinson, G. A. (1989). Curricular considerations: A life skills orientation. In G. A. Robinson, J. R. Patton, E. A. Polloway, & L. R. Sargent (Eds.), *Best practices in mental disabilities.* Des Moines: Iowa Department of Education, Bureau of Special Education.

Patton, J. R., Kauffman, J. M., Blackbourn, J. M., & Brown, B. G. (1991). *Exceptional children in focus* (5th ed.). New York: Macmillan.

Paul, J. L., & Epanchin, B. C. (1991). *Educating emotionally disturbed children and youth: Theories and practices for teachers* (2nd ed.). New York: Merrill Publishing.

Pervasive Developmental Disorder. (2003, September). *An AskERIC InfoGuide.* (On-line). Available: www.askeric.org/Old_Askeric/InfoGuides/alpha_list/ppd12_96.html;

Peterson, N. L. (1987). *Early intervention for handicapped and at-risk children.* Denver, CO: Love Publishing.

Phi Delta Kappa Commission on Discipline. (1982). *Handbook for developing schools with good discipline.* Bloomington, IN: Phi Delta Kappa.

Phillips, V., & McCullough, L. (1990). Consultation based programming: Instituting the collaborative work ethic. *Exceptional Children, 56*(4), 291–304.

Piaget, J. (1950). *The psychology of intelligence.* New York: International Universities Press.

Polloway, E. A., & Epstein, M. H. (1985). Current issues in mild mental retardation: A survey of the field. *Education and Training of the Mentally Retarded, 20,* 171–174.

Polloway, E. A., Patton, J. R., Payne, J. S., & Payne, R. A. (1989). *Strategies for teaching learners with special needs* (4th ed.). Columbus, OH: Charles E. Merrill.

Poplin, M. S. (1989). The reductionistic fallacy in learning disabilities: Replicating the past by reducing the present. *Journal of Learning Disabilities, 21*(7), 389–400.

Prater, M. A. (2003, May/June). She will succeed! Strategies for success in inclusive classrooms. *Teaching Exceptional Children, 35*(5), 58–64.

Pressley, M., & Harris, K. R. (1990). What we really know about strategy instruction. *Educational Leadership, 48*(1), 31–33.

Price-Bonham, S., & Addison, S. (1978). Families and mentally retarded children: Emphasis on the father. *The Family Coordinator, 3,* 221–230.

Pruchno, R., Patrick, J. H., & Burant, C. J. (1997). African American and White mothers of adults with chronic disabilities: Caregiving burden and satisfaction. *Family Relations, 46,* 335–346.

Przychodin, J. (1981). Improving classroom discipline. *Clearing House, 55*(1), 16.

Public Law 101–476 (1990). Individuals with Disabilities Education Act.

Pugach, M. C., & Johnson, L. J. (1989a). The challenge of implementing collaboration between general and special education. *Exceptional Children, 56*(3), 232–235.

Pugach, M. C., & Johnson, L. J. (1989b). Prereferral interventions: Progress, problems, and challenges. *Exceptional Children, 56*(3), 217–226.

Putnam, J. W., Rynders, J. E., Johnson, R. T., & Johnson, D. W. (1989). Collaborative skill instruction for promoting positive interactions between mentally handicapped and non-handicapped children. *Exceptional Children, 55*(6), 550–558.

Ramsey, R. S. (1981). *Perceptions of disturbed and disturbing behavioral characteristics by school personnel.* Unpublished doctoral dissertation, University of Florida, Gainesville.

Ramsey, R. S. (1988). *Preparatory guide for special education teacher competency tests.* Boston: Allyn and Bacon.

Ramsey, R. S. (1995a). Preparatory guide for special education teacher competency tests-revised. (formerly published by Allyn and Bacon, Inc.)

Ramsey, R. S. (1995b). Students with Learning Disabilities in College. Presentation to Andrew College Faculty, Cuthbert, Georgia, April 12 and September 6, 1995.

Ramsey, R. S. (1996). Working with college students with learning disabilities. Session Presenter at the Georgia Council for Exceptional Children State Conference, Columbus, Georgia, November 8, 1996.

Ramsey, R. S. (1997). *Learning Disabilities and Young Adults in College.* Unpublished manuscript.

Ramsey, R. S. (1998). *Co-teaching/collaboration.* A Session for the Block Academy, Muscogee County School District, Columbus, Georgia, June 11, 1998.

Ramsey, R. S., Dixon, M. J., & Smith, G. G. B. (1986). *Eyes on the special education: Professional knowledge teacher competency test.* Albany, GA: Southwest Georgia Learning Resources System Center.

Ratekin, N. (1979, March). Reading achievement of disabled learners. *Exceptional Children, 45*(16), 454–458.

Redl, F. (1971). The concept of the life space interview. In N. Long, W. Morse, & R. Newman (Eds.), *Conflict in the classroom.* Belmont, CA: Wadsworth Publishing.

Redl, F., & Wineman, D. (1951). *Children who hate.* Glencoe, IL: The Free Press.

Redl, F., & Wineman, D. (1957). *The aggressive child.* Glencoe, IL: The Free Press.

Reed, S., & Sauter, C. R. (1990). Children of poverty, the status of 12 million young children. *Phi Delta Kappan,* K1–K12.

Reid, D. (1978). *Toward the application of development epistemology to the education of exceptional children.* Proceedings of The Eighth Annual Conference on Piagetian Theory and the Helping Professions (8th). Los Angeles, California.

Reid, D. K., & Hresko, W. P. (1981a). Thinking about it in that way: Test data and instruction. *Exceptional Education Quarterly, 1*(3), 47–57.

Reid, D. K., & Hresko, W. P. (1981b). *A cognitive approach to learning disabilities.* New York: McGraw-Hill.

Reif, S. (1998). Redefining "structure" for students with AD/HD. Reclaiming Today's Youth: *The Journal of Emotional and Behavioral Problems, 2*(2), 24–28.

Reinert, H. (1976). *Children in conflict.* St. Louis, MO: C. V. Mosby.

Renzulli, J. S., Reis, S. M., & Smith, L. H. (1981). *The revolving door identification model.* Mamsfield Center, CN: Creative Learning.

Reschly, D. J. (1989). Incorporating adaptive behavior deficits into instructional programs. In G. A. Robinson, J. R. Patton, E. A. Polloway, & L. R. Sargent (Eds.), *Best practices in mild mental retardation.* Reston, VA: The Division of Mental Retardation Council for Exceptional Children.

Research Brief for Teachers (1988). *Curriculum based assessment.* (ERIC/OSEP Special Project). Reston, VA: The Council for Exceptional Children.

Restak, R. M. (1984). *The brain.* New York: Bantam Books.

Reynolds, W. M., & Miller, K. L. (1985). Depression and learned helplessness in mentally retarded and non-mentally retarded adolescents: An initial investigation. *Applied Research in Mental Retardation, 6*(3), 295–306.

Rezmierski, V. E. (1987). Discipline: Neither the steel nor the velvet, but the maturity inside the glove, that makes the difference. *The Pointer, 31*(4), 5–13.

Rhodes, W. C. (1967). The disturbing child: A problem of ecological management. *Exceptional Children, 33,* 449–455.

Rhodes, W. C., & Tracy, M. L. (1972a). *A study of child variance: Conceptual models* (Vol. 1). Ann Arbor, MI: University of Michigan.

Rhodes, W. C., & Tracy, M. L. (1972b). *A study of child variance: Interventions* (Vol. 2). Ann Arbor, MI: University of Michigan.

Rich, H. L., & Ross, S. M. (1989). Students' time on learning tasks in special education. *Exceptional Children, 55*(6), 508–515.

Ritschl, C., Mongrella, A. J., & Presbie, R. L. (1972). Group time out from rock and roll music and out of seat behavior of handicapped children while riding a school bus. *Psychological Reports, 31*, 967–873.

Roberts, M. (1986). Three mothers: Life span experiences. In R. Fewell & P. Vadasy (Eds.), *Families of handicapped children: Needs and supports across the life span* (pp. 193–218). Texas: Pro-Ed.

Roberts, S. (1983). A focus on learning disabilities at the college level. *Times-Argus, 89*, 90.

Robinson, G. A., Patton, J. R., Polloway, E. A., & Sargent, L. R. (Eds.) (1989). *Best practices in mild mental retardation*. Reston, VA: The Division of Mental Retardation Council for Exceptional Children.

Robinson, S. M. (1989). Oral language: Developing pragmatic skills and communicational competence. In G. A. Robinson, J. R. Patton, E. A. Polloway, & L. R. Sargent (Eds.), *Best practices in mild mental retardation*. Reston, VA: The Division of Mental Retardation Council for Exceptional Children.

Robinson, W. A. (1965). The elaborated code in working class language. *Language and Speech, 8*, 243–252.

Rogers-Dulan, J., & Blacher, J. (1995). African American families, religion, and disability: A conceptual framework. *Mental Retardation, 33*, 226–238.

Roit, M. L., & Pfohl, W. (1984). The readability of P.L. 94–142. Parent materials: Are parents truly informed? *Exceptional Children, 50*(6), 496–504.

Rosenberg, M. S., Wilson, R., Maheady, L., & Sindelar, P.T. (2004). *Educating students with behavior disorders* (3rd ed.). Boston: Allyn and Bacon.

Rosenshine, B., & Stevens, R. (1984). *Classroom instruction in a reading research*. New York: Longman.

Rothstein, L. F. (1995). *Special education law* (2nd ed.). New York: Longman Publishers.

Rubin, R., & Balow, B. (1971). Learning and behavior disorders: A longitudinal study. *Exceptional Children, 38*, 293–299.

Rutter, M., Giller, H., & Hagell, A. (1998). *Antisocial behavior by young people*. New York: Cambridge University Press.

Ryan, E. B., Short, E. J., & Weed, K. A. (1986). The role of cognitive strategy training in improving the academic performance of learning disabled children. *Journal of Learning possibilities, 18*, 521–529.

Safran, S. P., & Oswald, K. (2003). Positive behavior supports: Can schools reshape disciplinary practices? *Exceptional Children, 69*, 361–373.

Salend, S. J. (1987). Contingency management systems. *Academic Therapy, 22*(3), 245–253.

Salend, S. J. (2001). *Creating inclusive classrooms: Effective and reflective practices* (4th ed.). Upper Saddle River, NJ: Merrill/Prentice Hall.

Salend, S. J., & Lutz, J. G. (1984). Mainstreaming or mainlining: A competency based approach to mainstreaming. *Journal of Learning Disabilities, 17*, 27–29.

Sandford, J. A. (1987). Putting parents in their place in public schools. NASSP *Bulletin*, 47.99–103.

Sarason, S. B., & Doris, J. (1979). *Educational handicap, public policy, and social history*. New York: Free Press.

Satcher, D. (2000). Available: *http://www.surgeongeneral.gov/library/speeches/ChildMentalHealth.htm*.

Scanlon, D. M., Vellutino, F. R., Small, S. G., & Fanuele, D. P., & Sweeney, J. (2003). *The short and long term effects of different types of early literacy intervention on reading comprehension*. Paper presented at the annual conference of the Society for the Scientific Study of Reading. June, 2003, Boulder, Colorado.

Schloss, P. J., & Smith, M. A. (1998). *Applied behavior analysis in the classroom* (2nd ed.). Boston: Allyn and Bacon.

Schroeder, C. S., & Riddle, D. B. (1991). Behavior theory and practice. In J. L. Paul & B. C. Epanchin (Eds.), *Educating emotionally disturbed children and youth: Theories and practices for teachers* (2nd ed.). New York: Merrill Publishing.

Schultz, E. W., & Heuchen, C. M. (1983). *Child stress and the school experience*. New York: Human Sciences Press.

Schulz, J. B., Carpenter, C. D., & Turnbull, A. P. (1991). *Mainstreaming exceptional students: A guide for classroom teachers*. Boston, MA: Allyn and Bacon.

Schumaker, J. B., & Hazel, J. S. (1984). Social skills assessment and training for the learning disabled: What's on second? Part I. *Journal of Learning Disabilities, 17*(7), 422–431.

Schumaker, J. B., Pederson, C. J., Hazel, J. S., & Meyen, E. L. (1983). Social skills curricula for mildly handicapped adolescents: A review. *Focus on Exceptional Children, 16*(4), 1–16.

Schwartz, L. W. (1979). *Psychopathology of Childhood*. New York, NY: Holt, Rinehart & Winston.

Scott, M. E. (1988). Learning strategies can help. *Teaching Exceptional Children, 20*(3), 30–34.

Scruggs, T. E., & Mastropieri, M. A. (1986). Improving the test-taking skills of behaviorally disordered and learning disabled children. *Exceptional Children, 53*(1), 63–68.

Seldes, C. (1985). *The great thoughts*. New York: Ballantine.

Seligman, M. (1999). Childhood disability and the family. In V. L. Schwean & D. H. Saklofske (Eds.), *Handbook of psychosocial characteristics of exceptional children* (pp. 111–131). New York: Plenum.

Selman, R. L. (1980). *The growth of interpersonal understanding: Developmental and clinical analysis*. New York: Academic Press.

Seyle, H. (1975). *Stress without distress*. New York: Signet.

Sherry, L. (1982). Non-task oriented behaviors of educable mentally retarded, emotionally handicapped, and learning disabled students. *Educational Research Quarterly, 4*, 19–29.

Shriner, J. G., & DeStefano, L. (2003, Winter). Participation and accommodation in state assessment: The role of individualized education programs. *Exceptional Children, 69*(2), 147–161.

Sigmon, S. B. (1989). Reaction to excerpts from *The Learning Mystique*: A rational appeal for change. *Journal of Learning Disabilities, 22*(5), 298–300, 327.

Silver, H., Strong, R., & Perini, M. (1997). Integrating learning styles and multiple intelligences. *Educational Leadership, 55*(1), 22–27.

Silver, L. B. (1975). Acceptable and controversial approaches to treating the child with learning disabilities. *Pediatrics, 55*(3), 406–415.

Silver, L. B. (1989). Frequency of adoption of children and adolescents with learning disabilities. *Journal of Learning Disabilities, 22*(5), 325–327.

Silverman, R., Zigmond, N., & Sansome, J. (1981). Teaching coping skills to adolescents with learning problems. *Focus on Exceptional Children, 13*(6), 1–20.

Siperstein, G. N., & Goding, M. J. (1985). Teachers' behavior toward LD and non-LD children: A strategy for change. *Journal of Learning Disabilities, 18*(3), 139–144.

Skinner, D., Bailey, D. B., Correa, V., & Rodriguez, P. (1999). Narrating self and disability: Latino mothers construction of identities vis-à-vis their child with special needs. *Exceptional Children, 65*, 481–495.

Slavin, R. E. (1989). Students at risk of school failure: The problem and its dimensions. In Slavin, R. E., Karweit, N. L., & Madden, N. A. (Eds.), *Effective programs for students at risk* P. 319. Boston: Allyn and Bacon.

Slavin, R. E., Madden, N. A., & Leavey, M. (1984). Effects of cooperative learning and individualized instruction on mainstreamed students. *Exceptional Children, 50*(5), 434–443.

Smith, C. R. (1983). *Learning disabilities: The interaction of learner, task, and setting*. Boston: Little, Brown.

Smith, C. R. (1991). *Learning disabilities: The interaction of learner, task, and setting*. Boston: Allyn and Bacon.

Smith, J. E., & Patton, J. M. (1989). *A resource module on adverse causes of mild mental retardation*. (Prepared for the President's Committee on Mental Retardation).

Smith, R. A. (1987). A teacher's views on cooperative learning. *Phi Delta Kappan, 68*(9), 663–666.

Smith, S. (1980). *No easy answers: The learning disabled child at school and home*. New York: Bantam Books.

Smith, S. (2005). *The Lab School of Washington*. www.labschool.org

Smith, S. L. (1979). *No easy answers*. Cambridge: Winthrop.

Smith, T. E. C., Finn, D. M., & Dowdy, C. A. (1993). *Teaching students with mild disabilities*. Fort Worth: TX: Harcourt Brace Jovanovich.

Smith, T. E. C., Price, B. J., & Marsh, G. E., II. (1986). *Mildly handicapped children and adults*. St. Paul, MN, West Publishing.

Smith-Davis, J. (1989a, April). *A national perspective on special education*. Keynote presentation at the GLRS/College/University Forum, Macon, Georgia.

Smith-Davis, J. (1989b). Exceptional children in tomorrow's schools. In E. L. Meyen (Ed.), *Ex-*

ceptional children in today's schools. Denver, CO: Love Publishing.

Smothers, R. (1987, November 13). Jailed for paddling the paddler. *The New York Times*, A1.

Solnit, A. J., & Stark, M. H. (1961). Mourning and the birth of a defective child. *Psychoanalytic study of the child, 16,* 523–537.

Speece, S. L., McKinney, J. D., & Appelbaum, M. I. (1986). Longitudinal development of conservation skills in learning disabled children. *Journal of Learning Disabilities, 19*(5), 302–307.

Spence, S. H., & Marzillier, J. S. (1979). Social skills training with adolescent male offenders: Short term effects. *Behavior Research & Therapy, 19,* 349–368.

Sperry, R. W. (1968). Hemisphere deconnection and unity in conscious awareness. *American Psychologist, 23,* 723–733.

Stafford, P., & Klein, N. (1977). Application of Piaget's theory to the study of thinking of the mentally retarded: A review of the research. *The Journal of Special Education, 11*(2).

Stagg, V., & Catron, T. (1986). Networks of social supports for parents of handicapped children. In R. R. Fewell, P. F. Vadsay (Eds.), *Families of handicapped children: Needs and supports across the life span.* Austin, TX: Pro-Ed.

Stainback, D., Stainback, W., & Forest, M. (1989). *Educating all students in the mainstream of regular education.* Baltimore, MD: Brookes.

Stainback, W., & Stainback, S. (1984). A rationale for the merger of special and regular education. *Exceptional Children, 51*(2), 102–111.

Staub, D., & Peck, C. A. (1994). What are the outcomes for nondisabled students? *Educational Leadership, 52*(4), 36–40.

Stein, K. S., Leinhardt, B., & Bickel, W. (1989). Instructional issues for teaching students at risk: In R. E. Slavin, N. L. Karweit, & N. A. Madden (Eds.), *Effective programs for students at risk.* Boston: Allyn and Bacon.

Stephens, R. J., & Slavin, R. E. (1991). When cooperative learning improves the achievement of students with mild disabilities: A response to Tateyama-Sniezek. *Exceptional Children, 57*(1), 9–23.

Stephens, T. (1977). *Teaching skills to children with learning and behavior disorders.* Columbus, OH: Charles E. Merrill.

Stephens, T. M., Blackhurst, A. E., & Magliocca, L. A. (1988). *Teaching mainstreamed students* (2nd ed.). New York, NY: Pergamon Press.

Sternberg, R. J. (1990). Thinking styles: Key to understanding performance. *Phi Delta Kappan, 71*(5), 366–371.

Strauss, A., & Lehtinen, L. S. (1947). Psychopathology and education of the brain injured child. New York: Grune & Stratton.

Strong, R. W., Silver, H. F., Hanson, J. R., Marzano, R. J., Wolfe, P., Dewing, T., & Brock, W. (1990). Thoughtful education: Staff development for the 1990s. *Educational Leadership, 47*(5), 25–29.

Sugai, G., & Horner, R. (2001). *School climate and discipline: Going to scale.* Eugene, OR: Center on Positive Behavioral Interventions and Supports.

Sugai, G., and Horner, R.H. (1999). Discipline and behavioral support: Practices, pitfalls, promises. *Effective School Practices, 17*(4), 10–22.

Swanson, J. M., McBurnett, K., Wigal, T., Pfiffner, L. J., Lerner, M. A., Williams, L., Christian, D. L., Tamm, L., Wilcutt, E., Crowley, K., Clevenger, W., Khouzam, N., Woo, C., Crinella, F. M., & Fisher, T. D. (1993). Effects of stimulant medication on children with attention deficit disorder: A "Review of the reviews." *Exceptional Children, 60*(2), 154–162.

Sylwester, R. (1994). How emotions affect learning. *Educational Leadership, 52*(2), 60–65.

Sylwester, R. (2000). Unconscious emotions, conscious feelings. *Educational Leadership, 58*(3), 20–24.

Tarver, S. G. (1986). Cognitive behavior modification, direct instruction and holistic approaches to the education of students with learning disabilities. *Journal of Learning Disabilities, 19*(6), 368–375.

Tateyama-Sniezek, K. M. (1990). Cooperative learning: Does it improve the academic achievement of students with handicaps? *Exceptional Children, 57*(2), 426–427.

Taylor, S. J., & Searle, S. J. (1987). The disabled in America: History, policy and trends. In P. Knoblock (Ed.), *Understanding Exceptional Children and Youth.* Boston: Little, Brown.

Thomas, A., & Chess, S. (1977). Temperament and development. New York: Bruner/Mazel.

Thomas, C. C., Correa, V. I., & Morsink, C. V. (2001). *Interactive teaming: Enhancing programs for students with special needs* (3rd ed.). Upper Saddle River, NJ: Merrill/Prentice Hall.

Todd, A. W., Horner, R.H., Sugai, G., and Sprague, J.R. (1999). Effective behavior support: Strengthening school-wide systems through a team-based approach. *Effective School Practices, 17*(4), 23–27.

Tomlinson, C. (2000). Reconcilable differences? Standards-based teaching and differentiation. *Educational Leadership, 58*(1), 6–11.

Torgesen, J. K. (1977). Memorization processes in reading disabled children. *Journal of Educational Psychology, 69*, 571–578.

Treible, C. (1996, February). Unpublished interview with Director of Learning Disability Support Services, Andrew College, Cuthbert, Georgia.

Tucker, J. (1985). Curriculum-based assessment: An introduction. *Exceptional Children, 52*, 199–204.

U.S. Bureau of the Census. (1995). Health insurance coverage: 1994. *Current Population Reports, Series* P60–P190, November, U.S. Government Printing Office: Washington, D.C.

U.S. Department of Education. (1990). *To assure the free appropriate public education of all handicapped children: Twelfth annual report to Congress on the implementation of The Education of the Handicapped Act.* Washington, DC: Office of Special Education Programs.

U.S. Department of Education. (1993). *Fifteenth annual report to Congress on the implementation of the Individuals with Disabilities Education Act.* Washington, DC: Author.

U.S. Department of Education (1996). *Eighteenth annual report on the implementation of the individuals with disabilities education act.* Washington., D.C: Author.

U.S. Department of Education (1997). *Nineteenth annual report to Congress on the implementation of the Individuals with Disabilities Education Act.* Washington, DC: Author.

U.S. Department of Education (1998). *Twentieth annual report to Congress on the implementation of the Individuals with Disabilties Education Act.* Washington, DC: Author

U.S. Department of Education (2000). *A guide to the Individualized Education Program.* Washington, DC: Author. Available on-line: *www.ed.gov/offices/OSERS/OSEP/IEPGuide/.*

U.S. Department of Education. (2000). *Twenty-first annual report to Congress on the implementation of the Individuals with Disabilities Education Act.* Washington, DC: Author.

U.S. Department of Education. (2001). *Twenty-second Annual Report to Congress on the Implementation of the Individuals with Disabilities Education Act.* Washington, DC: Author

U.S. Department of Education. (2002). *Twenty-third Annual Report to Congress on the Implementation of the Individuals with Disabilities Education Act.* Washington, DC: Author.

U.S. Department of Education. (2003). *Twenty-fourth annual report to Congress on the implementation of the Individuals with Disabilities Education Act.* Washington, DC: Author.

U.S. Office of Education (1977). *Assistance to states for education of handicapped children: Procedures for evaluating specific learning disabilities.* (Federal Register, 42:65081–65085.

U.S. Office of Special Education Programs. (2002, Nov./Dec.). *A new resource to help IEP teams.* Idea Partner

Uecker, A., & Nadel, L. (1998). Spatial but not object memory impairments in children with fetal alcohol syndrome. *American Journal on Mental Retardation 103*(1), 12–18.

Umbreit, J., & Ostrow, L. S. (1980). The fetal alcohol syndrome. *Mental Retardation, 18*(3), 109–111.

Utley, C. A., & Obiakor, F. E. (2001). *Special education, multicultural education, and school reform: Components of quality for learners with mild disabilities.* Springfield, IL: Charles C. Thomas.

Vadasy, P. F. (1986). Single mothers: A social phenomenon and population in need. In R. Fewell & P. Vadasy (Eds.), *Families of handicapped children: Needs and Supports across the life span* (pp. 221–249). Austin, TX: Pro-Ed.

Valentine, M. (1994). Paper presented at the Convention of National Association of School Psychologists. San Francisco, CA.

Van Sickle, J. H. (1908–1909). Provision for exceptional children in the public schools. *Psychological Clinic, 2,* 102–111.

Vaughn, S., Bos, C. S., & Lund, K. A. (1986). But they can do it in my room: Strategies for promoting generalization. *Teaching Exceptional Children, 18*(3), 176–180.

Vaughn, S., Bos, C. S., & Schumm, J. S. (1997). *Teaching mainstreamed, diverse, and at-risk students in the general education classroom.* Boston: Allyn and Bacon.

Vaughn, S., Schumm, J. S., & Arguelles, M. E. (1997, November/December). The ABCDEs of co-teaching. *Teaching Exceptional Children, 30*(2), 4–10.

Villa, R., Thousand, J., Stainback, W., & Stainback, W. (1999). Restructuring for caring and effective educators, (2nd ed.). Balitimore, MD: Brooks Publishing.

Wagmeister, J., & Shifrin, B. (2000). Thinking differently, learning differently. *Educational Leadership, 58*(3), 45–48.

Wagner, M., Carneto, R., & Guzman, A. (2003). Who are secondary students in special education today? *Reports from the National Longitudinal Transition Study, 2*(1) www.ncset.org/publications/viewdesc.asp?id=1008.

Walker, H. M., & Severson, H. H. (1999). *Systematic screening for behavior disorders (SSBD): User's guide and administration manual* (2nd ed.). Longmont, CO: Sopris West.

Walker, H., Ramsey, E., & Gresham, F. (2004). *Antisocial behavior in school: Evidence based practices.* (2nd ed.) Belmont, CA: Thomson Wadsworth.

Walker, J. E., & Shea, T. M. (1991). *Behavior management: A practical approach for educators.* New York: MacMillan.

Wallace, G., & Kauffman, J. M. (1986). *Teaching students with learning and behavior problems* (3rd ed.). Columbus, OH: Charles E. Merrill.

Wallace, H. (1972, October). The epidemiology of development disabilities. Paper delivered to the Annual Meeting of United Cerebral Palsy, Kentucky.

Wang, M. C., & Baker, E. T. (1986). Mainstreaming programs: Design features and effects. *The Journal of Special Education, 19*(4), 503–520.

Warner, I. (1991). Parents in touch—District leadership for parent involvement. *Phi Delta Kappan, 72*(5), 372–375.

Warrenfleltz, R. B., Kelly, W. J., Salzberg, C. L., Beegle, C. P., Levy, S. M., Adams, T. A., & Crouse, T. R. (1981). Social skills training of behavior disordered adolescents with self-monitoring to promote generalization to vocational setting. *Behavior Disorders, 7,* 18–27.

Washburn-Moses, L. (2003, March/April). What every special educator should know about high-stakes testing. *Teaching Exceptional Children, 35*(4), 12–15.

Weatherly, C. L., Lewis, J. E., Dickson, T. W., & Fain, J. R. (2003, March). Reauthorization of the IDEA and the ESEA: No Georgia educator left behind. Paper presented to Georgia educators, 1–48.

Wehmeyer, M. L., Kelchner, K., & Richards, S. (1996). Essential characteristics of self determined behavior of individuals with mental retardation. *American Journal on Mental Retardation, 100,* 632–642.

Wehmeyer, M., & Schwartz, M. (1997). Self-determination and positive adult outcomes: A follow-up study of youth with mental retardation or learning disabilities. *Exceptional Children, 63,* 245–255.

Weller, C., Strawser, S., & Buchanan, M. (1985). Adaptive behavior: Designator of a continuum of severity of learning disabled individuals. *Journal of Learning Disabilities, 18*(4), 200–203.

Werner, H. (1944). Development of visuo-motor performance on the marble board test in mentally retarded children. *Journal of Genetic Psychology, 64,* 269–279.

Wesson, C. L. (1991). Curriculum-based measurement and two models of follow-up consultation. *Exceptional Children, 57*(3), 246–256.

WestEd. (2000). Improving student achievement by extending school: Is it just a matter of time. *http://web.wested.org/online_pubs/time-andlearning/TAL_PV.html.*

Westwater, A., & Wolfe, P. (2000). The brain-compatible curriculum. *Educational Leadership, 58*(3), 49–52.

White, M. A. (1971). The view from the pupil's desk. In M. L. Silberman (Ed.), *The experience of schooling.* New York: Holt, Rinehart, and Winston.

White, O. R. (1986). Precision teaching—precision learning. *Exceptional Children, 52,* 522–534.

Whiting, J., & Aultman, L. (1990). *Workshop for parents* (Workshop materials). Albany, GA: Southwest Georgia Learning Resources System Center.

Wickman, E. K. (1929). *Children's behavior and teachers' attitudes.* New York: The Commonwealth Fund.

Wiederholt, J. (1974). Historical perspectives in the education of the learning disabled. In L. Mann & D. Sabatino (Eds.), *The second view of special education.* Philadelphia: Journal of Special Education Press.

Wikler, L. (1979). *Single parents of mentally retarded children: A neglected population.* Paper presented at the American Association of Mental Deficiency, Miami, Florida.

Will, M. (1986). *Educating students with learning problems: A shared responsibility.* Washington, DC: U.S. Department of Education.

Williams, L. D. (1988). A parent's opinion: Exceptional teachers. *Teaching K–8, 9–10,* 88.

Williams, S. (2002). How speech feedback and word prediction software can help students write. *Teaching Exceptional Children. 34*(3), 72–78.

Wilson, C. R. (1983). Teaching reading comprehension by connecting the known to the new. *The Reading Teacher, 36*, 382–390.

Winick, M. (1976). *Malnutrition and brain development.* New York: Exford Press.

Winzer, M. A., & Mazurek, K. (1998). *Special education in multicultural contexts.* Columbus, OH: Merrill.

Wojnilower, D. A., & Gross, A. M. (1988). Knowledge, perception, and performance of assertive behavior in children with learning disabilities. *Journal of Learning Disabilities, 21*(2), 109–117.

Wolking, B. (1991). Personal correspondence.

Wong, B. Y. L. (1979). Increasing retention of main ideas through questioning strategies. *Learning Disability Quarterly, 2*, 42–47.

Wong, B. Y. L. (1985). Potential means of enhancing content skills acquisition in learning disabled adolescents. *Focus on Exceptional Children, 17*(5), 1–8.

Wood, M. (1986). *Developmental therapy* (2nd ed.). Austin, TX: Pro-Ed.

Wood, M. M., & Long, N. J. (1991). *Life Space Intervention: Talking with Children and Youth in Crisis.* Austin, TX: Pro-Ed.

Wyne, M. D., & O'Connor, P. D. (1979). *Exceptional children: A developmental view.* Lexington, MA: D. C. Heath.

Ysseldyke, J. E., & Algozzine, B. (1982). *Critical issues in special and remedial education.* Boston: Houghton Mifflin.

Ysseldyke, J. E., & Algozzine, B. (1984). *Introduction to special education.* Boston: Houghton Mifflin.

Ysseldyke, J. E., & Algozzine, B. (1990). *Introduction to special education* (2nd ed.). Boston, MA: Houghton Mifflin.

Ysseldyke, J. E., & Algozzine, B. (1995). *Special education: A practical approach for teachers.* Boston, MA: Houghton Mifflin.

Ysseldyke, J., Algozzine, B., & Thurlow, M. (1983). On interpreting institute research: A response to McKinney. *Exceptional Education Quarterly, 4*(1), 145–147.

Ysseldyke, J. E., Algozzine, B., & Thurlow, M. L. (2000). *Critical issues in special education* (3rd ed.). Boston: Houghton Mifflin.

Ysseldyke, J. E., Algozzine, B., Shinn, M. R., & McGue, M. (1982). Similarities and differences between low achievers and students classified learning disabled. *The Journal of Special Education, 16*(1), 73–85.

Zigmond, N., Levin, E., & Laurie, T. (1985). Managing the mainstream: An analysis of teacher attitudes and student performance in mainstream high school programs. *Journal of Learning Disabilities, 18*, 505–568.

Zinmeister, K. (1990). Growing up scared. *The Atlantic, 265*(6), 49–66.

Zucker, S. H., & Polloway, E. A. (1987). Issues in identification and assessment in mental retardation. *Education and Training in Mental Retardation, 22*(2), 69–76.

INDEX

WITHDRAWN

339404

Password LgadSA+1G

Current password
New password ✓

(4565341)
TORO